'A' Level Law

'A' Level Law

Third edition

Tony Dugdale   BA, BCL
Professor of Law, University of Keele

Michael Furmston   TD, BCL, MA, LLM
Professor of Law, University of Bristol

Stephen Jones   BA, Dip Crim
Lecturer in Law, University of Bristol

Christopher Sherrin   LLM, PhD
Professor of Law, University of Hong Kong

Butterworths
London, Dublin, Edinburgh
1996

United Kingdom	Butterworths a Division of Reed Elsevier (UK) Ltd, Halsbury House, 35 Chancery Lane, LONDON WC2A 1EL and 4 Hill Street, EDINBURGH EH2 3JZ
Australia	Butterworths, SYDNEY, MELBOURNE, BRISBANE, ADELAIDE, PERTH, CANBERRA and HOBART
Canada	Butterworths Canada Ltd, TORONTO and VANCOUVER
Ireland	Butterworth (Ireland) Ltd, DUBLIN
Malaysia	Malayan Law Journal Sdn Bhd, KUALA LUMPUR
New Zealand	Butterworths of New Zealand Ltd, WELLINGTON and AUCKLAND
Singapore	Reed Elsevier (Singapore) Pte Ltd, SINGAPORE
South Africa	Butterworths Publishers (Pty) Ltd, DURBAN
USA	Michie, CHARLOTTESVILLE, Virginia

A CIP Catalogue record for this book is available from the British Library.

First edition 1988
Second edition 1992

ISBN 0 406 04835 5

Printed by Clays Ltd, St Ives Plc

Preface

Our primary aim in writing the third edition of this book continues to be to meet the needs of students studying for 'A' level law syllabuses which address the study of law from a socio-legal perspective. The variety of topics covered by the different Boards makes it impossible for any book of reasonable length to cover every topic in every course. Nonetheless, we hope that students of any Board will find interesting material of use to their studies within this book.

We have tried to strike a balance between a description of the law in sufficient depth to meet the needs of an 'A' level student and a discussion of the law's working and the theoretical principles underlying it. At times the discussion in the text is placed in context by special sections dealing with cases or issues of particular interest. The study and practice of law is not just about rules but also about argument and throughout the text we have sought to encourage students to consider the arguments that surround the controversial issues in the law.

For the third edition we have thoroughly updated the contents in the light of rapid changes in the law in the 1990s. The sections on criminal law incorporate recent legislative changes such as the Criminal Justice and Public Order Act 1994, much new case law and discussion of new sentencing policies. In addition, to new case law, the contract section contains lengthy discussion of the Unfair Terms in Consumer Contracts Regulations 1994 which provide further control of exclusions. The extent of recent case law in the area of tort has been such that we have taken the opportunity to undertake a radical restructuring of the tort section of the book. The legal system part now includes an expanded section on the rule of law and a new overview chapter entitled 'Understanding Law'.

Whilst each author has had primary responsibility for different sections of the book, we have written to a common style and provided extensive cross-referencing between the sections of the book. Finally, we would like to thank the teachers who have written to us with comments about the book from which we hope that this third edition has benefited.

June 1996 AMD, MPF, SPJ, CHS

Contents

Table of statutes

References in this Table to *Statutes* are to Halsbury's Statutes of England (Fourth Edition) showing the volume and page at which the annotated text of the Act may be found.

Table of cases

PAGE

R

PAGE

Part I
The legal system

Chapter 1

The legal system

This chapter begins with some basic questions: Why does society need rules? What distinguishes the rules of a legal system from those of custom or morality? What makes a legal system work? From these general questions, the chapter moves on to consider the central features of the English legal system. How did they come about? What has enabled them to survive centuries of social change? Can they meet the needs of modern society? None of these questions can be answered simply but it is essential to think about them before embarking on any study of the English legal system.

Legal systems

Why rules?

All societies develop rules to govern the inter-relationship of their members. In his book *The Concept of Law*, the greatest English legal philosopher of the century, Professor Hart, argued that the reason lies in our knowledge of certain self-evident truths about human existence. We know we are all vulnerable to attack by others. We all have approximately equal physical and intellectual powers. We all have limited concern for others, and limited will-power. Finally, we know that we live in a world of limited resources. Given this knowledge and the natural desire to survive, human beings in any society will realise that they must have rules imposing self-restraint. The argument goes like this: Without such rules, we might succumb to temptation and take the property or even the life of someone in a weak position, conveniently forgetting that one day we too might be weak and vulnerable to the same treatment. The fighting and feuding would eventually lead to the break up of our society leaving its members to face the hostile world alone. It is this realisation which leads human beings in all societies to accept rules of self-restraint protecting the property and person of others and to accept that the observance of the rules must be guaranteed by some kind of penalty directed against the rule-breaker. Such rules, says Hart, are the minimum necessary content of law in any society.

What makes a legal system?

The fact that a society is governed by rules does not mean that we should describe it as having a legal system. Its rules system may be based on informal custom alone. Anthropological research has shown that small tribal societies can function perfectly well without any formal legal system. The customs to be followed may be complex but they will be well known throughout the group; disputes will be rare; group discussion will be a practicable means of settling disputes and of making such modifications in the rules as the slow pace of change requires. Such a system is appropriate to a society which has a simple economy and a cohesive structure. But once a society develops economically, politically and socially it both requires more complex rules and also loses the cohesion that supported the simpler rules system. Its people will no longer know all the necessary rules. Hence to avoid uncertainty the society will need to develop rules which will enable its members or at least the officials, to recognise the rules of conduct that govern the society – eg a rule demanding that the provisions of a code are to be recognized. Professor Hart calls these rules, rules of recognition. It will also need to be able to respond to economic and social developments by introducing new rules of conduct. To do this it will require rules of change specifying who has the authority to change the existing rules of conduct eg a rule that the governing body is entitled to change the code of conduct. As the degree of cohesion necessary to support informal methods of settling disputes no longer exists, the society will need to develop Rules of Adjudication defining the procedures to be followed in cases of dispute eg a court will adjudicate after hearing both sides.

Professor Hart describes these three types of rule, Recognition, Change and Adjudication, as secondary rules to distinguish them from the primary rules which directly govern the conduct of members of the society. He argues that this 'union of primary and secondary rules is at the centre of a legal system'. So, for Hart, the distinguishing feature of a legal system as opposed to a mere customary system, is the presence of these secondary rules. A customary system will have only primary rules but a legal system will have both. Other legal theorists take a less abstract approach and argue that the real hallmark of a legal system is the institution of a court. It is in the court that rules of recognition and change will be given effect. It is the court which operates the rules of adjudication. The rules are dependent upon the court – or is it the other way around ? There is no logical answer to the question. Whether one takes Hart's abstract and analytical approach or the so-called 'Realist' approach of those who emphasise the role of courts, is largely a matter of personal preference.

Legal systems and the principles of morality and justice

Appeals to morality are a familiar part of argument. To say that 'X's action is immoral' may be just an expression of general disapproval. But references to 'moral rights and obligations' are more specific. When we refer to the moral obligation not to commit adultery we are not referring to our own personal view but rather to the view generally supported by our society. This obligation is widely regarded as an important principle of behaviour without which social relationships would be less agreeable or secure. It is enforced by social pressures such as criticism of the culprit and sympathy for the victim. It is reinforced by religious teaching and by the media. The morality of our society consists of principles of behaviour like this.

Justice is an aspect of morality. It is concerned with how classes of individuals are treated. We would not regard a man who committed adultery as acting in an unjust way but we would regard it as unjust if his conduct was excused simply because he was famous whilst similar conduct by lesser mortals resulted in censure. Justice demands that like cases be treated alike. Similarly, we might regard it as unjust if the adulterous husband was allowed to leave his wife and children without any financial support. Justice demands that the victims be compensated.

In a primitive society, the customs which regulate its life have to be based on the morality of the group. Only in that way will they be followed and supported. But what about a society governed by a legal system? Does the legal system have to reflect the morality of that society? Does it have to be just? Professor Hart argues that there is no necessary relationship between the legal system and the ideas of justice or morality. In other words, a legal system can function effectively though it is neither just nor moral. The tyrannical legal system that operated in Germany during the latter years of the Nazi regime would be a good example of this point. It discriminated against individuals on racial grounds. Although we would argue that no civilised society should draw racial distinctions, it could be countered that if the morality of a society was such that racial distinctions were felt to be relevant, then it was entitled to discriminate and still claim it was treating like cases alike. The concepts of morality and justice are easily manipulated. But even so, the Nazi legal system sanctioned decisions which contradicted any notion of general morality or justice. Individuals were condemned on the whim of party officials. Individuals took to settling their private grudges against others by reporting them to officials for making anti-party remarks, with the result that they would be 'tried' and often executed. After the war some of the victims who survived brought the informers before the new German courts. The 'grudge informers' claimed that their action was lawful under the Nazi legal system. The new courts dismissed the defence on the ground that the Nazi laws were contrary to the 'sense of justice of all decent human beings'. To call the Nazi system 'legal' and to call its rules 'laws' was a false description of what they were. They were instruments of an arbitrary and tyrannical regime.

But is it sensible or helpful to refuse to treat such a system or its rules as being 'legal'? Professor Hart argues that the question of what is law must be separated from the question of whether it was moral or just. The post-war courts should have recognised the Nazi rules as laws and the post-war German legislature should then have faced the moral question and passed a statute instructing its courts to disregard defences based on Nazi laws. Retrospective legislation of this kind is undesirable but in this case it would be a lesser evil than leaving the informers unpunished. Other writers, such as the American Lon Fuller, have argued that law and morality cannot be so neatly severed and that the post-war courts were entitled to face the issue and hold Nazi rules not to be law. The 'grudge informer' problem illustrates a fundamental difference of view about the nature of law and its relationship with morality. However, on one point both Hart and Fuller would be in agreement: Immoral and unjust legal systems are unlikely to be stable and long-lived. Lacking morality and justice, they cannot command the allegiance of the people and must depend upon repression. When the repressive regime falls, its system falls with it. The complexity of the relationship between law and morality is a topic to which we return in Chapter 8 and there we also examine other functions played by law beyond providing rules of self-restraint. But for the present, it is sufficient to understand law as a system of primary and secondary rules.

The ideal legal system

Apart from the need for primary and secondary rules and the need for some relationship with the society's ideas of morality and justice, what else can be said about the essential or ideal nature of legal systems? Frederick the Great of Prussia, the enlightened despot par excellence, thought he had produced the ideal system for his citizens: a great Code of 17,000 provisions; the court to apply the Code and nothing else, any problems to be referred to the legislature for a ruling, neat rules of Recognition, Change and Adjudication of which a modern social planner would be proud. But this codified model of a legal system was soon criticised for being out of touch with the spirit of the people, the Volksgeist, as the nineteenth century writer Savigny called it. He wanted to see the German legal system based on a recognition of the customary rules of the people, to see it change through a process of unconscious growth rather than conscious decision. The ideals of Savigny and Frederick illustrate extreme models of a legal system. Neither proved to be workable. The best legal systems are not ideal models. They are those which have responded to the demands of society over the years, preserving successful features and discarding others. The English legal system is such a system. With over 900 years of unbroken development, it is rich in tradition. Its central features have stood the test of time. But here also lies its weakness. Tradition and complacency can be inhibiting. A legal system is only as good as its ability to respond to new pressures and circumstances.

The English legal system

What are the central features of the English legal system? How did they arise and what are their strengths and weaknesses? These questions provide a framework from which to view the history and structure of the system and the pressures facing it.

The centralised nature of the system

Prior to the Norman conquest in 1066, the legal system was decentralised. It consisted of local courts, the Borough, Shire and Hundred courts, each applying its own local customary law. The Norman king's could have adopted this system by allowing the Baron to whom a region had been given to run the court in that region. Indeed, by taking the office of Sheriff and with it the administration of the Shire court, some Barons tried to do just that. However, the fear that Barons would become provincial princes rivalling the power of the King was one of the main reasons which led to a strategy of judicial centralisation under Henry II (1154–1189). His reign saw the creation of a permanent royal court or 'King's Bench' as it became known, sitting in London and manned by specialist judges. In addition, the King commissioned officials, usually judges of the central court, to travel round a circuit of the regions hearing cases. These regional hearings were known as the 'Assizes' and dealt with both civil and criminal cases. Central control over the law was ensured by the procedure under which the legal issue in a case could first be decided by the royal courts in London and then the legal ruling would be taken by the travelling judge to the region concerned where the facts would be tried and the ruling applied to the facts found at the trial. This strategy enabled the royal judges to apply common legal principles to most parts of the land – hence the term 'Common Law' which is still used to describe our judge-made system of law. The existing local courts and laws were not abolished but, not surprisingly, litigants chose to use the royal courts with their professional judges and common law. This process of centralisation of the legal system and development of the common law was pursued by Henry II's successors, especially Edward I. By Tudor times local courts were hardly used for civil cases and the one local court which was widely used, the Sessions of the Justices of the Peace, had been specially created by the central government to deal with minor crime. It can hardly be considered an exception to the strategy of centralisation.

The modern pattern

The pattern of powerful central courts with travelling judges spreading its tentacles out to the regions, is one which has survived to the present day. The courts have changed their names. The King's Bench in London was merged with other royal courts in the last century to form a single court, the High Court which sits in different divisions for different types of case. King's Bench or rather Queen's Bench as it is under the present monarch, is now the name of one of these divisions. Assizes courts met their end at the hands of Lord Beeching in the 1970s. The Crown Court which sits in some 90 regional centres was created to take the criminal jurisdiction of the old Assizes. Its civil jurisdiction has returned to the High Court but to serve the regions, the High Court now sits in 24 regional centres as well as London. Minor criminal cases continue to be handled by Justices of the Peace but they are now usually referred to as magistrates and their courts sitting in all towns of any size, as magistrates' courts. In the last century a new court, the modern county court, was created to hear minor civil cases and that court too sits in most population centres of any size.

The court picture has changed. There are a large number of courts sitting in the regions. But the dominance of a small centralised judiciary remains. The 100 High Court judges still come on circuit to hear the most important criminal cases in the Crown Court and civil cases in the regional High Court. From their number the still smaller number of appeal court judges are selected – roughly two dozen in the Court of Appeal and less than half that in the highest court, the House of Lords. These appeal courts sit in London and to them may come not only appeals from the High Court but also those from the county court and by a less direct route, those from the magistrates court. Thus, this small group of judges based in London continues to dominate the system. They set the trends in both the theory and practice of law which will be followed by lesser judges in the regions.

The significance of the centralised system

The centralised nature of our system is striking when we compare it with systems in other countries. In France for example, each region has its own court structure. Their system has hundreds of judges of the same status and none with the pre-eminent status of our elite. If there is an elite court in France it is perhaps the Conseil d'Etat which sits at the pinnacle of a hierarchy of administrative courts, ie ones which review the administrative actions of government. Its prestige is necessarily limited to administrative law, ie the area of law concerned with the legality of government action. Our centralist tradition has inhibited the creation of a specialist court like the Conseil d'Etat. Arguably the development of our administrative law has suffered as a result but the counter would be that the system as a whole has gained from the over-view provided by our elite judges and from the fact that they have the opportunity to develop the principles of the common law through the full ranges of cases, be they criminal, civil or administrative.

But this centralised model with judges of universal competence is coming under increasing pressure. On the one hand, some areas of law are seen as so specialist in nature that they are thought to require specialist courts to handle them. Thus specialist courts usually called tribunals have been set up to hear cases concerned with welfare law, immigration law, employment law etc. Each tribunal has its own specialist jurisdiction and judges. On the other hand, there is a call for greater informality in the system so that the ordinary person can feel at home when using the system. Hence the demand for informal small claims courts divorced from the main court system or the experiments with mediation systems as an alternative to using the court system. There are other challenges. In his book, *English Law – The New Dimension*, Lord Scarman discusses the challenge of Welfare Law and Employment Law, and notes also that of Environmental law where there is a need for closer regulation of government power; and Human Rights law where the traditional role of our courts is in danger of being usurped by the fuller protection afforded by the European Court of Human Rights based in Strasbourg. He concludes: 'the common law system is in retreat: it is being remaindered to corners of the house which are unvisited by most members of society. The basis of the system is not only challenged: it is being abandoned. Yet the rule of law must be preserved if we are to have a just society.' To survive, he argues, both the common law system and the lawyers who operate it must respond to the challenges. If they fail, the universality of the common law will disappear. Our system will cease to move round a hub of common principles. Its different parts will be ruled by latter-day Norman barons, albeit without the same degree of baronial self-interest!

Equity and the law making role of the judges

A successful legal system must have the means of adapting its laws to meet changing social conditions. Superficially, it might seem that this is the job for Parliament and its legislation. Parliament does now play the leading role, but it is a central feature of the English legal system that for most of its existence the leading role was played by the judges. Indeed, they still play a vital role developing the law in those areas where legislation has not intervened or has proved inadequate. Initially, the ability of the judges to adapt the law rested on their control of the common law but as the potential of the common law waned, another avenue opened through the development of a system of equity.

Common law and equity

The centralised nature of the medieval legal system enabled the royal judges to apply a common law, but once that law was established it was not so easy to change. The judges, freedom to develop the law became circumscribed by the formality of the writ system and the rigidity of their own thinking. The writ system governed the work of the medieval courts. A person could not normally bring a claim before a royal court unless he could fit what had happened to him within the wording of one of the standard writs issued by officials of the King's Chancery office. Thus a thirteenth century trespass writ contained the words 'vi et armis' ie 'with force and arms', and that meant a civil wrong involving violence had to be alleged by a person wishing to claim compensation for trespass. When the Chancery officials stopped issuing new classes of writs in the late thirteenth century, the development of the common law was threatened. However, the judges were able to make slow progress by the use of fictions. Thus by the mid fourteenth century the judges were prepared to fictionally assume that a trespass was violent and the claimant would no longer have to prove that fact. The same technique was used with other writs and by the early seventeenth century the judges had managed to develop the outlines of much modern tort and contract law.

But the law developed by the judges was rigid and technical. Nowhere was this more the case than in relation to the ownership of land. The common law rules restricted a holder of land from determining who should have the land after his death. Such a freedom would have conflicted with the basic feudal notion that the permission of one's feudal lord was necessary for a transfer of land. Holders of land tried to avoid these rules by giving their land to a friend on condition that the holder could still use it and the friend would give it to a named person when the holder died. That worked if the friend was honest. But what if the friend kept the land for himself after the death? The named person was the intended beneficiary of the land but he would have no remedy under the common law rules. It was this kind of problem that led to the development of equity.

The broadest meaning of equity is simply 'fairness'. The notion of equity played an important role in the law of the Roman Empire. It was used to minimise the harsh results which could follow from the logical but strict rules of Roman civil law. In medieval England, equity also started life as a rather vague notion which could justify departure from the normal rules. Intended beneficiaries who had been cheated by so-called friends began to complain to the King's chief minister who was the Lord Chancellor. He had the power to override the common law rules and issue a royal decree granting the land to the beneficiary on the ground of fairness and conscience. During the fifteenth century this ad hoc system of granting a remedy in a specific case came to be heavily used. It became institutionalised with the cases being heard by a court, the Court of Chancery, and the decrees being granted in accordance with a growing body of rules known as the principles of equity. For a long period until the eighteenth century the growth of these principles enabled the Court of Chancery to adapt the law to changing conditions. Much of the structure of modern land law based on concepts such as the trust and the mortgage, was developed through Chancery during this period. The success of equity and the Court of Chancery also acted as a spur to the common law courts so that the common law too became revitalised and capable of responding to change. Indeed, by the time the courts were merged into the single High Court in the nineteenth century, it was equity rather than the common law which was showing signs of rigidity.

The need of a new equity

In 1952 Lord Denning, perhaps the most controversial judge of the century, delivered a lecture entitled 'the need of a new equity'. In it he regretted the fact that since the merger of the courts, equity seemed to have lost its power. The new courts applied principles of both common law and equity but neither seemed to enable the judges to adapt the law to changing conditions. Parliament was too slow and cumbersome to fill the gap. Lord Denning placed his hopes for the 'new Elizabethan era' upon the 'new spirit which is alive in our universities'. Looking back on this in 1984, he commented 'I can say that in my time the courts have discovered the new equity'. In the thirty year period, Lord Denning himself had played a major role in developing new principles such as promissory estoppel which introduces an element of fairness into contract law (see p 553). But the discovery is really much broader than Lord Denning suggests. Judges have developed new principles from the common law as much as from equity. What they have discovered seems to be a new found confidence in their law-making role. This central feature of the English legal system is no longer in danger.

Lay participation in the system

Until the nineteenth century the judges of the royal courts rarely exceeded 15 in number at any one time. Even today the professional judiciary is limited to a little over 100 High Court and appeal court judges supplemented by 350 or so circuit judges who sit in the county court and help out in the Crown Court, a few stipendiary magistrates sitting in city magistrates' courts and a number of full time chairmen of Tribunals. To run a legal system on so few professional judges is a remarkable achievement. Comparable countries operate their systems with up to 20 times the number of professional judges. The explanation lies in the participation of laymen in the working of the system and once again this is a tradition reaching far back into our legal history.

The magistracy

We have already noted the use of Justices of the Peace to deal with minor crime. This practice dates back at least 600 years. Today there are over 25,000 such lay justices and the magistrates' courts in which they sit try over one million minor criminal cases a year – twenty times the number managed by the Crown Courts. In addition, the magistrates deal with a million motoring offences, hear juvenile and domestic cases, take administrative decisions eg licensing pubs and betting shops, and finally exercise some control over the investigation of crime through the granting of warrants and bail, and their preliminary hearing of evidence relating to serious crimes (this happens at the transfer proceedings, see post, p 101). Magistrates are the workhorses of the legal system. To replace them we would need 4,000 professional judges costing well over £100 million a year in salaries let alone the cost of educating the additional lawyers necessary to fill a professional magistracy. But indispensability does not necessarily result in popularity. Magistrates have been criticised for being aged, incompetent and drawn from a narrow class background. As reforms introduced since the last war have gone some way towards meeting these criticisms, the attack has shifted to the procedure and atmosphere of the courts themselves. Lord Hailsham, who was Thatcher's Lord Chancellor in the 1980s, once defended the role of the lay magistracy as 'one of the characteristic institutions holding our society together' but it has to be conceded that this is not often the first thought that springs to mind when lawyers discuss the role of the magistrate.

The jury

Paradoxically, the lay jury is seen as playing a fundamental role in our legal system and our society although in practical terms its role is more restricted than the lay magistracy. Its use is limited to criminal cases tried in the Crown Court and the odd civil case such as a libel action. But it is credited with the development of the adversary system of justice and the protection of individual liberty under the law. Its original function promised none of these things. Juries were groups of laymen sworn (iurati in latin – hence jury) to tell the truth about events in their locality. The Normans gathered information for the Domesday survey in this way. Later, juries were assembled to give information to Assize judges about local crimes. Under Henry II they were used for deciding the facts in trials concerning land seizure and when in the next century the Church withdrew its approval of the traditional form of criminal trial by ordeal, the jury was the obvious substitute. But the jury still functioned as part of an inquest. Its members would be asked what they knew about the land dispute or the particular crime alleged. The critical change of practice occurred in the fourteenth century. Juries were now asked not what they knew but what facts they thought had been established by the evidence of witnesses. Each of the adversaries in the case produced his own witnesses and questioned them and then those witnesses were cross-examined by the other party in an attempt to convince the jurors that they were lying. The judge acted as an umpire, seeing that the questioning was fair. At the close of the evidence, the jury was asked to come to a collective and unanimous decision on the facts and to encourage that process they were confined without food or warmth until agreement was reached. The requirement of a unanimous verdict provided some protection for the accused, much needed in an age when he had no right to be represented by a lawyer. Nevertheless, judges still sometimes tried to bully juries into convicting particularly where the crime had political overtones. It was not until *Bushell's* case in 1670 that it was clearly established that jurors were the sole judges of fact and could not be penalised for taking a view of the facts opposed to that of the judge. It is on this tradition of independence from both judicial and political pressure, that the jury's reputation for defending individual liberty rests. The tradition has continued into the 1990s. The jury acquittal of the two men who admitted helping the spy George Blake to escape is a recent example of this tradition. Whether in the words of the Daily Telegraph, it was a 'bad day for justice' or in those of the Guardian, a 'much-needed reaffirmation of the value of the jury system' is a matter or opinion.

In France and Germany also, group inquests became the normal form of trial after the disappearance of ordeals and battles. But instead of developing this system to allow laymen to determine the facts, continental procedure moved in an opposite direction. Responsibility for determining the facts lay with the professional judge. He conducted the inquest. He decided how to question the witnesses. This procedure based on the traditions of Roman law and the Canon law that followed in its wake, is known as inquisitorial. The contrast between this model and the adversarial model adopted in England appears great. Under the adversary model, evidence such as an accused's previous convictions cannot normally be presented at the trial because it would unfairly influence the jury. Such evidence can be investigated by the judge in an inquisitorial trial. The accused can remain silent in an adversarial trial for it is up to his adversary, the prosecutor, to make the case against the accused from his own evidence. In an inquisitorial trial, the accused is bound to answer the questions of the judge. Above all the accused does not have the protection of an independent jury. Modern continental procedures influenced partly by the English system, have introduced some adversarial elements and some lay participation in major trials. But the laymen work alongside the judge. They consider the facts together. They do not have the same opportunity to exercise independent judgment that is open to the English jury.

The significance of lay participation

Such then is our tradition of lay participation in the legal system, a tradition of great practical importance through the role of the magistrates and of great conceptual importance through the role of the jury. But as with the centralised nature of the system, it is a tradition under pressure. The common criticism is that both magistrates and juries produce 'amateur' justice, getting too many decisions wrong – though here the criticism divides, it usually being said that magistrates convict too readily whilst juries acquit too readily. To the extent that this is true, it is arguably the cost the system has to pay for the benefits of lay participation. In the case of welfare law tribunals the cost of incompetence proved too high: the lay panels which heard welfare appeals in the 1960s and 1970s were a disaster and had to be replaced by a panel of two laymen with specialist knowledge of welfare problems and a legally qualified, experienced chairman. This pattern which combines lay participation with professional legal competence, is commonly adopted for tribunals. Some would argue that the pattern should be extended to magistrates' courts. Even the use of the lay jury is being questioned: an official report recently suggested that in complex fraud trials the jury should be replaced by a judge and lay expert panel with some modifications to the adversary system, eg requiring the accused to co-operate with the prosecution in the preparation of evidence for the trial. In civil cases the jury is no longer much used but its legacy, the adversarial system has recently been criticised by another review (see post, p 61) and fundamental modifications to the system have been proposed. The outcry against both these proposals from the legal profession is testimony to the strength of the lay judgment/adversary trial tradition. The government has not accepted either the recommendation to abolish jury trial for fraud cases or that of fundamental change to the adversary system. The more fundamental question is whether our society can still afford to use the lay model of justice represented by magistrates and juries as against the more professional model exemplified by tribunals or indeed, the continental inquisitorial system.

Judicial independence and autonomy of the law

The fourth feature of our system, the tradition of judicial independence, is more recent in origin than the others. No one could describe medieval common law judges as being independent of government. It is true that they resisted the attempts of Henry VIII's Lord Chancellor, Cardinal

Wolsey, to assert the supremacy of equity over the Common Law. But the common law judges were acting in defence of the jurisdiction of their court and hence, their fee earning capacity rather than asserting any ideological independence from the crown. The dispute was soon over, leaving each system of law to go its own way; Equity being administered by the Court of Chancery and the common law by its own courts. A century after Wolsey, the common law judge were once again in dispute with other courts, Chancery again and also a relative newcomer, the court of Star Chamber. This court was firmly under the control of the Stuart Kings and through its judgments they sought to justify seizure of property, creation of monopolies and imposition of taxes. Resistance was led by Sir Edward Coke, the common law Chief Justice under James I. It was not simply a question of business and fees being lost to Chancery and Star Chamber; the dispute was ideological and with the common law being allied with private property and the free market against the monopolistic, interventionist policies of the King. Coke gave the common law a somewhat mythical quality. As Christopher Hill notes in *The Century of Revolution*, he believed 'that the common law had survived from the times of the ancient Britons, and that Roman, Anglo-Saxon and Norman conquests had left it virtually unchanged.' It was the birthright of every subject. To achieve his goal, Coke was prepared to ignore or twist common law decisions he did not like, stretch the meaning of statutes and even in *Bonham's* case (1610) hold that a statute contrary to common right and reason would be invalid at common law. His opposition to royal policy led to his dismissal in 1616. Ten years later Charles I dismissed his Chief Justice for similar reasons. By the civil war every King's Bench judge was either with the King or in prison. The royalist judges had relied on the marriage of law and politics rather than its separation. The victory of Parliament over the King in the civil war exposed the danger of such attitudes.

Royal attempts to influence judges continued after the Stuart restoration. The 'Glorious Revolution' of 1688 replaced the Stuarts with William of Orange and brought a Bill of Rights, but royal influence was still able to procure the deletion of a judicial independence provision from that Bill. It was only with the Act of Settlement of 1700 that the power to remove judges was transferred from the Crown to Parliament. The requirement of a petition from both Houses of Parliament for a judge to be removed gave the judiciary essential protection from the influence of the Crown and its ministers. The eighteenth century saw not only the protection of judicial independence but also the rise in the notion of the common law as an autonomous system of rules uninfluenced by political or other pressures. This image strengthened as the law itself became more complex in its doctrine and terminology, more and more the preserve of the developing legal profession. The eminent eighteenth century legal commentator, William Blackstone reflected these developments when he spoke of law as a 'mysterious science'. Blackstone's advocacy of the 'declaratory theory ' of law, according to which judges decisions do not make the law but simply declare what the law has always been, furthered the myth of the autonomous common law. The common law could be seen as an all embracing system of law based upon reason and binding monarch, judge and subject alike.

So we have an image of an independent judiciary declaring the common law. The pattern of that law becomes clearer through their decisions. It is an autonomous system and binding sovereign and subject alike. It can be strikingly contrasted with the image of some continental systems where judges are seen not as a small, detached elite but as a large corps of civil servants conforming to the service ethos or at worst, the political dogmas of the day; where instead of law being the creature of custom and reason as perceived by the judges, it comes in the form of a code laid down by a legislature. This contrast under-estimates the role of continental judges and over-estimates that of the common law judges. Nevertheless, it is the case that the popular image of the English legal system is largely founded on the prestige of its elite group of judges. The image is strong. Traditionally, governments of all persuasions have been careful not to interfere with the judiciary nor to criticise their decisions. Instead they have made use of the judiciary's reputation for neutrality and independence by appointing them to head inquiries. Indeed, they may hope that some of the judicial aura of respectability will rub off onto their legislation when it is interpreted and applied by the courts.

The rule of law

A final feature, more abstract than the others, is the Rule of Law. Its role as a key feature of the English legal system was extolled by the great Victorian jurist, AV Dicey. He analysed three different aspects of the concept. First, that no person 'is punishable except for a distinct breach of law established in the ordinary legal manner before the ordinary courts of the land'. Secondly, 'not only that no man is above the law, but that every man, whatever be his rank is subject to the ordinary law of the realm and amenable to the jurisdiction of ordinary tribunals'. Thirdly, 'the general principles of the constitution (for example the right to personal liberty) are the result of judicial decisions determining the rights of private individuals in particular cases brought before the courts; whereas under many foreign constitutions the security given to the rights of individuals results from the general principles of the constitution'. Dicey considered the English system with its rule of law to be much superior to continental legal systems such as that in France. He pointed out that whilst the 1791 French Constitution proclaimed liberty of the press and the right to public meetings, these rights had not been enforced because the French system had given insufficient attention to the remedies necessary to secure the rights. The English system by starting with remedies in particular cases, was able to develop a secure system of rights. Again, the first principle of 'punishment only by the ordinary courts' contrasted with the arbitrary powers invoked by the rules of much of nineteenth century Europe. The second principle, that of legal equality irrespective of rank, contrasted with the system in France under which state officials were 'exempted from the ordinary law of the land and subject in certain respects only to official law administered by official bodies'.

Dicey's criticism of the French system of administrative law and tribunals for dealing with the wrongs of officials now looks to be misplaced. Their 'separate' system seems to have provided an effective means of controlling and reviewing the actions of the executive whilst our 'universal' system strains to do the same job. The procedure for controlling the actions of our executive is to ask the ordinary High Court for judicial review of the conduct in question. If it is found to have been unlawful, the court may issue an order quashing the executive's decision (known as certiorari), or instructing it to take specific action (mandamus) or forbidding it from taking action (prohibition). But it has not proved easy to adapt this old system, medieval in origin, to control the all-embracing powers of the modern executive. The grounds for review which do not include general unfairness, and the remedies which do not always include damages, are perhaps too limited. Twenty years ago, some of the major procedural barriers in the way of bringing actions for judicial review were removed and, as a result, there has been an explosion of case law. But if anything this evidence of the real demand only strengthens the case for establishing a separate and effective legal system for controlling the executive.

It is Dicey's argument that the most secure rights are those derived from remedies given by the courts rather than principles enshrined in a written constitution, that still carries weight. After all, the twentieth century has seen written constitutions in Germany and Italy which were twisted to deny real rights to most of the people. A modern constitutional writer, John Waldron, illustrates Dicey's point by reference to the case of *Pedro v Diss* (1981). A man called Ya Ya Pedro was standing outside the door of his brother's house in London. Constable Diss walked up, identified himself as a police officer and asked Pedro what he was doing. Pedro told him to 'fuck off' and walked off. Diss grabbed him by the arm and Pedro punched him. He was convicted by the magistrates of assaulting a constable in the execution of his duty and fined £50. The High Court overturned the conviction. There were two stages in the court's reasoning. First, the law provided that a constable may only stop someone on grounds of 'reasonable suspicion' (see post, p 83) if he explains to the suspect why he is doing it. Diss gave no explanation and hence, he was not acting in the lawful execution of his duty. That meant that when he grabbed Pedro,

Pedro was entitled to resist just as he would be entitled to resist any other person who attacked him. For Waldron the message of the case is:

> 'the police officer has no special privileges; just like the lowly suspect, he is equally subject to the law of the land. Similarly, other officials, even ministers of state, must follow the law along with everyone else, even when they think they are acting high-mindedly in pursuit of the common good or the will of the people. This is why people think it is possible to be free and governed at the same time: they say they are subject to the rule of laws, not men.'

Postscript: the judicial challenges of the 1990s

As Robert Stevens pointed out in an article in 1994, the Act of Settlement of 1700 provided independence of individual judges by making their dismissal dependent upon the approval of Parliament. It did not provide an independent judiciary in the sense of an equal branch of government capable of controlling the legislature and executive. Instead, the judges are servants of the legislature and bound by its laws. The legislature itself is largely controlled by the government through its party machine and as a result the judges have little opportunity to control the executive as it can secure almost any legislation it needs to pursue its goals. That is the theory but something odd seems to be happening. The judiciary seems to be flexing its muscles.

The signs are there. Hardly a month seemed to go by in 1994/5 without the Home Secretary, Michael Howard, being subject to judicial review on issues such as the criminal injuries compensations scheme, the treatment of asylum seekers, immigrations decisions, eligibility for parole, rights to naturalisation etc. The Foreign Secretary has suffered the same ignominy in relation to his (unlawful) decision to fund the Pergau dam in Malaysia. Several ministers were severely criticised by Lord Justice Scott in his 1996 report on the Iraqi arms affair. 1996 also sees the judiciary continuing to speak out loudly against the Home Secretary's proposal to interfere with their power to decide on sentences by stipulating US-style minimum sentences. As for the proposals of Lord Chancellor Mackay, the government's law minister, to reform the courts and the system of civil justice (see post, p 61), judges have queued to express their criticisms through the media, one even detecting a similarity between Lord Mackay and Adolf Hitler. The senior judges of the early 1990s, Lord Taylor who was the Lord Chief Justice with responsibility for the criminal courts, and Sir Thomas Bingham who was the Master of the Rolls with responsibility for the civil courts, were both powerful advocates for a Bill of Rights which would limit the power of Parliament to legislate against rights and give greater power to the judges to control the executive. Stevens comments: 'The truth is that this would transfer more power from parliament to the judiciary than

Maastricht transferred from Westminister to Brussels, but such truth is hidden under the mystical incantation of the rubric of the Independence of the Judiciary.'

Stevens speculates on the reasons for the new judicial boldness. The abandonment in the 1980s of the Kilmuir Rules which deterred the judges from making public pronouncements, is undoubtedly one reason but perhaps the symptom rather than the cause. Arguably, the role and calibre of the legislature weakened during the Thatcher period and some may see the judiciary as moving to fill a power vacuum, as an essential counter-balance to the strength of the executive. What would be the consequence of such a shift in the role of the judiciary? Stevens suggests that the cost may be higher than judges realise: 'The views of the judges will become a matter of public interest'. We might need to consider following the US system under which, although federal judges are appointed for life, they and their views are examine carefully by a legislative committee and in a couple of recent cases, have retired hurt during this process (remember Judge Clarence Thomas and his alleged sexual harassment). There might have to be other changes. For example, the senior judges all sit in the legislative House of Lords and regularly make speeches. Should they be expelled from the legislature? Does not independence of the judiciary also imply a firm separation of the judiciary from the legislature? These are questions to consider as we move on to study the detailed structure of the legal system.

Chapter 2
The structure of the English legal system

In this chapter we consider two questions. The first is how does our legal system fits into the constitutional structure of the country? What is its relationship with the executive, with the legislature, and with the European Communities to which we now belong? From considering the external relationships of the legal system, we move to its internal relationships asking how its court structure fits together and what role is played by the various types of judge and lawyer. Other countries have used the opportunity provided by a revolution or some other major political upheaval, to plan the answer to some of these questions so that the court structure will have at least a logical appearance, or their constitution will define the relationship between judiciary, executive and legislature. The English legal system has had little in the way of such planning. Rather, its structure has evolved over centuries of unbroken development. Particular features can be explained as the response to some, often long-forgotten problem; but the whole is an interlocking web of institutions, personnel and relationships which defies simple explanation. Its rich complex structure, embroidered with tradition and ceremony, obscures one further question which must be asked: Is it adequate to meet the needs of the late twentieth century? This same question arises in relation to both its external and internal relationships.

External relationships: the legal system and the constitution

In the last chapter we described how the tradition of an independent judiciary had arisen from the political turmoil of the seventeenth century. That tradition took root across the Atlantic and flowered in the written constitution adopted by the newly independent United States in the late eighteenth century. This constitution enshrined what is known as the separation of powers. The powers are the executive, the legislature and the judiciary. The United States' Constitution separates both the membership and functions of these three bodies. Members of the executive headed by the President are not members of the legislature, the Congress. The executive cannot dictate to the legislature what laws it should pass but the President can veto Congressional legislation, although that veto can itself be overridden. Neither can the legislature tell the executive how it should govern within those laws although it has the ultimate power to impeach the President. The judiciary of the Supreme Court cannot be members of the executive or legislature. They are appointed by the President but need to be confirmed in their post by the upper House of Congress, the Senate. Part of their job is to see that neither of the other two branches of government exceeds its powers under the written constitution. In Britain there is no such clear separation of powers. Our system is based on the overlapping of powers and institutions rather than their separation. The resulting inter-relationships are governed not by the written rules of a constitution but by unwritten conventions accepted and developed over the centuries. It is a constitution of compromise. With that in mind, we will consider the relationship of our legal system with the legislature, ie Parliament, the executive and finally, the European Communities, before returning to the broader question of whether our constitutional compromise is adequate for the late twentieth century.

Parliament and the legal system

An Act of Parliament is the supreme law within our system. The courts will apply the provisions of an Act even if they are inconsistent with rules established by case law or contained in previous legislation. The courts may try to interpret the Act to make it fit with previous case law or legislation but where this is not possible they must accept that the previous law no longer has any validity. There is no constitutional document which stipulates that the courts must recognise the supremacy of parliamentary legislation, but it is accepted that 'the duty of the court is to obey and apply every act of Parliament ... As a matter of law the courts recognise Parliament as being omnipotent.' (Sir Robert Megarry V-C in *Manuel v A-G* (1982).)

Parliament makes the legislation. The judges interpret and apply it. Great importance is attached to keeping those two functions separate. When you come to the section on statutory interpretation and in particular, the speech of Lord Simon in *Stock v Jones* (1978) (see post, p 169), you will see that judges are conscious of the fact that, unlike the legislature, they are not answerable to the people and that therefore it would be quite wrong for them to twist the interpretation of a statute to make it say what they wanted. Equally, when creating new rules of common law, they are aware that they should not trespass upon areas of law where Parliament is taking the lead (see post, p 185). On the other side of the coin, the legislature is careful not to trespass on the judges' territory. Criticism of a judge or the way he has interpreted a statute is rarely heard in Parliament and although Parliament has the power to have a judge removed from office, it is inconceivable that this would be done because of the way in which the judge had interpreted legislation.

The complex relationship of the legislature and the judiciary is well illustrated by the conventions which apply to the House of Lords. That body has a legislative role as the second chamber of Parliament and a judicial role as the highest appeal court in the land. Its members include the senior appeal judges commonly referred to as the Law Lords, the Anglican Bishops, the hereditary peers and the life peers who are political appointees. However, by convention the non-judicial members of the House do not take part in its judicial work and the 'judicial' members of the House do not take part in its political debates. This latter convention does not mean a separation of the judiciary from the legislative process. The Law Lords occasionally introduce non-partisan legislation and more commonly propose technical amendments to legislation. The line between the political and non-political arena is fine but, with occasional lapses, the Law Lords tread carefully. None of these problems arise with the other chamber of Parliament, the House of Commons. Judges cannot be members of the Commons.

Whilst Parliament cannot question or influence the work of the judiciary save by legislating, it can exercise some influence over the operation of the legal system as a whole. This is because the executive ie the government, is answerable to Parliament. Indeed, if it cannot command majority support in the House of Commons, the government will fall. As the government is responsible for the administration of the legal system, it must answer questions about the system in Parliament. Government members such as the Home Secretary, the Attorney-General and the Lord Chancellor may be questioned about those aspects of the legal system for which they take political responsibility. However, the extent of their political responsibility is determined by the complex relationship of executive and legal system.

The executive and the legal system

The constitutional compromise of our system is nowhere better seen than in the roles of the Lord Chancellor and the Attorney-General. The Lord Chancellor has a foot in all three camps. He is the head of the judiciary, presiding over the House of Lords and being the theoretical head of both the Chancery Division and the Court of Appeal. He is a member of the legislature, chairing the debates of the House of Lords. But his main activity is as a prominent member of the Government. He is their chief legal spokesman and normally a Cabinet Minister. He is responsible for the operation of the Civil Justice System – it was in this context that John Major's Lord Chancellor, Lord Mackay, commissioned the 1995 Woolf Report on Access to Justice in the civil court which is discussed later in the book (see post, p 62). He is also responsible for appointing both judges and magistrates although in the case of appellate court judges it is the Prime Minister who makes the actual appointment after advice from the Lord

Chancellor. He can be questioned about his conduct in the House of Lords but given the gentile nature of that House, real probing is difficult. Furthermore, issues such as the system of judicial appointment which has been described as recalling the days of the 'Rotten Borough', can be protected from open discussion by invoking 'judicial independence' and the impropriety of doubting the impartiality or qualifications of the judiciary. The hazy line between the executive and the judiciary can provide an effective shroud. By way of contrast, executive appointments to the Supreme Court in the United States can be and are occasionally vetoed by the legislature.

The role of the Attorney-General is similarly ambiguous. His post involves serving both the interests of the government and those of the legal system as a whole. He is a member of the Government and acts as its chief legal adviser. It was in this capacity that he advised ministers to sign the immunity certificates in the Matrix Churchill prosecution of businessmen for exporting arms manufacturing equipment to Iraq. The immunity certificates covered evidence revealing that government agencies knew about the exports and were using the businessmen to gather intelligence about the Iraqi war machine. When the trial judge insisted on seeing the evidence, the truth was revealed, the prosecution collapsed and the Scott inquiry into the whole affair was established. Again, it was in this capacity that in 1987 he advised the government to take out an injunction against the BBC to stop them showing a film about the secret Zircon satellite. His broader public responsibility involves taking civil proceedings to enforce public rights eg in public nuisance cases, and on the criminal side, the supervision of prosecution policy. Thus he has overall responsibility for the way the Director of Public Prosecutions (commonly referred to as the DPP, and a civil servant rather than a politician) runs the prosecution system. Specifically, his consent is necessary for the prosecution of many sensitive offences such as those relating to terrorism, public order and state secrets. He may take an active role in prosecuting such offences. It was in this capacity that he decided to investigate the leaks which had led to the making of the Zircon film with a view to prosecuting the culprits. As the Zircon affair illustrates, there is a fine but important line between the Attorney's political and public responsibilities. The Attorney is normally a member of the House of Commons and is answerable to the House for both his own governmental responsibilities and those of the Lord Chancellor. He has a deputy who carries the title of Solicitor-General, and together they are referred to as the Law Officers of the Crown.

The third member of the executive carrying some responsibility for the legal system is the Home Secretary. His 'law and order' brief carries with it the conduct of the police, the working's of the magistrates' courts and the reform of the criminal law. He is frequently subject to vigorous questioning both in the House of Commons and before the Commons' Home Affairs Committee. It has been suggested that matters falling under the responsibility of the Lord Chancellor or the Law Officers might also be brought within the jurisdiction of this Committee so that there might be more effective parliamentary scrutiny, but the 'threat to judicial independence' seems to have blocked this proposal.

The European Communities and the legal system

Our membership of the European Communities has had an impact upon the legal system at two levels. It has added a new law-making body and a new mechanism for interpreting those laws. The European Communities Act of 1972 provides that all rights, obligations etc created by or arising under the EC Treaties are part of UK law. Later, in Chapter 7 (post, p 182), we consider European law-making in more detail, but in outline what this means is that the Community institutions such as the European Commission can make laws which apply within the UK. Legal disputes arising under the Treaties are resolved by the European Court of Justice, commonly referred to as the ECJ. This court has repeatedly held that Community laws must take precedence over the internal laws of a member state. If Parliament were to pass legislation inconsistent with a Community law, the ECJ would refuse to recognise that legislation and would find the United Kingdom to be in breach of the Treaties if the domestic legislation was applied rather than the Community law. The ECJ would regard Parliament and not the Community to be the subordinate body. English courts too, have accepted that they should apply Community law rather than a later inconsistent legislation if the inconsistency seemed to be accidental. In the leading 1989 decision in *Factortame Ltd v Secretary of State*, Lord Bridge justified this on the basis that the 1972 Act writes into each subsequent Act of Parliament an implied provision that it will take effect subject to directly effective Community law. This 'implied provision' approach leaves open the possibility that Parliament might deliberately legislate contrary to Community law and that if it chose to do so and made its intentions clear, the English courts would give effect to the domestic legislation leaving the UK to face the consequences of breaking the Treaties. The ultimate consequence would be expulsion from the Community and few issues might be felt to justify that price.

The ECJ has a second important role. It is a court to which questions of interpretation concerning Community law may, and in some cases, must be referred. The ECJ will rule on the interpretation and leave it to the national court to apply the ruling to the particular case before it. Thus in some cases questions of interpretation may be referred by our highest court, the House of Lords, to the ECJ. This does not mean that the ECJ is the highest court in our system. It functions as a court of reference rather than as part of our hierarchy of appeal courts. The nature of this distinction and the operation of the reference system are explained in more detail when we come to consider the court structure (see post, p 36).

Internal relationships: courts, judges and lawyers

The court structure has evolved gradually over the centuries. It lacks the neat appearance one might expect from a planned structure. One cannot make simple divisions between trial courts and appeal courts or criminal courts and civil courts. The same court may have both a trial and an appeal jurisdiction or both civil and criminal jurisdiction. The jurisdictions of different courts overlap. The complexity is compounded by the fact that the same judges can appear in different courts judging different types of case. Finally, there are rules about what type of lawyer can appear in which type of court. Our consideration of these internal relationships starts with the courts. The diagram of the court structure at page 46 presents untidy pattern. As the criminal side of the diagram is marginally less complex, that is where we will start.

Courts having criminal jurisdiction

MAGISTRATES' COURTS

All criminal prosecutions start in the magistrates' court. Those accused of the most serious crimes such as murder, rape and robbery can only be tried in the Crown Court and hence the magistrates' function is limited to holding proceedings to decide whether there is sufficient evidence to justify transferring the case to the Crown Court for trial (see further p 101). The trial in the Crown Court is started by the reading of an Indictment ie a formal charge, against the accused. Hence, trial in the Crown Court is known as 'Trial on Indictment' and these serious offences are referred to as 'offences triable only on indictment'. At the other end of the scale are 'offences triable only summarily'. These are the minor offences eg threatening behaviour. These can only have a summary ie relatively swift, trial in the magistrates' court. Most offences are 'triable either way' and we discuss later in chapter 4 the procedure used to decide whether the accused should be tried in the magistrates' court or transferred for trial to the Crown Court.

Criminal Proceedings against a young person, ie a person aged 10 to 17, must normally take place before a special sitting of the magistrates' court known as the Youth Court. The magistrates who sit must be specially qualified for dealing with juvenile cases and the procedure of the hearing is less formal. Youth courts also hear Care Proceedings brought by a local authority on such grounds as the child being beyond the control of its parents. Magistrates' courts also have jurisdiction in some family matters eg payment of maintenance where a couple separate, and when hearing these cases they are known as domestic courts.

There are two routes of appeal from a criminal trial in the magistrates' court. The convicted accused has a right to appeal against his conviction or sentence to the Crown Court which will then rehear the facts of case and substitute its own decision for that of the magistrates' court. This can result in an increased sentence for the accused! Secondly, either prosecution or accused may appeal on a question of law by asking the magistrates to 'state the case' on the question to the High Court for a decision. The 'case stated' is heard by judges of the Queen's Bench Division of the High Court. Normally High Court judges hear cases sitting alone but 'case stated' proceedings must be heard by at least two judges and the sitting of the two or often three judges is known as a Divisional Court. So 'case stated' proceedings are heard by the Queen's Bench judges of the High Court sitting in a Divisional Court but for convenience lawyers usually refer to this mouthful as a hearing by the Divisional Court. From the Divisional Court there may be a further appeal to the highest appeal court, the House of Lords, but only if the Divisional Court certifies that the question of law is one of public importance and the Lords give permission for the appeal to be heard.

In addition to the two appeal routes, there is a third method of challenging the decisions of the magistrates' court. This is by an application for judicial review by the High Court. This procedure enables the High Court to review the proceedings of all inferior courts and tribunals to ensure that they have followed the rules of natural justice by giving a fair hearing, and have not acted outside their powers. As the magistrates' court has limited jurisdiction, it is classed as an inferior court. Either the prosecution or the accused may apply for judicial review. For example, the prosecution might apply on the ground that the magistrates' court had acted outside its powers in deciding to try a serious case itself rather than committing it to the Crown Court. The accused might apply on the ground that the prosecution had failed to tell him about a witness who would have supported the defence case and that as a result, he did not have a fair hearing. The application for judicial review is heard by the Divisional Court and if it upholds the complaint it will 'quash' ie cancel, the decision of the magistrates' court and order it to rehear the case. This procedure looks like an appeal. Technically it is not. In an appeal, the appeal court substitutes its own decision for that of the trial court. In judicial review, the reviewing court quashes the decision of the trial court and instructs it to do its job again.

Challenges to the magistrates' court present a complex pattern. As a generalisation it might be said that challenges to the sentence or conviction on the grounds of insufficient evidence, go to the Crown Court; those on the ground that the law was misunderstood, go to the Divisional Court by 'case stated'; and those on the ground that the wrong procedure was followed, go to the Divisional Court through judicial review. Whether the distinctions between the three types of challenge justify three different procedures is another question.

THE CROWN COURT

The Crown Court hears appeals from the magistrates' court. It also deals with transfers for sentence from the magistrates' court. These arise when the magistrates feel that their maximum six month sentencing power is insufficient, given what they have been told after the trial about the accused's background, previous convictions etc. (They will not normally be given this information before the trial for that might bias them against the accused.) Appeals and sentencing transfers from the magistrates' court are heard by a judge of the Crown Court often sitting with a small panel of magistrates who are supposed to contribute to the assessment of the appeal and learn from the experience.

Although its appeal and sentencing work is important, the main function of the Crown Court is to deal with those who are transferred for trial on Indictment by the magistrates' court. Trial on Indictment is conducted before a judge and jury. A High Court judge will try the most serious cases with lesser ones being tried by circuit judges who are full time judges or recorders who are solicitors or barristers appointed to act part time. The jury decides on whether the accused is guilty and the judge sentences if he is found guilty. The accused has a right to appeal to the Court of Appeal on a question of pure law eg an incorrect definition of the offence by the judge, but needs the permission or 'leave' of that court to appeal against the sentence or on grounds that involve the facts eg that the identification evidence was too weak to justify conviction. Furthermore, the Court of Appeal will only set aside a jury's conviction on the basis of insufficient evidence where it is clear that the conviction is 'unsafe or unsatisfactory'. To allow an appeal on lesser doubts might undermine respect for the institution of the jury. Only the accused can appeal to the Court of Appeal but from there, either side may appeal on a point of law to the House of Lords provided the Court of Appeal certifies the point as one of general public importance and that Court or the Lords grant leave to appeal. After these rights of appeal have been exhausted, it is still open to an independent body, the Criminal Cases Review Commission, to refer any conviction or sentence to an appeal.

THE COURT OF APPEAL

The same Court of Appeal hears appeals in both criminal and civil cases but it is organised into a Criminal Division and a Civil Division and the type of judge sitting in the court varies with the division. The ordinary members of the court are called Lords Justice of Appeal. Three Lords Justice will normally make up a sitting of the Civil Division with the more important sittings often headed by the president of the Civil Division who is the Master of the Rolls. The Criminal Division is presided over by the Lord Chief Justice. He frequently sits with two High Court judges. If the Lord Chief Justice is not available, a Lord Justice will sit with the High

Court judges. The reason for summoning High court judges to sit in the Criminal Division is obvious: they have a routine familiarity with criminal trials and in particular, current sentencing trends.

THE HOUSE OF LORDS

The House of Lords hears appeals from the Criminal and Civil Divisions of the Court of Appeal. It also hears appeals from 'case stated' decisions of the High Court and from the civil jurisdiction of the High Court where there are grounds for 'leapfrogging' the Court of Appeal ie missing it out of the stages of appeal. These grounds will be considered later. Finally, it hears appeals from the court system of Scotland and Northern Ireland. Their legal systems are separate from that of England and Wales. They have their own trial and appeal courts but they are joined at the top by having the House of Lords as the final appeal court.

An appeal to the House of Lords is usually heard by judges called Lords of Appeal in Ordinary or 'Law Lords' for short. The Lord Chancellor and Peers who have held high judicial office are also entitled to sit. In *R v Shivpuri* (1986), the criminal attempt case discussed at the end of Chapter 6, the court was made up of two Lords of Appeal in Ordinary, the Lord Chancellor, an ex-Lord Chancellor and a retired Law Lord. There may have been special reasons for having only two regular Law Lords in that hearing (read the background to the case) but it is not unusual for one member of the court in a hearing to be drafted from the ranks of the retired. A minimum of three Lords must hear an appeal but normally five Lords make up a sitting or 'Appeal Committee' as it is known. Each member of the Appeal Committee votes on the decision and is entitled to write a judgment which in this court is usually referred to as a 'speech' or an 'opinion'. It is an increasingly common practice for one member of the court to write an opinion justifying the decision with the others agreeing and only writing their own opinions if they vote against the majority decision. But in controversial cases such as *Gillick*, the under-age contraception case discussed in Chapter 8, one may find all the members writing lengthy opinions. *Gillick* illustrates one other point: Mrs Gillick's argument was rejected by the High Court Judge, supported by the three Lords Justice in the Court of Appeal and finally rejected by three votes to two in the Lords. Overall, a majority of judges supported her case but she lost by one vote in the crucial decision in the Lords. This may seem unfair but the appeal process has to stop somewhere, some court has to take the final decision.

Some critics have argued that the Court of Appeal can take the final decision and the system has no need for a second appeal to a third level court like the House of Lords. Others argue that the House of Lords should be 'judged' on its contribution to the system as a whole rather than to particular appeals. Being made up of only ten or so ordinary members, the House of Lords can give consistent leadership to lower courts which arguably, the Court of Appeal with its much higher membership, could not do. Of course, quality of leadership is also important and this leads to one final comment in relation to criminal appeals. In the House of Lords unlike the Court of Appeal, there is no functional specialisation. A criminal appeal may come before any group of five Law Lords. Criticism of the quality of their decisions in criminal appeals may not be unconnected with this lack of specialisation. The role of the House of Lords is discussed further in Chapter 6.

Courts having civil jurisdiction

In the case of courts having criminal jurisdiction, it is the appeal system that is complex. The trial system is simple to explain; all cases start in the magistrates' court and the more serious are committed for trial in the Crown Court. In the case of courts having civil jurisdiction the position is the reverse. The appeal systems are relatively straightforward but there is no simple pattern to the trial courts, no pattern of all cases starting in the same court. Instead there are a number of different courts having jurisdiction over different types of case and sometimes overlapping jurisdiction over the same type of case. The court with the widest jurisdiction is the High Court and this court with its appeal system will be considered first and then the role of the county court, magistrates' court and tribunals will be examined.

THE HIGH COURT

The High Court resulted from the nineteenth century merger of the older royal courts, courts with such Dickensian names as Chancery, Common Pleas and Exchequer. The High Court has unlimited jurisdiction over all civil claims except those which legislation has directed to be heard by specialist tribunals. It is staffed by some 100 or so High Court judges who are also known as Puisne judges – pronounced 'puny' and meaning 'junior'. Their task is anything but 'puny'. Civil trials are conducted by these judges sitting alone. With the exception of the rare cases where a jury is used eg libel cases, a single High Court judge will determine both the facts and law in the case before him. He has a position of great power and responsibility. To enable the judges to specialise somewhat, the work of the Court is split into three divisions, Queen's Bench, Family, and Chancery. Most sittings of the High Court take place in London but there are regular sittings in the major provincial centres. One final point of terminology: the nineteenth century merger legislation also created a new Court of Appeal to hear appeals from the new High Court and the legislation referred to the two new courts together as being the Supreme Court. Thus our Supreme Court is quite different in nature from that in the USA where it is the final appellate court. Here, the House of Lords performs that function.

Family

The Family Division is the smallest division with a President and 15 or so judges (in 1990 two of these judges were female and with one female judge in Chancery, three in Queen's Bench and one on the Court of Appeal, they break the otherwise male hegemony of the senior judiciary). The Division hears cases concerned with children eg wardship, adoption and guardianship, but its main business consists of defended divorce cases and related matters such as disputes over the division of family property or the access to children. These related matters are often dealt with by district judges attached to the Family Division.

Chancery

Chancery is the next largest in size with 18 or so High Court judges under the leadership of the Vice-Chancellor who deputises for the nominal head of the division, the Lord Chancellor. In the old independent Court of Chancery, the Lord Chancellor was the sole judge and under the influence of a line of great Chancellors the complex doctrines of equity were developed by the court. The concept of the trust is its best known legacy and still of great importance from a tax viewpoint. But equitable principles stretch much further, underlying much of the modern law of property and succession as well as influencing areas of law such as contract which are primarily based on the ideas of the common law. With the nineteenth century merger of the independent Chancery and common law courts into the High Court, equity and the common law were no longer treated as separate systems of law to be applied by separate courts. All Divisions of the High Court are to apply the principles of both equity and the common law with those of equity pre-vailing where there is conflict. However, the cases assigned to the Chancery Division mainly concern property, succession and taxation and hence Chancery judges are more likely to be applying principles of law based on equity than the common law. To that extent, the judges can develop an expertise in equity.

Queen's Bench

Queen's Bench is the largest division with more than 60 judges headed by the Lord Chief Justice. In London, they are assisted by court officials known as Masters who decide most of the interlocutory matters ie matters arising before the hearing of the case such as the exchange of documentary evidence between the two sides. They have the role of a judge in relation to the matters they decide. Indeed, the officials who do the job of Masters in the provincial High Court centres, are known as district judges. The division has jurisdiction over civil claims not assigned to the other two divisions. This means that contract and tort cases normally go to the

Queen's Bench. All such claims for more than £50,000 and all defamation claims (which require jury trial) must be tried in the High Court. All claims below £25,000 and all personal injury claims below £50,000 must be tried in the less formal county court and not the High Court. Non-personal injury claims between £25,000 and £50,000 are triable either way but, unlike the case with either way criminal offences, it is for the courts and not the parties to decide which is the most appropriate trial forum.

There are two specialist areas within the general jurisdiction of the Queen's Bench Division: Claims involving ships or aircraft and particularly those arising from collisions, go to the Admiralty Court those involving the commercial markets and the traders, shippers, bankers insurers etc who operate in them, go to the Commercial Court. These two courts are not independent. They are organisational sub-divisions of the Queen's Bench Division of the High Court. As such, they have been able to develop specialist procedures suited to the type of case involved and the Queen's Bench judges assigned to them have been able to develop specialist expertise in the areas of law involved. A final sub-division within Queen's Bench is that of the Divisional Court whose role in respect of 'case stated' appeals and judicial review has already been noted.

Appeals

Any case decided by any Division of the High Court may be appealed to the Civil Division of the Court of Appeal. Whether the ground of the appeal is that the trial judge got the law wrong or the facts wrong, the losing party has a right to appeal. No permission is necessary. In practice, appeals are expensive and, with the loser of the appeal normally having to pay the winner's costs, most parties will think carefully before appealing particularly if the only ground is that the judge got the facts wrong. The Court of Appeal is generally reluctant to over-turn the trial judge's findings of fact. The reason for this is that unlike the Crown Court hearing appeals on the facts from magistrates' courts, the Court of Appeal does not hold a complete rehearing of the case. It examines the transcript of the trial. It does not rehear the witnesses. Hence, it is not in any position to over-turn the trial judge's view of who was telling the truth etc. The most it can do is decide whether the trial judge drew the right inferences from what the witnesses said. The appeal will normally be heard by three Lords Justice, although in cases raising particularly difficult issues of principle and practice such as *Davis v Johnson* (1979), the case concerning the domestic violence legislation considered later in the book (post, p 154), the head of the Civil Division ie the Master of the Rolls, has been known to summon a court of five Lords Justice.

From decisions of the Civil Division of the Court of Appeal a further appeal on questions of law or fact may be made to the House of Lords. But at this stage there is no right to appeal. The party wishing to appeal must obtain 'leave' ie permission, from the Court of Appeal or the House of Lords itself. Permission is less likely to be granted if the decision of the Court of Appeal judges was unanimous or the ground of appeal is one of fact rather than law. In one situation an appeal on a point of law can be made direct from the High Court to the House of Lords, leapfrogging the Court of Appeal. This can be done where the High Court judge concerned certifies that the point of law was one of public importance and one on which he was bound to take the view that he did because a previous decision of the Court of Appeal or House of Lords had stated that this was the view to be taken. In this situation there would be no point appealing to the Court of Appeal for it too would be bound to follow the same view and reject the appeal. Only the House of Lords has the freedom to decide the point in a different way and hence if the appealing party will be taking the point to the Lords anyway, it makes sense to allow him to leapfrog the Court of Appeal thus saving time and expense. The point of the 'leapfrog' should become a little clearer after you have studied the rules of binding precedent (see post, p 149).

THE COUNTY COURT

The county courts were established in the nineteenth century to provide a cheap local means of deciding minor civil claims. Today there are some 300 county courts. They have jurisdiction over claims of up to £50,000 in common law matters such as personal injuries or contract, and of up to £30,000 on equity matters such as those relating to mortgages. Cases are tried by circuit judges. These are the same judges who try middle range criminal cases in the Crown Court. In the Crown Court they sit with a jury but in the county court they hear civil cases sitting alone. There is a special arbitration procedure for non-personal injury claims below £3,000 and personal injury claims below £1,000. The nature of this procedure will be described later but here it may be noted that the arbitration is frequently conducted not by a circuit judge but by a district judge of the court. Some 170 of the courts are designated as a 'divorce county court' and have jurisdiction to hear undefended divorces and also cases concerning adoption and guardianship although here again the jurisdiction overlaps with that of the High Court.

Appeals on law or fact lie to the Civil Division of the Court of Appeal but permission to appeal is generally necessary where the claim is at the lower end of the court's jurisdiction. Appeals from a Registrar's decision have to go first to a circuit judge sitting in the particular county court. From the Court of Appeal there may be a further appeal with leave to the House of Lords. The 'leapfrog' provision does not apply to appeals from the county court so there is no way of cutting out the middle stage in an appeal even if it is bound to end up in the House of Lords. As the county court is an inferior court ie one of limited jurisdiction, it is theoretically subject to judicial review in the same way as a magistrates' court but in practice little use is made of this alternative to appeal.

MAGISTRATES' COURTS

Magistrates' courts have to be considered in this section because they have a civil jurisdiction over domestic matters such as maintenance orders or the guardianship and adoption orders. Their jurisdiction overlaps considerably with that of the county court and High Court. Some uniformity of approach is encouraged by the fact that appeals from this jurisdiction of the magistrates' court have to go to the Family Division of the High Court, but this does not solve all the problems resulting from the overlapping jurisdictions. Depending on the court chosen, the same type of case may be dealt with by a different procedure and in some cases, by different substantive law. In 1974 the Finer Committee recommended the establishment of a single Family Court to bring all family issues under a common jurisdiction, procedure and substantive law. The single court recommendation was not accepted but the rationalisation of much of the law and procedure has been accomplished by the Children Act of 1989.

TRIBUNALS

There are over 50 different types of tribunal each with its own limited jurisdiction over a particular type of claim. Both the tribunals and the claims they consider are the product of legislation. The interventionist philosophy which prevailed until recently, resulted in an ever increasing number of legislative schemes designed to regulate relations between social groups such as employers and employees or between the state and its citizens as in the welfare system. Inevitably the administration of these schemes will produce disputes, eg an employee may claim that her dismissal was not legally justified under the term of the employment legislation or a welfare claimant may claim that the reduction in his benefit was not legally justified under the terms of the welfare legislation. The legislation could provide that such disputes should be settled by ordinary courts and this has been done in some cases, eg cases under the Domestic Violence Act 1976, which was passed primarily to protect women from such violence, are heard by the county court. But in many situations it has been felt that the ordinary courts lack the necessary expertise or are too formal, slow and costly to hear claims arising under a particular scheme and hence the legislation has established a tribunal to do the job. Many tribunals have expert assessors sitting alongside a legally experienced chairman to make up the judging panel. Thus an industrial tribunal which hears unfair dismissal cases consists of a lawyer, usually an experienced solicitor, sitting with one person drawn from a panel of TUC nominees and another drawn from a CBI panel. The industrial tribunals function in a fairly formal way but many tribunals particularly those dealing with welfare claims, are very informal in approach.

Little else can be said about tribunals by way of generalisation. They vary enormously in the caseload handled from the welfare tribunals handling over 100,000 cases a year to the Crofters Commission handling less than 100 a year. There is no consistency in the nomenclature: most tribunals are called tribunals but some are called 'commissions', others are called 'committees' eg the Education Appeal Committee which is a tribunal hearing appeals against the allocation of school places, others still are called 'courts' eg the Local Valuation Courts which hear appeals against rating assessments. Their legal function also varies. Some such as the industrial tribunal apply a fairly complex set of legal rules to the facts of cases, others such as the Education Appeal Committee have few rules and a lot of discretion in reaching their decisions. Their appeal systems usually match their caseload and function. Thus, there is no appeal from the Education Appeal Committee but from the industrial tribunal either side may appeal on law to the Employment Appeal Tribunal, a very formal body made up of High Court judges, and from there a further appeal lies to the Court of Appeal. Most tribunals will come between these two extremes, having some appeal system but perhaps not as formal as that for the industrial tribunals. One common feature of almost all tribunals however, is that they are subject to judicial review by the High Court. The Tribunals and Inquiries Act of 1958 required most tribunals to give reasons for their decisions and this gives judicial review something on which to bite: it will often be clear from the reasons given that the tribunal has exceeded its statutory powers by taking a decision on the wrong grounds and in that case its decision can be 'quashed' on review. The same 1958 legislation established a Council on Tribunals to act as a watchdog over tribunals, checking that their procedures are characterised by 'openness, fairness and impartiality'. But it is a watchdog with a bark and no bite. It has no power and can only advise the government of problems. In the words of one leading commentator, its role is 'inconspicuous'.

One final comment on tribunals: from the point of view of the ordinary citizen they are among the most important courts in the country but from the point of view of the lawyer they are perhaps the least important element in the court system. Lawyers rarely appear before many of the tribunals and as a result are not familiar with the kind of law they apply or procedures they employ. The reasons for this are complex, in part it may be due to the 'trivial' nature of the claims, in part to the lack of legal aid from the state to pay for lawyers services in tribunal work, in part to an attitude that law and lawyers have little role to play in the tribunal system.

Courts having influence but no jurisdiction

This rather odd classification is used to group four courts whose decisions may influence law in England, although they have no jurisdiction within the English legal system. The four courts are the Privy Council, the International Court of Justice, the European Court of Human Rights and the European Court of Justice.

THE PRIVY COUNCIL

It is not strictly true to say the Privy Council has no jurisdiction within our system for it does hear appeals from church courts and certain professional disciplinary bodies such as the General Medical Council. But its main role is to act as the final appeal court for the legal systems of some 25 of the smaller Commonwealth countries. Membership of the Judicial Committee of the Privy Council to give its full title, is limited to the Lord Chancellor, the Law Lords and privy councillors who hold judicial office in Commonwealth countries, eg six New Zealand judges are members. The Privy Council hears both criminal and civil appeals and its decision is binding on the Commonwealth court from which the appeal has come. It is not binding on any other Commonwealth country. Nor does it bind the English courts. But because the decision is given by largely the same judges who sit in the House of Lords, it does provide good guidance as to how they might decide a similar case on appeal from an English court. Hence its decisions are influential within the English legal system. But that influence is declining as the number of countries which use it as a final appeal court declines. India, Canada and many other Commonwealth countries have cut the link with the Privy Council, sometimes for symbolic reasons to assert the end of the colonial era, and sometimes simply because they have adequate legal resources to staff their own appeal systems.

THE INTERNATIONAL COURT OF JUSTICE

This court, established by the United Nations Treaty, sits in the Hague and is staffed by 15 eminent judges drawn from around the world. Indeed, is often called the 'World Court'. Despite these credentials it might well be said that it has neither jurisdiction nor influence. Its jurisdiction is limited to hearing disputes between states on questions of International law where both states consent to the hearing – not a common occurrence. Its decisions bind only the states and are enforceable if at all through the international community and not through the domestic courts of the states concerned. Thus, were the court to rule that our government had wrongly nationalised a foreign firm without compensation, neither that firm nor the state which brought the case on its behalf, would be able to enforce the judgment in the English courts. However, international law which is based on custom is usually regarded as being automatically part of English law. It is a source of English law. Hence, inasmuch as a judgment of the World Court establishes the customary international law on a particular point it could conceivably be said to have some influence over an English court.

THE EUROPEAN COURT OF HUMAN RIGHTS

This court was established by the European Convention on Human Rights, a Treaty signed in 1950 by 21 European States including the UK. The court which sits in Strasbourg, has a judge from each state. Under the terms of the Treaty the signatory states undertook to secure to everyone within their jurisdiction certain defined civil and political rights. Where one state alleges that another has broken the Treaty, the allegation is investigated by the European Commission of Human Rights and from there the case may be taken to the court if the state concerned has accepted the compulsory jurisdiction of the court. Almost all the signatory states have done this and most including the UK have also made an additional declaration that they will accept jurisdiction where the complaint is made by an individual as well as a state. The Treaty leaves enforcement of the court's judgments to political pressure.

Unlike customary international law, the international law established by a particular Treaty is not part of English law even thought the Treaty has been signed by the UK. Its provisions only become part of English law if they have been enacted in an English statute. This has been done in some cases, eg the European Communities Act 1972 enacts into English law the provisions of the Community Treaties. But it has not been done in the case of the Human Rights Treaty. Thus although the Treaty contains a 'Right to Privacy', this is not part of English law and when in 1979 an English judge had to consider the legality of telephone tapping by the police he disregarded the Treaty right to privacy and followed the English common law in holding the tapping to be lawful. But the affronted citizen took his complaint to the Commission. From there it went to the court where the UK was held to be in breach of the Treaty. Fear of the political repercussions swiftly led the UK government to introduce legislation controlling police tapping. This is just one of several instances of legislation being introduced to meet a judgment of the court. Clearly this court has a considerable influence over the development of English law and the operation of the English legal system.

THE EUROPEAN COURT OF JUSTICE

The role of this court which sits in Luxembourg, is to decide questions and disputes arising from the operation of the European Communities. Because the Communities system has been enacted into English law by the 1972 Act, the rulings of this court unlike the Human Rights Court, have direct authority within the English legal system. The court is an integral part of our legal system and not just an influential spectator. However, its original jurisdiction is limited. It hears disputes between member states and also between the states and Community Institutions such as the Commission. But an individual can only originate a case in the court when challenging the legality of Community decisions which affect him. This jurisdiction is rather similar to that of the High Court when conducting a judicial review of the validity of decisions given by inferior bodies in the UK. Its main influence stems not from this jurisdiction but rather from its role in deciding questions of Community law referred to it by national courts. The Treaty provides that any court or tribunal may refer such a question to the ECJ if it considers that 'a decision on that question is necessary to enable it to give judgement' and that such a reference must be made if the national court is one from which there is no further appeal. Thus the Court of Appeal would normally have a discretion in deciding whether to make a reference but the House of Lords would not. The object of this reference system is to attain uniformity of interpretation of the law throughout the Community. Clearly it would be absurd if the English courts were interpreting and applying a Community provision in one way, the French courts in another, the Germans in a third way etc. The reference system is designed to overcome this problem. Whether the question of interpretation arises in an English, French or German court, it should be referred to enable the ECJ to give an authoritative ruling. The ruling itself will be given to the national court referring the question and that court will then apply the ruling to the case before it and reach a decision on that case; but the ruling will also guide all other national courts in how to answer the particular question. It should be clear from this, that the ECJ does not function as a Court of Appeal. It does not substitute its own decisions for those of a lower court. It is a Court of Reference and as such it will assist a national court at any level in reaching a decision but the actual decision remains the responsibility of the national court.

The success of the reference system obviously depends upon the co-operation of the national courts. In the early days of our membership, English courts showed a certain reluctance to make references and English lawyers certainly lacked familiarity with the court and its procedures. The court does have an unfamiliar look to it: It consists of judges nominated by each of the member states but those eleven judges are assisted by five Advocates-General. Their task is to write an opinion on the arguments presented in a case before the court and suggest a ruling that the judges might adopt. In the majority of cases, the opinion of the Advocate-General is followed by the court and often their lengthy opinions are rather more helpful to legal advisers than the typically terse judgment delivered by the court itself.

The judges

In describing the courts we have said something about the different types of judges. In this section we will consider the judges in more detail. Two features of the judiciary should be clear from the diagram on p 47. First, there is no great distinction between criminal and civil judges. Most types of professional judge work in both criminal and civil courts. Secondly, judges are organised on a hierarchical basis. There are first and second division appeal judges and trial judges. There is a minor league taking in the tribunals and stipendiary magistrates, and a large amateur league of lay tribunal members, magistrates and jurors. In many continental legal systems where there are similar judicial hierarchies, a judge will begin his career in a bottom division and, depending upon his ability, gradually work his way up through the divisions. Our system does not have a judicial career structure of this kind. Unlike their continental colleagues, our professional judges are not career judges. A continental judge will frequently choose to be a judge at the outset of his legal career. He will be appointed to a minor court at an early age and will acquire experience of the inquisitorial technique of judging as he climbs through the hierarchy. Our judges are appointed in middle life after having acquired years of experience as a barrister, or in the case of the lower judiciary, as a barrister or solicitor. Such experience is thought to be an essential qualification for judging in an adversary system. Once appointed to a post, they will frequently remain there until retirement. A promotion ladder really only operates at the lower levels from recorder to circuit judge, and at the higher levels from High Court judge to Lord Justice in the Court of Appeal and from there to Lord of Appeal in the House of Lords. High fliers have been known to reach the House of Lords within ten years of their High Court appointment. But few High Court judges will be promoted to the Court of Appeal and fewer still will be promoted from there to the House of Lords. Promotion is the exception. We will start our section on judges at the top and work down.

LORDS OF APPEAL IN ORDINARY

They are appointed by the Prime Minister after consultation with the Lord Chancellor. They sit in the House of Lords and because that court hears appeals from Scottish as well as English courts, two of the eleven Lords are normally appointed from the Scottish Judiciary. The remainder will normally have been Lords Justice of Appeal before promotion. Theoretically, they are presided over by the Lord Chancellor who is also a member of the Court of Appeal and head of the Chancery Division of the High Court. In addition he carries heavy political and administrative responsibilities (see ante, p 22). Not surprisingly, all this prevents him from playing much of an active role in the House of Lords, although the Lord Chancellor for most of the 1990s, Lord Mackay, did take part in a number of cases eg *Pepper v Hart*, the case on the use of Parliamentary debates discussed in Chapter 6.

LORDS JUSTICE OF APPEAL

They sit in the Court of Appeal and are appointed in the same way as Lords of Appeal. They will normally have had a spell as a High Court judge before promotion. The Criminal Division of the Court of Appeal is presided over by The Lord Chief Justice. He is next in judicial rank to the Lord Chancellor, and he also presides over the Queen's Bench Division of the High Court. He is appointed on the recommendation of the Prime Minister after consultation with the Lord Chancellor. He has no political role and hence, unlike the Lord Chancellor, will remain in post when governments change. The present occupant, Sir Thomas Bingham, and his immediate predecessors have all shown their ability for the post through a successful career as a Lord Justice. The position and status of the Lord Chief Justice give him a key role in the development of the criminal law through case decisions.

The Civil Division of the Court of Appeal is presided over by the Master of the Rolls. He was originally the keeper of the rolls or records of the Chancery Court but later became a judge in that court. He is president of the Civil Division, largely because at the time that court was created in the nineteenth century the then occupant of the position was the best civil judge available and the obvious man to preside over the new court. The status of Master of the Rolls enables the judge to play the same role in developing the civil law as does the Lord Chief Justice in respect of criminal law. Lord Denning did that during his long tenure through the 1960s and 1970s. His successor Lord Donaldson MR was perhaps more interested in developing the efficient management of the court system than in developing the substantive law. The present incumbent, Lord Woolf, seems to combine both interests. The Master of the Rolls is appointed in the same way as the Lord Chief Justice and although some of his predecessors moved to the post from the rank of a Lord Justice, Lord Woolf moved from being a Law Lord.

HIGH COURT JUDGES

They sit in the High Court and also hear the most serious cases in the Crown Court. They are appointed on the recommendation of the Lord Chancellor and must have been barristers for at least ten years to be eligible for appointment. Solicitors cannot be appointed to the High Court Bench. The Lord Chief Justice heads the Queen's Bench Division of the High Court. The Chancery Division is headed by the Vice-Chancellor. The present occupant of the post is Sir Donald Nicholls. His predecessors were Sir Robert Megarry and Sir Nicholas Browne-Wilkinson, both known for the quality of their judgments. The Family Division is headed by the President of the Family Division. The judges of the High Court are supported in their work by Masters and Registrars of the Supreme Court. These are primarily administrative officers of the Court but they do judge some interlocutory matters, ie those arising before the full trial such as the disclosure of documents.

CIRCUIT JUDGES

They sit in the county court and also hear middle ranking criminal cases in the Crown Court. There are about 350 such judges. Six of them are appointed to conduct 'official referees' business which mainly consists of complex building disputes. These six are generally regarded as having a status above the rest but not as high as a High Court judge. All circuit judges are appointed on the recommendation of the Lord Chancellor but unlike High Court judiciary, being a barrister for ten years is not the sole means of qualifying for appointment. An alternative qualification is having held the office of recorder for five years and this means that solicitors can work their way up to the position of circuit judge.

DISTRICT JUDGES

They are attached to both the High Court and the county court and assist the judicial work of the courts particularly in relation to procedural matters.

RECORDERS

They are part-time judges of the Crown Court hearing the least serious criminal cases sent for jury trial in that court. They are appointed on the recommendation of the Lord Chancellor and qualify for appointment by having been a barrister or solicitor for ten years. If they make a success of their period as a recorder, promotion to the position of circuit judge is quite likely to follow. There are almost 500 recorders. Because of the pressure of cases on the Crown Court system, the Lord Chancellor now appoints assistant recorders to help out and in some cases may bring back a retired judge to the position of deputy circuit judge. There are now over 500 of these temporary assistants and deputies helping to keep the system going.

TRIBUNAL CHAIRMEN

These are generally appointed by the Lord Chancellor or the government department responsible for the area of administration concerned eg the DSS for welfare tribunals. Most tribunal chairmen are lawyers but unlike the higher judiciary, they may be selected from the ranks of the academics as well as practitioners.

STIPENDIARY MAGISTRATES

These are full-time professional magistrates appointed by the Lord Chancellor from those who have been barristers or solicitors for at least seven years. There are about 100 or so stipendiaries and they act as sole judge in their particular magistrates' courts which are mostly to be found in the large cities and London in particular. They rank at about the same level as Masters of the Supreme Court or Chairmen of the important tribunals.

LAY TRIBUNAL MEMBERS

In most tribunals a legally qualified chairman sits with two lay tribunal members who have an equal right to take part in deciding the cases. As with the chairmen, the lay members are generally appointed either by the Lord Chancellor or the responsible government department. In many cases they are appointed because they have some special experience of the type of problem that will be heard by the tribunal.

LAY MAGISTRATES

Otherwise known as justices of the peace, they sit in magistrates' courts generally in groups of three, and occasionally in the Crown Court with a judge to hear appeals. They are appointed by the Lord Chancellor on the recommendations of a local advisory committee which interviews candidates who in turn are usually put forward by the local political parties. No knowledge of the law is required for appointment and although they are given some limited training after appointment, their role is essentially to bring lay experience to the job of judging. Although they are advised on matters of law by a justices' clerk, they alone decide the facts, the law and the sentence. The 25,000 part-time lay magistrates, trying over 90% of all criminal cases, undoubtedly form the backbone of our criminal justice system.

JURIES

Juries are a group of twelve laymen who judge the factual question of guilt or innocence in Crown Court trials. They are also used to judge the facts in civil cases where there is an allegation of fraud or libel against one party. High Court judges have a discretion to use a jury in other civil cases but their use is almost unheard of. Jury members are selected at random from those on the electoral register.

ARBITRATORS

Arbitration is a private means of settling a dispute. It does not form part of the public legal system although legislation provides that the arbitrators' award may be enforced in the same way as a High Court judgment and may be appealed to the High Court on a point of law provided the parties agree to the appeal or the court gives permission. The parties choose their own arbitrator and pay him for his work. He works in accordance with the terms of reference set by the parties. He is in effect, a private judge.

Arbitration is widely used for settling commercial disputes. The reasons for parties choosing private arbitration rather than public litigation will be examined later.

The lawyers

The picture of the internal structure of the legal system is completed by a brief description of those who provide legal services. Fuller discussion will be found in Chapter 5. We will consider first, the two types of lawyers in private practice, barristers and solicitors; then, the most important group of public service lawyers, the Crown Prosecutors; and finally, the range of 'para-legals' who provide specialist services of one kind or another.

BARRISTERS

Barristers have the right to argue cases in all courts from the lowest to the highest. Each barrister practices on his own, sharing neither his work nor his income. However, they usually share a set of offices known as chambers, and will all contribute to common expenses such as the employment of secretaries and a managing clerk who plays an important role in organising the work of his barristers. Cases are brought to barristers by solicitors. The solicitor may come to the barrister for specialist advice on a case or to retain him to conduct a case in court – this is known as 'briefing the barrister'. Sometimes the solicitor will go directly to one particular barrister and sometimes he will go to the managing clerk and ask for the work to be passed to a suitable member of the chambers. A layman cannot go directly to a barrister, he must go to a solicitor who will consult the barrister on behalf of his client and chaperone his client at any meeting with the barrister. This system is supposed to protect the barrister from being over-influenced by his client, thus enabling him to take a detached view of the case and, if the case goes to court, present the facts fairly without distortion.

SOLICITORS

Solicitors normally practice in partnerships some of which are very large, employing many assistant solicitors and hundreds of support staff worldwide. They deal directly with lay clients and may now advertise their services. Much of their work for clients is not concerned with litigation but rather with organising the legal affairs of the client, his conveyancing, will, company and tax structure etc. If this work is very complex or financially very significant, the solicitor is likely to take advice from a specialist barrister. Normally, the solicitor will have to retain a barrister if his client is involved in a case in the Crown Court, High Court or appeal courts for the solicitor himself has no general right of audience in these courts ie he cannot present his client's case. He can appear for his client in the lower courts but may well decide to retain a barrister to do the job. The barrister is likely to have had more experience at appearing before a judge but also an appearance in court may disrupt the solicitor's office routine.

Not surprisingly there are far more solicitors than barristers, about 55,000 as opposed to 6,000 barristers. But the Bar remains the elite of the legal profession. With the limited exception of recorders and circuit judges, the judiciary must be drawn from the Bar. The Bar maintains a separate training and apprenticeship system and is steeped in traditions of one kind or another. The division of the legal profession into barristers and solicitors is pretty well unique to the English legal system. Comparable common law countries have a single legal profession. Whether anything other than tradition justifies the divided profession with its separate system of qualification etc is an issue to be considered at length in Chapter 5.

CROWN PROSECUTORS

The Crown Prosecution Service was established by statute in 1985 following the recommendations of a Royal Commission on Criminal Procedure. The function of Crown Prosecutors is to take over the prosecution of cases which have been initiated by the police. Previously the police had been responsible for both the decision whether to prosecute a suspect and the conduct of the prosecution itself. They had to engage lawyers for cases going to the Crown Court and often used them to prosecute in the magistrates' court as well, but the lawyers acted for the police and it was up to the police to decide whether to drop a case for lack of evidence. Now, once the police have taken the decision to prosecute and started the proceedings in the magistrates' court, the case will be taken over by the independent Crown Prosecution Service. They will decide how or whether to pursue the prosecution.

The Service is headed by the Director of Public Prosecutions (DPP) and organised around 29 local areas each headed by a Chief Crown Prosecutor and employing a large number of prosecutors. Prosecutors can be barristers or solicitors but only those that are qualified as barristers will be able to conduct cases in the Crown Court and consequently the Service will still need to engage outside barristers to conduct most Crown Court cases. All prosecutors work under a Code of Guidance issued by the DPP. In addition, the police must refer evidence in the most serious cases eg murder, or sensitive cases eg rape or abortion, to the DPP so that he can decide whether prosecution of a suspect is justified. The DPP also has the power to stop prosecutions commenced by the police or by private individuals.

PARA-LEGALS

Para-legals is a term used to describe those other than private firms of solicitors, who provide legal services of one kind or another. A variety of persons and organisations can be listed under this heading:

Licensed conveyancers are licensed to carry out conveyancing. The licensing system was created by legislation passed in 1985. Prior to this legislation, only solicitors were permitted to carry out conveyancing work for a fee. Now they have to share their monopoly with licensed conveyancers.

Law centres provide free legal advice to citizens living in the locality of the centre. Centres are usually situated in areas where there are few private solicitors eg deprived inner city areas. The centres handle the kind of problems faced by people living in those areas eg welfare and housing cases. The large centres employ full-time lawyers to give the advice. Others operate on a part-time basis usually in the evenings and are staffed by volunteer lawyers. These smaller centres are usually referred to as Legal Advice Centres.

The Citizens Advice Bureaux offers both legal and financial advice on all matters to members of the public. It also assists members of the public before tribunals.

Other agencies such as Consumer or Housing Advice Agencies, offer advice to the public on one particular type of problem. Some other bodies offer legal advice to just their members eg Trade Unions, the AA, the Consumer Association.

Representation agencies provide people to represent those involved in certain types of case, usually cases coming before tribunals. The Child Poverty Action Group and Claimants' Unions are the best know examples of agencies providing a representation service. Such a service cannot operate in the higher courts as only barristers have rights of audience and it is doubtful whether there is much scope for it to operate in the lower courts such as the magistrates' or county courts. This issue is discussed further in Chapter 5.

Postscript: who is in charge of the administration of the court system?

The ten years up to 1996 have seen a series of radical proposals to improve the efficiency of the legal system. A scrutiny of the legal aid system in 1986 led to major changes in the Legal Aid Act of 1988 and a further Green Paper in 1995 suggests more changes for the late 1990s. The 1989 Green Paper on the legal profession was quickly followed by a White Paper and then the Courts and Legal Services Act 1990 which introduced a new organisational structure. Both these developments are discussed in detail in Chapter 5. In 1985 the Civil Justice Review was established to examine the organisation and procedures of the civil courts. Some of its proposals were implemented by the Courts and Legal Services Act. The interim Woolf Report in 1995 has proposed further radical changes to improve the delivery of civil justice and a further, final report is awaited. In the next chapter we will consider the proposals relating to civil procedure but in this postscript we concentrate on a more fundamental question: Who should be in charge of the administration of the court system?

In an article in 1993 Sir Francis Purchas, a retired Court of Appeal judge, launched an attack on the 'executive-centred model' for the administration of the court system which he believed was being pursued by the civil servants working in the Lord Chancellor's Department. He speculated that their aim was the fusion of all civil work into the county court and the removal of High Court judges from the Crown Court. All work would then be done by circuit judges who would be under the control of the executive and could be dismissed without reference to Parliament. Others have gone further, suggesting that by giving rights of audience in all courts to solicitors, the executive would be able to undermine the role of barristers and cut off the supply of independent-minded judges at source: and by giving control of the resources and, in particular the number of judges allocated to the courts, to a new 'privatised courts agency' the executive would complete the process of putting the administration of justice on the same footing as the administration of other social benefits such as health or social security. In the view of Purchas and his fellow critics, the executive model, driven in the name of efficiency, would destroy judicial independence in the short term and threaten basic human freedoms in the long term.

The alternative, he suggested, was a 'judicial-centred' model of control under which the judiciary had complete control over the administration of the courts as is said to be the case in the US. The judiciary would then be able to determine the number of judges required in the light of the needs of the system rather than by reference to external economic constraints. They would also determine rights of audience in courts and the qualifications required to become a judge. Such a system would preserve the independence of the judiciary. Purchas recognised that the Lord Chancellor as a member of the executive and head of the judiciary, was rather caught in the middle. Hence, he suggested that matters relating to the independence of the judiciary should be the responsibility of the Lord Chief Justice. The Lord Chancellor could then be seen for what Purchas clearly considered him to be, a member of the executive. The tensions discussed here reappear in the next chapter concerned with civil process. It might be noted that the 1995 Woolf Report on civil justice does recommend that the High Court should be retained rather than merged with the county courts and that the system should be headed by a senior judge with overall responsibility for civil justice.

ENGLISH COURT STRUCTURE

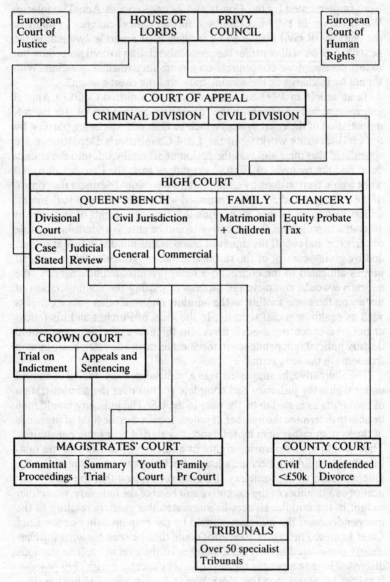

European Court of Justice	HOUSE OF LORDS	PRIVY COUNCIL		European Court of Human Rights

COURT OF APPEAL

CRIMINAL DIVISION	CIVIL DIVISION

HIGH COURT

QUEEN'S BENCH				FAMILY	CHANCERY
Divisional Court	Civil Jurisdiction			Matrimonial + Children	Equity Probate Tax
Case Stated	Judicial Review	General	Commercial		

CROWN COURT

Trial on Indictment	Appeals and Sentencing

MAGISTRATES' COURT				COUNTY COURT	
Committal Proceedings	Summary Trial	Youth Court	Family Pr Court	Civil <£50k	Undefended Divorce

TRIBUNALS

Over 50 specialist Tribunals

CRIMINAL JURISDICTION	CIVIL JURISDICTION

JUDGES

TYPE OF JUDGE	CIVIL COURT	CRIMINAL COURT
Lord of Appeal	House of Lords	
Lord Justice of Appeal	Court of Appeal	
High Court Judge	High Court	Crown Court
Circuit Judge District Judge	County Court County Court	Crown Court
Stipendiary Magistrate		Magistrates' Court
Tribunal Chairmen	Tribunals	
Lay Magistrates	Family Proceedings Court	Magistrates' Court
Lay Tribunal Members	Tribunals	
Jurors	High Court Libel and Fraud	Crown Court

Chapter 3

Civil process

What should be the aim of the legal process for dealing with civil claims? Should it be to discover the truth, to find whether the 'true' facts support the claim? But discovering the truth is often an elusive and usually an expensive task. Should it be to provide a fair system in which each side has a full opportunity to present its case and challenge that of the other? But that too can be expensive and also time consuming. Should it be to provide an efficient system under which the resources of time, money, judicial expertise etc made available for a particular type of claim are proportionate to the importance of the claim? But an efficient system would find it difficult to accommodate claims for small sums which, although subjectively important to the parties involved, do not objectively justify the allocation of legal resources. Should it be to provide an effective system which all claimants are able to use and which will provide some kind of resolution of the issue? Yes, but an effective system may not be perfectly fair or cost efficient etc.

It is not possible to fully satisfy all these aims. A balance has to be achieved between them. Where the balance lies will depend upon the type of claim involved. It must be remembered that civil claims come in all shapes and sizes: some for a few pounds eg small consumer cases, other for millions eg major shipping cases; some involving bitterly disputed facts eg libel or big business cases, others where the facts are agreed and only a ruling on the law is required eg many cases concerning property rights; some enforcing private rights against other citizens eg contract cases, others enforcing public rights against the state eg tax and welfare claims.

As one might expect, different types of process have been developed to deal with the different types of claim. This chapter will start by examining the traditional model, the adversarial process of the High Court and county court. This is best illustrated by personal injury litigation: A high percentage of cases reaching trial are personal injury claims and the social implications of the procedure are most marked in this type of case. From there, the chapter will consider how the model has been modified to meet the needs of other types of claim. For example, debt claims have required a swifter process, commercial claims have often required a more private and expert process, consumer claims a cheaper process, welfare claims a more informal process, family claims a more conciliatory process, employment or housing claims a more socially aware process etc. Different requirements have led to different modifications to the basic adversarial model.

Personal injury litigation in the High Court and county court

The adversarial process

Adversarial process is based on the principle that each party to the case is responsible for collecting its own evidence, interviewing witnesses, finding supporting documents and retaining experts to give favourable reports. When the parties are fully prepared, they will appear in court to present their own evidence and to attack that of their adversary by cross-questioning his witnesses and experts. The role of the judge is limited to ensuring fair play eg by disallowing trick questions, and to giving judgment to the party whose evidence and arguments were the more convincing. The judge may believe that neither party has painted an accurate picture of the facts, but his job is simply to find for the plaintiff if on the balance of probabilities his picture is the more accurate, and otherwise to find for the defendant. He cannot say 'I need more evidence before I can find what truly happened'. His job is not that of discovering the truth but that of judging on the evidence presented to him by the parties. This is quite different from the inquisitorial procedure which has prevailed in most of mainland Europe. Under that system, the judge plays the dominant role in collecting the evidence. During the course of a lengthy investigation, he will interview the witnesses, demand to see the documents and take the advice of experts. The discovery of the truth is the object of his endeavours. The litigants and their lawyers play a subordinate role, cooperating with the enquiry and making submissions which they hope the judge will follow up.

As adversarial ideas influence continental procedure and English procedure gives more power to the judge to manage the case, the contrast between the procedural models has become less marked but it remains fundamental. Litigation in the High Court or county court cannot be understood or assessed unless it is appreciated that the object of the exercise is not the discovery of the truth but the promotion of a fair trial in open court before an independent judge. In the inquisitorial model, the purpose of the final hearing of a case before the judge is often just to rubber-stamp his conclusion or at the most to resolve a question that the earlier investigation has been left unanswered. It cannot really be called a trial. Rather, the whole lengthy process of investigation constitutes the trial. In the adversarial model, the hearing before the judge is the centrepiece of the procedure. Until this hearing the parties will be able to keep secret much of the detail of their evidence and argument. They have to exchange some information about their case in the pre-trial procedure but the object of this exchange is not so much to resolve the dispute as to identify those issues which are in dispute and need to be judged, so that costly trial time is not taken up with points that are irrelevant or agreed between the parties. However, the lengthy time taken up by this pre-trial exchange of information does give the parties an opportunity to settle their disputes avoiding the cost of a trial. Indeed, less than 1% of personal injury cases go through to trial.

Lord Scarman has said of civil procedure: 'To be acceptable to ordinary people, I believe legal process in litigation must be designed to encourage, first, settlement by agreement; secondly, open and speedy trial if agreement is not forthcoming. In other words, justice, not truth is its purpose.' It is against the criteria of justice and fairness that the system must be assessed. Does it produce just settlements and failing that, fair trials? To answer these questions in the context of personal injury litigation, we will consider the theory and reality of pre-trial and trial procedure.

Pre-trial procedure

The stages through which a case passes on its way to trial in the High Court are set out in the diagram on p 79 which is designed to complement the explanation in the text.

DECIDING TO START LEGAL PROCEEDINGS

This is not a simple as it sounds. People suffering injuries do not immediately commence legal proceedings against those they feel were to blame for the accident. In the first place, they will need legal advice. Then they will need to make sure that they have some evidence to support a claim that those to blame were legally at fault ie they were negligent or in breach of some duty imposed by statute. Just as important is making sure that the claim is financially viable ie they can meet the costs of suing and those to be sued will have the money to pay compensation. If there is some evidence against those alleged to be to blame and they have some money, then in most cases it will be sensible to try to reach a settlement with them rather than starting legal proceedings right away. Finally, where legal proceedings are going to be necessary a decision must be taken as to whether to start in the High Court or the county court.

Advice

Only about one in ten of the three million people suffering personal injuries in accidents each year make any kind of claim for compensation against others involved. Research in the 1970s by a Royal Commission on Personal Injury Compensation and in the 1980s by the Oxford Centre for Socio-Legal Studies has shown that although in the majority of cases the failure to claim may be due to the minor nature of the injury or the lack of anyone to claim against, this did not explain all cases. Both research surveys showed that in perhaps a quarter of all cases the reason was ignorance or fear; ignorance of the means of claiming and fear of the costs, both legal expenses and lost earnings. Fear of immediate high costs are unfounded for many solicitors offer a £15.00 fixed fee interview which should be sufficient to decide if there is a chance of claiming. Clearly, many victims need to be told or persuaded to take legal advice. Left to themselves, they would accept their fate and place their faith in the Welfare State and its benefits. Often it is family, friends or the doctor who persuade victims to take advice. The first step may well be advice from a Citizens Advice Bureau which will usually be able to arrange a free 'diagnostic' interview with a solicitor. If the victim was injured at work and is a member of a union, then that union may put the victim in touch with its own solicitors.

The evidence

The legal adviser cannot effectively negotiate a settlement unless there is some evidence to support a claim. The victim's word is unlikely to be sufficient. Independent evidence in the form of witness statements or documents, photographs etc will be necessary. The problem with witnesses is that although a claimant can force a witness to appear at the trial, he cannot force the witness to give him a statement before the trial and without such a statement calling the witness at the trial is very risky: he might give evidence against the claimant which it would be difficult to contradict. So obtaining statements from witnesses is vital and the advisers of the victim and potential defendant (often an insurance company) may compete to get the relevant statements. The victim may have some additional help in the case of a road accident for the police report on the accident including statements they have taken from witnesses, will be made available to the victim. Unfortunately, help to the same extent is not forthcoming from the factory inspectors who investigate work accidents. Their reports do not include the names of witnesses, let alone their statements. There is a statutory procedure under which the victim can inspect and photograph things involved in the accident eg the brake system of a lorry or safety system of a machine. There is also a procedure for obtaining documents from potential defendants eg the service record of the lorry or machine, but only where the victim has made a specific allegation eg brake failure was due to lack of servicing. The victim cannot use this procedure to go through documents to find something to allege, to 'fish' for information on which to base his claim. Neither can he use it to get witness statements from potential defendants nor documents from third parties eg a garage servicing a car involved in the accident. These statutory procedures give the victim some assistance but collecting the evidence remains very much his or his legal adviser's responsibility.

Financial viability

There is no point claiming against someone when there is no money available to pay any compensation awarded. A High Court action against the average 'mugger' might produce a handsome award but no payment. The victim's compensation if any, is likely to come from a tribunal, the Criminal Injuries Compensation Board dispensing state money to victims of crime. Fortunately, unlike muggers, the motorists and employers against whom most claims are likely to be brought, have to be insured against liability for personal injuries. Their insurers have a duty to meet any award of compensation but they also have a right to manage the defence and can be tough opponents. Just as important as the potential defendant's ability to pay is the victim's ability to foot the costs of legal action, costs which will normally include those of the defendant should the victim lose his case or abandon it. Some victims will be backed by Trade Unions or motoring organisations. A few may have had the foresight to take out litigation expenses insurance. But for many the obvious solution lies with the legal aid scheme. This scheme is discussed in detail later, but basically it means that where the victim has reasonable grounds for bringing a claim his solicitor will be able to obtain legal aid for him which will cover all the costs subject to the victim having to contribute a limited amount based on a means test. So if legal aid is granted the victim is in a strong position to negotiate. Conversely, if it is refused his position is weaker. Somewhat surprisingly, the Oxford research showed that few solicitors did apply for legal aid for their client before starting negotiations (and most clients did not know if an application had been made for them!) The researchers inferred that solicitors confidently expected insurers to pay all the costs in a settlement and that they might have been put off the legal aid scheme by the form filling involved and lower fees payable to themselves under the scheme. The 1990s have seen the introduction of a new scheme intended to give some further financial security to the plaintiff. This is the conditional fee scheme under which the plaintiff's lawyers will only charge a fee if they win the case. Under this scheme, the plaintiff may also insure for a modest premium against the risk of having to pay the defendant's costs if the case is lost. This scheme is discussed in more detail in Chapter 5 (see post, p 142).

Negotiation and settlement

The Oxford research showed that negotiations and settlements were centred around three areas of uncertainty: whether the victim could prove the potential defendant was at fault; whether the victim was also at fault; in such a way that a court would reduce his compensation; and the medical prognosis for the victim. The negotiations may also be influenced by factors such as financial pressure on the victim and the experience of his legal adviser – the research showed that first offers of compensation to the victim were more likely to be accepted where the adviser was a small firm of solicitors, whereas big firms were more likely to hold out for an increased second or third offer. During the negotiations the sides may make concessions to help produce a settlement eg both sides might agree that they were at fault in an effort to reach a compromise. Such concessions would be dangerous if they could be used against a party if negotiations break down and the case goes to trial. To overcome this problem, there is a rule that concessions which are stated to be 'without prejudice' cannot be used in evidence in a court case. They are said to be privileged documents. The nature of the uncertainties and tactics involved may often lead to protracted negotiations but there is a time limit for the victim: He will normally lose his right to start legal proceedings three years after he incurred the injury. If his advisers have not received an offer or one they consider satisfactory as this time limit approaches, they must consider formally starting proceedings. The statistics show only 55,000 of the 300,000 claims made each year reach the stage of starting proceedings. Of the remainder, 85% are settled and the rest are abandoned usually for lack of evidence or finance to fight the case.

Going to court
Once the decision to go to court has been taken, proceedings will be started in either the High Court or the county court depending upon the amount claimed. Claims below £50,000 will generally have to start in the county court although they may be transferred up to the High Court where appropriate. As far as the procedure goes, there is little difference between the two courts. Proceedings are started in the High Court by issuing a writ and in the county court by taking out a summons. The county court staff fill in the summons form on the basis of information given by the plaintiff. The writ form is prepared by the plaintiff's solicitors and then stamped by the High Court staff. The summons or writ is then 'served on' ie delivered to, the defendant. Within 14 days of the date of service, the defendant must inform the court whether he intends to defend the case. If he fails to notify the court within the 14 days, the plaintiff can have judgment against him and this means he will no longer be able to deny liability but will have to submit to the amount or quantum of damages fixed by the court. If the defendant does give notice that he will defend, battle is joined and the case moves to a new stage.

INTERLOCUTORY PROCEEDINGS

The legal proceedings prior to the trial are known as interlocutory. The major interlocutory stages are the exchange of pleadings which is designed to clarify the issues in dispute, followed by the exchange of documents which is designed to simplify the process of trial. In fact there is often a considerable delay between the issue of the writ/summons and the start of the exchanges. There are official time limits eg a writ must be served within four months of issue, notice to defend must be given within 14 days of service and the plaintiff must send first pleading within 14 days of receiving notice; but the parties frequently do not enforce the time limits, preferring to proceed at a slower pace. Research for the Lord Chancellor's Civil Justice Review in 1986 revealed an average delay of about one year in provincial High Court actions and two years in London actions. The parties will use this time to assemble more evidence. Now that the action has started, they have a right to obtain documentary evidence from third parties eg the hospital records on the plaintiff's condition, and the defence will also have a right to have the plaintiff examined by its own experts. Both sides make take advice from a barrister on the strength of their case, their chances of success at trial, and whether further evidence might be needed. As all this goes on, the parties are likely to be negotiating. The service of the writ or summons is likely to have convinced the defendant or his insurers that the plaintiff is serious and the collection of more evidence and advice will give the parties new bargaining counters.

Exchange of pleadings

This process starts with the plaintiff sending the defendant a 'statement of claim' (known as 'particulars of claim' in a county court action). This will state the facts of the accident, the respects in which the defendant is said to be at fault and the damage suffered. It will not state the evidence by which the facts are to be proved. Neither will it indicate the amount of compensation sought. That is left unfixed ('unliquidated' in legal terminology) for the judge to decide at trial unless the case is settled earlier. The defendant will reply by sending back a pleading known as the 'defence' in which he may deny the plaintiff's allegations putting forward his own version of what happened eg the accident was all the plaintiff's fault, or refuse to admit the allegation leaving it to the plaintiff to prove eg that he suffered injury. In simple cases, these two documents, the 'statement of claim' and the 'defence' make up the pleadings. In more complex cases, there may be other pleadings: the plaintiff may want to counter an allegation made in the defence and he can do this by sending a pleading known as a 'reply'. This will add to the allegations contained in the original statement of claim. The defendant cannot reply to the 'reply', but he can complicate matters by himself making a claim against the plaintiff and this is common in motor accidents where both parties were injured and both might have been fault. The defendant's claim against the plaintiff is known as a 'counterclaim' and the plaintiff must respond to this with a 'defence'.

The date 14 days after the service of the last of these pleadings – usually a 'defence' – is known as the close of pleadings. It is a significant date because the parties can now embark on the stage of exchanging documents. But it certainly does not mark the end of the pleading process. The information provided by the exchange of documents may lead the parties to change their allegation and this they can do by amending the pleadings.

Again, the pleadings may be vague is some respect and to obtain clarification the parties will request from each other 'further and better particulars' of the matter in doubt. If sufficient information is not forthcoming a master or registrar will decide whether it must be given. In the light of the further information, further amendment of the pleadings may be required. Traditionally, the first amendments to pleadings are made in red, re-amendments are in green, re-re-amendments are in violet, then yellow. The final versions in a complex case may have a rainbow like quality and a pot of gold may well have been spent to achieve that effect.

Exchange of documents
This exchange is started 14 days after the close of pleadings by the process known as 'discovery'. Each party compiles a list of all the documents it has relating to the dispute and gives it to the other so that each discovers what documents are held by the other. From discovery the parties move to 'inspection'. Each party is allowed to inspect those documents on the list which are not marked as privileged. As we noted earlier, documents marked 'without prejudice' are privileged, but more important in this context is the fact that all documents prepared for the purpose of fighting the case are privileged. Hence, one party cannot inspect the witness statements taken by the other side nor reports that it has obtained from experts eg a technical report on a car or a medical report on the condition of a plaintiff. The secrecy afforded to expert reports causes problems. Without knowing whether their experts and those of the other side were in agreement or disagreement, parties often found it very difficult to negotiate a settlement and might well end up going to trial only to find when reports were revealed, that very little really divided them or that they had completely misunderstood what the case was about. Consequently, some years ago a rule was introduced providing for disclosure of experts' reports. However, it only applied to reports that the party intends to use at trial. Reports that are not going to be used eg because they are unfavourable, do not have to be disclosed. In the late 1980s the same principle was applied to statements that each side had taken from witnesses, so that one side intended to call a witness at trial it would have to supply the other with the written statements it had taken from that witness when preparing its case.

Pre-trial tactics
An outside observer might be tempted to ask why the process is so complex. Would it not be simpler and cheaper for each side to state precisely what it alleges in the pleadings so that no further particulars would be needed, for each side to fully disclose all the documents it holds, for each side to give the other copies of its witness statements, for the two sides to co-operate? Perhaps so, but that is not the way in which the adversary system has operated in the past. It has been seen as encouraging

tactical manoeuvring rather than co-operation. The pressure group Justice, reporting in 1974, graphically compared the strategy of pleading with 'naval warfare before the advent of radar, when each side made blind forays into the sea area of the other, while giving away as little as possible about the disposition of its own force.' If you tell the other side too much, you give them an opportunity to devise counter strategies and find contradicting evidence. Exactly the same tactic applied to documents, expert reports and witness statements. Give away as little as possible and find out as much as possible of the other side's strengths and weakness. That tactic helped both in bargaining for a settlement and failing that, at trial. Attitudes are slowly changing. Ten years ago in a medical negligence case, Sir John Donaldson MR stated that:

> 'We have moved far and fast from a procedure whereby tactical considerations which did not have any relation to the achievement of justice were allowed to carry any weight... nowadays the general rule is that, whilst a party is entitled to privacy in seeking out the 'cards' (ie evidence) for his hand, once he has put his hand together, the litigation is to be conducted with all the cards face up on the table. This is ... the product of a growing appreciation that the public interest demands that justice be provided as swiftly and as economically as possible.'

Certainly some of the rules eg on expert reports and witness statements have changed in recent years and there is less scope for tactical manoeuvring but old attitudes die hard and Sir John may be over-optimistic in his views. What is clear, is that High Court litigation is not a game for the inexperienced and that is why solicitors normally retain the specialists in litigation, the barristers, to draft the pleadings and advise on the evidence. Hence, it is also an expensive game.

The tactics are not limited to pleadings and evidence. A key factor is the costs rules. The basic rule is that the loser at trial pays the costs of the winner as well as his own. In personal injury cases this means that the victim will normally only be able to risk legal action if he is certain to win or has the financial backing of a private organisation such as a trade union or the public legal aid scheme. Such financial backing gives him some bargaining strength but it does not amount to a blank cheque enabling the victim to hold out for the maximum offer he could hope for. The backers, whether they be trade unions or the legal aid fund may withdraw their support if the victim refuses a reasonable settlement. Moreover, the defendant has one powerful costs card to play: he can deposit the amount he is offering in settlement with the court. This is known as making a payment into court. The costs rules provide that if the plaintiff refuses to accept the payment and at the subsequent trial, is awarded less than the amount paid in (the judge at trial will not have been told about the payment into court), then he must pay both his own and the defendants costs from the date of payment into court. Imagine a legally aided plaintiff expecting to win between £20,000 and £50,000 at trial depending upon whether he is found partly at fault or not and on how bad his injuries are found to be. Now suppose that the defendant pays £25,000 into court and that the estimated costs from the date of payment to the end of trial will be £10,000 for each side – not an impossibly high figure. What should the plaintiff do? If he rejects the payment and goes on to win the minimum £20,000 he will have to pay £20,000 of costs leaving him with precisely nothing to compensate for his injuries. Although there may be a 75% chance that he will recover more than £25,000, it will still take a strong plaintiff to reject such a payment into court. Once again, the experience and judgment of a barrister or solicitor specialising in litigation will be of vital importance to the victim.

One final tactical point. Insurance companies are in the business of handling claims. They can afford to take a percentage view of cases. They can afford to take risks, losing some and winning some, provided they get the right balance in the long run. Victims cannot put their case in such a long term perspective. For them it is a unique chance to recover some much needed compensation for an injury. One cannot ignore the resulting psychological pressure on the victim. Writing in the 1980s, the leader of the Oxford research team, Donald Harris, compared their position to runners in a compulsory long-distance obstacle race:

> 'The victims, without their consent, are placed at the starting line, and told that if they complete the whole course, the umpire at the finishing line will compel the race promoters to give them a prize; the amount of the prize, however, must remain uncertain until the last moment because the umpire has the discretion to fix it individually for each finisher. None of the runners is told the distance he must cover to complete the course, nor the time it is likely to take.... In view of all the uncertainties, and particularly the difficulties which could be presented by the unknown, future obstacles, many runners drop out of the race at each obstacle.... At any stage of the race, the promoters alongside the race-track are permitted to induce a runner to retire from the race in return for an immediate payment which they fix at less than the prize which they expect to be awarded by the umpire. After waiting to see how many runners drop out at the early obstacles without any inducement, the promoters begin to tempt the remaining runners with offers of money to retire: the amounts tend to increase the longer the runner stays the race. In view of the uncertainties about the remaining obstacles, their ability to finish the course, and the time it might take, most runners accept the offer and retire.'

Going to trial

The pre-trial stage is certainly an effective means of eliminating runners. Of the 30,000 High Court actions started each year, only 9,000 complete the 'exchange' section of the course and are set down for trial ie the date and venue of the trial is fixed. During the waiting period between the setting down and the trial itself (about one year), 7,000 of those cases will settle leaving under 2,000 to complete the course to trial. Settlements are made up to the last moment, the morning of the first day of trial, 'before the door of the court' as lawyers put it. Not surprising, as the parties know well, the trial itself will add between a half to two thirds to their existing costs bill. By this time too, the parties endurance may begin to crack. On average, the date of a High Court trial will be some three years after starting proceedings and five and a half years after the accident. The figures for the county court of almost two and three and a half years respectively, are not much comfort given the relatively minor nature of many of the injuries likely to fall within the £50,000 jurisdictional limit. Indeed, what is perhaps surprising in view of all these pressures, is that any cases go to trial. In some cases questions of law may arise eg the extent of a doctor's duty to warn patients of risks. In other cases the parties may view the case as raising a matter of principle eg the surgeon being adamant that he was not at fault. In most cases, it may be due to over-optimism by one or both parties as to the chances of winning a trial which means that they cannot agree on a compromise settlement. Such over-optimism may result from having incomplete information about the other side's case and this in turn, is a product of the adversary nature of the system.

THE TRIAL PROCESS

The evidence
After the years spent by the parties assembling paper work, pleadings, documents, statements etc, it used to be the case that the judge hearing their case might not have read any of the information before the case starts. This might have been partly due to lack of time on the part of the judge but also to the tradition of adversary trial that evidence is best presented orally in court where it can be questioned. At the trial not only will witnesses state what they saw etc, but documents too will be read out and those responsible for them will be questioned about their contents. Indeed, unless the expert or other person responsible is present to be questioned, the document will not normally be admissible as evidence for there will be no way of orally testing the truth of its contents. For exactly the same reason, witnesses cannot give evidence of what they heard another person say. This 'Hearsay Rule' means for example that the statement of a nurse that she heard a doctor say that X happened in an operation, could not be taken as evidence that X did happen. Only the doctor can give evidence that X happened and he can then be questioned about it. The emphasis on 'orality' dates from the time when High Court cases were tried before a lay jury who would find it easier to follow and assess the strength of oral evidence. Now that almost all civil trials are conducted before experienced judges, attitudes are changing. In 1986 it was decided that the written statements of witnesses could be accepted as evidence. In 1987 the Civil Justice Review conducted by the Lord Chancellor's Department suggested

that the hearsay rule should be abolished and judges should read the information about a case before the trial starts. The 1995 report of Lord Woolf recommends active management of the case by the judge prior to trial. The pressure to modify the emphasis on orality is likely to continue in an effort to make the trial process more efficient.

Whatever changes are made to the trial process, barristers are likely to continue playing a key role in questioning the witnesses. They have to be engaged for a High Court trial unless the litigant is bold or foolish enough to do the questioning himself. Solicitors have a right of audience in the county court, but in a disputed personal injury case they would normally retain a barrister for the trial. The barrister calling the witness, questions first but is not permitted to ask questions which lead the witness to an answer eg 'you did X, didn't you?'. The opposing barrister then cross-examines. He is allowed to ask 'leading questions' eg 'you could not have done X could you?', but a better tactic may be to trap the witness by asking seemingly innocent questions and gradually building on his answers to show that he must have been mistaken in his earlier evidence eg questioning an eye witness about the weather conditions and visibility before turning to what the witnesses said he saw. The judge's role should be limited to supervision eg disallowing leading questions or hearsay evidence. It is not his role to pursue his own view of the case by asking questions and interrupting those of counsel. His job is to listen, not to lead. If he oversteps the line, he provides ground for the losing party to appeal. Whether this process of questioning and cross-questioning by counsel provides the judge with reliable evidence is another matter. There is clearly a danger that an ordinary witness giving evidence years after the events occurred, will be so intimidated by the nature of the questioning and formality of the proceedings that his evidence will appear far less credible than is should be the case. Conversely, the evidence of an expert witness familiar with court room antics may well have an aura of authority which it does not deserve.

Judgment and appeals

After each side has presented its evidence (plaintiff first, then defendant) and summed up its case on the facts and law (defendant first this time), the judge will give judgment. He will go through the evidence, stating which facts he finds proven and why. Where the rival versions of the facts are evenly balanced, he will find for the defendant for it is the plaintiff who bears the onus of proving that on the balance of probabilities, his version is correct. Having found the facts, the judge will state the legal principles to be applied and in the case of disputed law, explain why one principle was preferred to another. Finally, he will apply the principles to the facts and give judgment for one side or the other. In a simple case he may give his judgment immediately the counsel have finished their submissions. In a case of any complexity the judge is likely to 'reserve' his judgment, taking time to consider the arguments and reconvening the court some days or weeks later to deliver his judgment.

Judgment in the High Court or county court does not necessarily end the trial process. Either side can appeal to the Court of Appeal on a question of fact or law or both. An appeal on the fact does not involve a rehearing of the witnesses but rather a review of the trial judge's findings in the light of the transcript of the evidence presented at trial. Consequently, the Court of Appeal will not interfere with the judge's finding of facts observed by witnesses, the so-called primary facts, because where there is dispute between witnesses the judge's finding is likely to be based on their relative credibility and only the judge has had the opportunity to assess this. However, where the judge's finding is based on inference ie by a process of reasoning from the primary facts, then the court will interfere if it considers that the judge drew an unreasonable inference. Medical negligence cases often raise inferred or secondary fact issues. Thus in *Maynard v West Midlands Regional Health Authority* (1985), the primary facts that the def-endant's surgeons decided on a particular exploratory operation after examining the patient's medical history and X-Rays, and that the operation caused permanent injury, were all undisputed. The appeal concerned the judge's finding of secondary fact that the surgeons chose the wrong type of operation. The Court of Appeal had no hesitation in overturning that finding on the ground that the judge had completely misunderstood the medical evidence and made quite the wrong inference from it. When an appeal raises legal issues, the court will rehear the legal arguments often at considerably greater length than that taken by the trial judge and unlike the latter, the appeal judges will have the advantage of being given a 'skeleton' outline of the barrister's arguments in writing before the appeal starts. Appeals are very expensive. Where legal issues are involved both sides will commonly retain a team of two or more barristers, each headed by a Queen's Counsel who will charge very high fees. Obviously parties must consider that they have strong ground before appealing although there maybe an element of 'in for a penny in for a pound' to their decision ie with so much at stake in terms of costs etc, one might as well spend a bit more on the chance of winning a lot more.

It is possible to appeal from the Court of Appeal to the House of Lords with leave from either court. Appeal to this level should not be regarded as part of the ordinary trial process. Leave is only likely to be granted where the case raises an issue of law of public importance where there is need for the House of Lords to clarify the point. In *Maynard* the Lords were asked to rule whether a judge was legally entitled to find a surgeon negligent if there was one body of medical opinion which considered his decision to be wrong, but another which considered it to be correct. Giving the judgment of the House, Lord Scarman stated that a finding of negligence could not be legally justified on such grounds. The function of the House in such case has been described as one of supervision rather than review ie the object is not so much to review the particular case as to supervise the development of the Common Law by clarifying or if necessary, modifying it principles. The nature and significance of this function will be considered later in Chapter 7.

Personal injury litigation: problems and solutions

The problems created by the present system are clear. Research carried out in 1986 for the Lord Chancellor's Civil Justice Review found that the time period from accident to trial in the London High Court averaged five years, and that from accident to settlement was even longer, just under six years. Ten years later, the delays are slightly longer. Although some of the delay can be attributed to external factors such as waiting for the victim's medical condition to stabilise sufficiently for his permanent injuries to be assessed, much of the responsibility lies with the system. In particular, apart from the three year time limit for issuing the writ or summons and the 14 day time limit for the defendant to respond to it, all other time limits can be waived by the parties' lawyers. They are waived to create time for negotiation, time which the tactics and sometimes the incompetence of the negotiators can extend without any effective control by the system. The result of such delay was, in the view of the Lord Chancellor's research team, to place intolerable psychological and financial burdens on the accident victim, undermine the justice of the trial by reducing the availability and eroding the reliability of the evidence, and to lower public estimation of the legal system as a whole.

The second major problem highlighted by the research was that of costs. In a High Court action the average combined costs of plaintiff and defendant was as much as 75% of the average compensation awarded. Costs were only half as much where cases were settled but would still amount to a sizeable percentage of the compensation agreed. In most cases the costs are paid directly by institutions, insurers, unions and the legal aid fund, but it is the public who pay indirectly through higher premiums, taxes and subscriptions. Furthermore, the high costs form part of the public image of the system, an image which deters many from making any use of it.

The system hardly meets Lord Scarman's criteria of justice and fairness. Few even amongst lawyers, would deny that there are serious problems. The difficulty lies in finding solutions. Not simply solutions which are sensible or just, but solutions which are acceptable to the public and lawyers alike. There have been some 35 reports on civil procedure this century, most suggesting solutions and most leading nowhere. But in the 1990s the pressure for change has become irresistible. It is not simply that the pressure groups representing the 'consumers' of the civil justice system have become more vocal. The key element has been the response of the senior judges. The Lord Chancellor undertook a major review of the civil justice system which reported in 1987 and followed that by commissioning a further investigation by Lord Woolf which led to an interim report in 1995. These two reports lay the foundations for a reform of the civil justice system to take it forward into the next millennium.

REFORMING THE CIVIL JUSTICE SYSTEM

Five different types of reform proposal have been put forward: structural changes to the court system to promote more efficient handling of cases, schemes to reduce the impact of the high costs, greater exchange of evidence to promote settlements, more judicial management of cases to reduce delay and promote settlement, and special procedures for dealing with smaller claims. On the structural side, the Civil Justice Review conducted by the Lord Chancellor's Department had suggested that there should be a merger of the High Court and county court creating a one court entry for all cases but with major cases being tried by the most experienced judges. However, fear that this would lower the status of senior judges led to this proposal being dropped in favour of one reallocating business between the two courts so that all personal injury claims for less than £50,000 should normally be heard in the county court. The Woolf report has now recommended that there should be a single set of procedural rules for both courts and a single method of starting cases replacing the old writ/ summons distinction. The impact of costs has been reduced by the 'conditional fee' system under which nothing is paid to the lawyer if the claim fails and a higher than usual fee if it succeeds. The Woolf report has recommended that more help should be given to litigants who conduct their own cases rather than using lawyers. This could be done by providing a Citizens Advice Bureau at each court to assist such litigants. The Woolf report also recommends that all litigants should be required to consider making use of Alternative Dispute Resolution (ADR) facilities. ADR describes a number of different techniques including 'mini-trials' in which the parties are given a single day in which to argue the guts of their case before an arbitrator, conciliation procedures, independent investigations and complaints procedures. Much has been done to develop such cheaper procedures in the United States and it is possible that ADR will come to play a significant role in civil justice over here.

Failure to exchange evidence before the trial is a major cause of problems. In one recent medical negligence case, *Wilsher v Essex Area Health Authority* (1987), the Court of Appeal noted that not only had the case taken over seven years to reach trial but the failure to disclose evidence meant that 'the parties realised, soon after the case began, that they had misunderstood what the case was about ... it was fought 'in the dark' ... it lasted four weeks instead of the allotted 5 days'. To meet this problem, the Civil Justice Review recommended full exchange of witness statements prior to trial, arguing that this would not only improve the conduct of trials but also lead to more settlements. A party who is fully informed of the other side's case is more likely to avoid an over-optimistic view of his own chances of winning at trial and is more likely to reach an earlier, cheaper and realistic settlement. The proposal has now been implemented by a change in the procedural rules. The Woolf report goes further recommending improved procedures for discovery and the use of US style 'case management conferences' and 'pre-trial reviews' to clarify the issues in dispute, facilitate settlement and if that fails, smooth the way to trial. Woolf also proposed a 'plaintiff's offer' scheme under which a plaintiff could state the figure at which it would be willing to settle and if this was not accepted by the defendant, it would have to pay the costs were a greater amount to be awarded at trial. This scheme, an equivalent for the plaintiff of the defendant's 'payment into court', would add to the pressures for settlement.

To reduce delay, the Civil Justice Review suggested a complex system for monitoring the progress of cases, imposing timetables where necessary. But this proved difficult to implement and the Woolf Report has recommended a system of case management under which the procedural judges, Masters for the High Court and district judges for the county court, would control the progress of the case providing individual hands-on management for the most difficult cases. As the report suggests, this proposal would result in 'a fundamental transfer in the responsibility for the management of civil litigation from litigants and their legal advisers to the courts'. Finally, the Woolf report suggested special procedures for the smaller claims. It recommended that the informal arbitration procedure in the county court which then applied to claims for up to £1,000 should be extended to cover all non-personal injury claims for up to £3,000 and this was implemented in 1995. For personal injury claims up to £10,000, it recommended the introduction of a new 'fast track' procedure with a fixed timetable of 30 weeks to trial, fixed costs and limited procedures, for example, involving the exchange of summaries of the evidence of witnesses rather than full, lengthy statements.

The proposals in Lord Woolf's interim report are radical. Inevitably, there are concerns and criticism. At a practical level, it has been questioned whether the district judges are sufficiently trained to take on the role as case managers and whether there are sufficient resources to appoint all the new procedural judges needed to operate the system. At a more fundamental level, there are concerns about introducing US practices with their emphasis on aggressive promotion of settlements. As we have seen, the pressure to settle often favours the institutional defendant rather than the individual plaintiff. Again, the Woolf proposals might be seen as producing a cut-down and speeded-up adversarial process which would simple exacerbate the existing resource inequalities between the parties to the settlement process. One leading critic, Professor Zander, has suggested that 'the only clear winners from the Woolf reforms would be the judges'. There would be many more of them with much more power. Time will tell whether these concerns are justified.

Of course, an alternative to reforming the system of personal injury litigation would be to abolish it entirely. Some have suggested that the tort action for personal injuries should be abolished and the financial savings should be used to provide improved welfare benefits for all those injured by accidents. New Zealand has adopted such an approach. A tribunal is still necessary to decide whether the injury has been caused by an accident but it is not necessary to decide whether someone was to blame for the accident. It is a 'no fault' system of state compensation. Others have suggested an even simpler form of abolition under which we would all be encouraged to take out personal insurance policies (rather like the standard holiday insurance) to provide compensation for any injuries suffered. Advocates of both the state compensation and private insurance schemes point to the vast costs savings that would be made by abolishing personal injury litigation. Lawyers tend to oppose such proposals, for obvious reasons. We return to this issue in Chapter 16.

Other tort claims

Personal injury claims based on the law of tort have been used to illustrate adversary procedure in the High Court. Other negligence claims eg for property damage/economic loss are litigated in the same way. Plaintiffs in such cases tend to be businesses and ineligible for legal aid, but the stakes often justify them spending considerable sums of their own money. If anything, litigation on these claims may be more protracted and bitterly fought than personal injury litigation. Other types of tort claim may involve additional procedural steps. In cases involving interference with property eg nuisance claims (see Chapter 17), the plaintiff may well require an interlocutory (pre-trial) injunction to stop the interference pending the trial decision as to its legality. In defamation cases too there are special procedures and rules governing when a plaintiff can obtain an interlocutory injunction to prevent publication pending trial and the trial itself follows what is now an exceptional procedure in civil cases, it involves a jury whose function is to decide the questions of fact, leaving the law and its application to the judge. But in all these types of claim the basic procedure is the same. When we turn to claims based on the law of contract – the other main civil law area discussed in this text – the position is different. Although some contract claims are litigated through the same adversary procedure, many are treated in an entirely different way.

Contract claims

The vast majority of contract claims are for debt ie money due under a contract for delivery of goods etc. These claims are brought in the High

Court or county court but as they are generally not disputed, the court functions more as an administrative agency than an adjudicator. The majority of disputed contract claims are not taken through the normal court procedures at all. Large claims are often taken to private arbitration. Small claims may also go to private arbitration although most probably go to the special arbitration procedure operated through the county court. In this section the procedures used for handling these different types of claim will be considered.

Debt claims

Debt claims start in the same way as personal injury claims ie with the issue of a writ or summons. In practice most debtors will have no defence and will either fail to respond or admit liability. The creditor may then proceed directly to judgment. As the claim will be for a liquidated (ie specified) sum, there is no need for the court to hold a hearing to determine the quantum (ie amount) to be awarded. Judgment is given for the liquidated sum and the whole process is a swift administrative formality. Where the debt is large it will clearly be in the debtor's interest to delay judgment and increase the time during which he can earn interest with the money, by purporting to dispute the debt even if he has no genuine grounds. There is a special procedure to counter this ploy. If the debtor puts in a defence to county court claim or simply indicates that he will defend a High Court claim, the plaintiff creditor may use what is known as the Order 14 procedure for summary judgment. (The procedural rules of the High Court and county court are organised under headings called 'orders'. Order 14 contains the rules for obtaining summary judgment – summary means after a brief procedure.) Under the procedure, the plaintiff must apply to the court with an affidavit ie a sworn statement, that he believes there is no defence to the claim. The defendant must then show that there is a triable issue and if he fails, judgment will be given for the plaintiff. In the rare case where there is a triable issue eg the defendant refuses to pay the debt on the ground that the goods or services supplied were useless, the claim will follow the same procedural course as was charted for personal injury claims.

Obtaining judgment in a debt claim presents little problem. The procedure is efficient and quick. The difficulty comes in trying to enforce the judgment against a debtor who will not pay up voluntarily. There are several different types of enforcement order that the courts can issue but it is up to the plaintiff (referred to as the judgment creditor once judgment is obtained) to choose the order and chase the debtor to see the order is effective. The commonest method chosen is seizure of the debtors goods under a writ of fieri facias from the High Court or a warrant of execution from the county court. The courts issue over a million such writs or warrants a year. In most cases, getting the order is sufficient to frighten the debtor into payment. In very few cases goods are actually seized. One reason for this may be that the tricky business debtor will not own the goods or plant he uses (it will be owned by an 'associated' company or hired) and the petty non-business debtor may not have any goods to own. Where seizure fails, the judgment creditor is likely to try other methods. In the case of a business debtor it may be possible to get payment through a garnishee order which usually attaches to the debtor's bank account giving the creditor a right to payment of the credit balance in the account; or through a charging order which attaches in a similar way to the debtor's interest in land and shares. However, the sophisticated business debtor is likely to anticipate these orders and ensure that he has no credit balance or land etc in his own name – in his wife's maybe, but not his own. In the case of a petty debtor it may be possible to get payment through an attachment of earnings. An order to this effect will require the debtor's employer to make regular deductions from his earnings and pay them to the creditor. Over 100,000 such orders are made each year by the courts. Of course, this method is no use for the petty debtor who is in debt because he is unemployed and research by the Lord Chancellor's Civil Justice Review team has shown that 40% of debtors fall into this unfortunate category.

The difficulty of enforcing judgment debts through the legal machinery may lead to other responses from the creditor. In the case of business debtors, the creditor may well threaten to report the debt to a credit rating agency or publicise it amongst the debtors other trading partners. Such tactics may well induce the debtor to settle with the creditor, albeit at less than the judgment for the creditor knows that the full amount is unobtainable. In the case of the petty debtor, institutional creditors eg utilities, may just not bother to enforce the debt. Research has shown that a third of county court debt judgments are not enforced and it has been suggested that institutional creditors go to court not so much with the idea of enforcing the debt but for the sake of appearance, to let it be seen that debtors will be taken to court. Less reputable creditors may not be content with appearances and may resort to more direct methods of enforcement against the petty debtor. Harassment of debtors is a criminal offence but it goes on although no research statistics are available!

All in all, the system is unsatisfactory. The law seems to make little effort to help the judgment creditor. The adversary principle under which the conduct of litigation is the responsibility of the parties, is carried to its conclusion and responsibility for enforcement is left to the parties. In 1969 the Payne Committee recommended that the legal system take more responsibility with the establishment of an enforcement office which would select the most appropriate method of dealing with the debtor. The proposal has not been implemented mainly it seems, because of the cost. The Civil Justice Review reporting in 1987 also considered an enforcement officer system to be 'expensive and inefficient' but suggested that more effort should be made to gather information about debtors' financial circumstances. But perhaps the most interesting suggestion was that made to the research team by a number of court officials, namely that 'credit is too readily obtainable and the law should be changed to make credit givers more liable for their bad debts if they have not carried out sufficient checks before giving the credit'. Unlike many of the review proposals, to no one's surprise this one has not been implemented.

Large disputed claims

Disputed contract claims for very large sums of money frequently arise in business. But managers know that High Court litigation is a very costly means of resolving such disputes, costly in terms of legal expenses and costly too, in terms of trading relationships. They may wish to preserve a trading relationship with the party in dispute but few such relationships can survive the public confrontation of a High Court trial. Hence, there is a strong desire to resolve disputes by other means. Where the parties do not have a close relationship but contract with each other only occasionally and for standard items or services, they are likely to negotiate against the background of market forces. The party allegedly in the wrong will often agree a compromise rather than run the risk of loosing future business in a competitive market place. Where the parties have a close relationship either because they regularly contract with each other eg in the shipping or commodity markets, or because their contract is highly specialised and long term eg civil engineering or defence contracts, the parties may devise their own means of resolving disputes. This is likely to involve an arbitration procedure under which disputes are referred to an outside arbitrator chosen by the parties, but it may also involve mechanisms under which disputes can be resolved by changing the terms of the contract itself ie by legislating rather than adjudicating. Thus an engineer in charge of a civil engineering contract will have the power to vary the contractual obligations as well as a power to decide disputes between the employer and the contractor. These governance structures as they are called, can be very complex, mini-legal systems in their own right.

Commercial arbitrations are governed by the provisions of the Arbitration Acts. These give the arbitrator the power to conduct the proceedings in the same way as a court case eg with pleadings, discovery etc, and provides that the arbitrator's award can be enforced just as if it were a High Court judgment. Private commercial arbitration is simply a private equivalent of public litigation. It is adversary in nature. It is not at all like the highly publicised arbitrations of industrial disputes where the aim often seems to be finding an acceptable compromise. The attraction of commercial arbitration is partly its privacy, partly the fact that the arbitrator can be chosen for his expertise and hence fewer expert witnesses and less explanation of the problem may be necessary, and partly the limited rights of appeal. However, there used to be a wide right of appeal to the High Court and to some extent this undermined the advantages of arbitration for there was always the possibility that the award would be reversed by an inexpert judge at great expense and with considerable publicity. This problem has been met by the 1979 Arbitration Act, which provides that awards can only be reviewed by the High Court on a question of law and with the leave of that court. Following a case called *The Nema* (1980), it is clear that leave will only be given where the arbitrator was obviously wrong on a point of law or where there was a point of law which will affect many other contracting parties eg the interpretation of a term in a standard form of commercial contract. In recent years the legal system has responded to the needs of commerce and business in other ways. Official Referee's business and Commercial Court business has increased greatly as procedures have been improved and judges have developed expertise. Still, the number of cases heard each year under both those systems only amounts to a couple of hundred or so whereas over 10,000 arbitrations are held in London each year. The business and commercial community seem to have voted with their feet.

Small claims

The county court operates a special arbitration scheme for claims of less than £1,000, typically claims by consumers against suppliers of goods or services. Under the scheme the claimant starts proceedings in the normal way by taking out a summons but if the defendant responds with a defence, the case is referred to the district judge of the county court for arbitration rather than to a circuit judge for trial. The district judge will then hold a preliminary discussion with the parties to get agreement on as many facts as possible and advise them as to what they should do to prepare for the arbitration itself eg obtaining an expert's opinion as to the cause of the defect in the goods purchased. Simple claims may settle at this stage. Complex claims involving difficult questions of law or evidence may be referred back to a trial before a circuit judge. Most cases will go on to arbitration which tends to be an informal and fairly short – statistics show that 60% last less than 30 minutes. The district judge's award can be set aside but only on the ground that he acted contrary to the rules of natural justice in not granting the parties a fair hearing, or that the record of the proceedings showed he made an error of law. As records of arbitrations are brief and do not usually state the reason for the award, the proceedings rarely go any further.

The small claims arbitration has two big advantages over the trial procedure. It is informal. The district judge will not allow a claim to get bogged down in pleadings, requests for further and better particulars etc. It is cheap to use. The claimant has to pay a small sum, based on the amount claimed, to the court to cover its costs but he does not have to fear having to pay the defendants legal costs if he loses the case. The rule of the loser paying winner's legal costs has been dropped for small claim arbitrations. Additionally, no legal aid is available to pay for the costs of legal representatives appearing at the arbitration. Thus both parties know that they will have to pay their own legal costs if they choose to retain a lawyer. The aim is to deter the parties from engaging legal representatives so as to keep down the overall cost and also to preserve the informality of the arbitration itself which might be undermined by the presence of lawyers. But here the system faces a dilemma. Lawyers are deterred from appearing but are not banned. It would be improper to ban them because the arbitration follows an adversary process ie each side is allowed to question the other's evidence. It would clearly be absurd to allow one side to engage say a part-time journalist to do the questioning but not allow him to engage a lawyer. If lawyers are to be banned from questioning so should others with experience of questioning and then where would you draw the line? The problem is that so long as the procedure is based on the adversary questioning system, lawyers cannot be banned and some degree of formality is bound to creep in to the proceedings. *Chilton v Saga Holidays* (1986) illustrates the problem. Dissatisfied with his holiday, Chilton brought a small claim against Saga. Saga retained a solicitor who wanted to cross-examine Chilton at the arbitration hearing. The judge refused to allow this and required all questions to be put through him ie he would rephrase the question and put it to Chilton, as would a judge operating under a continental inquisitorial procedure. Chilton won. Saga appealed on the grounds of natural justice and the Court of Appeal set aside the arbitrator's award on the ground that in an adversary system each party is entitled to cross-examine the other. It is the adversary nature of the proceedings that creates the problem and it is a real problem: research by the National Consumer Council in 1979 indicated that fear of the formality and atmosphere of the courts was a major reason why consumers did not pursue small claims. The county court officials help as much as they can with form filling etc but all this may be of little effect if the consumer feels he may have to face awesome cross-examination by a Kavanagh QC. The suggestion of the Woolf report that agencies such as the CAB should have offices at the courts to assist unrepresented litigants, might be one way of providing sufficient reassurance to the small claimant.

An alternative approach to small claims would be to use an inquisitorial procedure. In the 1970s voluntary small claims courts adopting such a procedure were set up in Manchester and London. The courts were unofficial so that there was no way in which a defendant could be forced to appear before them but if he did voluntarily agree to appear he would contract to observe any award made against him. Under these schemes the claimant made his complaint and it was then the responsibility of the scheme to get all the necessary information from the parties and obtain expert reports where necessary. The procedure was purely inquisitorial. Legal representation was banned but the normal type of representation would have been irrelevant anyway – there were no questions to ask, no evidence to prepare. The two schemes ceased to operate when their funding ran out but they survived long enough to indicate that an inquisitorial procedure can work successfully and may be less off-putting to ordinary claimants. The 1979 proposal of the National Consumer Council that there should be a separate Small Claims Division of the county court with a procedure under which an arbitrator would be able to commission evidence herself and conduct the hearing in any way she thought fair, reflects this kind of thinking. Critics argue that it did not go far enough towards an inquisitorial system. For some, it obviously went too far. Its proposals were not implemented. But the pressure for a more inquisitorial approach remains. The Civil Justice Review recommended that the *Saga Holidays* decision should be overturned. The Courts and Legal Services Act 1990 has done this with the result that if lawyers appear in small claims cases, their questioning is subject to the court's control.

The small claims problem cannot be left without brief mention of some other possible solutions. Under the provisions of the Fair Trading Act 1973, trades are encouraged to establish codes of practice and private arbitration schemes for dealing with consumer complaints. About 20 or so trades have done so. Chilton could have complained to the Association of British Travel Agents arbitration procedure. This provides cheap, independent arbitration and the statistics show that Chilton would have had a 50% chance of winning his case and getting on average half what he claimed. The record of that scheme is good but research has shown that some other schemes are rather slow in producing decisions and many are badly publicised. Consumers usually find out about them through advice agencies such as the Citizens Advice Bureaux or Trading Standards Departments. So the role that can be played by these schemes is very much tied to the extent to which advice is available to the public – a problem which is discussed fully in Chapter 5. In the cases of financial services such as pensions and insurance, the ombudsman approach has been adopted. The ombudsman is charged with investigating complaints by individuals against companies supplying the type of service and, if the complaint is upheld, can recommend the payment of compensation. The Courts and Legal Services Act 1990 has created a Legal Services Ombudsman with similar powers to investigate complaints. Again, a similar investigatory procedures operates for the privatised utilities through the office of the regulator, Offwat, Offgas etc. Another strategy is to make more use of the criminal law. Traders can be prosecuted under legislation such as the Trade Descriptions Act for much of the conduct which frequently gives rise to consumer claims. The problem here is that the regulatory agencies charged with enforcing this kind of legislation have neither the time, money or perhaps the will, to take on such a task in a comprehensive way. This problem is discussed further in Chapter 26. Finally it is sometimes suggested that allowing consumers to group together and bring a single legal action on behalf of their whole class or group, might be an effective strategy. Class actions are permitted in the USA and in a few well publicised cases, consumers have brought major corporations to their knees. Whether class actions really have a role to play in the average small claim problem is very doubtful.

Tribunal process

The growth in the number of tribunals is one of the most striking features of the-post war legal system. It stems from the growth of state intervention in social and economic affairs and the belief that the disputes that might arise under the new legislative schemes were not best dealt with by the ordinary courts. Special tribunals it was said, would provide a cheap, informal, quick and expert means of resolving such disputes. But in the rush to create these new tribunals relatively little thought was given to whether their procedures were as just as they were efficient. Each tribunal had a different procedure and no one took an over-view of the whole process until, ironically, a breakdown in government administrative efficiency in the Crichel Down scandal of 1954, led not only to a ministerial resignation but also to an investigation into the working of Inquiries and Tribunals by the Franks Committee. In 1957 Franks reported recommending that Tribunal procedures should be governed by the principles of 'openness, fairness and impartiality' and that a Council on Tribunals should be established with powers to supervise tribunals to ensure that these principles were observed. The Tribunals and Inquiries Act 1958 which followed did establish the Council but gave it advisory rather than supervisory powers. Government departments are supposed to consult with the Council about the tribunals for which they are responsible eg the DSS should consult about welfare tribunals, and the Council can itself advise the Lord Chancellor of problems. When in 1980 it advised that it should be given some power, it was ignored! In these circumstances, one might ask what has happened to Franks' three principles. With over 50 different types of tribunal, each with its own procedure, it is difficult to generalise. In this section we will compare industrial tribunals where the requirements seem to have been met without difficulty, with social security tribunals where there have been considerable problems.

Industrial tribunals

These tribunals hear workers' claims to compensation from their ex-employers on the ground that they have been unfairly dismissed from their jobs. The hearings of the tribunal are chaired by a lawyer who sits with two lay experts, one drawn from a panel of employers' nominees and the other from a union panel. Franks suggested that openness meant sitting in public and giving a reasoned decision and the tribunal meets both these criteria, although to save time it has recently decided to give full reasons for its decisions only when asked. It follows an adversary procedure under which it is for the parties to call and question the witnesses but in practice, if the worker is unrepresented the members of the tribunal will themselves ask questions of witnesses. The pre-trial procedure is similar to that of ordinary litigation with an exchange of the allegations to be made and any relevant documents; but in addition conciliation officers will attempt to settle the case, if possible through re-instatement of the worker in his job. The procedure combines the adversary model of fairness with an emphasis on informality and conciliation. Impartiality is secured not only by having a balanced tribunal membership but also by an appeal structure that links the tribunal to the ordinary court system. Appeals go to the Employment Appeal Tribunal which normally consists of a High Court judge sitting with two lay members, and from there appeals on a point of law may be taken to the Court of Appeal.

Industrial tribunals are a perfect advertisement for Franks' principles. They could easily fit into the court structure as say, the 'employment division' of the county court. But curiously, their court-like perfection only serves to emphasise their major deficiency. Legal aid is not available to pay for parties to be legally represented at the hearing. Such legal aid is confined to the proper courts. And yet the factual and legal issues raised in industrial tribunals are no less complex that those raised in many High Court cases. The procedure is modelled on that of the ordinary courts albeit with some greater informality. The argument against providing legal aid seems to rest on the doctrinal assertion that 'the tribunal is not a court', combined with a 'thin end of the wedge' argument that once granted for this tribunal it will have to be granted for all others. For union members the lack of legal aid for representation is not too serious as their union is likely to supply a representative. For non-union workers who are perhaps the category more likely to be unfairly dismissed, the absence of a representative can put them at a considerable disadvantage when facing the employer's experienced lawyer at the tribunal hearing.

Social security tribunals

The social security system presents a different story altogether and one complicated by the fact that there are two different benefit regimes, one which is rule based and subject to a tribunal system and one which is discretionary and subject to a system of review. The rule based system itself comprises two different types of benefit. First, the non-means-tested benefits such as unemployment, incapacity, industrial injury, maternity, pension and widow's benefits. These benefits are payable to those who have made the required national insurance contribution to the state. Under the post-WWII Beveridge scheme, these benefits were genuinely an insurance payment being paid from an insurance fund created by the contribution paid by workers. Now, they are paid from tax revenues and are seen as just part of the welfare system. But their insurance legacy lives on in the sense that the system is very rule based. The rules specify exactly what must be paid and under what circumstances. We explain some of the rules in Chapter 16 dealing with compensation for injury at work. Any such rule based system will inevitably give rise to dispute about whether the facts fit the rules and about what the rules mean. More recently a new system of means-tested benefits has been developed including such schemes as Income Support providing benefit to the unemployed with low incomes, Family Credit providing benefit to low-paid workers with children, and the regulated social fund which makes payments for maternity expenses, funeral expenses and cold weather expenses. These means-tested benefits are also rule based. For example, the cold weather rules provide that a qualifying period of cold weather is one of 'seven days during which the average daily mean temperature forecast for the region (the country is divided into 63 regions) is equal to or below 0 Celsius'. The discretionary system covers discretionary social fund payments. These can cover such items as the cost of domestic assistance, optical and dental services, the cost of work clothes necessary to get a job, council tax and most types of housing cost. Payments are usually made by way of a loan although a non-repayable grant is possible. The decision as to payment is discretionary, left to the local office of the Benefits Agency and limited by the overall budget given to each local office.

In the case of rule-based benefits, the initial decision as to disputed claims is taken by the adjudication officer (AO). If the claimant is dissatisfied with this decision, she can demand a further review by the AO or appeal to a social security appeal tribunal (SSAT). This is chaired by a lawyer sitting with two lay members, one of whom should be the same sex as the claimant. Like an industrial tribunal, an SSAT sits in public, gives reasons for its decisions and has an appeal system. An appeal may be made to a Social Security Commissioner. There are a dozen or so Commissioners. They must have had at least ten years' experience as a barrister or solicitor before appointment and but for the fact that they are not actually called judges, one could roughly equate them with circuit judges in the judicial hierarchy. The commissioners hear cases sitting singly and from their decision there is a further right of appeal on a point of law to the Court of Appeal. The complexity of the rules governing benefits ensures that the appeal system is well used.

There is no doubt that the SSATs are as open and impartial as industrial tribunals. The problem comes with the requirement of fairness and it stems from the fact that SSATs follow an inquisitorial rather than an adversary process. The adjudication officer who took the original decision will supply written details of the case to the tribunal and a different AO, known as the presenting officer, will appear at the hearing to summarise the case. The presenting officers see their function as one of assisting the tribunal to investigate and not as one of arguing against the claimant. This inquisitorial approach is something which must be taken into account when the criterion of fairness is applied. The fairness issue usually arises as a result of the claimant asking the High Court for judicial review of a tribunal decision on the ground that it contravened the natural justice requirement of a fair hearing. Thus for example, in 1965 Mrs Moore, who claimed that her slipped disc was a result of her work as a crane driver, sought review of a tribunal's decision that it was due to illness and no insurance benefit was payable. She argued that the decision contravened natural justice because she had not been allowed to question two doctors whose written opinions had been considered by the tribunal. Had the tribunal been governed by adversary principles, she would undoubtedly have succeeded in her argument. However, the Court of Appeal in finally disposing of the request for review, held that in the context of the tribunal's inquisitorial process, there had been no unfairness. But what is fair in an inquisitorial context? In 1974 Mr Viscusi sought review of a decision on the ground that the tribunal had not investigated all the possible explanations for his injury but had accepted a consultant's view that he was malingering. Dismissing his case, Lord Denning said 'the tribunal should make due enquiry, but I do not think this means they should follow up every suggestion. They must do what is fair but need go no further.' Rather vague, but then that is the problem with the notion of 'fairness'. In fact, there are grounds for concern about the inquisitorial process adopted by the tribunals. Research has shown that claimants who are legally represented fair much better than those that are not. This does not seem to 'fit' with a purely inquisitorial process. Neither does the fact that the tribunals investigatory powers are limited in some respects eg it cannot force employers to appear at a hearing. Perhaps it would be better to regard the process as a 'mixed' one with elements of both models within it. If that is correct, then the fundamental unfairness may be that no legal aid is available to pay for a claimant to be legally represented.

The system for discretionary benefits is different and has a troublesome history. In the 1960s and 1970s the discretionary system had a much wider scope covering such items as payments for a winter coat or children's shoes. During that period, a claimant who was dissatisfied with a benefit decision could appeal to a supplementary benefit appeal tribunal (SBAT). The SBAT was composed of three laymen. It held hearings in private. This was justifiable if the claimant did not wish his poverty to be aired in public but not justifiable as a blanket rule protecting the tribunals from public scrutiny. The tribunal did give reasons for its decisions but it has been said that it would require 'telepathic powers' to understand them. Its process was best described as 'informal', all around a table rather like a social work case conference. The officers representing the DSS were often able to dominate the proceedings. Research indicated that the rules of natural justice were frequently ignored, if that is, anyone knew what they were. Claimants were interrupted when they tried to put their case. Allegations of bias against the claimant might not have been difficult to substantiate. The tribunal procedure could not be described as fair and nor could it be described as impartial in the broad sense of freedom from the influence of the administering government department, the DSS. Research showed that the vast majority of tribunal members thought that, provided the authorities had followed their own internal code of guidance in refusing a payment, any appeal had to be disallowed. This was quite wrong in law as the tribunals were supposed to review the merits of the decision and not confine themselves to considering whether an unofficial code had been observed. As there was no appeal from the SBAT, little could be done about these problems.

In the later 1970s an effort was made to 'clean up' the SBATs. Legally qualified chairmen were brought in along with a panel system for selecting lay members designed to provide membership with some expertise in poverty matters. A right of appeal to the ordinary courts was added. But finally in the 1980s, the system was abandoned. Many types of discretionary payments, such as those for children's clothes, were abolished leaving the poor to claim under the rule-based systems and appeal to SSATs. For the limited discretionary system that remained, a budget and review system was introduced. Each district office of the Benefits Agency is given an annual budget for discretionary payments, known as the social fund. This budget must not be exceeded and most payments from the fund have to be on a loan basis. The initial decision as to payment is taken by the social fund officer (SFO). If the claimant asks for a review of that decision, it is reconsidered by the same SFO. If the claimant is dissatisfied with the outcome of that review, the case will be reviewed further by a social fund inspector and from his decision, there is no appeal. Each district office will issue local guidance for its SFOs but because this is a discretionary system, one cannot really talk about appealing on the ground that the local guidance was not followed. All one can say is that the best tactic when asking for a review is to rely on the code of guidance. When the original SBAT appeal system was abandoned, the council on tribunals was very critical, arguing that 'it is perfectly feasible to have independent appeal against discretionary decisions. In some ways it is even more important with discretionary decisions.' But the appeal system did face a challenge not only in dealing with a discretionary area but also one in which the pressure to cut public spending was heavy. The SBAT experience did show that it was possible for a tribunal to deal with discretionary matters but it also perhaps illustrated that the more a tribunal deals with such matters, the more difficult it may be to maintain the traditional approach to fairness and impartiality. Whether the introduction of the review system for discretionary payments should be seen as a wise retreat for the tribunal system or as a failure to allow it to respond to a challenge, whether it should be seen as a defeat or victory for the spirit of Franks, these are not easy questions to answer.

Tribunals and courts

The requirements of openness, fairness and impartiality are met fully by industrial tribunals but only partially by SSATs and not at all by the social fund system. But perhaps the real problem was that Franks grouped all tribunals together. Whether one can meaningfully lay down common requirements for tribunals whose function differs so much as the ones discussed in this section is debatable. At one end of the spectrum are industrial tribunals which can be equated with courts. At the other end is the internal review system which applies to social fund discretionary payments. In between lie the SSATs with their inquisitorial process. Grouping all tribunals systems together not only creates a false unity between them but also a false distinction from courts. This is most apparent in the context of legal aid for representation at tribunal hearings. It is difficult to argue that such aid should not be available for industrial tribunal hearings and those of other tribunals which function in an adversary fashion, but the fact that these bodies are called tribunals rather than courts still seems to block the way. The time has come to examine the procedures of tribunals not as a group but as individual parts of the legal system. In 1986 the Lord Chancellor's Civil Justice Review decided to examine the workings of Rent Assessment Committees (the tribunals which deal with rent disputes) alongside the workings of the High Court and county court in other types of housing case. This integrated approach based upon the nature of the dispute to be adjudicated rather than the name of the adjudicating body, points to a better way forward than pursuit of such vague principles as openness, fairness and impartiality. It avoids the danger of treating tribunals as a second class legal system for those with second class legal problems.

Postscript: civil process and the *Opren* case

Law students tend to regard civil process as a rather tedious subject made up of a mass of rules and concepts of which they have no experience and to which they find it difficult to relate. In comparison, the substantive law eg the law of tort or contract, appears interesting and significant. But to an observer of our legal system, almost the reverse is the case. The substantive law of tort etc is of relatively little significance. Few claims will ever raise interesting questions of law. Rather, it is the way the system processes claims which is crucial. This, rather than the substantive law, determines how the system operates. Research carried out by bodies like the Oxford Centre for Socio-Legal Studies constantly bears out this fact, but law students often remain unimpressed! Perhaps where statistics fail, a single illustration may succeed. Almost every year some example of civil litigation will hit the headlines. In the mid 1980s the case making the news was that concerning the anti-arthritis drug, Opren. In the 1990s there are similar well-publicised cases concerning tranquilisers and contraceptives. We will examine the Opren case, simply because it is now over.

Opren was manufactured by an American drug company and marketed in the early 1980s as a wonder drug for the treatment of arthritis. The drug was subsequently withdrawn when fears grew that it might have serious side effects such as making the skin very sensitive to sunlight. In 1984 many of the, mainly elderly, patients who had taken Opren began a legal action against the manufacturers for compensation for what were alleged to be the injuries they had suffered as a result of taking the drug. To succeed at trial each plaintiff would have to prove two things: first, that in some way eg in testing the drug, the manufacturer had acted negligently; and secondly, that the particular condition from which they suffered was actually caused by the drug. To persuade the manufacturers to settle, the plaintiffs would have to show that they had some chance of winning a trial on those two issues. The substantive law of tort has little relevance to this case. Everything turned on whether, within the framework of civil procedure, the 1,500 plaintiffs could build sufficient evidence to support their claims.

That was not to be easy. For a start there were estimated to be some 1.2 million documents relevant to the claims. Many of these were of a technical and scientific nature and not easy for the solicitors representing the plaintiffs to understand. The plaintiff's solicitors grouped together to pool resources and in late 1984 engaged an investigative journalist specialising in medical and drug issues, to help interpret the evidence and liaise with the expert advisers who would be needed to support the case. The manufacturer was reluctant to permit this journalist to inspect documents at the discovery stage, but after a three day hearing in early 1987 Sir John Donaldson gave permission, commenting that 'litigation is not a war or even a game. It is designed to do real justice between opposing parties'. There were further problems with discovery and two separate hearings were necessary to establish that the manufacturers had waived privilege on one important document and that a plaintiff was entitled to discovery of his hospital records from the health authorities.

The next problem faced by the plaintiffs was one of costs. The position was eased somewhat by the decision of the judge assigned to try the case, that a group of test cases should be taken to a single trial hearing in the hope that settlement in the rest would follow a resolution of the test cases. But the estimated cost of trying the test cases was over £5 million. It seems that the plaintiff's advisers originally thought that this problem could be met by choosing as test cases plaintiffs who were legally aided so that the huge cost of the action would be born by the legal aid fund and those plaintiffs who were not legally aided would be able to await the outcome of the test cases without having to spend their own money. There were catches with this plan. In the first place, even if the legally aided plaintiffs won damages they would be unlikely to receive money. The reason is complex: If the manufacturers lost they would have to pay the costs of the plaintiffs, but not all the costs. In any case a percentage of the plaintiff's costs will be irrecoverable against the defendant and small percentage of £5 million is a lot of money. The legal aid fund will meet those irrecoverable costs but it will then recover the money from the damages awarded to the plaintiff. In the Opren case the irrecoverable costs would have exceeded the amount of damages that would have been awarded. The second catch was the court. In mid 1987 the judge decided that the plaintiffs plan was unacceptable, partly because of the problem facing the test case plaintiffs and partly because it seemed wrong that the other plaintiffs should not contribute. As a result of the judge's ruling, it was said that nearly half of the plaintiffs would have to drop their claims because without legal aid they could not afford to bear a share of the enormous trial costs. The manufacturer's lawyers withdrew the offers of settlement that they had previously made to many of the plaintiffs. The plaintiffs appealed against the judge's ruling on costs. The Court of Appeal upheld the judge's decision but did urge the parties to settle as soon as possible and suggested that the parties might appoint a judge to arbitrate a settlement.

A settlement did not follow but an anonymous benefactor stepped in and offered £2 million to finance the claims of the 500 plaintiffs without legal aid. Following this, in late 1987, the manufacturers made offers of settlement to some of the plaintiffs. However, pressure groups campaigning for the plaintiffs feared that if the strongest runners were tempted out of the race by a settlement, the rest of the field would be in a weak position. Consequently, they began an advertising campaign appealing to the manufacturers to settle all claims and stated their intention to escalate the campaign to expose the inadequacies of the legal system. They were met by a warning from the court that their campaign was not far from the dividing line between legitimate comment and illegitimate pressure, punishable for being in contempt of court ie prejudicing the proper administration of justice.

The case was eventually decided by an arbitration hearing under a judge. It was obviously unusual for the media interest it aroused and its complexity – the number of court hearings on preliminary matters reached double figures. But the problems it highlights such as analysing the evidence and meeting the costs, are common to many civil actions and they are problems more related to the process for handling claims rather than the substantive law. Is there a fair, efficient and effective means of processing such claims? Would a tribunal system or an inquisitorial system produce better results? Does the answer lie with improvements in the provision of legal services rather than in civil process? These questions underlie the superficially dry study of civil procedure. The answers are vital to the way in which our legal system delivers its goods to the people.

HIGH COURT PERSONAL INJURY LITIGATION

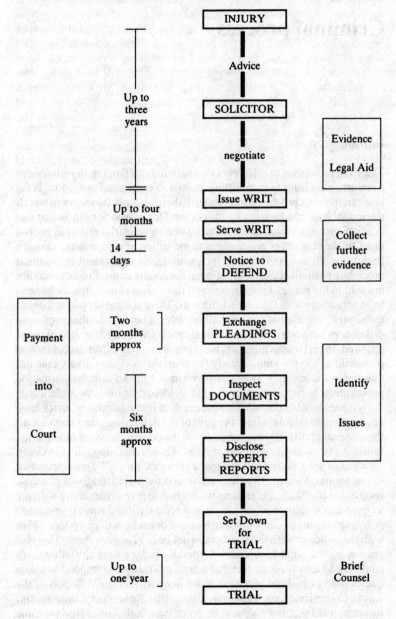

Chapter 4
Criminal process

Introduction

There are thousands of different criminal offences ranging in seriousness from dropping litter to committing murder. Yet criminal procedure is far less varied than civil procedure: indeed, there are only two ways in which a criminal case can be tried by the courts. One reason for this is that our criminal process, which is based on the same adversarial model as in civil cases, makes far fewer concessions to mediation or compromise than are found in civil cases. There is, for example, no equivalent in criminal procedure to small claims arbitration in the county court. Prosecutions are brought in the name of the Crown, and the Crown cannot openly be seen to be bargaining with the alleged criminal! There is some scope for 'behind the scenes' negotiation, as we shall see later. There are further important differences between civil and criminal cases. One is the standard of proof required. In civil cases plaintiffs must prove their cases 'on the balance of probabilities', ie they must satisfy the court that it is more likely than not that the evidence they have put forward is true. In criminal cases the prosecution is required to prove the evidence against the defendants 'beyond reasonable doubt'. This means that, if magistrates or juries have any 'reasonable doubt' about the guilt of the defendants, they must acquit them. Another difference can be seen in the consequences of defendants' refusing to co-operate with the proceedings or remaining silent in court. As we have seen, defendants can lose a civil case simply by not responding to the formal documents which are issued by plaintiffs. Even if a case reaches the trial stage, defendants who refuse to give evidence are unlikely to have much chance of success. Until recently there was an important principle in criminal cases that the failure of defendants to co-operate either with the police or with the court could not be held against them. This was known as 'the right to silence'. Generally judges were not allowed to comment adversely on the fact that defendants refused to respond to police questioning or had not given evidence in court. The 1993 Report of the Royal Commission on Criminal Justice (the Runciman Commission) recommended that there should be no change in this rule. However, the Government disagreed, and the Criminal Justice and Public Order Act 1994 provides that a court or jury 'may draw such inferences as appear proper' where suspects have refused to answer police questions or defendants have not given evidence in their own defence. This is discussed in greater detail at the end of this chapter.

Who can start criminal proceedings?

The general rule is that any private individual can bring a prosecution even if the individual has no particular interest in the case. This is usually referred to as a 'private prosecution'. The individual must persuade a magistrate to issue a summons, a document which orders the accused to appear at a magistrates' court. A magistrate is likely to be very wary of doing this, far more so than if a summons were requested by the police. Individuals will have to pay their own costs although these may be recouped in part if the prosecution succeeds. If it fails, they may have to pay some of the defence costs. The Director of Public Prosecutions (DPP) or Serious Fraud Office (SFO) can take over any case and effectively stop it by offering no evidence. An example of this occurred in October 1995 when the SFO stopped a private prosecution against the former Barings Bank trader Nick Leeson by holders of £100 million worth of Barings bonds. The Attorney-General can also stop a prosecution. A study done for the Royal Commission on Criminal Procedure (the Phillips Commission) showed that private prosecutions comprised 2.4% of the overall number. Most of these were for domestic assaults although some were shoplifting cases, as in some areas the police leave it up to the aggrieved shopkeeper to institute proceedings (this is because shopkeepers frequently failed to turn up in court to give evidence). Evidence given to the Phillips Commission was generally in favour of maintaining the right of private prosecution. It is seen by some as an essential civil liberty, providing the right to take action in cases where the police are reluctant to intervene or consider the evidence to be too weak. Others allege that private prosecutions simply provide scope for personal vendetta or revenge, and that the police are in the best position to determine if the public interest would be served by a prosecution. Some statutory offences in 'sensitive' areas, such as under the Obscene Publications Acts and the Theatres Act can only be prosecuted by 'named' officials, such as the Attorney-General or the DPP. Government departments, local authorities, nationalised industries and other public bodies also bring prosecutions. The Inland Revenue does not make frequent use of prosecution, preferring to reach an 'amicable' agreement for voluntary repayment. This is an exception to the avoidance of mediation in criminal cases: it reflects society's peculiar attitude towards tax evasion as well as the fact that such people (unlike social security claimants) can usually afford to pay the money they owe.

The greatest number of prosecutions, however, are brought as a result of action instigated by the police. Society recognises this in that the police are given greater powers than the private individual in relation to the apprehension of offenders and the investigation of crime (some individuals such as Customs and Excise officials and tax inspectors are also given greater powers). The use of these powers must be carefully controlled and in recent years there has been much discussion about the correct 'balance' between, on the one hand, the duty of the police to detect crime and, on the other hand, the right of individuals to go about their everyday business without being bothered by the police. Predictably opposing views are put forward from the likes of Tory MPs and the civil liberties organisation 'Liberty', but the incident which started a chain of events which led to major changes in the law was the murder of Maxwell Confait in Lewisham. Three boys were wrongly convicted of Confait's murder and in the subsequent enquiry under Sir Henry Fisher, serious irregularities in the conduct of the police came to light. Fisher's report recommended an enquiry into police powers – 'something like a Royal Commission' – and soon afterwards in June 1977 the Phillips Commission was set up. Its report was published in 1981 and the Government's response was the highly controversial Police and Criminal Evidence Act 1984 (PACE). This Act clarified and extended the powers of the police while at the same time introducing some of the safeguards against oppressive police conduct which had been recommended by the Phillips Commission. There are two ironies concerning the enactment of PACE. The first is that its genesis was a report which was strongly critical of police behaviour. The second is that in 1983 a report by the Policy Studies Institute (PSI) commissioned by the Metropolitan Police itself into policing in London showed that police officers frequently acted improperly, thus suggesting that even stronger safeguards might be necessary.

We shall now consider the various powers available to the police in order to assist their investigation of crime. It is important to note that the word reasonable, which occurs throughout PACE is to be interpreted objectively, ie judged by the standards of the reasonable police officer and not by the standards of the particular officer under consideration.

The power to stop and search

Prior to PACE, the power of the police to stop and search a suspect, which only exists under statute, was rather confused, with a mixture of local and national provisions. The best known national provision was that in the Misuse of Drugs Act 1971 relating to possession of drugs. There was no national provision for the stop and search of a person suspected of possessing stolen goods, although the London area was covered under the notorious section 66 of the Metropolitan Police Act 1839. Now section 1 of PACE provides that a police officer may stop and search any person or vehicle in a public place if the officer has reasonable grounds to suspect that the person possesses, or the vehicle contains, stolen goods or certain other prohibited articles. Such articles include offensive weapons, and articles made or adapted for use in connection with a burglary, theft, taking of a motor car or obtaining of property by deception. The requirement of 'reasonable suspicion' is supposed to be important and receives elaboration in one of the codes of practice issued by the Home Secretary under the provisions of PACE. It is emphasised that the power to stop a person should not be used simply to establish grounds for a search. Nor should people be stopped because of their appearance, race, or because they were a member of a group or community which has an image of being likely to commit offences.

The requirement of 'reasonable suspicion' existed before PACE but the PSI report showed that the Metropolitan Police frequently ignored it. In 33% of the cases observed, the researchers could see no possible grounds for the requirement to stop. Overall, certain characteristics seemed likely to increase the chances of a person's being stopped. Young people are eleven times more likely to be stopped than older people; men are likely to be stopped twice as often as women; and Afro-Caribbeans are more likely to be stopped than whites and, indeed, to be stopped more frequently. Even the evidence of police forces to the Phillips Commission showed admissions that individuals were stopped and searched without authority. The point was made that most of the people had no objection to being stopped. Yet, bearing in mind the fact that only 5% of those stopped and searched are arrested, the view expressed in the PSI report should be noted:

> 'Even if these people have no objections to the way a particular stop is handled, they will come to object to being stopped at all, bearing in mind that most of them are innocent.'

PACE does provide a number of safeguards. Under section 2, officers wanting to carry out a stop and search must give their name, police station and indicate the purpose of the search. Plain clothes officers must provide written evidence that they are members of the police. Under section 3, a police officer is required to make a written record of the search immediately or, if this is not practicable, as soon as possible. But if it is not practicable to make a record at all, as for example with a group of football supporters, then the officer is relieved of the requirement to do so. A copy of a search record must be made available on demand for up to twelve months. It is important to note that these safeguards only apply where a search follows a stop: no record need be made of questions which satisfy the officer that no search is necessary.

It remains to be seen how effective these safeguards will be. In a Home Office Research and Planning Unit study published in 1983, it was shown that the requirement to record a stop and search which existed in London prior to PACE was met in less than half of the cases. Many police officers found it difficult to give reasons why they stopped certain individuals. The success rate of stops and searches carried out by the Metropolitan Police is not significantly greater now than it was before PACE: in 1979 about one in eight stops resulted in an arrest, whereas in 1989 the figure was one in six.

The power of arrest

Lord Dilhorne has described the test to determine if a person has been arrested as ascertaining 'whether he has been deprived of his liberty to go where he pleases'. The fact of an arrest is not usually difficult to establish – what can be more troublesome is determining if it is lawful. If an arrest is unlawful, an arrested person is entitled to use reasonable force to resist it, although this is generally not an advisable course of conduct. The powers of lawful arrest are contained in both statute and common law.

Arrest under warrant

Under section 1(1) of the Magistrates' Courts Act 1980, a magistrate, on receiving written information on oath 'that any person has, or is suspected of having, committed an offence', may issue a warrant for the arrest of that person. A warrant cannot be issued unless the offence is indictable (see below), or punishable with imprisonment, or the address of the person is unknown.

Arrest without a warrant under statute

Section 24 of PACE provides that the police may arrest without a warrant for an arrestable offence and a number of other offences. An 'arrestable offence' is one for which the sentence is fixed by law (in effect, murder and treason); an offence which carries a maximum penalty of at least five years' imprisonment; or an offence deemed by PACE to be an arrestable offence (including offences under the Official Secrets Acts, taking a motor vehicle without authority and attempts to commit such offences). Private individuals may also make an arrest under section 24 but their powers are rather more restricted than police officers.

The situation is as follows:

(a)   Any person (ie a police officer or a private individual) may arrest without a warrant anyone who is in the act of committing an arrestable offence, or whom the person has reasonable grounds for suspecting to be committing such an offence.

(b)   Where an arrestable offence has been committed, any person may arrest without a warrant anyone who is guilty of the offence or anyone whom the person has reasonable grounds for suspecting to be guilty of it.

(c) Where police officers have reasonable grounds for suspecting that an arrestable offence has been committed, they may arrest without a warrant anyone whom they have reasonable grounds for suspecting to be guilty of the offence. The difference between (b) and (c) is important. A private individual (which includes a store detective) can only make a lawful arrest under (b) where an arrestable offence has actually been committed by someone, not necessarily the accused. If no such offence has been committed, the private individual will be liable for the tort of wrongful arrest. However, under (c), police officers are protected from liability as long as they had reasonable grounds for suspecting an arrestable offence had been committed.

(d) Police officers may arrest without a warrant anyone who is about to commit an arrestable offence or whom they have reasonable grounds for suspecting to be about to commit an arrestable offence. This power is not available to a private individual.

Under section 25, the police may arrest without warrant for non-arrestable offences if at least one of the 'general arrest conditions' is satisfied. The officer must have reasonable grounds for suspecting that any offence has been committed or attempted. The conditions are that the officer does not know and cannot find out the name and address of the suspect (or has reasonable grounds to suspect that a false name and address have been given); there are reasonable grounds to think that the suspect might cause harm to himself or others, cause loss or damage to property, commit an offence against public decency or obstruct the highway; or that a child or other vulnerable person needs to be protected from the suspect.

This provision goes much further than the recommendation of the Phillips Commission – which would only have applied where the officer did not know the suspect's name and address – and provides a significant extension to police powers.

Arrest without a warrant at common law

Any person may make an arrest without a warrant where a breach of the peace has been committed, or there is reasonable ground to suspect that it will continue or recur, or is about to take place.

Powers of entry, search and seizure

The police are given certain powers under PACE to search arrested persons and premises they have occupied. Section 32 allows arrested persons to be searched where an officer has reasonable grounds for thinking that they may be a danger to themselves or others. An officer may also search an arrested person for articles which might be used to escape from custody, or provide evidence relating to an offence. An officer may also enter and search any premises in which an arrested person was present immediately prior to arrest. The officer may seize any articles found on individuals or in premises if it is reasonably thought that they are evidence of any offence and seizure is necessary to prevent their concealment, loss or destruction. Under section 18, a search can be made of any premises occupied or controlled by a person arrested for an arrestable offence if the police have reasonable grounds to think that they will find evidence of the offence concerned or a related arrestable offence. Once the suspect has been taken to the police station, written authorisation must be obtained from a senior officer before any search is made.

There is no general power for police to enter premises; they can only do so in accordance with a specific legal provision. Usually, a warrant is necessary (other than for the situations described in the previous paragraph). A number of statutes, such as the Misuse of Drugs Act 1971, allow magistrates to issue search warrants to the police for special purposes. Section 8 of PACE for the first time provides a general power for magistrates to issue search warrants where there are reasonable grounds for believing that a 'serious arrestable offence' has been committed. This term has a rather complicated definition but basically includes offences such as murder, manslaughter, rape, and offences involving explosives and possession of firearms. In addition, the category includes an offence which is arrestable and has led, or is likely to lead to serious harm; to breaches of national security; serious interference with the administration of justice or police investigations; death or serious injury; or serious financial loss. The police must also have reasonable grounds to think that admissible evidence concerning the offence can be found on any premises, and that one or more of the following conditions applies:

(a) It is not reasonably practicable to contact any person who could give permission to enter the premises.
(b) Such a person has unreasonably refused to allow the police to enter the premises or hand over the evidence.
(c) Evidence would be hidden, removed or destroyed if the police sought access without a warrant.

The Phillips Commission recommended that permission for such warrants must be obtained by circuit judges but this view was rejected by Parliament. However, this requirement does apply when the police want to search for certain personal or business records, body samples held for medical purposes and confidential journalistic material. The circuit judge must be satisfied that there are reasonable grounds for thinking that the evidence is there and would be of major value to the police in investigating the commission of a serious arrestable offence; that unsuccessful attempts have been made to obtain the evidence or that no attempts have been made because they would be bound to fail; and that the public interest requires that the evidence be handed over. When searching premises, police officers can seize any items not covered by privilege (ie between solicitor and client) which they reasonably believe to be evidence of *any* offence. The police must also consider that it is necessary to take the items to prevent their being removed, hidden or destroyed. Yet again, this is a wider power than that recommended by the Phillips Commission which would have restricted the seizure of items not relevant to the offence being investigated to those concerning 'grave offences' (a similar category to 'serious arrestable offences'). Section 17 of PACE abolishes all common law powers of entry save one. A police officer has power to enter a building to prevent or deal with a breach of the peace.

Powers to detain and question suspects

PACE includes a number of innovations to try and meet criticism that, once suspects are taken to the police station, the police have virtually unfettered control over what happens to them. A new position, that of custody officer, was introduced. The custody officer, who must be un-connected with the case, has to ascertain if there is enough evidence to charge the suspect as soon as is practicable following the suspect's arrival at the police station. If there is enough evidence, the suspect should either be charged or informed that a prosecution may follow. The suspect should then be released with or without bail unless the custody officer reasonably believes that detention is necessary to secure or preserve evidence or to obtain evidence by questioning the suspect. A custody record must be kept containing all the details of how the suspect was treated at the police station. The suspect is entitled to a copy of the record.

Continued detention is subject to review at regular intervals. The first review should be not later than six hours after the detention was authorised, but this can be extended if it is considered that it would prejudice the investigation to break off the questioning at that stage. Subsequent reviews should take place at intervals not exceeding nine hours. Twenty-four hours after the arrest an officer not below the rank of superintendent must carry out a review. This officer can then authorise detention up to 36 hours from the arrest if the investigation is into a serious arrestable offence; if it is proceeding properly; and if continued detention is necessary to secure or preserve evidence concerning the offence or to obtain evidence by quest-ioning the suspect further. Any detention beyond 36 hours must be authorised by two magistrates sitting otherwise than in open court. At this stage the suspect can make representations. The magistrates can authorise detention for up to a further 36 hours. After the expiry of this period, the suspect must be brought before magistrates again, who can then authorise a further period of detention for up to 36 hours. However, the overall period of detention at the police station must not exceed 96 hours from the time of arrest (or arrival at the police station, if that was earlier). The suspect must then be either charged or released.

There will be little justification for most suspects to be detained beyond a fairly short period of time. Research for the Phillips Commission showed that three out of four suspects are held for less than six hours. Only one person in 20 is detained for more than 24 hours. Nevertheless, it is the conditions of detention and nature of questioning that can prove more oppressive than the length of time spent in custody. There is a large body of psychological research, including some commissioned for the Phillips Commission, which shows that statements made after lengthy or probing questioning can be highly unreliable. Before PACE, the situation concerning such aspects as cautioning and notification of the right to silence was covered by the Judges' Rules and the Administrative Directions to the Police. These had no legal force and the sanctions for their breach were internal disciplinary action by the police and the refusal by the judge to admit evidence obtained thereby at the trial. Judges had a discretion to exclude most types of evidence which had been illegally obtained. In practice such evidence was rarely excluded. But, if the evidence was in the nature of a confession, the judges had to exclude it. One example is *R v Hudson* (1981). The defendant, who was detained by the police for five days and four nights, was asked around 700 questions. Some of his answers contained admissions of guilt. The Court of Appeal quashed his conviction as the nature of the questioning was oppressive. PACE is accompanied by a number of 'codes of practice' one of which covers the detention, treatment and questioning of suspects. The Phillips Commission, which recommended the codes of practice to replace the judges' rules, suggested that they should be statutory instruments. The Government has not followed this advice and the codes, although far more detailed than their predecessors, are really of the same status. Any breach by a police officer cannot lead to prosecution. The sanctions remain the same; possible disciplinary action and possible exclusion of any resulting evidence by the courts. Section 76 of PACE contains the rules concerning the admissibility of confessions. The court should exclude any evidence obtained by oppression or as a result of anything said or done 'which was likely, in the circumstances existing at the time, to render unreliable any confession which might be made by [the suspect] in consequence thereof'. Oppression is defined as including 'torture, inhuman or degrading treatment, and the use or threat of violence (whether or not amounting to torture)'. Section 78 deals with other evidence. It provides that the court should exclude evidence if, in all the circumstances, its admission 'would have such an adverse effect on the fairness of the proceedings that the court ought not to admit it'. This retains a discretion, which under the old law was rarely exercised in favour of the accused.

Evaluation of PACE

Predictably the enactment of PACE attracted widespread criticism. Civil libertarian groups claimed that the Act considerably extended police powers and went even further than the recommendations of the Phillips Commission. More extreme opinion asserted that it was a step on the road towards a police state. On the other hand, senior police officers have said that PACE acts as a major constraint on effective policing and that the large amount of paperwork involved keeps officers off the beat and thus has led to a decline in the crime clear-up rate. Which of these views represents the true situation? The views of David J Smith, one of the researchers who compiled the PSI report previously referred to, invite the conclusion that the answer lies somewhere in between. It is simplistic, says Smith, to assume that the enactment of a piece of legislation is going to change the way in which the police go about doing their job. There are three main reasons for this. First, some of the important powers given to the police have been deliberately defined in vague terms. One example is the offence of 'threatening, abusive or insulting behaviour with intent to provoke a breach of the peace, or whereby a breach of the peace may be occasioned'. Even the requirement of reasonableness, which is found throughout PACE, is vague enough to pose few problems for officers who have acted improperly. Secondly, although the law is one source of rules for the police, there are others which in practice are equally important; for example, supporting a colleague. Thirdly, a small number of police officers have their own aims which are not provided by any law at all. The attack by several Metropolitan Police officers on five boys in 1983 and the fact that it took so long to identify the culprits are good illustrations of the last two reasons. In any event, Smith considers that PACE does not significantly affect police powers: 'Mostly it is just a combing out of snags and a tying up of loose ends that leaves unaltered the basic conditions and constraints within which the police operate and which shape their behaviour'. According to Smith, the one provision in PACE which may prove significant is the introduction of tape-recording interviews with suspects in police stations. Following successful trials in several areas, tape-recording has been mandatory (save in exceptional circumstances) since the beginning of 1992.

The Runciman Commission made a number of recommendations concerning safeguards for suspects. They approved of the growth in tape-recording interviews with suspects and considered that this might be extended to cover interviews outside the police station. Video recording should be used to monitor the custody officer and video recordings or colour photographs should be taken of all identification parades. The Commission were uncertain about the video recording of interviews, but thought the matter should be investigated. If a suspect waived the right to legal advice, this should be recorded on tape at the custody desk.

Bail from the police station

The question of bail arises twice, first at the police station and then when the defendant appears before a court. The granting of bail means that a person suspected or accused of a crime is released from detention until the case is heard. Bail is extremely important to a suspect. Apart from the obvious unpleasantness of being locked up, the suspect may become unemployed and will find it difficult to consult with lawyers and thus prepare an adequate defence. In fact, the refusal of bail can have a significant effect on the outcome of the case. Research suggests that suspects detained in custody pending trial are more likely to plead guilty, to be convicted, and to be imprisoned than suspects who were granted bail.

If a person has been arrested under a warrant, the warrant itself will state whether bail is to be granted – in other words, the decision is made by a magistrate rather than by the police. Otherwise, the police have to act under statutory provisions. The custody officer can only order the further detention of a person brought to the police station, but not yet charged, if the officer reasonably thinks that detention is 'necessary to secure or preserve evidence relating to an offence for which he is under arrest or to obtain such evidence by questioning him'. In most cases custody officers would have little difficulty in justifying this. A person who has been charged must be released unless

(a) the police cannot discover the person's name and address or reasonably think that the information given is false,
(b) the police reasonably think that detention is necessary for the person's protection or to prevent the person causing harm to someone else or interfering with property, or
(c) the police reasonably believe that the person will 'jump' bail, interfere with witnesses or otherwise obstruct the course of justice.

In addition, a juvenile can be detained in custody 'in his own interests'. Any person kept in custody after charge must be brought before a magistrates' court 'as soon as is practicable'. Following a recommendation of the Runciman Commission, the Criminal Justice and Public Order Act 1994 allows the police to grant bail subject to conditions. Police bail is particularly important as there is evidence that courts are influenced in their decisions about granting bail by whether the accused was granted bail by the police (see, for example, the 1973 Cobden Trust Report *'Bail or Custody'*). The criminal statistics show that a large majority of people arrested and charged are given bail by the police: in 1994 the figure was 88%.

The decision to prosecute

Many criminal offences that are committed never come to the attention of the authorities. This is often because there is either no victim to report the offence (eg personal use of illicit drugs) or else the victim does not bother to report the offence (eg minor cases of vandalism may not seem worth reporting). Such offences are said to comprise 'the dark figure' of crime. Yet even those offences which do come to the attention of the authorities are not necessarily proceeded against. As far as the police are concerned, the decision to prosecute is taken at two different stages. The first stage is where the police on the street, or in a patrol car, observe a crime being committed. They have to decide whether to report the incident. They may simply administer an informal caution, in which case the matter will be taken no further. The second stage occurs where the officer on patrol reports the incident and the decision is taken by a senior officer.

Formerly the police made the final decision to prosecute in the cases they were dealing with. Moreover, the police effectively controlled the prosecution, and in some magistrates' courts police officers actually appeared as advocates. This practice was diminished by the appointment of prosecuting solicitors by many police forces, but even this arrangement was perceived to be far from ideal: solicitors had to act in accordance with the instructions of chief constables, even if the solicitors felt that a prosecution was unwise. In short, the system was criticised for its lack of independence. The police, having investigated the case and brought the prosecution, would have a strong interest to be successful in court – far stronger, it was alleged, than in the normal adversarial relationship found in civil cases. The police, for example, might be unwilling to reveal to the defence all the information they had obtained while investigating the charge.

The pressure group 'Justice' published a report in 1970 calling for an independent prosecution service which would separate the investigation of crime from its prosecution. The report pointed out that the system in England and Wales was different from that operated in many other countries, and particular reference was made to Scotland. In that country there is a long-established system whereby the police have to report crimes to local officials known as procurators-fiscal who study each case and make the decision to prosecute. In minor cases they conduct the prosecutions themselves.

The matter was considered by the Phillips Commission. It concluded that the existing arrangements were unsatisfactory, giving rise to a possible conflict of interest on the part of the police between the collection of evidence and the prosecution of the case in court. The Phillips Commission considered submissions as to what form a new prosecution service should take. The main area of disagreement was as to whether it should be run on a national or local basis. The particular advantages of the latter approach were said to be that it would cause less drastic upheaval of the existing system and could be more adaptable to local variations in prosecution policy. On the other hand, such local variations were observed by some critics as a major drawback of the existing system. In the end the Phillips Commission recommended the local scheme. The Government, however, decided to reject the recommendation of the RCCP and adopt a nationally-based system of independent prosecution. It has been suggested that they were largely influenced in this decision by the perceived threat of local councils wanting to interfere in prosecution policy. The Crown Prosecution Service (CPS) was created by the Prosecution of Offences Act 1985 and came into effect nationally on 1 October 1986. It is under the control of the DPP. The police still investigate criminal offences and initially prefer charges but from then on the case is handed over to the CPS. It may decide to amend or drop any or all of the charges.

The Phillips Commission also noted wide variations in the prosecution policies of police forces. This can be seen in the level of formal police cautioning. Statistics cited by the Phillips Commission showed that, for example, the Suffolk police cautioned 22% of offenders over 17 whereas several forces, including the Metropolitan Police, cautioned less than 3%. As a response to the Phillips Commission's criticisms, the Attorney-General in 1983 published the guidelines on prosecution which he had previously circulated to all chief constables. No such official pronouncement had ever been made before. These have now been replaced by a Code for Crown Prosecutors. No prosecution should be brought unless 'there is a realistic prospect of a conviction'. Even if such a prospect exists, consideration should be given to 'whether the public interest requires a prosecution'. The more serious the charge, the more likely it is that the public interest will make such a requirement. Otherwise consideration should be given to the likely penalty (eg would it be only a conditional discharge?); the 'staleness' of the offence; the age of the offender (old age can also be relevant); the offender's mental or physical condition; the special nature of sexual offences (eg was the 'victim' a willing party?) and the attitude of the complainant.

Most of these criteria suggest that factors peculiar to the offender are the most important in determining whether a prosecution is necessary in a 'minor' case – one where the 'public interest' (or perhaps the public) does not demand a punishment. However, it seems unlikely that the increased use of cautioning in recent years has resulted from greater attention being paid to the views of criminologists (except, perhaps, in the case of juveniles). The criminal justice system is becoming greatly overburdened at almost every level and there is growing pressure to reduce the number of cases coming before the courts.

The CPS certainly experienced 'teething troubles'. Two reports have been published on its workings, one by the National Audit Office in 1989 and the other by the House of Commons Public Accounts and Home Affairs Committees in 1990. These suggested that staff shortages, insufficient time for training and serious under-funding were responsible for the service's initial problems. The overall situation, however, appeared to be improving. The salaried employees of the CPS have the same rights of audience in court as practising solicitors. These can be extended by the Lord Chancellor and there have been calls for CPS lawyers to be allowed to appear as advocates in Crown Court trials. Indeed, this is one possible means whereby the Bar's monopoly in that court could ultimately be removed (see Chapter 5) and it would lead to notable financial savings. Nevertheless, there is some evidence that the CPS is already achieving one of its main objectives – the sifting out of weak or unnecessary prosecutions and the resulting easing of pressure on the overburdened criminal justice system. In 1995 about 12% of all cases were discontinued.

Finally, it is worth noting that research into the Scottish system shows that procurators-fiscal prosecute in 92% of cases referred to them by the police and do not exercise a fully independent role (Moody and Tombs *'Prosecution in the Public Interest'* (1982)).

Magistrates

Once a decision to prosecute an offender has been taken, a case will be prepared and eventually it will be heard in court. As we shall see below, all criminal cases start in a magistrates' court. No less than 98% of them finish there as well. Magistrates therefore play a crucial part in our criminal justice system and it is to the institution of the magistracy that we now turn.

The position of magistrate or justice of the peace, dates back to the Justices of the Peace Act 1361, which makes it one of the oldest remaining features of our legal system. Their main function has always been to deal with criminals, although over the centuries they acquired a number of additional administrative functions (one of these which remains is their power to grant liquor licences) and magistrates' courts nowadays have statutory jurisdiction in certain family law matters. The zenith of the magistracy's power and influence was in the eighteenth century when the typical justice portrayed in the writings of such people as Henry Fielding (himself a magistrate) was the influential local squire. But the corruption of the magistracy soon became apparent and this had two significant consequences: discontent which helped Robert Peel found the Metropolitan Police in 1829, and the creation in London and other major cities of 'stipendiary magistrates', or salaried professional magistrates who, sitting alone, have the full powers of a bench of magistrates.

To what extent are magistrates in the later years of the twentieth century different from those described by eighteenth century novelists? Despite the vast social changes that have occurred in the past two hundred years, there are still allegations that the basis of the magistracy has not significantly changed, especially in rural areas; that the typical magistrate is still upper or upper middle class. There is a certain amount of evidence which sheds some light on this. The 1948 report of the Royal Commission on Justices of the Peace showed that about three quarters of all magistrates came from professional or middle class occupations. Studies published in the 1970s suggested that the situation has hardly changed. A 1985 Cobden Trust report found evidence of racial prejudice and racial discrimination amongst the magistracy. Moreover, the proportion of black magistrates in many areas was below that of black people in the local community. Skyrme has researched the party political affiliations of magistrates appointed in 1983. He found that 41% claimed to be Conservative, 28% Labour, 11% Liberal, 1% SDP, 0.3% Plaid Cymru and 18.7% either independent or not known.

The evidence, then, tends to indicate that the allegations are true. But the question must be asked: does it matter? There are two opposing schools of thought. The two Royal Commissions which have reported on magistrates (in 1910 and 1948) were set up by governments which were concerned about a strong Conservative bias on the benches. Both concluded that magistrates should come from varied social backgrounds. On the other hand, some people might agree with the views of Professor Rupert Jackson in his book '*The Machinery of Justice in England*'; 'Benches do tend to be largely middle to upper class, but that is a characteristic of those set in authority over us, whether in town hall, Whitehall, hospitals and all manner of institutions.' Bond and Lemon carried out a survey of 160 newly appointed magistrates in 1975/6. They found that on appointment there were no significant differences on the basis of social class in attitudes to penal philosophy, sentencing practice, the causes of crime, court procedure and the role of the magistrate. Some differences appeared on the basis of political affiliation, with Conservatives likely to have a more punitive penal philosophy. Bond and Lemon's survey does not show if particular attitudes are reflected in behaviour on the bench, although they speculate that it might be. Earlier research on this question is inconclusive. It seems that the particular bench a defendant appears before can be of far greater importance than the precise composition of the court and this brings us to the second major criticism levelled at magistrates' courts, namely the inconsistency between different benches.

Under the 'neo-classical' model on which our criminal justice is based (this is discussed in Chapter 13), similar crimes committed in similar circumstances by offenders with similar backgrounds should receive a similar punishment. At the Crown Court level, it is easier to achieve this consistency for various reasons: the trial judge is more knowledgeable about sentencing, the court proceedings are fully recorded and there is close control applied by the Court of Appeal, Criminal Division. Magistrates, however, are amateurs with relatively little guidance on sentencing. They have a Home Office booklet, '*The Sentence of the Court*', to guide them and they can always seek advice from their clerk. They do not receive much guidance from the Crown Court. All magistrates appointed since 1 January 1966 have to undergo basic training and those appointed since 1 January 1980 have to receive further training comprising twelve hours every three years (magistrates on youth court or domestic court panels receive additional training). The compulsory require-ment therefore is hardly very great and is probably inadequate; but there is evidence that some magistrates do not even bother to complete it. In October 1986, the Lord Chancellor told the annual meeting of the Magistrates' Association that a number of senior magistrates were not bothering to attend the training courses and, if they continued like this, they could not expect to chair benches. Evidence of inconsistency between different magistrates' courts appeared in the 1985 Home Office publication, '*Managing Criminal Justice*'. The Home Office admitted that, while the benches strove for internal con-sistency, there was little effort to attain consistency with neighbouring courts. Further evidence is found in the 1989 Consumers' Association survey: for example, the average fine for speeding imposed by Atherstone and Coleshill magistrates was more than double that of the nearby bench at Sutton Coldfield. The Home Office figures were further analysed by the National Association of Probation Officers. One interesting finding was that magistrates in urban areas tend to be less punitive than those in neighbouring rural areas: for example, in 1983 Bristol magistrates imprisoned 14% of males found guilty of indictable offences, whereas Weston-super-Mare magistrates imprisoned 22% (these figures include suspended sentences). It has been suggested that magistrates in inner city areas have a better understanding of the causes of crime than their rural counterparts.

Is the system of lay magistrates justifiable? Suggestions have been made over the years that the stipendiary system should replace the lay magistracy or that a stipendiary should sit together with lay magistrates on each bench. Whatever merits these proposals may have, there seems no prospect of their coming to fruition. The lay magistracy has the emotional appeal of involving the ordinary person in the administration of justice and the practical appeal of dealing with the vast majority of criminal cases relatively cheaply. This is surely an unassailable combination.

Appearance before the magistrates

All criminal cases start in a magistrates' court. There are three ways in which accused persons can come before the court. They can be arrested either with or without a warrant and granted bail by the police; they can be arrested either with or without a warrant and be brought before the court by the police; or they can be summoned by the police. This last device, which in 1994 was used in 61% of cases disposed of in magistrates' courts, simply orders the accused to turn up at the court at a particular time. The first question the magistrates will consider will be the mode of trial. For procedural purposes, criminal offences are divided into three categories: offences triable only on indictment, offences triable only summarily and offences triable either way. Offences triable only on indictment must be tried at the Crown Court by judge and jury. As the other two categories were created by statute, the easiest way to define offences triable only on indictment is by exclusion, ie they are offences which statute law does not make triable summarily or triable either way. In practice, they are serious criminal offences such as murder, manslaughter, rape and robbery. Offences triable only summarily must be tried at a magistrates' court. These include many small crimes such as minor motoring offences. The third category, offences triable either way, can be tried either on indictment by judge and jury or summarily by magistrates. The magistrates may insist on a trial at the Crown Court, but they cannot insist on trying the case themselves if the defendant wishes to be tried at the Crown Court. The DPP, Attorney-General or Solicitor-General, if involved in the case, can insist on trial at the Crown Court. Many offences under the Theft Acts come in this category. In recent years a number of offences which were triable either way have been made triable only summarily to ease the pressure of work on the Crown Court. Most of these have been non-controversial, but one proposal which continues to arouse hostility is that trial by judge and jury should cease to be available for small thefts, say under £10. As yet, no government has dared to adopt this proposal. The Runciman Commission proposed that the mode of trial for either-way offences should be decided in two stages. If the prosecution and defence can reach agreement, that would be binding. If they cannot agree, the magistrates should decide. The defendant would thus lose the right to elect jury trial in these cases.

After the mode of trial has been determined, there are two other important decisions for the magistrates. One is whether to grant the accused legal aid. This is discussed in the next chapter. The other depends on whether the case can be dealt with there and then. This may be possible if the charge involves a simple summary offence. If it is not possible, the question of bail will arise.

Bail from the court

The granting of bail to an accused by a court is important for the same reasons as the granting of bail to a suspect by the police; but, due to the greater periods of time involved, the importance will be even greater. Unlike police bail, the granting of bail by a court is not governed by PACE but is contained in the Bail Act 1976. This Act was designed to place restrictions on the wide discretion formerly held by magistrates in the granting of bail and at the same time to increase the number of defendants released on bail before trial. This means that a court should consider the question of bail even if the defendant does not specifically ask for it. This presumption in favour of bail has been partly eroded by the Criminal Justice and Public Order Act 1994. Following concern expressed by some senior police officers that too many offences were being committed by suspects already on bail (so-called 'bail bandits'), section 26 of the 1994 Act states that the presumption should not apply when such a person is charged with a non-summary offence (see below). Furthermore, section 25 provides that a person charged with murder, attempted murder, manslaughter, rape or attempted rape should not be granted bail if the person already has a conviction for one of these offences. However, this is unlikely to make much difference in practice, as it is unlikely that such a person would have received bail before.

The Bail Act 1976 itself is subject to a number of exceptions which are contained in Schedule 1. The exceptions are divided into two lists: the first list applies if the defendant is charged with an offence which carries a possible prison sentence (an imprisonable offence) and the second list applies if the offence charged does not carry a possible prison sentence (a non-imprisonable offence).

For imprisonable offences, a court does not have to grant bail if it is satisfied that it is probable that the defendant, if released on bail, would (a) fail to surrender to custody, or (b) commit an offence while on bail, or (c) interfere with witnesses or otherwise obstruct the course of justice. In addition, bail need not be granted if the court has not had enough time to obtain sufficient information to reach a decision. Finally, a defendant charged with an imprisonable offence whose case has been adjourned for a report need not be granted bail if the court thinks it would be impracticable to complete the report without keeping the defendant in custody.

The grounds on which a court can refuse bail to a person charged with a non-imprisonable offence are, not surprisingly, more restricted. Indeed it was unsuccessfully argued when the Bail Bill was before Parliament that bail should be automatically available for an offence which was not even serious enough to carry a possible prison sentence. Bail can be refused if the defendant has previously 'jumped bail' and the court considers that, in view of this, it is likely to happen again. For both imprisonable and non-imprisonable offences, bail need not be granted where courts consider defendants should be kept in custody for their own protection (or, if juveniles, for their own welfare); where the defendants are already serving a custodial sentence and are before the court for some other offence; or where defendants have already absconded on the present charge.

A court which decides to grant bail has the option of imposing conditions on the defendant. If it decides not to impose any conditions, the defendant only has to turn up at court on the specified day. Failure to do this constitutes an offence. The Act itself does not give any examples of what would be acceptable conditions but those commonly imposed include reporting to the police at regular intervals, residing (or not residing) at a particular place, and surrendering one's passport. If the police reasonably consider that a condition has been, or is about to be, broken, they are able to arrest the defendants and bring them before a magistrate. The Act abolished the notion of 'personal recognisance', whereby a defendant who failed to turn up as required had to pay a sum of money, but a court can require a defendant to provide a monetary security if it considers there is a danger the defendant will go abroad. A court is still allowed to require sureties. A 'surety' is a person who undertakes to pay a sum of money to the court should the defendant not appear. No money needs to be handed over in advance. If the defendant does not turn up, the court has a discretion whether to 'estreat', or order the payment of, the sum. All decisions concerning bail must be recorded and, if it is refused or conditions are attached, the reasons must be given to the defendant. A court must now also give reasons if it does grant bail to an accused charged with murder, manslaughter, rape, attempted murder or attempted rape. If a defendant who is not legally represented is refused bail, the court must inform the defendant of the right to apply to a higher court.

From the outset, the Bail Act 1976 was criticised. Its main critics were the police, who considered that its provisions would result in more defendants being granted bail and a corresponding increase in criminal offences. But although the level of reported crime has greatly increased since the Bail Act came into force (and was increasing before), there is no evidence that this is attributable to the Act itself. In fact, the percentage of defendants granted bail by magistrates has remained fairly constant for the past ten years. One factor that has changed – although not caused by magistrates – is that defendants remanded in custody now spend far longer awaiting trial: in 1975 the average time on remand in prison was 25 days, whereas by 1994 it had risen to 59 days for males and 44 days for females. This is another consequence of the severe pressure of numbers on the courts. The Prosecution of Offences Act 1985 introduced a scheme throughout most of England and Wales whereby, if a defendant in custody is not brought to trial within a specified period, release on bail will be ordered. However, the courts can grant the prosecution extensions to these time limits, and the scheme does not operate as well as in Scotland where limits have existed for a long time.

Whatever criticisms can be levelled at the bail system, therefore, are not attributable to the introduction of the Bail Act. What are the main criticisms? Although the rate of granting bail is slowly increasing, many people consider that considerably more defendants could be safely released into the community pending trial. It is also worth noting that in 1994 23% of defendants who had been remanded in custody at some stage were acquitted (or their case was not proceeded with) and a further 34% ultimately received a non-custodial sentence. Was it really necessary to lock these people up? In relation to the granting of bail, magistrates' courts show the same inconsistency that we have already seen in sentencing. For example, in 1985 magistrates' courts in Hampshire granted bail in 89% of cases it considered, whereas in the adjacent county of Dorset magistrates' courts only granted bail in 63% of cases. There are many variations of this magnitude and, bearing in mind the statutory criteria that magistrates have to consider in making their bail decision, it seems difficult to justify them: presumably Dorset people are no more likely to 'jump bail' than those from Hampshire! There is growing evidence that magistrates are increasingly less likely to 'rubber stamp' police objections to bail; this view was confirmed in Doherty and East's study of Cardiff magistrates' courts. One way in which the quality of magistrates' bail decisions could be improved, and hopefully more consistency introduced, would be through the increase of bail information schemes, which at present operate in over 100 courts. These schemes allow the probation service to provide verifiable information to the CPS in cases where the police are likely to object to bail. A Home Office Research and Planning Unit evaluation has indicated that the schemes are successful in increasing the use of bail.

What can an accused do if bail is refused? One course formerly available was to apply to another bench of magistrates. But in *R v Nottingham Justices, ex p Davies* (1980) the Divisional Court ruled that, after two unsuccessful applications, no further application for bail could be made to magistrates unless there had been a change of circumstances. This has been broadly codified in section 154 of the Criminal Justice Act 1988. Moreover, section 155 of the Act allows for the introduction of a power whereby a court can order a remand in custody for up to 28 days without the accused's consent. The accused does, however, have a right of appeal against a refusal to grant bail. An application can be made to a judge in chambers, but this is expensive as a lawyer must be used and criminal legal aid is unavailable for this purpose. Alternatively, an application can be made to the Official Solicitor (a court officer). This is purely a paperwork application which is given (together with many others) to a judge. There is no charge involved but the chances of success are slim. The third method is an application to the Crown Court. Criminal legal aid is available for this purpose.

The police's concern with 'bail bandits' (see above) has led to provisions allowing the granting of bail to be challenged. The Bail (Amendment) Act 1993 gives the prosecution the right to appeal to a judge in chambers where bail has been granted to a person charged with an offence carrying a possible prison sentence of at least five years, or with 'joyriding'. The Criminal Justice and Public Order Act 1994 has inserted a provision into the Bail Act 1976 which allows prosecutors to ask magistrates' courts to reconsider their decision to grant bail.

Summary trial

If an accused is charged with a summary offence, or is charged with an offence triable either way but decides against trial by judge and jury, the trial will take place at a magistrates' court, either before a bench of magistrates (a minimum of two but usually three) or in some parts of the country before a stipendiary magistrate. How does a person accused of an offence triable either way decide which court to be tried in? A trial by magistrates should take place sooner and magistrates have more limited powers of sentencing than a Crown Court judge (usually a maximum fine of £5,000 and/or six months imprisonment for a single offence). On the other hand, there has been a widely-held belief that defendants stand a better chance of being acquitted by a jury than by magistrates and this was confirmed by the Home Office Research and Planning Unit study *'Managing Criminal Justice'* published in 1985. A Crown Court trial is conducted with greater formality and points of law are likely to receive more consideration. Legal aid is nearly always available for Crown Court trials but is more difficult to obtain for trial by magistrates.

The defendant who is tried by the magistrates will be asked by the court clerk to make a response to the charge: this is called a plea. If a guilty plea is made, the prosecution lawyer will briefly describe the facts of the case and details of the accused, including any previous convictions. The defendant or the defendant's lawyer will then make a plea in mitigation. This consists of the defendant's explanation for the crime and reasons, including personal circumstances, why any punishment imposed should be as light as possible. The magistrates will then pass sentence. If the defendant pleads not guilty, the prosecution has to prove guilt beyond reasonable doubt. The prosecution may make an opening speech, and then witnesses will be called. Each will be examined (ie questioned) by the prosecution and then may be cross-examined by the defence. The prosecution may re-examine the witness, but this should be confined to dealing with points raised in the cross-examination. At the end of the prosecution case the defence can submit that there is no case to answer. The defence are here alleging that no reasonable court could possibly convict the defendant on the basis of the prosecution's evidence. This submission is infrequently made and is even less frequently successful. It is then the defence's turn to present their case. They do not in fact have to present any evidence at all but if, as usually happens, they choose to do so, the examination, cross-examination and re-examination of witnesses will take place in the same way as in the prosecution case, except, of course this time the defence will be conducting the initial examination. At the end of the defence evidence, the defence lawyer can make a closing speech to the magistrates. The magistrates will then decide on their verdict, if necessary by a majority decision. If they find the defendant guilty, the prosecution will read out any previous convictions and the defence will make a plea in mitigation. Sentence will then be passed. A defendant in any criminal trial is arguably at a disadvantage to the prosecution; this will be discussed later. One particular disadvantage in summary trials that is not present in trials on indictment is that the defence has no prior notice of the prosecution case against them. The Criminal Law Act 1977 provided for prior notice to be given but for several years the section was not brought into effect. However, rules were introduced in 1985 stating that the prosecution must provide advance disclosure of its case to the defence in the summary trial of offences triable either way.

The Runciman Commission recommended that, after the prosecution case has been disclosed, defendants should be required to inform the prosecution of the substance of their defence, or indicate that they will not be calling any evidence. A failure to do this would render a defendant liable to adverse comment from the prosecution or the judge.

Transfer proceedings

All criminal cases start in a magistrates' court but not all of them finish there. For over four hundred years magistrates' courts have had a second function in addition to that of holding summary trials. They have also acted as examining magistrates to provide a filter to ensure that there is enough evidence for a case to go to the Crown Court for trial on indictment. This procedure is known as committal proceedings. There are two types of committal proceedings: 'old style', or 'section 6(1)' committal proceedings and 'section 6(2)' committals (both types of proceedings are now contained in section 6 of the Magistrates' Courts Act 1980). The section 6(1) proceedings were the only type possible until the enactment of the Criminal Justice Act 1967. These involved a full exposition of the prosecution's case. Prosecution witnesses gave their evidence and were liable to cross-examination by the defence. The evidence had to be written down and read back to the witness. The defence had to decide whether to call any of its own witnesses or to reserve them until the trial. Witnesses were usually only called if the defence felt they had a good chance of persuading the magistrates that the case was too weak to go to trial. The Criminal Justice Act 1967 provided that in certain cases the oral statements could be replaced by written depositions. This could save considerable amounts of time but the overall procedure remained slow and was arguably un-necessary where the accused intended to plead guilty at the trial anyway or had decided not to challenge the prosecution evidence at that stage. Section 6(2) committals were introduced by section 1 of the Criminal Justice Act 1967 to cover these cases. This form of committal could be used when all the prosecution evidence was in the form of written statements, the accused was legally represented and the defence did not allege that the statements contained insufficient evidence to justify committing the accused for trial. In recent years about 98% of committals have been of the 'section 6(2)' type.

Section 6(2) committals, although administratively desirable, could raise problems. The situation arose that nearly all committals were largely unconsidered by magistrates and this placed a heavy duty on lawyers to give the fullest consideration to the case. This appears not to have happened in the '*Confait* case', referred to above. The convictions of the boys were quashed by the Court of Appeal in 1975 as there were serious discrepancies in the evidence. A subsequent inquiry under a former High Court judge, Sir Henry Fisher, was critical of the fact that the lawyers had not discovered these discrepancies at the committal stage. The committal had been of the 'old style' but with written statements instead of oral testimony. Fisher concluded that, if there is an argument for committal proceedings, they may be unreliable unless accompanied by oral testimony.

The Runciman Commission noted the criticisms of committal proceedings and recommended that they should be abolished. This was enacted in the Criminal Justice and Public Order Act 1994, which provides for their replacement by 'transfer for trial arrangements'. A notice of the prosecution case must be served on both the magistrates' court and the accused, who may accept it or apply for it to be dismissed. The court will reject an application for dismissal if it considers that there is sufficient evidence to put the accused on trial by jury. However, transfer proceedings have not been brought into effect and it has been reported that solicitors and some magistrates are unhappy with the new scheme.

Plea bargaining

Although plea bargaining can take place before a summary trial, it is of greater significance for trials on indictment. Plea bargaining refers to a process whereby a defendant agrees to plead guilty to a charge in return for some sort of advantage such as a withdrawal of police objection to bail or another charge being dropped. A variation of this occurs where a defendant agrees to plead guilty to a less serious charge, for example theft rather than robbery. Plea bargaining appears to have originated in the USA where, not only is it conducted far more openly, but it has also been approved by the Supreme Court. The American criminal justice system differs from ours in two important respects which help to explain this.

Prosecutions are conducted by elected officials known as district attorneys, who may be under considerable pressure to obtain convictions. They also make a recommendation on sentence to the trial judge. In addition, many crimes in the USA carry high mandatory prison sentences, thus increasing the attraction of pleading guilty to a less serious offence.

Plea bargaining can take two forms: agreements between prosecution and defence lawyers and agreements between the lawyers and the trial judge. Both types are found in the USA. In England, the former appears to take place without any judicial criticism whereas the latter has been closely restricted by the courts. The existence of plea bargaining among lawyers, which has long been suspected of taking place, was confirmed in research during the 1970s by John Baldwin and Michael McConville into criminal trials in Birmingham. The question of plea bargaining involving the trial judge was considered in the case *R v Turner* (1970). The Court of Appeal laid down five guidelines:

1 Counsel should be free to advise defendants to plead guilty and point out that doing so may attract a lighter sentence. Counsel must emphasise to defendants that they should not plead guilty unless they are guilty.
2 Defendants should have complete freedom of choice over plea.
3 There should be free access between counsel and judges. Any discussions that take place should include counsel for both sides. Discussions should normally take place in open court but in special circumstances it may be necessary for them to be in private.
4 Judges should not indicate the type or length of sentence they are minded to impose unless they can indicate the nature of the sentence irrespective of the defendant's plea.
5 Counsel should tell defendants the content of any discussion that has taken place with judges.

These guidelines are not free from difficulty. The first one refers to the well-established sentencing principle established by the Court of Appeal in cases such as *R v de Haan* (1967) that, if a defendant pleads guilty, the sentencer should make a reduction from the sentence that would have been imposed had the defendant been convicted following a not guilty plea. It has since been shown that this reduction can be about 25-30%. Yet the fourth guideline states that the judge should not give any indication that the sentence will be affected by the pleas. These two guidelines appear to be inconsistent.

The Runciman Commission recommended that courts should give a graduated sentence discount for pleading guilty: a full discount of one-third should be given for a plea of guilty at the committal stage, a reduced discount for such a plea at a preparatory hearing, and only a small discount for a guilty plea on the day of the trial. As a result, the Criminal Justice and Public Order Act 1994 provides that the stage in the proceedings at

which the offender indicated an intention to plead guilty, and the circumstances in which this indication was given, shall be taken into account in
determining what sentence to pass.

Supporters of plea bargaining claim that it has a number of advantages.
In the Crown Court about 70% of defendants plead guilty. If this figure were
to be reduced by much, the system would become overloaded. It is therefore
desirable for administrative purposes that defendants are encouraged to plead
guilty. It is also cheaper because it saves the expense of trials. Defendants
will be spared the trauma of going into the witness box.

Yet plea bargaining has many critics. There is a growing amount of
evidence, including the study in Birmingham by Baldwin and McConville,
that innocent people sometimes plead guilty and that plea bargaining can
persuade them to do this. Plea bargaining can also make a mockery of
sentencing. What would be the point of a man who had committed an
indecent assault, and was in need of some sort of treatment, being convicted
of battery or assault occasioning actual bodily harm? Whichever philosophy of sentencing one subscribes to, it is surely necessary for people to
be sentenced for what they have done. Moreover, it is not necessarily true
that plea bargaining saves money. Plea bargaining often occurs at the last
moment and this can cause considerable disruption and expense.

The Runciman Commission considered the question of plea bargaining.
They thought that the guidelines in *R v Turner* should be altered by the
introduction of a 'sentence canvass'. This would involve five stages. First,
it should only occur at the request of defence counsel acting on instructions
from the defendant. Second, it could take place at a preparatory hearing,
at a hearing called specially for the purpose, or at the trial. Third, both
sides should be represented and either a note or a recording should be made.
Fourth, the only question the judge may answer is 'What would be the
maximum sentence if my client were to plead guilty at this stage?' Fifth,
the judge may decline to answer the question if it is very difficult to do so
or might prejudice others, such as co-defendants.

Trial on indictment

If the magistrates commit the accused for trial, it will be held at the Crown
Court before a judge and jury. It should be noted in passing that there are
two alternative ways of bringing a defendant to trial at the Crown Court.
People charged with serious fraud offences may be brought before the
Crown Court by the Director of the Serious Fraud Office. There is also a
little-used procedure known as a voluntary bill of indictment. Any person
can apply to a High Court judge in writing for permission to prefer a
voluntary bill of indictment and must give reasons for wishing to do so. It
is difficult to justify the existence of the voluntary bill of indictment; its
procedure seems inherently secretive.

The term 'indictment' refers to the formal document which contains the charge or charges the accused will face at the Crown Court. An indictment may contain several different charges. Each one is called a 'count'. The trial procedure at the Crown Court is similar to that in a summary trial before magistrates. If the defendant pleads guilty the procedure is almost the same, the main difference being that, if the defendant in the Crown Court is represented, it must be by a barrister. If the defendant pleads not guilty to any of the charges on the indictment, a jury is sworn in. The indictment is read to the jury and then prosecuting counsel makes a speech setting out the case against the defendant. The prosecution witnesses then give evidence and are subject to cross-examination and re-examination. At the end of the prosecution evidence defence counsel may make a submission of no case to answer. If this is unsuccessful, the defence present their case. Defence counsel can only make an opening speech if at least one witness (other than the defendant) is to give evidence about the facts of the case. After the defence witnesses have appeared, prosecution counsel and the defence counsel make closing speeches. The judge sums up the case to the jury which then retires to consider its verdict. If the accused is found guilty, details of any previous convictions are given together with other personal information about the accused. The defence can then make a plea of mitigation.

The role of the jury

The different functions of judge and jury can be simply stated: the judge is concerned with questions of law and the jury is concerned with questions of fact. Like many simple definitions, however, this one contains hidden complexity. For example, to find a person guilty of theft, the jury must find an 'appropriation' of the item in question took place. But they cannot do this until the judge tells them what is the legal definition of appropriation in the Theft Act 1968 and the cases decided under it. Indeed, in the relationship between judges and juries, judges hold a very influential position. They conduct the trial and control the evidence the jury is allowed to hear. If it becomes apparent during a trial that the evidence cannot support a conviction (something which should have been ascertained either by the Crown Prosecution Service or at the committal stage), a judge can direct a jury to acquit the accused and they must follow this instruction. If the trial runs its full course, the judge will sum up the case to the jury before they retire to consider their verdict. But once this stage has been reached, there is nothing more the judge can do: however perverse the jury's verdict might seem, it has to be accepted. If the verdict is an acquittal, it is unchallengeable. There is no appeal against an acquittal at the Crown Court and, once acquitted, the accused cannot be charged with the same offence again.

Over the years juries have shown their independence by acquitting defendants apparently in the face of the evidence. Historically this often happened in the case of the many crimes which carried the death penalty. The offence of causing death by dangerous driving was created because juries were reluctant to convict motorists of manslaughter. In recent years juries have shown their dislike of prosecutions in particular cases by returning not guilty verdicts. The civil servant, Clive Ponting, was acquitted in 1985 of charges under the Official Secrets Act of passing classified information to a Member of Parliament in what many people considered a politically-motivated prosecution. In 1991 Patrick Pottle and Michael Randle were acquitted of helping the Soviet agent George Blake escape from Wormwood Scrubs prison in 1966, even though they had admitted the facts. They claimed, however, that their actions were justified given the length of Blake's prison sentence of 42 years. The jury may have felt that such a trial was unjustified 25 years after the event.

Trial by jury is held in high esteem in this country and controversy usually arises whenever there is any discussion about tampering with it. To what extent is this esteem justified? To decide this, more detailed consideration of the jury system is called for.

Any person aged between 18 and 65 whose name is on the electoral register and who has lived in the UK for at least five years since the age of 13 is, subject to exceptions, eligible for jury service. The Criminal Justice Act 1988 (section 119) increased the maximum age to 70, while allowing excusal as of right to those aged over 65. This reflected the Government's view that the average age of a jury had become too low. Yet there is no evidence that age has any significance for jury decision-making. The exceptions referred to above divide into three categories: those who are disqualified, those who are ineligible, and those who may be excused as of right. Certain people with criminal convictions are disqualified for either five years, ten years or life, depending on the sentence they received. A person who is on bail at the time of the trial is now also disqualified. Those who are ineligible include lawyers, policemen and, perhaps more surprisingly, the clergy. The Runciman Commission recommended that the clergy should be removed from this category. People entitled to be excused include members of parliament, members of the armed forces, doctors, veterinary practitioners and – following a recommendation of the Runciman Commission – practising members of certain religious bodies whose beliefs are incompatible with jury service. In addition, anyone who has performed jury service in the previous two years, or has been excused for life by a judge (usually following a long and arduous trial) is entitled to be excused. Courts have a general discretion to excuse anyone else who can put forward a good reason. The Runciman Commission considered that, in exceptional cases, either side should be allowed to apply to the judge to authorise the selection of a jury which contained up to three persons from ethnic minority communities.

There has been much discussion in recent years about the extent to which the barristers in a case should be able to influence the final composition of the jury. This reflects a tension between two requirements that we expect from trial by jury: that the jurors are selected randomly and that jury verdicts should be accurate. Historically, jurors were selected because they had special knowledge of the facts of the case; they were more like witnesses. But by the eighteenth century there had been a complete turn around: jurors were supposed to know nothing about the case and this is the situation that exists today. The notion of 'trial by one's peers' precludes trial by a panel of experts or people having particular qualities – such as high intelligence – that may increase the chances of obtaining the right verdict. The composition of the jury can be influenced either by the right of challenge or the prosecution's right to ask a juror to 'stand by' for the Crown. There are three types of challenge. Either side can 'challenge the array', or suggest that the whole jury panel has been improperly assembled. This is virtually obsolete. Either side can 'challenge for cause' or suggest that a particular juror should not sit in the case for some reason such as disqualification, physical disability or insufficient understanding of English. There was another type of challenge, the 'peremptory challenge'. This right only belonged to the defence, who could challenge up to three jurors without having to give any reason at all. The defence only had a limited amount of information to go on: the name, address and appearance of the juror. Until 1973 jurors' occupations were also revealed. Generally defence counsel were not allowed to question the jurors. This contrasts sharply with the situation in the USA where lawyers can spend days on end questioning jurors until a jury acceptable to both sides is assembled. Peremptory challenges were used by defence counsel to try and create as sympathetic a jury as possible. It is generally considered, for example, that women are less likely to convict than men (except for sexual offences) and that younger people are less likely to convict than older people. These views are not borne out by research. Baldwin and McConville's study of juries in Birmingham found that there were no particular social factors which influenced juries' verdicts.

Nevertheless, the Government wanted to abolish the right of peremptory challenge and this was carried out by section 118 of the Criminal Justice Act 1988. Many sections of the legal profession were opposed to this, claiming that the ancient right of defendants to have some control over the group of people who try them is of great constitutional importance. The Government clearly considered that juries which have been subject to challenge are more likely to acquit. However, Home Office evidence published in January 1987 suggests that there is no link between peremptory challenges and a reduced likelihood of conviction.

The prosecution (but not the defence) can ask a juror to stand by for the Crown. In practice, the effect is the same as for a peremptory challenge, although in theory a juror asked to stand by could be recalled if the prosecution had worked its way through the whole panel: otherwise there is no limit to the number of jurors who can be asked to stand by. This right has not been abolished, although guidelines issued by the Attorney-General in 1989 provide that its use should be restricted. It may be used, however, in jury vetting. This procedure, usually conducted by the prosecution, involves checking the list of those summoned for jury service to see if anyone appears to be 'unsuitable'. The matter first came to the attention of the public in 1978 in the 'ABC trial', a case under the Official Secrets Act 1911. It emerged that vetting was authorised by guidelines drawn up by the Attorney-General. These were eventually published in 1980. They stated that vetting was only justifiable in exceptional cases such as those involving terrorism, the Official Secrets Acts, and 'professional' criminals. Vetting should be carried out through checking one or more of the Criminal Record Office records, Special Branch records, and the knowledge of local CID officers. The consent of the DPP is needed and the Attorney-General should be informed. Even then, the information should not be used to exercise the right to stand by for the Crown unless there are serious doubts about the juror's impartiality. The defence do not need to be told the reasons why a juror has been asked to stand by but the defence should be told of any information indicating that a juror may be prejudiced against the defendant.

Two cases in 1980 considered the practice of jury vetting. In *R v Crown Court at Sheffield, ex p Brownlow* Lord Denning and Lord Justice Shaw stated obiter dictum that the practice was unconstitutional. Nevertheless, in *R v Mason* the Court of Appeal upheld as lawful the practice of Northamptonshire Police of checking to see if any members of a jury panel had a criminal record and cast doubt on the view expressed in *Brownlow*. After these two cases, the Attorney-General issued a statement confirming the previous guidelines subject to three main revisions: first, checks on Special Branch records would only be allowed on the authority of the Attorney-General following the recommendation of the DPP; second, no vetting would take place in cases of strong political motives unless they involved terrorism; and third, cases involving security would only be checked where there was a threat to national security. Whether or not these guidelines are strictly adhered to will probably never be known. In 1985 a civil servant, Clive Ponting, was acquitted under section 2 of the Official Secrets Act 1911 after he had passed confidential information to a Labour MP. It was revealed that 60 potential jurors were vetted by MI5. No threat to national security appears to have been involved. The development of jury vetting, together with the abolition of peremptory challenges and the removal of the right to jury trial from a growing number of offences are seen by some people as indicators of a growing attack on trial by jury. A development some years ago which was seen in the same light was the introduction of majority verdicts. The Criminal Justice Act 1967 allows a verdict from ten jurors where the jury consists of eleven or twelve people, or nine where the number of jurors has fallen to ten. The allegations of 'jury nobbling' which led to this development were never substantiated.

Even after changes made in the selection of jurors, there are still critics who say that the system does not 'work'. By this, they usually mean that juries are inconsistent in their decision-making and, more importantly, they acquit 'too many' people. This latter argument in particular was emphasised by the former Metropolitan Police Commissioner, Sir Robert Mark, in the 1973 Dimbleby Lecture. His arguments were subject to criticism by, among others, Michael Zander. Sir Robert had referred to half the defendants tried by jury being acquitted but, as Zander pointed out, the statement taken in isolation could be misleading because it fails to indicate the large number of defendants who plead guilty at the Crown Court. In recent years about 70% of defendants have pleaded plead guilty, 12% have been found guilty by the jury and 6% have been acquitted by the jury (the rest have been formally acquitted through lack of evidence). In any case the rate of acquittal is not surprising when one considers the high standard of proof that the prosecution has to satisfy. As we have seen, there are pressures on defendants to plead guilty, and those who resist are likely to have the strongest cases.

Sir Robert Mark was also sceptical about the academic research into jury decision-making. The leading American study, published in 1966, was the Chicago Jury Project which was based on 3,576 trials and replies to questionnaires from the 555 trial judges in the cases. These showed that the judges agreed with the juries' verdicts in 75% of these cases. The Oxford Penal Research Unit have carried out two studies. The first, published as *'The Jury at Work'* in 1972, concerned 115 jury acquittals from a sample of 475 defendants. It was found that most of the acquittals were attributable to the failure of the prosecution to present a good enough case rather than any perverseness on the part of the jury. The second study, published as *'The Shadow Jury at Work'* in 1974, involved the interesting idea of using second juries to listen to real cases and then comparing their decisions with those of the real juries. There was an agreement rate of 75%. A survey for the Royal Commission on Criminal Justice found that 80% of jurors and 79% of judges rated jury trial as a good or very good system. However, Baldwin and McConville's study of trials in Birmingham has presented a less favourable view of jury decision-making. Baldwin and McConville concluded that juries were sometimes too ready to acquit people who appeared to be guilty and to convict people who may be innocent. The Home Office Research and Planning Unit Report *'Managing Criminal Justice'*, suggesting that juries are twice as likely to acquit defendants than magistrates, has been held up as evidence by some critics. But it could be the case that it is magistrates who are convicting innocent people rather than juries who are acquitting the guilty.

If the jury system is considered inadequate, with what could it be replaced? The Report of the Fraud Trials Committee in 1986 recommended that jury trial be abolished for serious fraud cases and replaced by a panel of financial experts. This proposal has not been accepted by the Government. As we have seen, jury trial is being removed from certain offences by re-classifying them as summary. This seems to be the likely way in which trial by jury will be eroded. It is unlikely that systems found in other countries involving a single judge, a bench of judges or a panel with a judge and lay people will be introduced here, although at present a Crown Court judge sits with magistrates when hearing appeals from a magistrates' court.

Appeals

The grounds and procedures for appealing against conviction have been discussed in Chapter 2. In this section three particular problems concerning appeals will be discussed.

New evidence

The first of these relates to the introduction of new evidence at the appeal stage and the question of a retrial. Formerly, the test was that, if new evidence were offered to the Court of Appeal it must accept it if the evidence was credible, it would have been admissible at the trial and a reasonable explanation is offered as to why it was not produced at the trial. The Runciman Commission recommended that 'credible' should be replaced by 'capable of belief' and this has been enacted in the Criminal Appeal Act 1995. Having listened to the evidence, the Court can allow the appeal, dismiss it, or order a new trial. Formerly, a court could only order a retrial following the production of fresh evidence, but since the Criminal Justice Act 1988 it can now order one if it thinks it is in the interests of justice to do so. In the past the Court of Appeal has been reluctant to accept fresh evidence or to order a new trial. Until the case of *Stafford v DPP* (1974) the test had been that the court should have asked itself if the jury, having heard the fresh evidence, would still have convicted the defendant. In *Stafford* the House of Lords decided that the Court of Appeal should decide whether the conviction had now become unsafe and unsatisfactory. The difference is that, rather than consider the effect of the evidence on the jury, the Court of Appeal must assume the function of the jury – a subtle but significant difference. Most Commonwealth countries, as well as Scotland and Northern Ireland, still have a wider power to order a retrial.

The Runciman Commission felt that the court should take a broader view of what amounts to fresh evidence and whether there was a reasonable explanation for the failure to present the evidence at the trial or for a witness's subsequent departure from the evidence given at the trial. Where a retrial to test fresh evidence would be impracticable or undesirable, the Runciman Commission considered that the court should continue to apply the *Stafford* test. However, the Commission was divided on how to deal with cases not involving fresh evidence where a retrial is impracticable: six members thought that the court should automatically allow the appeal and five members felt that the court should choose between upholding the conviction and quashing it.

Miscarriages of justice

The question of whether the Court of Appeal is the best tribunal to deal with miscarriages of justice had been debated for more than 20 years before the appeals in the 'Guildford Four', 'Maguire Seven' and 'Birmingham Six' IRA bombing cases were finally allowed in 1990 and 1991. The previous appeal by the 'Birmingham Six' had been rejected by the court as recently as 1988. The provision which allowed cases to be referred to the court after the normal appeal process had been exhausted was section 17 of the Criminal Appeal Act 1968. The Home Secretary could either refer the whole case to the court, in which event the reference would be treated as an appeal, or just a particular point. The view became widespread that the Home Secretary, as a senior government minister, was not an appropriate person to be involved in making such a decision. The Runciman Commission recommended that the Home Secretary's power should be removed and given to a new body, the Criminal Cases Review Authority. The Authority, which should comprise a mixture of lawyers and lay persons, should be able to require that appropriate cases be investigated by the police. This has been enacted in the Criminal Appeal Act 1995. The Criminal Cases Review Commission (CCRC) will consist of at least eleven people, of whom at least one third should be legally qualified and at least two thirds should have knowledge or experience of the criminal justice system. The CCRC may refer any conviction or sentence (other than one fixed by law) either from the magistrates' court to the Crown Court or from the Crown Court to the Court of Appeal. The reference should then be treated by the court as an appeal. The CCRC will only make a reference if it thinks there is a real possibility that the verdict or sentence will not be upheld because an argument or piece of evidence was not put forward at the trial, and either an appeal has already been determined or leave to appeal has been refused. The Act also allows a reference in 'exceptional circumstances'. The CCRC may decide to carry out an investigation into the case, or it may be directed to do so by the Court of Appeal. Investigating officers (including a chief police officer) may be appointed for this purpose.

Prosecution right of appeal

Another problem concerning appeals has been whether the prosecution should have the right to appeal against an acquittal or a sentence. The

English legal system traditionally stood firm against prosecution appeals. The prosecution has been able to state a case for consideration by the Divisional Court of the Queen's Bench Division of the High Court following the acquittal of a defendant at a magistrates' court but this is restricted to a point of law and is not technically an appeal. The prosecution has also been able to appeal, with leave, to the House of Lords against a decision of the Court of Appeal. One way in which the prosecution can refer a point arising from an acquittal at the Crown Court to the Court of Appeal was introduced by section 36 of the Criminal Justice Act 1972. This provides for what is known as an 'Attorney-General's Reference'. The Attorney-General can ask the Court of Appeal to rule on a point of law which arose in a case where the defendant was acquitted. However, this is a hypothetical judgment intended for future guidance; even if the point of law goes against the defendant, it makes no difference to the acquittal.

Although there has been no serious discussion about a prosecution appeal against an acquittal (which exists in other countries, such as Canada), arguments began to emerge that the prosecution should be able to appeal against a sentence. The Prosecution of Offences Bill (which created the Crown Prosecution Service) contained a provision for the Attorney-General to refer sentences to the Court of Appeal for the Court to lay down guidelines for future cases. This would have been similar to an 'Attorney-General's Reference' under the Criminal Justice Act 1972 in that the sentence in the actual case would not be affected. The proposal was rejected by the House of Lords and not re-introduced by the House of Commons. A similar provision was included in the Criminal Justice Bill 1987. Following allegations of over-lenient sentencing in a rape case early in 1987, there were demands that the prosecution be given a full right of appeal against a sentence in a particular case.

Many other countries allow a prosecution right of appeal against sentence but there was strong opposition here, even to the suggestion of an 'Attorney-General's Reference' on sentencing. Supporters of the proposal claimed that there was strong public disquiet about over-lenient sentencing and that any guidelines for the future would not correct any injustice that had occurred in a particular case. Opponents argued that so-called 'public opinion' should not be the overriding determinant of a sentence. It is a cliche that public opinion is volatile; on this question public opinion is often very badly informed. There would be a real danger that prosecutors would find themselves under pressure from the press to appeal in a particular case. The number of cases that had led to informed public criticism had been very small and did not merit the introduction of such a provision. Another objection to the introduction of a prosecution right of appeal was that for the first time it would involve the prosecution in the sentencing process. The prosecution is not allowed to make a recommendation of sentence to the trial judge.

The arguments in favour of a full prosecution right of appeal against sentence finally prevailed and the power is contained in sections 35 and 36 of the Criminal Justice Act 1988. If the Attorney-General considers an offender has been sentenced too leniently at the Crown Court, the case may be referred to the Court of Appeal with its leave for the sentence to be reviewed. The provision only applies to indictable offences and certain offences triable either way. The Court of Appeal may substitute any sentence it considers appropriate, provided it was one the Crown Court had power to make.

Conclusion

Our study of the criminal justice system in this chapter will have shown that, like the civil justice system outlined in the previous chapter – and perhaps even more so – it has grown increasingly distant from the classic adversarial system. A clear majority of defendants, for whatever reason, plead guilty and thus by-pass the adversarial system altogether. The outcome of more and more cases seems to be determined before the case comes to court; at the police station or in conversation with defence counsel. Changes appear to reflect the growing pressures of increased crime on a system which lacks the resources to cope, rather than the development of principle.

But on what principle or principles does our criminal justice system operate? One view was expressed by both the Phillips Commission and the Runciman Commission which claimed that there should be a balance between, on the one hand, the rights and freedoms of the individual and, on the other hand, the importance of bringing offenders to justice. The Police and Criminal Evidence Act 1984 was criticised on the grounds that the Government upset the balance created by the Phillips Commission.

In order to try and assess the basis of our criminal justice system, it is useful to consider the work of the American writer, Herbert Packer. He argued that criminal justice systems basically either correspond to a 'due-process model' or a 'crime-control model'. A due-process model is founded on the belief that an accused is innocent until proved guilty beyond reasonable doubt. At every stage there are formal procedures which the police and prosecution must adhere to and the accused is protected from self-incrimination. The trial forms the focal point of the proceedings: strict rules of evidence prevent the introduction of material which is prejudicial to the defendant without having any clear value to the case. Protecting the innocent from conviction is such an important consideration that the price to be paid will be that the guilty are sometimes acquitted.

On the other hand, the most important purpose of the crime-control model is the prevention of criminal behaviour. The presumption is that this can be achieved by the conviction and sentencing of offenders, and this becomes the dominant aspect of the system. Informal procedures of fact-finding are very important and the discoveries made by the police at the stages of detention and interrogation have more significance than the proceedings in court. There is no effective presumption of innocence: on the contrary, the criminal justice system becomes a means of dealing with criminals (not 'defendants') as efficiently, in terms of administration and cost-effectiveness, as possible.

The English criminal justice system is generally supposed to reflect Packer's due-process model. In view of what we have seen in this chapter, this is open to severe doubt. Increased crime and lack of resources are said to be responsible for the growth of informal decision-making and negotiation in our system. Yet one cannot help wondering if, now that these devices have become almost institutionalised, they would be ended or reduced even if greater resources were to become available. American research by Nardulli has shown that bargains are made in under-utilised courts with the same frequency as they are in over-worked courts.

Postscript

The right to silence

As stated at the beginning of this chapter, it was formerly the case that persons accused of criminal offences were not obliged to say anything in their own defence either at the police station or in court, and judges were not allowed to comment on their remaining silent. Proposals had been made on several occasions since the early 1970s that, although accused persons should be able to remain silent, the prosecution should be allowed to bring this to the attention of juries, who would presumably then infer that the accused persons were concealing their guilt. The Criminal Law Revision Committee had made such a proposal in 1972 but it had been rejected by Parliament. The matter was considered again by the Phillips Commission but it did not recommend any change. In 1986 Douglas Hurd, the Home Secretary, suggested that the debate should be reopened and this was endorsed in 1987 by the new Metropolitan Police Commissioner, Peter Imbert.

Various reasons were put forward as to why this change in the law should be made. It was said that the enactment of PACE was of particular importance, as the safeguards it introduced, such as right of access to a solicitor, have removed – or at least greatly reduced – the likelihood of improperly obtained confessions. In addition, the Crown Prosecution Service would be able to pinpoint weak cases. Senior police officers clearly thought that innocent persons are always keen to protest their innocence and it is only the guilty who remain silent. PACE was seen as a measure which had tipped the scales firmly in favour of the accused and a rebalancing exercise was therefore necessary. Mr Imbert was quoted as saying that '. . . the removal of the privilege against self-incrimination would be the most important step legislators could take to control and reduce crime'.

Many people remained unimpressed by these arguments, and the assumption that PACE had removed the possibility of police officers coercing suspects into making false confessions was viewed with scepticism. We have already seen that the 'safeguards' in PACE are by no means watertight and determined police officers would be able to avoid them. Although most of the defendants in the 'Guildford Four' and 'Birmingham Six' cases signed confessions which were crucial to the case against them, the police have been quick to point out that this occurred before the enactment of PACE. Yet the 'Tottenham Three', who had been convicted of the murder of a police officer on the Broadwater Farm Estate, had their convictions quashed by the Court of Appeal in 1991 on the ground that their 'confessions' had been tampered with by the police. The 'confessions' had been made under the provisions of PACE. It may be that the tape-recording of interviews now provides some protection for the suspect but the danger remains that coercion might take place before the tape-recorder is switched on.

The eventual granting of the appeals of the 'Guildford Four' in 1990 and the 'Birmingham Six' in 1991 raised important questions about the propriety of our criminal justice system at virtually every level. Immediately after the Birmingham case, the Government announced the establishment of the Runciman Commission to look into every aspect of the criminal justice system from the time of arrest through to the end of the appeal process. The Commission published its report in July 1993 and, as we have seen, the Government has adopted some of its recommendations.

However, one recommendation that the Government has chosen to ignore was the Runciman Commission's view that the right to silence rule should not be altered. The Commission was concerned that 'the possibility of an increase in the convictions of the guilty is outweighed by the risk that the extra pressure on suspects to talk in the police station and the adverse inferences invited if they do not may result in more convictions of the innocent'. Furthermore, research carried out for the Commission by Roger Leng showed that the exercise of the right by suspects is not so great an obstacle to conviction as is commonly supposed. But by the time the Commission's report was published the impact of the Guildford and Birmingham cases had begun to fade and the Government, faced with the political embarrassment of sharply rising crime figures, had become even more strongly committed to a 'hard-line' criminal justice policy. As we have seen, the Criminal Justice and Public Order Act 1994 finally allows inferences to be drawn from silence.

As the Phillips Commission pointed out, the type of criminal justice system we have is ultimately a political choice.

CRIMINAL PROCESS FOR ADULTS

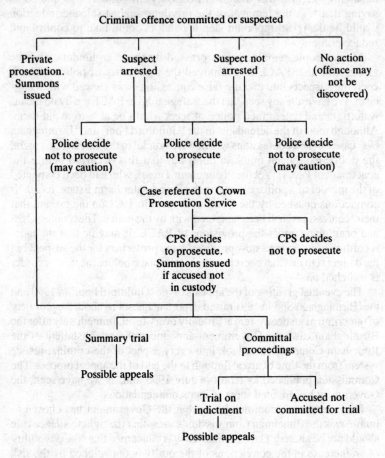

Juveniles (ie under 18) are normally tried by a youth court, which is a branch of a magistrates' court. However, if they are tried jointly with adults they must be tried by a magistrates' court, and if they are charged with murder or manslaughter they must be tried at the Crown Court.

Chapter 5
Legal services

The legal profession

The legal profession in England and Wales is divided into two branches: there are about 6,000 practising barristers and about 55,000 practising solicitors. The two branches organise themselves and operate in quite different ways.

The bar

There are two levels of barrister: Queen's Counsel ('QC' or 'silk') and junior. Any barrister, of whatever age, who is not a QC is technically a junior. Queen's Counsel, who comprise about 10% of barristers, are appointed by the Queen on the advice of the Lord Chancellor. It is from their ranks that judges are usually selected. Other reasons for a barrister's applying to 'take silk' are the enhanced status and the reduction in the amount of paperwork. Queen's Counsel take on fewer cases than juniors but their cases will be far more remunerative. Hence there is always a risk-element in becoming a QC. They are restricted to larger cases and are more expensive; a QC is usually accompanied by a junior in court.

All barristers must belong to an Inn of Court. There are four Inns, the Inner Temple, the Middle Temple, Lincoln's Inn and Gray's Inn. Barristers are one of three categories of Inn members; the others are students and benchers. The benchers, who comprise retired and active judges and senior practitioners, control the Inns. The Inns have a number of functions. They rent out property which they own to barristers and other people. Most of their income is obtained from this activity. They provide libraries and facilities for their members. They are involved in the training of students through the organisation of talks and practical exercises. The tradition of dining is said to fall into this category (see below). Inns are also playing an increasingly important role in the provision of scholarships.

Overall control of practising barristers is in the hands of the Bar Council. Its members come from all sections of the Bar. Its functions include making general policy decisions for the Bar as a whole, determining the consolidated regulations of the Inns of Court, dealing with disciplinary matters and making provision for the education and training of barristers.

117

What, then, is the function of barristers? Many people picture them, bewigged and robed, making passionate speeches in court. Advocacy is an important part of many barristers' work, but not the only part. Much time is spent drafting documents and writing opinions for solicitors. Indeed, some barristers spend virtually all their time doing this, seldom if ever appearing in court. As we shall see below, barristers have the sole rights of audience in the higher courts, other than the litigant. Some barristers specialise, but many practise in criminal law, family law and general tort and contract actions. Although barristers are self-employed, they have to work in 'chambers' (a set of offices) with other barristers. They share the expenses of running the place. Until recently, the Bar has prohibited the sharing of fees but, as a means of encouraging younger barristers, this restriction has been lifted. There are about 300 sets of chambers, about two-thirds of which are in London near the Inns of Court. Each set of chambers must have a clerk. This menial-sounding position is, in fact, one of extreme importance. Barristers' clerks not only control the administration of the chambers, but also act as agents for the barristers working there. They deal directly with the solicitors who contact the chambers seeking a barrister. If the desired barrister is unavailable, the clerk will suggest an alternative. The clerk is usually paid by commission, a percentage of the gross income of the chambers. Not surprisingly, some barristers' clerks can become very wealthy.

Detailed criticisms of the Bar's practices will be considered below. At this stage, it is worth observing that the structure of the Bar is based very much on tradition. Like so many aspects of our legal system, it has evolved over a long period of time. This appeal to tradition has been a major stumbling-block in effecting change at the Bar. Another problem has been that barristers have usually been prominent in high positions of government and thus very influential. This influence, however, is beginning to decrease.

Solicitors

The modern solicitor dates from the Judicature Act 1873 which merged the professions of solicitor, attorney and proctor. The solicitors' profession is under the control of the Law Society and the local law societies. The Law Society has a dual function: it promotes the interests of the solicitors in the same way as the Bar Council and it also deals with disciplinary matters and complaints. The Solicitors Complaints Bureau has recently come in for strong criticism and pressure is growing to replace it with a fully independent body. In addition, the Law Society issues practising certificates, arranges compulsory insurance for practitioners and operates a compensation fund to deal with claims against fraudulent solicitors. The Law Society has an educational role, running courses for those intending to qualify as solicitors, and continuing education courses for those who have already qualified. The local law societies, which are autonomous bodies, arrange lectures, deal with complaints from the public and respond to policy discussion documents sent out by the Law Society in London. The Law Society is run by the Council, which is elected by the solicitors themselves. A solicitor does not have to belong to the Law Society, although most do; but all solicitors come under the authority of the Law Society. It is also necessary to be a student member of the Law Society in order to qualify as a solicitor.

Solicitors can practise by themselves but most of them do so in firms, either as partners or as salaried employees known as assistant solicitors. Traditionally most firms have been quite small: the Royal Commission on Legal Services report in 1979 showed that about half had no more than four partners. However, with increased competition between firms, there is a growing number of mergers. The present number of solicitors has increased rapidly since 1960 when it was about 19,000. This has resulted largely from the fact that, until recently, solicitors have had a monopoly in conveyancing (the legal side of the buying and selling of houses) and during this period there has been a large increase in home ownership.

For many people, conveyancing is their only contact with solicitors and they consider that this is the main type of work that solicitors do. This assessment is fairly accurate for many firms. A survey commissioned by the Law Society indicates how solicitors derived their income in 1985: domestic conveyancing 29%, company and commercial 25%, probate (dealing with the property of deceased persons) and wills 9%, other non-contentious 5% matrimonial 7%, crime 5%, and other contentious 20%. Some firms, especially in the City of London, specialise in company or commercial work, whereas some provincial firms do little else but conveyancing. Solicitors, however, are not wholly office-bound. In quantitative terms they do more advocacy than barristers; as we have seen, 98% of criminal cases are tried in magistrates' courts and solicitors represent defendants in the vast majority of these. Solicitors do not generally have rights of audience in the Crown Court or any of the higher courts.

The Royal Commission on Legal Services produced some interesting statistics about solicitors, based on a random sample survey. The age group most likely to use solicitors was between 25 and 34. Use of solicitors varied according to socio-economic group: in 1977 a solicitor was used by 25% of the professional class but by only 10% of unskilled manual workers. This is not necessarily a reflection of a greater willingness on the part of the better-off to use solicitors: it could be a reflection of the fact that they are more likely to be involved in the buying and selling of property.

On the face of it, therefore, the situation appears to be that there are a large number of solicitors offering a wide range of legal services to the population as a whole. But, as we shall see later in this chapter, this is far from the case.

The social background and training of lawyers

Lawyers are mainly middle class. In evidence to the Royal Commission on Legal Services, the College of Law stated that the parental occupation of 60.9% of its solicitor students and 67.3% of its bar students (the College no longer teaches bar students) was either professional or managerial. In only 8% of cases was the parental occupation manual. Other evidence suggests that a similar situation exists in relation to university law undergraduates who enter the legal profession. Women are under-represented in the legal profession, although the situation has been improving: in 1996 women comprised 30% of all practising solicitors and 52% of practising solicitors under the age of thirty. In 1975 11% of all new barristers were women: in 1995 the figure was 44%. Sex discrimination occurs in that many sets of chambers and solicitors are more reluctant to take on women than equally well-qualified men. In 1995 the Bar Council recognised that female pupil barristers are sometimes sexually harassed by senior male barristers. Racial discrimination is also a serious difficulty. The Commission for Racial Equality threatened to investigate the Inns of Court School of Law after 45% of its black students failed the examinations in 1992. The Royal Commission, which had acknowledged these problems, made a number of recommendations, including that women's return to work from motherhood should be made easier, and that the Bar and the Law Society should strongly encourage racial equality in the profession.

Nowadays only graduates (not necessarily in law) and mature students can enter the Bar. There are two stages to the education. The first consists of obtaining a law degree recognised by the Council of Legal Education, or passing the Common Professional Examination (CPE), or obtaining a diploma in law. The second involves taking the Bar Vocational Course (BVC) for a year. Before being called to the Bar, the student must join an Inn of Court and dine there three times a term for eight terms. This is to encourage the students to mix with practising barristers, but it does not work as few barristers bother to dine and they often sit together. The Royal Commission recommended that compulsory dining by students should be abolished unless greater steps are taken to encourage mixing with the barristers. Once called, new barristers are not allowed to practise until they have been a pupil of another barrister for twelve months. After this, the barrister will have to obtain a 'tenancy' in a set of chambers and, due to the scarcity of such positions, this is often the most difficult stage of all. Grants from local education authorities are only discretionary and, although the Inns are providing an increasing number of scholarships and the Bar Council is encouraging chambers to fund pupillages, students who can be financially supported by their parents will find it much easier to qualify as a barrister.

Becoming a solicitor also involves two educational stages. The first is usually completed either by obtaining a recognised law degree or by passing the CPE. The second stage is the vocational course, known as the

Legal Practice Course (LPC). After this, the student must then spend two years as a trainee in a firm of solicitors before being admitted. About 90% of people admitted as solicitors are graduates. Discretionary grants may be awarded by local authorities but the Law Society offers little in the way of scholarships.

There have been three major enquiries into legal education in recent years: the Ormrod Committee, which reported in 1971, the Royal Commission on Legal Services in 1979, and the Marre Committee in 1988. The Ormrod Committee's report did lead to certain changes but a number of key proposals were not implemented. Ormrod envisaged greater integration between the academic and vocational stages and less emphasis than is now found on substantive law at the vocational stage. The Royal Commission's proposals were fairly mild, although they did suggest a greater emphasis on in-training. The Marre Committee considered that both the academic and vocational stages of legal education should be developed so as to give the students a better training in essential legal skills. Both the Bar and the Law Society have made their courses more skills-based.

Monopolies and restrictive practices on the legal profession

THE DIVISION BETWEEN BARRISTERS AND SOLICITORS

The division, which dates back only to the nineteenth century, has been controversial almost from its creation. The Bar agreed to give up direct access to clients and conveyancing to solicitors in return for sole rights of audience in the higher courts and the provision of judges. Thus, the polarity between the two branches of the profession was established and to a large extent still remains today. Clients do not have direct access to a barrister; a solicitor must be approached first. Barristers and solicitors may not work together or form a partnership. Judicial appointments still come from the Bar. The rigour of these principles has been slightly relaxed in recent years: hence barristers can now deal directly with clients in law centres (see below) and solicitors can in due course become circuit judges, although very few have done so.

The only occasion that the problem has been considered in a large-scale enquiry was by the Royal Commission on Legal Services. Neither branch of the legal profession wanted any substantial change in the existing arrangements. All the familiar arguments were put in evidence to the Royal Commission and these should now be considered; firstly the arguments for the fusion of the two branches of the profession and then the arguments against.

1 Fusion would prevent the unnecessary repetition of work that now occurs. A client instructs a solicitor who considers the problem. If the problem leads to litigation the solicitor will have to prepare a brief for the barrister. Even if it does not, the solicitor may require a barrister's opinion. (The barrister may be a genuine expert or the

solicitor may wish to take advantage of barristers' immunity from negligence claims in respect of their opinions.)

2 If the work is done by one lawyer, or within a firm, the quality may be better. Solicitors are responsible for the preparation of the facts without any assistance from the barrister who is going to have to argue them in court. In some cases, especially involving crime, the barrister is not selected until the last moment. Moreover, in the course of instructing the barrister, some points may be inadvertently passed over or misunderstood.

3 The problems of last-minute selection or change of barrister and the last-minute giving of instructions by the solicitor would be greatly reduced, or even disappear, if the case could be handled within one firm. Research by Bottoms and McLean in Sheffield showed that defendants saw their barristers for the first time on the morning of the trial in 96% of cases where there was a guilty plea, and 79% of cases where there was a not guilty plea.

4 Costs would be reduced if only one lawyer, or even one firm is involved in a case, rather than a firm of solicitors and at least one barrister. As Zander has put it, 'To have one taxi meter running is less expensive than to have two or three'. The larger the case, the more apparent this duplication of costs becomes, especially if a QC is involved. If a barrister is appearing in court, a representative from the instructing firm of solicitors should be present, even if there is nothing for that person to do. On the other hand, the Royal Commission on Legal Services report contained figures showing that solicitors' overheads are about double those of barristers, and some people argue that the savings in costs would be far less than suggested by a casual look at the system, or even non-existent.

5 The existing division is wasteful of talent. Students have to decide at a fairly early stage whether to become barristers or solicitors and, if solicitors subsequently discover they have a talent for advocacy, they are confined to the lower courts.

6 A unified profession would increase the scope for the selection of judges. It seems strange that there are plenty of able solicitors who are effectively prevented from becoming High Court judges. If they were able to practise advocacy in the higher courts, there would be no reason for this to continue.

The following are some of the main arguments which have been put against the fusion of the two branches of the legal profession:

1 Fusion would result in a body of expert and specialist skills, which is available to every solicitor in the country, being abolished. Moreover, barristers are far more easily identifiable than specialists would be in a unified profession.

2 The overall standard of advocacy would be reduced by fusion. If any lawyer could appear in court, there would be a greater risk of incompetence. Moreover, even the regular advocates in a unified system may have to spend more time in their offices, thus possibly reducing their effectiveness in court.

3 There could be a lowering of the standards of ethical behaviour which are so important in the conduct of a court case. This could result from the abolition of a relatively small, homogeneous body which is known to, and more easily under the supervision of, the judiciary.

4 Lawyers in a unified profession may be inclined to keep clients rather than direct them to specialists in other firms for advice.

5 Specialists would come to be employed by the large firms, thus leaving many smaller firms without specialist advice and facing the risk of losing their clients.

6 At present, barristers must adhere to what is called the 'cab rank' principle, which means that barristers, if offered a proper fee and not otherwise engaged, cannot refuse to take a case within their sphere of work. Barristers therefore cannot refuse to accept a case because it is repugnant or because they feel they have no chance of winning. It would be difficult to adhere to this principle in a unified profession.

The members of the Royal Commission on Legal Services were unanimously in favour of keeping the divided legal profession. The main argument which influenced them was that fusion would lower the quality of advocacy, which it is so important to maintain in our adversarial system. The existence of the specialist Bar and its availability to all solicitors was also a significant factor. The Royal Commission considered that the number of firms would be reduced by fusion as the small firms would be unable to compete and this would worsen the present uneven distribution of solicitors' firms throughout the country. Fusion would not remove other problems identified in the system: there could still be difficulties of communication within a firm and problems over dates. Costs at present are often kept down by an independent barrister being able to recommend a settlement.

After such a strong endorsement of the status quo by the Royal Commission, it seemed unlikely that the question of fusion would be raised again for some time to come. In January 1986, however, the Contentious Business Committee of the Law Society published a discussion document entitled *Lawyers and the Courts; Time for Some Changes*. The Committee reiterated many of the familiar criticisms of the present division and pointed out the particular difficulties for law students in having to decide on their chosen career at such an early stage. The Committee did not recommend total fusion of the system, but put forward what could be described as a compromise set of proposals. All lawyers should undergo the same training. After at least two or three years in 'general practice', lawyers could become barristers, in the same way that doctors can become hospital consultants. Some criteria would have to be established to assess their competence to act as barristers. Lawyers in general practice would have rights of audience in tribunals and lower courts for the first two or three years, but would thereafter be under no restrictions other than to act within their competence. In effect, the Bar would become a body of specialist advocates. The Committee added, as additional encouragement, that all existing barristers and solicitors would be entitled to keep their existing status, unless they chose otherwise.

The Bar published its response in June 1986. Predictably, it was opposed to the Law Society's proposals. Their implementation would lead to the end of the Bar. The Bar relied on the views of the Royal Commission to support its case.

If the view that extending rights of audience in the higher courts to solicitors would lead to the demise of the Bar is correct, fusion could still come in by the back door. As we shall now see, solicitors' rights of audience have been gradually increasing in recent years and there is mounting pressure for an even greater extension.

RIGHTS OF AUDIENCE

The Bar has had the sole right of representation in the higher courts since the last century. One long-standing exception has been a small number of courts, which were considered too far away from any practising barristers. Solicitors have also been allowed to appear before judges in chambers in certain cases. The question of the Bar's monopoly was raised before the Royal Commission on Assizes and Quarter Sessions, whose report was published in 1969 ('The Beeching Report'), recommending the replacement of Assizes and Quarter Sessions by the Crown Court. Beeching did not accept the Law Society's arguments for rights of audience in the new Crown Court and the only concession made was that the Lord Chancellor was given power to allow solicitors rights of audience where there are insufficient barristers to do the work. In 1972 the Lord Chancellor issued a Practice Direction which stated that solicitors could appear before the Crown Court in appeals from magistrates' courts or for committals from magistrates to the Crown Court for sentence, provided the solicitor or the solicitor's firm had acted for the client in the magistrates' court.

The establishment of the Royal Commission on Legal Services re-opened the issue. The Law Society argued that solicitors should have rights of audience in the Crown Court for appeals and committals for sentence from magistrates, cases which were triable either way and 'Class 4 offences' (these are generally the least serious of offences triable in the Crown Court). The Law Society claimed that this would give the client a choice of advocate; would in some cases prove cheaper; and would reduce the pressure on the overstretched resources of the Bar. The Law Society also considered that solicitors should have rights of audience in the High Court in a limited number of cases, including the announcement of agreed terms of settlement and unopposed petitions for the winding-up of companies. Extended rights of audience in all these cases should only apply to solicitors experienced in advocacy in the lower courts.

The Bar strongly opposed the Law Society's suggestions, in particular those relating to the extension of solicitors' rights of audience in the Crown Court. It stated that not only could this lead to a reduction in standards of advocacy, but it would be financially disastrous for the junior Bar who rely heavily on this type of work.

The Royal Commission on Legal Services recommended that there should be no change in existing rights of audience – but only by an 8 to 7 majority. The majority accepted the Bar's arguments, but the minority felt that solicitors should be able to represent clients pleading guilty. Three members of the minority felt that solicitors should be allowed to appear in committals for sentence and Class 4 work. The Royal Commission did recommend, however, that solicitors should be allowed to deal with formal or unopposed petitions.

The narrowness of the vote made this endorsement of the 'status quo' less authoritative than the unanimous rejection of fusion and, not surprisingly, the debate has continued. A Home Office proposal in 1984 that solicitors employed by the Crown Prosecution Service should have rights of audience in the Crown Court led to such opposition from the Bar that it has not been proceeded with. In November 1985 the case of *Abse v Smith* came before the Court of Appeal. Cyril Smith MP was challenging the refusal of a High Court judge to allow his solicitor to read a seven-line agreed statement in open court in settlement of a libel action. This was precisely the sort of case in which the Royal Commission thought that solicitors should be allowed to appear, but this recommendation was never implemented. The Court of Appeal upheld the judge's ruling. The Master of the Rolls, Sir John Donaldson, said that it was for the judges to decide whom they would hear as advocates. He said that the High Court and Court of Appeal judges would meet to consider the situation for the future. Sir John seemed to indicate that he was against major changes. He said that the body of advocates should not be allowed to become too large so that the present high level of skill could be maintained.

The argument continued with the publication of *Lawyers and the Courts; Time for Some Changes*. Following the publication of this document a joint committee from both sides of the profession has been established to consider matters arising from it. The Bar, meanwhile, has incurred the wrath of the Law Society by suggesting that it may be prepared to deal directly with certain clients, such as accountants, without involving solicitors. The Director-General of Fair Trading, Sir Gordon Borrie, has also questioned the Bar's exclusive rights of audience in the Crown Court. The Legal Aid Scrutiny Report published in 1986 considered that there was no good reason why solicitors should not be allowed to have rights of audience for guilty pleas in the Crown Court and that such an extension could save the legal aid fund about £1 million a year. However, the 1987 Legal Aid White Paper stated that the Government had no intention of extending rights of audience in the Crown Court.

CONVEYANCING

One of the most interesting and unexpected developments in the provision of legal services in recent years has been the abolition of the solicitors' conveyancing monopoly. The monopoly, which had existed since 1804, made it a criminal offence for an unqualified person to carry out the actual conveyancing transaction for gain. Thus it was not an offence for people to do their own conveyancing or someone else's without charge. Moreover, it was not an offence to carry out the preliminary stages of the transaction for gain and this led to a number of 'cut-price' conveyancers operating with a solicitor to draw up the vital documents. These made very little impact on the market.

The Royal Commission on Legal Services by a 10 to 5 majority agreed with the Law Society's arguments that the monopoly should continue. They accepted the view that, as conveyancing is a crucial transaction involving large sums of money, it is vital that it is carried out by a fully-qualified solicitor with the backing of insurance and the Law Society's compensation fund. There was no need for extra competition as solicitors' charges were now becoming competitive. Any system of licensed conveyancers would be very expensive to set up. In any case, it was doubtful if sufficient numbers would be interested to justify this. The minority view on the Royal Commission was that competition would be beneficial; that it was unfair that profitable conveyancing work should subsidise other solicitors' services; and that most conveyancing transactions were routine and would not prove too difficult for licensed conveyancers. In 1980 the Royal Commission on Legal Services in Scotland recommended that there should be no monopoly in conveyancing north of the border.

The manner in which the conveyancing monopoly was broken in England was unexpected. A private member's Bill to abolish the monopoly was given a second reading in the House of Commons. The Government agreed to adopt the terms of the Bill in its own legislation. In the event, it went even further. The Administration of Justice Act 1985 provided for the establishment of a Council of Licensed Conveyancers. The Council arranges for tests of competence for would-be licence holders. They must have had at least two years experience of conveyancing before being allowed to obtain a licence. Insurance must be arranged. Licensed conveyancers have been allowed to operate since May 1987. There are now more than 250 licensed conveyancers in practice and about 500 more in employment. With all the difficulties involved in setting up a business and becoming established, it may be several years before solicitors face any substantial challenge from licensed conveyancers. A potentially more serious threat appeared to be offered by the Building Societies Act 1986 which allowed solicitors employed by building societies to undertake conveyancing. These provisions, however, were not brought into force and have been superseded by provisions in the Courts and Legal Services Act 1990 (infra).

Even by 1987, it was clear that developments thus far had been beneficial for the consumer. Solicitors firms, helped by a reduction in the restrictions on advertising, had become far more competitive among themselves and reduced their conveyancing fees. A survey by a firm of management consultants engaged by the Law Society was published in January 1987, showing that solicitors were earning up to 30% less from conveyancing than they did five years previously.

THE COURTS AND LEGAL SERVICES ACT 1990

The 1988 Marre Committee Report into services provided by the legal profession was not a radical document, although it did recommend that certain approved solicitors should have extended rights of audience in the Crown Court and that professions other than solicitors should be allowed direct access to barristers. The real impetus for change came with the appointment of Lord Mackay of Clashfern as Lord Chancellor. As a Scottish lawyer, Lord Mackay has not felt bound to uphold the monopolies and restrictive practices of the English legal profession, but is prepared to allow market forces to provide the best service for the consumer.

In 1989 Lord Mackay published three Green Papers, '*The Work and Organisation of the Legal Profession*'; '*Contingency Fees*'; and '*Conveyancing by Authorised Practitioners*'. Later in the year these were followed by a White Paper, '*Legal Services: a Framework for the Future*', which adopted recommendations from the Green Papers and from the Civil Justice Review. This formed the basis of the Courts and Legal Services Act 1990. The Act contains major changes in the provision of legal services. It establishes the Lord Chancellor's Advisory Committee on Education and Conduct. It creates the post of Legal Services Ombudsman to deal with complaints concerning legal services which are not already being dealt with by a court, a tribunal or the appropriate professional body.

The Act provides for the extension of rights of audience in all courts and the right to conduct probate work to all suitably qualified persons, whether or not barristers or solicitors. Such a person, unless a party to the proceedings, must generally have a right of audience in a court approved by 'the appropriate authorised body'. The rights of audience held by barristers and solicitors prior to December 1989 are deemed to have been granted by the Bar Council and the Law Society respectively and therefore approved for present usage. Any extension of these rights, however, must be sent to the Lord Chancellor's Advisory Committee. The Committee reports to the Lord Chancellor, who also seeks the advice of the Director General of Fair Trading. An application needs the consent of the Lord Chancellor and each of four 'designated judges': the Lord Chief Justice, the Master of the Rolls, the President of the Family Division and the Vice-Chancellor. These judges, therefore, would have to approve any extension of solicitors' rights of audience. Originally it was proposed that the Lord Chancellor would have the sole power of approval, but it was objected that this would challenge the independence of the legal profession from the government. It is not clear to what extent these judges could prevent such an extension as they would be required to give reasoned decisions. The Act also contains new regulations requiring certain qualification standards for advocacy and litigation.

Banks, building societies and any other interested bodies are now able to provide a conveyancing service to borrowers. The provision of such a service is open to any practitioner authorised by the Authorised Conveyancing Practitioners' Board. The Board must be satisfied that the practitioner knows about conveyancing services, connected financial arrangements and commercial or consumer affairs. The practitioner must be a 'fit and proper' person; the Board must consider that the practitioner will be able to meet any claims made in relation to the service; and the practitioner must be a member of the Conveyancing Ombudsman Scheme established by the Act. The Lord Chancellor may make regulations governing standards of competence and to ensure that there is fair competition in the provision of conveyancing services and no conflict of interest. The Act prohibits loans for the purchase of residential property being made subject to a provision that the borrower should use other services (such as conveyancing) provided by the lender, and vice versa.

The Act also deals with the problems of multi-disciplinary and multi-national practices. Hitherto solicitors have not been allowed to form partnerships with members of other professions. The Royal Commission on Legal Services considered this position and approved of it. The Commission felt that forming partnerships with, for example, estate agents may result in sole practitioners and small firms being absorbed into large firms of estate agents and restrict the choice of legal services in rural areas. However, a report by the Director General of Fair Trading in 1986 considered that multi-disciplinary practices should be encouraged, and the National Consumer Council in 1989 considered that the consumer could benefit by having all the necessary transactions in a house purchase dealt with by one firm. The Law Society has not been so keen on the idea. It agrees with the Royal Commission's argument and is also concerned about maintaining the independence of the solicitor's position in view of the possible conflicts of interest that could arise.

The Courts and Legal Services Act has provided something of a compromise, abolishing the outright restrictions on multi-disciplinary practices while at the same time allowing the Law Society to make rules controlling their operation. The Act also abolishes statutory inhibitions on multi-disciplinary practices.

The state funding of legal services

Some people seeking legal advice will approach a Citizens' Advice Bureau, or a trades union representative (these are considered below). Others, especially those with more serious problems, will go straight to a solicitor. Many people are deterred from approaching solicitors by the thought of the expense involved. Yet, since the end of the Second World War, the state has provided a comprehensive system of free or subsidised legal representation and, more recently, free or subsidised legal advice from solicitors. We shall now consider the extent to which these schemes contribute to the provision of legal services.

The legal advice and assistance scheme

The Legal Advice and Assistance Act 1972 (now consolidated in the Legal Aid Act 1988) set up a scheme whereby any person could visit a participating solicitor and, providing that the person's finances came within the limits, the solicitor could provide £25 worth of work, including the giving of advice, writing of letters and the drafting of documents. This figure was raised to £50, or £90 for undefended divorce cases (although it could be extended with permission from the local legal aid office). It became increasingly apparent that these amounts were too low and that there should be a mechanism allowing them to be raised more frequently. Consequently since 1989 the amount available in divorce and judicial separation cases is three times the sum for preparation for magistrates' courts criminal proceedings, and in other cases twice the sum. The Legal Aid Act 1979 gave the Lord Chancellor power to order that the scheme could cover representation in certain cases. This 'assistance by way of representation' (ABWOR) is commonly found in domestic cases in magistrates' courts and also applies to mental health review tribunals, prison disciplinary cases, and for applications for warrants of further detention (or extensions) under PACE. It is designed to facilitate and expedite the funding of representation in relatively simple cases. It is useful as far as it goes, but its critics say it does not go far enough and would have to be extended to far more cases to make any real impact.

The legal advice and assistance scheme – known as 'the green form scheme' because of the colour of the form – does not have a 'merits test' as required for legal aid. If the solicitor agrees to deal with the problem, the only remaining question is the client's financial state. The 'means test' applies to both disposable income and disposable capital. The word 'disposable' indicates the amount remaining after deductions have been made for items like tax, national insurance, allowances for dependants (income), and house, furniture, clothes and tools of trade (capital). In 1996 an individual would need to have a weekly disposable income not exceeding £75 and disposable capital not exceeding £1,000 to be entitled to advice. No contributions are required and people receiving certain state benefits (including income support) automatically satisfy the disposable income test.

The main problem with the green form scheme can be seen in its usage. It was envisaged on its introduction in 1973 that the scheme would bring into solicitors' offices a whole new range of work, particularly in the area of welfare law. In fact, for many years about 40% of the cases have involved matrimonial disputes and about a further fifth have involved crime. Only about 2% of cases have involved problems which would be dealt with in tribunals and about 6% of cases have concerned landlord and tenant disputes. Although the past few years have seen a major increase in the number of immigration and nationality cases dealt with, welfare cases in general have scarcely increased. This suggests that many people with everyday problems are still not visiting solicitors. Maybe it is their image that is the problem, or maybe it is the lack of publicity about the scheme. Restrictions on solicitors' advertising are slowly being removed by the Law Society but there is still a considerable way to go.

In June 1986 a Legal Aid Scrutiny Report was published, recommending the abolition of the green form scheme. It suggested that legal advice in civil matters should be provided by advice organisations such as the Citizens' Advice Bureaux and that the Government should spend £25 million on such bodies. These proposals have been strongly criticised from all quarters. The Law Society pointed out that in many cases advice agencies direct clients to solicitors because they lack the expertise to deal with the problem themselves. If the advice agencies were to be enhanced to a comparable level to solicitors, the cost would be more than £360 million. The result would be two parallel services which would be wasteful of resources. The National Association of Citizens' Advice Bureaux claimed that the proposals would challenge their independence and undermine their relationship with the legal profession. In view of the criticisms it is not surprising that the Scrutiny Committee's proposals were not fully endorsed in the Government's 1987 Legal Aid White Paper or enacted in the ensuing Legal Aid Act 1988. The new Legal Aid Board, which was set up by the Act to administer legal aid instead of the Law Society, has been given powers to make new arrangements for certain categories of work, which would take these categories outside the scope of the green form scheme. One suggested category has been the provision of advice for welfare benefits. The Legal Aid Act 1988 has removed the making of wills (except for the over 70s) and conveyancing (except as a result of a court order) from the scheme.

The Legal Aid Board, although of the view that the green form scheme on the whole works well, has introduced the specialist franchising of services. This involves identifying firms of solicitors, law centres, advice agencies and other organisations who are competent and reliable, and encouraging them by removing some of the present administrative restrictions. For example, firms can be allowed to have devolved powers to exceed the green form limits, accept monthly payments on account and advertise that they hold a franchise. The franchisees are re-imbursed at a slightly higher rate than other solicitors' firms.

Legal aid in civil proceedings

State-funded representation in civil court cases was introduced in the Legal Aid and Advice Act 1949 on the basis of recommendations made by the Rushcliffe Committee. The current provisions are contained in the Legal Aid Act 1988. Civil legal aid was formerly administered by the Law Society, but since the 1988 Act it has been run by the new Legal Aid Board. Individual applications are considered by an Area Director, and an appeal from the Director's refusal to grant legal aid goes to an area committee.

To obtain legal aid, the applicant must pass both a merits test and a means test. The merits test is that the applicant has to show 'he has reasonable grounds for taking, defending or being a party' to an action and an application may be refused if the Director considers it would be unreasonable to grant it 'in the particular circumstances of the case'. This has generally been interpreted as a consideration whether a reasonable solicitor would advise a reasonable client, who could afford to spend his or her own money on the case, to proceed. The aid has usually been unavailable for small claims in the county court, as few solicitors would consider them worth contesting. The Royal Commission proposed that matters taken into consideration should include the applicant's reputation and personal dignity, even where only small sums of money are in question.

As with the green form scheme, the means test for civil legal aid is based on both disposable income and disposable capital, and the allowances made in calculating these figures are similar. On the latest figures, no person whose annual disposable income exceeds £7,403 (£8,158 for personal injury cases) can obtain civil legal aid. Any person whose annual disposable income does not exceed £2,498 is, subject to the capital limit, entitled to legal aid without contribution. In between these two figures is a sliding scale of contributions depending on disposable income. The capital limits are between £3,000 and £6,750 (£8,560 for personal injury cases).

The consequence of these figures is that only the poor, through legal aid, or the comparatively well-off, through private means, can afford to use a solicitor. Large sections of the population cannot bring or defend a civil action in court without incurring severe financial difficulty. If one adds to this the fact that, as we shall see below, many poorer people who could make use of legal aid and advice will not go to a solicitor, the situation is even worse.

The Royal Commission on Legal Services recommended that anyone who would otherwise suffer undue financial hardship should have a right to legal aid. There should be large increases in the rates and the upper limit should be abolished. The contribution acts as a significant deterrent and should be reduced. The Royal Commission also recommended an extension of legal aid to certain types of case in tribunals. At present, legal aid only applies to a handful of tribunals. The only change since the Royal Commission's report has been the addition of mental health review tribunals to the list.

There seems no prospect of a massive increase in legal aid – in fact all the indications point to cut-backs. The net annual expenditure on legal aid in 1989 was £537 million. By 1995 it had almost doubled, reaching £1,036 million. During that year the Lord Chancellor published proposals which would put a limit on the legal aid budget. Encouraged by the success of franchising, the Government plans to introduce a system of 'block contracts' which would cover the type, quality, volume and price of services to be provided. The contract holders would be responsible for delivering the stipulated services for an agreed price. Targetting of legal aid funds to areas of special need would be introduced. Advice agencies would be encouraged to bid for contracts and the use of alternative dispute resolution (such as mediation) would be encouraged.

Legal aid in criminal proceedings

This is administered by the Lord Chancellor's Department, although before 1980 it was operated by the Home Office. The change resulted from a recommendation of the Royal Commission and has had the effect of making criminal legal aid subject to greater scrutiny. Application is made to the court clerk. If the clerk feels unable to grant legal aid, the decision is taken by the court. The Legal Aid Act 1988 provides a right of appeal against refusal to criminal legal aid committees. At the moment this only applies to indictable offences and offences triable either way. A defendant charged with a summary offence can make repeated applications to the magistrates but these are unlikely to be successful.

As with civil cases, criminal legal aid is granted subject to a merits test and a means test. The Legal Aid Act 1988 states that the merits test is whether 'it is in the interests of justice' to grant legal aid. This has been interpreted subject to the so-called 'Widgery criteria' (recommendations of a committee in 1966 under the chairmanship of Mr Justice Widgery), which are now contained in the 1988 Act. If the means test is satisfied, legal aid should be granted where a court considers that one or more of the following apply;

(a) that the charge is a grave one in the sense that the accused is in real jeopardy of losing his liberty or suffering serious damage to his reputation;
(b) that the charge raises a substantial question of law;
(c) that the accused is unable to follow the proceedings and state his own case because of his inadequate knowledge of English, mental illness or other mental or physical disability;
(d) that the nature of the defence involves the tracing and interviewing of witnesses or expert cross-examination of a witness for the prosecution;
(e) that legal representation is desirable in the interest of someone other than the accused as, for example, in the case of sexual offences against young children where it is undesirable that the accused should cross-examine the witness in person.

One particular problem with these criteria is that it is difficult for a clerk or a court to know if several of them apply until the case has actually started, by which time the defendant may already have been disadvantaged. One possible way round this would be to require criminal legal aid applications to be made in advance, as in civil cases, but this would frequently be impracticable. The Legal Aid Efficiency Scrutiny Report recommended that the Lord Chancellor's Department should issue new guidelines on the 'Widgery criteria' in an effort to obtain standardisation of practice. In some cases, the 'interests of justice' test is deemed to be satisfied. These include charges of murder; where the prosecution wish to appeal to the House of Lords; where the accused appears before magistrates in custody, may well be remanded in custody and wants legal representation; and where the accused is detained in custody following conviction for reports to be made.

In recent years both the Home Office and the Lord Chancellor's Department have urged courts to consider the current constraints on public spending in deciding whether to grant legal aid.

The means test used to be applied in a fairly haphazard way. It was (and still is) applied by court clerks and they were supposed to apply similar financial tests as in civil cases. There was, however, no upper financial limit. Contributions could be requested but this was entirely at the discretion of the court and there were fairly wide variations in practice. The overall result was that some fairly well-off defendants were able to obtain legal aid. The Royal Commission on Legal Services considered there should be a statutory right to legal aid for charges of indictable offences and offences triable either way. For summary offences, legal aid should be provided unless the magistrates considered that (a) the defendant would not receive a custodial sentence, deportation order or (for a juvenile) care order, or suffer any major damage to his or her livelihood or reputation; and (b) representation was not necessary for the case to be properly put forward. In addition, contributions should be abolished in magistrates' courts.

However, the Legal Aid Act 1982 has not followed these recommendations and has laid down stringent tests to ascertain the defendant's income and capital. Contributions remain payable. Once again, the motive behind this change appears to be to reduce the amount of money the state spends on legal aid.

The statistics show that 97% of defendants tried at the Crown Court receive legal aid. In magistrates' courts the situation depends on the nature of the proceedings; for summary trial of an offence triable either way the figure is about 71%, but for the trial of summary offences it is only 5%. There are also considerable variations among magistrates' courts in granting legal aid – the sort of variations that were shown in other areas of magistrates' activity in Chapter 4. In 1983 the Lord Chancellor's Department published a *Report of a Survey of the Grant of Legal Aid in Magistrates' Courts* based on a sample of 60 magistrates' courts and about 3,000 cases. The Report confirmed the commonly-held view that wide discrepancies exist. It also revealed that many defendants do not even bother to apply for legal aid. The percentage varied according to the offence; in drug cases it was 25% and for assaults on the police it was 76%.

Duty solicitor schemes in court

The problem of unrepresented defendants in magistrates' courts had been apparent to criminal law practitioners for some time. One suggestion to deal with this was the establishment of duty-solicitor schemes, whereby solicitors on a rota basis would be present at the courts to see the defendants in the cells, provide legal advice, and if necessary appear in court to ask for an adjournment and bail. The Widgery Committee in 1966 said it would be both impracticable to introduce such schemes on a nationwide basis and 'unnecessarily wasteful of public funds'. However, in 1972 the Bristol Law Society started the first scheme and they soon began to escalate; by the middle of 1975 there were 29 schemes in operation and in 1984 the figure was over 130. By 1995 more than 97% of magistrates' courts were covered. All these schemes operated on a purely voluntary basis. In 1975 the Law Society drew up guidelines for running a 'model' scheme. Solicitors were advised that, if the circumstances allowed, they could invite the accused to fill in a green form and thus obtain some remuneration for their work, but this was not to be made a condition of providing advice.

No doubt, duty solicitors hope that, if the accused's case goes to a higher court, the accused will choose the solicitor or the solicitor's firm to act on his or her behalf.

The Royal Commission on Legal Services thought that duty solicitor schemes should continue and that the Law Society should set up schemes in courts where the amount of work justified it. The Legal Aid Act 1982 contained provisions enabling this to be put into effect. The Legal Aid (Duty Solicitor) Scheme 1983, made under the authority of the 1982 Act, created a nationwide structure of committees to identify areas where schemes should be created and make sure that they function properly (regional committees); and to choose the solicitors to take part in the schemes (local committees). The existing schemes were encouraged to come within this organisation by the solicitors being offered better rates of remuneration than are available under the green form scheme. There are rules on the level of experience a participating solicitor must have and rules on how the schemes should operate: for example, a duty solicitor should only exceptionally help a person who is charged with a non-imprisonable offence.

Duty solicitor schemes have had their critics. It has been alleged that they lead to a reduction in the quality of work provided and are a useful device for firms of solicitors to obtain lucrative criminal legal aid work. Research has suggested that the existence of a scheme in a court can lead to an increase in the number of guilty pleas. Other research, however, has suggested an increase in the granting of bail and legal aid. Perhaps the greatest danger would be if duty solicitor schemes, which can only provide an emergency service, were expanded at the expense of criminal legal aid.

Duty solicitor schemes in police stations

As we have seen in Chapter 4, the Police and Criminal Evidence Act 1984 (PACE) provides that suspected persons arrested and detained at police stations or persons attending police stations voluntarily have the right to legal advice. The Code of Practice states that such persons may consult their own solicitor, the duty solicitor, or one selected from a list of available solicitors. This resulted from discussions between the Government and the Law Society. In return for special funding, the Law Society agreed to extend the duty solicitor scheme to police stations. Section 59 of PACE strengthens this by providing that taking part in the police station schemes may be a requirement for solicitors wishing to become involved with the duty solicitor schemes in courts. The green form scheme is used at police stations but the service is provided entirely free to the suspect.

The scheme came into operation on 1 January 1986. Research commissioned by the Lord Chancellor's Department has shown that there has been an increase in the proportion of suspects receiving advice at the police station, although the figures are still relatively low. Duty solicitors provide over one third of all advice given at police stations. However, solicitors still regard the remuneration rates as low, and the withdrawal of firms in certain areas has led to the collapse of some schemes. Recent research has been critical of the service provided by duty solicitors: standards of recruitment and discipline were rather low and many relied on giving telephone advice rather than actual attendance at the police station.

The unmet need for legal services

So far, we have considered the provision of legal services by the legal profession and the extent to which this is assisted by state funding in the form of the legal aid and advice schemes. Already it will have become apparent that the situation is unsatisfactory in several respects. The financial limits of legal aid and advice schemes and the high cost of lawyers mean that large areas of the population are unable to use the services of solicitors. Even those who seek help do so for a fairly narrow range of subjects, in particular divorce and crime. It seems there are many people with legal problems who are not obtaining any advice at all. This is what is usually referred to as 'the unmet need' for legal services.

The phrase is not free from controversy: some people argue that it has no meaning. Nevertheless, Richard White in 1973 offered a number of examples which would seem to fall within it:

(a) a person does not realise that a problem is a legal one, so does not seek legal advice;
(b) a person realises that a problem is a legal one but is unaware of the appropriate legal service or the entitlement to use it;
(c) a person realises that a problem is a legal one and knows that a particular legal service will give advice, but does not approach it for some reason such as fear of expense or ignorance of the legal aid scheme;
(d) a person realises that a problem is a legal one and wants legal advice but cannot find a developed legal service available.

These problems cannot be solved in the same way. Problems (b) and (c) could be alleviated, if not eradicated, by an improvement in the provision of information. Problem (d) requires that lawyers or other agencies offering legal advice should offer a wider range of services. Problem (a) involves the difficulty of defining a 'legal problem'. For some people, a problem may not be worth a legal solution or attempting to solve at all. Anyone who buys a cheap cassette tape in London and takes it home to Bristol is unlikely to take any action if the record turns out to be faulty. But what about a compact disc bought in the local town centre? The impoverished student may rush back to the shop whereas the wealthy businessman may not bother. Most disputes allow for a legal solution, but for some people the need to pursue it is far greater than for others.

How great, then, is the unmet need? The 1973 book *Legal Problems and the Citizen* by Abel-Smith, Zander and Brooke, contained a study which compared people's perception of needing legal advice in certain areas with the steps they actually took to obtain such advice. In a large number of cases no action was taken. The study also supported the view discussed above that people usually approach solicitors on a fairly narrow range of matters. Nearly all the respondents who needed legal advice in connection with buying a house consulted a solicitor but only 3% sought advice on social security law. 16% looked for such advice from other sources and 81% sought no advice at all even though they considered they had a problem.

The Royal Commission also looked for evidence in a specially-commissioned Users' Survey. As well as confirming that respondents did not consult solicitors about such matters as employment and social security law, the Survey revealed that a third of respondents did not use solicitors because they thought they were too expensive. The Royal Commission appears to have concluded from this that the causes of the unmet need are poverty and the inability of lawyers to deal with a wide enough range of areas. The answer, however, is not that simple. All sections of society, including the poor, use solicitors for divorce and criminal work. At the same time, the middle class do not use solicitors for consumer or employment problems. Zander, in his 1978 book *Legal Services for the Community*, is attracted by the 'social organisation' theory set out by the American sociologists Mayhew and Reiss. Certain types of work are related to social contact. Everyone assumes that lawyers deal with matters like land law, wills and divorce, and it is easy to find someone who has used one of these services. On the other hand, in some less popular areas, such as personal injury claims, it is more difficult to find someone who has used a particular service. As lawyers also adjust the nature of their work to the demand, the provision of services becomes something of a self-fulfilling prophesy. Zander emphasises the importance of the advice given by the lay person as to whether the problem should be referred to a solicitor.

As we have seen, some people who, for whatever reason, are unwilling to approach solicitors are prepared to seek specialist advice elsewhere. Several bodies have come to provide this and first of all we shall consider the development of law centres.

The provision of legal services outside the profession – the rise of law centres

In its evidence to the Rushcliffe Committee, whose proposals formed the basis of the present legal aid scheme as enacted in the Legal Aid and Advice Act 1949, the Law Society proposed that a system of advice centres with salaried solicitors should be created to provide legal advice in those parts of the country where existing provisions were poor. The 1949 Act contained a provision to deal with this but the provision was never brought into force. The Law Society was no longer advocating this proposal at the time of the introduction of the green form scheme, but instead was suggesting the appointment of advisory liaison officers, salaried solicitors whose function would be to advise members of the public about the availability of services under the legal aid scheme. A provision based on this proposal was contained in the Legal Advice and Assistance Act 1972 (now consolidated in the Legal Aid Act 1988) but this provision too has never been brought into force.

Meanwhile, the extent of the unmet need for legal services was becoming increasingly apparent to young lawyers in this country. In the 1960s a system of neighbourhood law offices began to be developed in the USA and pressure grew for a similar development in England. The Lord Chancellor's Advisory Committee on Legal Aid rejected the idea in its reports for 1966 and 1967 but the following year the Society for Labour Lawyers published its influential pamphlet *'Justice for All'*. Although receiving official rejection, this publication appeared to be the catalyst for the start of the law centre movement. The North Kensington Law Centre opened in 1969 and others soon followed. By the end of the 1980s there were about 60 centres. Most are funded by local or central government. Because of cutbacks in government funding, several are now in severe financial difficulty and threatened with closure. Law centres usually employ a number of qualified lawyers, several (usually unqualified) assistants and administrative staff. They tend to specialise in welfare law, in particular housing, employment, social security, family problems and immigration. Many of the centres use the legal aid and advice scheme where possible.

The Law Society was initially opposed to the development of law centres. It argued that their creation was unnecessary and that the legal aid scheme should be improved to cover the sort of work the centres would be dealing with. It is also likely that the Law Society feared competition but, as many people predicted, these fears have proved groundless. Not only do law centres largely deal with people who would not approach solicitors, but in some cases they have actually generated work for solicitors by being able to refer clients to them for more specialist advice. The Law Society has had some involvement in the development of law centres. The centres have had to advertise their services and this is in contravention of the rules prohibiting solicitors unfairly attracting work. However, the Law Society is allowed to waive these rules if it wishes and, after some early difficulties, a standard waiver form has been produced. Until 1990 law centres were allowed to advertise in return for not undertaking work typically done by solicitors in private practice such as conveyancing, wills, divorce, commercial work and adult crime. These restrictions have now been removed. The Law Society has now come to terms with the existence of law centres and even tried to persuade the Royal Commission to put them under its control, but without success.

The Royal Commission on Legal Services was fulsome in its praise for law centres. It was, however, unhappy with one aspect of their work. Many law centres have gone beyond concentrating on the traditional adviser-client relationship and extended their activities as a pressure group in the local community. The reasoning behind this may seem sensible to many people: it is a waste of time and resources to keep dealing with the same recurring problem (eg poor housing), albeit manifesting itself in different cases, when the problem should be tackled at source. The Royal Commission said that the first ten years of law centres had been a time for experimentation and the time had come to move away from the disparity among the centres and offer a new single type, the Citizens' Law Centre. These would operate in much the same way as the existing law centres, except that they would not be allowed to engage in 'general community work': there should be no pressure brought on central or local government, or private landlords. The Law Centres Federation, which represents the centres, reacted very strongly against these proposals. In fact, no changes have resulted and law centres operate much as they did before. As was pointed out above, they now face a far greater threat of withdrawal of funding resulting from Government expenditure cuts.

Other organisations providing legal advice

The legal profession could not cope with providing legal advice to everybody who needs it and it is inevitable that other organisations will play a part. We have just seen how law centres, employing both qualified lawyers and lay persons, play an invaluable role in the provision of legal services. Other bodies, usually comprising mainly lay persons, also play an important part in giving advice. The largest and most important of these are Citizens' Advice Bureaux. Created in 1938 to provide assistance in a national emergency, the Bureaux declined in the post-war period only to receive the stimulus of fresh government funding in the 1960s. There are now over 1,000 Bureaux outlets and they deal with nearly 8 million enquiries a year. About 10% of the staff are salaried and the rest are volunteers. Free advice is offered on a variety of areas, the most popular now being social security. The Bureaux are all registered with the National

Association of Citizens' Advice Bureaux and have to comply with its rules and standards. The Royal Commission on Legal Services described Citizens' Advice Bureaux as '. . . the best placed organisation to provide a primary or first tier service' and felt that they should maintain this role rather than specialise in particular areas and employ solicitors. In fact, a number of Bureaux do employ solicitors and in others solicitors offer their services free on a rota basis.

Other organisations offer more specialist advice. Some local authorities operate Consumer Advice Centres to provide both advice and a mechanism for dealing with complaints. These operate closely with Trading Standards Departments. Local authorities are also involved with many of the Housing Advice Centres that now exist. There are also charitable organisations such as Shelter, the Child Poverty Action Group and the National Association of Victims Support Schemes. Some organisations offer specialist legal advice to their own members. These include the trade unions; the Consumers' Association, which provides the magazine 'Which?' and runs several legal advice centres; and the motoring organisations. Finally, we must not overlook the role played by the media, especially radio and television, in the provision of legal advice.

The services offered by these organisations are not without their problems. Greater co-ordination between them would be an advantage, in particular for the public who may sometimes be at a loss as to which organisation to approach. In addition, if the Government's plans to give advice bodies a greater role at the expense of the green form scheme come to fruition, their lack of expertise in specialist areas may be revealed.

Conclusions

In the first part of this chapter we considered the structure of the legal profession in England and the restrictive practices which have developed around it. These restrictive practices, such as the solicitors' conveyancing monopoly, have started to break down and this process is likely to continue. The one seemingly unchangeable aspect of our legal profession has been its division between barristers and solicitors. Yet even this is under threat, not as a result of the Royal Commission on Legal Services, which adopted a generally timid approach in its recommendations on the legal profession, but from a growing intrusion by solicitors as advocates in the higher courts as a result of the pressure to make savings in the State's expenditure on legal aid. Another development which may hasten the demise of the Bar is the growth of the London 'megafirm' resulting from the amalgamation of big commercial solicitors' practices in the City. These firms have specialist departments and, because they are able to pay attractive salaries to young lawyers, obtain the best graduates. Thus, not only is the Bar being deprived of the best brains, but it is also going to lose a lot of its specialist advisory work. We have also seen the deficiencies in legal education: how the student must choose between solicitor and barrister at too early a stage and how the lack of state funding means that students from better-off backgrounds have a distinct advantage in qualifying as solicitors, or especially barristers. The law is indeed a predominantly white male middle-class profession.

This causes particular problems in relation to the unmet need for legal services, which was considered in the second part of the chapter. Many people do not visit solicitors because they think that they cannot afford to. People who do go to solicitors usually do so in relation to conveyancing, matrimonial problems and criminal cases. Solicitors are not commonly approached on matters of welfare law. Many solicitors are considered too remote, not only in a physical sense but also in their attitude to poorer clients. This view may be unfair, but the fact that it is held shows that solicitors still have a lot to do in terms of public relations. The Legal Aid and Advice schemes cannot in themselves deal with this problem. In any case, those people who do approach solicitors soon discover that the financial limits in the schemes are such that most people, apart from the fairly poor, are excluded.

It is interesting to note, therefore, that many people who approach law centres are eligible to use the green form scheme. Law centres have gone out of their way to make themselves accessible to the public not only in their location but also in the approach of their workers. The Law Society's restrictions on advertising have been waived: it remains to be seen how crusading solicitors' firms will become now that the restrictions are being relaxed for them also. It seems likely that law centres, despite their funding problems, will continue and even expand: the 1988 Legal Aid Act, the creation of the Legal Aid Board and the Lord Chancellor's desire to extend franchising make it clear that the Government envisages a greater role for legal advice organisations, and law centres could benefit from this. Voluntary organisations could well have an important part to play in the provision of legal services, but it seems clear that the envisaged shift of work to them is only a cost-saving device rather than a commitment of principle, and it is unlikely that they will be adequately funded for this purpose.

The Royal Commission on Legal Services proposed that a Council for Legal Services should be established. The Council should conduct research into the provision of legal services, recommend and perhaps carry out any necessary changes. The Council would be under the overall control of the Lord Chancellor. Unfortunately, this idea was rejected by the Government, but the Legal Aid Board set up under the Legal Aid Act 1988 is required to ensure that advice, assistance and representation are available as specified by the Act and supply information to the Lord Chancellor. This may go some way towards dealing with the problem: much will depend on the extent to which the Board is able to remain independent of the Lord Chancellor.

Postscript: alternative methods of financing civil litigation

How can the legal system best help people like the victims of the 'Opren' drug who are ineligible for civil legal aid but cannot afford to bring a High Court action? One way would be through a contingency fee arrangement. Contingency fees are the normal means of financing litigation in the USA. Litigants only have to pay their lawyers if they win their cases; the lawyer usually takes a percentage of the damages. In England the system had been rejected on the ground that it is improper for a lawyer to have a financial interest in the outcome of the case: some unscrupulous lawyers might resort to unethical conduct to increase their chances of winning. The Royal Commission on Legal Services was convinced by these objections and recommended that the prohibition on the use of contingency fee arrangements should be continued. The Civil Justice Review, however, considered that the Law Society was in a much better position to regulate such arrangements and considered that the prohibition should be reconsidered. The Courts and Legal Services Act 1990 authorised conditional fee agreements. This is an agreement in writing between a person providing advocacy or litigation services and a client which provides that either a whole or a part of the client's fees or expenses shall only be payable in specified circumstances. The agreement must comply with any requirements imposed by the Lord Chancellor, and cannot apply to certain matrimonial or child proceedings.

Another way of dealing with the problem would be to abolish the rules which restrict actions brought by groups of plaintiffs. The advantage of such actions is that the costs can be shared among the group. At present, such actions are only allowed in very limited cases, but the Civil Justice Review recommended that the whole question should be reconsidered.

Legal expenses insurance is a further method of financing civil litigation. It now has the support of the Law Society in this country, having been used in Europe for a number of years. It is not widely used at present but it is likely to become more popular.

Another interesting suggestion that has been put forward is that some civil cases involve such important questions of law, which it is in the general interest to have determined, that cases ought to be taken to the higher courts, and particularly the House of Lords, at public expense. Sometimes points of law decided on appeal are so narrow that it seems unfair that the 'loser', who may have had the support of judges in lower courts, has to pay the whole costs of the case.

Chapter 6
Sources of law

The expression 'source of law' can be used in a number of different senses. At the most general level it could be used to refer to the underlying reason for law – the 'why' of law. In this sense our need for order, perhaps based on the reasoning of Hart discussed in Chapter 1, could be said to be a 'source of law'. At a more functional level, it could be used to refer to what provides the rules which judges and lawyers apply. In our system the rules are provided by the common law or legislation and they are often referred to as the two sources of law. They are the 'what' of law. At a still narrower level, it can be used to refer to the process by which judges and lawyers identify what rule is applicable. In this sense the sources are the principles of common law reasoning which guide him as to how to formulate common law rules, and the principles of statutoryinterpretation which guide a lawyer as to how a legislative provision should be applied. This chapter discusses common law reasoning and statutory interpretation. It considers the 'how' of the law, the process by which the particular rules are formulated. The next chapter will take a broader view, examining the relationship of the common law and legislation and the respective roles each should play in the law making process.

Common law reasoning

If the law on a particular issue is not contained in legislation, it will be found through the process of common law reasoning. That process provides the all embracing source of law. As Sir John Donaldson MR, the head of the Court of Appeal, has observed: 'As a matter of legal theory the common law has a ready-made solution for every problem and it is only for the judges, as legal technicians to find it.' But he went on to add 'the reality is somewhat different'. In reality, the judge is a designer as much as a technician. He creates the common law in the process of seeking it. The raw material for the process is previous case law. From a consideration of previous decisions, the judge has to be able to find a rule to provide a solution to the case before him. The process works at two levels. First, the judge must find and follow the rules established by previous decisions of higher courts. This is known as the doctrine of binding precedent. Second, where the facts do not fall squarely within the rule established by a binding precedent, the judge will draw more broadly from the fabric of the case law to find principles that may cover the particular facts, situation or rules that may be extended to do so. By this process the judge will justify his decision and justify creating new case law.

Case law as binding precedent

A judge is bound by a rule of law where it is the basis of a court's decision in a previous case and that case was decided by a court which has authority to bind the judge. A rule on which a court's decision is based is known as the ratio decidendi of the case. In a complex case there may be several ratios as the judge may have to decide several different issues each with a ratio, in order to reach his final decision. The rules which determine which courts have authority to bind others are usually referred to as the rules of stare decisis which means 'stand by what has been decided'. There is no simple explanation of how to identify a ratio or how stare decisis operates. Both concepts embody a complex balance between the need to preserve, on the one hand, some consistency in the way in which the law is applied and, on the other hand, sufficient flexibility to allow the law to develop in a coherent way. That need for balance should be borne in mind as the workings of the two concepts are discussed.

Ratio decidendi

It would be very helpful if judges were to say in their judgments 'these are the ratios of my decision'. But generally they do not. Why? Because unless they happen to be a Law Lord giving judgment in the House, their primary concern is not going to be with laying down a rule to be followed in the future, but rather with justifying the decision they propose to make in the case before them. When justifying a decision on a particular issue, a judge will often not give just one reason. Instead he will employ a number of supporting reasons. At one end of the scale, he may argue that the particular facts of the case justify a particular decision. At the other end he may appeal to some broad legal doctrine which can be shown to support the decision. In between he may examine rules applied in previous similar cases or he may digress, explaining what he would have decided if the facts had been different in some way. The judgments, as law students soon discover, can be complex, intricately argued affairs. Even a relatively short two or three page judgment can contain half a dozen supporting arguments each at a different level of generality, some very fact specific and others very abstract.

Extracting ratios from this mass of argument is an exercise in finding the right level of generality. If the ratio selected is too closely tied to the facts of the particular case, the law may become fragmented, consisting of innumerable little rules of law each tied to its particular fact situation. Judges in future cases would have to consider dozens of these narrow rules before finding the right one. They would, in Lord Denning's colourful phrase, 'be crushed by the weight of their own reports'. If, however, the ratio selected is fairly abstract it may well be applicable to a fact situation never really considered by the judge when he made his statement. What is wrong with that? One of the strengths of the common law system lies in the way in which the particular fact situation before the court is put under the spot light so that the judge is then able to see the situation and the right solution with clarity. But the corollary is, as Lord Simon has put it, 'the beam of light which so illuminates the immediate scene seems to throw the surrounding areas into greater obscurity; the whole landscape is distorted to the view.' To select an abstract ratio which applies to the surrounding areas as well as the immediate scene is risky. When a later case throws the light on that surrounding area the judges may discover that the wide ratio thought to be established by a previous case is totally inappropriate. Here, the danger to the judges would be that of being trapped rather than crushed by their own reports.

So, the first point to bear in mind is that the ratio selected should be neither too fact specific nor too abstract. But there is a second important point to remember about the process of selection. It is an on-going process. There is no one point in time when judges, lawyers or academics etch it in stone, as it were. Judges will make a selection when the case in question is argued before them in some subsequent case. Lawyers will make the selection when they are advising their client on some matter to which the case is relevant. Academics will make their selection when writing books about the area of law involved. Not only are the selections made at different times but they are made for different purposes. The judge may wish to select a narrow ratio to give him freedom to reach a different conclusion in the case before him. The lawyer may search for a wide ratio to reduce the element of uncertainty in the advice he gives his client. The academic may select the ratio which best suits his intellectual theme. Selection is thus both a backward and forward looking process, backward to the facts of the case and words of the judgment, forward to the reason for which the ratio is being selected. In simple cases everyone may agree on the ratio from the start but in other cases a consensus may take time to emerge as the on-going process of selection gradually narrows down the range of acceptable choices.

The ratio of a case is not like the DNA of a cell. It cannot be found by employing some magical test although that has not stopped some academics trying. It emerges through a process of argument fuelled by the experience and objectives of lawyers and judges. One cannot define the concept only describe the process. That is best done by illustration and for this purpose a leading tort case has been selected.

THE RATIO OF *RYLANDS V FLETCHER* (1868)

Rylands is no ordinary case. It gave rise to a new type of tortious liability. One hundred and twenty years later tort textbooks still have a chapter entitled 'The Rule in *Rylands*' and the case is discussed at length in this text (see post, p 426). But in the present context it is used because it is a good illustration of both the difficulty of selecting and defining a ratio and of the on-going nature of the process.

The facts were as follows: Both parties to the case were tenants of a local landowner. Fletcher owned a mill on the land that he leased. With the landlords permission, he hired an apparently competent contractor to construct a reservoir. The contractor carelessly failed to sufficiently block off old mine shafts cut into by the reservoir diggings with the result that when it was filled with water, the weight of the water burst through into the shafts. The shafts were disused but they joined onto shafts then being worked by Rylands who operated a mine on an adjacent piece of leased land. Rylands mine was flooded. He sued Fletcher for the considerable financial loss he suffered and was victorious in the House of Lords.

What was the ratio of the decision? One possibility can be excluded right away and that is the suggestion that Fletcher was liable because his contractor was careless. It can be excluded because the judges either failed to mention the negligence or expressly stated that it was irrelevant. A ratio must be based on facts that the judges expressly or impliedly indicated were material to their decision and the negligence of the contractor was clearly not treated as a material fact. If one looks at what the judges actually said, then three possibilities seem to emerge. The first is the proposition put forward by Blackburn J in a lower court and repeated by Lords Cairns and Cranworth in the House of Lords, namely that 'the person who brings on his land anything likely to do mischief if it escapes, must keep it at his peril, and if he does not do so, he is prima facie liable for all the damage which is the natural consequence of its escape'. Lord Cranworth went on to say that Blackburn's doctrine was founded on the wider principle that 'when one person in managing his own affairs causes, however innocently, damage to another, it is obviously only just that he should be the party to suffer.' That principle he said, was 'applicable to cases like the present' and is therefore, a second, wider candidate for the ratio. Lord Cairns supplied the third but narrower candidate. He repeated the Blackburn formula but noted that previous cases showed that a users of land would only be liable if 'not stopping at the natural use of their close, had desired to use it for any purpose which I may term a non-natural use, for the purpose of introducing onto the close that which in its natural condition, was not in or upon it.'

Which of these three contestants would emerge as the winner? The principle suggested by Lord Cranworth was really too wide. It would have led to liability in tort being based on causing loss rather than being at fault.

Such a 'strict liability' approach is too radical for the modern law to accept (see post, p 146) let alone for Victorian law. In any case judges prefer to move in a gradual way, gingerly stepping forward whilst preserving a line of retreat in case they have made a mistake. The Cranworth principle offered no line of retreat. It would have taken a very bold judge to have selected it as the ratio and there was no such judge around in the late nineteenth century. The formula suggested by Blackburn J was an attractive middle position. Blackburn's reputation as a great commercial judge would have added weight to his suggested ratio. Had later judges wanted to construct an area of strict liability within the law of tort, his ratio would have provided a suitable foundation stone. But by the end of the century it had become clear that the judges had no such interest. Whether for economic concerns about the impact of strict liability on Victorian manufacturers or for a moral concerns about the importance of fault as the basis of liability, the late Victorian judges soon made it clear that they had selected the more qualified suggestion of Lord Cairns. The ratio of *Rylands* was accepted as including a requirement that there be a non-natural user.

DISTINGUISHING CASES AND DEFINING OBITER DICTUM

Simply selecting the ratio does not end the problems. Judges are not like parliamentary draftsmen preparing legislation. They do not always express themselves in very precise language nor do they seek to provide an answer to every possible question that might arise as a result of their decision. Hence, their ratios will often be imprecise and incomplete statements of the law and this was the case with the *Rylands* ratio. The imprecision lay in the phrase non-natural user. Lord Cairns illustrated the phrase with the example of something not naturally on the land. He was thinking of non-natural in a physical sense. But could it be used in another sense? He did not say. In *Rickards v Lothian* (1913) Lord Moulton decided that it should be used in a social sense, that it meant 'some special use bringing with it increased danger to others and must not merely be the ordinary use of the land or such a use as is proper for the general benefit of the community.' Hence he decided that piping water to an upper floor of a building was a natural use and therefore there was no liability under the *Rylands* ratio for the escape of that water to lower floors as a result of a blocked sink. He restrictively defined the terms of the ratio so that it did not apply to the facts before him.

Lord Moulton gave a second reason for his decision, namely that the blockage and therefore the escape had been caused by a stranger for whom the owner was not responsible. *Rylands* had been concerned with a situation where the owner was responsible for the person causing the escape. The judges had not had to decide whether their ratio would apply to situations where the owner was not so responsible. Blackburn J had wisely taken the view that this kind of question could be left to future cases. His ratio was deliberately left as an incomplete statement of the law. In *Rickards* the court filled in one of the blanks in the statement. The ratio would not apply where a stranger was responsible for the escape. The technique used by Lord Moulton in *Rickards* is known as distinguishing. He distinguished *Rylands* on the ground that its ratio did not apply to cases of ordinary social user nor to cases of escape caused by a stranger.

One can see from these cases that judges may have a considerable discretion in selecting the ratios from previous cases and in defining the terms and scope of that ratio. However, gradually the way in which that discretion will be exercised is likely to become clearer. By the date of the *Rickards* decision it was evident that a restrictive view of *Rylands* was likely to be taken and *Rickards* re-inforced that impression. That trend reached its highpoint with the decision of the House of Lords in *Read v Lyons* (1946) and in particular the judgment of Lord Macmillan. The case concerned an explosion in a munitions factory which injured the plaintiff who was visiting the factory. All the Law Lords agreed that the plaintiff could not recover under the *Rylands* principle and they all gave as one reason for this, the fact that the injury had not been caused by an escape of something dangerous from the defendant's land. The plaintiff had been injured whilst on the defendant's land and not by an escape from it. Lord Macmillan suggested two further grounds for the decision: first, that a plaintiff ought not to recover for personal injuries under the *Rylands* principle and secondly, he said that 'were it necessary to decide the point, I should hesitate to hold that in these days and in an industrial community it was a non-natural use of land to build a factory on it and conduct there the manufacture of explosives'. However, neither of these statements formed part of the ratio of the case. Why not? The proposition that the manufacture of explosives was not a non-natural use could have been a reason for deciding the case against the plaintiff. But Lord Macmillan did not want to use it as a basis of the decision. This is clear from his intro-ductory phrase 'were it necessary to decide the point'. It was not necessary because he was prepared to rest his decision on other grounds. His statement is what lawyers call an obiter dictum ie a statement of law which is not part of the ratio of the judgment and is not binding on future courts. A statement of law may be regarded as an obiter dictum because the judge expressly states, as did Lord Macmillan, that it is not a reason for the decision. Or it may be obvious that it is not a reason, as where the statement of law relates to a fact situation not before the court. A statement in *Read* that the *Rylands* principle did or did not apply to escaping animals, would fall into that category. It might be an interesting statement but it could not be a reason for a decision about munition factories.

Lawyers also use obiter dictum to refer to statements which might have been candidates for the ratio, but have subsequently been regarded as too wide. Thus Lord Cranworth's wide principle in *Rylands* might now be described as obiter. Lord Macmillan's other statement about the inapplic-ability of *Rylands* to personal injuries would not seem to be an obiter dictum. It was relevant to the facts. It was not put forward in a tentative manner. It was not too wide. It seems to be a ratio of Lord Macmillan's judgment but it is not regarded as a ratio of the case. To understand why, we need to consider the problems presented by both multiple ratios and multiple judgments in the same case.

MULTIPLE RATIOS AND JUDGMENTS

An issue in a case may be determined by reference to more than one ratio. Thus in *Rickards v Lothian* Lord Moulton gave two reasons for his decision: the definition of non-natural user and the defence of act of a stranger. Both were intended to be ratios and both have been accepted and followed as ratios in subsequent cases. Indeed, it is not unknown for additional ratios to be 'discovered' in a case years after it was decided by a creative appeal judge looking for authority to support his views. So multiple ratios do not present a problem. The problem comes with multiple judgments in the Court of Appeal or House of Lords. Dissenting judgments are ignored, but what if the other judgments rely on different ratios? The general approach is to accept as a ratio of the case any ratio which has majority support. Thus, in *Read v Lyons* where there was unanimous support for 'lack of escape' as a ratio but only Lord Macmillan gave 'personal injury' as a ratio, it is only the former that is accepted as a ratio of the case. Where there is no majority in favour of any particular ratio (and it can happen), it seems a later court is free to follow any reasoning compatible with the actual decision in the troublesome case.

CONCLUSION

The difficulty of determining the ratio, the wide scope for re-interpretation and distinguishing, the problems caused by multiple judgments etc have led some critics to conclude that it is not worth drawing distinctions between ratios and obiter, that the concept of a ratio does not really exist. It is like buried treasure, providing an expectation that can never be fulfilled. Obviously there is some truth in this but like buried treasure, the concept of a ratio exerts a powerful influence on the minds of the seekers. Read any decision of an English judge and you will find that he is constantly seeking the ratios of previous cases. The reality of the concept lies in the fact that it is sought.

Stare decisis

Why is it important to search for the ratios of previous cases? The answer lies in the second latin phrase, stare decisis meaning stand by what has been decided. It is necessary to find the ratio of a past decision in order to know by which rule of law future courts must stand. The reason for standing by rules of law decided in past cases is obvious. It is an elementary principle of justice that 'like cases must be treated alike', that the law be applied in a consistent and impartial way. We may all disagree about what the rules of law should contain, about the substance of justice. But we can all agree that the form of the law would be unjust if say, a judge was permitted to apply different rules to the same factual situations depending upon whether he liked one party or not. Formal justice requires consistency, requires that the courts stand by rules of law decided in previous cases unless and until those rules are changed in some accepted way. This idea is so fundamental that it does not need to be set out in legislation or formal instructions from the Lord Chancellor. It can safely rest on the attitudes of the judges and the resulting practice of the courts. Two principles of practice have evolved to create the doctrine of stare decisis: the first is that lower courts must follow the ratios laid down by higher courts. This creates order and consistency within the hierarchy of courts. The second principle is that judges should respect and in some cases follow, decisions of other judges in the same level of court. This ensures order and consistency as between judges operating in different sittings of the same court.

HIGHER BINDS LOWER

A judge is bound by the ratio of a case decided by a higher court. Thus Court of Appeal judges are bound by the ratios of House of Lords decisions and High Court judges are bound by ratios of both Court of Appeal and House of Lords decisions. Which should a High Court judge follow in the case of conflict between Court of Appeal and House of Lords ratios? In theory this problem should not arise. If say, the Court of Appeal ratio on a particular matter is rule X and the House of Lords later decides that the relevant rule is Y, then ratio X is said to be overruled by the later House of Lords decision. It is said to be expressly overruled if the Law Lords said 'X is wrong' and impliedly overruled if they did not consider X but it follows from their adoption of Y, that X must be wrong. Overruling a ratio removes it from the list of precedents. Overruling does not affect the actual outcome in the case decided by ratio X. If the plaintiff lost that case in the Court of Appeal because they decided it on the basis of ratio X, it will make no difference if a year later the Lords in another case overruled X and substituted Y under which the plaintiff would have won. He would only win if he appealed to the Lords and in his case they held X to be wrong and substituted ratio Y. If this happens the decision of the Court of Appeal is said to be reversed. A court reverses a decision of a lower court in the same case and overrules a ratio of a lower court in a different case. So, the effect of overruling ratio X will be to remove it from the list of precedents that can be cited to the High Court judge, leaving only ratio Y for him to follow with no problem of conflict.

Subsequent Court of Appeal decisions should also follow ratio Y with the result that no further conflicts will arise, but here problems can develop. For a period in the 1970s, Lord Denning was trying to establish a practice under which the Court of Appeal could disregard House of Lords ratios if they were based on ignorance of the law (per incuriam being the latin tag) or were out of date (cessante ratione, cesset ipsa lex). Such a practice would have placed High Court judges in the difficult position of having to choose between conflicting ratios of the two higher courts. Despite Lord Denning's prestige as head of the Civil Division of the Court, his colleagues failed to follow him and his superiors in the House of Lords rebuked him. It is now accepted that the Court of Appeal cannot refuse to follow a House of Lords ratio. A conflict between two ratios cannot be deliberately created. However, this does not dispense with the problem for the court may still accidentally fail to follow such a ratio. The barristers arguing the case may not refer the House of Lords ratio to the court, or the court may totally misunderstand the ratio and whilst believing it was reaching a compatible decision, reach one that in fact established a conflicting ratio. This kind of thing can happen but very rarely. So rarely, that there is no real consensus as to what a High Court judge should do when confronted with a House of Lords ratio and a later conflicting Court of Appeal ratio. Which should he follow? Logically one might suggest the House of Lords as being the higher court. Practically, it might be best for the High Court judge to follow the Court of Appeal and then to allow a 'leapfrog' appeal to the Lords to enable them to decide whether to overrule the Court of Appeal ratio or alternatively, affirm it and overrule their own previous ratio. In the only House of Lords decision to consider the problem, one Law Lord adopted the 'logical' approach, another adopted the 'practical' approach, and the others did not comment! However, the nature of the common law system might be said to favour practical rather than logical solutions.

RESPECT FOR SAME LEVEL RATIOS

In theory, any inconsistency between the ratios of different cases decided by the same court can be resolved when the issue appears before a higher court, or in the case of inconsistent ratios in the House of Lords, reappears before that court. Unfortunately, litigants cannot be relied upon to spend their money taking cases to higher courts for the greater good of the legal system. Any inconsistencies which do emerge between same level ratios may remain unresolved for a considerable period and make if difficult for lawyers to give reliable advice on the matter in question. Hence, there is a strong case for avoiding inconsistency between same level ratios.

The House of Lords

The problem is most easily managed at House of Lords level. The low caseload – less than 100 a year, the strong peer pressure amongst the dozen or so judges and the fact that they can only staff two sittings at any one time, all help to ensure consistency. There is really no need to enforce consistency with a practice rule that House of Lords ratios must be followed in subsequent House of Lords decisions. Nevertheless, from the late nineteenth century until 1966, the House of Lords did follow such a rule. Because the House of Lords is the highest court within the system, the rule had the effect of stifling its ability to respond to changed social conditions. In theory, a Victorian decision of 1900 would still have to be followed 60 years later even though it might produce a totally inappropriate result in the changed conditions. In practice, the Lords might be tempted to 'distinguish' such a decision on some fairly transparent ground. This might produce the right decision in the particular case but at the expense of the consistency that the practice rule was supposed to promote. The unity of the common law within the Commonwealth was also at risk, for by the 1960s it was clear that top appeal courts such as the Supreme Court in Canada or the High Court in Australia, unfettered by such a stifling rule, were prepared to diverge from House of Lords decisions in order to update the common law within their countries. Awareness of all these problems led the Lord Chancellor to issue the 1966 Practice Direction under which the Lords are now free to depart from their own previous decisions. In fact, in the first 30 years after it was issued, the House of Lords have used it on only half a dozen or so occasions, most recently in *Murphy v Brentwood District Council* (1990 see post, p 443) where it departed from a previous 1976 decision holding a local authority liable to a subsequent purchaser of property for negligent failure to inspect foundations with the result that the property subsequently suffered from subsidence. The Lords stressed the change in the was one law which would have some significance in disputes between insurance companies as to responsibility for subsidence but little significance for the way the individual citizen ordered his affairs. Whether this is correct is another matter, but it does illustrate that the Lords are still very conscious of the need for consistency, particularly where the law affects the individual. Often the problem is that the law cannot be satisfactorily updated by simply overruling an old decision. The complexity of modern conditions demands a more thorough review and reform than can be provided by substituting one ratio for another. It demands legislation rather then judicial law reform. The proper balance between the two is a topic to which we return in the next chapter.

The High Court

At the opposite end of the scale, consistency is very difficult to achieve within the High Court. With more than a 100 judges delivering thousands of decisions a year most of which will be unreported, it is quite impractical to have a rule that one High Court judge is bound by the ratios of cases decided by other High Court judges. The best that can be done is to avoid too public an inconsistency. To achieve this one High Court judge has recently suggested that where the ratio of one High Court decision has been fully considered but not followed in a second High Court decision, then if a third case arises on the same issue the High Court judge in the third case should follow the second ratio unless he is convinced it is wrong. This suggestion would limit the extent of public inconsistency pending a final decision on the matter by the Court of Appeal. Without such a practice, the judge in the third case could follow the first ratio with the judge in a fourth case following the second ratio etc. However, as another High Court judge has subsequently pointed out, this suggested practice cannot be binding for the High Court is only bound by the rulings of an appellate court and not by the rulings of its own judges! But despite this technical point, the suggested practice does seem common sense.

Court of Appeal
In neither the House of Lords nor the High Court is there a rule that judges are bound by same level ratios. In the House of Lords, this is for reasons of principle ie that the court must be free to adapt the common law to changed conditions. In the High Court, it is for reasons of practicality ie such a rule could never be observed in practice. Neither reason applies to the Court of Appeal. It does not need to be free to change the common law because the House of Lords can do that job. Although its 20 or so judges operating in six or seven different sittings produce some 1,000 decisions a year, less than half of these are likely to contain significant ratios and most such decisions will be published in a law report of some kind. A rule that same level ratios must be followed is a practical proposition provided it allows for the possibility of some ratios being missed by the judges. Such is the compromise which does apply in the Court of Appeal. It is known as the rule in *Young v Bristol Aeroplane Co Ltd* (1944), that being the case in which the rule received its modern formulation. The rule provides that Court of Appeal judges are bound by the ratios of previous Court of Appeal decisions except where: (1) there are conflicting Court of Appeal ratios on the same issue; or (2) the decision has been impliedly overruled by a later House of Lords decision; or (3) the ratio has been given per incuriam.

The second exception is not really one at all but an application of the higher binds lower rule. The first exception is inevitable. Given the number of judges in the court and the number of cases it decides, sooner or later the judges in one case will misinterpret or be unaware of a previous relevant ratio and will deliver a decision based upon a conflicting ratio. When these conflicting ratios are put before the court in a subsequent case, the judges may follow one and overrule the other. The third exception gives rise to the most difficulty. Literally, per incuriam means 'through want of care'.

But because it would be too easy for a judge to hold ratios to be carelessly decided, badly argued etc simply because he thought they were wrong, the phrase is given a narrower meaning. As a general rule, it can only be applied where the court has reached a decision unaware of a binding rule contained in legislation or case law and it can be shown that, had the court been aware of the rule, it must have reached a contrary decision. To some extent per incuriam overlaps with the first exception as conflicting Court of Appeal ratios may arise from ignorance; but it would also apply to ignorance of a previous House of Lords decision and to situations where the court was unaware of a crucial statutory rule. In exceptional circumstances it may be given a wider scope and applied where there has been some manifest error in the reasoning of a prior decision. An example is provided by *Williams v Fawcett* (1985) where the Court of Appeal realized that in a line of four previous cases it had misunderstood the affect of the County Court Rules (technically these are a form of subordinate legislation) dealing with the procedure for committing to prison those who break court undertakings. As a result of this misunderstanding, the court had held committal orders to be invalid. In *Williams*, the court, led by Sir John Donaldson MR, refused to follow the ratio of these previous decisions on the ground of per incuriam. The exceptional circumstances justifying this use of the principle included the fact that many of the committals were for domestic violence and that such cases were most unlikely to be taken to the House of Lords which was the only other way of correcting the error. This 'manifest error' ground in a couple of subsequent cases where both large numbers of litigants were affected by the 'erroneous' ruling and its appeal to the House of Lords was very unlikely. It provides the rule in *Young* with a safety valve.

In the *Williams* case, Sir John Donaldson MR stressed the great importance of the rule of stare decisis 'particularly in an appellate court, such as this, which sits in six or seven divisions simultaneously. But for this rule, the law would not only bifurcate; it would branch off in six or seven different directions.' His cautious attitude contrasts strikingly with that of his predecessor as Master of the Rolls, Lord Denning. In another domestic violence case, *Davis v Johnson* (1978), he had gone so far as to say that the Court of Appeal should follow the example of the 1966 House of Lords Practice Direction and 'be at liberty to depart from (a previous decision) if we think it right to do so'. In *Davis*, Lord Denning thought it right to depart from the ratio of a previous Court of Appeal decision which gave a restrictive interpretation to the protection afforded to women by the 1976 Domestic Violence Act. Two of his colleagues on the court voted with him but on the narrower ground that there should be a fourth exception to the rule in *Young v Bristol Aeroplane Co Ltd* where it could be shown that the previous ratio interpreted legislation in a way contrary to the clear intention of Parliament. The final two members of the five man Court of Appeal (an unusually large sitting of the court reflecting the importance of the case) decided that they were bound to follow the restrictive interpretation embodied in the previous ratio. The case was appealed to the House of Lords which held that the Court of Appeal should have followed its own previous decision and that Lord Denning and the majority were wrong to add to the exceptions laid down in the *Bristol Aeroplane* case. Ironically, having admonished Lord Denning and his other colleagues for having refused to follow the previous restrictive ratio, the Lords then overruled that ratio. Changing the common law or changing the previous interpretation of a statute should be left to the 'big boys' in the House of Lords, was very much the message. Judging from Sir John Donaldson's comments, it is a message that has been understood.

Who is right, Denning or Donaldson? Would Lord Denning's approach lead to Donaldson's 'six or seven different directions' for the law? One suspects that peer pressure would prevent such a parting of ways but in any case differences could be resolved by calling special sittings of the court with more judges than normal. The five man court assembled for the *Davis* case is an example of this technique. Indeed, before the establishment of the modern appeal courts, controversial issues were decided by a gathering of all the judges of the relevant court, a sitting in banc as it was called. But if this solution were to be adopted, why keep the House of Lords? Its function is to supervise the system as a whole, resolving disputes over the interpretation of statutes and adapting case law to modern conditions. Could not this function be performed just as well by the Court of Appeal sitting in banc or at least in a special five man court? Perhaps not. The great strength of the House of Lords lies in the fact that its judges are able to specialise in hearing cases that raise fundamental issues. Their timetable is organised to enable them to consider such cases in depth. Their experience enables them to develop an overview of the role of the judiciary in the process of law-making. It is true that before the 1960s there was not much evidence that they had the insight or ability to perform their task, but that has changed. The House of Lords is now providing leadership and it is doubtful whether Court of Appeal judges able though they are, would be able to perform that role as effectively. The hurly-burly of processing every day appeals as fast and efficiently as possible would be likely to prevent them devoting the time or developing the over-view that is required. Equally, there would be practical problems in deciding which cases required a larger supervisory sitting of the Court. The fundamental nature of the case might become apparent only during argument before a normal sitting. Would it then be transferred to a different sitting? These problems do not arise under the present structure. Cases which are identified as raising fundamental issues in the Court of Appeal can be appealed in the House of Lords. Of course, going to the House of Lords costs the litigants a lot of money. But the solution to this problem does not lie in abolishing the Lords or giving the Court of Appeal greater freedom to act in a supervisory way. It lies in providing a public subsidy to enable the few cases raising fundamental issues to be litigated before the House of Lords. The Royal Commission on Legal Services (1979) recommended such a 'suitors fund' but failed to persuade the government.

Lord Denning's apparently simple suggestion that the Court of Appeal should follow the example of the 1966 House of Lords Practice Direction, raises some complex issues of principle about the structure and role of the appeal system. In practice, however, the rule that the court is bound by the same level ratios gives rise to few problems. The choice that the judges have when selecting the ratio of a previous case means that in most situations they will be able to distinguish a precedent they do not like. Admittedly, this is more difficult when it comes to decisions involving statutory interpretation but in few cases will the court find itself stuck with a rule or interpretation it considers to be wrong. Indeed, many legal issues that reach the courts will not be covered by binding precedents or legislation at all. One of the reasons for bringing such cases to court is to obtain a judgment as to what rule should apply in the absence of any binding case law or legislation. In providing the answer, judges use previous case law in a rather different way. They use it to justify their decision.

Case law as justification

In *Parker v British Airways* (1982), Sir John Donaldson MR had to decide who should be given possession of a gold bracelet: British Airways, in whose departure lounge it was found or Mr Parker, who found it. There were no binding precedents dealing with the issue and hence, Sir John took the view that the court had 'the right and the duty to extend and adapt the common law in the light of established principles and the current needs of the community.' He continued: 'This is not to say that we start with a clean sheet. In doing so, we should draw from the experience of the past as revealed by the previous decisions of the courts.' He went on to discuss 15 previous cases, starting with a 1722 decision and ending with a 1977 decision of the Manitoba Court of Appeal. These were the building blocks of his decision. But the design, the way in which the blocks were fitted together to justify the decision, was provided by Sir John himself. He extracted what he considered to be the guiding principles from the cases. He considered whether giving possession to the finder or the occupier would be more likely to lead to lost goods being returned to their true owner, that being the general community need. He concluded that case law, principle and policy all justified a rule giving possession to the finder. Without such a rule, he thought it likely that finders would conceal their finds and prevent any chance of the true owner recovering his lost goods.

Parker is a good example of justification but what it does not show is that different judges approach the task in different ways. For a more detailed illustration of the different approaches, we will turn again to a leading tort case, but this time from the twentieth century. The case is *McLoughlin v O'Brian* (1982) and it shows the House of Lords justifying the extension of recovery for nervous shock to what are called 'immediate aftermath' situations.

MCLOUGHLIN V O'BRIAN

Mrs McLoughlin's family were injured in a road accident for which O'Brian was responsible. An hour after the accident, she was told of it and taken to visit the family in hospital. Her daughter was dead, her son screaming with pain and her husband sobbing with grief. This experience 'in the immediate aftermath' of the accident caused her to suffer nervous shock resulting in organic depression and a change of personality. She sued O'Brian for compensation for that injury to herself. There was no binding authority dealing with liability for nervous shock suffered in the 'immediate aftermath'.

Lord Wilberforce gave the first judgment in the House of Lords. He examined eight previous cases including ones from Australia and Canada and then reasoned as follows:

> 'Throughout these developments the courts have proceeded in the traditional manner of the common law from case to case, on a basis of logical necessity. If a mother, with or without accompanying children, could recover on account of fear for herself (step 1, permitted in a 1901 case), how can she be denied recovery on account of fear for the accompanying children (step 2, permitted in 1925)? If a mother could recover if she had witnessed a serious accident to her husband and children, does she fail because she was a short distance away and immediately rushes to the scene? I think that, unless the law is to draw an arbitrary line at the point of direct sight and sound, these arguments require acceptance of such an extension [of recovery] in the interests of justice (step 3, permitted in a 1972 Australian case). If one continues to follow the process of logical progression, it is hard to see why the present plaintiff also should not succeed. If from a distance of some 100 yards she had found her family by the roadside (facts of Australian case) she would have come within the principle [of recovery]. Can it make any difference that she comes on them in an ambulance, or, as here, in a nearby hospital? To allow her claim may be on the margin of what the process of logical progression would allow. But where the facts are strong and ... fairly analogous, her case ought, prima facie, to be assimilated to those which have passed the test.' (In this extract we emphasised the nature of the reasoning by noting the steps in brackets.)

Lord Wilberforce used the previous case law to show how one could move step by step to justify recovery in the immediate aftermath situation. This type of argument is know as reasoning by analogy. It rests on showing how similar one fact situation is to another. It is the form of argument used by most judges to justify decisions. Its attraction lies in the cautious case by case approach. Using this technique a judge never extends the law further than necessary to decide the particular case before him. Its limitation lies in the absence of guidance as to whether or not to draw the analogy. Lord Wilberforce recognised this problem when he continued:

> 'To argue from one factual situation to another and to decide by analogy is a natural tendency of the human and legal mind. But the lawyer still has to inquire whether, in so doing, he has crossed some critical line behind which he ought to stop.'

Whether this was so, he said, depended upon arguments of policy. He then considered four policy arguments against extending recovery to immediate aftermath cases, namely, that it would lead to a proliferation of possibly fraudulent claims, that it would impose a greater burden on defendants, insurers and indirectly road users as a class, that it would increase evidentiary difficulties, and finally, that such an extension should only be made by the legislature after careful research. He concluded that although these arguments justified a limit to recovery eg no recovery by an ordinary bystander as opposed to a relative, they did not justify excluding recovery simply because the shock was suffered in the immediate aftermath.

The other Law Lords also allowed recovery but Lord Scarman in particular, reached his conclusion by a different path, by emphasising the importance of principle:

> 'it (the court) starts from a baseline of existing principle and seeks a solution consistent with ... principles already recognised. The distinguishing feature of the common law is this judicial development and formulation of principle. Policy considerations will have to be weighed; but the objective of the judges is the formulation of principle. And, if principle inexorably requires a decision which entails a degree of policy risk, the court's function is to adjudicate according to principle, leaving policy curtailment to the judgment of Parliament.'

We will consider Lord Scarman's views about the ability of the judiciary to assess policy matters and its role in relation to Parliament, in the next chapter. For the present, it is the technique of advancing the law through the formulation of principle that is significant. After citing a few of the leading cases, Lord Scarman concluded 'common law principle requires the judges to follow the logic of the "reasonably foreseeable test" so as, in circumstances where it is appropriate, to apply it untrammelled by spatial, physical or temporal limits.' As it was reasonably foreseeable that Mrs McLoughlin would suffer her injury, she was entitled to recover.

The attraction of this type of justification by reference to principle, is that it appears to give the common law both coherence and direction. The limitation of the technique is that it will only work if the principle has been chosen at the right time and with the right content. In perhaps the best known of all common law decisions, *Donoghue v Stevenson* (1932), Lord Atkin laid down the principle that recovery for ordinary physical injury was to be governed by 'reasonable foreseeability'. He chose precisely the right time to pronounce the principle. The courts had decided enough cases on a step by step, analogical basis, for it to be clear how the case law could be welded into a coherent whole under a guiding principle. The content of the principle was right. It dealt with physical injuries directly caused by a negligent wrongdoer and did not purport to cover such problem situations as nervous shock or economic loss which had not been previously explored on a case by case basis. It worked, as a reading of the tort section of this book will reveal. But if the timing and content are wrong, a pronouncement of principle will not work in the long term and may even lead to a retrenchment in the development of the law. A judge needs to be sure of his ground before citing principle as the main justification for his decision. In the nervous shock context, the subsequent House of Lord decision in *Alcock v Chief Constable of South Yorkshire* (1991) decided that the cautious approach of Lord Wilberforce rather than the principled approach of Lord Scarman should set the pattern for future case law (see post, p 386).

The principles of equity

There is a group of principles to which judges frequently resort when justifying decisions. The group consists of those principles which historically were developed by the Court of Chancery. Some are referred to as maxims of equity, others as the Doctrines. But they all function as principles justifying particular decisions or rules of law. Since the nineteenth century merger of Chancery and Common Law courts, they can be used in any type of case although their appeal is most powerful in the areas of law traditionally dealt with by Chancery. Some are vague in nature eg the well known maxim 'He who comes to equity must come with clean hands' – used for example, to prevent one party taking advantage of another's illiteracy; or the sweeping 'Equity will not suffer a wrong to be without a remedy' to which Lord Denning tended to resort when there was no other available justification for an innovative decision. Some are more technical in nature, such as the doctrine of part performance. This enables a court to accept oral evidence of a contract to transfer land even though statute provides that such contracts must be evidenced in writing. The doctrine applies where there is an act of part performance of the contract by one party and that act is 'unequivocally referable to the contract'. The meaning of this requirement has given rise to much case law and the doctrine is still developing in scope. In a recent case, it was described as 'one of the great judicial creations of English law' and 'lending itself to judicial development'. This is true of most of the principles of equity. They lack precise limits. In the words of Lord Scarman, 'This is the world of doctrine, not of neat and tidy rules'.

In a book of this length and content it is impossible to do justice to the contribution made to our law by the principles of equity. We do not deal with the law of property which is the area in which the principles have had their greatest impact. The concept of a trust and rules which govern the modern mortgage were developed through principles of equity. Again, we do not deal with remedies in any great detail and hence little can be said about two other products of equity, specific performance and the injunction. However, in the section of the book on the law of contract there are examples of equitable principles. If you read the discussion of estoppel (p 553) you will get some idea of the significance of one particular equitable principle. You will also see how that principle has been developed on a case by case basis. Justifying a decision by the principle of estoppel usually requires a process of reasoning similar to that undertaken by the judges in *McLoughlin*.

Conclusion: principles, policy and pragmatism

Arguments of principle like those of policy are not a substitute for the experience of previous case law. They can guide a court as to how that past experience should be interpreted, as to how the building blocks of past precedents should be put together. But judicial reasoning whether concerned with the common law in the narrow sense of issues decided by the old common law courts, or in the wider sense of all judicially created law including equity, is essentially concerned with the adaptation and extension of previous case law to new fact situations. This is what the skill and experience of a judge primarily equips him to do. He is essentially a pragmatist, concerned with finding the right solution to the case before him rather than creating a logical framework of law built around principle and still less, policy. This pragmatic approach has important implications for the role of the judge as a law-maker which we consider in the next chapter.

Statutory interpretation

It is understandable that there may be problems discovering and interpreting the ratio of a case. Although judges will consider the future implications of their judgments, their primary purpose in drafting judgments is to justify their decision in a particular case. But statutes are drafted with the sole purpose of establishing clear rules for regulating future conduct. Unlike judgments, they are wholly forward-looking. Furthermore, they are normally drafted by expert lawyers known as 'Parliamentary Counsel', who take great care to ensure that the meaning of each provision is absolutely clear. Their drafts are dissected in the debates of Parliament, many of whose members are experienced lawyers. Parliamentary committees spend hours scrutinizing each provision. One might have expected the product of this labour and expertise to be foolproof so that it would be clear how the statutory provisions should be applied to a situation. Unfortunately this is not the case. Sometimes problems result from drafting errors. More often they are the result of two inherent difficulties facing the draftsman. The first is the indeterminate nature of much of our language and in particular, the way in which we phrase rules. As Professor Hart has observed, rules often have a core of certainty and a penumbra of doubt. A rule 'prohibiting vehicles from entering the park' has at its core a motor car, but at its penumbra will be say, a child's pedal car. You could solve the problem by specifying in the rule the types of vehicles prohibited eg motor car, pedal car etc. But that raises the second problem, inability to anticipate and indeterminacy of aim. You would be almost certain to forget some type of vehicle when writing the list – perhaps one failed to anticipate the arrival of skate boards. Even if you had the foresight to think of skate boards, it is quite likely you would not know whether to ban them. You would be safer opting for the indeterminate classifying word, 'vehicle'.

'No vehicles in the park' provides a simple illustration of the problem. The case of *R v Bloxham* (1982) provides a more complex illustration in the context of the wording of section 22(1) of the Theft Act 1968. The relevant part of this provides:

> 'A person handles stolen goods if ... he dishonestly undertakes or assists in their ... disposal by or for the benefit of another person...'

Bloxham had purchased a car for £500 cash down and a further £800 to be paid when the seller delivered its registration document. That document was never produced and after a few months Bloxham realised that the car must have been stolen. He drove it for a bit longer and then sold it for £200 to someone willing to take it without the document. Somehow these facts came to light and Bloxham was prosecuted under section 22 on the basis that by selling it to X for the low price of £200 he was 'disposing of it for the benefit of another person' ie X. The problem is this: clearly the normal case envisaged by section 22 is that of B selling a car on behalf of X and handing some of the money back to X. X is the supplier of the stolen goods not the purchaser. But section 22 does not say 'for the benefit of a supplier'. Rather, it uses the general classifying term 'another person'. It is very unlikely that the draftsman of the section foresaw the *Bloxham* situation or could have anticipated the problem that would be caused by use of the general term. This is the kind of interpretation problem that is constantly arising. Not that one must imagine that every statutory provision is fraught with such difficulties; the vast majority give rise to no issue of interpretation whatsoever. But those that do can be both difficult and important. Thousands of people may do what Bloxham did each year. For them the interpretation of section 22 determines whether they are classed as criminals or not. The difficulties involved frequently mean that the cases will go to the Court of Appeal or even as in *Bloxham*'s case, to the House of Lords. Indeed, the majority of cases heard by the Lords involve issues of statutory interpretation. The importance and difficulty of these cases has led the higher courts to develop principles to guide lower courts and officials in the task of interpretation. These are often referred to as 'the rules of statutory interpretation' but there is really little that is precise enough to merit description as a 'rule'. Rather what has to be described is a general approach with some principles and few rules. The next section will describe this approach using *Bloxham* as the main illustration, and a further section will discuss the limits and problems of the approach.

Approaches to interpretation

Giving the leading judgment of the House of Lords in *Bloxham*, Lord Bridge said of the phrase 'another person': 'But the words cannot, of course, be construed in isolation. They must be construed in their context.' In isolation and read literally, the words do appear to cover a purchaser. Indeed, judges in the early part of this century have been criticised for taking such isolationist approaches to interpretation, an approach the critics have often dubbed the 'literal rule' of interpretation. But from the 1970s onwards, judges in the House of Lords in particular, have stressed the need to interpret words in their context. They have accepted that words have no plain literal meaning in isolation and that meaning must be related to context. This new approach requires the judge to consider the context before making any decision about the 'plain meaning' of the words. The judge can discover the context by looking at evidence inside and outside the statute. These so-called internal and external aids to construction give the judge a lot of help but there are limits.

INTERNAL AIDS

The first step is to set the problem words in the context of the particular statutory provision. In *Bloxham*, Lord Bridge reasoned that section 22 created an offence that could be committed in two ways: assisting in the disposal for the benefit of another person, or assisting in the disposal by another person. Then he argued that the phrase 'another person' must have the same meaning for each of the two ways. Now clearly you cannot be said to 'assist in the disposal of goods by a purchaser'. That does not make sense. A purchaser buys goods. He does not dispose of them. Hence, you cannot assist him to dispose when he is buying. If a purchaser cannot be within the scope of the phrase 'another person' for the 'by way' of committing the offence, neither can he be within the scope of the phrase for the 'for way' of committing it. Thus read in the context of the section, the plain meaning of 'another person' excludes a purchaser. Clever, intricate reasoning and perhaps, not very appealing. From this narrow approach, Lord Bridge moved to setting the word in the context of the statute as a whole and here the argument was simpler. Section 3 of the Theft Act 1968 provides that an innocent purchaser of goods who subsequently discovers that they are stolen, does not commit theft by keeping the goods without trying to find the true owner. As Lord Bridge commented, it would hardly be consistent with this protection if the same person were to commit the offence of handling were he to sell the goods rather than keep them.

The best internal aids will often be provided by the scheme of the section and statute in which the problem words are to be found. There are other internal aids. Judges may be able to find some clues as to the proper context from the long title of the Act (ie the explanation of the object of the Act which is normally to be found right after the title itself) or the subheadings within the Act. These were no help in *Bloxham*. The long title said 'An Act to revise the law of England and Wales as to theft' and the subheading under which s 22 was grouped, read 'Offences relating to goods stolen, etc'. But sometimes there may be clues, particularly in the case of older statutes passed when there was a tradition of including a longer explanation of the statute's purpose in what was known as the 'preamble' to the Act. It has been suggested that modern draftsman should develop this old tradition by providing an official explanatory document with each statute to assist judges and lawyers in finding the context, but the proposal has not been acted upon: Such an explanation might not make things clearer than the Act itself and might add to the difficulties by giving the judge a second document to interpret.

The final type of internal aid is provided by certain 'Rules of Language' developed by lawyers. Perhaps the most used of these is known as Eiusdem Generis under which a general phrase following a list of specific items all belonging a class or genus, is to be interpreted as limited to items of the same type (eiusdem in latin). In *DPP v Jordan* (1976) for example, the House of Lords had to decide whether the defence of justification to a charge of publishing obscene material could apply where the public good was said to be the psychotherapeutic value of sexual fantasy to the reader. The statutory provision referred to justification 'as being for the public good on the ground that it is in the interests of science, literature, art or learning or of other objects of general concern.' Should 'objects of general concern' be interpreted to cover the psychotherapeutic value? The prosecution argued that 'other objects' should be limited to the genus of intellectual or aesthetic values to which the listed items belonged. The House was not convinced by this argument alone, but given the overall context of the statute and particularly the fact that its long title included the phrase 'to provide for the protection of literature', they concluded that psychotherapeutic value fell outside the scope of 'objects of general concern'. Like the eiusdem rule, the other linguistic rules are really common sense and as in *Jordan* one finds them being used in a supporting role, to bolster the court's view of the plain meaning of the word in its context. If the linguistic rules pointed in an opposite direction from that provided by the overall context, they would be disregarded.

EXTERNAL AIDS

The court can seek external assistance from the legislative background of the statute, the social background against which it was passed, the broad principles of the legal system into which it must fit, and finally in the case of statutes passed to honour an international obligation of the UK, the nature and background of that obligation. For the most part these aids play a supporting role being used to justify an interpretation that the judge already favours. Thus in *Bloxham*, Lord Bridge supported his contextual interpretation by reference to the legislative background, the report of the Criminal Law Revision Committee which led to the passing of the Theft Act 1968. In the section on handling, the report spoke of the object being to 'combat theft by making it more difficult to dispose of stolen property'. Commenting on this, Lord Bridge said that there was 'no hint that a situation in any way approximating to the circumstances of the instant case lay within the target area of mischief which the Committee intended their new provision to hit.' Lord Bridge did not consider any of the detailed comments of the Committee on the draft provision which eventually became section 22. He said that he was not entitled to take account of what the Committee thought its draft Bill meant but could only consider what they thought was the 'mischief' its provisions were designed to cure. In other words, he could look at the report to discover the broad object of the Bill but no more. There are important practical and theoretical reasons for this restriction. The practical reason is that were consideration of the detail permitted, lawyers would have to argue over and courts would have to interpret, two documents rather than one, the Act and the Commentary on the draft. In so doing they might well find the Act had not included part of the draft or that the draft commentary had not discussed a provision that was in the Act etc. The theoretical reason is that it is the constitutional function of the courts to interpret the words of a statute, to ascertain the intention of Parliament and they would not be exercising this function if they simply mirrored the interpretation put forward by another agency such as a law reform body.

What about Parliamentary debates? If the court examined what MPs said about the provisions of the Bill as it went through, surely it would be ascertaining the intention of Parliament in the most direct way. In *Davis v Johnson* (1978), Lord Denning in the Court of Appeal did use the debates concerning the Domestic Violence Act 1976 as an aid to interpretation, saying that to ignore them would be to 'grope about in the dark for the meaning of an Act without switching on the light.' Indeed, there is evidence that failure to examine the debates has resulted in judges reaching an interpretation of an Act quite opposed to that intended by Parliament. Nevertheless, the House of Lords in *Davis* admonished Lord Denning and instructed judges to put on their blinkers and ignore debates. Why? Two reasons were put forward by the Lords. First, the evidence might not be reliable. What was said in the cut and thrust of public debate was 'not always conducive to a clear and unbiased explanation of the meaning of statutory language' argued Lord Scarman. Second, if debates were to be used, there was a danger that the lawyers arguing a case would devote a lot of time and attention to ministerial statements etc at the expense of considering the language used in the Act itself. However, fifteen years later in *Pepper v Hart* (1993), the House of Lords relaxed the prohibition and allowed reference to debates where three conditions were satisfied: First, the legislation was ambiguous or obscure or its literal meaning led to an absurdity; second, the statements referred to were those of the minister or other promoter of the Bill; and third, those statements were clear. The Lord Chancellor, Lord Mackay, dissented on the ground that practically every question of statutory interpretation coming before the courts would involve an argument as to whether the case fell under the *Pepper* exception and the result would be an unnecessary increase in the cost of litigation. Experience since the decision in *Pepper* suggests that the exception provides a workable compromise between no consideration of debates and unlimited consideration. Lord Mackay's fears do not seem to have realised.

The social background of a statute can provide a guide as to the way in which its words should be read. Unfortunately, not all statutes have one clear social purpose. Many reflect a complex interplay of social interests and aims. Neither the politicians nor their advisers may have a clear idea of which interest should have priority in a case of conflict and the resulting legislation may employ vague wording to leave such issues unresolved. In this situation, it is asking a bit much to expect a judge to solve the problem by identifying the true social purpose of the statute and giving the words the appropriate meaning. Nevertheless, judges and particularly Law Lords, do attempt this task when they have nothing else to go on. An example is provided by the 1977 Homeless Persons legislation. This implemented the policy of housing the homeless by imposing on local authorities a duty to provide them with permanent housing. However, to ease the financial burden on the authorities, the statute also provided that the duty would not apply where the persons were 'intentionally homeless'. The meaning of this phrase was left vague by the statute. Inevitably, the judges had to face the problem of interpretation. The nature of the problem is clear from the House of Lords decision in *Din v Wandsworth London Borough Council* (1979), in which the court gave a three against two decision in favour of the authority. Lord Wilberforce for the majority, emphasised the importance of the 'intentionally homeless' qualification for both authorities and those on their housing waiting lists who might be queue jumped by the homeless. Against this background he argued, the qualification should not be interpreted narrowly. Lord Bridge for the minority, emphasised the priority need of the homeless and argued that the qualification should not be interpreted in such a way as to treat them unjustly. Both judges agreed that the social context of the legislation was relevant to its interpretation. They disagreed about the nature of that context. Such disagreements are not uncommon and are hardly the judges' fault. It is in precisely those situations where the social policy is unclear, that the legislature may use vague wording and the problem may end up in the House of Lords. Where the policy is clear, the wording will usually reflect this and problems will not come before the courts.

The third external aid is provided by the context of the legal system as a whole, its fundamental nature and principles. These are often expressed in the form of presumptions of interpretation. In *Bloxham* for example, Lord Bridge referred to the presumption that 'ambiguities in a criminal statute are to be resolved in favour of the subject, in favour of the narrower rather than the wider operation of an ambiguous penal provision.' In past centuries this approach reflected the libertarian and humanitarian policy of the law. In a twentieth century democracy with no capital punishment or torture, such an approach is less necessary and many would say that the protection of society demands that penal provisions should be interpreted in the light of their social purpose and where appropriate, given a wide meaning. Lord Bridge placed little weight on the presumption and perhaps it should now be regarded as out-dated. Much the same could be said of other presumptions of interpretation mentioned in the books eg that taxes were not to be imposed or property rights taken away without clear words. As Lord Devlin has suggested, the nineteenth century judges who developed these and other presumptions were really applying their own 'Victorian Bill of Rights' to the interpretation of legislation. There is a case for a modern Bill of Rights to control both the interpretation and content of legislation but such control is now beyond the powers of the judges. It is a matter for politicians.

The final external aid is the international background to legislation passed to honour a treaty obligation. In *Garland v British Rail* (1982), Lord Diplock stated that the principle of interpretation to be applied was:

> 'that the words of a statute passed after the treaty has been signed and dealing with the subject matter of an international obligation of the United Kingdom, are to be construed, if they are reasonably capable of bearing such a meaning, as intended to carry out the obligation and not to be inconsistent with it. A fortiori is the case where the treaty obligation arises under one of the Community (EEC) treaties.'

In *Garland*, the House of Lords gave a restrictive interpretation to one of the qualifying provisions of the Sex Discrimination Act 1975 so as to make the Act fit with Article 119 of the EC Treaty which provides that 'men and women should receive equal pay for equal work'. One problem in achieving a fit in this kind of case is that EC obligations like Article 119 are frequently framed in terms of broad principle, the 'European fashion' as Lord Denning has called it, whereas the English fashion is to frame legislation with detailed specific rules. This means that the court must decide how the broad principle would apply to specific situations dealt with by the rules and this in turn requires an examination of the purpose of the principle. In the case of EC obligations this job can be done for the English court by the European Court of Justice. In *Garland* the House of Lords referred Article 119 to the ECJ asking how it applied to concessionary travel facilities for retired employees, and then interpreted the Sex Discrimination Act to fit the answer given by the ECJ.

In the case of other international obligations the English court will have to interpret the provision itself and that may require it to look at the background to the obligation. Thus in *Fothergill v Monarch Airlines* (1980), the House of Lords had to decide whether the phrase 'damage to baggage' included loss of baggage. The phrase appeared in the Warsaw Convention on air travel and the exact wording of that treaty was contained in domestic legislation passed to implement our obligation to honour the treaty. To find the meaning of the phrase, the Law Lords examined what are known as the travaux preparatoire ie the documents and conference debates which led to the treaty, and they also considered the views of the leading textbooks on the question. They would not have consulted any of this material had the legislation been purely domestic in character. It was consulted because, in the words of Lord Diplock, the language of the convention was 'neither couched in the conventional English legislative idiom nor designed to be construed exclusively by English judges.' The language lacked the technical precision of English drafting and hence a purposive interpretation was required. That interpretation would be provided by courts in all the countries honouring the treaty and in civil law countries these courts would routinely use travaux preparatoire and textbooks to assist legislative interpretation. By taking the same approach, the House of Lords was merely keeping in step with the rest of the world. After all, the purpose of treaties like the Warsaw Convention is to secure uniformity in the treatment of the matter in question. After consulting the relevant materials, the House concluded that 'damage' was to be interpreted as including 'loss' although 'loss' would not have been within its plain, literal meaning.

Problems and rules

Most statutory interpretation cases come before the courts because there is no plain meaning to the words they use. Rather there is a choice of meanings. After examining the context, the court will make its choice. In

Bloxham, the House of Lords chose the narrow meaning of 'another person' excluding the purchaser and quashing Bloxham's conviction. After reading the judgment of Lord Bridge one is tempted to think there was no other possible outcome. In fact the Court of Appeal had previously reached just the opposite outcome, applying a wide interpretation and affirming the conviction. The choice was always there and only the skilful reasoning of Lord Bridge disguised that fact. Exercising choice where the words are vague or ambiguous is clearly a proper function of the court. A far more difficult problem is raised when the statute contains words which seem to have a plain meaning, but one which appears to produce an unreasonable result. Here the court may be asked not so much to choose a meaning but to rewrite the words so as to produce a sensible result. The question to be asked is whether and to what extent it is part of the proper function of a court to rewrite statutes passed by Parliament. It is a question of fundamental constitutional importance.

This question is traditionally discussed in terms of the so-called 'rules of statutory interpretation'. Historically the first of these was the mischief rule under which medieval judges would do what they felt was necessary to make the statute 'suppress the mischief' that Parliament had intended to remedy. The medieval judges were competent to do this; they often drafted the statutes for the King who had them rubber-stamped by Parliament. After the constitutional settlement of 1689, this rather 'cavalier' attitude to statutory interpretation gave way to what is known as the literal rule according to which, as one leading nineteenth century judge put it, 'If the words of an Act are clear, you must follow them, even though they lead to a manifest absurdity.' But even nineteenth century judges felt there must be limits to this rule, and consequently they developed the golden rule under which a court may depart from the plain wording of a statute if that wording creates an anomaly which defeats the intention of the statute, which could not have been envisaged by Parliament and which can be cured by a simple modification of the words used as opposed to a redrafting of the whole statute.

Behind this talk about the three rules, about precisely when the mischief or golden rules can be used to qualify the literal rule, lies the constitutional question. The fundamental nature of this question was brought out into the open in 1950 with the clash of Lord Denning in the Court of Appeal and Lord Simonds in the House of Lords. The case which provided the battleground involved a statute which contained plain wording but wording which seemed to produce a degree of injustice. Lord Denning avoided the injustice by ignoring the plain wording and justifying his stance with great rhetoric:

'We do not sit here to pull the language of Parliament to pieces and make nonsense of it. That is an easy thing to do, and it is a thing to which lawyers are too often prone. We sit here to find out the intention of Parliament and carry it out, and we do this better by filling in the gaps and making sense of the enactment than by opening it up to destructive analysis.'

All to no avail. Leading the Lords, Lord Simonds was prepared to accept the comment about finding the intention of Parliament as an 'echo' of the old Mischief rule but of 'filling gaps' he said 'It appears to me to be a naked usurpation of the legislative function under the guise of interpretation ... If a gap is disclosed, the remedy lies in an amending Act.' This case marked the beginning of an era in which Lord Denning battled for a more active judicial role in the interpretation of statutes, a battle he was still fighting and losing 30 years later when in *Davis v Johnson* the House of Lords rejected his view that judges could consult parliamentary debates.

Although Lord Denning failed to persuade the House of Lords to accept his views, his campaign undoubtedly contributed to the more liberal and open approach to interpretation which the House pursued from the early 1970s. Lord Simon was a leader of this new approach and in a series of cases he emphasised the importance of interpreting a statute in its full context and particularly, its social context. His judgments gave a new vitality to the mischief approach to interpretation. But he combined this liberal approach with a perceptive appreciation of the proper function of the judge within the constitution. In *Stocks v Jones* (1978) where he refused to read extra words into a piece of employment legislation to give it an effect that would have been fair for an employer, he drew attention to the following eight factors:

1 The judge cannot match the experience and vision of the legislator.
2 Unlike the legislators, the judge is not answerable to the people.
3 Under the rule of law, citizens are entitled to regulate their conduct according to what a statute has said rather than what a judge says it is meant to say.
4 Searching for the 'spirit of the law' should be left to peoples' courts in totalitarian regimes.
5 Parliament may wish to tolerate an anomaly in legislation in order to achieve a broader objective.
6 What strikes a lawyer as an injustice may appear as a correction of an unjustifiable privilege to the legislature.
7 Rejecting the ordinary meaning of statutory words may only lead the draftsman to use more complicated wording in his next statute.
8 Finally, quoting rather than paraphrasing 'an unlooked-for and unsupportable injustice or anomaly can be readily rectified by legislation; this is far preferable to judicial contortion of the law to meet apparently hard cases with the result that ordinary citizens and their advisers hardly know where they stand.'

These are powerful arguments. As Lord Simon said, they advocate not 'judicial supineness' but rather 'commend a self-knowledge of judicial limitations, both personal and constitutional.' They require the judges to think carefully before adding to the plain words of a statute. Such a step must be carefully justified rather than being swept along by rhetoric or hidden away by reference to traditional rules. The process and the problems are well illustrated by the abortion case, *Royal College of Nursing v DHSS* (1981). The Abortion Act 1967 provided that an abortion was lawful if the pregnancy 'is terminated by a registered medical practitioner' ie a doctor. In 1967 the only method of producing an abortion was surgical and hence it would have been envisaged that hospital abortions under the Act would have been performed by doctors. However, by the 1980s the standard method was medical induction ie drip feeding a drug which induces discharge of the foetus. The routine steps in the method are carried out by nurses acting on doctors' instructions. Were these abortions unlawful? The pregnancies were actually terminated by nurses not doctors. The case went to the House of Lords. The majority of the Law Lords were prepared to treat the words of the Act as meaning 'is terminated by treatment of' a doctor. They were influenced by what they considered to be the policy of the Act namely, broadening the grounds of lawful abortion and ensuring that it was carried out with proper skill. The minority, Lords Wilberforce and Edmund-Davies, felt that the Act should not be rewritten in this way. It should not be given a purposive construction,. Rather it should be 'construed with caution' because it dealt with 'a controversial subject involving moral or social judgments on which opinions strongly differ.' If it was sought to render medical induction lawful, 'the task must be performed by Parliament'. There is much to be said for both majority and minority arguments. This and the sensitivity of the particular issue, highlighted the more general importance of judges justifying rather than disguising a decision to reword a statute. Whether such rewording can be justified as part of the judicial function is a question for the next chapter.

Postscript: errors and attempts

The examples used in this chapter show the judges making sensible or at least, justifiable decisions when developing case law or interpreting a statute. But judges can make mistakes and it may be salutary to end this chapter with a brief discussion of the problem of criminal attempts. It is a good example of the scope for error open to the judges, of the danger of such errors being entrenched by precedent, and of the difficulty of achieving an effective reform of the law on an issue which is both technical and important.

The problem appears simple: can a person be convicted of attempting to commit a crime when the attempt was in some way impossible of being successfully carried out? For example, if a pickpocket puts his hand into an empty pocket, should he be regarded as guilty of attempting to steal?

In the 1960s it appeared that the common law had reached the conclusion that the answer was 'yes'. But then in 1973, the House of Lords decided that this was the wrong answer and held that a person is not guilty of attempting to handle stolen goods if in fact the goods were not stolen although he believes them to be so. The decision was justified on the basis of nineteenth century authority and common sense. To find such a person guilty would be to punish him for his guilty intention and although in the words of Lord Reid, 'the law may sometimes be an ass, it cannot be as asinine as that'. To many of those responsible for law enforcement it was this 'not guilty' decision that was asinine. Despite the criticism, the House of Lords confirmed its view five years later. After considerable pressure from Professor Glanville Williams and other academic criminal lawyers, the Law Commission was persuaded to examine the problem (the role of the Law Commission is explained in detail in the next chapter, see post, p 180). The Commission recommended that the defence of impossibility be abolished and drafted a Bill to achieve that object. However, when the Bill was introduced into Parliament its wording had been weakened in an effort to achieve a compromise on the problem. Fortunately, after hearing evidence from Professor Williams, the House of Commons Committee reviewing the Bill decided to substantially reinstate the Law Commission's draft and that was then passed as the Criminal Attempts Act 1981. Section 1 of the Act provides:

'(1) If with intent to commit an offence, a person does an act which is more than merely preparatory to the commission of the offence, he is guilty of attempting to commit the offence.

(2) A person may be guilty of attempting to commit an offence to which this section applies even though the facts are such that the commission of the offence is impossible.

(3) In any case where – (a) apart from this subsection a person's intention would not be regarded as having amounted to an intent to commit an offence; but (b) if the facts of the case had been as he believed them to be, his intention would so be regarded, then ... he shall be regarded as having an intent to commit that offence.'

In *Anderton v Ryan* (1985) the House of Lords had to decide whether a woman who bought a cut-price video recorder thinking it to be stolen when in fact it had been damaged, could be convicted of attempting to handle stolen goods. The Law Commission had recommended guilt in such circumstances and had drafted its Bill to achieve that result. Unfortunately, the House of Lords, seeing that the Act was not drafted in quite the same terms as the Law Commission's Bill, decided to ignore the Commission's views and in the words of Lord Bridge, approached the question of interpretation with 'no pre-conceived view of the legislative purpose intended'. Lord Bridge had his own pre-conceived view of the scope of the criminal law, and this was that a person should not commit an offence by doing an 'objectively innocent act' but with a guilty mind. As the Act did not make it absolutely clear that a guilty mind alone justified conviction, Lord Bridge held that section 1(3) should be read as subject to the requirement that there be some 'guilty act'. On this interpretation the purchaser of the video committed no offence. Neither did the man who had sexual intercourse with a girl over 16 believing her to be under that age – Lord Bridge thought it impossible to believe that Parliament intended such a person to be convicted. But the man who put his hand in an empty pocket did commit an offence for his conduct was 'objectively' guilty. Lord Roskill took a similar view, invoking Lord Reid's call to avoid asinity and promote common sense. The majority of the House of Lords agreed with this compromise interpretation of the Act.

The critics led again by Professor Williams, disagreed. They argued that whether conduct should be regarded as innocent or guilty turned on the state of mind of the actor and could not be determined 'objectively'. Whether purchasing a cheap video or putting a hand in a pocket was an innocent act or not depended upon the intention of the person doing it. In *R v Shivpuri* (1986) the House of Lords had an opportunity to reconsider. The accused had thought he was smuggling heroin into the UK. On investigation it turned out that the powder found on him was ground cabbage leaves. Was he guilty of attempting to deal with illegal drugs? Lord Bridge was once again to make the key speech in the House of Lords. This time he had noted the Law Commission's recommendation and had also read Professor Williams biting attack on *Anderton*. Lord Bridge conceded that the concept of 'objective innocence' was unworkable, invoked the 1966 Practice Direction to overrule *Anderton* and held that the wording of the Act meant someone could be guilty on the basis of a preparatory act and subjective intent alone. Shivpuri was guilty. So too would have been Ryan and the man mistakenly thinking he was having intercourse with an under age girl. The other Law Lords, none of whom had taken part in the *Anderton* decision, agreed. Professor Williams had triumphed.

What can be learnt from this episode? That the judges' desire to reach what seemed to them to be a common sense solution guided their approach to both the old common law and the new legislation. That our technical approach to drafting legislation can sometimes fail to impress upon judges that there has been a change of principle in the law. That the judges reluctance to make full use of the travaux preparatoire can blinker their interpretation of legislation. That the 1966 Practice Direction is a vital safeguard for without its use the judges could have been stuck with an unworkable interpretation for years. It must be remembered that the unworkable, compromise interpretation of the 1981 Act was the ratio of the *Anderton* decision and as such it was binding on all courts unless and until overruled by the House of Lords or superseded by new legislation. Finally, that the final outcome owed much to an academic, a point to be considered when we examine the nature of the law-making process in the next chapter.

Chapter 7

The law-making process

This chapter considers the process by which law is created and in particular, the respective roles of the legislature and judiciary. The need to examine and balance their roles is a relatively modern problem. For most of the history of our legal system the judges have dominated the law-making process.

Custom

It has been said that in early Norman times 'custom of the realm' was what made the law, that judges' decisions and royal statutes merely gave formal recognition to general custom. In fact, it is doubtful whether such general custom ever existed. Sir Henry Maine, a great nineteenth century scholar who studied the evolution of legal systems, observed that in all the Indo-European societies he studied be they Roman or Hellenic, Persian or Indian, customary law was kept in the custody of a privileged order who were assumed to know its rules. In England that privileged order was the small number of judges and lawyers who operated the London based court system. The custom was that of the courts not the people. Although accepted patterns of social behaviour must have influenced the judges, in reality it was their decisions which created the so-called custom. It was only a matter of time before their decisions were openly recognised as the root of the law-making process and custom was relegated to a backwater. It came to be regarded as a source of local law only eg that fishermen could dry their nets on local land. In 1275 the Statute of Westminster provided that such local custom must have continuously existed since 1189 to be valid. That would have been difficult to prove in 1275, let alone today. In a broader sense, customs may still influence the law-making process. Trade customs for example, are sometimes incorporated in both legislation and case law. But it is the legislation and case law, not the custom that is the law. In the narrow sense of being law itself, custom has little role to play. Modern courts will rarely encounter valid local customs. They are very much the endangered species of the source world.

173

Judge-made law

The medieval judges of the common law courts were initially somewhat handicapped in their ability to create new law by the writ system under which a plaintiff had to bring his allegation within the wording of the standard writs issued by royal officials. Thus a thirteenth century trespass writ contained the words 'vi et armis' ie force and arms, and that meant forcible trespass had to be alleged. But before long the judges began to develop the law by the use of fictions. Thus by the fourteenth century it was fictionally assumed that a trespass would be forcible and the plaintiff would not have to prove that fact. In time, the 'vi et armis' wording itself was dropped from the relevant writ. This same technique was used on other writs and through this process the judges were able to develop the basic principle of modern tort and contract law. The process took time: the modern law of contract founded on the doctrine of consideration, did not emerge until the early 1600s. At the same time as the common law judges were using fictions to get round the writ system, the Lord Chancellor and the clerks in the Chancery office were developing the principles of equity to provide a fairer system for settling land rights than that allowed by the writ system. Again, by the seventeenth century many of the central concepts of modern land law and in particular, the idea of the trust, had been developed by Chancery. Against this background of slow but steady law-making by the judiciary, statutes played a minor role. They might be needed to clarify particular points eg the date from which customs must have existed, or for blocking tax loopholes devised by clever lawyers (a problem then as now). But they were regarded as a subsidiary source of law to be fitted in to the greater common law and equitable background by judges accustomed to a 'mischief' approach to interpretation. They were islands in an ocean of judge-made law.

Legislation

With the industrial and social revolution of the nineteenth century, this pattern of law-making underwent a radical change. The regulation of trade and transport, factory safety and sanitation all required new legislative frameworks. Legislation swiftly became the major law-making process. In the twentieth century legislative intervention in social and economic matters has continued apace with a proliferation of tribunals to apply the new laws, but legislation has also moved into areas formerly the preserve of judge-made law. Statutes such as the Unfair Contract Terms Act 1977 or the Defective Premises Act 1972 have had a major impact on the law of contract and tort. Landlord and tenant legislation now forms a major part of the land law system. Far from being islands, statutes have come to form vast continents with the judge-made law being trapped in inland seas. It is against this background that the role of the legislature and judiciary in the law-making process needs to be examined. This chapter considers first the nature of legislative law-making, and then in the light of that, the proper role of the judiciary.

Legislative law-making

In this section we will consider law-making by Parliament and by the European Communities. In both cases, we will consider the types of legislation, the technical procedures by which it becomes law and the practical pressures which determine its content.

Parliament: types of legislation

When we think of legislation, we normally think of an Act of Parliament which alters the general law of the land, an Act such as the Theft Act or the Unfair Contract Terms Act. Acts which are intended to alter the general law, are known as Public Acts. The procedure for passing such an Act is complex. It starts with the presentation of the bill ie the draft legislation, to the House of Commons or possibly in the case of less controversial legislation, to the House of Lords. The title of the bill is read out to the House and this constitutes what is known as the first reading. The object of this stage is simply to give notice of the proposed measure. Next comes a full debate on the principles of the legislation followed by a vote on whether the bill should proceed. This is known as the second reading. If the bill has been introduced in the Commons, it will then be referred to a committee of the House for detailed consideration and amendment. The committee reports back to the House of Commons and if necessary, any amendments are debated and voted upon. This is known as the report stage. Finally, the bill is given a third reading at which stage there may be a brief debate and then a vote on whether to accept or reject the bill as a whole. If the bill was introduced in the Commons, it will then pass to the House of Lords where it will be given a similar three readings. If the Lords alter clauses accepted by the Commons, the bill will return to the Commons for further consideration. If the bill started in the Lords, it has to receive three readings in the Lords (there is no committee stage in the Lords, detailed amendments being considered by the whole House at the second reading stage), then move to the Commons for three readings, and then return to the Lords if there is disagreement between the two Houses. At one time the agreement of both Houses was necessary before a bill could receive the Royal Assent and become an Act of Parliament. As a consequence, the House of Lords was in a position to block legislation desired by the Commons. However, Lloyd George's Parliament Act of 1911 provided that the Lords could delay a 'money' bill for only one month, and other legislation for a little longer. The provisions of this Act have rarely had to be used. The most recent example was in relation to the War Crimes Act 1991. The Act dealt with war crimes which had been committed abroad by those who were not British citizens at the time. Prior to the Act, such individuals would not have committed an offence under English law. The Act applied retrospectively to make their conduct criminal. The majority of the House of Lords considered that the retrospectivity of the Act raised such an issue of conscience that they had to oppose both it and the Commons even if that hastened the replacement of the House by an elected second chamber.

There are other types of legislation. A Private Act is one which deals with a local or personal matter. There was a time when divorce was only possible through a Private Act of Parliament legislating for the couple involved. Now Private Acts are mainly used by local authorities or companies to acquire special powers eg to use land as an oil refinery. Private bills are scrutinised to see that notice of the bill has been given to all those affected by its provisions. Once this has been done, they go through the same three reading procedure, usually with little debate. A Private Members' Bill refers to something different. It means a bill introduced into Parliament by an individual MP as opposed to a government minister. It will be intended to alter the general law and will be a Public Act if passed. It must go through the same three reading procedure but faces two further problems; the MP must find an opportunity to introduce the bill eg by winning a ballot with other MPs for the right to introduce legislation, and secondly, the MP must persuade the government to allow enough parliamentary time for the bill to go through its readings. Despite these hurdles, important legislation does result from private members' bills. The Abortion Act 1967 introduced by David Steel, is an example.

A 'consolidation' is an Act which brings together all the existing legislation on a topic into a single statute. Because they do not change the law, such Acts are passed by an accelerated procedure which cuts out any debate. A 'codification' is different. It is an Act which replaces all the existing legislation and case law on a topic with a single set of provisions. The Theft Act 1968 is an example of such a code. It passes through the same procedure as any other Public Act.

In many ways the most important type of legislation is that known as delegated legislation. This describes legislation made by a subordinate body authorised to legislate by an Act of Parliament. The Health and Safety at Work etc Act 1974, for example, authorised a government minister to make new safety laws by issuing regulations. Safety laws have to be complex and may need frequent updating. It would have been impractical to put every complex change in the law through the full three stage

Parliamentary procedure. Hence, Parliament delegated the power to legislate on these matters to a member of the executive. Technically, regulations of this kind are known as statutory instruments. They have to be laid before Parliament so that all MPs can read them, but provided there is no objection they will become law with all the binding force of an empowering Act itself. Given the complexity of modern society, it is not surprising that the output of delegated legislation vastly exceeds that of Acts of Parliament.

PRESSURES PRODUCING LEGISLATION

Two types of pressure need to be considered: that resulting directly from politics and that resulting from independent investigation of one kind or another.

Political pressure
The simplest illustration of political pressure is that of legislation passed to implement a party's election manifesto commitments eg to privatise or re-nationalise. In fact, only 10% of legislation results from this kind of party political commitment. Problems often arise during a party's period of office and these may also lead to pressure to legislate eg the violence of the 1984 miners' strike led to political pressure which resulted in the 1986 Public Order legislation giving the police much greater powers to control demonstrations. Sometimes the response to a problem is led by outside pressure groups. These groups may represent particular sections of the community eg the construction industry persuaded the government to include provisions regulating its use of contracts in the 1995 legislative programme. They may be concerned with a particular interest eg Shelter concerned with housing conditions or the Legal Action Group concerned with the operation of the legal system particularly in the welfare law area. Some of these sectional or interest groups may be highly organised. Others, like the coalition which mounted a successful campaign against the government's Sunday trading reforms in 1986, may be a loose and temporary grouping. As in that instance, the success of such a grouping against the forces of government and commerce, may be short lived. Sometimes the pressure is very much the creation of one person. Mary Whitehouse was almost single-handedly responsible for the Protection of Children Act 1978. She wrote letters to numerous newspapers exhorting readers to stamp out 'kiddie porn', found an MP to sponsor a private members bill, lobbied MPs, spoke of the widespread public concern etc. The legislation emerged although whether there was ever a serious 'kiddie porn' problem is uncertain. A final important source of pressure is the civil service, unseen but powerful. Civil service departments will have their own internal view as to what kind of legislation would enable them to achieve their goals most efficiently. Thus, Home Office civil servants will

develop strategies for controlling the prison population etc (see post, p 330) and the Lord Chancellor's Department is as we have seen, busy reviewing the efficiency of the court system. Much of the content of the criminal and civil justice legislation which seems to be passed almost every year, stems from such civil service pressures.

These illustrations may give the impression that particular kinds of legislation emerge from particular kinds of pressure. This is true in some cases but in others a combination or even conflict of pressures produces the legislation. Take the housing legislation of 1977 which imposed a duty on authorities to house the homeless unless they were intentionally homeless. That resulted from a combination of pressures: the concern of Department of Environment officials to give guidance to local authorities; a campaign by Shelter; the determination of a liberal MP able to exploit the Lib-Lab pact on which the government was then based. All these contributed to the emergence of the legislation. This may suggest that legislation often emerges from a consensus. Emile Durkheim, the famous French sociologist writing at the turn of the century, saw modern society as being increasingly based upon cohesion or 'organic solidarity' as he called it. Consensus based laws would be a reflection of that social cohesion. But others see society rather differently. Marxist theory at its crudest, would see all laws as directly or indirectly benefiting the ruling class. Nineteenth century factory safety legislation is often used to illustrate the point. Outwardly it appears to benefit the working class but Marxists would argue that it was never effectively enforced and was never intended to be. It was there simply to give the workers the impression that their interests were being promoted and to take the steam out of their militancy. However, research has shown that this is far too crude a picture. The promoters of the legislation were genuinely concerned to produce change, to protect workers. There was pressure from large manufacturers for the enforcement of the legislation because safety requirements would put up the costs of their smaller rivals – clearly the ruling class was by no means united! The position is a lot more complex than a crude Marxist theory would suggest and that becomes even more apparent if one examines the background to the passing of the modern 1974 safety legislation. One finds a combination of civil service pressure to update the legislation, sectional group pressure from the TUC campaigning for recognition of union safety committees, and public concern heightened by such tragedies as Aberfan. To this must be added two human factors: Barbara Castle, a fiery employment minister determined to do something and Lord Robens who she appointed to head an investigating committee, a man with great leadership qualities who also had the misfortune to be NCB chairman at the time of Aberfan. The report of his committee was implemented by the 1974 legislation.

Perhaps a pluralist rather than a consensus or Marxist model provides the best explanation of this kind of complexity. A pluralist model would see law-making as being the product of a struggle between a plurality of competing groups with different interests and power bases, with sometimes one and sometimes another group being victorious on a particular issue. Sometimes there may be consensus on a particular issue but society itself is not based on any general consensus other than an acceptance that it is made up of diverse groups each trying to further their own interests. We will return to these broad issues in the next chapter, Understanding Law, but one final point may be made here. There is a danger with all theories of society whether consensus, pluralist or Marxist; it is that they tend to neglect the role of the individual. As a leading modern writer on the sociology of law, Roger Cotterrell has put it, they tend to reduce 'the individual to a mere unit in a system, an actor whose actions are determined by social structures which exist quite independently of him.'

Independent investigation
Independent investigations often results from political pressures as we have seen with the Robens' examination of safety laws. However, although the decision to investigate may result from political pressures, the investigation itself may be conducted in a fairly non-political way with every attempt being made to find a consensus amongst interested groups. Thus Robens' recommendations were accepted by both the TUC and CBI and the major political parties. The Robens Committee was an example of an ad hoc body established to look at a particular problem. Another example is the 1984 test tube baby inquiry headed by Dame Mary Warnock. Her understanding of the ethical issues amply qualified her to lead that inquiry just as Robens' experience at the Coal Board qualified him for the safety inquiry. Where the problem is one on which a wide range of public opinion may need to be considered, the government may entrust the ad hoc investigation not to a committee headed by an expert individual but to a group of experienced non-experts who will be given a Royal Commission to investigate the problem. The Royal Commission not only gives them prestige but also financial and human resources. They will have a team of civil servants working on the investigation. The result is usually a thorough review of the problem in question although the recommendations tend to be in the nature of a compromise. This is not surprising. The membership of the Commission is usually itself a bit of a compromise with the interests and views of its members being balanced eg Northerners and Southerners, left and right, male and female, and preferably no one likely to stand out against a consensus compromise. Ironically, the compromise nature of some Royal Commission reports may result in a lack of political support for their recommendations and a failure to implement them. The report on Accident Compensation under Lord Pearson's chairmanship is perhaps an example of the dangers of compromise. On the other hand the Royal Commission on Criminal Procedure also produced something of a compromise series of recommendations and they have been largely implemented in the Police

and Criminal Evidence Act (PACE) which was discussed in Chapter 4. After the Thatcher decade in which Royal Commissions were regarded as an ineffective means of achieving reform and none were appointed, 1991 saw their rehabilitation with the appointment of the Commission on Criminal Justice under Lord Runciman. The pressure for its appointment came with the release from prison of the Guildford Four, then the Maguire Seven, and finally, the Birmingham Six. All had been convicted in connection with terrorist bombing incidents. All were released following findings by the Court of Appeal that there had been a miscarriage of justice in the convictions, largely stemming from the weaknesses in the police and forensic evidence. The report of the Commission has led to further changes in both law and practice (see ante, p 111).

PERMANENT LAW REFORM BODIES

In addition to ad hoc investigating committees or commissions, the government also receives recommendations from three permanent advisory bodies. Two, the Law Reform Committee (LRC) and the Criminal Law Revision Committee (CLRC), date from the 1950s. The LRC considers problems of civil law referred to it by the Lord Chancellor. The problems are often fairly narrow and call for technical rather than radical solutions. The report on limitation periods which resulted in the Latent Damage Act 1986 (see post, p 404) is a good example of the LRCs work although the outcome, in spite of making technical sense, has given rise to such practical problems that the whole area of law is now under review once again. The CLRC performs a similar role in respect of criminal law and the Theft Acts are its main achievement. The third body is the Law Commission established in 1966 as part of the Wilson government's attempt to modernise the structure of the nation. Its brief was to produce a systematic programme of law reform. Whereas the LRC and CLRC are staffed by part-timers and investigate only issues referred by government, the Law Commission has a full time staff headed by five Commissioners (in practice two academics, two practitioners and a judge who for the crucial early years was Lord Scarman) and furthermore, it can itself decide what problems to investigate (subject only to the Lord Chancellor's veto). It will have its own programme of issues to investigate but it may also respond to pressure eg the report on criminal attempts made in response to academic pressure (see ante, p 171). It works by a process of selective consultation, issuing to interested parties a working paper with tentative proposals on a particular topic and, in the light of the responses, producing a final report often with draft legislation for the government to introduce to Parliament.

The Law Commission has had considerable success producing around 100 major law reform recommendations in its first 25 years, 80% of which have resulted in legislation. Its reports have ranged from the very technical area of contribution actions in contract and tort to the highly charged atmosphere of the law of blasphemy. It has consolidated and clarified family law, radically interfered in contract law with recommendations which led to the control of exclusion clauses, and is currently engaged in an extensive review of issues relating to tortious damages. Its achievements have been great. It is true that some of its recommendations have been messed around by parliament eg the Criminal Attempts Bill, and others have not been accepted by government, but that has usually been for sound political reasons: Take the rule that interest is not payable on a contract debt unless the parties have agreed otherwise. In 1978 the Commission recommended that this rule should be changed and that interest should be paid at a rate to be fixed by legislation. That seemed a fair proposal and it received the enthusiastic support of the Law Lords in the *President of India* case (1984). But it has still not been implemented. This is because a number of powerful groups such as consumer organisations, the CBI, engineering contractors and others, lobbied against the proposal and the government listened. Of course, the Commission also listened to these views but it is more concerned with the fairness than with the politics of law reform. The government is still trapped by the politics and although in 1996 it promised to take action to secure speedy payment of debts, it still fights shy of the obvious means of securing such payment ie automatic interest on over-due payments.

As well as considering particular problems, the Law Commission has also examined the possibility of codifying whole areas of law. The attraction of codification is that it brings together all the law in a particular area and presents it in a organised way. Instead of having to consult several different statutes and cases, all the law can be found in one place. It is accessible to the layman and comprehensible to the lawyer. That is the theory. The reality is somewhat different. In the first place, codification would have to be reconciled with our common law tradition under which judicial decisions are of central importance. The experience with the Sale of Goods code dating from 1893 suggests that judicial interpretation of the code would soon become as important as the code itself and that unless the code was updated to meet changed conditions, the judges would themselves add to the law. Judicial recognition of a third species of contractual term, the innominate term, in addition to the two species defined in the 1893 code, is an example of this process (see post, p 493). A second difficulty arises when codification of a common law area is considered. The Commission attempted a codification of the law of contract but soon found that no agreement could be reached on what rules should replace the common law. As you will see from the section on contract, the case law is often confused, conflicting, inconclusive and constantly changing. Finding a consensus on which to base a detailed code was impossible. One could have drafted a code which relied on telling the judge to do what is reasonable whenever problems arose. In New Zealand much of the common law of contract has been replaced by legislation of this type. If anything it has made the law more unpredictable and has helped neither lawyer nor layman. Even where there is substantial agreement on the nature of the necessary rules, detailed codification requires an immense amount of work and resources. The attempt to codify landlord and tenant law had reached 650 of its projected 880 rules before the draftsman died and the Commission suspended work realising that there was no realistic prospect of either completing it or getting parliament to implement it in legislation.

The Commission has learnt from experience. Work on family law, for example, has proceeded on the basis that it is better to take one topic at a time, investigate, recommend and legislate on that topic with the end aim of gradually covering the whole area and bringing it together in a code. Work on codifying criminal law, started in the mid 1980s, seems set to follow the same path. For the 1990s it has embarked on a topic by topic examination in the common law area starting with the law of damages and considering such issues as structured settlements, exemplary damages, non-pecuniary loss, contributory negligence and joint liability. Professor Stephen Cretney, who as a Law Commissioner was responsible for much of the family law work, has concluded that

> 'the Commission's most useful function has been to deal, sometimes on an ad hoc and pragmatic basis with perhaps limited areas of the law where reform has been shown to be necessary. Its distinctive contribution to the development of the law has in fact been to open up to serious public analysis and discussion the implications of reform, and the formidable difficulties of policy which are often involved.'

The controversy in 1995 concerning its proposals for no-fault 'quickie' divorce (see p 207) and procedures for terminating support for patients in a persistent vegetative state (see p 218), simply demonstrates how formidable these difficulties may be.

The European Communities

The European Communities Act 1972 provides that all rights, obligations etc created by or arising under the EC Treaties are part of UK law. The Articles of the Treaties themselves create some rights and obligations. Thus Article 119 of the EC Treaty which provides that 'men and women shall receive equal pay for equal work', creates rights and duties for individuals within the UK. Thus, in *Macarthys v Smith* (1979) Article 119 was held to give a woman the right to claim from her employer the same wages as were paid to the male predecessor in her job although she had no such right under the domestic equal pay legislation passed in 1970 before the UK joined the Communities. The affect of Article 119 was clear enough in the situation which arose in *Macarthys* and hence it could be directly enforced in the UK, but in other situations that would not be possible. If, for example, the woman was claiming that she did equal work to a higher paid male employee doing a different job for the same employer, Article 119 could not be directly enforced for it contains no definition of 'equal work'. Many of the articles of the Treaty need filling out with more detail before they can be enforced. They are statements of intent requiring much more work before implementation.

To meet this problem the Treaties provide for regulations and directives to be issued. Regulations are directly applicable in all the member states and are thus a means of achieving uniformity of law within the community. If a regulation had been issued defining equal work as being work of equal value as measured by a particular formula, all women whether in France, Germany, the UK etc would have been able to enforce that same provision. However, uniformity may not be possible or desirable given the different national traditions and systems of law. To meet this kind of difficulty, a directive may be issued. This will require each member state to achieve a particular result within a set time limit, but leaves some degree of choice of method and detail to the states. Directives are intended to achieve harmonisation not uniformity. This was the strategy adopted for equal work. A 1975 Directive required states to see that their domestic law treated equal work as extending to work to which an equal value can be attributed. After being taken to the European Court of Justice for failing to implement this Directive within the time limit, the UK finally passed the appropriate legislation in 1984: An independent expert is to assess whether the work is of equal value.

The legal system of the Communities is organised around four institutions, the European Assembly, the Council of Ministers, the Commission and the Court of Justice. The European Assembly is normally referred to as the Parliament and like the House of Commons, it is composed of elected representatives. Like the UK Parliament, it is a forum for debating policies and problems. But unlike the UK Parliament, it has no legislative power. The reason is simple: the governments of the individual states that make up the Community are not prepared to give legislative power to a body over which they have no control. Instead, the major legislative power in the Community lies with the Council of Ministers which is made up of ministers from each of the national governments. Through this body, national governments can assert their own national interests. Although it is the Council which has the power to issue regulations and directives, in most cases it cannot act on its own initiative but must wait for proposals from the Commission. The Commission is the central institution of the Community. Like a Civil Service, it is responsible for the day to day running of the Community but its role in formulating new policies and the regulations and directives to give effect to those policies makes it appear more like a government. It is also responsible for enforcing

Community laws and may bring member states refusing to comply before the European Court of Justice. As we noted in the last chapter, the ECJ also pays an important role in interpreting Community legislation.

Hundreds of regulations and directives are issued each year. Many of the regulations are of a transitory nature eg fixing this month's wheat price, but a considerable number of regulations and many directives are of fundamental importance. They emerge from a process of political bargaining just as intense as that which applies to domestic legislation and more difficult to control because of its multi-national character. The process can best be illustrated by taking an example, the Products Liability Directive which finally emerged in 1985. It had started life ten years earlier as a Commission proposal. The Commission felt that the Treaty goal of fair competition would be furthered if the principles of product liability in all the member countries were roughly similar and that proper protection for consumers required those principles to be based on the strict liability of a producer for damage done by his goods to a consumer. As required by the Treaties, the draft proposal was submitted to the Council of Ministers and the European Parliament for consideration. At this stage pressure groups came into their own. There are around 500 Europe-wide pressure groups and those representing consumers, manufacturers and insurers would have been active in lobbying the Parliament on the products liability draft. At this stage also, national pressures may emerge. In the UK, a House of Lords Select Committee evaluates Community policies and draft proposals, hears evidence from pressure groups and reports. Groups such as the CBI may also put direct pressure on the government and it in turn can exert pressure in the Council of Ministers. After all this consultation, the Commission submitted a revised draft to the Council in 1979 and here it stuck. It stuck because of fundamental differences between the legal traditions of the member countries. The Italians objected to strict liability. The Germans accepted strict liability but wanted a limit to the amount of liability. The French and Belgians wanted strict unlimited liability. The British and Irish wanted some special protection for so-called development risk situations. Each government was subject to its own domestic pressures and it is perhaps not surprising that agreement took six years. The Directive gives governments a good deal of discretion. It allows them to restrict liability both in amount and in respect of development risks. But it does impose minimum levels which must be met by domestic legislation. Finally, it allows a ten year transitional period for implementation. The ball is now back in the court of the member states. They must decide how to implement the directive. The UK did this through the Consumer Protection Act 1987 (see post, p 394). Not all EC legislation will be as controversial as the Products Liability Directive or take as long to emerge. But the impression that EC legislation is forged by technocrats closeted in Brussels is false. The process by which it emerges is open and political.

Judicial law-making

Legislative law-making whether initiated by the government, the Law Commission or the European Commission involves policy problems and political pressures. As we know from the last chapter, judges also make law. They make it when they extend the common law as they did with nervous shock in the case of *McLoughlin v O'Brian*, or when they update a statute through interpretation as they did with the Abortion legislation in the *Royal College of Nursing* case. They are not subject to direct political pressure when they make law but they cannot avoid the policy problems. The most fundamental of these is whether the court ought to make law on a particular issue or whether that job ought to be left to the legislature. In this part of the chapter, we will consider that fundamental question. Three aspects of the question need to be considered: the first is whether there are any constitutional limits on the role of the judiciary which preclude it from making law on a particular issue. The second is whether the nature of the law in question is such that any changes are best left to the legislature. The final aspect is whether the characteristics of the case law process are suited to law-making on the particular question.

Constitutional limits

Judges sometimes appeal to constitutional propriety in support of a conservative view of their function. Thus, when justifying a refusal to extend the duty of care in relation to economic loss (on which see generally, Chapter 19) in a case called the *Aliakmon* (1985), Lord Justice Oliver described the judicial development of new concepts as 'an abandonment by the court of its proper function of interpreting and applying the law and an assumption by it of the mantle of the legislator' and concluded 'that is not a role that this or any other court is empowered to adopt.' Most judges and commentators would probably agree that Oliver's view was too restrictive. An opposing view was put by Lord Scarman in *McLoughlin v O'Brian* (1982): ' The court's function is to adjudicate according to principle ... If principle leads to results which are thought to be socially unacceptable, Parliament can legislate to draw a line or map out a new path.' This described 'the true role of the two law-making institutions in our constitution.' He concluded 'The real risk to the common law is not its movement to cover new situations but lest it should stand still, halted by a conservative judicial approach.' The philosopher Hayek, whose libertarian philosophy underlay much 1980s monetarist thinking, would go much further. He has argued that there should be as little legislation and as much common law as possible. The strength of judicial law-making, he argues, is that it allows the law to evolve in the light of experience. It creates a 'free market' in legal ideas. If the ratio of a case is not seen to work it will be abandoned. If it works, it will be followed. Legislative law-making by contrast, is the work of the social planner, imposing his views on society whether they work or not. That, and not judicial law-making, is what threatens the liberty of the individual.

Whether one accepts Hayek's view depends upon one's political persuasion. Hayek is to the right of the spectrum. What can be accepted, however, is that there is nothing inherently anti-democratic in delegating to wise men, the judges, the job of fixing the starting points for the law provided they respect the overriding power of the legislature elected by the people. The need for respect is particularly important when it comes to the interpretation of statutes. The eight point warning of Lord Simon in *Stock v Jones* (1978) must be heeded (see ante, p 169). When Parliament has legislated, citizens are entitled to regulate their conduct in accordance with the terms of the statute rather than the views of the judges. And it is not only where Parliament has legislated that respect may be necessary. In the *President of India* case (1984), the Law Lords felt that there was a strong case for overruling the nineteenth century decision which had held that no interest was payable on a contract debt. But they were also aware that the Law Commission had recommended the abolition of this rule and that the legislators had deliberately decided not to implement this recommendation (see ante, p 181). In such circumstances, said Lord Brandon giving the leading judgment, to overrule the nineteenth century case 'would be an unjustifiable usurpation of the function which properly belongs to Parliament.' Lord Radcliffe, a distinguished Law Lord of the 1960s, put the point more broadly when he said that there were 'certain areas of public interest which at any one time can be seen to be a matter of its (the legislature's) current concern... In those areas I think that the judge needs to be particularly circumspect, not because the principles adopted by Parliament are more satisfactory or more enlightened, but because it is unacceptable constitutionally that there should be two independent sources of law-making at work at the same time.' Such sensitivity to the role of Parliament rather than a sweeping assertion that the judicial function is interpretive rather than creative, is the right way to approach the constitutional aspect of the problem.

Nature of the law

Other judges have sought to limit judicial law-making by reference to the kind of law involved. Lord Reid, another Law Lord of the 1960s, took the view that lawyers' law ie the basic areas of common law, was best developed by the judges subject to the qualification that a high degree of certainty was necessary in the law of property and contract, and that the criminal law should be left to Parliament although the judges should remain the guardians of mens rea ie the requirement of a mental element in criminal conduct (see post, p 236). Lord Devlin, who with Radcliffe and Reid completes the triumvirate of great Law Lords of the 1960s, took a slightly different position. He argued that a line could be drawn between acceptable activist law-making and unacceptable dynamic law-making. Activist law-making involves the judge in developing the law in line with the consensus view of society whereas dynamic law-making involves creating an idea outside the consensus, taking sides where there is no consensus. To indulge in dynamic law-making would put at risk the judiciary's reputation for independence and impartiality and that reputation was, he felt, an asset not to be plundered.

Lords Reid and Devlin are quite right. The judges are on much safer ground if they make law in areas of lawyers' law or where there is at least consensus. The problem is that judges may have no choice but to make law in other areas. In *Gillick v West Norfolk Health Authority* (1985), the Law Lords had to decide whether Mrs Gillick was right to demand that doctors only supply contraceptives to girls under 16 with their parents' consent. The case raised fundamental issues of policy and morality on which there was no consensus and on which Parliament had given no clear guidance. The Lords had to decide between giving priority to the rights of the parent or the child. By a majority of 3 to 2 they decided that a girl under 16 did not have to have parental consent if she was mature enough to make up her own mind. Controversy followed. Among other questions, it was asked how such a decision came to be made by five elderly men. The answer is simple. Parliament and the government were not prepared to give a lead and hence the matter was left to the courts. As the Tony Bland case (for detailed discussion, see post, p 216) illustrates, even if legislation on such a 'moral' issue is recommended by the Law Commission, the controversy may be such that the government will be unable to see its implementation and the problem will remain with the courts.

The tube fares case, *Bromley London Borough Council v GLC* (1982) is another much publicised example of a controversial decision the judges could not avoid. Legislation had imposed on the labour-run Greater London Council (GLC) a duty to run its transport system in an 'economic' way. The problem lay in the word 'economic'. Bromley, a conservative led borough, argued that it meant 'business like' and that therefore the GLC's policy of cutting fares and subsidising the system through an extra rate demand from London boroughs was illegal. Bromley applied for judicial review to quash the rate demand. The GLC argued that the word meant 'cost effective' in the sense of giving value for money and that their fare cutting strategy did just that. On review, the Divisional Court upheld the GLC view but the Court of Appeal and House of Lords voted for the business interpretation. Inevitably the decision was seen as political, as allied to the government's general attack on the GLC, a body it subsequently abolished. Lord Denning's protestations that as a ratepayer and tube traveller he was on both sides of the dispute, did not convince the critics. But again, these problems were not of the judges' making. They became embroiled in politics because they were asked a question the answer to which would have major political implications. Professor Griffith in his controversial book, *The Politics of the Judiciary*, has argued that 'judges cannot be politically neutral because they are placed in positions where they are required to make political choices' and further, that their political position 'is part of established authority and so is necessarily conservative and illiberal.' Whether justified or not, the fact that such assertions can be made is an indication that the Reid/Devlin view of the limits of judicial law-making, desirable though it might be, is unrealistic.

The characteristics of case law

In practice the characteristics of the case law process impose the most important limitations on judicial law-making. The process is unpredictable, based on limited evidence and is incremental in nature.

UNPREDICTABILITY

It is unpredictable in the sense that the judges depend upon litigants bringing cases and taking them on appeal, for the opportunity to make the law. For example, from the 1960s onwards it was pretty clear that the judges felt that the old rule under which a builder of property owed no duty of care in tort to a person to whom he sold the property, needed to be changed. In *Dutton v Bognor Regis UDC* (1971) Lord Denning stated that the builder did owe such a duty but his statement was only obiter. The opportunity to make the change did not arise until 1978 with the case of *Batty v Metropolitan Property* (1978). In the meantime the Law Commission and legislature had moved and the Defective Premises Act 1972 was introduced to provide a statutory remedy against builders and others (see post, p 446). Subsequently, the House of Lords used the introduction of this statutory remedy to justify its decisions in *D & F Estates Ltd v Church Comrs for England* (1988) and *Murphy v Brentwood District Council* (1990) in which it over-ruled *Dutton* and *Batty* and held that no common law duty of care was owed to the purchaser by the builder. Judicial and legislative law-making on this topic does not present a neat co-ordinated picture and in part this is due to the fact that the courts cannot choose their time.

More important than the fact that appearance of case law before the judges is unpredictable, is the fact that it produces results which are unpredictable for those relying on the law to organise their affairs. This is because changes in case law have a retrospective effect. The point is best explained by an example, the problem of the 'matrimonial car' raised in the case of *Morgans v Launchury* (1973). The car in question was owned and insured by a woman who allowed her husband to use it and he in turn loaned it to a third person who caused an accident. Those injured sued the woman because she had the insurance. The question was whether she was legally responsible, 'vicariously liable' is the term, for the actions of the third person. The existing law said she was not as she had not given permission to the third person. Lord Denning in the Court of Appeal introduced the idea of the matrimonial car under which permission given by one partner would bind the other. Here, the husband's permission would bind the wife and hence, her insurers would have to pay. The House of Lords rejected this view and upheld the existing law. The retrospective effect of changing the law was one of the reasons for their decision. The matrimonial car concept would have applied retrospectively. It would have applied not just to accidents occurring after the *Morgan's* decision but to those occurring before. As there is a three year limitation period for bringing personal injury claims, insurance companies would only really have to worry about post 1969 accidents and earlier ones for which writs had been issued. Nevertheless, they would have fixed insurance premiums for the years in question on the basis that the insured was not responsible for permission given by a matrimonial partner. If the House of Lords changed the law, it would in effect be saying to the insurers ' Through no fault of your own you got the law wrong, fixed your premiums too low and are going to suffer a loss. Sorry, you are suffering for the good of judicial law-making.'

Legislation applies prospectively. If a 1996 Act were to introduce the idea of the matrimonial car, it would apply only to post 1996 accidents and insurers would be able to adjust their premiums to the new risk. Clearly, the retrospective characteristic of case law makes it a less appropriate method of law-making in circumstances where parties may have based commercial arrangements on the previous law. The American Supreme Court has sought to overcome this problem on occasion by changing case law prospectively. It has been suggested by some judges and commentators that the House of Lords should follow this example. Lord Devlin has criticised the suggestion on the ground that 'it turns judges into undisguised legislators' and he went on to comment 'it is facile to think that it is always better to throw off disguises. The need for disguise hampers activity and so restricts the power (to make law).' It is undoubtedly true that the principle of retrospectivity does restrict the judges' law-making power. But that does not make it desirable. It might be argued that judicial law-making power is sufficiently restrained by other considerations such as the limited evidence available to the judge and the incremental nature of case law.

LIMITED EVIDENCE

The second restraining characteristic of the case law process is the limited nature of the evidence that the courts can consider. Again the point is best illustrated by a case. In *Lim v Camden Health Authority* (1979) the courts had to consider the method of calculating damages in the case of severe personal injury (for detailed discussion of the case, see post, p 414). The trial judge applied the normal principles and awarded what was then a record sum of £243,000. In the Court of Appeal, Lord Denning suggested that instead of awarding a single sum as 'once and for all' compensation for the injury, the victim should be given an interim award of £136,000 and should be able to come back to the court for more if it was needed eg if she lived longer than expected. The House of Lords rejected this suggestion and Lord Scarman commented:

> 'It is an attractive, ingenious suggestion, but, in my judgment unsound. It raises issues of social, economic and financial policy not amenable to judicial law reform, which will almost certainly prove to be controversial and can be resolved by the legislature only after full consideration of factors which cannot be brought into clear focus, or be weighed and assessed, in the course of the forensic (ie court room) process. The judge, however wise, creative, and imaginative he may be, is "cabin'd, cribb'd, confin'd, bound in" not, as was Macbeth, to his "saucy doubts and fears" but by the evidence and arguments of the litigants. It is this limitation, inherent in the forensic process, which sets bounds to the scope of judicial law reform.'

The judge is not only limited to the evidence presented by the litigants, but also to arguments which are legal in nature and presented orally – although recent practice has sanctioned the submission of a written skeleton argument to appeal court judges. Arguments dealing with the social or economic implications of a particular judicial change in the law are not generally permitted by the judges and this necessarily restricts their ability to make law on issues where such factors are relevant. In the USA this problem is met by allowing the litigants to submit written arguments containing socio/economic material. Such arguments are known as 'Brandeis briefs' after the name of the counsel who first used them. Lord Simon has suggested that the problem might be met in the UK not by inviting the litigants to put forward such arguments as their view of the socio/economic implications would be necessarily biased; but by inviting the state to send a law officer to put forward such arguments in an objective way. Neither solution seems likely to be adopted. Some would support the restrictive UK rule, arguing like Lord Devlin, that depriving the courts of such information hampers their law-making power and is therefore, desirable. Others would support it, arguing that judges and barristers who are highly experienced in oral argument on legal issues, should stick to what they know best and not claim to assess matters outside their area of expertise. It may perhaps be added that academics whose suggestions can greatly influence the view of practising lawyers and judges (see for example, the influence of Professor Williams in relation to criminal attempts, ante, p 171), have often been similarly blinkered. Until the 1970s, few law academics showed much interest in looking at legal problems in their economic or social context.

INCREMENTAL NATURE

The third and perhaps most important restraining characteristic is that judicial law-making is incremental in nature. Judges can only make law on the facts of the particular case before them. They cannot lay down a comprehensive code to govern all analogous fact situations. Lord Goff, one of the new Law Lords appointed in the mid 1980s, has described judicial law-making in terms of forming a mosaic: 'It is the judges who manufacture the tiny pieces of which the mosaic is formed, influenced very largely by their informed and experienced reactions to the facts of cases.' Unlike the legislature, they are not able to provide the complete mosaic at one go. This characteristic is both the strength and weakness of the case law process. There are some areas of law well suited to this pragmatic, case by case approach. The development of the law of negligence through the concept of the duty of care (see post, p 382) is a good example. There are others. In a 1984 tax case, Lord Scarman observed that what constituted 'unacceptable tax evasion' was ' a subject well suited to development by judicial process' and one 'beyond the power of the blunt instrument of legislation'. Judicial law-making can accommodate fine distinctions, can balance conflicts of interest in a way that legislation is unable to do.

Conversely, the case by case approach is not appropriate where a comprehensive or detailed change in the law is required. By placing the emphasis on principle rather than on the particular facts of a case, a bold judge like Lord Scarman may be able to provide guidance for future cases, but the detail will still be missing. Thus in *Pirelli v Oscar Faber* (1983) where the House of Lords had to consider changing the law on when limitation periods start running (see post, p 403), Lord Scarman commented:

> 'It is tempting to suggest that, in accordance with the practice statement of 1966, the House might consider it right to depart from (their previous decision on the matter). But the reform needed is not the substitution of a new principle or rule of law for an existing one but a detailed set of provisions to replace existing statute law. The true way forward is not by departure from precedent but by amending legislation.'

A similar point arose in the *President of India* case (1984). One reason for refusing to change the 'no interest on contract debts' rule was constitutional, but another was the fact that judicial law-making would not be able to 'incorporate the many detailed qualifications and refinements' necessary to make the change work. Neither is the case by case method of law-making suitable for areas such as the criminal law where both the public and the law enforcers need to know where they stand. The pragmatic, common sense approach of the House of Lords towards criminal attempts, discussed at the end of the last chapter, is a good illustration of this point.

The incremental nature of case law is a major restriction on judicial law-making. One often finds that a whole series of rules and assumptions have been built up on the back of an old case law decision. If the court makes law by overruling that decision, the superstructure it supports will collapse like a house of cards. In some areas of law, the judges may feel able to rebuild the house case by case over a number of years but when dealing with issues like limitation periods or interest payments where certainty is a priority, that approach would be irresponsible in the extreme. This is one of the reasons for the limited use by the House of its freedom under the 1966 practice direction. In the half a dozen or so cases in which it has overruled its own previous decisions, the point of law has been fairly narrow and the effect of overruling has been to replace one rule with another rather than to demolish a whole structure which will then take time to rebuild. Of course, this point applies equally to the overruling of a Court of Appeal decision if it supports a whole superstructure of law which would require time to rebuild in a different form.

Postscript: reform of medical accident compensation

This chapter has considered the various law-making processes and their limitations. Perhaps the best way to pull the different strands together is by taking one particular reform problem and considering how the different processes might apply to it. The problem is that of compensation for medical accidents. At present some 35,000 persons per year suffer injury as a result of a medical accident. The accidents are diverse, ranging from incidents which affect many such as that concerning the drug Opren which we discussed in an earlier postscript, to the individualised tragedy of the childbirth that goes wrong. There is a common factor. The victim can only obtain compensation if it can be shown that negligence caused the injury. As we noted in Chapter 3, proving this sufficiently to persuade the doctor or hospital or those insuring them against liability to settle or a court to award damages, is a very expensive and time-consuming business. The vast majority of victims fail to obtain compensation. Victims and medics alike agree that the present system for obtaining compensation needs changing. But what are the most appropriate means of producing change?

The government could take a political decision to back legislation reforming the law such as Rosie Barnes' 1990 private member's bill which would have provided low level compensation for all medical victims. But it did not and no government is likely to. Such a scheme would cost money and win few political points. Victims of medical accidents would be grateful but victims of other forms of accidents would complain. Appointing a Royal Commission would avoid the immediate financial and political difficulties but there is a risk that it would produce a useless compromise as did the broader Accident Compensation Commission in the late 1970s or, much more embarrassingly, recommend a scheme that the government could not support. Asking the Law Commission to undertake a narrower, technical investigation of the problem is a much safer bet and, indeed, the Lord Chancellor has asked the Commission to consider whether the litigation process in medical negligence cases could be improved. But whatever the procedural improvements, the need to prove negligence and causation would remain. It would be improvement not reform.

What about judicial reform? After all, the law of tort which is what governs compensation for negligence, is lawyers' law. There could be little constitutional objection to the judges developing the law in a way more favourable to the victims. Certainly, this is what has said to have happened in the United states. For a time it did appear as if this would happen. The courts began to hold that rather than proving that medical negligence actually caused the damage to the victim, it was enough to show that it had increased the risk of the damage occurring. Similarly, it was held that it was sufficient to show that the victim might have had a chance of recovering if treated properly rather than having to show a probability of recovery. It was even suggested that in some circumstances negligence as well as causation could be inferred. All these developments favoured the victim, making it easier to claim compensation. But in the late 1980s in the cases of *Hotson v East Berkshire Area Health Authority* and *Wilsher v Essex AHA* the House of Lords rejected this pro-victim approach. The details are discussed in Chapter 15. Here the problem is addressed from the law reform perspective.

In the past the House of Lords has expressed the fear that a pro-victim approach might lead doctors to adopt 'defensive medicine' as is alleged to have happened in the United States. Clearly, this kind of argument is one that it would be difficult to support with the limited evidence available to the British courts and it did not feature in *Hotson* or *Wilsher*. What did concern the judges was the uncertainty which would result from changing the rules of causation. Lord Bridge put it this way in *Wilsher*: 'We should do society nothing but disservice if we made the forensic (ie court room) process still more unpredictable and hazardous by distorting the law to accommodate the exigencies of what may seem hard cases.' The uncertainty would not be limited to medical cases either. The principles of negligence law are universal. The new approach to causation would have applied to all injury victims and those suffering other types of loss eg damage to their property. Common law principles are universal in effect and this makes it very difficult for judicial law reform to achieve particular social goals such as assisting the victims of medical accidents.

One possible source of change is the European Community. As we noted (p 184), it was a Directive from the Commission which required the UK legislature to pass the Consumer Protection Act 1987 providing for strict liability for injuries caused by defective products. In 1990 the Commission issued a draft directive providing for strict liability for injuries caused by services and this would include medical services. But the proposal has now been dropped following lobbying. As President Clinton has discovered, it is much easier to propose health care reform than to carry it through.

One final thought: changing the law is not necessarily the best way of protecting the interests of those using medical services. Improving those services through better organisation or financial support might be an answer. Better health education might lead to less reliance on medical services. Better legal education might lead to a greater willingness to assert rights to compensation. Another approach would be for the users to help themselves by taking out insurance against medical accidents, a point to which we return at the end of Chapter 16.

Chapter 8
Understanding law

In this part of the book we have examined the rules and institutions which govern the operation of our legal system. In the following parts we will be concerned with the substance of the law which is applied by this system. Three areas of law are covered, criminal law, torts or civil wrongs, and contract law, but your syllabus may require study of only one or two of these areas. The aim of this chapter is to provide a bridge between the study of the system and the substance. It considers three key questions. First, *what* does law do, what does it contribute to society? Under this head we will consider its role in resolving disputes, its role in regulating society and the way in which it enables society to set and realise goals. Second, *why* do individuals accept law? Is it because of the power of the law enforcers or is it more to do with our rational acceptance of the law or respect for its moral authority? Third, *how* should you evaluate law? On what basis can one criticise law? What criteria of good or bad should be used? In answering these questions, we will reflect on the nature of the legal system but also anticipate some issues relating to the substantive law. In a single chapter, it is only possible to sketch the possible answers to these questions. Students wishing to go further are advised to read *Understanding Law* by Professors Adams and Brownsword, published by Fontana.

What does law do?

It is easy to think of the function of law as being simply to sentence those who commit crimes in the hope of deterring further criminal conduct, and to provide a remedy to the victims of civil wrongs in the hope of undoing the wrong. The analysis of the mid-twentieth century American scholar, Karl Llewellyn, makes us take a broader perspective. He studied the way in which the society of the Cheyenne Indians worked and from that, concluded that there were four 'law-jobs' that had to be performed in any society. The first was the obvious one of dispute resolution. He likened this to the 'garage-repair work' necessary to deal with car breakdowns. The second was the regulation of the society with the aim of preventing disputes arising. This too is a vital job. Without it the courts would be overloaded with too much repair work. The law performs this second job by providing a regulatory and conceptual framework within which relationships can be structured. The third was the allocation of authority, necessary to ensure that someone is recognised as being in the position to resolve disputes or make regulatory rules. The fourth and final function was that of enabling society to set goals and directions for its development. We will follow this fourfold analysis of law's function and add one more.

Dispute resolution

We have examined at length the forms of process ranging from formal litigation to informal conciliation, provided by the law for the resolution of civil disputes. The fact that it is the state that normally prosecutes someone for a crime, tends to disguise the fact that criminal process is also concerned with dispute resolution. In Anglo-Saxon times, 'crimes' were essentially a private matter with the law providing that the 'criminal' should pay the victim or his family a tariff figure for each wrong, for example, three shillings compensation for a punch on the nose with extra if the victim was a priest. The purpose of the scheme was to prevent disputes between families growing into mafia-style blood feuds by providing reparation. The state or rather, the king, had little interest in such a criminal process. Today, the state has assumed responsibility for maintaining order and for prosecuting criminals. The aim is to provide retribution against the criminal rather than reparation for the victim (see p 318). But an underlying objective, perhaps clearest in rape prosecutions, remains the resolution of any dispute as to the facts between accused and victim. However, in this section our primary concern will be with the ways in which the law provides for the resolution of civil disputes.

Many disputes will simply turn upon the facts. The parties will agree on the rules that are to be applied but dispute the facts eg the goods were or were not defective or the car driver was or was not careless. Ultimately a court can resolve that dispute by deciding which view of the facts is to be accepted. The losing party will not like the decision but if he accepts the authority of the legal system, he will have to accept that the dispute has been resolved. However, in more difficult cases the parties may disagree about the rules. Their disagreement is likely to arise because they have conflicting interests: The manufacturer does not want a rule providing for unlimited product liability but the consumer does. The tenant may want a rule giving him security in his home but his landlord may not. The landowner may want a rules controlling industrial pollution but the manufacturer may not. In many cases the line between the conflicting interests has been drawn by the legislature in accordance with what it sees as the interests of the community. Thus we have legislation which defines the extent of a manufacturer's responsibility for products and defines a landlord's responsibility to his tenant. As we have seen in the last chapter, this kind of legislation is often influenced by the views of pressure groups representing the conflicting interests and will usually embody a compromise of some sort. Sometimes the legislation may leave the precise line between the conflicting interests to be drawn by the courts. Thus the Unfair Contract Terms Act 1977 fixes the ground rules of the balance by providing that an exclusion clause in a contract is ineffective if it is unreasonable, but leaves it to the courts to decide what is unreasonable on the facts of the particular case (see p 538). In other areas, the legislature may not intervene at all. Thus, the question when pollution of land is so unreasonable that the landowner may obtain an injunction to prevent it, is left entirely to the common law of nuisance and the judgment of the courts.

BALANCING INTERESTS

In resolving disputes about the rules or their application, courts are inevitably engaged in balancing the interests of the parties. This balancing exercise is often hidden by a fog of precedent but it is sensible to recognise that it may lie at the heart of the court's decision. In the early part of this century the American legal academic, Roscoe Pound, produced a detailed analysis of the types of interest that came before the American courts and the way in which conflicts between them were balanced and resolved. He divided interests into categories. His two main categories were those of individual interests such as the interest in owning property, making contracts and having personal privacy, and social interests such as protecting the security of the state and its institutions, conserving resources and promoting public morality. He argued that an interest could only be properly balanced against another interest in the same category; a social interest could be weighed against another social interest but not against an individual interest. The point can be illustrated by a leading tort case, *Miller v Jackson* (1977) (see further p 424). Mr Miller owned a house bordering the village cricket club ground and after a season in which several balls had been hit into his garden, he brought an action against a club representative for an injunction to stop the playing of cricket. He argued that the playing of cricket constituted a nuisance ie an unreasonable interference with his enjoyment of his land. Lord Denning approached the problem in terms of a conflict of interest: 'There is a conflict here between the interest of the public at large; and the interest of a private individual. The public interest lies in protecting the environment by preserving our playing fields ... The private interest lies in securing the privacy of his home.' Having posed the problem in this way, it is not surprising to discover that Lord Denning refused to grant the injunction. Denning's public interest (Pound would have called it a social interest) was almost bound to outweigh the private interest. If both interests had been presented at the Individual level eg Mr Miller's interest in privacy against Mr Jackson's personal interest in playing cricket; or both had been presented at the social level eg protecting general domestic privacy against protecting the environment, then the court could have engaged in a genuine balancing exercise.

That is Pound's point and it is a good one. When it came to deciding how to carry out the balancing exercise, Pound's analysis was less helpful. He argued that courts do it by reference to the 'Jural Postulates' that is the fundamental values of the legal system such as the protection of property, the protection of the person, the value of keeping promises, of taking reasonable care etc. These are rather vague and Pound did not suggest any magic formula to deal with the case where there was a conflict of values as well as interests eg where personal and property values conflicted. It is easy to criticise him on this score. His view of society seemed to assume that it was founded on a general consensus within which court could work out which value and interest should prevail. He believed that by analysing interests and values, courts could act as 'social engineers' achieving a balance between interests which would allow society to run in a friction-less, efficient way. This may seem a little naive but it has to be remembered that Pound was writing at a time when courts were reluctant even to admit that there was a problem of balancing interests, let alone that of irre-concilable conflict. The fact that we now think of balancing interests as being an obvious and central function of the law owes a lot to Pound.

We have noted the balancing exercise in the nuisance case of *Miller v Jackson*. Nuisance claims inevitably involve the court in such an exercise for liability only arises when one land owner unreasonably interferes with another's use of his land. One cannot sue for nuisance simply on the basis that the factory on the neighbouring land causes some pollution or some noise. The pollution or noise must be unreasonable. In deciding what is unreasonable, the court will look at a number of factors, the gravity and duration of the interference, the importance of the interfering activity, its social acceptability etc, but essentially the exercise is one of balancing competing claims to land use. In other areas of tort law the balancing exercise may not be so obvious but it is nevertheless at the heart of the courts' function. In deciding whether a defendant owes a plaintiff a duty of care which can give rise to liability for negligence (see post, p 382), a court has to balance the interest of the plaintiff in being compensated for foreseeable and avoidable damage against those of the defendant who may face the prospect of very wide and possibly uninsurable liability if there is no policy limit to the scope of his liability. For example, unless there was some limit to the scope of his duty, an auditor might be liable to thousands of people who invested in a firm in reliance upon his widely publicised audit report.

The courts' approach to balancing interests often seems rather crude. In an audit case, the judges might refer to the interests of the particular type of plaintiff or the more general social interest in the reliability of published information; or on the other hand, to the particular liability problems of auditors or to the more general fear that the 'floodgates' holding back masses of negligence claims might be released were a duty to be imposed. But such references rarely form part of a structured balancing exercise of the kind Pound was advocating. Some American academics and judges now argue that the best way to go about a balancing exercise is by reference to economic theory. This 'economic approach to law' as it is called, suggests that economic criteria can be used to determine the most appropriate liability rules. The extent of an auditor's liability for a negligent report can be used as a simple illustration of these economic techniques. Two economic arguments can be used. First, the argument that liability should be placed on the person who at the least cost, could have avoided the loss producing activity eg in the audit case, relying upon an unreliable audit report. Would it have been cheaper for the auditor to check out his figures or for the investor to make a direct check of his own? The second argument is based on the economics of production. The auditor sells his audit information to his client ie the firm being audited. He can take account of the risk of liability to the client when fixing the price of his services. If he is held liable to investors who have read his information in the financial press but have not paid him for it, how will he react? If he is not able to take account of this liability risk because he cannot charge the investors, will he seek to reduce the amount of information he provides? Will a wide liability rule result in the under-production of valuable audit information? These are the kinds of question that might be asked by someone following an economic approach to law. Whether questions such as these can produce clear answers is doubtful. Much effort has been put into applying the approach to the law of nuisance but it does not seem to have produced agreement on the most appropriate liability rules. Whether the approach itself is appropriate raises even more questions. Many would argue that the primary concern of the law must be with justice rather than economic efficiency. If justice demands that the investor should recover from a negligent auditor that should be the prevailing consideration. However, one can at least say that the economic approach has provided an interesting tool for analysing the balance achieved by liability rules.

Regulatory framework

Llewellyn saw that a second vital role of law was that of channelling people's conduct towards one another so that common goals can be achieved without disputes arising. The law performs this second job by providing an institutional and conceptual framework within which relationships can be structured and regulated. Thus for example, the law of wills enables individuals to organise the distribution of their property after death and the law of marriage enables them to organise their family relationships around a particular framework. In this way the law provides individuals with facilities for realising their wishes and this type of law is sometimes described as being 'facilitative'. The rights and duties created by the will or marriage can, in the last resort, be enforced by a court of law. But the primary function of the law is facilitative rather than coercive.

Contracts are a good example of Llewellyn's point. One function of contract law is to provide a remedy when the contract is broken. The victim may take the guilty party to court and thereby recover damages. Without this ultimate sanction individuals would be reluctant to rely on promises made by others. But going to court is usually the last thing businessmen intend when they enter in to a contract. They use the contract to plan their relationship so that they will not need to go to court. For example, they may try to reduce the chance of disputes about defects by agreeing terms that provide for performance tests eg AA tests on used cars or operating tests on new power stations. They may also plan exactly what is to happen if a problem does arise by say, a term that late delivery of goods may be catered for by a system of graduated payments eg so much per day of delay. Research has shown that businessmen rarely think of enforcing such clauses through the courts. Rather, they view their purpose as being to impose a structure and discipline on their relationships. Indeed, on some matters eg what is to happen on cancellation of the contract they may not plan at all, being content to let the general rules of contract law govern the situation. Again, in a simple consumer transaction, rather than negotiate special terms for defects etc, the parties will rely on the general rules of contract as codified in the sale of goods legislation. So, both the terms of the contract and contract law itself enable the parties to organise and channel their relationships.

Much of the modern regulatory framework is provided by legislation. For example, the Companies Act 1980 and the Financial Services Act 1986 regulate important areas of commercial activity, whilst the Children Act 1989 provides the framework for the protection of children. But whether the legal framework is provided by such legislation or by the common law in areas such as contract, it is expressed in terms of legal concepts. These are the organising ideas of the legal world, generating rules which specify both the means of acquiring the particular conceptual status and the consequences of having obtained it. We will examine two of the most important organisational concepts, that of a right and that of legal personality.

THE CONCEPT OF A RIGHT

Legal relationships are frequently expressed in terms of rights and duties. The parties to a contract owe each other a duty to perform what they have promised and have a right to the performance of promises by the other. If A has promised to pay B £10 in return for B's promise to give him a book, then A has a duty to pay £10 and B has a right to £10, and conversely, B has a duty to give the book and A has a right to the book. Yet another

American academic, Wesley Hohfeld, has provided the leading analysis of rights and duties. He described the relationship of rights and duties as being 'correlative' ie each duty owed by one person correlates with a right possessed by another person. Hohfeld also pointed out that the term 'right' is often used where there is no correlative duty but some other kind of correlating concept and he provided a scheme for understanding these correlatives. A brief analysis of this scheme is a useful way of illustrating the complexity of the relationship that the law can provide for parties.

Hohfeld's scheme started with the simple pair of correlatives, right and duty. They fit our example of the book. B owes a duty to give A the book and A has a right to claim the book. This kind of right could be described as a claim/right.

The second use of the concept of a right is in the sense of a liberty eg when we say a person has a right to work, we do not normally mean he has a claim/right with someone being under a duty to give him a job, but that he has a liberty/right with others, such as unions, having no claim/right to stop him. No claim is the correlative of a liberty/right. It may not always be true that an individual has a liberty/right to work. If a solicitor's contract with his firm includes a term that on leaving employment with the firm he will not go to work for another firm in the same area, then if that term is valid (see p 546), he will not have a liberty/right to work in that area and if he breaks the term his firm will have a claim against him. His liberty/right to work is qualified by the extent of his ex-employer's claim/right.

The third category of right is a power. If someone offers to sell you goods, you have a power/right to accept that offer thereby creating a contract between you. The other person is liable to have his legal relationship with you changed if you exercise the power. Liability is the correlative of power. In the ordinary case, the offeror is free to withdraw his offer at any time before it is accepted (see p 466). Withdrawing the offer will remove the offeree's power and the offeror's own liability. If, however, he contracted with the offeree that he would not withdraw the offer for a certain period of time, then he is under a duty not to withdraw. If he does withdraw the offer then, although the offeree will no longer have a power, he will have a claim/right against the offeror for breach of the duty. Think it through. In this example, the power-liability relationship may be replaced by a claim-duty relationship. The whole relationship is what contract lawyers call an 'option'.

Hohfeld's fourth and final type of right is an immunity. For example, in *R v Cambridge Health Authority, ex p B* (1995) it was held that a hospital which refused to give bone-marrow treatment to a ten year old girl suffering from leukaemia because it had less than a 5% chance of saving her life and would cost £75,000, was immune from legal action. The girl was unable to use the law to force the hospital to provide the treatment. In Hohfeldian terminology, she was under a disability in relation to the hospital. Disability is the correlative of immunity. But the hospital is not totally immune. It is under a duty to properly consider her case for treatment. For example, if it refused the treatment simply because she was female and its priority was to treat males, then she would have a right to a court order requiring the hospital to reconsider the matter. So the scope of the immunity is limited by a duty-right relationship.

Hohfeldian analysis enables one to slice up relationships into their component parts. The structure of relatively complex concepts such as an option, can be seen with clarity. It is a useful analytical technique but it is no more than that. It does not tell a court whether it should hold hospitals to be immune in respect of refusal to treat on resource grounds, but only what this will mean in terms of the structure of the relationship. As an analytical technique its use is limited. It does not fit all situations. For example, we talk of a person owing a duty not to break the criminal law but where is the correlative claim/right? We could say that the state has a claim/right but that seems a rather artificial and unhelpful analysis. Or again, consider Lord Scarman's opinion in *Gillick v West Norfolk Health Authority* (1985), the case about whether doctors could supply contraceptives to girls under 16 without their parent's consent (see p 187). Lord Scarman started from the proposition that 'parental rights are derived from parental duties and exist only so long as they are needed for the protection of the child'. Is the parent's right matched by a correlative duty or liability on the part of the child or possibly, the doctor? Who has the claim/right which should correlate to the parent's duty to protect the child? The answers are not obvious and Hohfeldian analysis is not helpful.

Lord Scarman used his proposition to argue that, as parental rights were derived from the duty to protect the child, it followed that once a child was properly capable of making up her own mind about contraception there was no need for parental protection and consequently, no parental right to be consulted by the girl's doctor. In this argument, the supposed purpose of the rights and duties was used to justify a conclusion. Indeed, judges commonly use assertions about rights to justify a conclusion that a particular remedy should or should not be available. Ubi ius ibi remedium, meaning roughly 'where there is a right, the law should give a remedy' has been a popular slogan with creative judges like Lord Denning. Cynics might say that it is only used where the judge can find no better case law or statutory authority to support his view about the proper remedy. But the slogan does illustrate that lawyers use concepts such as rights in a dynamic way, to justify new rules as well as to analyse existing rules.

The point is important. The legal system, its rules and concepts do not just provide static structures within which social and economic structures can be organised. They also provide responsive structures which can change to meet the needs of society. Both qualities can be seen when we examine the concept of legal personality.

LEGAL PERSONALITY

Viewed from a Hohfeldian perspective a legal personality is an entity to which rights and duties can attach. The concept includes both human persons and artificial persons such as corporations. But that tells us very little about what precise rights and duties should attach, about the extent of the legal personality. Return to the problem in *Gillick*. Clearly, a girl under 16 has a legal personality to some extent. In some circumstances she can enter into contracts creating rights and duties. She can sue and be sued for negligence although she cannot settle an action without an adult acting for her. But one thing she has no legal power to do is to give consent to sexual intercourse with a man. The man will always be committing a criminal offence however much consent there was from the girl. In *Gillick*, the dissenting Law Lords argued from this, that the girl could not give consent to being supplied with contraceptives either. Only her parents could give that consent. It seems a plausible argument. If the girl does not have the legal personality to consent to intercourse, she should not have it to consent to contraception. The majority Law Lords refused to draw the analogy. They relied instead on social factors. As Lord Fraser put it: 'Social customs change and the law ought to, and does in fact, have regard to such changes when they are of major importance.' Lord Scarman identified three changes: contraception was now a subject for medical advice; young people were more independent; and the status of women had changed. With these factors in mind both he and the other majority Law Lords took a purposive view of parental rights and came to the conclusion that a girl under 16 had the capacity to consent to contraception provided she had sufficient understanding of what was involved.

Gillick shows that social policy may be just as important as arguments based on analogy or logic when determining the extent of legal personality. The importance of policy is also evident when we consider the controversial question whether an unborn child has any legal personality. The question surfaced in the litigation surrounding the Thalidomide tragedy for one of the issues was whether the manufacturers could be said to owe a duty of care to a foetus. The litigation was settled and it was left to legislation to give the answer to the question by providing that if the negligence affected the parents ability to have a healthy child, then the disabled child could sue after birth. The child's rights are derived from the parent rather than any legal personality possessed before birth. The general question arose again in *Paton v British Pregnancy Advisory Service* (1979) when the judge in dismissing a husband's application to stop his wife having an abortion, said: 'a foetus cannot in English law have any right of its own at least until it is born.' A pregnant woman's drug addiction raised the problem yet again in *Berkshire County Council v D-P* (1986). The child was born with severe withdrawal symptoms. The legislation allowed a child to be taken into care if its health was being avoidably impaired. A child was defined as 'a person under the age of 14'. The court concluded that an unborn child could not fall within that definition and impairment to an unborn child could not of itself justify a care order although impairment after birth resulting from the mother's conduct prior to birth could justify the order. The trend seems to be against recognising the unborn child as having any personality. But consider this problem: suppose a pregnant woman is in labour and the unborn child is found to be in a transverse lie such that both it and the mother will die unless she has a Caesarian operation. Suppose she refuses consent because she is a 'born-again Christian' who believes that God will intervene. Can a court override her wishes and authorise the surgeons to operate? This was the question in *Re S* (1992). The judge decided that the interests of the unborn child prevailed and authorised the operation. Was he right? The critics say that he paid insufficient respect to the personality of the mother.

CORPORATE PERSONALITY

In the changing approach to the legal personality of women and children we see the law responding to social pressures. In the development of the concept of corporate personality we can see it responding to economic pressures. In 1612 a judge declared that corporations 'cannot commit treason, nor be outlawed, nor excommunicated, for they have no souls.' However, by the twentieth century they seem to have acquired all the other attributes of human personality. Lord Denning has described a corporation as having a 'brain and nerve centre which controls what it does' and he went on: 'some of the people in a company are mere servants who are nothing more than hands to do the work. Others are directors and managers who represent the directing mind and will of the company and control what it does. The state of mind of these managers is the state of mind of the company and is treated by law as such.' By using the fiction that a corporation has a mind, courts have been able to convict them of offences which require mens rea ie guilty intent (see p 236). But the main significance of corporate personality lies in the fact that it enables the law to separate the company from those who operate or own it. *Salomon v Salomon* (1897) is the classic illustration of this point. Mr Salomon sold his business at a grossly inflated purchase price to Salomon & Co in which he and his family were the only shareholders. The company went bankrupt still owing the purchase money to Salomon and large debts to other creditors. It couldn't pay both Salomon and the creditors. The creditors argued that Salomon was disqualified from claiming because he was the company and the sale was a sham. Not so, said the House of Lords; the company was a separate person and Salomon was entitled to be paid.

The reason that the company's separate personality is so important is that it can provide investors with a limit to their liability on behalf of the company. If an investor decides to buy part of a firm which has not been formed as a company, he will become a partner in the firm with the other owners. In law, the partners are the firm. The firm has no separate legal personality. If the firm loses say £10,000 on a particular contract, that loss must be met by all the partners however much they invested in the firm. An investment of £100 may result in liability for debts of ten times that amount. However, if the firm was formed as a company, the investors will own not the company itself but shares in the company; and where the firm was incorporated with limited liability, the investor's liability to contribute to the company's debts is limited to the amount of their shareholding. If the investor's shareholding consisted of one hundred £1.00 shares in the company, then his liability to meet the company's debts would be limited to £100, however much the debts. The company might go bankrupt but the shareholder would not. Furthermore if the company turns out to be highly profitable then it can pay out those profits to the shareholder in dividends. Thus if a company's annual profits were double the money invested in it, it could pay out a £2.00 dividend for each £1.00 share. The prospect of further high dividends would also raise the market price of the shares so that the value of the shareholder's investment would also increase. This simplified explanation of the system shows how the concept of the separate corporate personality enables the law to provide an incentive to investment. Without this structure, with its safeguards and benefits for shareholders, few would invest in anything but the safest of enterprises and the pace of economic development would slow to a crawl.

The twentieth century has brought further changes in the character of corporations. In the nineteenth century, investors played a crucial role in the management of companies. The annual shareholders meeting enabled them to control the management and change directors if they were dissatisfied. But now many corporations, swelled by take-overs and operating through subsidiary companies, are too large and complex for shareholders to control. The nature of shareholding has also changed. The majority of shares in large companies are usually owned not by individuals but by institutions such as pension funds who are primarily concerned with the investment value of their shareholding rather than the management of the company. With the collapse of shareholder power over company management, many companies now seem to function as bureaucratic organisations, able to move their money and influence around the world at the touch of a computer button. The problem is to find some means of effective control over this power. Much company and financial legislation is now concerned with the regulation of corporate power. Soulless, corporations may be; but their religion, the philosophy of the free market, is potent. Controlling and channelling this force is a challenge for any society and its legal system.

Allocation of authority and setting goals

As we have seen, many of the rules of the legal system are concerned with identifying the courts and judges with authority to resolve particular kinds of disputes and the process by which courts and legislatures are entitled to make law. As we noted in Chapter 1 (p 4), Professor Hart argued that rules concerning what is recognised as a law, who is authorised to adjudicate and who is authorised to change laws, are the distinguishing characteristic of a legal system as opposed to a customary system. The legal system must provide such rules otherwise the society will remain at a rather primitive level. In particular, it must identify who has the authority to set the goals of the society. In our constitutional structure, it is essentially the executive which has this authority. Parliament has limited control over an executive cabinet commanding a substantial parliamentary majority. Whist in political terms it may be unhealthy for a small body of ministers to wield so much power, in practical terms it does ensure that goals can be set and efforts focused on their achievement. Constitutional systems which are based on proportional representation and produce coalition governments lacking control over their legislatures, are arguably more democratic but less effective in fulfilling Llewellyn's fourth law job.

Maintaining social values

There is a final more controversial function of law not mentioned by Llewellyn and that is its role in supporting the moral values of a society and the institutions such as the family, around which those values are centred. Obviously the law provides a framework within which social institutions like the family can function. Rules on marriage and divorce, on parental rights etc all shape family relationships. But from time to time it is suggested that it is part of the essential function of law to go further and support the moral ideas that surround institutions like marriage and the family. Thus, it is argued that homosexuality and prostitution should be punished by the law because such practices weaken the web of morality protecting marriage and the family. When, some forty years ago, the Wolfenden Committee (1957) recommended that homosexuality and prostitution should be legalised there was an outcry. In a forceful and eloquent article, Lord Devlin argued that unless the law supported the 'seamless web' of morality surrounding marriage, there was a great danger that society itself would disintegrate. In other words, the system for maintaining values required legal support and without it, the system and society would cease to operate efficiently.

Lord Devlin's views were opposed in equally eloquent terms by Professor Hart. He argued that enforcing moral values is first, unnecessary as moral fragmentation will not cause society to disintegrate; second, undesirable as it will freeze morality at a time when our society is becoming increasingly multi-cultural; and third, and above all, morally unacceptable for it will infringe the liberty of the individual. Hart followed the thinking of the great nineteenth century philosopher, John Stuart Mill, who in his essay *On Liberty* argued that a person should be free to do as he wished unless his conduct harmed others. Thus Hart would say that bigamy should remain a crime because the bigamist harms others by his deception, desertion etc. Supporters of Lord Devlin responded by arguing that individual liberty can only flourish in a stable society and that disintegration of our society may be upon us before we know it. As one writer put it: 'People on the edge of a landslide may truly say that at that precise moment collapse has not occurred'.

Although forty years have elapsed since the legalisation of homosexuality, there is not a great deal of evidence that moral standards or the institution of marriage have been undermined. Attitudes to marriage may have changed, but that would seem to be more a result of women's greater financial and biological freedom than of any failure by the law to support morality. This does not mean that supporting values is not an important function of the law but just that our value system is a lot stronger than Lord Devlin might have supposed and is supported by several 'socialising' processes of which law is only one and education and the family are more important. But despite this lesson, it is still the case that any proposal perceived to weaken the legal support for the institution of marriage is likely to meet with resistance. Thus, in 1995, the Daily Mail led a successful campaign to persuade the government to drop proposals to provide unmarried women with the same protection against violence from partners as that available to married women. The argument was that by treating 'live-in lovers' in the same way as married couples, the law would be subverting family values. Similar pressure led to a government defeat in 1996 on a proposal emanating from the Law Commission, to allow 'quickie' divorce after a year's separation. On a free vote MPs, influenced by the media campaign, voted for an eighteen month period.

Why is law accepted?

One answer is that the legal system mirrors the division of power in a society and is accepted because it is supported and enforced by those having the power. A Marxist would take that line. An alternative explanation is that law is accepted as authoritative because it provides a rational rule system. This approach is associated with the analysis of the sociologist, Max Weber. A third view is that the authority of the law must rest on its moral force, that law and morality cannot be separated in practice. This is the view held by natural law theorists. In this section we will examine these three approaches.

Marxism and law as power

Marx constructed a theory to explain the way in which the social system for producing goods and wealth had developed. He charted the progress from a slave economy to a feudal economy, from that to a capitalist economy, and from a capitalist economy he predicted that society would progress to a socialist economy. The slave, feudal and capitalist economies were each so flawed that they were bound to collapse. The flaw in the capitalist economy was the fact that it was based on a society divided into two main classes, the capitalists who owned the means of production eg the factories, and the workers. The capitalist exploited his workers by giving them just enough to live off, whilst keeping all the surplus value of their output for himself. Ultimately, the workers were bound to react against this exploitation, seize power and change this system to one of socialist production. However, for the short term the capitalist was able to maintain the exploitive relationship partly by controlling the state and the means of repression ie the army, police etc, but partly also, by establishing a dominant ideology, that of capitalism. An ideology is a framework of ideas and values which an observer uses to interpret what he sees. It is like the coloured lenses of glasses, tinting what is observed. A number of ideas like individualism ie interpreting everything in terms of individual rights and responsibilities, go to make up what Marx saw as the ideology of capitalism. He argued that so long as that ideology was dominant, it would be difficult for the working class to become sufficiently aware of their exploited position to rise up and seize power. To Marx, it was essential to promote a rival ideology to raise the working class. Hence the importance to the Marxist of ideology and propaganda.

What are the implications of this theory for the role of law? To some extent Marxists have seen the law as being directly influenced by capitalist ideology. Thus it is argued that judges have always regarded trade union action as bad because it threatens the free market economy on which capitalism depends. True, unions are no longer outlawed as they were by the Combination Act 1800, but their ability to organise is still undermined by legislation prohibiting the closed shop. The problem with this view is that it has to explain away an equally consistent pattern of legislation benefiting the working class, a pattern running through from the original factory safety legislation in 1802 to modern welfare legislation. Rather than seeking to explain this legislation as in some way repressive, Marxists have concentrated on arguing that law plays a more subtle role, contributing to the ideology which helps to maintain the existing social order. This ideology is promoted by a number of different systems, education, politics, the media etc. But because law is so central to the organisation of society, it has a particularly important contribution to make.

How does the law contribute towards the dominant ideology? Our legal system is often regarded as embodying certain key values and ideas: it expresses the idea that society is made up of free and responsible individuals. It emphasises the concept of the rule of law according to which all these responsible individuals are equal before the law. It guards the value of judicial independence, promoting the image of the law as being neutral and autonomous ie separate from the political system. Through the rules of precedent, it reinforces the idea of an unchanging autonomous legal doctrine. It has embraced the idea of liberalism under which a major function of law is seen as the promotion of a fair, liberal society by such measures as anti-discrimination legislation. To a Marxist these ideas and values could all be seen as linked and contributing to an overall ideological framework which serves to hide the reality of capitalist society. A reality in which only the powerful and rich can make full use of the law, and in which 'neutral' judges apply biased anti-working class legislation. A reality in which apparently unchanging legal doctrine is in fact used to achieve different ends eg the rules of property which in a pre-capitalist society gave protection to the worker, now give the corporations the power to control and exploit the worker. A reality in which liberal legislation on discrimination, safety, consumer protection etc is largely symbolic in effect when measured against the way in which society actually operates.

How accurate an explanation of the relationship of law, ideology and society is that provided by Marxist analysis? Some evidence about the way in which the law is enforced does seem to provide disturbing evidence for the Marxist case. The enforcement of factory safety laws is a classic example. At first sight the passing of the Factory Act 1833 regulating work safety, making it a criminal offence for employers to break the regulations and establishing an inspectorate to enforce the law seems to refute the Marxist thesis. Here surely legislation was in the interests of the worker and against those of the capitalist. Yet research has shown that the pressure for legislation came not only from social reformers like Lord Shaftsbury, but also from large manufacturers who feared cost-cutting on safety matters by their smaller rivals, and from those who feared that unless the law provided some protection, the workers would take action themselves. Furthermore, the evidence is clear that the legislation was rarely enforced: There were far too few inspectors to undertake the job of enforcement and in any case, the magistrates were very reluctant to find 'respectable' manufacturers guilty of breaking the law. The pattern of limited prosecution remains true today. Although there are now over 1,000 inspectors, fewer than 1% of detected offenders are prosecuted. Is the explanation that the law is playing a symbolic role? Is it helping to create the ideology of equality before the law whilst in reality workers are disciplined or dismissed for misconduct and nothing nasty happens to employers when they are to blame?

One can see the force of this kind of argument, but there are other more functional explanations for the failure to prosecute employers. Most offenders are 'good' businessmen and to prosecute might alienate them thereby lessening the likelihood of future co-operation, and alienate the public thereby lessening their support for the safety cause. Many of the offences are defined in vague terms eg failure to do what is 'reasonably practicable'. This gives the inspector considerable discretion in deciding whether there has been an offence but, equally it means the court has a discretion and therefore the success of prosecutions cannot be guaranteed. In any case, prosecutions are time consuming and there may be a feeling that it is not worth missing several inspections just to spend a couple of days in court dealing with just one offender. The relationship between the inspectors and firms is continuing in nature. Firms may be visited by the same inspector a number of times over a period of years. This may lead to the feeling that long-term pressure and persuasion is a better tactic than the short-term shock of prosecution. The inspector may prefer the role of expert adviser to that of crude law enforcer. Finally, there is a question of resources. With limited staff, time and money it is simply not possible to adopt too aggressive an enforcement strategy. Safety prosecution policy represents a compromise in which the interests of firms, workers and inspectors have to be balanced. Prosecution will often follow if there is blood ie a severe injury to a worker. Otherwise the strategy is likely to be one of seeking to persuade firms to comply with the law. Indeed, the 1974 safety legislation has recognised the importance of this compliance strategy by giving inspectors the power to order an offender to improve his machines as an alternative to prosecution.

The picture looks a good deal more complex than Marxist analysis allows. If we recall from the last chapter (see p 178) the pressures which led to the 1974 safety legislation, the same point is apparent. It is difficult to make either the origin of modern safety legislation or its enforcement strategy fit the Marxist explanatory scheme. One reason may be that the scheme is too simple. It reduces the analysis of all social change to just one formula based on class conflict. It ignores the fact that modern society houses a range of competing interest groups, consumers, women's, environmentalists, etc. All these groups have an influence and hence as we noted earlier in Chapter 7 (p 179), power in society is divided amongst a plurality of such groupings. It also ignores the role played in society by co-operative relationships, by consensus between individuals and groups. Finally, it ignores the individual, treating him as a pawn in a game being played between social structures and their ideologies. But, if the basis of people's acceptance of law is not that it is imposed by the powerful nor being duped by an ideology promoted by the powerful, then we must look elsewhere for the answer.

Weber and the rational domination of law

In contrast to Marx, Weber based his explanation of society on the reasons individuals have for acting in particular ways. Applying this approach to the acceptance of law, Weber concluded that there were three reasons why authority might be accepted in a society, three different forms of domination to adopt Weber's terminology. The first was through the charisma of the person responsible for the law. Historically, there are plenty of examples of such charismatic domination from biblical figures onwards. Today, we can see charismatic authority playing a role in the way in which legal systems operate in some Islamic states. The second form of domination was through tradition. Thus for much of our medieval history, the King's law was accepted not so much because of his charisma but because tradition laid down that as the eldest son of the previous ruler, he was to be recognised as having legitimate authority. However, Weber concluded that modern western society was typified by rational domination under which a law or a legal decision was accepted as legitimate because it was recognised as forming part of a rational system of law. Weber argued that it was the predictability provided by such rational systems which enabled commerce and society to flourish and provided the reason for the acceptance of the system. He was thinking primarily of the codified systems of the continent with their highly structured provisions but his explanation applies equally to the common law with its more fluid rules of recognition. He put forward these three forms of domination as 'ideal types' in the sense that they provide models against which the practice of any legal system can be judged. For example, although the legitimacy of the common law system may be based to a large extent on rational acceptance of its complex rules of recognition, it also relies to an extent on the traditional authority of its elite corps of judges, chosen for office in a self-perpetuating way by their own predecessors.

The difficulty with Weber's analysis is that by focusing on the position and reasoning of the individual, it neglects the relationship between that individual and his society. In particular, it does not recognise the role that ideas of justice and morality play in binding the individual to the society. As we saw in Chapter 1, Professor Hart in his analysis of law as a system of rules, goes further and argues that there is no necessary relationship between the legal system and ideas of morality and justice. Against this view, we must now examine that of the so-called 'Natural Law' analysts who believe that it is precisely the relationship of law and morality which explains the legitimacy and acceptance of law.

Law and morality

In Chapter 1, we noted that the views of Hart on the separation of law and morality were opposed by the American jurist, Lon Fuller. Fuller argued that because law was dependent for its success on the intelligence and conscientiousness of those involved, it had to incorporate an 'inner morality' by which he meant procedural principles such as being of general application, being publicised, not being retrospective, being clear and non-contradictory. In addition, it had to be possible to comply with the law and there had to be congruence between the official rules and the rules actually applied by officials. Without these features, a so-called law would be neither effective nor fair. Indeed, in Fuller's view, it would not constitute law. Thus, he argued that the edicts of the Nazi regime, often retrospective, secret and discriminatory, did not constitute law. However, it is clear that compliance with the requirements of inner morality does not guarantee that the legal system will be just or moral in any wider sense. The South African legal system of the apartheid era probably satisfied the requirements of inner morality but could not be described as moral or just. What can be said about such systems?

One answer was provided in the fifth century by St Augustine: 'What are states without justice, but robber bands enlarged?' He did not regard unjust laws as being 'law' at all because they conflicted with the natural law as set out in the scriptures. A much more sophisticated version of the natural law theory was put forward in the thirteenth century by the Dominican Thomas Acquinas. He argued that laws which conflict with the requirements of natural law lose their power to bind morally. On this reasoning an unjust system, such as that based on apartheid, has forfeited any right to be obeyed because it lacks moral authority. As acceptance of the system breaks down, progressively more repression will be needed to impose order on the society. In the end those in power may recognise that a fresh start based on principles of justice is required and this is what happened in South Africa. Following the general approach of Acquinas, the contemporary philosopher John Finnis has developed a natural law theory which identifies the basic human goods such as life, sociability etc and then argues that to enable those goods to flourish, a legal system must embody certain natural rights such as not to have one's life taken as a means to further any end, not to be lied to, not to be deprived of one's capacity to procreate. It is a complex theory but rests on the simple proposition that unjust legal systems lose their direct moral authority to bind individuals.

If the morality of a legal system is central to its acceptance by the people, what of the justice of individual laws? It is clear that in an open society like ours, a law which is widely perceived to be operating in an unjust way may prove difficult to uphold. The widespread protests against the community charge or poll tax resulting in its abandonment after only a couple of years, is a good example. Another example from the 1990s is provided by the Child Support legislation requiring fathers to continue providing support for their children after a separation. The particular aspect of this scheme which provoked an outcry was its application to fathers who had entered into 'clean break' settlements with their ex-partners prior to the introduction of the new scheme. This retrospective element was perceived as unjust and political pressure led to a relaxing of the original scheme to allow such settlements to be taken into account.

How should law be evaluated?

Clearly, a law providing for torture as a method of extracting evidence or providing for arbitrary discrimination on racial grounds as under the apartheid system should be regarded as a bad law and perhaps not even a law at all if one follows the reasoning of the natural lawyers. But beyond such obvious examples, how should one evaluate the merits of a law? This section will examine two different approaches to evaluating laws: Utilitarian theories which evaluate laws in the light of their broad social goals and consequences; and deontological or rights based theories which focus on the position of the individual and his rights. A simple way of putting the contrast is that the former approach leads to a conclusion that the law is 'good or bad' whilst the latter leads to the conclusion that it is 'right or wrong'. There may be a tension between the two approaches. For example as we will see in Chapter 14, one goal of the law of torts may be that of distributing the losses caused by accidents across a wide group by holding those who will be insured to be liable for the loss irrespective of whether they are at fault. And yet if they were not morally responsible, this approach seems to treat them wrongly. Indeed, in some cases there may a direct conflict. A law may be perceived as good in its social goal but wrong in the way in which it sacrifices an individual's rights to that goal. A sensible evaluation of a law has to take into account both approaches and seek a balance.

Utilitarian theory

The classic exposition of Utilitarian theory was provided in the early nineteenth century by Jeremy Bentham. According to the theory, a society is just when its institutions and laws are arranged so as to achieve the greatest net balance of pleasure over pain. The theory says nothing about how the pleasures should be distributed between individuals. There would be nothing to say that a system of slavery was unjust if it could be shown that the pleasure provided to the slave owners outweighed the pain borne by the slaves. One might think it unlikely that such an argument could be upheld on the facts but the important point is that Utilitarian theory allows the argument to be made. It is concerned with what is good for society and not what is right for the individual. Of course the two are not always in conflict, indeed rarely so. Thus, John Stuart Mill who wrote the essay *On Liberty* in defence of individual liberties, was a utilitarian who viewed liberty as a pleasure in itself and as a means of securing other pleasures. Securing the individual's right to liberty would also secure the maximum net pleasure within society.

In so far as the theory points us towards examining the consequences of particular kinds of law, it has a useful role to play. Thus, if we considered that a ban on abortion was desirable on the utilitarian ground that it would protect the pregnant from the mental pain of abortion and provide the childless with the pleasure of being able to adopt, it would be important to know what the real affect of such a ban might be. The evidence from past times when there was a ban on abortions in most circumstances, was that there were very large numbers of 'back-street' abortions often resulting in death or serious injury to the pregnant. A utilitarian argument for a ban would have to take account of that evidence. Again, it is perfectly proper to justify particular legal principles on the ground of social utility. Thus, the principle of vicarious liability under which an employer is held liable to compensate the victim of wrongs committed by its employees, can be justified on the ground that this enables the victim's loss to be re-distributed to the employer and then onto his insurer and to the wider group of employers who pay the insurance premiums (see p 391). Such loss spreading is often said to be one of the social goals of the law of torts and its utility is said to outweigh the unfairness of holding the employer liable despite the fact that he not to blame.

But there must be doubts whether a theory of justice based on the achievement of the greatest net balance of pleasure over pain is either workable or acceptable. Great efforts have been made to develop a cost-benefit analysis of law by American lawyers, such as Judge Richard Posner, who have applied economics to the study of law. They argue that a just law is one which maximises the wealth of society. They suggest, for example, that liability will be justly placed upon a manufacturer in respect of defective products only where it would be economically more efficient for it to bear the cost of improving product quality than for the consumer to guard against defects in the product. A major problem with this approach is that there is often no precise data for calculating costs and no agreement on the appropriate economic model for comparing costs and benefits. But even if the theory were to be workable, there would be major reservations about its acceptability in all situations. To take an example, would it be acceptable to allow a car manufacturer to produce a car with a safety defect making it more likely to catch fire on impact, on the ground that the cost of caring for the victims of crashes would be less than the cost of rectifying the defect. Such a permissive rule might be said to maximise the wealth of society as a whole, allowing more people to buy more cars at a lower price. But would it be morally acceptable to sacrifice the protection of the minority who might burn in a car crash to the greater good of the majority? Fortunately, when facts such as these arose in American litigation in the 1970s, the outcome was determined by a lay jury rather than by expert economists and the jury held the manufacturer responsible.

Rights theories

Many approaches can be grouped under this head but perhaps the most influential in recent times has been that of John Rawls in his book *A Theory of Justice* published in 1972. Rawls criticises Utilitarianism for allowing the minority to be sacrificed to the greater good of the majority, and for potentially justifying great inequalities of wealth. As an alternative Rawls suggests a process of reasoning based on the notion of a social contract, that is an agreement we might all be willing to enter into as a just basis for governing our society. Of course, we might be tempted to agree to only those provisions which would be in our own interest. We might consider that government should fund only those areas of tertiary education which are 'useful' like the study of law and not those which are 'useless' like philosophy, or (assuming we are male) that funding should go to males but not females. To eliminate such partisan views, Rawls requires us to play a game, to imagine that we are entering this social contract whilst shrouded in a veil of ignorance. This notionally prevents us from knowing to which sex, class, religion, or social position we belong. From this 'original position' as Rawls calls it, we must agree the social contract. Given this veil, we would not agree to a system of slavery because we would not know whether, when the veil was lifted, we would turn out to be a slave or a slave owner. We would not take the risk of agreeing to slavery.

What would we agree? Rawls argues that we will rationally agree on two key principles of justice. First, that 'each person is to have an equal right to the most extensive total system of equal basic liberties compatible with a similar system of liberty for all.' These liberties he identifies as political liberty including freedom of speech, freedom of thought, freedom of the person and to hold property, and freedom from arbitrary arrest. Protection for these liberties must be secured before we can apply the second principle which is that:

> 'Social and economic inequalities are to be arranged so that they are both (a) to the greatest benefit of the least advantaged, and (b) attached to positions open to all under conditions of fair equality of opportunity.'

This is known as the difference principle and it allows for, say, the entrepreneur to be better rewarded than the ordinary worker because the extra incentives for the former lead him or her to create better opportunities and rewards for the latter. Rawls argues that this idea corresponds with that of fraternity in the sense of not wanting to have greater advantages unless this is to the benefit of others who are less well off.

Critics say that Rawls is simply using the original position to justify liberal welfare policies which redistribute wealth via a progressive taxation system. They argue people might be just as likely to opt for a system under which they have a right to keep much more of their earnings and rely on their own efforts to protect themselves from hardship. The 1980s saw such right-wing theories come to political prominence. Other theorists, like Adams and Brownsword, base their approach on the individual's right to freedom and well-being and the duty to respect the freedom and well-being of others. Whatever the basis of the rights theory, it provides a counter-balance to the Utilitarian stance. Perhaps the answer is to keep both approaches in mind when evaluating laws. One must also reflect on the function of law and what makes it acceptable. Finally, one must constantly reassess one's judgment in the light of these different perspectives. Adams and Brownsword put the point well when they conclude their book thus:

> 'Understanding law is rather akin to climbing a mountain: it is an uphill task; the views can be rewarding; on occasion, one may have to retrace one's steps to make a fresh ascent; and, above all, one must constantly be sceptical that one has actually reached the summit.'

Postscript: the Tony Bland case

The case of *Airedale National Health Service Trust v Bland* (1993) brings together some of the themes of this chapter. It concerned the withdrawal of treatment from a patient in a persistent vegetative state (PVS). It raises questions concerning the role of the law and the medical profession in regulating such questions, the relationship of legal and moral principles, the acceptability of judicial as opposed to legislative decisions on such matters, and, finally, the justice of the outcome when viewed from perspectives of the social good and individual rights.

Tony Bland was 17 when his lungs were crushed at the Hillsborough crowd disaster in 1989. By the time that his breathing was restored his upper brain had been severely and irreversibly damaged. For three years he remained at Airedale hospital in a persistent vegetative state. He could breath unaided but as he could not swallow, he was fed by pumping nutritive fluids down a naso-gastric tube. He had no cognitive functions and could not see, hear, smell or communicate in any way.The unanimous opinion of all the doctors was that there was no hope of recovery. The hospital asked for a declaration that it might lawfully discontinue feeding him. Such discontinuance would inevitably result in his death and would have amounted to the offence of murder unless the declaration was granted. The trial judge, three Court of Appeal judges and five Law Lords were all in favour of granting the declaration and as a result there is now a new common law exception to the offence of murder which applies where life support is discontinued with the consent of the court. However, despite the judicial unanimity as to the declaration, there was a major difference of approach between Hoffmann LJ in the Court of Appeal and the members of the House of Lords. It is this tension which we will explore.

Hoffmann and the moral equation

Hoffmann LJ saw the case turning on a moral equation. On the one side was the principle of the sanctity of life. This was relevant even though

Bland had no consciousness of his life. It was relevant because human life has an intrinsic value irrespective of whether it is valuable to the person concerned or anyone else. Hoffmann argued that its value was such that it was almost always wrong to cause the death of another and he illustrated the danger of treating lives as useless by reference to the extermination of the handicapped in Nazi Germany. But opposed to this principle was that of the right to self-determination. It is accepted that an adult is entitled to exercise this right and refuse treatment which would save his life. Thus, a Jehovah's Witness cannot be forced to have a life-saving blood transfusion. His right to self-determination prevails over society's broader interest in the sanctity of his life. In the case of a child, the law will act paternalistically and override its wish to refuse treatment in order to save its life. What of those incapable of exercising their right to self-determination, those such as Bland? If he had left an advance directive or 'living will' as to what should happen were he to be incapacitated, then that directive should be followed. But Bland, like most of us, had given the matter no thought. So instead, the court had to do its best to imagine what he would have decided. At this point in the argument, Hoffmann brought in a third principle, that of human dignity. It is this principle that leads us to pay respect to the dead and to the privacy and honour of the living. The principle may not be rational but it is deeply rooted in our ways of thinking. It was this principle which swayed the equation. Hoffmann concluded that had he known of his position, Bland would have chosen to put an end to 'the humiliation of his being and the distress of his family'. But Hoffmann was still concerned about the argument that the declaration would enable the hospital to starve Bland to death and would violate the principle of treating the helpless with humanity. He argued that the language of starvation should be disregarded as it was emotive and purely designed 'to evoke images of cruelty, suffering and unwelcome death'. As to humanity, he argued that it had no application where the treatment could no longer serve a humane purpose. Hoffmann stressed two points in relation to his general approach. First, the case had to be argued from 'moral rather than purely legal principles' and that a properly explained decision was required to reassure people. Second, the issue was one for the law to resolve and not one which required any medical expertise. The medical profession could tell the court about the patient's condition and might have views on whether to withhold treatment, but essentially the issue was legal/moral and one where 'medical ethics [should] be formed by the law rather than the reverse'.

The Law Lords and the patient's best interests

The general approach of the Law Lords differed fundamentally from that of Hoffmann in both respects. First, the Law Lords considered that the answer lay in legal authority, and in particular, their previous decision in *F v West Berkshire Health Authority* (1990). That case held that a mentally handicapped woman could be lawfully sterilised without her consent if such a course of action was in her best interests. Second, the Lords argued that 'best interests' must be determined by doctors acting in accordance with 'a responsible and competent body of relevant professional opinion'. Guidance as to such opinion could be found in the papers issued by the medical ethics committee of the British Medical Association. Lord Mustill stressed that the test was not the 'best interests' of the community for that would involve a cost-benefit analysis, for example, as to whether the resources being devoted to Bland 'might be more fruitfully employed in improving the condition of other patients. Only Parliament was competent to undertake such a utilitarian exercise. Indeed, Lord Mustill considered that 'the whole matter cries out for exploration in depth by Parliament and then for the establishment of a new set of ethically and intellectually consistent rules'.

Legislation: experts and the media

The Law Commission reported in 1995 on the Bland issue amongst others and proposed the enactment of a Mental Incapacity Bill. This would have allowed withdrawal of nutrition from a patient with no upper brain activity and no prospect of recovery if approval was given by the court, or an attorney previously appointed by the patient to take such a decision should the need arise, or an independent doctor. When giving permission the court, attorney or doctor would have to consider the patient's best interests. Not much of an advance on the position left by the Lords in *Bland* and certainly no reference to cost-benefit analysis, indicating perhaps that such analysis is not appropriate to questions of life and death. The proposal attracted the attention of the media. A Daily Mail writer regarded it as 'downright dangerous' for giving too much power to courts and doctors. It suggested that the only sensible reform would be the abolition of the Law Commission. Other experts are divided. John Finnis has suggested that the 'good' of human life gave Bland a right to be cared for. Ian Kennedy, perhaps the leading authority on medical law, has suggested the court should recognise 'that in carefully defined circumstances, the concept of treatment for the dying should extend to that which will kill the patient' ie legalised euthanasia. 1996 has seen some PVS patients awakening, in one case after seven years. The General Medical Council has issued some new guidelines designed to distinguish between persistent and permanent vegetative states. Early legislation on the issue does not seem likely.

Understanding law

What does this example tell us? That on critical issues what the law does, in this instance its regulatory function, is intertwined with what is acceptable to the people and that, in turn, is inevitably linked to the criteria on which we evaluate the law.

Part II
Criminal law

Chapter 9
General principles

Introduction

Criminal law is concerned with the liability of individuals for wrongdoing against other individuals, society or the state. But not every form of wrongdoing or anti-social behaviour constitutes a crime even if harmful consequences result: for example, adultery is not a crime, nor is the smoking of cigarettes in public places. Society through its law makers, has to decide what forms and types of conduct or activities are to attract the criminal process. Some forms of conduct are clearly accepted as criminal: murder, rape, theft; others are more controversial attracting differing views and attitudes: abortion, censorship, the smoking of cannabis. Others have been the subject of a change in attitude: homosexuality (which once was regarded as a crime but is no longer in certain circumstances) and the so-called marital exemption from rape, which has recently been removed. The criminal law must be dynamic, responding to changes in society both in the development of new offences to meet new situations and in the elimination of anachronisms and obsolete crimes. New developments sometimes require the creation of new crimes; the Computer Misuse Act 1990 is designed to tackle the misuse of computers, including computer 'hacking'.

Historical context

Although historically the King's Justices formulated the principles of the major crimes by case law development, it is now regarded that it is the role primarily of Parliament to decide whether particular conduct should or should not be a crime. The extent to which the courts should have a residual role to play in the creation of new offences is a matter for debate. Judicial law-making can be seen as undemocratic and retrospective, but the courts have not hesitated to intervene when this is thought to be essential. In 1736 a famous criminal jurist, Sir Matthew Hale, formulated the principle that a man could not be guilty of raping his wife since the wife had, by marriage, consented to all acts of sexual intercourse with her husband. This was unchallenged for 150 years before being considered

221

by the courts, when the rule was affirmed. But in 1991 the Court of Appeal decided that in certain circumstances a man could be found guilty of raping his wife when he had sexual intercourse with her without her consent. This ruling was upheld by the House of Lords in the historic decision in *R v R* (1991). Lord Keith stated that the common law is capable of evolving in the light of changing social, economic and cultural developments. Hale's proposition reflected the state of affairs in these respects at the time when it was enunciated. Since then the status of women, and particularly of married women, has changed out of all recognition, so that the denial of convicting a man for marital rape is no longer reasonable or tenable . Lord Keith agreed with the view of the former Lord Chief Justice, Lord Lane, in the Court of Appeal decision in the case:

> 'The remaining and no less difficult question is whether, . . . this is an area where the court should step aside to leave the matter to the Parliamentary process. This is not the creation of a new offence, it is the removal of a common law fiction which has become anachronistic and offensive and we consider that it is our duty having reached that conclusion to act upon it.'

Thus the House of Lords thought that, where the common law no longer even remotely represented what was the true position of a wife in present-day society, the duty of the court was to take steps to alter the rule if it could legitimately do so in the light of any relevant Parliamentary enactment.

Sources

The sources of the criminal law are mainly statutory at the present day, although some crimes, of which murder is the most obvious example, still lack statutory definition and are termed common law crimes as originating in custom and being defined by the cases in which they were judicially formulated. The substantive criminal law is thus largely a law of crimes in the sense of being made up of a large number of specific offences each of which consists of specified physical conduct, done with a particular accompanying mental state. Criminal law also embodies ancillary rules relating to, for example, aiding and abetting crime, attempting crime and recognises several defences to apparent criminal conduct.

Definitions

It is fundamental to English law that there is no single definition of a crime but rather multiple formulations of individual crimes. The definition of 'crime' and the reasons why some conduct is regarded as deserving of criminal sanction and other conduct is not is discussed in a later chapter. We are concerned here not so much with the criteria which underlie criminality, as with the substantive principles of the criminal law. A useful starting point is the following statement by Lord Diplock, in a case concerning a prosecution for blackmail (*Treacy v DPP* (1971)).

'The Theft Act 1968 is a code of criminal law; and criminal law is about the right of the state to punish persons for their conduct, generally where that conduct is undertaken with a wicked intent or without justificatory excuse. A code of criminal law defines offences; ie the kinds of conduct which render the person guilty of it liable to punishment. Conduct which constitutes a crime consists of a person's doing or, less frequently omitting to do physical acts; and the definition of the crime always contains a description of physical acts or omissions, though it may and in English law generally does, also require that the physical acts or omissions which constitute the described conduct should be done with a particular intent either expressly stated in the definition or to be inferred from the mere fact that Parliament has made the described conduct punishable.'

Thus the crime of rape is statutorily defined and consists, in essence, of unlawful sexual intercourse by a man with a woman without the consent of the woman in circumstances where the man knows (or is reckless) that the woman is not consenting.

Actus reus and mens rea

The physical elements referred to are collectively called the actus reus and the accompanied mental state is called the mens rea. A criminal offence is thus committed when the defendant is proved to have satisfied both the actus reus and the mens rea of the alleged offence. It is the fundamental duty of the prosecution to prove both of these elements of the offence to the satisfaction of the judge or jury beyond reasonable doubt. In the absence of such proof the accused will be acquitted since in English law all persons are presumed innocent until proved guilty (see *Woolmington v DPP* (1935)).

The function of the criminal process is to determine with reference to the stated definitions whether an individual has or has not committed the offence charged. It is characterised by enquiry, trial and sentence. The substantive criminal law will indicate what has to be proved; the rules of evidence will determine how the relevant facts can be proved and with what degree of certainty and the rules of procedure will provide the forum and framework within which those issues can be contested and resolved. When an individual has been convicted the rules and principles governing sentencing will be regarded to determine what punishment or treatment is appropriate. It is the purpose of this, and the next two chapters, to consider the substantive criminal law and to provide guidance on how the court answers the first question above, namely what has to be proved. Subsequent chapters will consider some of the other related questions.

The physical element: the act

Most crimes require some positive conduct, some activity or act by the accused as an essential element in the offence. However, exceptionally a person can be criminally responsible for an omission, a failure to act; and for some crimes it will suffice if a 'state of affairs' exists with the accused as a passive participator. Both of these exceptional cases are discussed later.

Actus reus

Actus reus means literally 'prohibited act' but few crimes can be adequately described simply by reference to the act; most require proof of accompanying circumstances and some proof of a particular consequence. Consider the crime of rape. The act is sexual intercourse but that alone is not a crime; it is only a crime when the act of intercourse is accompanied by the circumstance of the woman not consenting to the intercourse (see Sexual Offences (Amendment) Act 1976, section 1, post). Likewise in criminal damage the offence consists of destroying or damaging any property (the act) which belongs to another and for which act there is no lawful excuse (the circumstances). Further, in this crime it is essential that the property be actually destroyed or damaged; in other words that a particular consequence follows the act and the circumstances (Criminal Damage Act 1971 section 1, post). Similarly, the actus reus of the offence of unlawful wounding is defined by section 20 of the Offences Against the Person Act 1861 as 'whosoever shall unlawfully and maliciously wound or inflict any grievous bodily harm upon any other person . . .'. The requirements here are a physical act of aggression which in the circumstances is unlawful (eg not in self defence or in proper chastisement of a child) with the consequence that someone is wounded or caused grievous bodily harm. A similar analysis will be apparent with the offence embodied in section 20 of the Sexual Offences Act 1956: 'It is an offence for a person acting without lawful authority or excuse to take an unmarried girl under the age of sixteen out of the possession of her parent or guardian against her will.' Taking the girl is the act; without lawful excuse, that the girl is under sixteen and in the possession of her parents are all essential circumstances and the consequence is the removal of the girl from her parent or guardian.

A package

Thus strictly the concept of 'actus reus' is a package which embraces acts, circumstances and consequences which collectively constitute the physical elements of a crime. The formulation of particular crimes is largely concerned with the statement of these elements. But the conduct prohibited is often only simply stated, leaving problems of construction and definition to be resolved with reference to particular factual situations.

For example, the Criminal Damage Act 1971 refers to a person who 'destroys or damages any property belonging to another'. These are alternatives and the former is clearly more comprehensive than the latter. Whether property is 'destroyed' depends on the nature of the property, but the usual acts include, burning, breaking, killing, demolishing, and consuming. Some kinds of property can be destroyed by being mixed with other property, some by being immersed in water, and some by simply being used as intended. Most acts of destruction involve some fundamental change in the physical condition of the object and can be a matter of degree. Is a picture destroyed by being wholly painted over? But a few additional marks merely damage? If the picture is completely burned or torn into shreds it will be destroyed, but what if it is merely singed or cut with a knife? Intangible property is excluded from the definition of property for the purposes of criminal property so that a patent is not destroyed by being copied or a trade secret by being published. But is a computer program destroyed by being erased although the disk is physically undamaged? Or is an undeveloped film destroyed by being exposed although the film is physically undamaged? (See *Cox v Riley* (1986)). 'Damage' is more difficult to define. Most acts which damage property involve some permanent degradation of the object, but is it still damage if the interference can be easily reversed? Is a car damaged by loosening the wheel nuts? Or by being covered in mud which can be washed off without leaving a trace? Is a battery damaged by being used so that its power is reduced? Or does it depend on whether the battery is rechargeable? Does the concept require some reduction in value or usefulness of the object to the owner? Is an egg damaged by having its shell painted? Is a pencil damaged by being sharpened? Such questions must be answered with reference to the crime charged, by applying strictly the definition of the prohibited conduct as stated in the formulation of the offence, with the assistance of judicial decisions in analogous cases where available.

A voluntary act

It is perhaps obvious that the act involved must be a voluntary willed act of the accused. If in an assault case the accused's arm was physically forced by another to strike the victim, or if the accused was pushed against the victim by another, then there would be no crime by the accused, although it is probable that the perpetrator of the force in these examples would be guilty of crimes against both the accused and the victim.

DURESS

A related discussion is the extent to which duress can be pleaded as a defence and whether such a plea negates the actus reus as opposed to the mens rea, of the offence. In these cases there is no direct physical compulsion by one to another but a threat of death or serious injury to the accused or to his family if he does not participate in a crime, which it is alleged negates the freedom of choice to the accused. In the leading case of *DPP for Northern Ireland v Lynch* (1975) (discussed more fully in Chapter 11) the accused alleged that he was forced by an armed terrorist to drive him and two armed accomplices of the terrorist to the place of work of the victim. At the scene the accused remained in the car and the armed terrorists murdered the victim. The accused sought to negate his criminal responsibility for the killing by pleading that he had been an unwilling participator who had been forced, in effect at gun point, to drive the car. Lord Simon recognised that there will be situations where a person has no freedom of choice – the classic example being where A by irresistible force directs B's hand holding a knife to stab C; that is not B's act. But the plea in the case above is more difficult. Lord Simon thought that:

> '...duress is not inconsistent with act and will, the will being deflected not destroyed; so that the intention conflicts with the wish – a legal situation correctly described by the phrase coactus volui.'

Lord Wilberforce agreed that duress does not destroy the act; the accused completes the act and knows that he is doing so; but the addition of the element of duress will excuse some crimes, short of murder. Essentially in such cases the accused is saying 'Yes, I did the act by my own physical volition but I had no wish to so act'. In effect that his freedom of choice has been overborne so that he has been forced in a mental rather than a physical way to so act. Much the same attitude will be apparent in cases where the accused pleads necessity as a defence. In the case of *R v Martin* (1989) the defence of necessity was said to arise most commonly, from the pressure on the accused's will from the wrongful threats or violence of another. In that case the accused had driven his stepson to work despite being disqualified from driving. His defence was that he had been forced by necessity to do so, because his wife had threatened to commit suicide if he did not. The Court of Appeal held that this defence should have been left to the jury. But the law, as a matter of policy, limits the scope of this plea, denying any place for it where the consequences of yielding to the pressure exceeds or equals the possible result of not acting. Thus the defence cannot be pleaded to a charge of murder. In the celebrated case of *R v Dudley and Stephens* (1884) the accused were shipwrecked and cast adrift in an open boat. They were starving and conspired to kill the weakest member of their party so that they could eat his flesh. They were charged with, and convicted of, his murder. Their actions although prompted by the necessity of their circumstances were still their own free voluntary acts.

AUTOMATISM

These situations must be distinguished from true cases of involuntary conduct sometimes called automatism; ie cases where the accused has no control over his physical movements, where there was a total destruction of voluntary control (see *A-G's Reference (No 2 of 1992)*). Examples that readily come to mind are muscular spasms brought on by fits and seizures, and actions committed whilst unconscious such as when under an hypnotic trance. The law is justly suspicious of such pleas since the time honoured 'I had a black-out and can remember nothing about the incident' is easy to raise but difficult to prove or disprove. Similarly, the court was reluctant to accept a plea of automatism where the accused alleged that the offence occurred whilst he was sleepwalking (*R v Burgess* (1991)). Where the defence is successfully raised then there will be no criminal liability because there will be no voluntary conduct to constitute the actus reus of the offence. The defence was successfully pleaded in *R v Quick* (1973) where a nurse in a mental hospital was charged with assaulting a patient and pleaded that he was a diabetic and was suffering from hypoglycaemia, a deficiency of blood sugar after an insulin injection, at the time of the offence. He alleged that this condition caused him to have violent outbursts over which he had no control. The trial judge sought to deny Quick the defence of automatism ruling that the condition amounted to insanity and should be pleaded as such. On appeal it was held that the accused's condition was due to the injections of insulin and thus the malfunctioning was caused by an external factor and not by the disease, accordingly the accused was entitled to plead the defence of automatism. But where a lorry driver crashed into a vehicle parked on the hard shoulder of a motorway killing two people he sought to plead a defence of 'driving without awareness' which he alleged was analogous to a state of automatism. The court rejected the plea insisting that automatism involved a total destruction of voluntary control (*A-G's Reference (No 2 of 1992)*).

State of affairs crimes

It is necessary to note in brief here that some crimes are defined not in the sense of the accused doing a positive act but of consisting in the accused 'being found', 'being in possession', 'being in charge', etc. In some such cases all the prosecution needs to prove are the existence of the factual circumstances which constitute the crime – the existence of the state of affairs. In the case of *R v Larsonneur* (1933), the conviction was for 'being found' in the UK as an illegal alien. Another example, frequently cited, is the offence provided in section 4(2) of the Road Traffic Act 1988 expressed in terms of being in charge of a motor vehicle whilst unfit through drink or drugs. There were few, if any, such crimes at common law but Parliament has not hesitated to create them in the twentieth century. For example 'being in possession' offences have increased with reference to drugs, explosives and fire arms. The offence described as going equipped for burglary or theft (Theft Act 1968, section 25) also comes to mind. In some of these offences the scope of the actus reus is cut down by a required mens rea such as 'knowingly' in possession or 'with intent to. . .' and such limitations are clearly desirable to prevent the creation in effect of absolute offences.

Crimes of omission

The question to be considered here is the extent to which a person can be held criminally responsible for a failure to act. In general the common law does not penalise omissions and when liability does arise it can be said to be exceptional.

A contractual duty

First, a person can commit a crime by failing to act in circumstances where he has a contractual duty to act. Thus in the leading case of *R v Pittwood* (1902) a man was employed by a railway company to operate a level crossing gate. He opened the gate to let a vehicle cross the line on the road and then omitted to close it. Later a second vehicle passed through the open gate and attempted to cross the line; it was struck by a train and the driver was killed. The court expressly stated that a person might incur criminal liability from a failure to carry out a duty arising out of contract.

A statutory obligation

Second, statute can make certain omissions an offence. Failure to wear a seat belt in a car, and failure to stop after or to report a vehicle accident are two that come readily to mind. However, many crimes expressed as omissions require positive conduct to be liable: thus driving without insurance or failing to observe a stop sign on the road. Consider also those cases where someone is advantaged because of another's mistake, where for example someone finds that they have been overpaid their wages or salary by their employers. The Theft Act 1968 contains a special provision for cases such as this in section 5(4), the effect of which is to impose an obligation on the recipient to make restoration of the money. Applying that provision, where a woman was overpaid £74.74 by salary payment into her bank, the Court of Appeal thought the woman could be guilty of stealing the money if she dishonestly appropriated it instead of returning it or notifying her employers of the overpayment. However, it will be noticed that this is not really a case of liability for a pure omission since some positive act of dishonest appropriation is required to make the offence. If goods are wrongly delivered to your house and you put them to one side, do not use them but ask the sender to collect them, you do not steal them by passively keeping them.

Other statutes make it an offence in defined circumstances to fail to act. An obvious example is provided by section 1(1) of the Children and Young Persons Act 1933:

'If any person who has attained the age of sixteen years and has the custody, charge, care of any child . . . under that age, wilfully . . . neglects . . . him, or causes . . . him to be . . . neglected . . . in a manner likely to cause him unnecessary suffering or injury to health . . . that person shall be guilty of an [offence].'

The House of Lords has stated that the actus reus of the offence is simply the failure, for whatever reason, to provide the child whenever it was necessary, with the medical care needed. However, the offence is not one of strict or absolute liability (which is discussed later) since the neglect must be 'wilful' which the House of Lords stated required proof either that the accused was aware at the time that the child's health might be at risk if medical aid was not provided, or that the accused's unawareness of that fact was due to his not caring whether the child's health was at risk.

Assumption of duty

Third, an analogous liability can arise where a person assumes the duty to care for an aged or infirm person. The principle was pronounced in the nineteenth century case of *R v Instan* (1893) but can be illustrated graphically by the facts of *Stone and Dobinson* (1977). They were an unmarried couple who lived together and who were described respectively as being of below average intelligence, partially deaf and almost blind, and of being ineffectual and inadequate. Stone's middle-aged sister came to live with them and assumed an eccentric, withdrawn and bedridden existence in their house. Although Stone and Dobinson were aware that the woman was totally neglecting herself and was rapidly deteriorating in condition they did little if anything to assist her or to summon outside help. Three years after the woman came to live in the house Dobinson found her dead in her bed. She was naked, emaciated, her body was ingrained with dirt and she was lying in a pool of excrement. The cause of death was toxaemia from the infected bed sores and prolonged immobilisation. Stone and Dobinson were convicted of her manslaughter. The appeal court thought that they had assumed the duty of caring for her, a duty which they could have discharged either by summoning help or by caring for her themselves. Further the court was satisfied that they had either been indifferent to an obvious risk of injury to the infirm person's health or had actually foreseen the risk of injury and had determined to run that risk.

Minimising your own act

Fourth, it is possible to incur criminal liability by failing to prevent or minimise the harmful consequences of your own act. A good factual

illustration can be found in the case of *R v Miller* (1983) where the accused
was charged with arson contrary to section 1(1) and (3) of the Criminal
Damage Act 1971. His own version of the events was that he returned to
the house where he had been sleeping and

> 'I lay on my mattress and lit a cigarette. I must have fell to sleep because I
> woke up to find the mattress on fire. I just got up and went into the next room
> and went back to sleep. Then the next thing I remember was the police and fire
> people arriving. I hadn't got anything to put the fire out with so I just left it.'

Lord Diplock had no doubts that he had been correctly convicted because
the actus reus of the offence of arson is present if the defendant accidentally
starts a fire and thereafter, intending to destroy or damage property
belonging to another or being reckless whether any such property would
be destroyed or damaged (as here), fails to take any steps to extinguish
the fire or prevent damage to such property by that fire. It will be noticed
that by his own admission the accused became aware of the fire and chose
to do nothing; the case is not suggesting liability for purely accidental fires.

Apart from such exceptional circumstances it remains true to say that
in general no criminal responsibility attaches to failures to act however
morally reprehensible such failure might be. Thus the classic example of
the fit young man who is an excellent swimmer failing to rescue a child
whom he observes drowning in a lake, unless the man has (as a parent for
example) some responsibility for the care of the child. Similarly, failing
to warn a passer-by that they are about to be struck by a runaway car or
falling building – unless the accused is the creator of the risk. You can
ask whether such clearly reprehensible conduct should be subject to
criminal sanctions and this question should be considered in the context
of the later discussion relating to the definition of the act.

Causation

Many crimes require proof of a particular consequence as an essential
ingredient: in murder you must prove that the victim died; in section 18
of the Offences Against the Person Act 1861 that the victim was wounded
or caused grievous bodily harm, and in criminal damage that the property
was destroyed or damaged. The apparently simple proposition to be stated
here is that in such crimes it is essential to prove that the accused's act
caused the consequence or in other words that the accused is liable as a
matter of causation for the crime.

An example

In many cases such proof will be obvious: A shot a gun at B, the bullet
entered B's heart and B died; A caused B's death. But consider some other
situations.

Suppose that A pointed a gun at B and B died of a heart attack?

Suppose that A knocked B unconscious and left him lying in the road where he was run over, and killed by a bus?

Suppose that A injured B who was being taken by ambulance to the hospital when the ambulance crashed killing all the occupants?

Suppose that A injured B who was taken to the hospital where he subsequently died because: he received no medical treatment; he received the wrong medical treatment; he refused all medical treatment; he died in a fire which burnt down the hospital; or he was stabbed to death by a fellow patient after a quarrel?

Suppose that A knocked B unconscious who remained lying in the street for several hours and she was robbed, raped or further assaulted?

Suppose that B had a toddler at home whom she had meant to leave only for a minute but who because of the attack is left alone for hours and who knocks over an oil fire and is burnt to death?

Suppose that B has an aged mother who dies of a heart attack or commits suicide on hearing the news of B and the baby's death?

SINE QUA NON

In these cases it could be argued that A caused each of the consequences on the basis that none of them would have happened but for the initial attack on B. However, there is a danger in such 'sine qua non', 'without which it would not have happened', reasoning because it will often be possible to find a causal link however tenuous in very remote circumstances. If A had not stolen B's car then B would not have had to walk home late at night and B would not have been raped. Further if C had not invited B out to the cinema she would not have taken the car out, therefore it would not have been stolen etc! But no one would conclude, as a matter of common sense that A or C caused or was criminally responsible for the rape of B. In *R v Watson* (1989) two burglars entered the house of an elderly woman at night. They abused her but left without taking anything. Shortly after, the police arrived and council workmen to board up the broken window. An hour and a half after the burglary, the woman suffered a heart attack and died. Which of the three visitations to the woman's house, all of which caused her stress, was the immediate precipitating cause of her heart attack? Or was the heart attack the result of the cumulative effect of all three? It could be said that the burglary was the initiating cause of the whole sequence of events, but the Court of Appeal felt obliged to quash the burglar's conviction for manslaughter. In the criminal law, and in particular in the law of homicide, whether the death of a deceased was the result of the accused's criminal act is a question of fact for the jury, but it is a question of fact to be decided in accordance with legal principles explained to the jury by the judge (*R v Cheshire* (1991)). Where the law requires proof of the relationship between an act and its consequences as an element of responsibility, a simple and sufficient explanation of the basis of such relationship has proved notoriously elusive.

POSSIBLE TESTS

A possible approach would be to say that A is liable for all the natural and probable consequences of his actions and indeed there is authority to support such a proposition, see for example the decision of Lord Bridge in *R v Moloney* (1985) (discussed later). But this approach was immediately departed from by the House of Lords in *R v Hancock, R v Shankland* (1986) on the grounds that it would link together too remotely connected events. The House thought that any such formulation must be expressed with reference in addition to the degree of probability that one event will lead to another.

An alternative formula is to borrow the concept of foreseeability from the law of tort and to say that the accused will be liable for all events which are 'reasonably foreseeable'. But the Court of Appeal has pointed out the difference in policy between the approach of the civil and the criminal law to the question of causation and warned of the dangers of importing the language of the one to the other (*R v Cheshire* (1991)).

It can be said that the question of causation remains a basic question of, should this person be held criminally responsible for this event? Are his act and the consequence sufficiently closely linked to justify a criminal prosecution?

Two case law examples

Most of the reported cases are concerned with murder since this is the most important crime in which it is necessary to prove a result or consequence of the accused's act. In *R v Blaue* (1975) the appellant attacked an 18 year old girl with a knife causing a serious stab wound which pierced the lung. She was taken to hospital where she was told that as she had lost a large quantity of blood she needed a blood transfusion. The girl was a Jehovah's Witness and pursuant to her religious beliefs, she refused to have the transfusion. She was told that if she did not have the transfusion she would die. She persisted in her refusal and died. Blaue was convicted of the girl's manslaughter on the grounds of diminished responsibility and he appealed on the grounds that it was the girl's own act which caused her death. The court dismissed his appeal. First, Lawton LJ confirmed the age old maxim that 'you must take your victim as you find him'. Thus if you attack a person who proves to be unusually frail it is no defence to argue that most people being more robust would have survived the attack. In the same way Blaue had to accept the fact that his victim had religious beliefs which prevented her from receiving the appropriate medical treatment. The court refused to accept an argument that the attitude of the girl in this case was unreasonable and should therefore have been taken into account. Secondly, the Lord Justice returned to the basic question, what caused the girl's death? As a matter of medical fact it was the bleeding into the pleural cavity arising from the penetration of the lung, in other words the stab wound. Blaue had caused the stab wound and thus the girl's death. 'The fact that the victim refused to stop this end coming about did not break the casual connection between the act and the death.'

A more difficult case is that of *R v Pagett* (1983). The defendant armed with a shotgun shot at police officers who were attempting to arrest him. He had with him a sixteen year old girl and he forcibly used her body as a shield in front of him to prevent the police officers from shooting him. She was killed by shots fired at the defendant by the officers in instinctive reaction to his firing at them. The defendant was charged with murder and convicted of manslaughter. On appeal he argued that it was the police officer who shot the girl not he (as indeed was the case) and that this constituted a novus actus interveniens breaking the causal link between his act and the girl's death. This does, as a matter of causation, look convincing but the court were content with the good sense of the jury's verdict. The accused was guilty of two unlawful and dangerous acts. First the act of firing at the police; secondly the act of holding the girl as a shield in front of him when the police might well fire shots in his direction in self defence. Either act could constitute the actus reus of manslaughter and thus justify his conviction.

Improper medical treatment

There have been a number of interesting cases where it has been alleged by the accused as a matter of defence, that the victim's death has been caused by negligent or improper medical treatment, so that it is the treatment and not his act which caused the death. In *R v Cheshire* (1991) the accused shot the deceased in the leg and stomach seriously wounding him. The deceased was taken to hospital where he was operated on and placed in intensive care. While in hospital he developed respiratory problems and a tracheotomy tube was placed in his windpipe to assist his breathing. The tube remained in place for four weeks. The deceased suffered further chest infections and other complications and complained of difficulty in breathing. Over two months after the shooting, while still in hospital, the deceased died because his windpipe had become obstructed due to narrowing where the tracheotomy had been performed, such a condition being a rare but not unknown complication arising out of the operation. The accused was charged with murder. The trial judge directed the jury that the accused was responsible for the deceased's death even if the treatment given by the hospital medical staff was incompetent and negligent and that it was only if they had been reckless in their treatment of the deceased that he was entitled to be acquitted. The accused was convicted and appealed. The Court of Appeal dismissed the appeal:

> 'It seems to us that (cases cited) demonstrate the difficulties in formulating and explaining a general concept of causation but what we think does emerge from this and other cases is that when the victim of a criminal attack is treated for wounds or injuries by doctors or other medical staff attempting to repair the harm done, it will only be in the most extraordinary and unusual case that such treatment can be said to be so independent of the acts of the accused that it could be regarded in law as the cause of the victim's death to the exclusion of the accused's acts.'

The court ruled that where a judge has to direct a jury on causation it is sufficient to tell the jury that they must be satisfied that the Crown have proved that the acts of the accused caused the death of the deceased, adding that the accused's acts need not be the sole cause or even the main cause of the death, it being sufficient that his acts contributed significantly to that result. Even though negligence in the treatment of the victim was the immediate cause of his death, the jury should not regard it as excluding the responsibility of the accused unless the negligent treatment was so independent of his acts and in itself so potent in causing death that they regard the contribution made by his acts as insignificant. The earlier case which were referred to in *R v Cheshire* were: *R v Jordan* (1956), *R v Smith* (1959), *R v Malcherek* (1981), and *R v Evans and Gardine (No2)* (1976).

The case of *R v Malcherek, R v Steel* (1981) provided the answer to the previously mooted question of the position when the victim was being kept alive by a life support machine in hospital and the doctors decided, after a time during which no recovery was apparent, to switch the machine off. Could the assailant plead 'novus actus interveniens', a new act intervening, and point to the switching off of the machine as the operative cause of death? The Court of Appeal decided against the assailant. Where by generally accepted medical criteria the victim was dead, the switching off the life support machine could not exonerate the assailant from responsibility for the death, if at the time of death the original injury was a continuing or operating cause of the death, for the disconnection of the machine did not break the chain of causation between the infliction of the original injury and the death. Few would argue with that conclusion.

Frightening your victim

Non-fatal injuries

There is authority to the effect that an assailant will be liable for the consequences where he so frightens a victim that he or she takes actions to escape and thereby injures himself or herself. A nineteenth century Chief Justice stated:

'If a man creates in another man's mind an immediate sense of danger which causes such person to try to escape, and in so doing he injures himself, the person who creates such a state of mind is responsible for the injuries which result.'

That was a case where a husband so threatened his wife that she climbed half out of her bedroom window to escape. Her daughter got hold of her to prevent her falling. Halliday shouted at her in a threatening manner to let the wife go. She did so, the wife fell to the ground and broke her leg. The husband was convicted of wilfully and maliciously inflicting grievous bodily harm on his wife. This decision was founded on earlier authorities to the effect that in such cases the victim's actions were not voluntary acts; the threats operating on her free will as effectively as physical compulsion. Similarly in *R v Lewis* (1970) where a woman jumped out of a window following a threat through the locked door that the accused would kill her. *R v Roberts* (1971) establishes that an alternative conviction in such cases could be assault occasioning actual bodily harm.

Fatal injuries

It would seem that if the deceased was forced as the only means of escape from the accused's threats or actual violence to jump from a window and dies from the injuries received from such a fall, then the attacker will be guilty of manslaughter. *R v Hickman* (1831) provides a further example. There the deceased was riding a horse and in order to escape from a violent attack by the accused, spurred his horse which reared up and threw him. He died from the injuries received in the fall and the attacker was held to be guilty of manslaughter.

The matter has been revisited more recently in *R v Williams* (1992) which considered situations where a person was injured or killed while attempting to escape from violence or after threats were made against him. It was thought that there were two requirements for a conviction. The first, which applied whether or not the injuries were fatal, related to whether a reasonable and responsible person standing in the assailant's shoes would have foreseen the victim's conduct, while the second, which applied only if the victim was killed, related to the quality of the unlawful act, which had to be such that all sober and reasonable people would have inevitably recognised that it would subject the victim to some physical harm resulting therefrom, albeit not serious. This formulation can be referred to the discussion on manslaughter in the next chapter. Consider now the relevance and effect of the following matters: the nature of the threat; whether the deceased's conduct was proportionate to the threat; whether the deceased's acts could amount to a novus actus interveniens; the chain of causation.

Consider also the application of the principles set out in *R v Williams* to variations of the facts of *Hyam v DPP* (1974) which will be considered post. Suppose that the children who died in the fire caused by Pearl Hyam had died because they had jumped out of the upstairs windows in panic to avoid the flames? If the taxi driver in the striking Welsh miners case had seen the falling concrete block and had swerved to avoid it, lost control of the car and crashed into the bridge supports and been killed by the impact, would the men have been found guilty of his murder or manslaughter?

The mental element

In addition to the physical elements discussed above most crimes require proof of some accompanying mental element referred to as 'mens rea', which is often loosely translated as meaning guilty mind. In many cases the proof of the required mens rea is the crucial element in the prosecution and the determinate of the criminal liability. Further it will be the mens rea of the accused that will often differentiate between serious and less serious crimes, as with murder and manslaughter, for example, or between causing grievous bodily harm contrary to section 18 of the Offences Against the Person Act 1861 or unlawful wounding contrary to section 20 of the same Act. Both murder and section 18 require proof of the state of mind as to 'intention' whereas 'recklessness' will suffice for manslaughter and acting 'maliciously' for section 20.

Intention and recklessness

The common law formulation of the more serious crimes such as murder or rape was usually with reference to proof of an intention to do the act and intention remains a crucial concept as the epitome of mens rea. However, increasingly crimes are defined by statute and in the modern law there is a tendency to include recklessness as an alternative ground of liability. Thus the offence of criminal damage will be committed if the actus reus (discussed above) is accompanied by the accused 'intending to destroy or damage any such property or being reckless as to whether any such property would be destroyed or damaged' (Criminal Damage Act 1971, section 1(1)). Further, in addition to this basic offence there is a more serious offence which is committed by proof of an additional mens rea, where the accused is shown to have been 'intending by the destruction or damage to endanger the life of another or being reckless as to whether the life of another would be thereby endangered' (Criminal Damage Act 1971, section 1(2)). Consider the following cases. A is trying to make a call from a public phone box but he hasn't got the correct coins. He slams the handset down onto the rest in frustration breaking it. A simple case of criminal damage? Suppose that there is another person waiting outside the box who tells A that he has to phone for an ambulance as his father has just had a heart attack. A slams the phone down breaking it, the next person cannot make his call and the father dies. A case of the aggravated offence? An additional mental element is also present in the basic definition. It must be shown that the destroying or damaging was 'without lawful excuse' and section 5(2)(a) of the 1971 Act provides that a person is deemed to have such lawful excuse:

> 'if at the time of the act or acts alleged to constitute the offence he believed that the person or persons whom he believed to be entitled to consent to the destruction of, or damage to the property in question had consented ....'

Proof of this belief can affect liability. Thus a fireman is entitled to break into a house whilst the owner is away in order to extinguish a fire. Can he break into the house next door in order to better tackle the fire even if he is told by another neighbour that the next door neighbour hated the other and would never do anything to assist him?

Dishonesty

In the crime of theft defined by section 1 of the Theft Act 1968 the basic required mens rea is that the appropriation should be done 'dishonestly'. This mental state is not defined by the Act but section 2(1) limits it to some extent by enabling the accused to negate dishonesty by proof of various 'beliefs'. For example, that he believes that he has in law the right to deprive the owner of the property, or that the owner would consent to the taking if the circumstances were known to him. In addition, in theft the accused must be shown to have intended permanently to deprive the owner of the property and this requirement is amplified in section 6 of the 1968 Act.

Murder and manslaughter

The distinction between murder and involuntary manslaughter is almost entirely dependent on the mens rea which accompanies the actus reus. Thus murder is a crime of specific intent, ie an intention to kill or an intention to cause grievous bodily harm, whereas manslaughter is a crime of unlawful killing where the specific intention is absent but some serious fault lies on the accused. Unfortunately such a simplistic formulation will not suffice, since although homicides at the most serious, and the least serious, ends of the spectrum of responsibility will easily fall into their respective categories of murder or manslaughter, the precise demarcation of the boundary in border line cases is notoriously difficult to draw. This is very largely because in recent years the cases have failed to provide a clear statement of the required mens rea of murder and the legislature has not yet provided any statutory formulation.

Consider the case of *R v Hancock, R v Shankland* (1986), which was concerned with the accused's liability for the death of a taxi driver taking a miner to work during the 1984 miners' strike. The facts were not in dispute. A concrete block of considerable size and weight fell from a bridge over a roadway and struck the windscreen of a taxi travelling along the road and killed the driver. At the same time a large concrete post also fell from the bridge on the road and hit the taxi a glancing blow. The accused admitted that they had placed the objects on the parapet of the bridge and awaited the arrival of the taxi. Hancock admitted that he had pushed the block from the bridge when he saw the vehicle approaching and Shankland admitted that he had 'flipped' the post over the parapet at the same time. These admissions established that the dropping of the objects had not been an accident or the result of merely negligent conduct, the actions had been deliberate. Further it seems clear that both accused were aware that the car was approaching and that it was occupied. Neither accused could deny that they had been responsible for the death and they could hardly plead that the falling of the objects had been an accident. But the question remained, was it murder or was it manslaughter? The answer to this question depended on the state of mind which accompanied their actions, or in other words on their mens rea.

At first instance they were convicted of murder but on appeal this was reduced to manslaughter. The crucial questions for the jury at first instance and for the judges in the appeal courts were – first, did the men cast the objects from the bridge intending them to strike the occupants of the car, and thereby intending to kill or to cause serious injury to the occupants? This was the prosecution case and if proven would result in a conviction for murder. Alternatively, did the men intend to frighten the occupants by wilfully exposing them to the risk of death or injury? – such a finding might also suffice for murder. The accused denied any such intention stating that they merely intended to block the road with the objects and thereby to prevent the miner from going to work. Further questions are relevant with reference to their foresight of probable consequences. Did they realise that what they were doing was highly dangerous and involved the probability of death or injury to the occupants of the car? And did they perceive this probability as being inevitable, highly likely, likely, possible, remote, or impossible? On such questions relating to intention, knowledge and foresight will their criminal liability depend. Further since in many cases the accused are unlikely to admit to their state of mind at the time of the offence the jury will have to infer the correct state of mind from the facts and circumstances surrounding the crime, and on this they are likely to seek the guidance of the judge. These matters will form the basis of the following discussion, but first a brief discussion of the relevance of motive in the criminal law.

Motive

Motive answers the question why someone does something. In the case involving the two Welsh striking miners discussed above the motive for their actions was no doubt to stop the working miner from reporting for work and to deter others from so doing. Perhaps in their hearts they thought this was justifiable since the victim was strike breaking and thereby prejudicing the chances of a successful outcome to their actions which had involved them and others in great hardship. No doubt anger and frustration also played a part but fundamentally they probably thought that they had a 'good' motive – just as the mercy killer will justify his actions or the puritan will justify the destruction of another's pornographic book, or a poor socialist revolutionary will justify stealing from the rich. However, most motives for crime are 'bad' and may stem from the seven deadly sins: pride, covetousness, lust, anger, gluttony, envy and sloth. But good or bad motive in this sense is in general irrelevant to the proof of mens rea since the law is not so much concerned with the emotion which prompted a particular course of action as with the intent or foresight with which the action is done.

Illustrative case law

Consider the case of *Hyam v DPP* (1974) which will need to be fully discussed post. Pearl Hyam deliberately set fire to a house and caused the death of two children who were asleep in the house. Her intention which accompanied the act of setting fire to the house was to cause a fire that would frighten the occupants by exposing them to danger. Her motive for so acting was sexual jealousy since the woman who lived in the house had supplanted her in the affections of her erstwhile lover. The former state of mind was crucial and resulted in her conviction for murder. The latter motive was irrelevant. Lord Hailsham, LC commented that motive can be used in two senses but that he preferred to restrict the meaning to the 'first sense' which he defined as follows (at p 51):

> 'In the first sense motive means an emotion prompting an act. This is the sense in which I used the term when I said that the admitted motive of the appellant was jealousy of Mrs Booth. The motive for murder in this sense may be jealousy, fear, hatred, desire for money, perverted lust, or even, as in so-called "mercy killings" compassion or love. In this sense motive is entirely distinct from intention or purpose. It is the emotion which gives rise to the intention and it is the latter and not the former which converts an actus reus into a criminal act.'

The relevance of a secret motive to prove a requisite intention, was fully discussed by the House of Lords in *R v Court* (1988), prompting a dissent by one of the Law Lords. The appellant pulled a 12 year old girl visitor into the shop in which he worked across his knees and smacked her with his hand 12 times on her bottom outside her shorts. There was no apparent reason for this action but the appellant admitted to the police that he had a 'buttock fetish'. When charged with an indecent assault he pleaded that this statement should be excluded as evidence because it was merely a secret motive which was not communicated to the victim and it could not make indecent an act which was not overtly indecent. The majority of the House of Lords disagreed. A person was guilty of indecent assault if he intentionally assaulted the victim and intended to commit an assault which any right-minded person would think was indecent. Any evidence explaining the defendant's conduct was admissible to establish whether he intended to commit an indecent assault. Lord Goff dissented, on the basis that the prosecution cannot illegitimately fortify what is assumed to be a doubtful case of an objectively indecent assault by calling evidence of a secret indecent intention on the part of the accused.

Intention

Many crimes require proof that the accused intended to do a particular thing or intended a particular consequence. Intent can be said to be the primary state of mind constituting mens rea. However, description or definition of the concept is notoriously difficult although philosophers and judges have not hesitated to try. A famous definition (see Lord Bridge in *R v Moloney* (1985)) was given by Asquith LJ in *Cunliffe v Goodman* (1950):

> 'An "intention" to my mind, connotes a state of affairs which the party intending
> – I will call him X– does more than merely contemplate. It connotes a state of
> affairs which, on the contrary, he decides, so far as in him lies, to bring about
> and which, in point of possibility, he has a reasonable prospect of being able
> to bring about, by his own act of volition.'

Hyam v DPP

A celebrated case where the issue of intention arose in the context of the mens rea of murder was *Hyam v DPP* (1974) where Asquith LJ's statement cited above was referred to. It will be recalled that Pearl Hyam was jealous of a Mrs Booth whom she feared was about to marry her erstwhile lover Mr Jones. She went to Mrs Booth's house at night and taking care not to disturb anyone she set fire to the house. Mrs Booth and one of her children escaped but the other two children died in the fire. Pearl Hyam was undoubtedly guilty of the manslaughter of the children but was she guilty of their murder? This question raised specifically the required mens rea for murder, but more generally also provoked a discussion of what would suffice to prove an intentional state of mind. Mrs Hyam intentionally, in the sense of deliberately, set fire to the house, but did she intend to kill the children? She would protest that she did not. Her intention was to frighten Mrs Booth and that object could have been achieved by the conflagration without anyone being injured. The House of Lords was divided on the issue. Lord Hailsham thought that her intention was made apparent by two sets of facts. First, that prior to setting in train her criminal plan, Mrs Hyam first ascertained that her former lover was not in the house and therefore safe, thus making it plain that her intention was to expose those who were in the house to danger to their lives. Second, that she took elaborate precautions to make sure that her actions did not awake the sleepers in the house, thus making it doubly clear that her intention was to expose them to whatever danger would be involved in the fire.

Viscount Dilhorne also thought that 'no reasonable jury could on the facts of this case have come to any other conclusion than that she had intended to do grievous bodily harm, bearing in mind her knowledge and the fact that, before she set fire to the house she took steps to make sure that Mr Jones was not in it as she did not want to harm him'. Lord Diplock also was prepared to equate the state of mind of one who does an act because he desires it to produce a particular evil consequence and the state of mind of one who does the act knowing full well that it is likely to produce that outcome although it may not be the object he was seeking to achieve by doing the act. These comments give a potentially wide meaning to intention and thus in consequence a wide embrace to the crime of murder. In a later House of Lords case, *R v Moloney* (1985) the House of Lords restricted the definition. The House made it clear that foresight of consequences is no more than evidence of the existence of the intent. Foresight does not necessarily imply the existence of intention, though it may be a fact from which when considered with all the other evidence a jury may think it right to infer the necessary intent. The probability of the result of an act is an important matter for the jury to consider and can be critical in their determining whether the result was intended.

Proof of the intention

But even if one can arrive at an acceptable definition of intention the difficulty still remains of explaining and understanding the concept. Simply telling a jury to find the accused guilty of murder if they are satisfied that he intended to kill or cause really serious injury to the victim rather begs the question and the jury are likely to respond with a request for guidance on what is meant by 'intention'. In *Moloney* Lord Bridge attempted to provide some assistance with that question as follows:

'In the rare cases in which it is necessary to direct a jury by reference to foresight of consequences, I do not believe it is necessary for the judge to do more than invite the jury to consider two questions. First, was death or really serious injury in a murder case (or whatever relevant consequence must be proved to have been intended in any other case) a natural consequence of the defendant's voluntary act? Second, did the defendant foresee that consequence as being a natural consequence of his act? The jury should then be told that if they answer Yes to both questions it is a proper inference for them to draw that he intended that consequence.'

The jury in the *Hancock* case were advised in these terms and brought in verdicts of murder. On appeal these convictions were quashed and convictions for manslaughter were substituted. This was because both the Lord Chief Justice in the Court of Appeal and the House of Lords were not happy with this formulation expressed without qualification. Lord Scarman pointed out that Lord Bridge had omitted any reference in his guidelines to probability, and commented:

'He did so because he included probability in the meaning which he attributed to "natural". My Lords, I very much doubt whether the jury without further explanation would think that "probable" added nothing to "natural". I agree with the Court of Appeal that the probability of a consequence is a factor of sufficient importance to be drawn specifically to the attention of the jury and to be explained. In a murder case where it is necessary to direct a jury on the issue of intent by reference to foresight of consequences the probability of death or serious injury resulting from the act done may be critically important. Its importance will depend on the degree of probability: if the likelihood that death or serious injury will result is high, the probability of that result may, as Lord Bridge noted and Lord Lane CJ emphasised, be seen as overwhelming evidence of the existence of the intent to kill or injure. Failure to explain the relevance of probability may, therefore, mislead a jury into thinking that it is of little or no importance and into concentrating exclusively on the causal link between the act and its consequence.'

The House of Lords emphasised that the greater the probability of a consequence, the more likely it is that the consequence was foreseen and that if that consequence was foreseen the greater the possibility that that consequence was intended.

Section 8 of the Criminal Justice Act 1967

The proof of a mental state will be difficult as it is impossible to look into the mind of man, and so in the absence of an admission, the accused's state of mind is inferred from the circumstances. If a man places a large bomb on an aircraft timed to go off when the plane is in flight which it does causing the death of all the passengers no amount of denial will prevent a jury from concluding that the accused intended to kill the passengers. This is because their death is a virtual certainty from his actions. Other cases are not so clear. In *DPP v Smith* (1960) the accused was in a car when he was approached by a policeman. In order to prevent apprehension he drove off. The policeman clung to the bonnet of the car and Smith drove in a manner to shake him off. The policeman fell off into the path of another vehicle, was run over and killed. Smith protested that he did not intend to kill the policeman but merely to escape, an object that he could have achieved equally well if the policeman had suffered no harm. However, injury or death to the policeman was a highly likely consequence to his actions and the House of Lords in confirming his conviction declared in effect, an irrebuttable presumption that a man intends the natural and probable consequences of his acts. This was immediately criticised as basing liability for murder on objective criteria, ie dependent not on what the accused foresaw but on probable consequences assessed as an objective fact. Statutory intervention followed. Section 8 of the Criminal Justice Act 1967 provides:

'A court or jury, in determining whether a person has committed an offence –

(a) shall not be bound in law to infer that he intended or foresaw a result of his actions by reason only of its being a natural and probable consequence of those actions; but

(b) shall decide whether he did intend or foresee that result by reference to all the evidence obtaining such inferences from the evidence as appear proper in the circumstances.'

The effect of this provision has been considered by the House of Lords in *DPP v Hyam* (supra), *R v Moloney* (supra) and in *R v Hancock* and there seems no doubt that the objectivity in *Smith* has been removed. Proof of an intention is to be achieved by reference to subjective criteria, ie by what the accused foresaw or knew and there is no place in the modern law for a presumption that a man is taken to have intended the natural and probable consequences of his actions.

Specific or ulterior intent

Some crimes are categorised as offences which require proof of a specific or ulterior intent going beyond the mens rea which accompanies the actus reus. This somewhat troublesome doctrine is relevant to the application of the defence of drunkenness and is considered post in that context.

Transferred malice

Any first year law student knows (according to Lord Bridge in *R v Moloney*) the answer to the question, what is the position if the accused shot at A and killed B? Guilty of the murder of B if he intended to kill A because, as the law says, the malice against A is transferred to B. This is established by *R v Latimer* (1886) where the accused in striking at a man, struck and wounded a woman beside him. But the intention can only be transferred to a like result; if A strikes at a window intending only to damage the building and strikes B then the intention to damage property cannot be transferred to become an intention to injure a person. Likewise when A strikes at B, misses and damages the building. However in these cases if A is shown to have been reckless vis a vis the actual victim then that might be sufficient mens rea directly attributable to the offence committed. In other words if A throws a stone at B and misses and breaks a window he intends to injure B but may be reckless as to whether he damages the building.

Recklessness

The mens rea of many statutory crimes, and some common law offences, can be proved by establishing a reckless state of mind. Few concepts in the criminal law have been the subject of such controversy and difficulty, as the meaning of recklessness. The House of Lords have considered the meaning and application of the term in several modern cases, *R v Caldwell* and *R v Lawrence* in 1982, *R v Seymour* in 1983, *R v Savage*, *R v Parmenter* in 1991 and *R v Reid* in 1992.

Objective or subjective?

The debate centres on whether the test to be applied to the proof of the required foresight should be subjective, ie did the accused foresee the consequences of his actions, or objective, ie does it suffice to show that a reasonable man in the circumstances of the accused, would have foreseen the consequences. The traditional attitude has been to require proof of subjective foresight as in the case of *R v Cunningham* (1957) which concerned a prosecution to '... unlawfully and maliciously administer to or cause to be administered to or taken by any other person any poison or other destructive or noxious thing so as to endanger the life of such person' contrary to section 23 of the Offences Against the Person Act 1861. The court declared :

> 'in any statutory definition of a crime "malice" must be taken not in the old vague sense of wickedness in general but as requiring either (a) an actual intention to do the particular kind of harm that was in fact done, or (b) recklessness as to whether such harm should occur or not (ie the accused has foreseen that the particular kind of harm might be done, and yet has gone on to take the risk of it). It is neither limited to nor does it require any ill will towards the person injured.'

This approach to recklessness was developed in subsequent cases, as in *R v Briggs* (1977) where it was stated:

> 'A man is reckless in the sense required when he carries out a deliberate act knowing that there is some risk of damage resulting from that act but nevertheless continues in the performance of that act.

A similar approach justified the quashing of the conviction for arson of a schizophrenic vagrant in *R v Stephenson* (1979). The court emphasised that the correct test of whether a person was 'reckless' for the purposes of that offence was the subjective test of whether the particular person (as opposed to a reasonable man) had knowledge or foresight of the risk of damage from his act. In this case the evidence suggested that the accused had lit a fire in a hay stack to keep warm without proof that he had foreseen that the whole stack would thereby catch fire. An understanding of that risk might have been obvious to a reasonable man, but the accused was not, by reason of his medical condition, a reasonable man.

A gloss was put on the *Cunningham* decision in *R v Mowatt* (1968) which was concerned with a prosecution for wounding with intent contrary to section 18 of the Offences Against the Person Act 1861. The Court of Appeal referred to the 'very special facts' in Cunningham, stating that no doubt upon these facts the jury should have been instructed that they must be satisfied before convicting the accused that he was aware that physical harm to some human being was a possible consequence of his unlawful act. Diplock LJ then stated that the word 'maliciously' did import upon the part of the person who unlawfully inflicts the wound or other grievous bodily harm an awareness that his act may have the consequence of causing some physical harm to some person, but that it was quite unnecessary that the accused should have foreseen that his unlawful act might cause physical harm of the gravity described in the section, ie a wound or serious physical injury. It is enough that he should have foreseen that some physical harm to some person, albeit of a minor character, might result.

THE HOUSE OF LORDS DECISIONS

The issue was reconsidered by the House of Lords in the somewhat controversial decision in *R v Caldwell* (1981). In that case the accused set fire to a residential hotel at night. It appeared that he had been employed at the hotel and nursed a grievance against the proprietor. The Criminal Damage Act 1971 creates two offences in section 1. First, the basic offence of destroying or damaging another's property either intentionally or 'being reckless whether any such property would be destroyed or damaged'. Second, a more serious offence is committed where the act is done with the further element that the accused at the time was 'intending by the destruction or damage to endanger the life of another or being reckless as to whether the life of another would be thereby endangered'. The accused pleaded guilty to the lesser offence but not guilty to the more serious charge, arguing that he was so drunk at the time that it never occurred to him that there might be people whose lives would be endangered by his act. His appeal against conviction was dismissed, the House holding that if a charge under section 1(2) of the Act was so framed as to charge the defendant only with the intent to endanger life, evidence of self-induced drunkenness could be relevant as a defence, but (by a majority), not when the charge included a reference to being reckless as to whether life would be endangered. The appeal was essentially concerned with the meaning of the word 'reckless' in the section and whether the defendant's state of mind at the time of the offence corresponded with the mens rea demanded by the word. The House of Lords reviewed the meaning of the word and Lord Diplock delivering the majority decision gave to it a meaning which surprised many commentators, and which could be regarded as being inconsistent with the previous understanding. Two of the judges, Lord Edmund-Davies and Lord Wilberforce dissented. Lord Diplock stated:

'"Reckless" as used in the new statutory definition of the mens rea of these offences is an ordinary English word, it had not by 1971 become a term of legal art with some more limited esoteric meaning than that which it bore in ordinary speech, a meaning which surely includes not only deciding to ignore a risk of harmful consequences resulting from one's acts that one has recognised as existing, but also failing to give any thought to whether there is any such risk in circumstances where, if any thought were given to the matter, it would be obvious that there was.

... in my opinion a person charged with an offence under section 1(1) of the 1971 Act is "reckless as to whether or not any property would be destroyed or damaged" if (I) he does an act which in fact creates an obvious risk that property will be destroyed or damaged, and (2) when he does the act he either has not given any thought to the possibility of there being any such risk or has recognised that there was some risk involved and has none the less gone on to do it. That would be a proper direction to the jury. Cases in the Court of Appeal which held otherwise should be regarded as overruled.'

This formulation does not confine the state of mind to subjective foresight. The reference to 'failing to give any thought to whether there is any such risk in circumstances where, if any thought were given to the matter, it would be obvious that there was' introduces objective criteria, ie obvious to a reasonable man. *R v Cunningham* was distinguished on the basis that the restriction on the natural meaning of recklessness was necessary to an explanation of the meaning of the adverb 'maliciously' when used as a term of art in the description of an offence under the Malicious Damage Act 1861, but it was not directed to and consequently had no bearing on the meaning of the adjective 'reckless' in section 1 of the Criminal Damage Act 1971. *R v Mowatt* was not considered. The objective approach of *R v Caldwell* has been subject to much comment and criticism both academic and judicial, but as a House of Lords authority, the case will be applied to cases directly covered by it, such as in prosecutions under the Criminal Damage Act 1971 (*R v Sangha* (1988)).

Subsequent decisions by the House of Lords in *R v Lawrence* (1982), a case concerning causing death by reckless driving contrary to section 1 of the Road Traffic Act 1972, and *R v Seymour* (1983) (a manslaughter case) are now of less relevance since the Road Traffic Act 1991 introduced a new section 1 offence using the word 'dangerously' rather than 'recklessly'.

Three case studies

The House of Lords appeal in *R v Savage*, *R v Parmenter* (1991) arose out of a trilogy of contemporaneous Court of Appeal cases on sections 20 and 47 of the Offences Against the Person Act 1861, namely *R v Spratt* (1991), *R v Savage* (1991) and *R v Parmenter* (1991). Section 20 refers to 'maliciously wound' and section 47 refers to 'assault', which is traditionally defined with reference to recklessness. The specific issues raised by these cases will be discussed in the next chapter, but the general question of the requisite mens rea can be noted here.

In the first of these cases, Spratt, the appellant, unaware that children were playing outside, fired an air pistol through a window in his flat. Two of the pellets struck a seven year old girl. He was charged with assault occasioning actual bodily harm contrary to section 47 of the 1861 Act. The conviction was quashed by the Court of Appeal because it was thought that the section required a subjective foresight of the risk of harm.

At the same time a different division of the Court of Appeal was considering the appeal in *R v Savage* where both section 20 and section 47 were in issue. In that case the appellant threw a glass of beer over the complainant, a former girl friend of the appellant's husband, in a public house. The complainant was injured by the glass or a splinter from it either when the glass struck a table and shattered while the appellant was throwing the beer over the complainant or when, the appellant having deliberately thrown the beer over the complainant or the table, the glass accidentally slipped from her grasp and struck the complainant. The Appeal Court quashed the conviction for unlawful and malicious wounding contrary to section 20 of the 1861 Act, since the judge had failed to direct the jury that they had to find that the appellant foresaw that some physical harm, apart from wetting the complainant with beer, would follow as the result of what she had done. But the court substituted a conviction for assault occasioning actual bodily harm contrary to section 47 of the 1861 Act, holding that no proof of foresight was required for that offence.

The inconsistency of approach thus revealed was considered in the third of these cases, *R v Parmenter*. The Court of Appeal chose to follow *R v Spratt* and disapproved of *R v Savage*, insisting that a defendant could not be convicted under section 20 unless he actually foresaw that physical harm to some other person would be the consequence of his act, although it was not necessary that he actually foresaw that the harm would be as grave as that which actually occurred. Further that the offence under section 47 was not made out if the defendant acted without intending or appreciating the risk of the possibility of physical harm. The House of Lords dismissed the appeal in the *Savage* case but allowed the appeal in *Parmenter*'s case. The House's general observations on the general meaning of recklessness will be noted here. Lord Ackner, delivering the judgment of the House thought that the *Caldwell* case accepted that *Cunningham* (subject to the Mowatt 'gloss' to which no reference was made) correctly stated the law in relation to the Offences Against the Person Act 1861. The word 'maliciously' in that statute was a term of legal art which imported into the concept of recklessness a special meaning, thus distinguishing it from 'reckless' or 'recklessly' in modern 'revising' statutes then before the House, where those words bore their then popular or dictionary meaning. Therefore in order to establish an offence under section 20 the prosecution must prove either that the defendant intended, or that he actually foresaw, that his act would cause some harm, but that it is unnecessary to prove that the accused should have intended or have foreseen that his unlawful act might cause physical harm of the gravity described in the section, namely a wound or serious physical injury. So far as section 47 is concerned the House thought that it is not necessary for the prosecution to prove that the defendant intended to cause some actual bodily harm or was reckless as to whether such harm would be caused.

Strict liability

Having declared initially that all crimes require proof of an actus reus and a mens rea it is now necessary to note that exceptionally some crimes can be committed without proof of mens rea. Such crimes are almost wholly statutory offences and are known as crimes of strict liability; they are also sometimes incorrectly, referred to as 'absolute offences'.

Public safety

Many are offences of a regulatory public safety type and the justification for the absence of mens rea is the necessity to ensure observance and enforcement. Thus in one of the recent cases (*Seaboard Offshore Ltd v Secretary of State for Transport, The Safe Carrier*, 1993) a provision of the Merchant Shipping Act 1988 was held to create 'absolute liability'. The section in question was aimed at the protection of life and property at sea which was of such importance that Parliament might well have thought it necessary to impose sanctions even on persons who were ignorant or forgetful, and assuming therefore, in the absence of express mention of any criminal state of mind, that failing 'to take all reasonable steps to secure that the ship is operated in a safe manner', did not require the implication of a criminal state of mind; the wording of the section defined all that was needed to be proved. To require prosecutors to prove knowledge or intention would in many such cases be a burden that would be very difficult to discharge. Additionally the real defendant in many of these cases is a business or trading organisation and the penalty is a fine.

There are many cases that could be referred to but a reference to a couple must suffice here. In the Privy Council decision in *Gammon (Hong Kong) Ltd v A-G of Hong Kong* (1984) the defendants were the registered contractor, the project manager and the site agents for building works on a site in Hong Kong. Part of a building in the process of construction collapsed and the defendants were charged with a breach of the building regulations. On appeal the Privy Council held that the relevant regulations (the details of which need not concern us here) created offences of strict liability and that the appellants were guilty. The following general principles were reiterated. First, there is a presumption of law that mens rea is required before a person can be held guilty of a criminal offence. Second, the presumption is particularly strong where the offence is 'truly criminal' in character. Third, the presumption applies to statutory offences and can be displaced only if this is clearly or by necessary implication the effect of the statute. Fourth, the only situation in which the presumption can be displaced is where the statute is concerned with an issue of social policy; public safety is such an issue. Fifth, even where a statute is concerned with such an issue, the presumption of mens rea stands when it can also be shown that the creation of strict liability will be effective to promote the objects of the statute by encouraging greater vigilance to prevent the commission of the prohibited act.

Drugs offences

Clearly in regulatory offences particularly those involving the processing or sale of food and drink the necessity to ensure maximum public protection can be regarded as a matter of policy as sufficient justification for the principle. However, much more controversy surrounds any such liability for more serious offences. In *Sweet v Parsley* (1969) the appellant took a sub-lease of a farm house outside Oxford intending to live in it herself and commute to her place of work. This proved impractical and so she sub-let the house. She retained one room in the house for herself and visited the house occasionally to collect letters, to collect rent from the tenants and generally to see that all was well. Whilst she was in Oxford the police no doubt pursuant to information, searched the house and found receptacles containing cannabis and LSD. Miss Sweet was found guilty of being concerned in the management of premises which were being used for the purpose of smoking cannabis, contrary to section 5(b) of the Dangerous Drugs Act 1965 (since replaced). She appealed, alleging that she had no knowledge of the circumstances and indeed could not be expected reasonably to have had such knowledge. The House of Lords allowed her appeal. Lord Morris reiterated the 'cardinal principle' of our law that mens rea, an evil intention or a knowledge of the wrongfulness of the act is in all ordinary cases an essential ingredient of guilt of a criminal offence. It is only if the words of the statute (or the nature of the subject matter) clearly displace this presumption that strict liability should be imposed. Looking at the wording of the statute, the subject matter with which it was concerned, the nature of the offence and the possible punishments that might follow, the House was confident that Parliament did not intend to make the offence with which Miss Sweet was charged an offence of strict liability. In contrast a pharmacist who supplied restricted drugs on a forged prescription, was found guilty of an offence although there was no knowledge or fault on his part (*Pharmaceutical Society of Great Britain v Storkwain* (1986)).

Coincidence of actus reus and mens rea

It is essential that the mens rea should accompany or coincide with the actus reus. This is particularly important where the actus reus consists of a single act rather than a series of repeated acts or a state of affairs. Suppose that A strikes B on the head and renders him unconscious. A then believes that he has killed him and so he pushes the 'body' over a cliff dressing up the scene to make it look like an accident. In fact the man is not then dead and medical evidence establishes that the cause of his death is exposure from being left unconscious at the foot of the cliff. A might argue that the striking over the head and the pushing over the cliff were two separate acts. The mens rea of intending to cause grievous bodily harm (sufficient for murder – see post) accompanied the first act but the consequence necessary for the actus reus of murder (ie the man's death) was not caused by that act. When A pushed the body over the cliff he caused the death but at that time he had no accompanying mens rea since he thought the man was already dead. Thus he will seek to avoid conviction by in effect pleading that there was no coincidence between the mens rea and the actus reus. Such were indeed the facts and the argument in the Privy Council case of *Thabo Meli v R* (1954). However, in that case the plea did not succeed because the court was not inclined to split up the acts into separate events. They thought that the accused's conduct was really one series of acts with sufficient coincidence of the essential elements of murder to justify the conviction. But consider what the position would have been if A had left B unconscious at the scene and returned several hours later to dispose of the 'body' and had thereby caused his death (see also *R v Church* (1965) discussed post).

Continuing actus reus

Crimes which have a state of affairs actus reus or a continuing actus reus cause less problem since the offence will be committed if the necessary mens rea is formed at any time the actus reus continues. It is not necessary that the mens rea should be initially present. In *Kaitamaki v R* (1984) the accused was charged with rape and he alleged that at the time of the initial penetration of the woman he thought the woman was consenting although he admitted that he was subsequently aware during the act of intercourse that she was not. He was held guilty; sexual intercourse was a continuing act which only ended after withdrawal.

Chapter 10

Offences against the person

Offences against the person fall into the two main categories of fatal and non-fatal offences. The offences of homicide will be considered first.

Homicide

Unlawful killings can be divided into the two main categories of murder or manslaughter but include also the offences of infanticide and child destruction and causing death by dangerous driving contrary to the Road Traffic Act 1991. This discussion will concentrate on murder and manslaughter; the latter being traditionally divided into voluntary and involuntary. Unlawful killings can cover a wide spectrum of culpability from cases of intentional cold blooded killing to cases which are 'nearly accidents' but where the circumstances involve sufficient fault to justify a criminal conviction.

Murder and manslaughter

Murder, which historically carried the death penalty and attracts a mandatory life sentence and restrictive rules for parole, is reserved for a narrow band of culpability at the top end of the spectrum of heinousness. It is traditionally characterised by an intentional state of mind.

Voluntary manslaughters are cases where a charge of murder is reduced to a conviction for manslaughter by virtue of one of three statutorily formulated mitigating factors. These three categories are fixed and there is no discretion in a court to reduce murder to manslaughter in other circumstances. Thus in the leading case of *R v Clegg* (1995) a British soldier serving in Northern Ireland shot and killed a civilian in circumstances which were not justifiable. His plea of self defence to a charge of murder failed because the force used was excessive and unreasonable and the House of Lords ruled that such a plea could not reduce a culpable homicide from murder to manslaughter.

Involuntary manslaughters cover a wide range of the other unlawful killings and can be considered under several heads but in the modern law tend to be categorised under the two principal heads of deaths consequential to an unlawful and dangerous act and deaths caused by gross negligence.

Murder and manslaughter share many common criteria with reference to the actus reus but are distinguished by the accompanying mens rea. Clear cases of each are readily identifiable but the distinction at the boundary can be difficult. This is partly because different judges have formulated the mens rea of murder in slightly different terms which leads to the possibility of different conclusions when applied to the more difficult factual circumstances, but also because even with an agreed and settled test the ascertainment of the mind of the accused, closed to all but himself, is difficult. Consider again the case of *R v Hancock, R v Shankland*, concerning the two Welsh miners who dropped a concrete block and a concrete post onto the taxi carrying a working miner to work and killed the driver. Was that a case of murder or of manslaughter? There is room for disagreement in such a case even among High Court and appeal judges.

In many such cases, there is no doubt that the accused was criminally responsible for an unlawful killing and was deserving of a custodial sentence. The two miners *Hancock* and *Shankland* (in the case discussed in the previous chapter) were, on their own case guilty at least of manslaughter by deliberately committing an unlawful and dangerous act which involved the risk of injury. Likewise Pearl Hyam who deliberately set fire to a house resulting in the death of two children. Although the death penalty has been abolished it is still crucial for the accused to seek to avoid a conviction for murder because the latter will result in a life sentence and will thus be subject to a more stringent procedure when the question of parole comes to be considered: only the Home Secretary can sanction release of life sentence prisoners. It has been proposed on several occasions, that the mandatory life sentence for murder should be abolished. But all such proposals have been rejected by the Government, who feel that public opinion demands some demarcation of the most heinous killings, and that this can best be done by having a distinct penalty for murder.

It can certainly be argued with some justification that the present apparently rigid (in consequence at least) distinction between murder and manslaughter should be abolished in favour of a simple offence of homicide, or unlawful killing. In cases where an unlawful killing is established the accused's state of mind and the circumstances would then be crucial not in order to determine the nature of the conviction but in order to determine the appropriate level of punishment. Such a proposal has been made by reformers and by judges but has not, for various policy and political reasons, been given legislative effect. A final word: voluntary manslaughter is a statutory creation and subject to statutory principles; murder and involuntary manslaughter are common law crimes and have no statutory definition.

Murder

ACTUS REUS

The act required is that the accused should do something which directly causes the victim's death; the circumstances are that the act was unlawful and that the victim was a living human being; the consequence is that the victim should die.

The act

The act which causes the death will generally be in the nature of a direct assault on the victim, whether with or without a weapon. Thus shooting, stabbing, clubbing, poisoning or strangling are clearly sufficient. But it will also suffice to show that the accused directly although not immediately caused the death. Thus pushing the victim over a cliff or into the path of a train; or placing a deadly snake in the victim's bed or cutting the brake cables on the victim's car. In all of these the accused's act, if accompanied by the requisite mens rea, could be a sufficiently direct cause of the death to amount to murder.

Indirect acts

Consider other indirect acts which have been held to be murder. There is an old case where a gaoler confined a prisoner in a dank room which was considered to be 'very unwholesome and most dangerous to the health'. The prisoner died and the court clearly thought that this could amount to murder. (Huggins, the warden of the gaol, was found not guilty because he was not present at or directly responsible for the confinement of the prisoner. The actual gaoler was found guilty.) 'Murder may be committed without a stroke.' The court referred to earlier cases where an infant was laid in a hog sty and a sow ate it; where an infant was laid under leaves in an orchard and a kite struck it; where a ferocious beast was let loose knowing that it would attack and kill someone: in all these cases it was thought to be murder if the mens rea was present.

In *Castell v Bambridge* (1729) it was declared that it would be murder for a gaoler to confine a prisoner in a room occupied by another prisoner with smallpox, so that the prisoner caught the disease and died. This seems correct provided that the gaoler knew of the smallpox and intended death or grievous bodily harm to the first prisoner. A more modern illustration would be where a person who knows that he is suffering from Aids, deliberately infects another with the virus. Such cases return us to the problem of causation considered above. The accused can certainly be guilty even if the victim or others contributed by their acts to the death. Thus *Blaue* and *Cheshire*, discussed above, were guilty. Consider also what would have been the position in *Blaue* if the girl had been raped, not fatally injured, and she had felt such shame over the incident that she had taken her own life. *Blaue* seems to suggest that the principle that 'you should take your victim as you find him' extends to beliefs, and thus to mental conditions as well as to physical ones.

SEPARATE ASSAULTS

Returning to more settled principles it is established that if it is shown that the accused was responsible for a number of separate assaults against the victim any one of which could have caused the death, then it is not necessary for the prosecution to show precisely which act was the immediate cause of death.

More difficult is the situation where it is shown that a number of persons assaulted the victim who died as a result of the combination of the injuries, as where a gang punch and kick a person to death. In such cases it is certainly not necessary to prove that the accused was the sole cause of death; it is usually expressed that it should be shown that his act was a significant or substantial cause of the death. The matter becomes one of fact and degree and evidence and will usually be left to a jury for their determination.

CONCERTED ACTION

It is of course clear that two or more persons can be jointly responsible for the death and jointly liable for murder. A useful ruling was given by the Lord Chief Justice in the case of *R v Hyde* (1990). If a secondary party realised, without agreeing to such conduct being used, that a fellow assailant in a fight might kill or intentionally inflict serious injury, but nevertheless continued to participate with the assailant in the fight, then that amounted to a sufficient mental element for the secondary party to be guilty of murder if the assailant, with the requisite intent, killed the victim in the course of the fight, since in those circumstances the secondary party had lent himself to the enterprise and by so doing had given assistance and encouragement to the assailant in carrying out an enterprise which the secondary party realised might involve murder. This formulation has been applied by the Privy Council in *Hui Chi-Ming v R* (1991) and by the House of Lords in *R v Roberts* (1993). In the former case the emphasis was put upon participating in the joint enterprise with foresight that the principal might commit the relevant act as part of the joint enterprise; the prior contemplation of the principal was not a necessary additional ingredient that had to be proved to render the secondary party guilty.

A person who is a party to a joint enterprise which resulted in the death of another could be liable for manslaughter even though he did not strike the blow if the relevant act was committed in the course of carrying out the joint enterprise (*R v Stewart* 1995). The House of Lords has stated as a principle of general application,that a person involved in a joint unlawful enterprise could be guilty of murder if he realised (without agreeing to such conduct being used) that the other party involved might kill or intentionally inflict serious injury but nevertheless continued to participate with the other party in the venture and the other party, with the requisite intent, killed in the course of the venture. One can test these formulations by asking some questions. Does it matter whether weapons were carried or not ? Or whether the object of the enterprise was to cause physical injury or to commit some other unlawful act such as burglary or robbery? What is the position if the secondary party fleetingly thinks of the risk of the principal using violence with murderous intent in the course of the joint enterprise only to dismiss it from his mind and goes on to lend himself to the venture?

A LIVING HUMAN BEING

It is an obvious and basic requirement that the accused should have caused the death of a living human being. Difficult questions are posed by the killing of unborn infants, in the course of being born or shortly after birth. Unborn infants are protected by section 58 of the Offences Against the Person Act 1861, section 1 of the Infant Life (Preservation) Act 1929 and by the Abortion Act 1967. It is clear on the older authorities that it can be murder to give a child a mortal wound whilst it is in the course of being born or shortly after it has been born. The difficulty lies in formulating a test of independent existence – is the test whether the baby has breathed, or whether it has been wholly expelled from its mother's body, or whether the umbilical cord has been severed? There is confusion evident in the older authorities and the matter is probably best left to the good sense of the jury guided by appropriate medical evidence.

LIFE SUPPORT MACHINES

It is impossible to murder a person already dead, even if the accused believes him to be alive, although such a circumstance might amount to an attempt to murder. At one time people were fairly confident that they knew whether a person was alive or dead. Breathing and circulation were regarded as the crucial test and if both were absent the person was declared dead. Any attack subsequent to that time could not amount to murder. However, advances in modern medicine have made the problem much more difficult since it is now recognised that death is a very complex process. A person who has stopped breathing can sometimes be made to breathe again by mouth to mouth resuscitation; circulation can sometimes be restored by manual manipulation or electric stimulation of the heart. Further, both functions can be supplied artificially by life support machines. It is accepted now that brain activity is a more vital and accurate determinant of life or death and this can be measured by electronic probes. If all brain activity has ceased then the person is dead even if their body is being kept functioning by artificial aids.

Consider again *R v Malcherek* and *R v Steel* (1981). The victim in the first case was stabbed, she collapsed in hospital, and shortly afterwards her heart stopped beating. Surgery was performed to remove a blood clot from the pulmonary artery and thereafter the heart, after not beating for thirty minutes, started to beat again. Because of the danger of brain damage resulting from the period when the heart was not beating, the woman was put on a life support machine. Three days later she was found to have suffered irretrievable brain damage. The next day the decision was made to disconnect the life support machine and shortly afterwards the woman was declared to be dead. In the second case involving Steel, the accused attacked a girl and caused her grave head injuries. On the same day she was taken to hospital and put on a life support machine. Two days later the doctors concluded that her brain had ceased to function and the machine was disconnected. Shortly after she was declared dead. Both accused were convicted of murder and their appeals were dismissed. The court stated that there was a body of opinion in the medical profession that there was only one true test of death and that is the irreversible death of the brain stem which controls the basic functions of the body such as breathing. The switching off of the life support machines and the consequent cessation of circulation and breathing by artificial means was not the cause of death. A similar approach was adopted in the decision in *R v Pagett* (1983) where the defendant armed with a shotgun had taken a sixteen year old girl as hostage. He fired shots at police officers using the girl's body as a shield from any retaliation by the officers. She was killed by shots fired at the defendant by the officers in instinctive reaction to his firing at them. It was held that the act of firing at the police and the act of holding the girl as a shield was the cause of the girl's death sufficient to constitute the actus reus of manslaughter even though the shot which killed her was fired not by the defendant but by a police officer. The shooting by the officers was a natural consequence of the defendant's actions and did not break the chain of causation.

Mens rea of murder

There are two clear and established states of mind that will justify a conviction for murder. First, an intention to kill, which needs little further elucidation. Second, an intention to cause grievous bodily harm, which simply means an intention to cause serious injury even if there is no intention to kill or to endanger life (see *R v Vickers* (1957)). *DPP v Smith* (1960) which although strongly disapproved of, and overruled in part by section 8 of the Criminal Justice Act 1967, remains good law on this point (see *Hyam v DPP* (1974)). The intention to cause grievous bodily harm, with death resulting, has traditionally been accepted as a sufficient mens rea for murder and can be justified on the grounds first, that proof of an actual intention to kill in all cases would place an intolerable burden on prosecutors; second, historically inflicting grievous bodily harm was tantamount to putting a person's life in danger – granted the then state of medical expertise. Lord Diplock in a dissenting speech in *Hyam* sought to justify a reformulation of the head in the modern law as an intention to endanger life but this was expressly rejected by the House of Lords in a subsequent case (*R v Cunningham* (1981)).

PROOF OF MENS REA

In many cases of murder the proof of the mens rea will not cause difficulties. If the defendant is proved to have deliberately shot or stabbed his victim the jury will conclude that he intended to kill or cause serious injury so that if the victim dies, the accused will be found guilty of murder. But difficulties arise in more oblique cases, where the primary motivation of the defendant is to achieve one purpose which results in the death of the victim. In such cases questions of foreseeability, probability and natural consequences arise which can cause difficult problems for the courts and for juries. The case of *Hyam*, supra, highlighted the difficulty. On the facts it could be argued that Pearl Hyam did not intend as a direct and primary motivation the death of the two children. Her intention was, immediately, to set fire to the house, and ultimately to frighten or terrorise the occupant Mrs Booth by the fire. The judge had directed the jury in the following terms:

'The prosecution must prove, beyond all reasonable doubt, that the accused intended to (kill or) do serious bodily harm to Mrs Booth, the mother of the deceased girls. If you are satisfied that when the accused set fire to the house she knew that it was highly probable that this would cause (death or) serious bodily harm then the prosecution will have established the necessary intent. It matters not that her motive was, as she says to frighten Mrs Booth.'

The jury convicted her of murder on this direction and the House of Lords in reviewing the case had to decide whether this was a correct direction or not. The crucial question under consideration was whether it sufficed for the crime of murder, if short of an actual intention to kill, that the accused knew that it was highly probable that the act would result in death or serious bodily harm. Viscount Dilhorne thought that it was; Lord Diplock dissented and would have allowed the appeal and Lord Kilbrandon (in a short speech adding nothing of substance to the issue in question) appeared to support Lord Diplock and certainly would also have allowed the appeal. Lord Cross's position on the wording does not appear clearly from his speech but he concluded in a qualified way that the answer to the question posed above should be in the affirmative and voted to dismiss the appeal. Lord Hailsham's speech as the leading judgment in favour of the majority conclusion is in many respects the most interesting. He did not specifically approve the formulation above but preferred to justify the conviction on the ground that it will suffice where the defendant knows that there is a serious risk that death or grievous bodily harm will ensue from his acts, and commits those acts deliberately and without lawful excuse, the intention to expose a potential victim to that risk as the result of those acts. Thus after *Hyam* there was little clarification but some confusion on the central issue of the required mens rea for murder to the consternation not only of law students but of judges charged with directing juries as well.

TWO ILLUSTRATIVE CASES

The House of Lords attempted to clarify the position in *R v Moloney* (1985). The appellant was at the time of the incident on leave from the army and living with his mother and stepfather, with whom he was by all accounts on the best of terms. A dinner party was held during which the appellant and the stepfather drank a large quantity of alcohol. They remained up after the other family members had departed or gone to bed. Shortly after 4 am a shot was fired and the appellant was heard to declare, 'I have shot my father'. Two shotguns were found at the scene, one of which had been fired resulting in the death. The actual circumstances of the shooting were not entirely clear but it would seem that the appellant and the stepfather had had a contest to see who could load their gun and be ready to fire first. The appellant won and stood pointing the gun at his stepfather when by his own admission he pulled the trigger and the gun fired, killing his stepfather instantly. There is no doubt that Moloney was criminally responsible for the death and certainly could not avoid a conviction for manslaughter. However, at first sight it looked like a case of murder; was it? The actus reus was admitted; the mental state of Moloney at the time of the killing needed further examination. He said, 'I didn't aim the gun. I just pulled the trigger and he was dead'. 'I never deliberately aimed at him and fired at him intending to hurt him or to aim close to him intending to frighten him.' 'In my state of mind I never considered that the probable consequence of what I might do might result in injury to my father. I never conceived that what I was doing might cause injury to anybody. It was just a lark.' The jury had been directed that it would suffice if the accused desired a certain consequence to happen or if he foresaw that it would probably happen whether he desired it or not. This direction was expressly disapproved of by the House who set aside the conviction for murder and substituted a verdict of manslaughter. Lord Bridge noted that the fact that when the appellant fired the gun the gun was pointing directly at his stepfather's head at a range of about six feet was not and could not be disputed. 'The sole issue was whether, when he pressed the trigger, this fact and its inevitable consequence were present to the appellant's mind.' Recognising the difficulty of proving a particular state of mind Lord Bridge thought that foresight of consequence as an element bearing on the issue of intention in murder, belonged not to the substantive law but to the law of evidence. It was said that the matter was best left to the good sense of the jury but where the judge feels it necessary to direct the jury he should invite them to consider two relevant questions. First, was death or really serious injury in a murder case a natural consequence of the defendant's voluntary act? Second, did the defendant foresee that consequence as being a natural consequence of his act?

The matter was re-examined in the more recent case concerning the two striking miners, *R v Hancock, R v Shankland* (1986). The basic facts were not in dispute and were summarised as follows by Lord Lane CJ. At about 5.15 am on 30 November 1984 a convoy taking a miner, David Williams, to work during the miners' strike was travelling in the nearside lane of the Heads of the Valleys Road and passing under Rhymney Bridge. The convoy comprised the following vehicles: first, a police motor cycle; next a police Land Rover with driver and observer; third, a taxi driven by David Wilkie with David Williams, the miner, as a passenger; and, finally, a police Sherpa van bringing up the rear. A concrete block weighing 46 lb and measuring 18 inches by 5 inches or thereabouts came from the bridge, struck the taxi's windscreen and killed Wilkie the driver. At almost the same time a concrete post weighing some 65 lb also came from the bridge, fell onto the inside lane of the carriageway and hit the taxi a glancing blow. Both appellants had, shortly before 5 am that morning, placed the post on the parapet rail of the bridge. The appellant Hancock placed the block on the rail. The two appellants waited for the arrival of the convoy. The appellant Hancock admitted in a written statement that he had pushed the block which killed Wilkie and he pleaded guilty to manslaughter. The appellant Shankland admitted in chief that he flipped the post over the rail with his fingers. He too apparently accepted that he was guilty of manslaughter. The Crown were not content with those admissions and the trial of the murder charge took place. Additional evidence in support of the prosecution case was that the police officers in the Land Rovers said that they saw two figures standing on the bridge in such a way as to make them fear that something was going to be thrown off the bridge at them. Further that there was evidence of ill-feeling between Hancock and the non-striking miner, Williams.

The trial judge adopted the *Moloney* guidelines in his direction to the jury who found both defendants guilty of murder. On appeal convictions for manslaughter were substituted because the appeal court was unhappy about some aspects of the *Moloney* decision. In particular the court did not think it correct to invite the jury to conclude that an accused intended a consequence merely because it was a natural consequence of his act. Quite improbable and remote results could be attributed to the accused on this test. What should be emphasised was the degree of probability of the consequence and the Lord Chief Justice thought that the jury should be told that 'natural consequences' means that it must have been highly likely that the defendant's act would cause death or serious injury before the inference can be drawn that he had the necessary intent. The verdict is, of course, a matter for the jury in the light of the guidance given by the judge in his summing up of the case. Juries are essentially arbiters of fact, of veracity of witnesses and of the cogency of evidence. They are unsuited to the determination of complex legal principles. The judge should seek to give them help on the practical problems encountered in evaluating the evidence of a particular case and reaching a conclusion. Lord Scarman in the House of Lords appeal in *R v Hancock, R v Shankland* thought it was preferable for the judge to follow the traditional course of a summing up:

> 'He must explain the nature of the offence charged, give directions as to the law applicable to the particular facts of the case, explain the incidence and burden of proof, put both sides' cases making especially sure that the defence is put; he should offer help in understanding and weighing up all the evidence and should make certain that the jury understand that whereas the law is for him the facts are for them to decide. Guidelines, if given, are not to be treated as rules of law but as a guide indicating the sort of approach the jury may properly adopt to the evidence when coming to their decision on the facts.'

AIMED AT SOMEONE

In *Hyam* Lord Hailsham had declared that the act must be 'aimed at someone'; the purpose of this requirement being to ensure that cases of motor manslaughter were not regarded as murder. However, the comment is not helpful and was disapproved in *Moloney*. The terrorist who plants a bomb in a shopping precinct intending to kill or injure members of the general public indiscriminately is undoubtedly guilty of murder if death results. A generic intention to kill or cause grievous bodily harm will suffice; it is not essential that a particular person is in mind as the victim.

Voluntary manslaughter

Under this heading the law includes three situations where a prima facie case of murder is reduced to manslaughter by reason of the successful invocation of a statutory defence. The cases fall under the heads of provocation, section 3 of the Homicide Act 1957; diminished responsibility, section 2 of the 1957 Act and suicide pacts, section 4 of the 1957 Act. It must be stated that these 'defences' are usually pleaded to avoid a conviction for murder and the mandatory life sentence that such a conviction now carries. If, as has been recently suggested by the House of Lords in its legislative capacity, the mandatory sentence for murder is abolished, then the relevance of these three pleas will be much reduced.

Provocation

The defence of provocation was developed by the courts to reduce a case of prima facie murder to one of manslaughter and thus to save the convicted man from the gallows. Where a person kills in response to provocation he will usually have the mens rea of murder, the intention to kill, but the law takes the view that because the killing took place whilst the accused had lost his self-control in response to proven provocation from the victim, that it is less heinous, less blameworthy than a premeditated or cold blooded killing. The classic illustration is when a man returning home unexpectedly finds his wife in the act of adultery and flying into an immediate and uncontrollable rage grabs the nearest heavy object and batters one or both of the guilty parties to death. The defence is now embodied in statutory formulation which supplants the common law definition.

Section 3 of the 1957 Act is in the following terms:

> 'Where on a charge of murder there is evidence on which the jury can find that the person charged was provoked (whether by things done or by things said or by both together) to lose his self-control, the question whether the provocation was enough to make a reasonable man do as he did shall be left to be determined by the jury; and in determining that question the jury shall take into account everything both done and said according to the effect which, in their opinion, it would have on a reasonable man.'

The essential elements of this provision can be examined in turn. The issue can only be pleaded as a matter of substantive defence on a charge of murder and if successful has the effect of resulting in an automatic conviction for manslaughter. The advantage being of course that the accused will escape a mandatory life sentence and will be sentenced as the judge feels appropriate for the conviction for manslaughter (which can include a sentence of life imprisonment). It is thus a limited defence, unlike for example, self-defence which if successfully pleaded will be a complete justification for the killing and result in an acquittal. It cannot be pleaded in, for example, physical or indecent assault cases; although where provocation from the victim was present in such cases it can be pleaded in mitigation of sentence.

It is for the judge to decide whether there was evidence, which must be more than slight or tenuous, on which the jury could find provocation. If there is such evidence the judge must put the matter for decision to the jury (*R v Cambridge* (1994)). It is for the jury to decide the issue and not for the judge to rule as a matter of opinion that the evidence is insufficient or to rule that for any other reason, the defence cannot be made out (see *R v Rossiter* (1992) and *Vasquez v R* (1994)).

ACTS OF PROVOCATION

The person charged must be provoked 'whether by things done or by things said or by both together'; so there must be acts of provocation. The earlier cases on the common law defence had decided, not altogether logically, that a person could be provoked by acts but not by mere words. So finding a wife in the act of adultery was sufficient; a mere confession of adultery was not. Insults alone would not suffice unless accompanied by assaults of some kind. Illustrative acts that could be regarded as provocation are striking, pushing, kicking, spitting, pulling hair or any other form of physical assault; any form of indecent assault; marital infidelity; insults whether racial, with reference to physical or mental characteristics or to a person's religion or nationality. In most cases the provocative act will stem from the victim and it is probably essential that some degree of provocation should be provided by the victim. But acts of third parties which are related closely to the victim, such as the conduct or words of a lover in a marital infidelity situation can be regarded so that the accused could plead the joint provocation by words and acts of his wife and her lover (*R v Davies* (1975)). A difficult situation is where the accused is to a large extent the author of the situation, where, for example, A insults B who responds by insulting and attacking A which causes A to lose his self-control and kill B. It is clear that a defendant can rely on 'self induced provocation', ie a reaction by another caused by the defendant's conduct which in turn led him to lose his own self-control, as a defence to a charge of murder (*R v Johnson* (1989)).

Loss of self control
It is essential to prove that the provocative conduct of the victim led to a sudden and temporary loss of self-control which resulted in the defendant being unable to restrain himself from doing what he did (*R v Richens* (1992), *R v Thornton* (1992) and *R v Ahluwalia* (1992) the last two being cases where battered wives killed their husbands). But it is not necessary to prove a complete loss of self-control (*R v Richens* (1992)). This is often referred to as the subjective element. No amount of provocation will assist the defendant if in fact he nonetheless managed to retain his self-control. The longer the delay in reacting and the stronger the evidence of deliberation on the part of the defendant the more likely it would be that the prosecution would be able to negate provocation. The essence of the defence is that the killing took place whilst the accused was temporarily (and to some extent understandably) not master of his actions.

It was suggested in a leading case on the common law defence called *Mancini v DPP* (1942) that 'the mode of resentment must bear a reasonable relationship to the provocation'. Thus an attack with a lethal weapon can be met with a like response but insults and blows with a fist would not justify shooting the victim to death. The comment was no doubt intended to reduce the scope of the defence to reasonable proportions but the illogicality is apparent. If on the one hand you require the accused to lose his self control you cannot on the other require him nicely to weigh the possible reactions that he might make. He either loses his self control or he does not. The statutory formulation in section 3 makes no reference to the reasonable relationship rule and the modern approach is to avoid any such specific direction but to make it clear to the jury that the manner of response can be relevant to both the subjective and the objective elements.

The objective criteria

The crucial element of the defence is that the jury must be satisfied that the provocation offered in the circumstances was not merely sufficient to cause the accused to lose his self-control but was also enough to make a reasonable man do as he did. This is the so-called objective element which was present in the common law formulation and is re-expressed in section 3. The purpose of the requirement is to provide some common sense limits to the invocation of the defence. The law does not intend to excuse deliberate killings simply because a person claims to have been provoked by, for example, the colour and style of the clothes that the victim was wearing. In a crowded society such as ours people are subjected to many small irritants such as being pushed or jostled by a crowd whilst waiting in a queue for a bus or in a shop; or by rude or aggressive driving on the road . The person of ordinary and acceptable standards of behaviour and self-control does not kill in response to such conduct and as a matter of policy the law is not inclined to excuse those who do. The difficulty with the rule is the familiar one – who is a reasonable man? Is he the 35 year old lower middle class English man who is married with two children and who lives in a semi-detached in Norwood? If so, consider the effects of a racial insult on an illegitimate 17 year old unemployed black youth. The word used might well have a very real and hurtful effect on the youth but is his reaction to be assessed according to the effect that the words would have on the reasonable man above? Such a conclusion seems ridiculous because the insult having no relevance to the man would evoke merely amusement or slight puzzlement. So is the reasonable man in this circumstance the reasonable 17 year old black youth etc?

The reasonable man

The House of Lords has considered this point in two leading cases where essentially the difficulty centred on the extent to which the court should invest the hypothetical reasonable man with the actual characteristics at the time of the offence, of the accused person, for example, sex and age (as in *R v Camplin* (1978)) or the fact that the accused was addicted to glue sniffing (as in *R v Morhall* (1995)).

These two decisions overrule the approach adopted in a pre-1957 Act case called *Bedder v DPP* (1954), where the court refused to take into account the fact that the accused was sexually impotent which was a significant element in the circumstances which led the accused to kill a prostitute. The emphasis in the statutory formulation on the role of the jury pointed to an alternative route which was taken in *DPP v Camplin* (1978). The accused aged 15 went to the house of one K. Whilst there K had buggered him in spite of his resistance and had then laughed at him, whereupon Camplin had lost his self control and hit K with a pan thereby killing him. The House of Lords ruled that for the purpose of the modern law of provocation the 'reasonable man' was not confined to the adult male.

The expression meant 'an ordinary person of either sex, not exceptionally excitable or pugnacious but possessed of such powers of self-control as everyone is entitled to expect that his fellow citizens will exercise in society today' (per Lord Diplock). The jury should be invited to consider physical characteristics of the accused which are not abnormal, such as age, sex, race or pregnancy. There are clear indications also that abnormal physical characteristics such as malformities should also be regarded; Lord Simon refers to the case of the hunchback, for example. However, what is less clear is the extent to which the accused's peculiarities of temperament can be taken into account.

R v Morhall

The relevance of non physical characteristics was considered by the House of Lords in *R v Morhall* in 1995. The accused had killed his victim in a fight after a long period of glue sniffing. At his trial he unsuccessfully put forward a defence of provocation; on appeal against his conviction for murder he contended that his addiction to glue sniffing was a special characteristic which should have been taken into account as affecting the gravity of the provocation. The Court of Appeal were not so persuaded, feeling that the appellant's addiction to glue sniffing should be excluded because it was a characteristic which was repugnant to the concept of a reasonable man.

The House of Lords disagreed. Where provocation is raised as a defence by an accused who claims that he was provoked by taunts about his addiction to drugs or alcohol or with having been intoxicated on some previous occasion the jury should be directed simply by reference to a hypothetical person having the power of self-control to be expected of an ordinary person of the age and sex of the defendant, but in other respects sharing such of the defendant's characteristics as they think would affect the gravity of the provocation to him. Lord Goff stated:

'It seems to me, with all respect, that this conclusion (ie that of the Court of Appeal) flows from a misunderstanding of the function of the so-called "reasonable person test" in this context. In truth the expression "reasonable man" or "reasonable person" in this context can lead to misunderstanding. Lord Diplock described it in *DPP v Camplin* ... as an "apparently inapt expression". This is because the 'reasonable person test' is concerned not with ratiocination, nor with the reasonable man whom we know so well in the law of negligence (where we are concerned with reasonable foresight and reasonable care), nor with reasonable conduct generally. The function of the test is only to introduce, as a matter of policy, a standard of self-control which has to be complied with if provocation is to be established in law: see *DPP v Camplin* ... Lord Diplock himself spoke of "the reasonable or ordinary person", and indeed to speak of the degree of self-control attributable to the ordinary person is (despite the express words of the statute) perhaps more apt, and certainly less likely to mislead, than to do so with reference to the reasonable person. The word "ordinary" is in fact the adjective used in criminal codes applicable in some other common law jurisdictions, as in New Zealand, ... and in Tasmania.'

By exploiting the adjective 'reasonable' it is easy to caricature the law as stated in section 3 of the 1957 Act by talking of the test of, for example, the reasonable blackmailer or, nowadays perhaps, the reasonable glue sniffer; indeed, the sting of the caricature is derived from the implication that the adjective 'reasonable' refers to a person who is guided by reason or who acts in a reasonable manner. Lord Goff thought this to be misleading. In his opinion it would be entirely consistent with the law as stated in section 3 of the 1957 Act, as properly understood, to direct the jury simply with reference to a hypothetical person having the power of self-control to be expected of an *ordinary* person of the age and sex of the defendant, but in other respects sharing such of the defendant's characteristics as they think would affect the gravity of the provocation to him.

In other cases it has been stated that characteristics relating to the mental state or personality of an individual, as well as physical characteristics, could be taken into account by the jury provided they had the necessary degree of permanence, in determining whether a reasonable person having the characteristicsof the accused would have lost his or her self-control in the face of the victim's provocation (*R v Ahluwalia* (1992)).Examples of such personal characteristics which have been accepted by the courts recently are; battered wife syndrome (*R v Thornton (No 2)* (1995)); obsessiveness and eccentricity (*R v Dryden* (1995)); and abnormal immaturity and attention seeking by wrist slashing (*R v Humphreys* (1995)).

Aimed at the condition

But this is not to say that alcohol or drugs can always be relevant in excusing a loss of self control; the condition of being drunk on alcohol or 'high' on drugs can only be relevant where the provocation is aimed at the condition causing loss of self control. Lord Goff in *Morhall* drew a distinction between two situations. The first occurs where the defendant is taunted with his addiction, for example that he is an alcoholic or a drug addict or a glue sniffer, which may, where relevant, be taken into account as going to the gravity of the provocation. The second is the simple fact of the defendant being intoxicated – being drunk or high with drugs or glue – at the relevant time which may not be taken into account, because that, like displaying a lack of ordinary self-control, is excluded as a matter of policy. Such an approach is not inconsistent with the authority of *R v Newell* (1980) where the accused killed a drinking companion who made homosexual advances to him. The accused sought to pray in aid of his plea of provocation his lack of sobriety, the fact that he had attempted suicide by taking an overdose of drugs a few days before, and his grief at the defection of the woman with whom he had lived for ten years as man and wife. The Court of Appeal rejected all of these since they were not matters which would be regarded as characteristics within the contemplation of the Law Lords in *Camplin* but were merely transitory states for which Newell had himself in part at least been responsible.

One can ask whether this is convincing and whether the narrow distinctions drawn by Lord Goff in *Morhall* will be correctly understood and applied by juries. At least one commentator has hoped for a complete review of the law of provocation, 'before it becomes so riddled with hairsplitting distinctions as to render it incomprehensible.'

DIMINISHED RESPONSIBILITY

The common law has always recognised that a person's culpable responsibility for a crime can be alleviated by proof of mental incapacity at the time. The general defence of insanity was evolved but it was formulated in unsatisfactory language requiring a very high degree of proof on the part of the defence (see Chapter 11). It was apparent that many defendants were suffering from some form of mental disability but could not satisfy the stringent particulars of the defence of insanity. Further, insanity resulted, historically, in a finding of 'guilty but insane' and that effectively meant it was only pleaded in capital murder cases. In order to save patently ill, but not criminally insane, defendants from the gallows the defence of diminished responsibility was introduced in 1957.

The Homicide Act 1957, section 2 provides:

'(1) where a person kills or is a party to the killing of another, he shall not be convicted or murder if he was suffering from such abnormality of mind (whether arising from a condition of arrested or retarded development of mind or any inherent causes or induced by disease or injury) as substantially impaired his mental responsibility for his acts and omissions in doing or being a party to the killing.
(2) On a charge of murder, it shall be for the defence to prove that the person charged is by virtue of this section not liable to be convicted of murder.
(3) A person who but for this section would be liable, whether as principal or as accessory, to be convicted of murder shall be liable instead to be convicted of manslaughter.'

It will be noticed that the defence can only be pleaded on a charge of murder and thus has no application to crimes of, for example, rape or assault. Further, if successfully pleaded the result is a conviction for manslaughter. The elements of the defence will be apparent from the above provision. An 'abnormality of mind' must substantially impair the accused's moral responsibility for his acts.

Abnormality of mind
The phrase 'abnormality of mind' means a state of mind so different from that of ordinary human beings that the reasonable man would term it abnormal (*R v Byrne* (1960)). It is wide enough to cover the mind's

activities in all its aspects, not only the perception of physical acts and matters, and the ability to form a rational judgment as to whether an act is right or wrong, but also the ability to exercise will power to control physical acts in accordance with that rational judgment. So that the crucial question becomes 'was the abnormality such as substantially impaired the accused's mental responsibility for his acts in doing or being a party to the killing?' It has been said that there must be aberration or weakness of mind, that there must be some form of mental unsoundness, that there must be a state of mind which is bordering on, though not amounting to, insanity (Lord Cooper in *HM Advocate v Braithwaite* (1945)). The defence of diminished responsibility had been available in Scotland, of course, for a hundred years before its statutory introduction into the law of England and Wales.

Substantial impairment of responsibility
It will be noted that the section refers to 'substantial' impairment of responsibility and *R v Lloyd* (1966) is an illustrative case where the defence failed to prove that the abnormality, depressive illness, was a substantial impairment of responsibility. Nor will emotional instability or gross personality disorders suffice. The defence will not be able to excuse an accused who has a very short temper or is unusually excitable or lacking in self-control. Voluntary drunkenness producing a loss of mental control cannot be relied on to establish diminished responsibility. For a craving for drink, in itself, to produce an 'abnormality of mind' induced by the disease of alcoholism, within the section, the alcoholism had to have reached such a level that the accused's brain was damaged so that there was gross impairment of his judgment and emotional responses or the craving had to be such as to render the accused's use of drink involuntary because he was no longer able to resist the impulse to drink (*R v Tandy* (1989)). Where it is shown that the defendant was intoxicated at the time of the killing, the questions for the jury were, whether, disregarding the effect of the intoxication, the defendant would have killed as he in fact did, if he had not been drunk and whether he would have been under diminished responsibility, ie more than a trivial degree of impairment of mental responsibility when he did so (*R v Egan* 1992). The defence has been successfully invoked by a psychopath, and in the leading case of *R v Byrne* (1960), by a sexual psychopath.

Irresistible impulse
'Irresistible impulse' is within the section for it has been stated that inability to exercise will power to control physical acts, provided that it is due to abnormality of mind from one of the causes specified in the section, is sufficient to entitle the accused to the defence. But mere difficulty in controlling his physical acts depends on the degree of difficulty that occurs, and whether such difficulty is so great as to amount to a substantial impairment of the accused's mental responsibility for his acts is a question

for the jury. The jury should approach the question 'in a broad common sense way'.

Burden of proof
The section clearly places the burden of proving the defence on the defendant and the evidence should be directed to the jury rather than the judge. In *Walton v R* (1978) the Privy Council emphasised that the defence is a matter for the jury to ascertain in a broad common sense way, whether at the time of the killing the accused was suffering from a state of mind bordering on but not amounting to insanity. In determining that issue, the jury could consider all the evidence but were entitled if they so wished to reject the evidence of a psychiatrist. In that case the jury returned a verdict of guilty of murder notwithstanding the clear evidence of a psychiatrist that in her opinion the accused was suffering from a mental illness which satisfied the definition in section 2.

Relationship with insanity
It sometimes happens that where the accused pleads diminished responsibility the Crown wish to respond by establishing insanity because the verdict in the latter event will clearly establish the necessity for some form of (possibly secure) psychiatric treatment. The Criminal Procedure (Insanity) Act 1964 resolves a previous controversy by expressly permitting this course, and also provides that where the defendant pleads insanity the prosecution can contend that the correct verdict should be guilty of manslaughter by reason of diminished responsibility.

Although the original rationale of the defence of ensuring that a capital sentence is not passed on someone patently suffering from mental illness no longer applies, the provision remains worthwhile. In practice it has supplemented the plea of insanity and can be regarded as being formulated in more satisfactory terms than the common law defence. If successfully pleaded it avoids the imposition of a mandatory life sentence and enables the court to give whatever sentence is regarded as appropriate. This can include a hospital order under section 7 of the Mental Health Act 1983 thus ensuring treatment not punishment in appropriate cases.

SUICIDE PACTS

Section 4 of the Homicide Act 1957, speaks for itself.

'(1) It shall be manslaughter, and shall not be murder, for a person acting in pursuance of a suicide pact between himself and another to kill the other or be a party to the other killing himself or being killed by a third person.
(2) For the purposes of this section "suicide pact" means a common agreement between two or more persons having for its object the death of all of them, whether or not each is to take his own life, but nothing done by a person who enters into a suicide pact shall be treated as done by him in pursuance of the

pact unless it is done while he has the settled intention of dying in pursuance of the pact.'

Involuntary manslaughter

Unlawful killings which do not fall under the heads previously discussed are included under the general umbrella of involuntary manslaughter. The cases are diverse and the culpability varies widely but all such cases have the characteristic that the law regards the accused as criminally responsible for the death of another. The traditional approach is to divide such cases into the two main and most important headings of, unlawful act manslaughter, and gross negligence manslaughter.

UNLAWFUL ACT MANSLAUGHTER

The essential characteristics of this offence have been consistently enumerated in a number of cases, and the decision of the Court of Appeal in *R v Mitchell* (1983) can be conveniently referred to. To establish the offence of manslaughter of this type the court stated that it had to be shown first, that the accused had committed an unlawful act; second, that the act was dangerous in the sense that a sober and reasonable person would inevitably recognise that it carried some risk of harm; third, that the act was a substantial cause of death and fourth that the accused intended to commit the act as distinct from intending its consequence. In that case the accused had an altercation with A. He struck A causing him to fall accidentally against B; B died of the injuries received. It was held that it did not matter that the act was aimed at some person other than the victim or that the death had not arisen due to some immediate impact on, or physical contact with, the victim since the primary question was one of causation, ie whether the accused's act caused the victim's death.

Excessive force
Another situation that has recently been presented to the court is where the defendant was justified in using some force but used a degree of force which caused the death of the victim. In such a case the defendant could only be guilty of manslaughter if he had committed an assault and the required mens rea was that he had intentionally or recklessly applied force to the person of another. So where the force used was excessive the defendant could not be convicted of manslaughter if he believed that the circumstances called for the degree of force used even if his belief was unreasonable (*R v Scarlett* (1993)).

Frightening your victim into causing his own death
See the discussion in Chapter 9.

Case-law illustrations

Let us consider some illustrations of this type of unlawful killing. In the classic case of *R v Church* (1966) the accused and a woman went to his van for sexual purposes but he was unable to satisfy her and she reproached him and slapped his face; they then had a fight which resulted in the woman being knocked out. The accused panicked and thinking that he had killed her he dragged her out of the van and put her in the river. It was established that she was alive when that was done and that the eventual cause of death was drowning. Church was convicted of her manslaughter. He had acted unlawfully towards the woman in a way that sober and reasonable people would appreciate involved risk of injury to the woman; it was not necessary to show that Church realised that what he had done was dangerous. Church could also have been convicted of manslaughter by reason of gross negligence since it was criminally negligent to jump to the conclusion on flimsy evidence that the woman was dead, and to put her body into the river.

In *R v Lamb* (1967) the court emphasised that the unlawful act had to be in the nature of an assault. Consider the facts. The accused pointed a revolver in jest and with no intention to harm his best friend. There were to the accused's knowledge two bullets in the chambers but neither was in the chamber opposite the barrel. The accused then pulled the trigger; this had the effect of rotating the barrel and thus placing a bullet opposite the firing pin. The gun discharged and killed the accused's friend. An assault involves the element of fear of force either actual or apprehended and this, since both parties treated the whole incident as a joke, was absent in the case. But it is criminally negligent to point guns which are known to be loaded at another person and deliberately to pull the trigger and on that basis Lamb could have been convicted. However, because of a defective summing up to the jury in the case, the conviction was quashed. In *R v Watson* (1989) noted above, it will be recalled that a burglar broke into an elderly woman's home late at night and verbally abused her. After the incident the police and council workmen attended at the house and an hour and a half after the break-in the woman suffered a heart attack and died. Given a correct direction to the jury, it is possible that the accused could have been convicted of her manslaughter on these facts.

Overdose of drugs

There are two contrasting cases in the Court of Appeal concerning deaths resulting from an overdose of drugs. In *R v Cato* (1976) two drug addicts injected each other a number of times with a powder believed to be heroin. The procedure was that each man prepared a mixture of the powder and water and loaded the syringe to his own liking and then gave it to the other to administer to the first party by injection. They continued so to give each other injections right through the night. By the morning they were both very ill; one man died, the other survived and in due course the survivor was charged with his friend's manslaughter. The conviction was affirmed.

Cato had caused the death either by an unlawful and dangerous act or by acting with gross negligence towards him. The fact that the friend had consented to the act was no defence to the charge of manslaughter but was a factor which had to be taken into account when the jury came to consider whether the accused had acted with recklessness or gross negligence.

In contrast a conviction for manslaughter was quashed in *R v Dalby* (1982). The appellant was a drug addict who lawfully obtained drugs on prescription. He gave some of the tablets to a friend, also known to be a drug addict. Each then injected himself intravenously with the drug and with other substances. The friend died. The unlawful act here consisted of supplying the drug to the friend and it will be noticed that in contrast to Cato the accused did not himself inject the friend with the drug. It was held that the unlawful and dangerous act had to be directed at the victim and that the mere act of unlawfully supplying the drug was not an act which was directed against the deceased or was likely to cause him direct injury.

Causing death by dropping objects
Finally, let us consider two cases involving similar facts in that death was caused by dropping or throwing things from an overhead bridge onto passing traffic below. In *DPP v Newbury and Jones* (1976) two fifteen year old boys were proved to have pushed a concrete slab off a bridge over a railway line directly into the path of an approaching train. The stone crashed through the front window of the driver's cab, struck the guard who was sitting next to the driver, and killed him. The boys were convicted of manslaughter. A clear case of an unlawful and dangerous act directed at someone and causing his death. The only issue was the boys' defence that because of their age and immaturity they did not realise how dangerous their act was. The House of Lords rejected the plea. In manslaughter there is no requirement of proof of subjective foresight; the criterion is whether sober and reasonable people would appreciate that what the accused did was a dangerous act. In the second case, *R v Hancock, R v Shankland* (1986) discussed above, concerning the two Welsh miners who caused the death of the taxi driver taking a working miner to work, the liability for manslaughter was never in doubt.

GROSS NEGLIGENCE MANSLAUGHTER

Consider the case of a doctor acting as an anaesthetist during an eye operation, who fails to notice that the supply of oxygen has become disconnected. As a result the patient dies. The anaesthetist must concede that he had been negligent; the question is whether he is criminally liable for the death. These facts were the basis of the appeal in *R v Adomako* (1994) where the House of Lords clarified the type of conduct which can be characterised as gross negligence manslaughter, returning the law to a more traditional formulation after a wrong turn had been taken in *R v Lawrence* (1981) and *R v Seymour* (1983) referring to a test of recklessness.

The classic formulation of liability under this head, expounded in a case called *R v Bateman* (1925), refers to 'gross negligence' by the accused as the basis of liability,Whatever the label which is attached, the matter remains one of degree; the test stated in Bateman was, 'does the conduct of the accused show such disregard for the life and safety of others as to amount to a crime against the state and conduct deserving of punishment?'

Similarly in *Andrews v DPP* (1937) Lord Atkin stated that where gross negligence manslaughter is charged, simple lack of care such as would constitute civil liability is not enough. For purposes of the criminal law there are degrees of negligence, and a very high degree of negligence is required to be proved before the crime is established.

Probably of all the epithets that can be applied 'reckless' most nearly covers the case. Illustrative situations could involve, drunken doctors performing operations; careless lift cage operators at a pit; careless construction workers working on a high building above a busy pavement and roadway; sleeping train drivers; negligent aircraft loaders carelessly closing cargo doors; the gossiping school teacher who is supposed to be supervising a swimming class. In each of these cases the person in question is prima facie lawfully performing his work but each involves a high degree of risk to others and thus each has a responsibility for their safety. It is not every slip or mistake that will render them liable but conduct which the jury as representatives of the public, feel was so negligent as to deserve punishment.

R v Adomako

Lord Mackay LC in *R v Adomako*, returning to the two earlier authorities referred to above, stated the guiding principles as a five stage sequential test.

1 The ordinary principles of the law of negligence apply to ascertain whether or not the defendant has been in breach of a duty of care towards the victim who has died.
2 If such breach of duty is established the next question is whether that breach of duty caused the death of the victim.
3 If so, the jury must go on to consider whether that breach of duty should be characterised as gross negligence and therefore as a crime.
4 This will depend on the seriousness of the breach of duty committed by the defendant in all the circumstances in which the defendant was placed when it occurred.
5 The jury will have to consider whether the extent to which the defendant's conduct departed from the proper standard of care incumbent upon him, involving as it must have done a risk of death to the patient, was such that it should be judged criminal.

The Lord Chancellor recognised that to a certain extent this test involves an element of circularity, and continued:

' ... but in this branch of the law I do not believe that is fatal to its being correct as a test of how far conduct must depart from accepted standards to be characterised as criminal. This is necessarily a question of degree and an attempt to specify that degree more closely is I think likely to achieve only a spurious precision.The essence of the matter, which is supremely a jury question, is whether, having regard to the risk of death involved, the conduct of the defendant was so bad in all the circumstances as to amount in their judgment to a criminal act or omission.'

Causing death by driving

The reckless motorist requires separate consideration. In principle he should be treated as any other person who causes death unlawfully but in practice juries have a reluctance to convict the errant motorist of so serious an offence and so obviously criminal an offence, as manslaughter. This led to the introduction of the offence of causing death by reckless driving, now replaced by an offence of causing death 'by driving a mechanically propelled vehicle dangerously' (Road Traffic Act 1991), which has its own sentence and, to some extent, its own criteria for liability. However, a charge of manslaughter is not excluded by the existence of this offence and in a particularly bad case of reckless driving a manslaughter conviction will be upheld. A topical illustration of such a case might be where so called 'joy riders' cause the death of others by particularly dangerous and reckless driving.

But cases of motor manslaughter will be rare and the statutory offence will usually be charged. The existence of a separate offence with a 'motoring' rather than a 'criminal' connotation, and, of course with a defined maximum sentence, can only be justified on policy grounds and is an illustration of the phenomenon which has been described as 'the twentieth century love affair'.

The earlier House of Lords cases of *R v Lawrence* (1981) and *R v Seymour* (1983), which were concerned with deaths caused by road traffic accidents, were respectively not followed, and overruled, by the House of Lords in *R v Adomako* (see above). Since the legislation which under-pinned these decisions has been changed by the 1991 Road Traffic Act, the decisions need no longer be regarded in this context.

Wilful neglect of others

A distinct category is liability for wilful neglect of others. We have already considered the distressing case of *R v Stone and Dobinson* (1977) where it will be remembered a couple were held responsible for the death of a helpless adult who was in their charge and whom they neglected. Refer again also to the negligent railway level crossing keeper: *R v Pittwood* (1902). Liability for neglecting children is the subject of statutory provision and the death of a child will usually be the result of both acts of commission and acts of omission. It is quite clear that wilful neglect of a child for which a person has responsibility resulting in its death can amount to manslaughter.

A classic case
Although we have, for convenience, discussed involuntary manslaughter under the two headings of 'unlawful act' and 'gross negligence' it will be appreciated that in some factual situations a conviction for manslaughter could be justified under either or both heads. Consider the classic manslaughter case *R v Kevin Goodfellow* (1986). The accused, who lived in a council house with his wife and three children, had been having difficulties with his neighbours and he wanted to move house. He was unable to persuade the council to exchange his house for another so he decided to try to force the decision. His plan was to set his own house on fire in such a way as to suggest that it had been caused by a petrol bomb thrown through the window by one of his neighbours. On the night in question his wife, a girl friend and his three children were in the house. The accused obtained some petrol from a friend to whom he outlined his plan to set fire to his house. His friend told him that it was a stupid idea, but the accused continued. He poured petrol liberally over the living room and deliberately set fire to it. His intention was that the adults in the house would rescue the children and that they would all escape unharmed. He thought it necessary that they should all be in the house at the time the fire started or else it would look suspicious. However, once the fire started it spread so rapidly and with such intensity, that the wife and the girl friend and one of the children were unable to escape and were killed. The two children were rescued by the accused. He was charged and convicted of three counts of manslaughter, one of arson and one of arson being reckless whether the lives of those in the house would be in danger. The convictions for manslaughter could be satisfied on either or both of two grounds. First, it was an unlawful and dangerous act to set fire to the house, and one that all sober and reasonable people would inevitably recognise as subjecting another reason to, at least, the risk of some harm resulting therefrom, albeit lot serious harm: unlawful act. Second, the accused had acted in such a manner as to create an obvious and serious risk of causing physical injury to some person, he had recognised that risk and had nonetheless gone on to take it recklessly.

Non-fatal offences

Some of the more important non-fatal offences against the person can be considered. Most of these offences are embodied in statutory provisions and can be initially divided into offences involving physical assault and sexual offences. The relevant statutory definition will be noted with some case law illustrations.

Assault and battery

'An assault is any attempt or offer with force and violence to do a corporal hurt to another, whether from malice or wantonness; as by striking at him or even by holding up one's fist at him in a threatening or insulting manner, or with such other circumstances as denote at the time an intention coupled with a present ability of using actual violence against his person; as by pointing a weapon at him within the reach of it. Where the injury is actually inflicted, it amounts to a battery, (which includes an assault); and this, however small it may be; as by spitting in a man's face or anyway touching him in anger without any lawful occasion.' (East PC 406.)

Although 'assault' is colloquially used to include a battery (see *R v Lynsey* (1995)) the offences are distinct as is shown by the definitions above, see *DPP v Taylor*; *DPP v Little* (1992).

Assault

The House of Lords has affirmed in *R v Savage, R v Parmenter* (1991) that the mental element of assault is an intention to cause the victim to apprehend immediate and unlawful violence or recklessness whether or not such apprehension be caused.

Consider an illustrative case: PC David Morris was on duty when he observed Vincent Fagan driving irregularly. He approached the vehicle and asked Fagan to pull into the side of the road so that he could ask him to answer some questions and produce his driving documents. Fagan stopped but didn't move as asked. The police officer indicated where he wished Fagan to park the car and Fagan made to comply but stopped a long way from the kerb. PC Morris then walked to a position one yard in front of the vehicle and pointed to the exact position against the kerb where he wanted Fagan to park the car. Fagan drove the car in the direction indicated and stopped it with its front offside wheel on the police officer's foot. The officer asked him to move the vehicle but Fagan said he could wait. The engine then stopped; whether by reason of being turned off or of stalling on its own account was not clear. PC Morris again asked the driver to move the car off his foot and slowly Fagan started the car and moved it. Fagan was charged with and convicted of an assault. The court stated that:

'An assault is any act which intentionally or possibly recklessly causes another person to apprehend immediate and unlawful personal violence. Although "assault" is an independent crime and is to be treated as such, for practical purposes today, "assault" is generally synonymous with the term "battery" and is a term used to mean the actual or intended use of unlawful force to another person without his consent. Where an assault involved a battery, it matters not whether the battery is inflicted directly by the body of the offender or through the medium of some weapon or instrument controlled by the action of the offender.'

Fagan argued that he had not intentionally or recklessly done any act that constituted an assault and pleaded the requirement that the mens rea should coincide with the actus reus. The court accepted that an assault requires some intentional act; a mere omission to act cannot amount to an assault. Fagan alleged that when he moved the car initially it accidentally came to rest on the officer's foot; that he had no intention (nor was he reckless) to put the car on the officer's foot. In other words that no mens rea accompanied the actus reus. Further that when he was aware that the car was on the officer's foot he did nothing positive to further the act; the car rested on the officer's foot by inertia and he had merely omitted to move it. This argument persuaded one member of the Appeal Court but the majority thought otherwise. They drew a distinction between acts which are complete and acts which are continuing; if the act is a continuing one (which they thought was the situation in this case) then the mens rea can be superimposed subsequent to the initial act to result in a sufficient coincidence of the mens rea and the actus reus (*Fagan v Metropolitan Police Comr* (1968)).

ASSAULT OCCASIONING ACTUAL BODILY HARM

Section 47 of the Offences Against the Person Act 1861 provides that any person convicted on indictment of 'any assault occasioning actual bodily harm' is liable to imprisonment for a term not exceeding five years.

'Actual bodily harm' means causing some injury to the victim but not necessarily injury that would be regarded as serious. Thus bruises and abrasions caused by punches and kicks would fall within the offence. The phrase is capable of including psychiatric injury but did not include mere emotions such as fear, distress, panic or a hysterical or nervous condition, nor did it include states of mind that were not themselves evidence of some identifiable clinical condition (*R v Chan-Fook* (1994)). In effect section 47 provides an offence of aggravated assault which embodies simple common law assault but which is rendered more serious by the consequence of actual bodily harm resulting.

In the controversial decision in *R v Brown* (1993) the House of Lords decided by a three to two majority, that consensual sado-masochistic homosexual encounters which occasioned actual bodily harm to the victim were assaults occasioning actual bodily harm (section 47) and unlawful wounding (section 20) notwithstanding the victim's consent to the acts inflicted on him. This case is considered further in the next chapter.

THREE CASES

Note the facts in three recent cases and consider whether each of the acts constitutes an assault.

In *R v Spratt* (1991), a young girl was struck twice whilst playing in the forecourt of a block of flats by two air gun pellets, which had been fired from a window by the appellant. He admitted to the police that he had fired a few shots out of the window, not in order to hit anyone, but to see how far the pellets would go.

In *R v Savage* (1991) the accused admitted throwing the contents of her beer mug over the victim in a public house altercation. The glass slipped out of her hand and broke and a piece of glass cut the victim's wrist.

In *R v Parmenter* (1991) the accused's baby suffered injuries as a result of the accused's rough handling of the child.

Mens rea

The mens rea of the offence can cause more difficulties. The section does not specifically define the mental element required which is supplied by the common law definition of assault. It is clear that either an intentional or a reckless state of mind will suffice, the problem centring on what is meant by 'reckless', and in particular whether it is necessary to show a subjective foresight of the consequences of the act, ie must the prosecution also prove that the defendant intended to cause some actual bodily harm or was reckless as to whether such harm would be caused. This question was explored by the Court of Appeal in the three contemporaneous cases noted above, where there was judicial disagreement. The matter has now been resolved by the House of Lords in the appeal in *R v Savage, R v Parmenter* (1991). Lord Ackner followed the earlier case of *R v Roberts* (1972). In that case the accused gave a girl a lift in his car late at night. He began to make unwanted advances of a sexual nature to her which alarmed her. She feared that he intended to rape her and as the car was moving, she opened the door and jumped out and injured herself. Roberts was convicted of causing her actual bodily harm because the victim's conduct was a reasonably foreseeable result of his actions, although he protested that he had not foreseen that the girl would act as she had. Applying that case, the House of Lords in *R v Savage, R v Parmenter*, ruled that once the assault was established, the only remaining question was whether the victim's conduct was the natural consequence of that assault. The word 'occasioning' raised solely a question of causation, an objective question which did not involve enquiring into the accused's state of mind. The House of Lords thought that the Court of Appeal had applied the wrong criteria in their decision in *R v Parmenter*. The verdict of assault occasioning actual bodily harm may be returned upon proof of an assault together with proof of the fact that actual bodily harm was occasioned by the assault. The prosecution are not obliged to prove that the defendant intended to cause some actual bodily harm or was reckless as to whether such harm would be caused.

Malicious wounding

Section 20 of the Offences Against the Person Act 1861 states:

> 'Whosoever shall unlawfully and maliciously wound or inflict any grievous bodily harm upon any person, either with or without any weapon or instrument, shall be guilty of an offence, and being convicted thereof shall be liable to imprisonment for five years.'

THE INJURY

'Wound' means a break in the continuity of the whole skin; it is not enough that there has been a rupturing of blood vessels or vessels internally (*JJC (a minor) v Eisenhower* (1983)). 'Bodily harm' needs no further explanation and 'grievous' means no more and no less than 'really serious'. Such has been the accepted position since *R v Vickers* (1957); through *DPP v Smith* (1960); *Hyam v DPP* (1974), and it has been recently affirmed in *R v Moloney* (1985). The difference between actual bodily harm (within section 47) and grievous bodily harm (within sections 20 and 18) is thus largely a matter of the degree of the injury. Attacks with deadly weapons such as knives, guns and clubs will nearly always result in wounds or grievous bodily harm. Fights with fists, so called punch-ups, are perhaps only actual bodily harm. Any injury serious enough to warrant hospital treatment will be regarded as serious, such as broken bones, cuts requiring stitches, ruptures of internal organs, etc.

MALICIOUSLY

It will be noticed that only the word 'maliciously' relates to the accused's mental state in this definition, and that there is no further elucidation in the statute as to the meaning of the word in this context. The mens rea of the offence has been the subject of several, somewhat inconsistent, judicial decisions, which have now been resolved by the House of Lords in *R v Savage, R v Parmenter* (1991). The House of Lords posed two questions. First, in order to establish an offence under section 20, must the prosecution prove that the defendant actually foresaw that his act would cause harm, or is it sufficient to prove that he ought so to have foreseen? After reviewing the cases of *R v Cunningham* (1957), *R v Mowatt* (1968) and *R v Caldwell* (1981), the House ruled that the prosecution must prove either that the defendant intended or that he actually foresaw that his act would cause harm. The second question posed was as follows: in order to establish an offence under section 20 is it sufficient to prove that the defendant intended or foresaw the risk of some physical harm, or must he intend or foresee either wounding or grievous bodily harm? On this issue the House preferred the view expressed in *R v Mowatt* (1968) to that of the Court of Appeal in *R v Parmenter* (1991). Lord Ackner stated:

> 'I am satisfied that the decision in *Mowatt* was correct and that it is quite unnecessary that the accused should have intended or have foreseen that his unlawful act might cause physical harm of the gravity described in section 20, ie a wound or serious physical injury. It is enough that he should have foreseen that some physical harm to some person, albeit of a minor character, might occur.'

A verdict of guilty of assault occasioning actual bodily harm is a permissible alternative verdict on a count alleging unlawful wounding contrary to section 20.

Causing grievous bodily harm

Section 18 of the Offences Against the Person Act 1861 provides:

> 'Whosoever shall unlawfully and maliciously by any means whatsoever wound or cause any grievous bodily harm to any person with intent to do some grievous bodily harm to any person, or with intent to resist or prevent the lawful apprehension or detainer of any person, shall be guilty of an offence, and being convicted thereof shall be liable to imprisonment for life.'

This crime is more clearly and precisely defined as one would expect with an offence of such potential seriousness. Note the 'wound or cause grievous bodily harm' part of the actus reus about which we need say no more than has been noted above. The differing factor from section 20 and the one which makes this a very much more serious offence is the specific intent spelled out by the statute. With such an intent, if the victim dies the charge could be murder: if he survives, the charge is section 18. Oddly enough, the alternative of attempted murder can, according to authority, only be charged if there is an intent to kill (see *R v Whybrow* (1951)). In *R v Belfon* (1976) the Court of Appeal emphasised that in order to establish the offence under section 18 it was essential to prove the specific intent; references to the accused foreseeing that such harm was likely to result or that he had been reckless whether such harm would result, are an insufficient direction.

A charge under section 18 is wide enough to embrace section 20 and so it is open to a jury to convict a defendant charged with causing grievous harm with intent, contrary to section 18, of the alternative offence of inflicting grievous bodily harm, contrary to section 20 (*R v Mandair* (1994)).

FRIGHTENING A PERSON INTO INJURING HIMSELF

See Chapter 9.

Sexual offences

There are a great many offences of a sexual nature mostly codified in the Sexual Offences Act 1956 (as amended by the Sexual Offences (Amendment) Act 1976). Of these the crime of rape is the most important and the only one that space permits a discussion of here.

RAPE

For centuries rape was a common law crime of imprecise definition that was summed up by the simple reference to sexual intercourse by a man with a woman without the woman's consent. Section 1(1) of the 1956 Act merely declared that it was an offence for a man to rape a woman. The necessity to define the offence more clearly was prompted by the House of Lords decision in *DPP v Morgan* (1975). Morgan invited three strangers to come to his house and to have sexual intercourse with his wife. He assured them that although his wife would protest this would be a pretence and that she was really quite willing to participate. The four men went to Morgan's house, awakened the unfortunate wife, dragged her into another bedroom and then each in turn had intercourse with her whilst the others restrained her. She struggled and protested throughout. The three men were charged with rape and all four including Morgan with aiding and abetting the rape by the others. At first sight the charges of rape seem irrefutable since clearly the men did have sexual intercourse with a woman who was not in fact consenting. The three men, however, raised a defence that they honestly thought that she was consenting. In support of this allegation they could pray in aid the statement by the husband that although she might struggle and protest she was in fact willing. In effect they were pleading an honest mistake. The response was simply that for such a mistake to amount to a defence must be a reasonable one, which theirs patently was not. The House of Lords decided that the crime of rape consisted in having sexual intercourse with a woman with intent to do so without her consent or with indifference as to whether or not she consented. If the accused honestly believed that the woman had consented then he could not be found guilty of rape. On the facts of the case before them the House thought that no reasonable jury could have believed the accused's story and could not have failed to convict them. Accordingly the convictions were affirmed.

Marital rape

It can be noted that at the time of the decision in *Morgan*, there was a rule that a husband could not be guilty of raping his wife. This was based on the notion that on marriage a wife consents to all acts of sexual intercourse with her husband. This has recently been changed by the House of Lords in *R v R* (1991), affirming the Court of Appeal decision in the case. The previous rule that a husband cannot be criminally liable for raping his wife if he forces her to have sexual intercourse against her will no longer forms part of the law of England, since a husband and wife are now to be regarded as equal partners in marriage for all practical purposes, and it is unacceptable that by marriage a wife submits herself irrevocably to sexual intercourse in all circumstances, or that it is an incident of modern marriage that a wife consents to intercourse in all circumstances, including sexual intercourse obtained by force. The time honoured rule to the contrary was thought no longer to be appropriate in modern circumstances. It has always been the law that a husband can be guilty of aiding and abetting another to rape his wife.

Reform
The decision in *Morgan* provoked great concern that it would facilitate a too easy excuse or response to a charge of rape and the Heilbron Committee was set up to investigate the law. The resulting report, which in fact substantiated the *Morgan* decision as a matter of law, led to the enactment of the Sexual Offences (Amendment) Act 1976:

'1(1) For the purposes of section 1 of the Sexual Offences Act 1956 (which relates to rape) a man commits rape if –
(a)   he has unlawful sexual intercourse with a woman who at the time of the intercourse does not consent to it; and
(b)   at that time he knows that she does not consent to the intercourse or he is reckless as to whether she consents to it.
(2)   It is hereby declared that where in a trial for a rape offence the jury has to consider whether a man believed that a woman was consenting to sexual intercourse, the presence or absence of reasonable basis for such a belief is a matter to which the jury is to have regard in conjunction with any other relevant matters in considering whether he so believed.'

The reference in the statutory definition to 'reckless' causes familiar difficulties: should it be construed analogously to the meaning given to the word in the Criminal Damage Act 1971 in *R v Caldwell* (1981) discussed above? Or should a more subjective awareness of the risk of non-consent be required? There is some authority that it will suffice if, with reference to the woman's consent, the accused was indifferent and gave no thought to the possibility that she might not be consenting in circumstances where, if any thought had been given to the matter it would have been obvious that there was a risk that she was not consenting or that the accused was aware of the possibility that she might not be consenting but persisted regardless of whether she did so (*R v Pigg*, supra). It is clearly not necessary to prove that the woman was overcome by force or by the fear of force but merely that for whatever reason she did not consent: *R v Olugboja* (1982).

Consent
The prosecution can prove that the woman was incapable of consenting by reason of her age, or moral or physical condition or drugged, etc,

condition. Although the *Morgan* defence of honest belief that the woman is consenting negates the mens rea and although there is no substantive requirement of reasonable grounds, it will be appreciated that as a matter of evidence the jury will usually require some substantiation of the accused's story if he is to be believed. Thus the accused were convicted in *Morgan*. The law has, as a matter of policy, always resisted drunkenness as a defence to rape, ie that it is no answer for the accused to say that he was so befuddled by drink that he did not realise that the woman was not consenting.

A man may commit the offence of attempted rape even though he is reckless whether the woman consents to sexual intercourse, *R v Khan* (1990).

The act of penetration
The actus reus of rape is clear. The act is the penetration by the man's penis, to whatever extent, of the woman's vagina. Sexual intercourse is a continuing act commencing with the initial penetration and terminating only after complete withdrawal. Thus where a man honestly believed that the woman was consenting when he initially penetrated her, but realised during the act of intercourse that she was not, and continued nevertheless, he was held to be guilty of rape. The necessary mens rea when formed corresponded with the continuing actus reus and he could only escape conviction if he desisted the moment it became clear to him that the woman was not consenting (see *Kaitamaki v R* (1984)).

Chapter 11

General defences

Introduction

In all cases where the accused pleads 'not guilty' to a criminal charge he
will raise issues by way of defence. In many cases he will claim, 'I did
not do it' and support that assertion by seeking to negate the prosecution
evidence which suggests that he did. Thus where the prosecution case rests
on eye witness identification of the accused at the scene of the crime, he
will seek to show that they are mistaken, or insufficiently certain, to identify
him beyond reasonable doubt. In other cases the defence might be one of
alibi, ie that the accused could not have committed the crime in question
because he can prove that he was elsewhere at the time. Or he might seek
to show that he is physically incapable of committing the act alleged, for
example. that he is impotent on a charge of rape. In all of these cases the
accused is essentially challenging the prosecution case in the ordinary
course of a criminal trial. We are not here concerned with such matters.
This discussion will note certain specific pleas which the law accepts can
give rise to substantive defences.

Substantive defence

A substantive defence is proof of certain circumstances which excuse or
justify actions which would otherwise be criminal and which operate by
way of negating the actus reus, the physical element, or the mens rea, the
mental element, of the crime. It has been shown in the preceding chapter
that in order to secure a conviction on a particular charge the prosecution
must prove all the elements of the particular crime. Evidence must establish
that the accused did the prescribed act, in the circumstances which render
that act criminal and with the required consequences and that these physical
elements were accompanied by the required mental state of intention or
knowledge or recklessness. A substantive defence if raised tends to negate
one or more of the essential elements of the crime and thus results, if
successful, in an acquittal. Consider for example a case where the accused
is shown by the evidence to have struck X and caused him injury. Prima
facie the accused is guilty of an assault. But he might allege that he struck

X during the course of an epileptic fit when he had no control over his physical movements, a plea of automatism. Or he might allege that X attacked him first and that he retaliated in justifiable self-defence. Where the accused is charged with rape he might admit the act of sexual intercourse but allege that he honestly thought that the woman was consenting, a plea which would negate the required mens rea that at the time of the intercourse he should know, or be reckless, that the woman was not consenting. A plea by way of substantive defence must thus be distinguished from challenges as a matter of fact to the evidence and to pleas in mitigation of sentence. Thus, for example, on a charge of assault the accused might deny that he was the assailant relying on an alibi and alleging mistaken identity of the witnesses for the prosecution; an evidential defence. Or he might admit that he struck the victim but allege that he did so as a matter of essential self-defence as the victim attacked him first; a substantive defence. Or he might admit the attack but plead that he had been sorely provoked by the words and actions of the victim so to act; a plea in mitigation.

Voluntary manslaughter

Provocation, diminished responsibility and being party to a suicide pact, can be pleaded as a defence to a charge of murder and if successfully pleaded will result in a conviction for manslaughter; see the previous chapter.

Burden of proof

The burden of proof in criminal cases remains throughout on the prosecution, who must prove beyond reasonable doubt that the accused had both the actus reus and the mens rea of the crime charged. Where a defence is raised there is an evidential burden on the defendant to introduce evidence which tends to substantiate the defence. If that has been successfully done the prosecution must in effect re-establish their case of proof of the mens rea and the actus reus of the crime by, in effect, negating the issues raised by the defence. For example, in the crime of rape the prosecution must prove, inter alia, that at the time of intercourse the accused knew that the woman was not consenting to the intercourse or that he was reckless as to whether she consented to it (Sexual Offences (Amendment) Act 1976, section 1). The prosecution prove the act of intercourse by the accused with the woman and that she did not in fact consent to such intercourse, and will invite the inference that the accused knew that she was not consenting. Prima facie they have established their case and without more the accused will be convicted. But the accused might allege by way of defence that he thought that she was consenting, ie that at the time he was mistaken as to whether she consented or not. He will introduce evidence, perhaps the testimony of other persons present at the time, to establish that she did appear to be consenting to the intercourse. Now since the prosecution must prove beyond reasonable doubt not simply that she did not in fact consent, but also that the accused knew (or was reckless) that she did not consent, the effect of the defence will be to cast doubts on the proof of this essential issue so that the prosecution will have to respond by reaffirming the matter in the minds of the jury.

The age of responsibility

No child under the age of ten years is deemed to be criminally responsible for his or her actions. But where a child commits an act at the instigation or under the control of an adult, the latter can be guilty of the criminal act through the innocent agent. This principle will cover the Fagin and Oliver Twist type of situation.

There is a presumption that a child over the age of 10 years and under the age of 14 years did not have 'mischievous discretion', ie that he or she knew and understood the wrongfulness of their conduct so as to be guilty of a criminal offence. Accordingly, in such cases the prosecution is required to prove, according to the criminal standard of proof, that a child defendant between the ages of 10 and 14 did the act charged and that when doing that act he knew that it was a wrong act, as distinct from an act of mere naughtiness or childish mischief. This knowledge could not simply be inferred from the acts done however horrifying or obviously wrong those acts might be. This rule was reaffirmed in these terms by the House of Lords in 1995 in *C v DPP*, reversing the Divisional Court who had thought the presumption to be outdated.

A person over the age of 14 years has potentially full criminal responsibility but, of course, the requisite intention or knowledge or foresight, etc, will need to be proved which might be very much more difficult in the case of a young person than in the case of an adult. It will also be appreciated that young people are subject to special forms of procedure and if found guilty of criminal offences are dealt with in a different way to adults.

Insanity

The criminal law has long recognised that persons truly insane should not be held criminally responsible for their actions. The substantive defence if raised successfully would historically result in the verdict 'guilty but insane' which obviously contained an inherent contradiction. The present verdict is the more properly expressed 'not guilty by reason of insanity' (Criminal Procedure (Insanity) Act 1964, section 1).

The issue can be raised either at a preliminary stage in the trial, a plea of unfitness to plead, or as a substantive defence to the charge. The evidential and procedural points relating to the defence have been amended by the Criminal Procedure (Insanity and Unfitness to Plead) Act 1991. It can be noted that under this Act a jury are not to return the special verdict of 'not guilty by reason of insanity', under section 2 of the Trial of Lunatics Act 1883, except on the written or oral evidence of two or more registered medical practitioners, at least one of whom is approved by the Secretary of State under the Mental Health Act 1983. There are new provisions in section 2 of the 1991 Act, regarding the issue of fitness to plead. There are new powers to deal with persons found not guilty by reason of insanity or who are found unfit to plead. Provision is also made for appeals.

McNaghten Rules

Despite repeated criticism the authoritative statement of the defence of insanity is still Tindal CJ's judgment in 1843 in *McNaghten's case* (1843):

> 'It must be clearly proved that, at the time of the committing of the act, the party accused was labouring under such a defect of reason, from disease of the mind, as not to know the nature and quality of the act he was doing; or if he did know it, that he did not know he was doing what was wrong.'

It will thus be seen that if an accused is successfully to raise the defence of insanity he must satisfy three requirements. First, he must be suffering from a disease of the mind; second, this must result in defect of reason, and third, he must either not know the nature and quality of the act he was doing, or, he must not know that what he was doing was wrong. Each of these elements will have to be considered in some detail.

DISEASE OF THE MIND

It will be noted that the statement of the defence of insanity refers to a 'defect of reason, from disease of the mind'. The phrase 'disease of the mind' has no precise medical definition and the legal meaning of the phrase has given rise to much difficulty and confusion. Whether a particular disorder is a disease of the mind within the M'Naghten rules is a question for the judge. Lord Denning has provided a useful definition of the phrase (*Bratty v A-G for Northern Ireland* (1961)):

> 'The major mental diseases which the doctors call psychoses, such as schizophrenia, are clearly diseases of the mind. But in *R v Charlson* (1955), Barry J seems to have assumed that other diseases such as epilepsy or cerebral tumour are not diseases of the mind, even when they are such as to manifest themselves

in violence. I do not agree with this. It seems to me that any mental disorder which has manifested itself in violence and is prone to recur is a disease of the mind. At any rate, it is the sort of disease for which a person should be detained in hospital rather than be given an unqualified acquittal!'

Case law illustration

In *Bratty* there was evidence that at the time of the attack the accused was suffering from psychomotor epilepsy, and all the Law Lords based their speeches on the assumption that Bratty was suffering from a disease of the mind.

But Lord Denning's formulation of the meaning of disease of the mind has not been universally accepted. Thus Lawton LJ in *R v Quick* (1973) thought that if he applied the formulation 'any mental disorder which has manifested itself in violence and is prone to recur' to the case before him, he would have to conclude that Quick, who was at the time of the attack suffering from hypoglycaemia, was suffering from a disease of the mind, which he was reluctant to do. Quick was a diabetic who contrary to medical orders consumed a quantity of alcohol on the day in question and very little food. This caused a severe fall in blood sugar resulting in an excess of insulin in his blood stream. When this imbalance occurs, the insulin has much the same effect as an excess of alcohol; the higher functions of the mind are affected; the sufferer may become aggressive and violent without being able to control himself or without knowing at the time what he was doing and ultimately the sufferer can relapse into a coma. Quick, who was a nurse at a mental hospital, was charged with assault occasioning actual bodily harm to a patient and pleaded not guilty on the grounds of automatism. The judge ruled that the evidence could only be relied on to support a defence of insanity since it indicated that the appellant was suffering from a defect of reason from disease of the mind within the M'Naghten rules. The question therefore arose whether Quick's alleged condition at the time of the attack could be said to amount to a disease of the mind and the Court of Appeal concluded that it did not. The mental condition from which Quick alleged he was suffering had not been caused by his diabetes but by the use of insulin prescribed by his doctor; the alleged malfunctioning of his mind had therefore been caused by an external factor and not by a bodily disorder in the nature of a disease.

In a later case, *R v Sullivan* (1983), the House of Lords had to consider the criminal liability of an epileptic who inflicted grievous bodily harm during a seizure. The epileptic wished to plead automatism, ie that at the time of the act he had no control over his actions and thus the conduct was not voluntary. If successful such a plea would result in a simple verdict of not guilty. The trial judge, however, ruled that the defence amounted to insanity. On appeal the question for consideration was whether the state of mind during the epileptic seizure amounted to a disease of the mind. It was held that it could and that the special verdict of not guilty by reason of insanity was appropriate. The House of Lords agreed that if the effect of a disease was to impair the functions of the mind so severely as to have the consequence that the accused did not know what he was doing, or if he did, that he did not know that it was wrong, he was insane in the legal sense and it mattered not whether the aetiology of the impairment was organic, as in epilepsy, or functional, or whether the impairment itself was permanent or was transient and intermittent, provided that it subsisted at the time of commission of the act. Lord Diplock commented:

> 'The purpose of the legislation relating to the defence of insanity, ever since its origin in 1800 (The Criminal Lunatics Act), has been to protect society against recurrence of the dangerous conduct. The duration of a temporary suspension of the mental faculties of reason, memory and understanding, particularly if, as in the appellant's case, it is recurrent, cannot on any rational ground be relevant to the application by the courts of the M'Naghten rules, though it may be relevant to the course adopted by the Secretary of State, to whom the responsibility for how the defendant is to be dealt with passes after the return of the special verdict of not guilty by reason of insanity.'

Hyperglycaemia and sleep-walking
This passage has been applied by the Lord Chief Justice in two further cases. In the first, *R v Hennessy* (1989), the accused was a diabetic and at the time of the offence claimed that he was suffering from hyperglycaemia and in a state of automatism. The trial judge rejected this plea, holding that his condition was caused by a disease, namely diabetes, and therefore fell within the legal definition of 'insanity' within the M'Naghten rules. Following this ruling the accused changed his plea to guilty. His appeal was dismissed since hyperglycaemia was caused by an inherent defect and not corrected by insulin was a disease and since the functioning of the appellant's mind was disturbed by disease and not by some external factor, the judge's ruling had been correct. In the second case, *R v Burgess* (1991) the accused sought to avoid a conviction for wounding with intent, by pleading that the assault was committed whilst he was sleepwalking, and that this amounted to non insane automatism. The Appeal Court in dismissing his appeal, took the view that a transitory abnormality or disorder caused by an internal factor, whether functional or organic, which manifested itself in violence and which might recur, amounted to insanity within the M'Naghten rules and was not merely non-insane automatism, even though the possibility of it recurring in the form of serious violence was unlikely. A decision which seems to owe more to policy than to logic, since it is difficult to see how a sleepwalker can be termed insane, an incongruity which the court itself recognised!

DEFECT OF REASON

The second requirement of the M'Naghten rules is that the accused should be suffering from a defect of reason. This means that the accused should by reason of a disease of the mind be deprived of the power of reasoning. The phrase does not cover those persons who retain the power of reasoning but who in moments of confusion or absent-mindedness fail to use their power to the full. Thus, the defence of insanity was not available for a woman charged with shop-lifting who retained the power of reasoning but who was momentarily absent-minded or confused and acted as she did by failing to concentrate properly on what she was doing and by failing adequately to use her mental powers (*R v Clarke* (1972)).

NATURE AND QUALITY OF THE ACT

'Nature and quality' are usually regarded as synonyms, and it is not correct to distinguish between the physical character of the act and the morality of the act, by contrasting 'nature' with 'quality'. The phrase simply refers to the physical nature of the act. It will be thus appreciated that only extreme behaviour will satisfy this requirement. Judicial examples are where at a christening, a drunken nurse puts the baby behind a large fire taking it for a log of wood; or where a man thinks that his friend lying in a bed is a theatrical dummy placed there, and stabs him to death.

The text book illustrations are similar; for example the madman who cuts a woman's throat under the idea that he was cutting a loaf of bread. In *R v Kemp* (1957), where the defence was made out, Kemp struck his wife, to whom he was devoted, with a hammer, not knowing anything about it, and not having any real memory of it, and not conscious that he picked up the hammer or that he was striking his wife with it.

DID NOT KNOW THAT WHAT HE WAS DOING WAS WRONG

Many of the problems presented by this requirement have been resolved. Thus, it has now been stated that in the M'Naghten rules 'wrong' means contrary to law and not 'wrong' according to the opinion of one man or of a number of people on the question of whether a particular act might or might not be justified. It is undesirable for juries to have to consider whether some particular act was morally right or wrong, since opinions can obviously differ for example with reference to the mercy killing of a terminal cancer patient, and so the test must be whether it is contrary to law.

Further, it is not necessary for the prosecution to prove that the accused knew of the particular law in question, for it is axiomatic that everyone knows the law. If the accused was conscious that the act was one which he ought not to do, and if that act was at the same time contrary to the law of the land, he is punishable. It has been further stated that whether the accused was 'conscious that the act was wrong' must be judged according to the ordinary standard adopted by reasonable men. Inevitably, the justification for this objective standard is that if the question was judged according to the standard of the accused, then it would 'excuse crimes without number and weaken the law to an alarming degree'.

Intoxication

Alcohol

The general principle of English law is that drunkenness is no defence to a criminal charge, nor is a defect of reason produced by drunkenness. The law recognises that the effect of alcohol may be to impair a man's powers of perception so that he may not be able to foresee or measure the consequences of his actions as he would if he were sober, but he is not allowed to set up his self-induced want of perception as a defence. Likewise he cannot plead as a defence that his judgment, the ability to judge between right and wrong, was affected by drink so that he did something whilst drunk that he would not dream of doing whilst sober. It is well known that the effect of alcohol is frequently to impair a man's power of self control, so that he gives way more readily to violent or sexual urges, but it is regarded as an aggravation rather than as a mitigation of the offence, see Lord Denning in *A-G for Northern Ireland v Gallagher* (1963). Nor can an accused rely on her voluntary state of intoxication as constituting an 'abnormality of mind' giving rise to the plea of diminished responsibility, *R v Tandy* (1989).

Crimes of specific or ulterior intent

It is, however, established that drunkenness can provide at least a partial defence in crimes which require a specific or ulterior intent. This is a troublesome doctrine necessitating a distinction between crimes which are said to have a specific or ulterior intent over and above the basic intention which accompanies the mens rea, and crimes of so-called basic intent. The best judicial statement of the distinction is that of Lord Simon in *DPP v Morgan* (1975):

> 'By "crimes of basic intent" I mean those crimes whose definition expresses (or more often, implies) a mens rea which does not go beyond the actus reus. The actus reus generally consists of an act and some consequence. The consequence may be very closely connected with the act or more remotely connected with it; but with a crime of basic intent the mens rea does not go beyond the act and its consequence, however remote, as defined in the actus reus.'

The offence of assault is such a crime since the actus reus of assault is an act which causes another person to apprehend immediate and unlawful violence and the mens rea corresponds exactly.

Lord Simon continued:

'On the other hand, there are crimes of ulterior intent "ulterior" because the mens rea goes beyond the actus reus. For example, in the crime of wounding with intent to cause grievous bodily harm, the actus reus is the wounding. The prosecution must prove a corresponding mens rea (as with unlawful wounding) but the prosecution must go further: it must show that the accused foresaw that serious injury would probably be a consequence of his act, or would possibly be so, that being a purpose of his act.'

MURDER

The classic illustration of a crime of specific intent is murder where it is necessary not merely to prove the deliberate striking or shooting or stabbing but also that it was done with the intention of causing death or really serious injury. It has been established by the case of *DPP v Beard* (1920) that drunkenness can be a defence where the accused was at the time of the offence so drunk as to be incapable of forming this specific intent. In that case the charge was murder in the course of rape and the House of Lords were satisfied that the accused was, at the time of the offence, incapable of specifically intending to kill the girl. His conviction for murder was quashed and a conviction for manslaughter substituted. It will be noted that drunkenness in these cases does not amount to a total defence but simply can negate the mens rea of a particular offence, typically murder, leaving the possibility of conviction for another offence, usually manslaughter, which does not require proof of a specific intent as part of the mens rea. This approach has been confirmed by the House of Lords case, *DPP v Majewski* (1977) which concerned a charge of assaulting a police constable in the execution of his duty (Criminal Justice Act 1967, section 8). Drunkenness at the time was pleaded as a defence but was not accepted. The offence charged required only proof of a basic intent, not a specific intent and thus drunkenness could be no defence. In contrast the offence embodied in section 18 of the Offences Against the Person Act 1861, unlawful and malicious wounding or causing grievous bodily harm, is specifically defined with reference to the need to prove the intent to cause grievous bodily harm.

CRIMINAL DAMAGE

A further illustration is provided by section 1 of the Criminal Damage Act 1971, which creates two offences, a basic offence in subsection (1) and an offence with a specific intent in subsection (2). Reference can be made to this provision which has been set out in a previous chapter. It will be noticed that the basic offence is damage to property which becomes a more serious offence when done with the intention of endangering the life of another.

The illogicality of this approach should be apparent. If it is recognised that drunkenness can negate a specific intent, surely it should also be capable of negating a basic intent. It can be said that drunkenness should either be relevant or irrelevant but not arbitrarily relevant for some aspects of some crimes but not all aspects of other crimes. The issue in all crimes is: did the accused have the required mental state to constitute the mens rea of the offence? If the accused was so drunk that he did not know, or foresee or intend, then he should strictly be acquitted as lacking the required mens rea whether that mental state is brought about by insanity, drunkenness or simply stupidity. But such an approach would permit too general a defence of drunkenness and the criminal law has firmly resisted any such general defence. As Lord Edmund-Davies commented in *Majewski*:

> 'Illogical though the present law may be, it represents a compromise between the imposition of liability on inebriates in complete disregard of their condition (on the alleged ground that it was brought on voluntarily) and the total exculpation required by the defendant's actual state of mind at the time he committed the harm in issue.'

POLICY CONSIDERATIONS

Thus the justification of the present position rests on policy, common sense and regard for the accumulated wisdom underlying the precedents. Nowhere is this attitude more graphically illustrated than with reference to the crime of rape. This offence is defined by the Sexual Offences (Amendment) Act 1976 to include the requirement that at the time of the intercourse the accused 'knows that she does not consent to the intercourse or he is reckless as to whether she consents or not.'

In terms of the analysis above, it could be said that the basic mens rea is the intention to have sexual intercourse, with the further additional specific knowledge or intent relating to the consent. But such an approach would permit a drunken rapist to plead that he was so drunk that he was not aware that the woman was not consenting possibly resulting in a conviction for a lesser offence of physical or indecent assault. Although *DPP v Beard* provides some support for the idea that rape is a crime of specific intent the House of Lords most recently in *DPP v Majewski* has expressly rejected such a conclusion. Little regard was paid to logic, policy being the overriding consideration recognising that 'the public is haunted by the spectre of the drunken rapist' and it is essential that he should be convicted.

Involuntary intoxication

The House of Lords has recently (somewhat surprisingly) held that there is no general defence of involuntary intoxication, ie where the intoxicated condition has been brought about by the strategem or fraud of another (see

R v Kingston (1994)). The exact ratio of the House, delivered by Lord Mustill, is somewhat obscure but the view seems to be that involuntary intoxication can be used as evidence by the jury in determining whether the accused possessed the mens rea but will not assist when the defendant is proved to have had the necessary intent. Nor will it assist to plead that the involuntary intoxication removed inhibitions as to committing the offence that he might have. It is probable that this area of law will be the subject of review by the Law Commission.

Drugs

If a man consciously and deliberately takes alcohol and drugs not on medical prescription, but in order to escape from reality, to 'go on a trip', or to become hallucinated, he cannot plead his self-induced disability as a defence to a criminal charge. This basic attitude of the law to the effect of drugs on criminal liability was reiterated by the House of Lords in *DPP v Majewski* (1977) which underlined the seminal decision in *R v Lipman* (1969). In that case the accused and a girl took a quantity of the drug LSD at the accused's flat. In the course of the hallucinatory experience which was the result of taking the drug the accused attacked the girl under the illusion that he was descending to the centre of the earth and was being attacked by snakes. The girl suffered two blows to the head causing haemorrhage of the brain but she died of asphyxia as a result of some eight inches of sheet having been crammed into her mouth. At his trial for murder the accused said that he had no knowledge of what he was doing whilst under the influence of the LSD and that he had no intention to harm the girl. He was acquitted of murder but his plea was not accepted as a defence to manslaughter. The Court of Appeal simply stated that when the killing results from an unlawful act of the accused no specific intent has to be proved to convict of manslaughter; self-induced intoxication is no defence and since the acts complained of were obviously likely to cause harm to the victim, the verdict of manslaughter was inevitable.

Valium

A rather different attitude is evident in the later case of *R v Hardie* (1984). The drug involved there was valium, a sedative or soporific drug that is frequently legally prescribed. The accused lived with a woman at her flat but the relationship broke down and she insisted that he leave. He became upset and took several tablets of the valium which had been prescribed for the woman. Later he started a fire in the bedroom of the flat whilst the woman and her daughter were in the sitting room. He was charged with damaging property with intent to endanger the life of another or being reckless whether another life would be endangered contrary to section 1(2) of the Criminal Damage Act 1971. The basic rule was reiterated: self-induced intoxication from alcohol or a dangerous drug could not be a defence to ordinary crimes which involved recklessness because the taking of the alcohol or drug itself involved an element of risk. However, it was thought that different considerations could apply where the normal effect of the drug was merely soporific or sedative. The Court of Appeal was unhappy with a ruling that there was a conclusive presumption that the drugs were irrelevant to the proof of mens rea, and thought that the jury should have been directed in this case that if, as a result of taking the valium, the accused was at the time unable to appreciate the risks to property and persons from his actions, they should then consider whether the taking of the valium had itself been reckless. The important factual elements in this case were that the drug was not unlawful in prescribed quantities; that the accused had no knowledge of the effects the drug might have; that he had been assured that it was old stock and that it would do him no harm; and that the normal effect of the drug is soporific or sedative. The denial by the courts that self-administered dangerous or unlawful drugs can negate mens rea and thus criminal liability, even where the effect of the drug is a complete disruption of the normal mental processes, can be criticised as illogical and inconsistent with the usual requirements of proof of a subjective mens rea.

Strict logic should not prevail

But the House of Lords has met the criticism head-on in *DPP v Majewski*:

'If, as I think, this long-standing rule was salutary years ago when it related almost exclusively to drunkenness, and hallucinatory drugs were comparatively unknown, how much more salutary is it today when such drugs are increasingly becoming a public menace? My Lords, I am satisfied that this rule accords with justice, ethics and common sense, and I would leave it alone even if it does not comply with strict logic. It would, in my view, be disastrous if the law were changed to allow men who did what Lipman did to go free. It would shock the public, it would rightly bring the law into contempt and it would certainly increase one of the really serious menaces facing society today. This is too great a price to pay for bringing solace to those who believe that, come what may, strict logic should always prevail.'

As to a drug affected condition which it is alleged was involuntary, ie caused by the act of another, see the previous section and the House of Lords in *R v Kingston* (1995).

Duress

The law has long recognised that duress can provide a defence to criminal offences (except treason or murder) if the will of the accused has been overborne by threats of death or serious personal injury so that the commission of the alleged offence was no longer the voluntary act of the accused. The defence has been described as a concession to human frailty in that it allows a reasonable man to make a conscious choice between the reality of the immediate threat and what he may reasonably regard as the lesser of two evils (Lord Hailsham LC in *R v Howe* (1987)). Where it is successfully pleaded it provides a complete defence, unlike provocation or diminished responsibility, for example, which operate to reduce a charge of murder to a conviction for manslaughter. It does not operate simply in mitigation but results in an acquittal. The precise jurisprudential basis of the defence has been a matter of debate but it now seems settled that it does not simply operate to negate the mens rea for the accused in such circumstances makes a calculated decision to do what he knows to be wrong and to that extent he has a 'guilty mind'. It seems that duress operates by being superimposed on the other ingredients which by themselves would make up an offence, ie on the act and intention. The accused knows what he is doing but the addition of the element of duress prevents the law from treating what he has done as a crime.

The threat or force

There are a number of aspects of the defence that require consideration, the first being the nature of the threat or force that will suffice. All the formulations of the concept would include fear produced by threats of death or grievous bodily harm to the accused so as to overbear his wish not to perform the act . Thus in *DPP for Northern Ireland v Lynch* (1975) the accused was ordered by a man who he knew to be a member of the IRA and to be a ruthless gunman to assist in a crime. The accused formed the view that if he did not agree he would be shot. However, one difficulty in the case was that there appeared to be no evidence that the accused was actually specifically threatened either physically or verbally with death or injury if he refused to participate; the accused thought the threat was obvious and implicit. This raises the question whether the test to be applied to establish the effectiveness of the threat should be an objective one or subjective to the accused? The suggestion is that it should be the latter, and that the effect of the threat on the actual accused should be considered. The vulnerable frail old person should not be equated with the robust physically and mentally strong person. In a recent relevant case the ruling of the Court of Appeal was that both elements have a part to play. The accused must satisfy the subjective requirement that he was impelled to act as he did because he had good cause to fear the other would kill him if he did not so act. However, public policy also required that a defendant should have the self control and steadfastness reasonably to be expected of the ordinary citizen in the defendant's situation so that the jury should also consider the objective test of whether a sober person of reasonable firmness, showing the defendant's characteristics would have responded in the way the accused did. One effect of this objective requirement is that it negates any consideration of the effect of drink or drugs voluntarily taken (see *R v Graham* (1982)).

Nature of the threat

Other difficulties centre on the nature of the threat. Would a threat of imprisonment suffice? Or a threat of damage to the accused's home or business or car or pets? Most formulations include threats to the accused or to members of his immediate family but obvious uncertainties arise. Granted that a spouse and children would be included, what about other family relationships? Would a fiance or a cohabitant be included? The cases provide no clear answer and the matter is probably determined by reference to the individual circumstances rather than by rigid rule. *R v Hudson* (1971) raised two further questions. First, whether the threat must be present and immediate and second, whether a right to plead duress may be lost if the accused has failed to take steps to remove the threat, as for example, by seeking police protection. The facts of the case were that the accused, who were both teenage girls, were the principal witnesses for the prosecution at the trial of a man charged with wounding. At the trial they both failed to identify the accused as the assailant and falsely testified that they did not know the accused. They were subsequently tried for perjury and admitted that their evidence at the trial had been false but set up the defence of duress. One girl alleged that she had been threatened with injury if she identified the assailant and the other girl said that she had also been warned by others to be careful what she said as she would be hurt. At the trial, one of the persons who had allegedly threatened the girls was seen by them to be present in the public gallery. Accordingly they said that they were frightened and had decided to tell lies at the trial. The prosecution submitted that the circumstances afforded no defence because at the time of the offence with which they were charged, the giving of the perjured evidence, there was no possibility of a present and imm-ediate resort to violence against them. They were convicted of perjury.

Their appeals were allowed by the Court of Appeal. What was essential if the defence of duress was to succeed was that the *threat* was present and immediate even if it could only be actually carried out at a later date. In this case there was evidence of a present threat operating at the time of the offence. It is open to the Crown to prove that the accused had failed to avail himself, or herself, of the opportunity to render the threat ineffective, for example, by resort to the police. Whether the circumstances were sufficient to negate the defence depended on whether such an opportunity was reasonably open to the accused having regard to the age and cir-cumstances of the accused, and to any risks to him or her, which might be involved in following that course of action. It is now clear (*R v Sharp*

(1987)) that the defence cannot be pleaded by a person who voluntarily joins a gang which he knows will expose him to pressure to act as a member of the gang.

Types of crimes

Duress has been successfully invoked as a defence to some forms of treason, in receiving, in stealing, in malicious damage, in arson, in unlawful possession of ammunition, and in perjury. Traditionally the defence has not been available to a person charged with murder as a principal and this was confirmed in Lynch. However, in that case the accused had merely driven the assailants to the place where they had murdered a man and had not himself participated in the actual shooting. It was held that it was open to a person accused as a principal in the second degree to plead duress. This view has now been overruled by the House of Lords in a later case, *R v Howe* (1987). It is now established that duress is not available to a person charged with murder whether as a principal in the first degree, the actual killer, or as a principal in the second degree, the aider and abettor. The House endorsed the view expressed in Hale's Pleas to the Crown that:

'... if a man be desperately assaulted, and in peril of death, and otherwise escape, unless to satisfy his assailant's fury he will kill an innocent person then present, the fear and actual force will not acquit him of the crime and punishment for murder, if he commit the fact; for he ought rather to die himself, than kill an innocent ...'

This is now the governing attitude although it is recognised that as a matter of common sense one participant in a murder may be considered less morally at fault than another, the youth who worships the gang leader and acts as a look-out man whilst the gang enter a jeweller's shop and kill the owner in order to steal is the obvious example. The solution, it is suggested, with more extreme examples such as the woman motorist being hijacked and forced to act as a getaway driver, is that such persons would not be prosecuted but would rather be called as principal witnesses for the prosecution. The degree of complicity and culpability in a murder cannot be reflected in the sentence since a conviction for murder attracts a mandatory life sentence. It will be small comfort in such cases to the accomplice who participated under threat of duress to be told that his case will be viewed more favourably by the parole board when in due course his application for release on licence is considered. It has been decided that duress is not a defence to attempted murder (*R v Gotts* (1992)).

The effect of the defence

An obvious compromise would be to treat duress analogously to provocation, providing a limited defence to murder resulting in a conviction for manslaughter. Such a change in the law would require statutory provision which although proposed has not yet found legislative expression.

Necessity

It has been said that duress is only that species of the genus necessity which is caused by wrongful threats. But the distinction is apparent: duress arises from wrongful threats or violence of another human being and necessity arises from any other objective dangers threatening the accused. In a necessity situation, the accused finds himself on the horns of a dilemma and must make a poignant and anguished decision (see Lord Hailsham LC in *R v Howe* (1987)).

An example

Consider the position of three men and a cabin boy adrift in an open boat after shipwreck. After many days they have no food, no water and no apparent prospect of rescue. The cabin boy is very weak and will inevitably die soon in the absence of assistance. The three men resolve to kill the cabin boy and eat his body in order to sustain their own lives. Can they plead, when charged with the murder of the boy, the defence of necessity? *R v Dudley and Stephens* (1884) ruled that they could not. The case suggests other moot questions. Can you justify on the grounds of necessity the death of one to save a great many? Can you steal to feed your starving children? Can you destroy your neighbour's house to provide a fire break to save your own house and others from being burnt? Can you exceed the speed limit (or go through a red light) in order to take a seriously ill patient to hospital? Can you justify breaking into an empty house to provide shelter for yourself and your family? English law has been very cautious in admitting a general defence of necessity. Lord Denning MR in *London Borough of Southwark v Williams* (1971) (a case concerning a homeless family taking possession of an empty local authority house) has explained the attitude as follows:

> '... necessity would open the door to many an excuse. It was for this reason that it was not admitted in *R v Dudley and Stephens*, where the three ship-wrecked sailors, in extreme despair, killed the cabin-boy and ate him to save their own lives. They were held guilty of murder. The killing was not justified by necessity. Similarly, when a man who is starving enters a house and takes food in order to keep himself alive. Our English law does not admit the defence of necessity. It holds him guilty of larceny. Lord Hale said that "if a person, being under necessity for want of victuals or clothes, shall upon that account clandestinely, and animus furandi, steal another man's food, it is felony". The reason is because, if hunger were once allowed to be an excuse for stealing, it would open a way through which all kinds of disorder and lawlessness would

pass. So here. If homelessness were once admitted as a defence to trespass, no one's house could be safe. Necessity would open a door which no man could shut. It would not only be those in extreme need who would enter. There would be others who would imagine that they were in need, or would invent a need, so as to gain entry. Each man would say his need was greater than the next man's. The plea would be an excuse for all sorts of wrongdoing. So the courts must, for the sake of law and order, take a firm stand. They must refuse to admit the plea of necessity to the hungry and the homeless; and trust that their distress will be relieved by the charitable and the good.'

Limits of the defence

The limits of the defence have been stated more fully in the case of *R v Martin* (1989). First, English law does, in extreme circumstances, recognise a defence of necessity. Most commonly this defence arises as duress, that is pressure on the accused's will from the wrongful threats or violence of another. Equally, however, it can arise from other objective dangers threatening the accused or others. Arising thus it is conveniently called 'duress of circumstances'. Second, the defence is available only if, from an objective standpoint, the accused can be said to be acting reasonably and proportionately in order to avoid a threat of death or serious injury. Third, assuming the defence to be open to the accused on his account of the facts, the issue should be left to the jury, who should be directed to determine two questions: the first, was the accused, or may he have been, impelled to act as he did because as a result of what he reasonably believed to be the situation he had good cause to fear that otherwise death or serious physical injury would result? The second, if so, would a sober person of reasonable firmness, sharing the characteristics of the accused, have responded to that situation by acting as the accused acted? If the answer to both of these questions is 'Yes', then the jury should acquit; the defence of necessity would have been established. See also *R v Conway* (1988): necessity can only be a defence to a charge of reckless driving where, objectively, the facts establish duress of circumstances, ie that the defendant was constrained to drive as he did to avoid the threat of death or serious injury to himself or some other person.

Mitigation

Even in cases where the substantive defence is denied such cases may not be visited with the full rigour of the law. In some cases the discretion not to prosecute at all will be the solution; in others the circumstances can be taken into account when considering what sentence would be appropriate.

Mistake

A mistake of fact, but not law, can sometimes constitute a defence to a crime by, in effect, negating the mens rea of the crime. Where, for example, the crime requires proof of knowledge, as for example in rape where the prosecution must prove that the accused knew (or was reckless whether) the woman was not consenting to the intercourse, it can be a defence for the accused to show that he honestly thought that she was consenting even if she wasn't. In other words that he made a mistake as to her consent (see *DPP v Morgan* (1975) discussed above). Similarly in crimes of dishonesty such as theft where the accused takes the object honestly believing that it is his own, when it is not, or that the owner has given it to him, when he has not. An honest, albeit mistaken, belief in facts which would justify the taking, negates the mens rea of dishonesty and thus provides a defence. Where the charge is assault then the accused might plead that he honestly thought that his actions were necessary for self-defence or for the defence of another person. Such a plea can succeed even though the victim shows that he was in fact acting in jest and that the accused was mistaken in thinking that some response was necessary.

Honest or reasonable?

One issue that has been considered by the courts is whether the mistake must not only be based on an honest belief in facts which if true would justify the action, but whether there must also be reasonable grounds to support that belief. The matter was explored in *DPP v Morgan* where the House of Lords concluded that the issue was whether the accused had the necessary mens rea for the offence (rape in that case) and that accordingly where mistake was pleaded to negate that mens rea it was the state of mind of the accused that was relevant, not that of a hypothetical reasonable man. Thus the accused could show that he did not know the woman was consenting by proof that he honestly but mistakenly believed that to be so. It was not necessary to show that there were reasonable grounds for the mistake, but it will be appreciated that the jury are unlikely to believe that the mistake was genuine if the circumstances are incredulous. Such indeed was the conclusion in Morgan where the court thought that no jury could possibly believe the accused's assertion that he thought the woman was consenting in view of the circumstances.

Consent

Consent to physical contact can provide a defence in sexual cases, where indeed in indecent assault or rape, the lack of consent is the essence of the crime.

Marital rape

It was for centuries the accepted view that a husband could not be guilty of raping his wife. This was founded on Sir Matthew Hale's view, expressed in 1736 that 'by their mutual matrimonial consent and contract the wife hath given herself in this kind unto her husband, which she cannot retract.' This view endured for centuries with only limited exceptions where, for example, there was a legal separation or the granting of a decree nisi. However, the law has now been changed by the case of *R v R* (1991). The House of Lords has now stated that the rule that a husband cannot be criminally liable for raping his wife if he has sexual intercourse with her without her consent, no longer forms part of the law of England. A husband and wife are now to be regarded as equal partners in marriage and it is unacceptable that by marriage the wife submits herself irrevocably to sexual intercourse in all circumstances or that it is an incident of modern marriage that the wife consents to intercourse in all circumstances, including sexual intercourse obtained only by force.

Physical assaults

Consent is generally no defence to a charge of physical assault. The matter was reviewed by the House of Lords in 1993 in *R v Brown* where it was held that sado-masochistic acts which inflicted injuries which were neither transient nor trifling, could amount to the crimes of assault occasioning actual bodily harm or malicious wounding under the 1861 Act. The plea that the activities were carried on in private with the consent of the victim was held not to constitute a defence. One can ask whether there is a convincing logical justification for this ruling; or does the explanation lie in policy?

Duels with deadly weapons are unlawful and provide no defence where injuries or death are inflicted; likewise where the persons quarrel and agree to settle their differences with their fists 'outside' (see *A-G's Reference No 6 of 1980*). A conviction has also been upheld where a girl was beaten as a form of sexual perversion and the court was deaf to the plea that she had consented to the conduct (*R v Donovan* (1934)). Similarly in the old law where persons have consented to mutilations so that they might beg more effectively.

Sports

But the necessity to render lawful the so-called manly diversions of boxing and rugby which involve frequent physical contact has ordained exceptions in favour of properly conducted sports and games. Policy also demands exception for lawful chastisement or correction by parents or school teachers of children, and for surgical interference. In these cases the consent of the victim will negate the unlawfulness of the force used (see *A- G's Reference No 6 of 1980*, supra). But that is not to say that the opponent has carte blanche to do what he wishes. In games such as rugby the common sense approach is to say that the players consent to such contact as is incidental and normal to the game. They do not consent to deliberate acts of violence 'off the ball'; as where a player kicks or pushes another not in the course of play (see *R v John William Billinghurst* (1978)). Boxing is more difficult to justify because the violence is not incidental but is the primary object of the event. The law has traditionally exempted such activity so long as it is properly conducted according to the Queens-bury Rules but the policy seems archaic and the present day justification is not apparent.

Other consents

Excessive force used in the correction of children can amount to assault but reasonable chastisement is permitted. It is probably true to say that the amount of force regarded as acceptable at the present day is considerably less than would have been tolerated a century ago. Consent to surgical treatment speaks for itself; virtually everyone has consented to the considerable discomfort inflicted by dentists and the hospital surgical consent form will be unhappily an experience for many. Emergency treatment without consent is justified on obvious policy grounds.

Self-defence

Where an attack of a violent, unlawful or indecent nature is made so that the person under attack fears for his life or safety of his person from injury, violation or indecent or insulting usage, then the person is entitled to protect himself and to repel such usage by force, provided that he uses no more force than is reasonable in the circumstances (see Lord Morris in *Palmer v R* (1971)). Whether justified self-defence can provide a complete defence to charges of murder or any of the non-fatal or sexual offences has been considered above. The defence operates by negating the unlawfulness of the assault; by rendering the circumstances which surround the act not unlawful.

Use of excessive force

Where the defendant was justified in using some force but used excessive force and killed his victim, his plea of self defence will fail altogether and he will be convicted of murder. There is no law enabling the court to reduce the conviction to one of manslaughter. The most celebrated case of this sort is *R v Clegg* in 1995, which concerned a British soldier who shot and killed a civilian while on patrol in Northern Ireland. The judge accepted that the first three shots he fired could have been in justifiable self defence but that this did not apply to the fourth shot, which was fired when the fleeing car was well past the defendant and moving away, so that the defendant was no longer in any danger. This shot constituted excessive force. The soldier was convicted of murder and the House of Lords rejected his appeal, on the basis of the ruling stated above.

Similar issues were raised in the much publicised case of the New York subway vigilante who shot four youths who he alleged were attempting to rob him. Evidence was rendered that the youths were not armed with guns and that in at least one case the victim was shot in the back. What should the verdict be in such cases ?

It will be appreciated that if the circumstances justify a plea of provocation, where it can be shown that the accused lost his self-control in response to the initial attack on him, then a conviction for manslaughter not murder will follow. Is this satisfactory ? Should the law be changed so that excessive force in self defence becomes a type of voluntary manslaughter ? See further discussion in the previous chapter.

Mistaken self-defence

If A is attacked by B with a knife in circumstances of obvious danger to himself then A can defend himself. But what if A honestly but mistakenly believes that B is about to attack him? In such cases the accused must be judged according to his mistaken view of the facts regardless of whether his mistake was reasonable or unreasonable (*R v Williams* (1987)). This ruling disapproves a suggestion in an earlier case (*Albert v Lavin* (1981)) that self-defence can only be relied on if the mistake was reasonable in the circumstances. It can be noted that the law has no sympathy with persons who are drunk so that an honest mistake resulting in fear from the accused's drunken condition will provide no defence (*R v O'Grady* (1987)).

Duty to retreat

Another issue considered by the courts in recent years is whether there is any duty on the accused to retreat; if the accused apprehends an attack or indeed is attacked, should he take steps to get away or can he stand his ground and repel the attack ? The answer is provided in *R v Julien* (1969) where Widgery L J said:

'It is not, as we understand it the law that a person threatened must take to his heels and run in a dramatic way suggested by counsel for appellant: but what is necessary is that he should demonstrate by his actions that he does not want to fight. He must demonstrate that he is prepared to temporise and disengage and perhaps to make some physical withdrawal; and to the extent that this is necessary as a feature of the justification of self-defence, it is true, in our opinion, whether the charge is a homicide charge or something less serious'.

However, in the latest case of *R v Bird* (1985) the court thought that expressed in that way, it placed too great an obligation on a defendant and Lord Lane CJ preferred to express it as follows

'If the defendant is proved to have been attacking or retaliating or revenging himself, then he was not truly acting in self-defence. Evidence that the defendant tried to retreat or tried to call off the fight may be a cast-iron method of casting doubt on the suggestion that he was the attacker or retaliator or the person trying to revenge himself. But it is not by any means the only method of doing that.'

It would seem that a person is not obliged to wait until he is being attacked before taking steps to protect himself. It has been said a person can in effect arm himself as a precaution against a real apprehension of attack. It is an offence to be in possession of an offensive weapon in a public place 'without lawful authority or reasonable excuse' (Prevention of Crime Act 1953, section 1(1)). Thus it may be a reasonable excuse for the carrying of an offensive weapon that the carrier is in anticipation of imminent attack and is carrying it for his own personal defence but the threat must be an imminent particular threat affecting the particular circumstances in which a weapon is carried. The same approach has been used to justify possession of an explosive substance, the threat of imminent apprehended attack being sufficient to constitute a 'lawful excuse within the statute' (*A-G's Reference No 2 of 1983*).

Self-defence or the prevention of a crime can amount to a lawful excuse to a charge of threatening to kill contrary to section 16 of 1861 Act, if it is reasonable in the circumstances to make the threat (*R v Cousins* (1982)). If a person is attacked in circumstances that would justify retaliatory self-defence then he should use only such force as is proportionate to the attack, such force as is reasonably necessary to protect himself. Thus if a strong man is attacked with fists by a puny man, he is not justified in shooting the attacker dead if there are other ways in which he could adequately protect himself .

Defence of others

An analogous defence extends to the defence of others so that a person can use reasonable force to prevent an assault whether physical or indecent, on another. In the famous case of *R v Rose* (1884) a son was held justified in shooting his father who was in the act of a murderous attack on his mother. Granted that one can act to protect members of one's own family, what is not clear is the extent to which one can intervene under this common law principle to protect total strangers. In practice this would now

be covered by the statutory provision in section 3 of the Criminal Law
Act 1967, which is discussed in the next section .

Defence of property

The law is much less sympathetic, at least in modern times, to force used
to protect property. The Englishman's home might be his castle but it is
unlikely that he could justify killing to protect it. In many such cases of
intruders breaking into a house or being discovered in a house, the owner
will be able to show a real apprehension of personal injury to himself or
to his family and thus will be able to justify the use of force against the
intruder on the grounds of self-defence or defence of his family. But the
home owner will not be justified in shooting his fleeing burglar dead, in
order to prevent him escaping with the family silver in circumstances which
pose no danger to himself. Again section 3 of the Criminal Law Act would
apply here and certainly a person would be justified in using reasonable
force to thwart the handbag snatcher.

Prevention of crime

Section 3 of the Criminal Law Act 1967 provides:

> 'A person may use such force as is reasonable in the circumstances in the
> prevention of crime, or in effecting or assisting in the lawful arrest of offenders
> or suspected offenders or of persons lawfully at large.'

The wording speaks for itself. Section 3 does not supplant the common
law defences noted above but supplements them and the overlap will be
apparent.

Superior orders

There is no general defence of superior orders, so that it will not assist a
defendant to try to justify a criminal act on the grounds that it was done in
obedience to superior orders. This has always been the policy of the law
and was re-stated most recently by the Privy Council in *Yip Chiu-cheung
v R* (1994).

Chapter 12

Crime and society

In the last three chapters we have considered the important principles of the criminal law itself: in what situations a person may be criminally liable and the defences that can be raised. In this chapter we are going to move away from the substantive law and look at some of the important questions underlying the state's attempts to deal with criminal behaviour.

The definition of crime

We have already referred to the difficulties in defining crime and seen Lord Diplock's view in *Treacy v DPP* (1971). Lord Diplock made the common error of giving a circular definition when he said, 'A code of criminal law defines offences, ie the kinds of conduct which render the person guilty of it liable to punishment'. Such a definition is also unsatisfactory for other reasons. As we shall see below, there is usually in any society a disagreement about the content of the criminal law. Moreover, the concept of crime is a relative one: whether behaviour is considered criminal or not can vary over a period of time. It has been estimated that 76% of the prisoners in the USA in 1931 had been convicted of offences which had not existed 16 years earlier. In this country, suicide ceased to be a criminal offence in 1960 and abortion and homosexuality were to some extent decriminalised in 1967. The variation also occurs among countries which, in other respects, have similar types of society. In some states of the USA adultery and prostitution are criminal offences, although neither is unlawful in this country. Variations occur between neighbouring countries: as the French philosopher Blaise Pascal wrote, 'Three degrees of latitude upsets the whole system of jurisprudence . . . a truth on this side of the Pyrenees becomes an error when we cross them'.

The exclamation 'It's criminal' is frequently heard in relation to conduct which does not in fact infringe the criminal law, but the speaker is perhaps suggesting ought to. Some radical criminologists consider that the term 'criminal' should be redefined to include behaviour which has severe consequences for human rights, such as the waging of war and the tolerance of poverty.

Why certain types of activity are regarded as criminal

Despite this view, the conventional scope of 'criminal behaviour' is usually confined to behaviour which is specifically prohibited by law and for which the state will bring court proceedings usually resulting in the punishment of the criminal. This raises an important question: why is some antisocial behaviour defined as criminal and yet other antisocial behaviour results in no more than social disapproval? We may be tempted to think that the difference is purely one of degree, but the answer is not that simple.

Morality

Most societies prohibit acts such as killing, stealing and raping (although the precise definitions of these crimes are likely to vary). This may be for religious reasons or simply because the society has realised that it cannot function if this sort of behaviour is allowed to occur. Christianity, for example, forms the basis of the morality in countries which have come under its influence. But this does not mean that Christianity and criminal law are co-extensive in these countries. In most states the criminal law will have been influenced by political development, especially if they have totalitarian regimes. In England, many acts which are contrary to the Christian ethic are not criminal offences. Adultery has never been a crime; nor has English law ever imposed a duty on people to assume the role of the Good Samaritan and help other people in distress (unless a special relationship exists between them). As we have seen, certain types of behaviour such as homosexuality and abortion have been largely de-criminalised.

The arguments that led to the decriminalisation of homosexuality and abortion started after the publication of the Report of the Committee on Homosexual Practices and Prostitution, known as the Wolfenden Committee, in 1957. In recommending that homosexual acts in private between consenting males aged 21 or over should be legalised, the Committee stated, 'Unless a deliberate attempt is to be made by society, acting through the agency of the law, to equate the sphere of crime with that of sin, there must remain a realm of private morality and immorality which is, in brief and crude terms, not the law's business'. This view clearly reflected the writings of the nineteenth century philosopher John Stuart Mill who wrote '(that) the only purpose for which power can be rightfully exercised over any member of a civilised community against his will is to prevent harm to others'. The opposing view can be seen in the writings of the judge Sir Patrick Devlin, who claimed in a lecture in 1959 that 'the suppression of vice is as much the law's business as the suppression of subversive activities'. His view, that the criminal law should cover immoral behaviour even if it does not harm other people, was given support by the House of

Lords in the case *Shaw v DPP* (1961). Their Lordships held that there is such an offence as 'conspiracy to corrupt public morals' and Lord Simonds stated that 'there remains in the courts of law a residual power to enforce the supreme and fundamental purpose of the law, to conserve not only the safety and order but also the moral welfare of the state'.

The law-morality argument is an interesting one which cannot be dealt with in any depth here but it does illustrate that even the oldest, and some would say the strongest, basis of our criminal law is not immune to change. The crime of bigamy was formerly punishable by death; nowadays it is rarely prosecuted. Notwithstanding *Shaw v DPP*, the change is likely to be in one direction. It seems inconceivable that, for example, the law on homosexuality could ever revert to its former state or that adultery could become a criminal offence.

Social development

Nowadays, there are thousands of different criminal offences on the statute book and few of these – except in a very broad sense – can be said to be directly related to the sort of moral basis that we have just considered. Indeed, many of these are 'strict liability' offences so that defendants may be convicted without being aware that they have done anything wrong. Most of these offences have been created in the last fifty years and can be seen to coincide with the rise of the welfare state. As our society has become more developed, it has been considered necessary to create criminal sanctions to deal with infractions of the ever-growing mass of rules and regulations. Laws concerning food, hygiene, trades descriptions and weights and measures also contain criminal offences. Other offences reflect the creation of new social problems: there is now a large amount of road traffic legislation to deal with situations which were unknown only several decades ago. The increasing threat to the Western world of dangerous drugs has led to new criminal offences to try and deal with it.

Much of this legislation is non-controversial in a political sense, but inevitably governments will create criminal offences which do not meet with general approval. The Criminal Justice and Public Order Act 1994 is an example of this. It is controversial because it has been seen by some as imposing unjustified restrictions on public marches and gatherings and has been widely condemned as restricting the freedom to demonstrate. The Act is also interesting in another respect. Governments seem increasingly prone to react to specific incidents of which they disapprove by immediately creating criminal offences to try and stop them. In the early 1990s there was a growing media interest in 'raves', which were reported to be keeping people awake at night. Under the Act a senior police officer, who suspects that people are gathering for a rave, can order them to leave the land. In addition, any person within five miles of the site who the police suspect is heading towards it can be stopped and forbidden to do so! Parliamentary drafters, who were left with the unenviable task of having to define the music played at raves, came up with 'sounds wholly or predominantly characterised by the emission of a succession of repetitive beats'.

The deviance perspective

Some sociologists, while not rejecting the above analysis, would maintain that it gives an incomplete explanation as to why some behaviour is made criminal and other behaviour is not. Preferring to use the wider concept of deviance, these sociologists argue that it is important to look at who has the power to determine what behaviour is considered deviant (or criminal) and the way in which similar acts may be reacted to differently depending on who has committed them. Thus, the enforcement of law becomes at least an equally important factor as its existence. For example, people who live in university cities are aware that 'high-spirited' behaviour by undergraduates frequently produces much less of a reaction from the police than the same 'loutish' behaviour perpetrated by the local youths. It was the American sociologist Howard Becker who made the self-evident, but often overlooked point when he wrote, 'Deviance is not a quality of the act the person commits, but rather a consequence of the appreciation by others of rules and sanctions to an offender'. Although some acts, such as killing and rape, are inherently deviant (although even killing is considered lawful in war), many other criminal offences are a reflection of the interests of powerful and influential groups in society. The same can be said for their enforcement: why is it that tax evasion is usually dealt with outside the criminal courts, whereas crimes involving far smaller amounts, such as shoplifting, are usually prosecuted?

Theories of punishment

When magistrates or judges sentence defendants following conviction in a criminal trial, they presumably ought to have some notion of what they are trying to achieve. As we shall see in the next chapter, sentencers are to a large extent restricted in what they can do by both statutory provisions and a large body of case law. But nowhere in these provisions can a clear statement be found of the different aims of sentencing and in what particular cases they should be applied. Sentencers must therefore turn to the established theories of punishment and, assisted by some of the case law, decide which of the theories they want to adopt in the case before them.

Writers classify the aims of sentencing in different ways. The division used here is between reductivism, retribution and denunciation.

Reductivism

The aim of reductivism seems simple enough; to take whatever steps are necessary to reduce criminal behaviour. But the reductivist is subject to certain constraints. Humanitarian considerations apply: executing all offenders or imprisoning them for the rest of their lives would be likely to reduce crimes as the criminals could not re-offend (except in prison), but this would be unacceptable in most societies. Disqualification from driving is a form of incapacitation, although the determined motorist may be prepared to take someone else's car. Moreover, the reductivist, unlike the retributivist or the denouncer, has to make a prediction about the future rather than simply deal with behaviour which has taken place in the past. The main forms of reductivist sentences passed in courts are those aiming to deter the offender, or other people, from committing offences and those aiming to reform the offender. Deterrent sentences can be divided into general and individual.

GENERAL DETERRENCE

The justification for passing such a sentence is that other people will be discouraged from committing the particular offence charged, or even other offences, by what has happened to the defendant. It is not necessary to study the law reports to see that sentencers consider this to be a very important part of their function; one can read it every day in the newspapers. For many years, it was generally assumed that sentencing had a deterrent effect, but more recently research has cast doubt on this. The notion of deterrence is often unpopular because it imposes the imposition of hardship on someone, and this would be exacerbated if it were shown that deterrents are ineffective. It is, therefore, necessary to look carefully at the available evidence in an attempt to unravel the problem.

There is some evidence to suggest that people can be deterred from offending by the prospect of facing criminal proceedings. In 1944, during the Second World War, the Danish police force was held under arrest by the occupying German army for seven months. During that period, there was a sharp increase in thefts and robberies but not in frauds. Similar occurrences have been reported elsewhere in cases of police strikes and power failures, thus suggesting that police presence has a deterrent value. Following the introduction of the breathalyser in Britain in 1967, there was a significant decrease in the number of serious road accidents, especially during the times when pubs are at their busiest. However, after a while the number of accidents began to increase again, possibly because drivers realised that their chances of being stopped by the police were not as great as they had thought. American research suggests that deterrence may even be operative for more contemplative crimes. Richard Schwartz and Sonya Orleans (1967) studied a group of taxpayers in Illinois. They were divided into four groups and each group was given a different interview. The 'sanction' group's interview reminded them of the penalties for tax evasion; the 'conscience' group's interview played on their feelings of civic sense and duty; the 'placebo' group were asked questions which raised neither of these topics; and the fourth group was not interviewed at all. The US Internal Revenue Service found that subsequently the reported incomes of the 'sanction' and 'conscience' groups increased, but those of the 'placebo' and uninterviewed groups showed a slight decrease.

The advocates of the view that deterrent sentences are ineffective usually point to government statistics which suggest a reconviction rate within two years of about 65% of people released from prison and similar figures for 'better risk' offenders who are given non-custodial penalties. Even if one accepts this argument, it could still be maintained that the 30% or so who did not re-offend (or, at least, were not reconvicted) might have been deterred by the sentence they received, so it cannot be said that deterrents are never effective. Another argument raised concerns the deterrent value of the death penalty. The evidence, which is not very strong, appears to indicate that homicide rates between different countries, or between different areas of the same country (eg the USA), do not vary in accordance with the existence of the death penalty. Some people have argued from this that the death penalty is not a deterrent, but all that can be claimed is that the death penalty is not a greater deterrent than the likely alternative punishment, which would be a long prison sentence. The death penalty may occasionally be a deterrent: some professional criminals have suggested that they would be less likely to carry firearms if it existed in this country. Yet the vast majority of homicides – and some other crimes as well – are committed without any premeditation, so in these cases the question of deterrence is irrelevant. It must also be the case that some people, including many recidivists in prison, are incapable of being deterred, either because of their mental or physical state, or because they are so experienced in their criminal ways that punishment is little more than an occupational hazard.

Courts sometimes pass an unusually severe sentence on offenders in the hope that, by making an example of them, others will be particularly deterred from acting in the same way. The effectiveness of this is unclear. A much-cited case is the sentencing of nine young men, all but one of whom had no previous convictions, to four years' imprisonment following attacks on black people in Notting Hill, London in 1958. It is said that this had the immediate effect of stopping racial violence there for a while, but it seems that other factors, such as an increased police presence, might also have been influential. Perhaps of more significance is a case in Birmingham during the 'mugging' scare of the mid-1970s. A young man was sentenced to twenty years' imprisonment after a violent attack. The case was given wide coverage by the media, both in Birmingham and nationally. But a study of the frequency in mugging in Birmingham, Liverpool and Manchester following the sentence showed there had been no decrease.

If deterrence is to have any effect, the mass media must play an important role. Few potential offenders read the annual Criminal Statistics and, although a certain amount of information is probably passed among professional criminals by word of mouth, it is unlikely that most other offenders learn much about the courts' activities by this method. Judges and magistrates, in passing deterrent sentences, may hope that they are given the widest possible publicity but they are unlikely to be reported by the national media unless the defendant is a public figure or there is something exceptional about the offence. Sentences which appear to be very lenient usually feature prominently, certainly more than those which seem too severe. The local media may pick up the story, but there is some evidence which suggests that the identity of the defendant and the circumstances of the offence are likely to make a greater impact than the sentence passed. However, there is evidence that the media can be useful in this respect. It is customary at Christmas for the Government to run campaigns against drinking and driving. These are given wide publicity by the media and usually lead to a decrease in the number of arrests, at least in the short term.

It is generally assumed that the threat underlying deterrent measures is that of some form of punishment but a Government Social Survey by Willcock and Stokes published in 1968 casts some doubt on this. Willcock and Stokes interviewed 80 young men between the ages of 15 and 22 about their views on criminal behaviour. There is always a risk that answers given to interviewers may be fabricated, but nevertheless some of the responses they received were very interesting. On being shown eight cards containing different consequences that would be feared from a court appearance, the one placed first by most interviewees (49%) was 'What my family would think about it'. This was followed by 'The chances of losing my job' (22%) and 'Publicity or shame of having to appear in court' (12%). Only in fourth place does one find 'The punishment I might get' (10%). Another interesting fact to emerge from the survey was that the respondents considerably overestimated their chances of being detected if they were to commit a crime.

INDIVIDUAL DETERRENCE AND REFORM

Individual deterrence involves doing something to offenders which is sufficiently unpleasant to ensure that they will not commit the offence – or maybe any other offence – again. Reform means changing the personality and character of offenders in such a way that they will genuinely not wish to commit the offence – or maybe any other offence – again. Unfortunately, with most types of sentence, it is virtually impossible to tell whether a person who does not re-offend has been deterred or reformed. The more personal attention to the offender a sentence involves (such as probation), the more likely it is that reform has taken place. Although some sentences, such as a fine, are highly unlikely to involve any element of reform, most have the potential to be a reforming influence. Imprisonment provides work and educational facilities, although nowadays these are often so depleted as to be almost useless. Community service is supposed to inculcate in the offender a desire to help the community but for many people it probably just appears as a burden they have to endure for as long as necessary. Probation, as we have seen, potentially involves a great deal of personal contact, but the resources of the probation service are so overstretched that the contact is often fairly minimal.

Are these sentences, which are aimed at the individual, successful? One difficulty is defining the criteria of success. The conventional means is to look at reconviction rates. However, reconviction rates are not the same as re-offending rates; there is a large 'dark figure' of crime which does not come to the attention of the authorities except in self-report and victim studies. This in itself only tells us that more crime is committed than we know about, but it does pose particular problems if one tries to compare reconviction rates following one type of sentence with those following another. There are also methodological problems involved in making such comparisons, especially in ensuring that the groups of offenders being compared are properly matched for age, background, number and type of previous convictions, and other important factors. All these problems render unreliable the superficial finding that, for many offenders, the type of sentence does not greatly affect the chances of reconviction. There is also the question of whether we should consider a reconviction for an offence of a completely different type to the original offence as a success or a failure. This probably depends on whether the deterrent or reforming influence operated specifically (you should not commit rape) or generally (you should not break the law). Nevertheless, it seems difficult to judge as a failure a rapist who within a couple of years after release from prison is convicted for shoplifting.

Some people have argued that reconviction is an inadequate test to measure the success of a particular sentence, and that, if an offender emerges better equipped to deal with relationships and cope with the stresses of everyday life, this shows that the sentence has served some purpose. In 1976 the Home Office Research and Planning Unit published the results of its 'IMPACT' study, which involved comparing reconviction rates of offenders given ordinary supervision on probation with a matched group of offenders given specially intensive supervision. Although the reconviction rates of those given the intensive supervision were actually slightly worse than those given ordinary supervision, the former did better in as much as they were better off than the others financially by the end of the probation period; most made better use of their leisure time; more had male friends who were not delinquents; and more had been discharged from the probation order early for making good progress. However, more of them had unsolved family problems (although, perhaps, they were more likely to be revealed through the greater supervision) and more of them had casual as opposed to steady employment.

A word of caution should be expressed about the idea of reforming offenders. Until about forty years ago, this aim was largely centred on young offenders, with the important exception of probation, which applies to adults as well. Since that time, more sentences have been introduced and existing sentences modified in an effort to try and reform adults. As we have just seen, it is questionable whether this aim has been very successful. Yet, it is arguably even more questionable whether we should be trying to reform offenders in the first place. If we attempt to deter a person by punishment, our intention is to affect behaviour, but not necessarily to change attitudes and beliefs. If we attempt to reform a person by punishment, the changing of attitudes and beliefs becomes an end in itself, in addition to a means of reducing criminal offences. Has society a right to try and change people's attitudes by punishment? Is it entitled to go beyond requiring offenders to cease acting in an antisocial way? It is not only in totalitarian regimes that allegations have been made about the brainwashing of prisoners. Hopefully, nothing of this kind occurs in the English penal system, but this is an important question to bear in mind when we are considering what we should be trying to do with our offenders.

Retribution

Retribution is an important feature in our sentencing practice. Retribution states that wrongdoers deserve punishment; that the penal system can demand atonement by way of punishment. In its pure form, retribution would demand that an offender be punished not only when such punishment would fail to reduce the frequency of the offence in question, but even if the punishment would be likely to increase it. It has been said that the imprisonment of homosexuals provided an example of this. In practice, few present-day retributivists would adhere to such an extreme position. As with reductivism, humanitarian considerations are bound to be significant.

There are several basic features of retribution. One is that a fixed sentence is passed by a court and this should not be altered to take account of a change in circumstances: if a sentence was retributively correct at the time it was passed, it cannot stop being so at some future date. The English penal system does have a system of appeals, but this is to deal with mistakes that were made at the trial or the sentencing stage, and not, for example, where the offender has suddenly become a reformed character. Even measures such as parole have been introduced primarily to ease the pressure on the prison system and encourage good behaviour in prisons. Another important feature of retribution is that similar wrongful acts should receive similar punishments. As we shall see in the next chapter, sentencers who pass individualised sentences are able to avoid this principle, but generally a very high regard is paid to consistency. A well-known example can be seen in the case of *R v Reeves* (1964). Reeves and another man were convicted of receiving stolen goods. The other man was tried summarily and fined £25. Reeves elected trial by jury and was sentenced to nine months' imprisonment. The Court of Criminal Appeal (as it was then called) thought that Reeves' sentence was about right and the other man's far too lenient. However, it reduced Reeves' sentence to enable him to be immediately released, so as to uphold the principle of consistency.

Retributive sentencing also requires that the severity of the punishment is related to the amount of harm that has been caused. This clearly applies in our legal system where it is common for sentencers to impose lesser penalties for attempts than for the full offence. Also, a thief or cheat who can claim in court that the money has been paid back to the victim may well receive a more lenient sentence. A difficult problem that retributivists have to face is how to determine the level of punishment that is appropriate for a particular offence. In principle, the easiest way would be to adopt the 'eye for an eye' doctrine, and the penalty (although not the method) of capital punishment is the clearest example of this. However, there are obviously practical and humanitarian objections to extending this much further and an alternative method must be sought. Judges largely rely on sentencing precedent which they themselves have established without any proper basis. Parliament is reluctant to interfere with 'judicial freedom' and statutes only provide maximum sentences. Critics of present sentencing levels often claim that more notice should be taken of public opinion but, apart from being difficult to gauge, it is notoriously fickle and levels of sentencing would be constantly changing.

The general requirement of criminal law that offenders cannot be convicted unless it is proved that they had the mens rea of the crime in question is in accordance with retributive principles. The notion of atonement can hardly be relevant to a person who has innocently caused a prohibited act. Yet this is not free from difficulty. English criminal law often punishes recklessness and, since the case of *R v Caldwell* (1981), this concept is sometimes defined in terms closely resembling negligence, which is arguably too low a level of culpability to require atonement. Furthermore, the only mens rea required for offences of strict liability is that the accused consciously performed the prohibited act, eg driving a motor vehicle without proper lighting, even if one of the bulbs had just gone and the accused could not possibly have known of the fact.

The following is an interesting problem. Suppose that it is virtually certain that a person is going to commit a serious criminal offence and the only way to prevent this happening is to put the person in custody. What should society do? A reductivist would feel justified in taking this action, but a 'pure' retributivist would have great difficulty, as the person has not yet broken the law. In practice, one suspects that the police would be likely to find some pretext to take action under a catch-all provision such as fearing a breach of the peace, but this does not really solve the retributivist's problem.

A further difficulty that retributivists face is the way in which the imposition of punishments, such as large fines or imprisonment, can result in hardship for the offender's family. The reductivist will consider that this is an unfortunate, but necessary consequence of the need to deal with crime. The retributivist, however, is bound to be unhappy at the extension of suffering beyond what is strictly necessary to deal with the offence in question.

'JUST DESERTS'

Rehabilitative sentences reached the peak of their popularity in the USA in the early 1970s. However, not only did reconviction rates fail to improve, but gross disparities in sentences resulted as different judges held different views as to what length of prison sentence was necessary to reform an offender. One by one the states began to reject this approach and adopt a 'just deserts' model which aims at uniformity in sentencing and severely restricts judicial discretion. California, which had been at the forefront of rehabilitative sentencing, reacted by fixing the penalties for most offences at three levels: if, for example, involuntary manslaughter were punishable with two, three or four years' imprisonment, the three year middle term should normally be imposed, with the four year term reserved for the presence of aggravating circumstances, and the two year term for mitigating circumstances. Most other states adopted a more flexible model. As we shall see in the next chapter, the judges have moved some way towards the American model by issuing sentencing guidelines in Court of Appeal decisions.

Denunciation

In the opinion of some people, one important aim of sentencing is to indicate both to the offender and to other people that society will not stand for the offender's criminal behaviour. This argument is not new; it can be traced back at least as far as the eighteenth century. However, it does appear to have come to the fore since the capital punishment debate began to be intensified in the 1950s. In his written evidence to the Royal Commission on Capital Punishment Lord Denning stated:

> 'Punishment is the way in which society expresses its denunciation of wrong doing: and in order to maintain respect for law it is essential that the punishment inflicted for grave crimes should adequately reflect the revulsion felt by the great majority of citizens for them.'

To some extent our court-room procedure already contains elements of denunciatory ritual. For a start, the very formality of a Crown Court case can be awe-inspiring: the judge, robed and wigged, is seated on something resembling a throne and is confronted by the defendant, who is often brought into the dock from below the court. Both the judge and defendant frequently occupy positions raised above the rest of the court. The passing of sentence is inevitably a solemn affair and many judges take the opportunity to accompany it with a homily. The defendant will then be led below to the cells.

An interesting aspect of denunciation is that, strictly speaking, it does not require that the sentence be actually carried out. Jeremy Bentham in his book '*The Rationale of Punishment*' (1830) envisaged the possibility of the public's being satisfied by mock executions. Nowadays, the total non-implementation of a sentence would be inconceivable, but it is worth bearing in mind that a number of existing sentences are not fully implemented: as we shall see in the next chapter, prisoners may be granted parole. Life imprisonment seldom means life and a suspended sentence has little more than denunciatory value at the time it is passed.

In practice it is difficult to distinguish denunciation from reductivism or retribution. If the denouncers are hoping that less crime will be committed in the future, then their aim is reductivist. Even if the denouncers feel that their words are important in their own right, the words are meaningless without an audience, and an audience which wants to hear denunciation is probably really thinking of retribution.

Reparation

Before the Norman conquest, English society ranked compensation and restitution to the victims of crime as a more important objective than seeking the punishment of the offender. With the development of a nationwide criminal law, however, the emphasis moved firmly behind dealing with the offender and victims were left to pursue their claims in civil courts.

This is broadly the position today. It is not an inevitable one; the French 'action civile' shows how courts can deal with criminal liability and adequately compensate the victim in the same hearing. English criminal courts have the power to make compensation and restitution orders and we shall consider these in the next chapter. This power has hitherto been operated in a rather haphazard way. In the last few years there has been a growing belief that criminal courts could do more for the victims of crime. The Criminal Justice Act 1988 provides that courts should give reasons for not making a compensation order in cases involving personal injury, loss or damage.

What we are concerned with here, though, is whether there are any types of case where a sentencer would be justified in making reparation the main or sole aim of the sentence. This is uncommon at present. Community service rarely involves offenders dealing directly with their victims. The disposition which probably makes most use of reparation is a deferment of sentence. Section 1 of the Powers of Criminal Courts Act 1973 provides that sentence on an offender may be deferred 'for the purpose of enabling the court to have regard . . . to his conduct after conviction (including, where appropriate, the making by him of reparation for his offence) or to any change in his circumstances'.

Yet this provision illustrates a fundamental difficulty in elevating reparation to a primary sentencing aim. Critics of deferment claim that it enables offenders to buy themselves out of trouble. This may be slightly unfair to deferment itself, as the courts usually accept any improvement in the offender's behaviour – even keeping out of trouble – as a reason for not imposing a custodial sentence when the offender returns to court. However, if reparation were the main or sole aim of a sentence, judges and magistrates would face severe problems in dealing with offenders of different means. For example, some offenders may already have sold the property they stole, whereas others may be on the point of doing so. The end result would be great inconsistency in sentencing. Not only would this be objectionable to retributivists, but reductivists may be worried that 'better off' offenders would be encouraged to commit crimes in the knowledge that, if caught and convicted, there would be a possibility that only compensation would be ordered.

Alternatives to prosecution for adults

In Chapter 4 we discussed the criteria which the Crown Prosecution Service and other prosecuting bodies consider in reaching their decision whether to prosecute in a particular case. What we shall now turn to are the alternative courses available should the decision be taken not to prosecute. A prosecution may not be undertaken because of lack of evidence and in these cases no further action can be taken. Where, however, there is sufficient evidence to justify a prosecution, but the decision is taken not to proceed for some other reason, it is uncommon for an offender to be let off without at least a formal police caution.

Police cautions

There are two types of police caution: the informal 'ticking-off' given by a police officer on the spot for very minor offences and the formal caution administered by a senior officer. Formal cautions for motoring offences are administered by letter. Research published in 1980 suggested that only about 38% of offences under the Road Traffic Acts where the police speak to the driver are prosecuted; about 44% receive a verbal warning and about 4% are cautioned in a letter. For non-motoring cases, the offender usually has to go to the police station. The caution will be administered by an officer of at least inspector rank and a record will be made of it. There is also a special cautioning system in section 2 of the Street Offences Act 1959, which deals with 'loitering or soliciting in a street or public place for the purpose of prostitution'. The caution is usually administered to the woman (the offence does not apply to men) and a record will be made. The police administer two cautions before prosecuting. A woman who disputes the caution can ask for it to be removed from the record by applying to a magistrates' court within fourteen days.

For what sort of crimes are offenders cautioned? The 1994 Criminal Statistics show that for indictable offences committed by people aged 21 or over, the greatest number of cautions was given for theft and handling stolen goods and the least number for robbery. One problem with police cautioning has been the wide variations in its use among different forces. The 1994 Criminal Statistics showed cautioning rates for indictable non-motoring offences ranging from 56% in Surrey to 21% in South Wales. In recent years the Home Office has issued a series of circulars and guidelines to police forces on the cautioning of juveniles and adults for non-motoring offences. The main purpose has been to standardise cautioning practices throughout the country. For adults, the earlier circulars made reference to the criteria laid down in the Attorney-General's guidelines on prosecution (now superseded by the 'Code for Crown Prosecutors'; see Chapter 4) and also dealt with several other points. It was stated that there should be no prohibition on cautioning offenders who had previously been cautioned or convicted. A caution should only be given:

(a) if the evidence was sufficiently strong to support a prosecution,
(b) the offender made an unequivocal admission of guilt, and
(c) the offender, having been told of what is involved, agreed to be cautioned.

Other relevant factors in making the decision were the offender's character and record; whether or not any agency such as the probation service should be consulted; the wishes of the victim (although these should not be paramount) and the necessity to prosecute in order to avoid retaliation; and the willingness of the offender to make reparation. Cautions should normally be administered at the police station unless the offender was too old or medically unfit to attend, in which case they may be administered at the offender's home. Local records should be kept and should be presented to the prosecution if the offender came to the notice of the police again. If the offender stayed out of trouble, three years should be long enough to keep the record. During that three year period, cautions should be mentioned in court if the offender were prosecuted for a subsequent offence. Care should be taken to ensure that cautions were presented separately and not confused with previous convictions. It was also pointed out that some police forces had special provisions to deal with drunkenness in public. This usually involved keeping offenders at the police station until they were sober and only prosecuting those who had been arrested more than three times in a month.

In 1994 the Home Office issued a new circular on cautioning. This adopts a tougher approach, seeking to 'discourage their use in inappropriate cases, for example for offences which are triable on indictment only'. Cautions should not be given in circumstances where there can be no reasonable expectation that they will curb offending, and 'It is only in exceptional circumstances that more than one caution should be considered'.

Voluntary settlements

Certain Government departments prefer to come to a settlement with an offender rather than prosecute. The Inland Revenue has operated this practice for many years. The Keith Committee on the Enforcement of Revenue Legislation (1983) approved the practice as being 'swift and economical'. The settlements involve payment of the tax due plus any interest that has accrued, and a financial penalty which will be less than that which a court would have imposed. Prosecutions are only brought in particularly serious cases. The Customs and Excise operate a similar policy in cases involving the evasion of controls on importing animals and dangerous drugs; people entering the country with small amounts of cannabis for personal use will usually be offered the option of a monetary penalty by customs officers. Cases involving non-payment of VAT may be prosecuted. The Department of Transport's Driver and Vehicle Licensing Centre is often prepared to allow car tax evaders to pay a penalty according to a fixed scale, but the National Television Licence Records Office usually prosecutes.

Opportunities to remedy defects

In certain cases, an alternative to prosecution is to allow the offender to remedy the defect which is contrary to the law. Certain police forces have adopted the policy of allowing the drivers of defective motor vehicles to avoid being summonsed by having the vehicle repaired at an authorised MOT test centre and producing evidence of the repair to the police. An inspector appointed under the provisions of the Health and Safety at Work etc Act 1974, who finds that a person has contravened the Act may, rather than prosecute the person, issue an 'improvement notice' which requires that the contravention be remedied.

Fixed penalties

These have existed for several years in this country for some minor road traffic offences, most notably illegal parking. A traffic warden or police officer places a ticket on the offender's car which states that payment of a fixed sum of money will avoid prosecution. Motorists have the option of not paying the sum and contesting the case in court. The fixed penalty scheme is really an administrative process and there is little use of discretion. Nevertheless, it has been invaluable in saving the time of both the police and the courts. The Interdepartmental Working Party on Road Traffic Law suggested in 1981 that the scheme be extended to other motoring offences. Provisions were inserted in the Transport Act 1982 and these were brought into force on 1 October 1986. The scheme now covers a wide range of endorsable (on the driver's licence) and non-endorsable offences including the use of a vehicle in a defective condition, speeding, and contravening a red traffic light or a no-entry sign. The motorist has 28 days in which to pay the sum or ask for a court hearing; if neither course is taken in that time, the sum is increased by 50%.

The fixed penalty scheme also applies to fare dodgers on London Regional Transport. The London Regional Transport Act 1984 enables inspectors to ask for a sum of money from anyone found travelling without a ticket. Refusal to pay can lead to a prosecution.

Assessment

Should greater use be made of the alternatives to prosecution? It is arguable that any extension would benefit both courts and offenders. The courts – and the Crown Prosecution Service – are becoming heavily overburdened with a steadily increasing number of cases. Offenders are having to wait for long periods of time before their cases come to court and this can put them under considerable pressure. Court appearances can have a stigmatising effect on individuals, which even many retributivists would concede is not supposed to be part of the punishment. In any case, the stigma can also extend to families. Some American sociologists have written about the consequences of 'labelling' offenders with a court appearance and conviction: offenders whose transgressions may have been fairly trivial can come to see themselves as 'real criminals' and behave accordingly.

It has been suggested that minor property offences – for example cases involving theft, fraud and criminal damage where the value is less than £50 – should be dealt with by a formal caution or a fixed penalty, coupled with compensation or restitution to the victim. Formal cautions would presumably be confined to cases with mitigating circumstances. It is becoming increasingly questionable whether the cost to the system of dealing with such cases in the courts can be justified. What would be the problems involved in taking such a step? Those people who believe in denunciation as an aim of sentencing would probably not approve. Retributivists would be unhappy if offenders received a lighter punishment than the crime deserved. But even now some of these cases are dealt with by small fines and others by probation or community service orders. Reductivists may fear a weakening of deterrence, but unless the appearance at court in itself is a significant deterrent, there is no good reason why this should be the case. One problem that may arise is that some offenders who would otherwise contest allegations against them in court may be prepared to take the 'easy way out' offered by a fixed penalty. The new road traffic fixed penalties could have this effect: not only will motorists who choose to go to court face the likelihood of an increased fine if convicted, but they will also probably have to pay a contribution to the cost of the case. Any extension to the fixed penalty scheme must, therefore, have a proper balance between the incentive to offenders to pay the sum and the reasonable availability of court proceedings for those who consider they are innocent.

Alternatives to prosecution for juveniles

The term juvenile is used to refer to children (under the age of 14) and young persons (14–17). For many years juveniles have been treated differently from adults in the criminal justice system, the view being that not only should greater allowance be made for their youth when sentencing, but also that reformative measures are more likely to have success. During the 1960s two further arguments were put forward: that juvenile delinquency should be understood as a symptom of some deeper maladjustment and that court appearances, especially in a criminal case, can cause stigma and should be avoided wherever possible. These views found expression in the Children and Young Persons Act 1969. However, some of the key sections of this Act were never brought into force. It was planned that they would be introduced in stages but, before this could happen, there was a change of government and the Conservatives refused to implement them. No action was taken by the subsequent Labour administration.

Two important provisions in the Act that were not implemented were contained in sections 4 and 5. The provisions have now been repealed by the Criminal Justice Act 1991 but, as we shall see below, it is still useful to consider them.

Section 4 states that 'A person shall not be charged with an offence, except homicide, by reason of anything done or omitted while he was a child'. Since 1963 the minimum age of criminal liability has been 10, although a child (ie under 14) can only be criminally liable if it has shown 'mischievous discretion' in committing an offence; a condition which is easily satisfied in the case of a reasonably intelligent child. Section 4 would have precluded any criminal liability (except for homicide) under 14 and thus brought this country more into line with the rest of Europe, where the minimum age of criminal liability is usually higher. Under section 5, the prosecution of young persons would only have been allowed for certain specified offences (the 1969 Act itself did not indicate what these would be) and could only be brought by 'a qualified informant' which would have been a police officer or employee of the local authority children's department. In any case, the qualified informant would have to consult the local authority before prosecuting, although there would be no obli-gation to follow the advice. Section 5(2) would have been of particular importance. The qualified informant should not have brought a prosecution unless satisfied that the case could not be adequately dealt with (a) by a parent, teacher or other person, or (b) by a police caution or (c) by instituting care proceedings under section 1 of the Act.

Unlike sections 4 and 5, section 1 was brought into force and has played an important part in dealing with a child or young person who is in need of care or control for various reasons, one of which can be the commission of a criminal offence. Care proceedings are civil proceedings but, if the allegation that the child or young person is in need of care and control was based on the commission of a criminal offence, that offence had to be proved to the court in accordance with the ordinary rules of criminal evidence. However, the law in this area has been considerably altered by the Children Act 1989: care proceedings can no longer be brought on the basis of the child or young person having committed an offence. We shall consider the sentences a youth court can pass in the next chapter.

To summarise, the situation concerning the prosecution of juveniles is the same as before the Children and Young Persons Act 1969. Any person aged 10 or over (subject to the 'mischievous discretion' requirement) can be prosecuted for any criminal offence (although boys under 14 are deemed incapable of committing certain sexual offences).

The discussion of section 4 and in particular, section 5 of the Act is necessary to understand the present situation concerning the prosecution of juvenile offenders. The 'welfare' approach, which was popular in the 1960s and 1970s, has now been largely superseded – at least in Government thinking – by a 'justice' approach, in which juvenile offenders are more likely to be considered responsible for their actions and sentenced accordingly. In this climate, it is not surprising that the view expressed in section 5, that care proceedings should be a preferred alternative to criminal proceedings, was never adopted by most police forces. However, adherents to both the 'welfare' and 'justice' approaches are generally in favour of police cautions: the stigma argument appears to have convinced both sides.

Police cautioning of juveniles had taken place before 1969, but following the Children and Young Persons Act, it became far more common. All English and Welsh police forces have a juvenile bureau or similar department to which the question of how to proceed against a juvenile offender will be referred. The juvenile bureau will be in close contact with the local social service and education departments and will consult them, although their advice does not have to be accepted. As with adult cautioning, discrepancies have emerged between different police forces. In 1994 the Surrey police cautioned 81% of males aged 14 but under 18 for non-motoring indictable offences; the corresponding figure for Durham was 37%. The Home Office circular and guidelines on cautioning referred to above suggested that, for juveniles, the first considerations should be the seriousness of the offence and the offender's record. If it is still not possible to reach a decision, regard should be had to other circumstances such as the attitude of the parents, the recommendations of the social services department and the interest of the victim. In any case, a caution should only be administered where there is enough evidence to justify a prosecution, the juvenile makes an admission of guilt and the parents consent to a caution. The citing of cautions in juvenile courts should continue.

The practice of cautioning juveniles is open to criticism. The large increase in cautioning in recent years has partly resulted from the cautioning of juveniles who, in earlier years, would have been let off without any action being taken at all. As cautions are recorded, juvenile offenders can be brought before the court at an earlier stage than in the past. Magistrates are likely to deal more severely with juveniles who have already been cautioned. Another criticism is one we have considered for adult cautioning: that some juveniles may be inclined to take the 'easy way out' rather than argue their genuine innocence in court.

The caution, which consists of a stern 'ticking off' by a senior officer at a police station, seems in itself to contain little by way of positive value. Some police forces, however, follow up the caution by keeping in touch with the juvenile and offering support where needed.

Victims

We have already considered the difficulties that could arise from making reparation to the victim the main or sole aim of sentencing. However, this does not mean that the plight of the victim should be ignored by our criminal justice system. The claim that in recent years far more attention has been paid to the offender than the victim is not wholly without foundation, although this argument could imply that attention has to be paid to either one or the other. The needs of the offender and the victim are different and there is no reason why greater consideration should not be given to both.

We shall consider three ways in which victims of crime can receive assistance: the powers of criminal courts to make compensation and restitution orders, the Criminal Injuries Compensation Scheme and victim support schemes.

Compensation and restitution orders

A criminal court can award compensation to the victim of a crime under section 35 of the Powers of Criminal Courts Act 1973. Indeed, a court is now under a statutory duty to give its reasons for not making a compensation award in an appropriate case. The victim must have suffered personal injury, loss or damage resulting from the offence. With the exception of claims arising from road accidents, compensation is now also payable to the victim's relatives for funeral expenses or as a bereavement award. The offender must either have been convicted of the offence or it must have been taken into consideration on sentence (the significance of offences taken into consideration is explained in the next chapter). Formerly, a compensation order could only be attached to another sentence, but now it can be a sentence in its own right. It is also no longer necessary for the amount of loss or damage to be proved to the court. If a court considers that both a fine and a compensation order are appropriate, but that the offender's means are insufficient to pay both, priority should be given to the compensation order. In *R v Miller* (1976) the Court of Appeal gave some directions on the making of compensation orders. They should only be made when the legal position is clear. The offender's ability to pay must be taken into account. If payment is to be made by instalments, the amount payable should be clearly specified and the instalments should not be spread over too long a period: the offender should not be encouraged to commit further offences in order to pay the compensation. There may be good moral grounds for making the order to remind the offender of the evil that has been caused. In 1988 a Home Office Circular set out guidelines for compensation awards in criminal courts, including tariff levels for personal injury cases.

Despite recent changes, there are still problems with compensation orders. Compensation can only be ordered following a conviction; it cannot be ordered when the offender has only been cautioned. This can lead to particular difficulty in cases involving juveniles. The level of compensation awarded has also been criticised. Although magistrates' courts can award compensation up to £5,000 and the Crown Court has no limit (although both must consider the offender's means), the amounts awarded can be small. The average amount of compensation in 1994 was £163 at magistrates' courts and £2,019 at the Crown Court. Since the introduction of the requirement on courts to give reasons for not making compensation orders, there has been a significant rise in the number of orders made. This is particularly the case for offences of violence against the person: in magistrates' courts the use of orders increased from 34% in 1988 to 59% in 1994. Compensation orders suffer from the same problems of enforcement as other financial orders: the court order does not guarantee that the money will be paid. Courts have a similar range of options as for the enforcement of fines, with the ultimate sanction being committing the offender to prison.

Under section 28 of the Theft Act 1968, courts have power to order any person, including an innocent party, who is in possession or control of stolen goods to make restoration to anyone entitled to them. If the goods have been sold or otherwise disposed of, the order can be made to cover either the proceeds, or any goods which directly or indirectly represent the stolen goods (for example, goods that have been exchanged or bought from the proceeds of the stolen goods). Otherwise, a court can order that any money taken from the offender on being apprehended can be used to pay the value of the stolen goods to any person entitled to them. It is necessary that the goods have been stolen and the person ordered to make restitution has either been convicted of an offence related to the theft, or had the offence taken into consideration on sentence for another offence. As with compensation orders, restitution should only be ordered by a court where the question of entitlement to the property is clear. It is also possible for a victim of crime to seek compensation in the civil courts. Details of the ways in which this can be done and the drawbacks involved are discussed elsewhere in this book.

The Criminal Injuries Compensation Board

The Criminal Injuries Compensation Board (CICB) was established in 1964 to make payments to the victims of personal injury caused either by a crime of violence or by trying to prevent a crime or apprehend a suspect. If the victim died, close relatives or dependants could be entitled to compensation. The victim had to provide information about matters such as the nature of the offence, the injuries received and their treatment, the financial loss and any compensation or benefits that have been received. On receipt of the application form, the CICB checked the information provided. The police were asked to verify the victim's account of the incident. They were asked if the victim's conduct contributed to the injuries received. If it appeared that there could be a lengthy delay in dealing with the application, for example, because the victim's medical condition could not yet be fully determined, the CICB had the power to make an interim award. When all the information was available, an application was considered by a single member of the CICB who could make an award for the amount claimed or a lesser amount, refuse to make an award at all, or pass the application on for consideration by a two or three member panel of the CICB. If the victim wanted to appeal, there would be a hearing at which the victim had to appear. The victim could also seek judicial review of the decision of the CICB.

There were certain restrictions on the availability of compensation from the CICB. If the total compensation payable after the deduction of social security benefits would be less than a specified figure, no award would be made. The CICB could reduce or withhold payment if the victim had not told the police of the attack within a reasonable period, if the victim had not helped the Board with its enquiries, or if there were a possibility that the person who caused the injury may benefit from the award. In addition, the Board could refuse to make or reduce an award because of the victim's criminal record or unlawful conduct connected with the injury.

In some cases compensation would also be refused if the victim lived in the same household as the offender. Legal aid was not available, but advice could be obtained under the green form scheme. Many victims appeared not to know of the existence of the CICB: research by Joanna Shapland showed that 39% of victims in her sample had never heard of it. The research also showed that the average time between the application and making of an award was just over nine months. The scheme was criticised for not covering property offences, but the Government considered that these should be dealt with by private insurance. The awards were also criticised as being too low.

The Criminal Justice Act 1988 contained a provision which would have put the CICB on a statutory basis, but this was never brought into force. In December 1993 the Government published a White Paper, 'Compensating Victims of Violent Crime: Changes to the Criminal Injuries Compensation Scheme'. It set out details of a new tariff scheme to compensate victims of violent crime with awards based on a flat-rate tariff according to the type of injury which the claimant suffered, instead of the former basis of common law damages. No special account was to be taken of special damages, loss of earnings, or the circumstances of the particular case. The Government claimed that this scheme would be quicker and cheaper to administer, and would not leave the average claimant any worse off. The criteria for eligibility would be broadly the same as before. The new scheme has now been put on a statutory basis by the Criminal Injuries Compensation Act 1995. The Act does, however, contain important changes from the proposals in the White Paper: in specified cases compensation will be payable for loss of earnings and special expenses.

Victims support schemes

There are several bodies which provide assistance for victims of crime on a voluntary basis. In 1980 the National Association of Victims Support Schemes (NAVSS) was established and there are 378 affiliated schemes in England, Wales and Northern Ireland (Scotland has a separate organisation). In addition there are 76 Crown Court witness schemes to provide support for people who have to give evidence. Each victims support scheme has a co-ordinator who is in daily contact with the local police. The police give the co-ordinator details of victims of crime in the area. The co-ordinator will then contact one of a number of volunteers who will visit the victim as soon as possible. The volunteers will provide practical support such as changing a lock, helping with insurance forms and giving legal advice. In some cases they will also be able to provide emotional support. The NAVSS receives funds from central government but these have been insufficient to enable the local schemes to function properly so they have had to raise money themselves. In 1994/95 the Home Office provided £10,600,000.

Other organisations which help victims include rape crisis centres and the National Women's Aid Federation, which provides refuges for women and their children.

Postscript: insider dealing

It was stated earlier in the chapter that most newly-created criminal offences were a reflection of 'social development' and it was unlikely that any behaviour would be criminalised in the future simply on the ground that it was immoral. The practice of 'insider dealing' is interesting to consider in this respect. Insider dealing occurs when people in the world of finance, such as company directors or stockbrokers, receive information in a situation where it would be improper to make personal use of it but then proceed to use the information for personal gain. The Companies Act 1980 made insider dealing involving transactions on the Stock Exchange a criminal offence punishable with a maximum of two years' imprisonment. Few prosecutions followed, apparently because it was difficult for investigators to obtain information about the transactions. However, the Financial Services Act 1986 gave Department of Trade and Industry inspectors wider powers to obtain documents and compel witnesses to give evidence. In 1987 Geoffrey Collier, the former head of Morgan Grenfell Securities, pleaded guilty to two charges of insider dealing. He was given a twelve month prison sentence, suspended for two years, and fined £25,000. He was also ordered to pay £7,000 costs.

The practice of insider dealing was officially disapproved, but by no means unheard of, before it became a criminal offence. It is no secret that the purpose in creating the offence was to maintain confidence in the Stock Exchange. The 'Big Bang' in the City brought with it more fears of sharp practice and the Criminal Justice Act 1988 raised the maximum sentence for insider dealing to seven years' imprisonment. The present law is contained in the Criminal Justice Act 1993. The maintenance of public confidence, which is necessary for the successful operation of a major wealth-creating institution, was openly admitted to be the main reason for creating this offence, whereas the fact that a businessman can make a personal gain of thousands of pounds by abuse of trust was only a secondary consideration. Thus, the offence of insider dealing is really a product of 'social development' rather than the criminalisation of immoral behaviour.

Chapter 13

The procedure and practice
of sentencing

In Chapter 4 we considered the working of the criminal process up to and including trial by jury. We then looked at some of the problems in the appeals system. In this chapter we shall consider the important area that comes between conviction and possible appeal – sentencing. The chapter is divided into three main sections: information for sentencers; the powers of the criminal courts; and the practice of sentencing.

Information for sentencers

Before judges or magistrates can pass sentence, they need to know a certain amount of information about the defendant. At the very least they will know the defendant's name, address and sex, and the circumstances of the offence(s) for which the defendant has been convicted. This information is hardly sufficient to form the basis of an appropriate sentence, unless the criterion of appropriateness is pure retribution, in which case the circumstances of the offence would probably be the only information required. However, as we shall see below, our sentencing process is not wholly based on retribution. Until recently there were no statutes or cases which stated that certain types of information should be considered before sentence could be passed; there were only a number of statutory provisions dealing with specific cases. The Criminal Justice Act 1991 (as amended by the Criminal Justice and Public Order Act 1994) provides that, in the case of an offender aged 18 or over, a court shall obtain a pre-sentence report (see below) before the passing of a custodial sentence or certain community sentences (see below), unless it considers that it is unnecessary to do so. The relevant community sentences are a probation order with additional requirements; a community service order; a combination order; or a supervision order with additional requirements. In the case of an offender aged under 18, a pre-sentence report must be obtained before the passing of a custodial sentence or the same community sentences, except for cases triable only on indictment where the court considers it unnecessary. For a custodial or a community sentence, where a pre-sentence report is required, failure to obtain such a report will not invalidate the sentence, but a report must be obtained for any appeal against the sentence.

There are a number of different sources of information and it will become apparent that this can lead to difficulties.

Antecedents

Courts usually receive information about the accused (known as 'antecedents') from the police, unless the offence is a very minor one or the offender has pleaded guilty by post, an option which is available for certain summary offences and is widely used for minor road traffic offences. The amount of information provided varies among different police forces but usually includes the age, education, and domestic background of the offender, as well as any previous convictions. Since 1985 cautions can also be mentioned.

The police may include with the report of the antecedents a list of any offences the defendant would like to have 'taken into consideration' (TIC) when sentenced. These offences are ones which the defendant is prepared to admit to, but which are not being charged. There are advantages for both the police and the defendant in this process. The police will have their numbers of unsolved crimes reduced and will not have to present cases for prosecution which may be difficult to prove. A defendant will have the slate 'wiped clean', with probably only a small resulting increase in sentence – certainly much smaller than if there had been separate convictions for the TIC offences. Strictly speaking, an offender could subsequently be prosecuted for a TIC offence, but the Court of Appeal has said this should not happen. The procedure is also used to deal with situations where, for example, a defendant admits to a hundred similar cases of defrauding the same employer. Several instances may be charged, with the rest as TIC offences.

The practice of taking offences into consideration has been subject to some of the same criticisms as plea bargaining. The increasing pressure on police forces to clear up crime could provide an incentive to some officers to persuade offenders to admit to other offences of which they are innocent, in return for some benefit such as the withdrawal of any objection to bail. In 1986 a former police officer in Kent made widely-publicised allegations of such deals being made in his force.

In her book '*Between Conviction and Sentence*', Joanna Shapland provides evidence of widespread variations in practice among police forces as to what is included in antecedents reports. Essential information is not always provided and there is little uniformity in the provision of information about previous convictions. One reason for this is that many police forces use a court liaison officer, whose job it is to read out information about defendants from documents which the officer probably played no part in compiling.

The prosecution's statement of the facts

If the defendant pleads guilty, the prosecution will outline the facts of the case to the court. In any case, the defence will usually mention the facts in its plea in mitigation (see below). However, each will do so in a different way. It is traditional in our criminal justice system that the prosecution, unlike in many other countries, makes no suggestion of a possible sentence to the court. The defence, on the other hand, is not only allowed but expected to urge the court to deal with the defendant as leniently as possible. Some people argue that this is likely to give an advantage to the defendant and that the prosecution, even if not allowed to recommend a sentence, should at least be able to remind (or acquaint) the court with the appropriate level of sentence for that type of offence recommended by the Court of Appeal. Others argue that, as the whole trial process is likely to present the defendant in a bad light anyway, it is not unbalanced to restrict the prosecution to a simple statement of the facts. The point about reminding the court of the appropriate level of sentence does have some validity: after all, Court of Appeal decisions on sentencing are law (although it may be argued that some of the 'guidelines' are obiter dicta) and it has always been the function of an advocate to remind the court of the law. Indeed, in *R v Panayioutou* (1989) the Court of Appeal stated that prosecution counsel should draw the trial judge's attention to any guideline cases. As we have seen in Chapter 4, the prosecution now has the right to appeal against sentence, but it is interesting to note that, in the debate so far, there has been no proposal to give the prosecution the right to *recommend* a sentence.

Pre-sentence report

A social inquiry report (SIR) was another, and much fuller, source of information about the defendant. The reports were compiled by probation officers. Generally, courts had no obligation to consider SIRs but there were specific cases when they were directed to do so, either by statute or by Home Office circular.

The Criminal Justice Act 1991 introduced the pre-sentence report, which effectively replaces the SIR. The Act defines a pre-sentence report as a report in writing containing information on certain matters prescribed by the Home Secretary, and which has been written by a probation officer or social worker with a view to helping the court determine the best way of dealing with an offender. We have seen above the circumstances where a pre-sentence report is required.

The compilation of SIRs took up a considerable proportion of the probation service's time and there were demands from probation officers that more selective use should be made of them. One contentious issue was the compilation of reports on defendants who intended to plead not guilty. There were problems in trying to provide an explanation for a criminal offence the client denied committing. Also, about half of jury trials end in acquittal (see Chapter 4), so a large number of reports were wasted. The Home Office urged probation officers to try and complete a report in such cases provided the defendant consented. If there were difficulties about compiling a full report, a short report would suffice.

There was certainly inconsistency among different probation services in the compilation of SIRs, and this was highlighted in research by Fred Perry (1974) and the Home Office Research and Planning Unit (1979). For example, some reports omitted important details which were considered potentially damaging to the recommendation the officer wished to make. Following a report of a Working Group on Services to the Courts, the Home Office produced a new circular on SIRs in 1983. The circular confirmed that they should include an assessment of the offender's personality and family background; relevant information about the offender's circumstances; the offender's employment (or employment prospects) and attitude to work; the detail of, and the offender's attitude to the offence(s); and the probation officer's opinion of the effect of any sentence which is recommended. The question of recommending a sentence in a SIR was itself a matter of some difficulty. About 80% of SIRs contained a recommendation as to sentence. Many probation officers felt unable to recommend a custodial sentence so they either recommended a non-custodial sentence or sometimes made no recommendation at all. In a number of cases in the Court of Appeal Lord Justice Lawton criticised probation officers for making 'unrealistic' recommendations (for example, *R v Blowers* (1977)). The Home Office re-affirmed the right of probation officers to make whatever recommendation they considered appropriate in the case. It was never clearly spelt out to probation officers whether their recommendations should be wholly based on what was most appropriate for the offender, or whether they should take into account the wider interests of the public.

About 70% of recommendations as to sentence made in SIRs coincided with the sentence actually passed. What is not clear is whether this reflected a genuinely high rate of agreement between probation officers and sentencers, or whether probation officers knew the sort of sentences their local judges and magistrates were likely to pass and, therefore, made realistic recommendations. There is no clear evidence to suggest that SIRs improved the quality of sentencing in terms of reconvictions. Reports with opinions or recommendations were more likely to be followed by non-custodial sentences. Probation officers increasingly came to present their own reports in court and some people considered that this increased the likelihood of the sentencer's accepting the report's recommendations.

The Government envisaged that the introduction of the pre-sentence report would result in a change in the role of the probation officer in this respect. The National Standards for Pre-Sentence Reports published in 1995 prescribes four main sections for each report. The first, 'offence analysis', should include discussion of the context in which the offence occurred. The second, 'relevant information about the offender', should deal with personal and social information, but should also examine the outcome of any earlier court sentences. The third section is 'risk to the public of re-offending, and the fourth, 'the conclusion', should explain why the report writer either does or does not recommend a community order. A Home Office data collection exercise published in 1994 revealed that about two-thirds of proposals in reports for magistrates' courts and about half of those in the Crown Court were in accordance with the sentence given. Almost 80% of proposals made to magistrates for a community sentence resulted in such a sentence, whereas the corresponding figure in the Crown Court was just over 50%. This suggests that there has not been a major difference between the success rates of proposals in SIRs and pre-sentence reports.

Medical reports

These are in practice nearly always psychiatric reports. Psychiatric examinations are always carried out on people charged with murder or manslaughter. Otherwise, they result from initiatives by the defence, by the court itself or sometimes by the probation service or police. Medical reports were made in about 13% of the cases studied by Shapland. However, there was not a single medical disposal (see below) in any of these cases. This does not mean that such reports are a waste of time; the sentencer will be able to take the defendant's state of mind into consideration in passing sentence and a non-custodial measure will enable out-patient treatment to be undertaken or continued.

Pleas in mitigation

These are speeches to sentencers made by defence advocates, or sometimes by the defendants themselves, pointing out reasons why defendants should not be dealt with too severely. Shapland's research included presenting 30 barristers with the facts of the same fictitious case (she played the role of client). There were considerable variations in both the amount of information selected by the barristers to use in the pleas in mitigation, as well as the particular facts of the case which the barristers felt to be important. Pleas in mitigation often contain more information than pre-sentence reports and are more up to date as defendants can advise their barristers of recent changes in their circumstances. Advocates are less likely to omit factors unfavourable to defendants. Experienced advocates will know the judge or magistrates they are addressing, whereas probation officers writing pre-sentence reports will have no way of knowing the composition of the courts their reports will be presented to. Pleas in mitigation rarely mention specific sentences; the appeal to the sentencer is usually more along the lines of 'avoiding a custodial sentence' or 'being lenient'.

Some people, including police officers and judges, are cynical about pleas in mitigation, taking the view that defence advocates will put forward any story for the benefit of their clients, even if this involves making unsupported allegations against victims. Lawyers can be in a difficult position here. The professional ethics of the Bar provide that counsel must put forward any explanation provided by the client, however unlikely it may seem, unless counsel knows that the explanation is false. If necessary, the judge could intervene and ask for some sort of proof but this does not often happen. Fortunately, counsel usually handle such matters with discretion as they do not wish to risk antagonising the jury.

Despite the fact that the Court of Appeal is establishing a large body of case law on sentencing, it is rare for a defence advocate to cite authority to the sentencer in the plea in mitigation. If the prosecution were able to cite authority in commenting on sentence, the defence would have to do so as well. However, this would also exacerbate the problem of unrepresented defendants. Shapland's research has shown that they already have a considerable disadvantage in that, when making their own pleas in mitigation, they often mention the wrong sort of factors and are not always fully prepared to accept the gravity of the case. Legal argument would be totally beyond the capacity of many of them.

Conclusion

The provision of information about the defendant before sentence is of considerable importance, but the present system can be criticised in that the duplication of information provided to the court (eg in the pre-sentence report and the plea in mitigation) is wasteful of increasingly scarce resources. The main justification for the existing system is that the effect of the imperfections in each of the sources of information is reduced by this duplication. Possible reforms would be a single court report, or an agreement between the existing agencies as to what information each should include in its report.

Powers of the criminal courts

In this section we shall consider the main powers available to criminal courts to deal with adult, young adult (18–20) and juvenile offenders.

Death

It is widely believed that the death penalty has been abolished in this country. For all practical purposes this is true, but it could still be imposed on anyone aged at least 18 convicted of one of a small number of uncommon offences including high treason and piracy with violence.

There have been several attempts in Parliament to re-introduce the death penalty for murder in recent years but they have all failed.

Imprisonment

Both magistrates' courts and the Crown Court have the power to imprison convicted offenders. Until recently, there has been little statutory guidance as to when a court should consider a custodial sentence appropriate or as to how long such a sentence should be. The Criminal Justice Act 1991 now provides some guidance. Except in the case of a defendant convicted of murder, a court should not pass a prison sentence unless it considers that the crime was so serious that only a prison sentence is justified or, in the case of a violent or sexual offence, that only a prison sentence would be adequate to protect the public from serious harm.

The Act also has something to say about the length of custodial sentences. They should be commensurate with the seriousness of the offence or, in the case of violent or sexual offences, for a longer term if the court thinks it necessary to protect the public from serious harm. The Government considered such a statement to be very important, but it is vague and does not seem to be having much influence on the practices of sentencers.

In April 1996 the Government published a White Paper, 'Protecting the Public: the Government's Strategy on Crime in England and Wales'. This document proposes two radical changes in our penal system: the introduction of a minimum sentence, and the abolition of parole.

At present, there is no minimum prison sentence in this country, although a magistrates' court cannot impose a sentence of less than five days. Provisions have long existed which permit the release of prisoners before the expiry of the period to which they were sentenced. Formerly, all prisoners could have up to one third of their sentence remitted on the grounds of 'industry and good conduct'. In practice, all prisoners received the full third remission unless any of the period had been lost through breaches of prison discipline (for prisoners serving 12 months or less, the remission period was up to one half). In addition, the Criminal Justice Act 1967 introduced the parole system. The Home Secretary had the power to release, on parole, any offender serving a prison sentence after a fixed period, which at the scheme's termination was six months or one third of the sentence, whichever was later. An offender released on parole remained on licence until the earliest date on which the offender would otherwise have been released. The licence could contain conditions. An offender could be recalled to prison at any time during the licence period, usually for committing another offence or for the breach of a licence condition. The parole system became complicated and gave rise to many anomalies and inconsistencies. Moreover, it seemed to belong to a bygone age of rehabilitative sentencing and did not fit well with the new 'justice' approach (see Chapter 12). A committee under Lord Carlisle therefore recommended its abolition and this was effected by the Criminal Justice Act 1991. 'Short term prisoners', serving less than four years, are released after serving half of their sentence, and 'long term prisoners', serving four years or more, are released after serving two-thirds of their sentence. In any case where the sentence was for 12 months or more the prisoner is released on licence, which expires after three-quarters of the sentence. Discretionary release after half the sentence may be ordered for long term prisoners at the discretion of the Home Secretary, having been advised by the Parole Board. The arrangements for the release of life sentence prisoners remained the same: the Home Secretary is advised by a special committee.

The 1996 White Paper proposes that parole should be abolished and that offenders should serve the full term of imprisonment ordered by the court, although prisoners aged over 16 will be eligible for a discount of 15-20% for good behaviour.

It is not envisaged that this change in itself will lead to an increase in the period of time offenders spend in prison, as judges will be asked to take account of these changes when sentencing. Minimum sentences are proposed for persistent adult drug dealers and burglars. A person convicted of trafficking in Class A drugs (including heroin and ecstasy), who has two or more previous convictions for similar offences, should receive a prison sentence of at least seven years, whereas a domestic burglar, with two or more previous convictions for similar offences, should have a minimum sentence of three years' imprisonment. In addition, an adult offender who is convicted for the second time of a serious sexual or violent offence should receive an automatic sentence of life imprisonment.

Since the abolition of the death penalty for murder, imprisonment has been the main sanction available to courts in this country. However, imprisonment has only been widely used since the nineteenth century. Previously, corporal and capital punishment were common and, later on, transportation. More recently, new sentences have been introduced which were designed to keep certain types of offender out of prison and deal with them in the community. There were two main reasons for this: first, prisons had become very overcrowded and, second, they were failing to deter or reform many offenders. However, the proposals outlined in the White Paper are in line with the new Government philosophy that 'prison works', a view which has – at least indirectly – led to an increase in the prison population from 40,606 in December 1992 to 53,974 in April 1996. The Government itself accepts that implementation of the White Paper's recommendations would add at least 10,800 to the prison population. This would be met by building new prisons. Is the Government's view that 'prison works' correct? The evidence is not encouraging. About 65% of offenders released from prison are reconvicted within two years. Keeping an increasing number of offenders off the streets may seem likely to reduce the level of crime, but evidence showing that fewer than 3% of offences result in conviction indicates that it would be more productive to concentrate resources on crime prevention and detection. It is clear that, although there is a small number of extremely violent individuals from whom the public needs to be protected, many prisoners have committed relatively minor offences and could be dealt with just as effectively (and far more cheaply) in the community. It is a sobering thought that the UK has a higher percentage of its population in prison than any other country in the EU. Is our society that much safer as a result?

SUSPENDED SENTENCE OF IMPRISONMENT

The suspended sentence was introduced in the Criminal Justice Act 1967. The relevant provisions are now contained in the consolidating statute, the Powers of Criminal Courts Act 1973. If a court passes a sentence of imprisonment of not more than two years, it may order that the sentence shall not take effect unless the offender commits another imprisonable offence during the 'operational period' fixed by the court. This must be not less than one, nor more than two years. If the offender is convicted (which does not include being given a discharge: see below) of an imprisonable offence during this period, a court, in addition to any sentence it passes for the subsequent offence, may order that the suspended sentence shall take effect either with the original term unaltered, or for a lesser term. Alternatively, a court may substitute a new operational period to take effect from the time of the hearing. A court may even make no order at all. However, a court should normally order that the sentence take effect with the original term unaltered unless it considers that such an action would be unjust. If the court varies the original order, or makes no order, it is likely to be when the subsequent offence was comparatively trivial or of a different nature to the original offence, but a defendant certainly cannot expect to be dealt with more leniently for these reasons. If a suspended sentence is brought into effect, it is normally consecutive (ie additional) to any term imposed for the subsequent offence.

A sentence of imprisonment of more than six months which is suspended may be accompanied by a suspended sentence supervision order. The offender is placed under the supervision of a probation officer for a specified period not exceeding the operational period of the suspended sentence.

An offender should not receive a suspended sentence of imprisonment unless imprisonment would have been appropriate if the power to suspend had not existed and the exercise of the power can be justified by the exceptional circumstances of the case.

The suspended sentence has been the subject of a number of criticisms. Many offenders consider that the order, which is in fact a suspension of the strongest sanction available to the courts, means they have been let off completely. Although the suspended sentence was introduced as an alternative to immediate imprisonment, there is evidence that the sentence has been imposed on offenders who, had the sentence not existed, would have been fined or placed on probation. As a result, subsequent offending has not only led to an immediate prison sentence, but has resulted in a longer period of imprisonment than would have otherwise been the case, as offenders then received two (or more) consecutive sentences. It has also been argued that the suspended sentence added nothing new to our 'penal armoury', as the same effect could be achieved by the imposition of other sentences such as a conditional discharge.

The power of a court to order that part of a prison sentence should be served immediately and the rest held in suspense has been abolished by the Criminal Justice Act 1991. Introduced in 1982, the order's rather complicated provisions resulted in its being infrequently used and ultimately thought to serve no real purpose.

DETENTION IN A YOUNG OFFENDER INSTITUTION

The Criminal Justice Act 1982 abolished the sentence of imprisonment for offenders under the age of 21. The sentence of borstal training was also abolished. Borstal training was originally an indeterminate sentence for boys specially selected as being likely to respond positively to its regime. However, by the late 1970s it was largely indistinguishable from a prison sentence and the reconviction rates were high. Moreover, as we saw in Chapter 12, indeterminacy in sentencing was becoming unpopular. The Government felt that, although the borstal sentence was unnecessary, young adults should still be dealt with separately and youth custody was introduced to replace borstal training and imprisonment for the under 21 age group. The other custodial sentence for this age group, the detention centre order, was retained in the 1982 Act with the maximum term fixed at four months. The detention centre order was always surrounded by controversy. It was introduced in the Criminal Justice Act 1948 to calm the fears of people who were unhappy about the abolition of judicial corporal punishment. There was always a tension between the punitive nature of the order and the training element which staff said they tried to introduce. The existence of detention centres came to owe a great deal to 'law and order' politics. When the much-publicised 'short, sharp shock' regime introduced in 1980 did not lead to any improvement in reconviction rates, the writing was on the wall and both the detention centre order and the youth custody order were abolished in the Criminal Justice Act 1988 to be replaced by a single sentence of detention in a young offender institution (YOI). Together with the sentence of custody for life for very serious crimes, this is now the only custodial sentence available for the 15–20 age group. The sentence can only be passed if the court is satisfied that the circumstances, including the nature and gravity of the offence, are such that, if the offender were 21 or over, the court would impose a prison sentence; and that 'the offender qualifies for a custodial sentence'. The maximum term that can be ordered for an offender aged 17 or above is the same as for an adult convicted of that offence but, as we shall see later, youth is considered a mitigating factor by courts and terms imposed are usually less. This is determined in accordance with the same criteria that must be satisfied before a custodial sentence can be passed on an adult (see above).

SECURE TRAINING ORDER

During the early 1990s a 'moral panic' developed as a result of reports in popular newspapers claiming that young children were increasingly responsible for crimes such as vandalism and 'joy riding'. Matters came to a head with the murder of a two-year-old boy, James Bulger, by two boys aged eleven. The Government's response was the enactment in the Criminal Justice and Public Order Act 1994 of a new custodial sentence called the secure training order. A court can impose an order of between six months and two years on an offender aged 12, 13 or 14. Half the sentence is to be served in a secure training centre and half under supervision in the community. To qualify for this order, the child must have been convicted of three or more imprisonable offences, and must (either on this or a previous occasion) have been found to be in breach of a supervision order, or have been convicted of a criminal offence while subject to a supervision order. At the time of writing, this sentence, which has provoked much opposition, has not been made available to courts. It is worth noting that, in several other European countries, there is no criminal liability under the age of 14.

ATTENDANCE CENTRE

Like detention centres, attendance centres were created by the Criminal Justice Act 1948 and are now governed by provisions in the Criminal Justice Act 1982. Any offender aged 10 to 20 can be sent to an attendance centre if the offender has been convicted of an offence punishable with imprisonment for an adult; or, if an adult, could be imprisoned for fine default or failing to obey a court order; or for having broken any of the requirements of a probation order. The number of hours an offender is required to attend at the centre is usually 12, but the maximum sentence available is 24 hours where the offender is under 16, or 36 hours where the offender is aged 16 to 20. Attendance centres are divided into junior and senior; there are no senior attendance centres for women. The centres are normally run by the police and usually involve attendance on Saturday afternoons for physical education classes or practical courses.

Fine

Any offender convicted on indictment of an offence for which the sentence is not fixed by law (in effect murder, for which there is a mandatory sentence of life imprisonment) may be sentenced to pay a fine and this can be in addition to another order (except a discharge; see below). A magistrates' court can impose a fine as the whole or part of a sentence following conviction for an offence triable either way and for many statutory offences. In the Crown Court there is no maximum limit to the amount of a fine, although both the Magna Carta 1215 and the Bill of Rights 1688 provide that a fine should not be excessive. Statutes restrict the amount of the fine that can be imposed for many offences. The maximum fine that can be imposed by a magistrates' court following conviction for an offence triable either way is £5,000. For most summary offences, the maximum fine is determined by levels on a standard scale, with different offences being allocated to different levels according to their gravity. This system was introduced because the maximum fines laid down in statutes were becoming unrealistic because of inflation, and the Home Secretary can now change the amounts for each level without the need for legislation. The present maximum for level 5 (the highest level) is £5,000. Magistrates' courts are limited to maximum fines of £1,000 for young persons and £250 for children following conviction for any offence.

When the Crown Court imposes a fine, it must make an order specifying a term of imprisonment not to exceed 12 months or a similar order for the detention of young adult offenders, which the offender may have imposed for non-payment of the fine. There are, however, certain restrictions on the order being carried out. A magistrates' court also has the power to imprison adults or order the detention of young adults for non-payment of a fine. A court should not impose a fine which the offender will be unable to pay; yet a court should not imprison an offender if a fine would have been the appropriate sentence had the offender been able to pay.

If it could be shown that fines are an effective deterrent in reducing crime, they would be a very useful penalty as, provided the offender is able to pay, a fine lacks the unpleasant side-effects of imprisonment and is very cheap to administer. The evidence is not easy to evaluate as – perhaps more than any other measure – the fine (especially in the Crown Court) is likely to be reserved for the 'better risk' offender who is less likely to re-offend. However, making all possible allowances for this, the evidence still suggests that offenders who are fined are less likely to reoffend than similar offenders given other sentences. One difficulty with fines is their enforcement. This may be partly because some people are given fines they have difficulty in paying. There is also a view that some people simply refuse to pay fines, and the Criminal Justice Act 1991 gives the Home Secretary power to make regulations enabling a fine imposed by a magistrates' court to be deducted from any income support the offender receives. Also, it seemed unfair that an affluent offender and a poor one were given the same fine for the same offence. For several years there was growing pressure to adopt the Scandinavian 'day-fine' system where the fine is calculated by multiplying a number representing the offender's daily income by a number representing the gravity of the offence. The Criminal Justice Act 1991 introduced a unit fine scheme which operated on a similar basis. However, reports in the press of very high fines being imposed for trivial offences led to severe criticism of the scheme, and in the Criminal Justice Act 1993 the Government took the unusual step of abolishing a provision less than twelve months after it had come into force.

Probation

The Crown Court or a magistrates' court can make a probation order in respect of any offender aged 16 or over who has been convicted of any offence except one where the sentence is fixed by law. The court must consider that the order is desirable either to secure the rehabilitation of the offender or to protect the offender from causing harm or committing further offences. The effect of the order is that the offender is placed under the supervision of a probation officer for a fixed period between six months and three years. The order usually contains conditions designed to ensure the good conduct of the offender; for example, that the offender should be of good behaviour and lead an industrious life and that the offender should keep in touch with the probation officer and notify the officer of any change of address or employment. Following consultation with a probation officer, a court can impose conditions requiring the offender to attend at a specified place and engage in specified activities for a maximum of 60 days, and a condition requiring the offender not to undertake specified activities for either the whole or part of the period on probation. Other orders that the court may make include the requirement that the offender lives in a specified approved residence such as a probation hostel, or undergoes psychiatric treatment. As the offender's co-operation is crucial to the success of probation, an order may only be made if the offender consents to it.

If an offender does not comply with a condition of a probation order and the probation officer decides that the offender should be brought before a court (which does not happen in every case), the court can either fine the offender or, in an appropriate case, make an attendance centre order. A court may even deal with the offender for the offence for which the probation order was made. An offender who commits another offence while on probation may be dealt with for both the subsequent offence and the original offence.

Probation is no longer used mainly for first offenders and this may partly explain why the re-conviction rates of people given the order are disappointing. Recent research has shown that offenders, other than juveniles and adult males with one to four previous convictions, are actually more likely to re-offend after being placed on probation than if they had been given some other non-custodial order. Moreover, offenders who were given specially intensive supervision as part of the IMPACT study had worse re-conviction rates than offenders in the study who had received ordinary probation supervision. Some probation officers argue that re-conviction rates are not the appropriate criteria by which to measure the effectiveness of probation. In the IMPACT study the offenders who received intensive supervision gained certain personal advantages; for example the majority of them made better use of their leisure time than those who had received ordinary supervision.

The National Standards for the Supervision of Offenders in the Community (1995) set out various objectives for the probation order. The offender should be given a copy of instructions detailing the required standards of behaviour. A supervision plan should be developed, which should seek to identify the causes of the offending behaviour; make offenders aware of the impact of their crimes on the victims; state the purpose and desired outcome of supervision; draw-up an individual programme for each offender; and set a timescale for achieving each of the objectives.

Community service order

This order was introduced in the Criminal Justice Act 1972 and the provisions are now consolidated in the Powers of Criminal Courts Act 1973. An offender aged 16 or over who has been convicted of an imprisonable offence may be ordered to carry out unpaid work in the community for a specified number of hours. The minimum number of hours is 40 and the maximum 240. As with probation, the offender must consent to it and the full implications of a community service order explained before consent is given. The court has to consider a report by a probation officer about the offender's suitability for community service and must also be satisfied that there are suitable arrangements in the area where the offender resides. The work, which is supervised by the probation service, should normally be carried out within twelve months. As far as possible, its performance should avoid conflicting with the offender's religious beliefs and work or educational requirements.

If the offender fails to comply with a condition of the order, and the supervising officer decides to bring the matter to the attention of a court, the court may impose a fine and allow the order to continue, or revoke the order and pass another sentence for the original offence.

From its introduction in 1972, it has been recognised that community service has a number of different appeals. For some it has the appeal of 'making the punishment fit the crime'; others are attracted by the idea of reparation to the community and the effect this may have on offenders' attitudes; and others again see it as a cheaper and more constructive alternative to short prison sentences. None of these purposes has ever been officially expressed as paramount although the magistrates' handbook '*The Sentence of the Court*' considers the greatest value of the order to be its constructive nature. Community service orders have not generally been used to replace imprisonment: there is evidence that they have frequently been made for offenders who would otherwise have been given another non-custodial sentence. Nor are re-conviction rates following community service particularly impressive: in one Home Office study, they were even higher in the case of young adult men than for those released from detention centres.

The National Standards require probation officers to give offenders a set of requirements, which are similar to those issued to offenders on probation. On average, the offender should work for no fewer than five and no more than 21 hours a week. Work placements should be 'demanding in the sense of being physically, emotionally or intellectually taxing'.

Combination order

Probation has traditionally been regarded as an alternative to punishment and so it was always felt inappropriate to combine it with any other order. This restriction has been abolished by the Criminal Justice Act 1991 which allows a probation order to be combined with a community service order, with a reduced maximum of 100 hours unpaid work. The court must consider that a combination order is desirable in the interests of securing the rehabilitation of the offender; or protecting the public from being harmed by the offender; or preventing the offender from committing further offences.

Curfew order

The Criminal Justice Act 1991 introduced a curfew order for offenders aged 16 or over. A court may order that, within a six month period, an offender should remain in a specified place or specified places for periods of not less than two hours or more than 12 hours in any one day. The order, which the offender must consent to, should avoid interfering with the offender's work or education, or causing conflict with the offender's religious beliefs or the requirements of any other community order. A specified person shall be made responsible for monitoring the offender's whereabouts. The meaning of the order and the consequences of failing to comply with it must be explained to the offender. A curfew order may contain an additional requirement for securing the electronic monitoring of the offender during the specified period, provided that suitable arrangements exist in the area.

The use of a curfew order is not new in our criminal justice system. It can be imposed as part of a supervision order made on young offenders. However, the police are worried about the enforceability of such a provision and youth court magistrates rarely use it. In the US city of Atlanta in Georgia there is a night curfew on anyone under 16. Although introduced to protect children, it has had the effect of considerably reducing juvenile crime. It remains to be seen how popular such an order will be in this country and whether enforceability will prove a problem.

Electronic monitoring, or 'tagging', is also found in the USA and has been a controversial issue in this country for several years. The main objections have been civil libertarian ones, such as the degradation involved in being constantly under surveillance. Supporters of tagging – including one or two well-known former prisoners – counter this by saying that imprisonment is even more degrading. This argument has force providing that tagging is only used as an alternative to imprisonment: its opponents, however, claim that it is likely to be used to replace other non-custodial measures. Home Office experiments which allowed tagging as a condition of bail have not been particularly successful: in Nottingham, for example, nine out of seventeen defendants breached their bail conditions. Nevertheless, the Government brought the relevant provisions into force in 1995 so that further trials could take place in Manchester, Norfolk and Reading.

Community sentence

The White Paper 'Crime, Justice and Protecting the Public', which preceded the Criminal Justice Act 1991, took the view that, while greater use of non-custodial measures was desirable, sentencers would need to be more confident about them; to believe that the measures would be properly enforced and that offenders would be seen to be receiving a degree of punishment. In short, a 'toughening up' of non-custodial measures was envisaged. It was considered that one way of doing this would be to combine existing non-custodial orders. A community sentence is defined in the Act as a sentence consisting of, or including one or more community orders. A community order is any of the following: a probation order; a community service order; a combination order; a curfew order; a supervision order; an attendance centre order. A court should not pass a community sentence unless the offence was serious enough to warrant it.

Where a court passes a community sentence, the order or orders involved must be considered by the court to be the most suitable for the offender, and any restrictions on liberty must be commensurate with the seriousness of the offence.

Supervision order

Supervision orders were introduced by the Children and Young Persons Act 1969 to replace probation for juvenile offenders. The orders are also available for juveniles made the subject of care proceedings. A youth court can make a supervision order in respect of any child or young person convicted of a criminal offence. The consent of a juvenile to a basic supervision order is not required. Children (ie under 14) will be placed under the supervision of the local authority and young persons (ie 14 to 17) can be placed under the supervision of either the local authority or a probation officer. As with probation, the supervisor must 'advise, assist and befriend' the offender and the order may contain requirements, for example, that the offender should keep in touch with the supervisor. An order can be made for up to three years, the commonest periods being one or two years. The 1969 Act contains special requirements that can be added to an order. An offender may be required to live with a named individual or submit to medical treatment. An offender may also be required to take part in 'intermediate treatment'. If this is the case, the supervisor has power to order the offender to do any or all of the following: to live in a specified place; to attend at a specified place; to take part in specified activities. The maximum period of such an order is 90 days. The purpose of intermediate treatment is to remove juvenile offenders from their home environment and make them take part in challenging activities such as canoeing, fell-walking or even simply attending a local youth club. Youth court magistrates, after consultation with the supervisors, can specify the activities they want the offenders to participate in, or activities the offenders should not participate in. In these cases consent must be obtained from the offenders, their parents or guardian. Youth court magistrates can also impose night restriction orders, which instruct offenders to be indoors during certain hours at night. If the offender is in breach of a requirement in the order and the supervisor brings this to the court's attention, the court, in addition to its power to discharge or vary the order, may fine the offender or make an attendance centre order. In some cases the court may discharge the order and sentence the offender for the original offence. However, unlike probation, an offender who re-offends while under supervision cannot be sentenced for the original offence.

The power of criminal courts to impose a care order, which placed the child or young person in the care of the local authority, was abolished by the Children Act 1989. However, the Act does insert in the Children and Young Persons Act 1969 a provision whereby, in certain circumstances, a supervision order may require a child or young person to live in local authority accommodation for up to six months.

Deferment of sentence

Like the community service order, deferment of sentence was introduced in the Criminal Justice Act 1972 and the provisions are consolidated in the Powers of Criminal Courts Act 1973. The Crown Court or a magistrates' court can postpone sentence on an offender for up to six months to see how the offender behaves. The only factors that should be taken into account then are post-conviction behaviour, such as the making of reparation for the offence, and a change in the offender's circumstances. Only one deferment is allowed and the offender must consent to it. If the offender is convicted of another offence during the period of deferment, sentence for the original offence may then be passed before the end of the period. In practice, an offender for whom sentence is deferred and who manages to keep out of trouble during the deferment period, will not receive a custodial sentence.

There have been two main criticisms of the power to defer sentence. One, which we have already considered, is that it enables better-off offenders to buy their way out of trouble. The other is that the order is a good example of the tendency to encumber our sentencing system with unnecessary measures: the Crown Court has the ancient common law power to bind over a convicted offender to come up for judgment when requested. Since the introduction of deferment of sentence it is rarely used but, had it been extended to magistrates' courts, it would have served more or less the same purpose.

Absolute and conditional discharge

If the Crown Court or a magistrates' court convicts an offender for any offence (except one for which the sentence is fixed by law) and considers that in the circumstances it is unnecessary to punish the offender and probation is inappropriate, then the court can discharge the offender either absolutely or conditionally. An absolute discharge means in effect that no action is taken at all and is often ordered where a court disagrees with the decision to prosecute. A conditional discharge means that no further action will be taken unless the offender commits another offence within a specified period not exceeding three years. A discharge cannot be combined with another sentence for the same offence although it can be combined with an award of costs or a compensation order. If an offender who has received a conditional discharge is convicted of another offence during the specified period, the offender may, in addition to any other punishment imposed, be sentenced for the original offence. A discharge does not generally count as a conviction other than for the proceedings in which it was imposed. Thus, it is possible to appeal against a discharge but a discharge will not activate a suspended sentence.

Binding over to keep the peace or be of good behaviour

These are very old powers: binding over to keep the peace dates back to the thirteenth century and binding over to be of good behaviour to the Justices of the Peace Act 1361. The Crown Court and magistrates' courts can bind over to keep the peace or be of good behaviour any person who 'is before the court'. This includes not only the defendant, but also any witness or person making a complaint, even if such a person has not been convicted of an offence. The order usually lasts for a year. People bound over have to enter into their own recognisances or find a surety (or sometimes both) for a fixed sum of money which will be forfeited if the undertaking is broken. A person who refuses to be bound over can be imprisoned.

Mental health order

Under the Mental Health Act 1983, the Crown Court may order an offender to be detained in a specified hospital where the offender has been convicted of any imprisonable offence (except one for which the sentence is fixed by law) if the court is satisfied that the offender is suffering from a mental disorder, the nature or degree of which makes detention in a hospital for medical treatment appropriate and, if psychopathic disorder or mental impairment is present, the court is satisfied that the treatment is likely to alleviate the condition or prevent its deterioration. The court must also consider that such an order is the most suitable way of dealing with the case. Alternatively, the court may place the offender under the guardianship of a local authority. If the Crown Court orders detention in a hospital and considers that the public needs to be protected from the offender, it can make an order restricting the discharge of the offender, either for a specified period or without limit. A magistrates' court can make an order for detention in a hospital when an offender has been convicted of an imprisonable offence, or even if the offender has not been convicted if the court is satisfied as to guilt.

Comment

The changes introduced in the Criminal Justice Act 1991 were made because both imprisonment and the existing non-custodial measures had not been particularly successful in preventing further offending. Of course, people who are imprisoned are unable to offend in the community, but the time comes when they have to be released and re-conviction rates following imprisonment have been particularly high. This is not surprising when one considers it is the worst (or, at least, most persistent) offenders who are sent to prison, but many people considered that we could make greater use of non-custodial punishments without increasing the threat to the community. Even before the changes in the 1991 Act, they were more successful than imprisonment for most offenders as well as being far cheaper and more humane. The 1991 Act contains provisions designed to reduce the number of offenders sent to prison, but the evidence suggests that, in this respect, they have not been very successful.

The practice of sentencing

Given that the courts have the powers which we have just outlined, how does a sentencer come to decide on the sentence in a particular case? The sentence is usually at the discretion of the judge or magistrates. As we have seen, the sentence for murder is fixed by law as life imprisonment. Also, conviction for certain motoring offences results in automatic disqualification from driving. Otherwise, criminal offences usually have a statutory maximum penalty, such as seven years for theft, ten years for burglary (other than from a dwelling) and life for rape. The appropriate levels of sentencing for particular cases are contained in decisions of the Court of Appeal. Dr David Thomas of the Institute of Criminology, University of Cambridge, made a detailed study of these cases, which he first published in his book *'Principles of Sentencing'* in 1970. Thomas identified certain principles underlying the Court of Appeal's decisions. These principles are often fairly broad and are not precedents in the strict sense described in Chapter 6. Indeed, it is possible to find many exceptions to them. Thomas's analysis has been criticised as being too rigid, but it was never intended to be so and, provided it is considered as no more than a loose framework, it is still valuable.

Two further points should be noted. First, the decisions of the Court of Appeal are still usually found in cases where the defendant has appealed, despite the prosecution right to appeal against sentence. Defendants are only likely to appeal against what they consider to be heavy sentences. There is evidence to suggest that for some offences the general sentencing level of the Crown Court is lower than that advocated by the Court of Appeal. Second, the decisions of magistrates' courts, which deal with 98% of all criminal cases, are not so greatly influenced by the Court of Appeal. Magistrates deal with a large number of relatively trivial cases which are not always covered by Court of Appeal decisions, as these are appeals from Crown Court cases. As we have seen, magistrates are more concerned with internal consistency within their own bench than with considering the decisions of other benches and this leads to considerable inconsistencies in sentencing.

According to Thomas's research, the first or primary decision that a sentencer has to make is whether to pass a 'tariff' sentence or an 'individualised' sentence. The idea of a tariff was certainly popularised by Thomas – even among the judiciary – although he claimed that he was simply describing a process which was already taking place. It does not mean that there is a rigid scale of penalties, such as one year's imprisonment for robbery of £100 and two years' imprisonment for robbery of £200. What Thomas stated is that for most types of criminal offence one can identify a scale or range of sentence within which sentences for different factual situations will occur. If the primary decision results in a tariff sentence being chosen, the secondary decision is where in the range to place the sentence for the particular offence under consideration.

Before we consider tariff sentences in more detail, let us look at the less common individualised sentences.

Individualised sentences

Tariff sentences are based on proportionality – that people with similar backgrounds who commit similar offences in similar circumstances should receive similar sentences. Individualised sentences are not based on this principle; they are generally aimed at dealing with individual offenders in the manner most appropriate to their needs. A sentence can sometimes be justified as an individualised measure when it would be inappropriate on tariff principles.

There are four main types of offender for whom individualised sentencing is used.

YOUNG OFFENDERS

The sentence of borstal training, which was abolished in the Criminal Justice Act 1982, was a good example of an individualised sentence: it provided a training regime and its length was (within limits) indeterminate, so it could involve offenders spending more time in custody 'for their own good' than would be appropriate for a tariff sentence. YOI sentences are operated on a tariff basis, so it is non-custodial sentences such as supervision or probation which provide the main individualised measures for young offenders. These can be found in quite serious cases if there is evidence that the offender is likely to respond to supervision.

INTERMEDIATE RECIDIVISTS

These are offenders in their late twenties or early thirties who have many previous convictions probably dating back to their childhood. If there is evidence to indicate that a new approach may work, the Court of Appeal will often be prepared to replace a custodial sentence with an order such as probation.

INADEQUATE RECIDIVISTS

The same approach may be adopted for middle-aged or elderly offenders who have a long history of relatively minor offences which have resulted in imprisonment and most other types of sentence. In one case the Court of Appeal quashed a five year prison sentence on such a man and imposed a probation order with a requirement of residence at a hostel.

OFFENDERS WHO NEED PSYCHIATRIC TREATMENT

As we have seen above, offenders may be detained in a hospital under the Mental Health Act 1983, or placed on probation with the condition that they undergo psychiatric treatment. These are both examples of individualised sentences. A further example is the use of life imprisonment in such cases. Life imprisonment, where allowed, is sometimes imposed on offenders to enable prison and Home Office officials to determine when it is safe to recommend their release. A fixed term sentence would not allow this flexibility and there would be a possibility of an offender having to be released before treatment had been completed, thus constituting a danger to the public. In some of these cases the application of tariff principles would require a fairly short fixed term sentence.

Tariff sentences

DEFINING THE RANGE

Once the primary decision has been taken to impose a tariff sentence, the secondary decision must be taken as to what is the appropriate place on the range to put the offender. At the outset this involves defining the range for the particular type of crime within the available scale of sentencing. As Thomas put it, 'The conventional relationships between frequently encountered factual situations and corresponding levels of sentence constitute the foundations of the tariff'. The maximum penalty provided by a statute does not necessarily represent the top of the scale. This is especially true in older statutes such as the Offences Against the Person Act 1861, as attitudes towards certain offences have changed over the last century. That statute makes the crime of bigamy punishable with a maximum sentence of seven years imprisonment: nowadays, it is rarely prosecuted. Some common law offences do not have a maximum penalty. In more recent statutes, such as the Theft Acts 1968 and 1978, the maximum sentence is more likely to be relevant. In these cases the Court of Appeal has made it clear that it should be reserved for the worst possible example of that crime.

Therefore, for each type of offence dealt with in the Crown Court, one can identify a series of ranges of sentence which are related to the variations of the offence most frequently encountered. Generally, such typical fact situations have upper and lower limits within which the sentence usually falls. Thomas has written of two parallel scales: one formed of typical fact situations, the other formed of the ranges of sentences usually associated with those fact situations.

How can these ranges of sentence be altered? For several years there was a growing concern about increasing levels of imprisonment and it was suggested that one way of dealing with this would be for courts to impose shorter prison sentences. In 1978 the Advisory Council on the Penal System published a report pointing out that prison sentences could be reduced across the board without affecting the re-conviction rates of those imprisoned. The report was widely criticised in Parliament; comments were made to the effect that in a period of rising crime it would be folly to reduce the punishments imposed on convicted offenders (perhaps it would be more accurate to say that it was perceived as political folly). In 1979 the Committee of Inquiry into the Prison Service (the May Committee) also stated that prison sentences were longer than they need be. The Government's view remained that the level of sentencing was a matter for the judges and in 1980 the then Lord Chief Justice, Lord Lane, took the initiative. In *R v Upton* Lord Lane said that courts should be sparing in their use of imprisonment, and sentences for non-violent petty offenders should be as short as possible. Not long afterwards, the Court of Appeal heard a number of cases on the same day in which it was more specific. The most important of these is *R v Bibi*. Lord Lane, echoing the view of the Advisory Council on the Penal System, said that many offences could be dealt with just as effectively by sentences of six or nine months' imprisonment as by 18 months or three years. This applies not only to first offenders but also to 'the less serious types of factory or shopbreaking; the minor case of sexual indecency; the more petty frauds where small amounts of money are involved; the fringe participant in more serious crime'. But there are still sentences which should remain in the medium to long range category: 'most robberies; most offences involving serious violence; use of a weapon to wound; burglary of private dwelling houses; planned crime for wholesale profit; active large scale trafficking in dangerous drugs'. The Court of Appeal is still laying down such guidelines, but it is interesting to note that the Government has at last been prepared to intervene in the determination of maximum sentences: the Criminal Justice Act 1991 reduced the maximum sentence for theft from ten years imprisonment to seven years, and for burglary (other than from a dwelling) from fourteen years to ten years. As we have already seen, the Act also contained provisions which were designed to restrict the length of prison sentences.

INITIAL TARIFF PLACEMENT

The initial tariff placement in the sentencing range shows the highest sentence that is appropriate for the case but it does not necessarily indicate the final sentence. As we shall see below, many initial placements are then lowered to reflect mitigating factors. It is important, however, that the initial placement is proportionate to the facts of the case and is not aggravated by other factors. The importance of proportionality is well-illustrated in a case in 1975 where a woman was convicted of damaging a flower pot valued at £1. She had a record of minor offences, many amounting to little more than a nuisance, and her sentences had included probation, borstal training and a hospital order. As there was no suitable psychiatric order available, she was sentenced to 18 months' imprisonment. The Court of Appeal reduced this to a £2 fine. Even if the offender is likely to receive treatment in prison for such problems as alcoholism or drug addiction which may require a reasonable length of time to have any chance of success, a court should still not pass a disproportionate sentence.

SECONDARY TARIFF PRINCIPLES

There are a number of 'secondary tariff principles' which should be considered. It is clearly established that a sentencer should not take account of the fact that the offender is likely to receive remission or parole in making the initial placement. Although a plea of guilty will usually be taken into account as a mitigating factor, a defendant who pleads not guilty should not be given a disproportionate sentence. If an accused is sentenced for two or more separate offences, the question has to be considered whether the sentences should be concurrent (ie they run side by side which means the effective length is that of the longer) or consecutive (ie the effective length is that of the sentences added together). If the offences are part of a single transaction, for example a number of burglaries committed in the same evening, the sentences are normally concurrent. But, if one of the burglaries were accompanied by personal violence on a house owner, the attack would be treated as a separate transaction. The imposition of consecutive sentences allows a court to exceed the maximum allowed for each offence. In 1962 the Court of Appeal upheld a sentence of three consecutive terms of 14 years (the maximum penalty) for espionage passed on George Blake. In 1986 sentences totalling 45 years were passed on the arab terrorist Nazir Hindawi; this is now the longest term of imprisonment imposed by an English court. The sentencer should also consider the 'totality principle'. The effect of this is that the aggregate of consecutive sentences should not be longer than is appropriate for the offender's conduct, taken as a whole. It has been said that the aggregate should not be substantially higher than would be appropriate for the most serious of the offences taken alone and that the sentence should not be wholly out of keeping with the offender's past record or prospects. If this is still the case, the decisions in *Blake* and *Hindawi* must be considered as exceptional.

MITIGATING FACTORS

The final stage in determining a tariff sentence is for the sentencer to decide if there are any mitigating factors concerning the offender which will enable the initial placement on the scale, as determined by the facts of the case, to be reduced.

The youthfulness of the offender often leads to an individualised sentence, but youth can also be a mitigating factor when a tariff sentence is passed. Old age is allowed as a mitigating factor in some cases. The offender's record will also be relevant. Previous good character is considered a mitigating factor (minor motoring offences are ignored) and allowance may be given for a gap since the offender's last conviction, and where previous convictions are for a different type of offence than the present conviction (eg a number of convictions for violence and the present conviction for theft). In addition, there is a principle known as the 'jump effect'. According to this, sentences on an offender should increase steadily rather than by large jumps.

The circumstances leading to the offence may also be considered in mitigation. These are generally the sort of points mentioned in pre-sentence reports and pleas in mitigation. Provocation, although a defence only in murder cases, is a mitigating factor for assaults, woundings and even some cases of manslaughter. Domestic and financial problems may be relevant and, to a lesser extent, drink and drugs. So much crime is alcohol-related that sentencers find it difficult to take it into account in differentiating sentences. The consequences of conviction, such as loss of job or the effect on the offender's family, are not commonly accepted as a mitigating factor. Ill-health is sometimes considered, and also any special hardship offenders may have to undergo in prison, such as having to be placed in solitary confinement for their own protection as informers or sex offenders. In recent years the Court of Appeal has been applying what has come to be known as the 'clang of the gates' principle. In a number of cases the court has reduced a prison sentence because it felt that the offender had suffered enough punishment through the shock of being locked up. The development of this principle has been connected with that enunciated in *Upton* and *Bibi*.

The offender's behaviour after committing the offence will sometimes be considered in mitigation. A plea of guilty is usually taken to be a sign of remorse (although, as we have seen in Chapter 4, this is not necessarily the case) and the initial tariff placement can be reduced by between one-quarter and one-third for this reason alone. Help given to the police in their enquiries may be ground for mitigation, as well as any efforts made to compensate the victim. The Court of Appeal may reduce a sentence if it considers that the offender has a justifiable grievance arising whether before or at the trial. The commonest ground is where a co-defendant of equal culpability and with a similar record has been treated more leniently.

Examples of tariff sentences

To illustrate the operation of the tariff in practice, three criminal offences will now be considered; burglary, wounding or causing grievous bodily harm with intent to cause grievous bodily harm, and rape.

BURGLARY

As we have seen, the maximum penalty for burglary has been reduced from 14 to 10 years' imprisonment, except for burglary from dwellings where it remains at 14 years. The Court of Appeal, however, was already making such a distinction.

The court considers that burglary from a dwelling is a particularly serious crime which should result in a custodial sentence. The fact that the offender is young, is of previous good character or the value of the property stolen is small does not make any difference. The reasons were given by Lord Justice Lawton in *R v Smith and Woollard* (1978): 'This court knows that when there is a burglary in a house great distress is caused. Not only is there a loss of property but there is induced a feeling of insecurity ... it has been said, and rightly said, that when a house has been burgled it never seems the same again'. The length of sentence approved by the court will depend on factors such as the number of burglaries committed, the value of the property stolen and the number of similar previous convictions. If burglary is committed with a weapon – which is uncommon – the offence becomes one of aggravated burglary for which the maximum sentence is life imprisonment. Otherwise, the court seems to approve sentences in the range of two to five years. Sentences of ten years or more have been confirmed for professional burglars who operate carefully planned schemes for entering large houses and taking items of great value. The extent to which the court considers a custodial sentence essential for burglaries of dwelling houses can be seen in *R v Viera* (1991). The appellant, who had no previous convictions, lived in the same block of flats as an 87-year-old woman. During a visit, he unbolted the back door, and subsequently returned and stole an envelope containing £1,500. The woman was initially unaware that any offence had been committed. However, the Court of Appeal only reduced the two year prison sentence to one of twelve months.

Burglaries from commercial premises are usually regarded as less serious than those from dwelling houses. There are no Court of Appeal decisions which say that custodial sentences should be imposed in these cases. If a custodial sentence is to be considered, courts should bear in mind the comment of Lord Lane in *R v Bibi* that 'the less serious type of shopbreaking' could be dealt with by a relatively short sentence. This should probably be in the area of six to nine months. If the offender is a professional burglar with a number of previous convictions, long terms may be approved. In *R v Cole* (1996) the appellant had travelled several hundred miles to commit a burglary at a restaurant. A sum of £6,500 in cash and some cheques were stolen. Less than a year had elapsed since the appellant had been released from prison after a long sentence for robbery. The Court of Appeal held that the five year prison sentence for the burglary was 'entirely appropriate'. In *R v Lawrence* (1982) a 23 year old man, who had kept out of trouble for a number of years since completing a sentence of borstal training, broke into an electrical shop. He was sentenced to 18 months imprisonment. The Court of Appeal replaced this with a community service order as the burglary had been an isolated lapse.

Sentencing for burglary in the Crown Court and magistrates' courts appears to be at a lower level than is recommended by the Court of Appeal. In 1994, of all offenders convicted of burglary, just over a third received an immediate custodial sentence.

WOUNDING OR CAUSING GRIEVOUS BODILY HARM WITH INTENT TO CAUSE GRIEVOUS BODILY HARM

This offence carries a maximum punishment of life imprisonment. The Court of Appeal considers that a sentencing range from three years to eight years is generally suitable, although there is a number of very bad cases where the sentence has exceeded eight years. The placement in the range will depend, in addition to the usual mitigating factors, on whether a weapon was used; the seriousness of the victim's injuries; whether there was any provocation and whether the attack was premeditated. Three common ways in which this offence is committed are by stabbing, 'glassing' and kicking. The court has upheld imprisonment for up to twelve years in cases of stabbing. In *R v McCarthy* (1986) the appellant, a woman aged 22, went to the home of the victim, whom she knew by sight, and asked for a loan of £500. When the victim said she did not have this amount of money, the appellant stabbed her hand with a pair of scissors, punched her, and struck her on the head several times with a vase and a kettle. The appellant pleaded guilty to robbery and causing grievous bodily harm with intent. The Court of Appeal saw no reason to interfere with the sentence of twelve years' imprisonment. On the other hand, the court takes a more sympathetic view in cases where there was severe provocation or when defendants were not fully in control of their actions. One example is *R v Haley* (1983). The defendant, said to have an excellent character, stabbed a person whom he believed to be having an affair with his wife. The court reduced a three year sentence to 18 months with half suspended (the partly suspended sentence has been abolished by the Criminal Justice Act 1991).

'Glassing' refers to the use of a broken glass or bottle to wound the victim, usually in the face. The court has indicated that a three year custodial sentence should be the minimum in such cases. This was stated by Lord Lane in *R v Harwood* (1979) – a typical case, where a fight in a public house led to Harwood's attacking the victim in the face with a broken milk bottle. In *R v Martin* (1991) the appellant, who had no previous convictions, pushed an unbroken glass into the face of his victim, causing severe lacerations which required 73 stitches. There had been no provocation. The Court of Appeal felt unable to interfere with a sentence of six years' imprisonment.

Kicking or stamping on the victim's head is also viewed seriously by the Court of Appeal. In *R v Ivey* (1981) the defendant became involved in an argument outside a club. He punched the victim, who fell to the ground, and then stamped on his head, causing considerable damage to his face and skull. Although Ivey had no previous convictions and had originally intervened to try and stop his brother-in-law fighting, the Court of Appeal approved the sentence of four years' imprisonment.

One case with rather unusual facts at the lower end of the scale is *R v Johnson* (1986). During a rugby union game the defendant, a police officer, bit off part of the ear of an opposing player. The Court of Appeal upheld a sentence of six months' imprisonment, Lord Lane commenting that it would only be in very rare cases that an immediate custodial sentence would not be appropriate.

Once again, there appears to be a divergence between the view of the Court of Appeal on the appropriate level of sentence for cases of violence and the practice adopted by Crown Court judges. In 1994 the average length of prison sentence for violence against the person was under two years.

RAPE

Sentencing levels in rape cases have been subject to a certain amount of controversy in recent years. Both rape and attempted rape are punishable with a maximum sentence of life imprisonment. Lord Lane, who during his term as Lord Chief Justice developed the practice of issuing sentencing guidelines, gave his views concerning rape cases in some detail in *R v Billam* (1986). He reiterated the Court of Appeal's view in *R v Roberts* (1982) that a rape conviction should result in an immediate custodial sentence save in very exceptional cases. He pointed out that Crown Court judges in 1984 gave immediate custodial sentences in 95% of cases; but, in his view, many of these sentences were too short. The starting point for an adult convicted of rape without any aggravating or mitigating circumstances should be five years imprisonment in a contested case. If the rape had been committed by two or more men acting together, or by a man who had broken into the victim's residence or by a man who had a position of responsibility towards his victim, the starting point should be eight years. At the other end of the scale one finds a defendant who has carried out a campaign of rape involving a number of victims. In such a case, a sentence of 15 years or more may be appropriate. If the defendant's behaviour had been such as to suggest that he suffers from severe psychological problems and that he may be a danger to women for a long time, a sentence of life imprisonment may be called for.

The crime can be aggravated by a number of factors: the use of violence beyond that which is necessary to commit the rape; the use of a weapon to frighten or wound the victim; the repetition or careful planning of the rape; the defendant having previous convictions for rape, or for other serious sexual or violent offences; the subjection of the victim to additional sexual indignities or perversions; and the victim's being either very old or very young. The physical or mental effect on the victim is of particular seriousness. If any of these aggravating factors were present, the sentence should be 'substantially higher' than the figures recommended at the starting point. A plea of guilty may lead to a reduction in what would otherwise have been the proper sentence: this may be more than usual because of the particular distress suffered by rape victims who have to testify in court. The victim's having acted incautiously (such as accepting a lift with a stranger) and the victim's previous sexual experience are irrelevant. But if the victim had acted in a way which was calculated to make the defendant think she would consent to sexual intercourse, some mitigation of the sentence should be allowed. The defendant's previous good character is of little importance.

The starting point for attempted rape should usually be less than for the full offence but, if aggravating factors are present, it may turn out to be an even more serious crime. Offenders under 21, who comprise about one third of those convicted of rape, should normally receive a sentence of detention in a young offender institution, although some reduction should be made from what would have been the appropriate sentence for an adult to reflect the offender's youth.

An example of an offence near the top of the scale is *R v Robinson* (1980). The defendant had advertised in an Irish newspaper on three occasions for a girl to work as a nanny and help with domestic chores. Three different girls came to London and Robinson violently raped each of them. Lord Lane said it was the worst case of rape the Court of Appeal had ever dealt with and upheld a total of 15 years' imprisonment. At the other end of the scale is *R v D* (1996). Over a period of seven years, beginning when he was aged 12, the appellant committed a number of sexual assaults on his sister, who was two years younger than him. These ended in 1992 and the victim told her parents about them in 1993. The appellant underwent counselling, but it was only when this broke down that the police were informed. The appellant, who pleaded guilty to indecent assault, rape and incest, was sentenced to four years' imprison-ment. The Court of Appeal felt that new evidence that the victim was being adversely affected by her brother's imprisonment was very important. Feeling able to take 'a more merciful course', the Court substituted a two-year probation order with the condition that the offender should undergo an extended group work programme for sex offenders.

Conclusion

In Chapter 4 it was stated that our criminal justice system is based on a 'neo-classical' model. What does this mean? The classical school of criminology developed in the eighteenth century from the social contract theories of writers such as Hobbes, Montesquieu and Rousseau, and became very popular throughout Europe. Criminal laws were vague and criminal process operated in an arbitrary fashion. Classical theory, how-ever, is precise and systematic. Its main tenets are simple. All people are self-seeking and, therefore, are liable to commit crime. It is in the interests of society to protect its members and their property from harm. Members of society enter into a social contract with the state, in which the state is given the power to punish individuals who break the rules. Punishments must be proportional to the amount of harm used. They should not be used for reformative purposes. There is a strong emphasis on due process. Individuals are considered responsible for their actions and no excuses or mitigating factors are allowed.

Although the influence of classical theory led to a reduction in arbi-trariness in the criminal justice system, it introduced rigours of its own. In particular, the emphasis on 'the criminal act' and the lack of con-sideration given to the circumstances of the actor became increasingly unacceptable to many people. This led to the 'neo-classical' revision of the nineteenth century. The main aspect of this was that allowance should be made for mitigating circumstances, in particular those arising from the offender's mental state, or lack of any previous convictions. Rehabilitation could be significant, but the main principle of classical theory, individual responsibility for one's actions, still remained.

This will be immediately recognisable as not only the basis of the English criminal process but also of its sentencing system. Even in-dividualised sentencing, although lacking certain important characteristics of neo-classical theory such as proportionality, is still based on the notion of individual responsibility. Individuals cannot be sentenced unless convicted of criminal offences (the binding over power is an historical anomaly). However, our consideration of juveniles showed that, in certain circumstances, diversion from court and treatment are preferable to formal proceedings. This reflects the influence of another important nineteenth century theory, positivism. The growing importance of scientific method at that time underlies the development of the positivist approach. Positivism is the antithesis of the free-will notion of classical theory. Human behaviour is governed by a range of factors, whether personal or environmental (or both), and the positivist seeks to study the problems and perhaps try to cure them. Positivism has been very influential in both the theory and practice of criminology throughout this century, but it is only rarely that it has had any significant impact on our criminal justice system. As we have seen with the non-implementation (and subsequent repeal) of important parts of the Children and Young Persons Act 1969, it did not have the expected influence in the area of juvenile delinquency.

As reform does not play a major part in tariff sentencing, and the length of a prison sentence does not seem greatly to affect its deterrent value, it could be argued that the question of length is decided more by retributive principles. Retribution certainly plays a part, but most sentencers still claim to pass deterrent sentences. They must, as intelligent people, be aware that such sentences usually do not work, and perhaps the truth really lies in their occasional comments that they are acting in accordance with public expectations. As in any democracy, this raises certain problems: as the public know next to nothing about our criminal justice system, how can they have any idea of what 'works', in a deterrent sense, or even what is retributively appropriate? Is there a case for judges leading public opinion? Judges did this in the Netherlands during the 1950s. The reduced levels of sentencing that resulted did not lead to an increase in crime. But is it right that sentencing levels should be determined by the judiciary? Those who believe that it is, usually refer to the constitutional independence of the judiciary to support their view. But many people think that it is the function of the Government to say what levels of sentence are appropriate in particular cases. This would be achieved by making sentencing provisions in statutes far more detailed: an example already exists in the Misuse of Drugs Act 1971, where different penalties are provided for dealing with different types of drug. But there is no reason why sentencing levels set by Government would be any better (in whatever sense) than those determined by the judiciary. A Government's view of public opinion would inevitably be affected by political considerations, and this brings us back again to the uninformed state of the public on penological matters.

Postscript: a Sentencing Council

We have already seen how, since the beginning of the 1980s, there has been a number of guideline judgments in the Court of Appeal in areas such as drug trafficking, rape and social security fraud. However, these judgments cover only a relatively small number of offences and have, as yet, not dealt with common offences such as theft, burglary and handling stolen goods. Few guideline judgments deal with non-custodial sentences, particularly in relation to magistrates' courts, where there is considerable inconsistency. The guideline judgments have appeared on an 'ad hoc' basis over a number of years and do not appear to be based on any particular policy in relation to the use of custody or, indeed, sentencing in general. It is with this background that calls for a Sentencing Council have been made.

The idea seems to have been first proposed by Professor Andrew Ashworth in 1983 and has been taken up by a number of organisations including JUSTICE, the Prison Reform Trust and the Labour Party. According to Ashworth, a Sentencing Council should consider sentencing practice, commission research to provide information about the reasoning of judges and magistrates, and then 'reformulate sentencing policy so that it is no longer excessively reliant on custodial measures'. Guidelines should be established for all categories of crime. The Council could set ceilings for different categories of offence, indicate the importance to be attached to such factors as guilty pleas, previous convictions and age.

An important element of a Sentencing Council is that it should include people who are not members of the judiciary so as to provide a wide range of expertise. Ashworth originally suggested that the Council should be chaired by the Lord Chief Justice and include magistrates, a judge, a probation officer, a prison governor, a Home Office official and an academic. Others may wish to cast the net even wider so as to include, for example, lay persons or clergy.

Objections have been raised to the creation of a Sentencing Council. The creation of sentencing guidelines in the USA has coincided with an increase in the use of custody. Yet, there seems no reason why this should be inevitable, particularly if it were made clear from the outset that the Council should be aiming at a reduction in custodial sentences. It has also been suggested that it would reduce or even remove the independence of the magistracy and the judiciary. However, given that the recommendations of the Council would probably be contained in some sort of legislation, it can hardly be argued that Parliament should not legislate on sentencing matters. In any case, no guidance offered by the Council would be so rigid as to prevent sentencers from having an element of discretion in dealing with the cases before them.

Part III

The law of tort

Chapter 14

The nature of tort law

A tort is a civil wrong. A car driver who carelessly causes an accident will be liable to those injured under the tort of negligence. A journalist who publishes an untrue story about someone damaging her reputation will be liable to that person under the tort of defamation. A manufacturer responsible for unreasonable pollution which prevents a farmer from growing crops, will be liable to the farmer under the tort of nuisance. The conduct may also amount to a crime, for example, under the road traffic or pollution legislation. The state may prosecute the offender for the crime and if he is found guilty, a court may impose punishment, a fine or even imprisonment. But the state has no interest in the fact that the conduct may be a civil wrong. It is left to the individual damaged by that wrong, the plaintiff, to take legal action against the wrongdoer, the defendant. If the defendant is found liable, the court will award the plaintiff a remedy such as compensation or an injunction forbidding future damaging conduct. As a tort claim is a private matter between the parties, there is no objection to them settling the matter before it reaches court. Indeed, less than 1% of negligence claims reach trial. But in the case of criminal charges, the public interest demands that they proceed to court. If the defendant paid the prosecution to drop the case that would be condemned as a bribe and not praised as a settlement. The limited plea bargaining that goes on in criminal cases (see ante p 102) is controversial and remains subject to control by the court.

The law of torts has grown over the centuries as the courts recognised different situations as giving rise to civil liability. Different legal names were given to the different fact patterns that gave rise to liability. Perhaps the earliest tort was 'trespass to land' which was the name given to liability which attached to invading another's land. Because there was liability in that situation, the courts eventually recognised liability where there was an indirect interference with another's land and this became known as the tort of nuisance. Again, from the early tort of trespass to the person, that is a deliberate touching of another, the courts developed liability where damage was caused to another negligently. A number of different negligence liability situations were developed and only in the 1930s did the courts finally recognise that they all formed part of the same tort of negligence rather than being separate torts of their own. But negligence is the only 'general tort' based on a type of conduct. Other torts remain limited

365

to particular fact situations. Thus, there are a number of different torts which involve intentional conduct, for example, trespass to land, trespass to the person, deceit, interference with a contract and several others. Again, there are several torts where the liability is based on the fact that the defendant has caused the damage irrespective of whether he was at fault by acting intentionally or negligently. For example, there can be liability for the tort of defamation which is committed by insulting another's reputation or the tort of nuisance, that is indirect interference with land, even though the defendant did not intend the insult or interference and was not negligent either. These torts are known as strict liability torts because the liability will be imposed irrespective of whether there was fault. One particular liability situation left the 'family' of torts centuries ago and that is liability for breaking an informal agreement. Originally, a person making such an agreement with another would sue him in a form of tort action but now this action is regarded as a distinct form of civil liability known as breach of contract. The last section of the book deals with this form of action. However, it is important to note that tort and contract liability can overlap: if a person negligently breaks a contract, he may be liable for both breach of contract and the tort of negligence.

The framework of tortious liability

The result of the centuries of development is a maze of over twenty different torts with only the tort of negligence being based on the type of conduct rather than the particular fact situation and damage. However, some threads run through the maze. One way of understanding the frame-work of liability is to look at the nature on the interest being protected, in other words, what kind of loss has been suffered by the plaintiff. There are four broad types of loss to be considered. The first is pure economic loss, that is financial loss suffered not as a result of physical damage to anything but simply because the defendant's conduct affected the plain-tiff's financial dealings in some way. The second is physical damage to the plaintiff's person or his property, for example, the kind of loss suffered in a road accident. The third is interference with the enjoyment of land, for example, by pollution, and the fourth is insult to the reputation of the plaintiff, most obviously by a defamatory statement. If we combine this analysis with one of the type of conduct which can give rise to liability, we can see a pattern emerging. Pure economic loss receives the least protection from the law of tort. In some circumstances there will be liability if the defendant acted deliberately to cause such financial loss and in much narrower circumstances, there may also be liability where he acted negligently. The main reason for this limited protection is that an individual can protect himself from financial loss by entering contracts with those providing services and suing them if their breach of contract causes him financial loss. There is wider protection against physical damage. Intentional physical damage will almost always give rise to liability through the tort of trespass to the person and negligently inflicted damage will normally give rise to liability. In addition, there are some limited circumstances where a defendant may be strictly liable for causing such damage. There is still more protection for enjoyment of land. There is liability in trespass for intentional interference with land and in negligence for careless interference but most significant is the semi-strict liability under the tort of nuisance. This liability arises whenever there has been an unreasonable interference and is not limited to situations where there has been negligence. This wider liability reflects the importance traditionally attached to ownership of land. But the greatest protection is afforded to a person's reputation. Here, liability can be absolute and not dependent on whether the defendant acted intentionally, negligently or unreasonably. The pattern of liability is be represented in the diagram on p 371.

The torts section of this book has been structured around the framework shown in this diagram. Some of the detail of the diagram will only become clear as you read the chapters and it is suggested that you refer back to the diagram when starting on each chapter. The next chapter considers what is now the most important interest protected by the law of torts, that of physical security. The chapter considers the areas of intentional, negligence and strict liability, considering in particular, the relative merits of negligence and strict standards as the basis of liability. The following chapter completes the picture in relation to physical damage by considering the rules governing the calculation of damages for personal injuries and comparing the tort system with both the state system of social security benefits and the no-fault systems which operate in other comparable countries. Chapter 17 examines interference with the use of land and the way in which the law of tort is adapting to meet new social and economic pressures. Chapter 18 is mainly concerned with the tort of defamation but also considers more broadly the problems of protecting individuals from infringement of their personality. Finally, Chapter 19 looks at the limited protection under the law of torts against pure economic losses. This leads on to the section of the book concerned with contract law which provides the primary protection against such losses.

The aims of the law of torts

The law of torts exists to protect the four kinds of interests identified above. But how does it aim to protect those interests? Is its primary purpose to deter or prevent wrongdoers from harming those interests or is it merely to compensate when those interests have been harmed? To the extent that its aim is compensatory, in what circumstances is it regarded as just to compensate for harm? These are the questions to be explored in this section.

Deterrence and prevention

Once harm has occurred, the law of tort may seek to prevent that particular harm from continuing by awarding the plaintiff an injunction ordering the defendant to stop the harmful activity. Thus, courts will normally award an injunction to stop activities which are continuing to cause a nuisance by unreasonably interfering with the plaintiff's enjoyment of his land. For example, where a plaintiff's peace has been shattered by the noise from a nearby go-kart club (see p 424), an injunction was granted ordering that activity to cease. Again, where the defendant is proposing to publish an article which is clearly defamatory of the plaintiff, the court will grant an injunction to prevent publication (see p 430). But most harm is not caused by a continuing activity nor by planned action like the publication, which can be prevented in advance. Most harm is caused by single unplanned acts whether deliberate, careless or even accidental. Such conduct cannot be prevented but might be deterred if the damages likely to be awarded for causing harm were sufficiently penal to persuade the defendant to alter its pattern of behaviour. However, the normal objective of awarding damages is to compensate the plaintiff and not to penalise the defendant. There are just two situations in which penal awards known as exemplary damages, will be made. The first is where the tort has been committed in an oppressive or unconstitutional way by government officials. The most common example is that of an unlawful arrest by a police officer which results in liability for the tort of false imprisonment (see post p 434). Here, the courts may award exemplary damages to the plaintiff going beyond any calculation of what he has lost. The purpose is to deter the state from infringing civil liberties. The second situation is where the defendant's conduct has been calculated to make a profit in excess of any compensation payable to the plaintiff. An example would be where a newspaper decides to publish a damaging article about a celebrity knowing that it is risking liability for defamation but calculating that the profit from increased sales will more than cover any damages awarded to the celebrity. In such cases exemplary damages, in addition to the normal compensatory damages, will be awarded to the celebrity plaintiff. In the Elton John case, for example, the award of £50,000 for exemplary damages exceeded that of £25,000 for compensation (see post, p 432).

In *AB v South West Water* (1993) the plaintiffs asked the Court of Appeal to extend the category of cases in which exemplary damages could be awarded. The defendant had carelessly allowed the drinking water in the Camelford area of Cornwall to become polluted with aluminium sulphate. Despite becoming aware of the obvious ill effects caused to the local population, the defendant compounded its error by deliberately misleading the public with statements that the water was perfectly safe. The plaintiffs claimed compensation for their ill effects on the ground that the defendant was liable for negligence and public nuisance (see post, p 429) but they also claimed exemplary damages arguing that the water company was equivalent to a government official and that the power to award such damages should extend beyond specific torts such as defamation and false imprisonment to broader areas of liability such as nuisance and negligence. The Court of Appeal rejected both arguments, holding that exemplary damages were exceptional and limited to the two recognised areas with no extensions. American courts have extended exemplary damages to many other situations of deliberate conduct and even careless conduct where there has been an element of recklessness. But there are two problems with such an extension. First, it is unclear whether exemplary damages do deter careless or reckless conduct. For example, it is difficult to see how they would deter reckless driving. If the prospect of injury to himself does not deter the driver, why should the prospect of exemplary damages. In any case, the driver is insured against legal liability. Exemplary damages would only 'bite' if the driver had to meet the award himself and could not pass it on to his insurers. But that raises the second problem. The exemplary damages would probably amount to a more severe punishment than the fine for dangerous driving likely to be imposed by a magistrates' court. Not only that, but it would also be a punishment imposed without a key safeguard provided for offenders by the criminal law, namely, that the prosecution must prove its case 'beyond reasonable doubt'. It would seem odd if the greater penalty of exemplary damages could be imposed on the basis of the lesser requirement in civil cases that the plaintiff proves its case 'on the balance of probabilities'. Indeed, this point perhaps suggests that it should not be any part of the function of the law of tort to punish and that exemplary damages should be abolished rather than extended. Punishment and deterrence should be left to the criminal law.

Compensation and justice

Compensation is clearly a proper aim of the law of torts. Justice requires that the victim of a wrong be compensated for his losses. But that simple proposition hides a problem: does justice demand compensation because the victim has suffered a wrong or sustained a loss? Focusing on the wrong concentrates attention on the moral responsibility of the defendant. That tends to suggest that the basis of liability should be fault whether in the form of intentional or negligent conduct, and that strict liability should be very much the exception. The concentration on moral responsibility is linked to one of the two classifications of justice developed by the Greek philosopher, Aristotle, that of corrective justice. Corrective justice provides the justification for restoring the position between plaintiff and defendant to that which existed before the wrong. The award of damages corrects or undoes the wrong suffered by the plaintiff at the hands of the defendant. However, if the focus is upon the loss rather than the wrong, different concerns arise. Attention concentrates on the most effective way of compensating for harm. That may well be through a system of strict liability imposed on those who can protect themselves from personal loss by taking out insurance against liability. It is this kind of thinking which is said to justify the strict liability imposed on an employer for injury to an employee caused by breach of a statutory duty (see post, p 393). The employer will be insured against such liability. Hence, the compensation to the employee will be paid by the insurance company and, in turn, it will spread the loss back to a larger group of employers through the premiums it charges for the insurance policy. The result will be that the loss suffered by the individual employee will have been distributed to a much wider group. Loss distribution in this way is often seen as a major social goal of the law of torts. It is also linked to the second category of justice identified by Aristotle, that of distributive justice. This is concerned with how the burdens and benefits of life may be fairly and justly distributed amongst individuals. In the context of employer's liability, it can be used to justify the conclusion that it is not just to place the burden of an injury on the industrial employee when the employer and society at large is benefitting from the products of the industry.

There are then two rival conceptual frameworks, that of fault-based liability linked to notions of moral responsibility and corrective justice one the one hand, and on the other that of strict liability linked to social goals and distributive justice. The tensions between these rivals underlie much of the law of torts concerned with physical damage. Neither can claim victory. Instead, the law represents a compromise between the two perspectives. Some would argue that the result is inconsistency and sometimes incoherence in the law. But others would suggest that practical justice is often achieved only by accepting contradictions and regarding rival approaches as being complementary with each being applied in the most appropriate circumstance.

The Framework of Tortious Liability

	Intentional Liability	Negligence Liability	Strict Liability
Economic Loss	Deceit etc	Limited Negligence Liability	*NO LIABILITY*
Damage to Person or Property	Battery etc	Under *Donoghue*	'No duty' situations: shock, omissions etc — Limited strict liability: animals, products, etc
Interference with Land	Trespass	eg *Miller*	Nuisance and *Rylands* [semi-strict standard]
Infringement of Personality	Malicious Falsehood	eg *Spring*	Defamation

(The chart is divided by a diagonal line: the upper-right region is marked **NO LIABILITY** *and the lower region is marked* **LIABILITY**.)*

Chapter 15

Physical damage: fault and strict liability

Compensating individuals for damage to their person or property caused by another might seem to be an uncontroversial objective of the law of tort. But, as we saw in Chapter 14, there is a problem: It is not clear whether the objective should be to compensate the victim for the wrong done by the defendant or, more widely, for the loss caused by the defendant. If the law focuses on moral responsibility and corrective justice, compensation should be limited to situations where the defendant has been at fault and has either intentionally or negligently caused the damage. If the focus is on social goals and distributive justice, compensation may be extended to situations where the defendant has simply caused the damage and particularly where he is likely to be insured against liability. Liability based on causation alone is known as strict liability. In fact the law adopts neither approach to the exclusion of the other. Although the concept of negligence provides the basis of recovery in the widest range of cases it is often applied in a rather strict way with the result that the defendant is deemed to be legally at fault even though he might not appear to be morally at fault. Furthermore, in a number of key areas the common law or legislation has introduced principles of strict liability to supplement recovery for fault. So the overall picture is one in which there is a balance between the two approaches, one in which they complement each other. This chapter considers the scope of fault liability based on intention and negligence, the scope of strict liability and finally, the defences available whichever form of liability is in issue.

Intentional liability

Assault and battery is a crime (see p 276) but it is also a tort. Indeed, technically the law of tort draws a distinction between the two: assault is an act which causes the plaintiff to fear the infliction of unlawful force and battery is an act inflicting such force. To shake a fist at someone is an assault. To hit them is battery. To be liable for either tort, the defendant must have intended his action but he need not have intended to injure the plaintiff. Thus, a surgeon will be liable for battery if he has operated without a patient's consent. He does not intend to injury the patient, quite the contrary. But when he cuts into the patient he is intending the infliction of force and without the patient's consent this will amount to battery. What about the 'social contacts', the minor inflictions of force that form part of everyday life such as pushing in a queue, slapping a friend on the back or the surprise kiss? Suppose the queue jostling injures an OAP, or the slapped friend falls over and breaks a bone, or the kiss was unwanted and affronts the girl. One approach has been to say that there should be no liability unless the defendant's intention was hostile. But that would mean no liability in any of those situations and that might not be thought right. An alternative and preferable approach is to say that there should be no liability for physical contact which is generally acceptable in the ordinary conduct of everyday life. On this approach, the OAP would not recover, the girl would, and the friend might, if the back slap was over-enthusiastic.

Assault and battery apply to actions which directly affect the plaintiff. If the defendant intentionally harms the plaintiff but does so by indirect means, there will be liability under the principle in *Wilkinson v Downton* (1897). In that case the defendant played a practical joke on the plaintiff by telling her falsely that her husband had broken both his legs in an accident. As the defendant intended, the plaintiff was shocked but as a result she suffered from a mental illness. She successfully sued the defendant for compensation in respect of the illness. The principle would apply in other 'indirect' cases such as spiking a plaintiff's drink with the indirect result that he crashes his car. Some situations lie on the borderline between direct and indirect. Would giving someone AIDS through un-protected sex give rise to liability under battery as in *Wilkinson v Downton*? Should it give rise to liability at all? Can the defendant argue that although he intended the unprotected sex, he hoped that he would not transmit the virus?

Negligence liability

To establish negligence liability the plaintiff must show that the def-endant's conduct fell short of the standard of care expected by the law and that this careless conduct was responsible for the damage. The principles concerning both standard of care and responsibility will be considered at some length. In some situations the law will not impose liability even though there is carelessness and responsibility. The reason for not imposing liability may be due to the practical difficulties of limiting the scope of liability, or to a moral feeling that liability should not be imposed, or to some reason of social or political policy. The concept that the law uses to distinguish between situations where there can be liability and those where there cannot be, is known as the duty of care. This will be considered in the final part of this section.

Carelessness

The test for whether the defendant has acted carelessly is to consider what would have been expected of a reasonable person in the defendant's position. This is an objective approach and the reason is obvious; it would be unsatisfactory if the defendant could escape liability simply by arguing that he had done his incompetent best. Carelessness is measured not by asking whether the defendant fell below his own standard of conduct but by asking whether he fell below the standard of the reasonable person. But sometimes this objective approach can produce a tension between the desire to compensate the plaintiff and the desire to limit liability to situations of moral fault. The case of *Wilsher v Essex Area Health Authority* (1988) illustrates the problem. The case concerned a premature baby who had been placed in a special baby care unit at the defendant's hospital. A junior and inexperienced doctor was on duty in the unit and he mistakenly placed an oxygen monitor in the baby's vein rather than its artery. As a result the monitor wrongly showed that the baby was receiving insufficient oxygen and that led to it being given more. In fact, the baby had sufficient oxygen and hence it was being given too much. Later it was discovered that the baby was blind which is one of the possible side effects of being given too much oxygen. One of the questions in the case was whether the junior doctor had acted negligently. In the Court of Appeal the judges disagreed in their approach. Browne-Wilkinson V-C said that 'so long as the English law rests liability on personal fault, a doctor who has properly accepted a post in a hospital in order to gain necessary experience should only be held liable for acts or omissions which a careful doctor with his qualifications and experience would not have done or omitted.' Judged against the objective standard of the inexperienced doctor, the junior doctor in this case was not careless. Instead, Brown-Wilkinson V-C suggested that the hospital itself might be held negligent if it had failed to provide doctors of sufficient skill to staff its specialist units. However, Mustill and Glidewell LJJ took a different view of the standard to be applied to the junior doctor. They held that he had to be judged against the objective standard of care to be expected from the post he occupied, that of someone providing a specialist service. The public should not be expected to put up with a lower a standard just to enable junior doctors to gain more experience. Glidewell LJ was clearly concerned that this approach was harsh in relation to the inexperience and he readily found that the junior doctor had done all that could be expected from his post when he showed the X-ray of the monitor's position to the supervising registrar. The experienced registrar failed to notice the misplacement and it was he who was negligent. Mustill LJ was less convinced that the junior doctor should escape liability but did not rule on the matter because the negligence of the registrar was sufficient to decide the case.

The tension in *Wilsher* between the concept of personal fault and the need to protect the public from inexperience, arises in other situations and in most it is the latter which prevails. Thus a learner driver is expected to match the standard of care of the experienced driver. Of course, what explains the decisions in hospital and driving cases is the fact that the defendants are insured against liability and will not personally have to pay the compensation. Where this is not the case, for example, where a typically uninsured child or old person has caused an accident through immaturity or immobility, the court may be more likely to apply the standard of care to be expected of children or the aged rather than that of the mature and mobile.

Having established the category of reasonable person against which the defendant's conduct falls to be evaluated, it is necessary to determine how that particular person would have behaved. The first general point to make is that a reasonable person can only be expected to take care in relation to harm which is foreseeable. There is no obligation to take reasonable care to avoid the unforeseeable. The best known example of this is *Roe v Minister of Health* (1954) in which the plaintiff developed paralysis after undergoing surgery and sought to hold the hospital liable in negligence for this. An inquiry into the accident revealed that the problem had been caused by the anaesthetic. This had been supplied to the hospital in sealed glass ampoules and had been stored, in order to minimize the risk of infection, in a solution of phenol. It was known that phenol was dangerous and the accepted procedure when anaesthetic was required was to wash the ampoules and to inspect them to ensure that they were free from cracks or breakages. This procedure had been used in this case. The inquiry revealed that it provided insufficient protection as it was possible for the phenol to penetrate the glass and contaminate the anaesthetic through microscopic flaws which were invisible to the human eye. This accident alerted the medical profession to this risk. At the time of the acts in question the risk was not within accepted medical knowledge. It was unforeseeable and there was therefore no obligation to guard against it. The doctors could not be criticised for failing to provide protection against a risk which they could not appreciate. As a result the individual who had been permanently paralysed by a medical accident went without tort compensation. A second important aspect of the reasonable care standard was emphasised in *Roe*. A defendant is entitled to be judged according to standards accepted at the time that he acted. The lessons of hindsight are not relevant. Once a risk has been publicised accepted procedures may change and the law will reflect this change. But, as Denning LJ said 'we must not look at a 1947 accident through 1954 spectacles'.

In medical cases such as *Roe* and other cases where the defendant is a professional, the courts will look to the standards of conduct accepted by the relevant profession. If such a case goes to trial on the issue of carelessness, the court will hear expert evidence to show what was acceptable common practice for the profession. In areas such as medicine, there may well be a number of approaches to a problem which are broadly acceptable. Provided the defendant followed one such approach he will not be regarded as having been careless despite the fact that hindsight shows that a different approach would have been better for the patient. Following a common professional practice does not always mean that the defendant will escape liability. On occasion, courts have been prepared to hold that the whole practice of the profession shows a lack of proper care for the interests of the client. Judges are most likely to reach this conclusion in relation to the legal practice about which they may consider themselves to be experts but they have taken the same stance in relation to other professional practices, most recently to the practice of Lloyd's agents. Their common approach to insurance underwriting resulted in the Names losing millions on the so-called LMX spiral in the Lloyd's insurance market. Obviously, evidence of common practice is easiest to find in the professional context where practice is based on expertise and is often set out in texts or codes of practice. But potentially it is relevant in all contexts. So, for example, the common practice of employers would be relevant when assessing whether a particular employer has taken reasonable care to prevent an injury to an employee.

In addition to looking for evidence of common practice, the courts may balance the risk of the damage against the level of precaution necessary to avoid the risk. In considering the risk, the court will take account of both the likelihood of an accident occurring if precautions are not taken and the severity of any injury or damage if an accident does occur. Assessing the level of precaution may require the court to consider both the financial cost of the precaution and the social cost in terms of the benefits which would be lost if the precaution were to be taken. The cases show the courts balancing these factors in order to make what is, in essence, a value judgment on the acceptability of the defendant's conduct. In *Bolton v Stone* (1951) a cricket club which had provided 17 foot high fencing around its ground was held not negligent in failing to eliminate the recognised, but small, risk that cricket balls would be hit into the neighbouring road and cause injury. The expense involved in taking this precaution was disproportionate to the risk. In *Daborn v Bath Tramways* (1946) it was held to be acceptable for the ambulance services to use, during the Second World War, American left hand drive ambulances which were not fitted with mechanical indicators. It was reasonable to use the only equipment available, even if this increased the risk of road accidents. These cases illustrate the distinction between strict liability and the standard of reasonable care. The latter standard does not make a defendant an insurer of all risks created by his conduct. The activities of a modern developed society create risks, but it is only those risks which society, as personified by the courts, deems unacceptable that attract legal liability.

There are few, if any, forms of medical treatment which do not carry the risk of side effects. Yet if an acceptable balancing of the potential benefits of the treatment against the risks has been carried out the decision to proceed will be unimpeachable. Severe, and inevitable, side effects, such as the amputation of limbs in order to save life, may be justifiable in extreme circumstances.

Finally, the characteristics of potential victims are relevant to the level of care required. Duties are not owed in the abstract but are owed to those individuals in classes who are known, or should be foreseen to be at risk. This rule may increase or decrease the level of required precautions. An obvious example of the former is that contained in section 2(3)(a) of the Occupiers' Liability Act 1957 'an occupier must be prepared for children to be less careful than adults'. The 1957 Act was passed to make it clear that occupiers owed a duty of care to everyone coming lawfully onto their land and the legislature simply took the opportunity to put in statutory form a number of obvious propositions concerning the standard of care to be expected. Section 2(3)(a) is one of them. Of course, the underlying principle applies to a broader category than children. For example, other cases have involved liability for failure to provide adequate protection to meet risks posed by blind or partially sighted individuals. Section 2(3)(b) sets out a converse proposition which is again of general application in all contexts and not just that of occupiers' liability. This is that a defendant is entitled to take account of the potential victim's capacity to avert risks. Thus, a householder can expect an electrician installing new wiring to decide for himself when to switch off the mains supply. Her duty to take reasonable care of visitors does not require her to advise the electrician about his job, however obvious that advice might seem. A final general proposition is to be found in section 2(4)(a) of the Occupiers' Liability Act which provides that sufficient care may be taken by warning a potential victim of a danger provided this enabled the visitor to be reasonably safe. A building contractor who cuts a trench through a pavement, puts a narrow plank across and then warns pedestrians to take care when walking the plank, will not escape liability if, say, an elderly person falls off and into the trench.

To summarise, courts will determine whether a defendant has been careless by asking whether his conduct fell short of what would be expected of the hypothetical reasonable person engaged in the activity in question. The defendant will be judged in relation to the foreseeable risks. The risks will be balanced against the ease of providing protection. Both common practice and commonsense propositions about behaviour, such as those relating to children, may also be relevant. But in the end, everything will turn on the particular facts of the case. The plaintiff must prove on the balance of probabilities that the defendant's conduct was careless. In practice this may be difficult to establish. In the leading medical negligence case of *Whitehouse v Jordan* (1981) for example, the trial occurred more than ten years after the events. Most of the witnesses could not be traced. The obstetrician who was alleged to have been negligent, could not really remember what happened and his post delivery notes were ambiguous. His female patient claimed to remember exactly what took place but her story was clearly an exaggeration. Such difficulties are not unusual and help to explain the failure of many accident victims to obtain compensation from the tort system. However, there are several devices which may reduce the burden. The most important is section 11 of the Civil Evidence Act 1968. This provides that the fact that a person has been convicted in criminal proceedings is admissible evidence in subsequent civil proceedings of the fact that he committed the offence and that some of the evidence on which the conviction was based is also admissible. It is obvious that this should be the case. The provision is an important weapon particularly in tort cases concerning road or industrial accidents. It means that an injured victim may obtain considerable assistance from criminal proceedings initiated against the driver by the police or against an employer by the Health and Safety Inspectorate. A conviction for careless or dangerous driving or breach of industrial safety legislation will virtually conclude the issue of civil liability.

A similar result may be obtained by the rule known as res ipsa loquitur. The reasoning underlying this is that certain kinds of accident do not happen unless there has been negligence. It follows that the simple occurrence of such an accident is evidence of negligence which assists the plaintiff in proving his case. Two conditions must be satisfied before this rule operates. First, on a common sense basis, the mere fact of the accident must point to negligence as the cause. If several possible causes can be postulated, only some of which involve negligence, the facts do not 'speak for themselves' and the rule does not apply. Second, the activity in question must have been under the exclusive control of the defendant. This arm of the test is satisfied if the defendant is an employer and hence, vicariously liable (see p 391) for the acts of all those who might have caused the damage. Examples of the operation of res ipsa have included items falling from buildings and the collision of trains. However, the exclusive control test has tended to stop the rule operating in relation to activities in which a number of people are involved such as medical procedures.

Responsibility

Proving that the defendant has been negligent is not enough. Negligence 'in the air', that which has no harmful consequences, is not actionable in tort. It must be shown that the negligence was responsible for damage to the plaintiff. This involves two different kinds of question. The first is whether the negligence was *factually responsible* for damage and this is often tested by asking whether the damage would have occurred 'but for' the negligence. If the answer is 'no', then the negligence was a factual cause of the damage. A second question then arises, which is whether the negligence was *legally responsible* for the damage. For example, the defendant's negligence might be the least important of several factual causes of the damage and so it might be unreasonable to hold the defendant legally responsible for that damage. Or some kinds of damage might be so unexpected a consequence of the negligence that it would again be unreasonable to hold the defendant responsible.

FACTUAL RESPONSIBILITY

A person cannot be liable unless the damage is linked, in terms of cause and effect, to the negligence in issue. In most cases this link is so obvious that it causes no difficulty. If difficulties do arise the normal approach is to use the 'but for' test. If the damage would not have occurred 'but for' the negligence, it has been factually caused by it. In other words the court considers a hypothetical set of facts identical to those at issue save that the negligence is removed. If, on this hypothesis, the plaintiff would have suffered the same damage, the defendant's negligence was not a cause of it. A number of cases illustrate this. A hospital which had failed to provide proper treatment for a patient escaped liability by showing that proper treatment could not have saved the patient's life and an employer in breach of duty by not providing essential safety equipment similarly escaped by showing, on the basis of previous experience, that it was certain that the employee would not have used the equipment if it had been available.

In most situations the 'but for' test poses an easily answered question of cause and effect. However, serious difficulties may occasionally arise. For example, the test presupposes that it is possible to decide what results would follow from the absence or presence of negligence. In practice this may be very difficult as there may be a number of possible explanations for damage, only some of which could be attributed to negligence. For example, it may be disputed whether a cancer is to be attributed to natural causes, to the fact that the victim was a heavy smoker or to the fact that someone's tort had exposed the victim to a dangerous chemical. Whether cause in fact is established in such a case may depend on how the rules on burden of proof operate. In practice, the courts have adopted rules which make it very difficult for plaintiffs to succeed in the problem cases. In *Wilsher v Essex Health Authority* (1988), the case concerning the premature baby found to be blind after having been given too much oxygen, the House of Lords held that the plaintiff bears the burden of proving that the defendant caused his damage or had made a material contribution to it. In that case it could only be shown that the over-oxygenation had increased the risk of blindness but it was still only one of a number of possible causes. The House of Lords held that this was not sufficient to establish liability. A variation of this difficulty arises in relation to loss of a chance. If negligent medical treatment turns a probability of permanent disablement into a certainty, should damages be awarded for the loss of the chance of recovery or be denied on the basis that the disablement would, on the balance of probabilities, have occurred in any case? In *Hotson v East Berkshire Area Health Authority* (1987) the House of Lords held that a finding that such a disablement was 75% likely to occur before the plaintiff arrived at the hospital amounted to a finding on the balance of probabilities that the damage was going to occur in any case. The hospital therefore escaped liability for its negligent treatment even though its conduct cost the plaintiff his 25% chance of recovery.

LEGAL RESPONSIBILITY

As indicated above, questions of legal responsibility are raised in two types of situation. The first concerns multiple causes where the question is whether the defendant's conduct should be legally responsible given the significance of other causes of the damage. This is sometimes referred to as a question of 'legal causation'. The second concerns unexpected damage where the question is whether the kind of damage is so unforeseeable that the defendant's conduct should not be regarded as responsible. This is sometimes referred to as a question of 'remoteness'.

The nature of the legal causation problem is well illustrated by *Wright v Lodge* (1993). With two girlfriends as passengers, Miss Shepherd was driving her rather old mini along a dual carriageway in foggy conditions with visibility of about 60 yards. The engine of the mini petered out and it came to a stop in the nearside lane of the carriageway. For three minutes she kept trying to start it and then the mini was hit in the rear by a Scania lorry being driven at about 60 mph by Lodge. The lorry went out of control, crossed the central reservation and hit Wright's car causing him injury. Lodge was found to have been driving not just carelessly but recklessly and he was obviously liable to Wright. But the difficult question in the case was whether Miss Shepherd was also liable to Wright. The judge found her negligent on the ground that she should have got her passengers to push the mini off the carriageway and onto the verge. Her negligence was undoubtedly a factual cause of Wright's injury because the lorry would not have crossed the central reservation had it not collided with the mini. But given that Lodge was driving so badly, was it reasonable to hold Shepherd responsible as well? The Court of Appeal held that the reckless driving of Lodge 'broke the chain of causation' from Shepherd's negligence and hence she was not responsible. Lodge's driving was so bad that it was quite outside the range of what might be expected. Had he been driving at a slower speed of say 40 mph, and carelessly failed to brake in time, then the court would probably have held that his conduct came within what might reasonably be expected and did not break the chain of causation. It is all a matter of degree. It is sometimes also a question of the responsibility of the defendant. For example, in *Home Office v Dorset Yacht Co* (1970) prison officers were held liable for deliberate damage done by prisoners they had carelessly allowed to escape. Normally, an act of deliberate damage would be regarded as so unreasonable as to break the chain of causation from any prior act of negligence. But here there was no break in the chain because it was the officers' job to prevent the prisoners from having the opportunity to escape and cause damage.

The law in relation to the second issue, remoteness, has been settled by the decision of the Privy Council in *The Wagon Mound* (1961). The defendants negligently allowed fuel oil to escape from their ship and spread in a thin film across the waters of the harbour in which it was moored. The oil needed to be raised to a very high temperature before it could be ignited and it was held to be unforeseeable that a fire would start in such oil when spread on water in this way. It was, nevertheless, foreseeable that the plaintiffs, who operated a wharf nearby, would be damaged in having to clear the oil off its property. In fact the oil did catch fire, probably as a result of sparks from welding igniting waste matter floating in the water and the plaintiff's property was destroyed by the fire. The Privy Council held that the defendant escaped liability. The court rejected earlier authority which had held that a defendant was responsible for all the natural and direct consequences of his tort, and held instead, that he was only responsible for those of a kind which is reasonably foreseeable. This test protects a defendant against the unfairness of being held liable for consequences which could not have been foreseen and avoids the difficulty involved in determining which consequences of a tort are direct and which are indirect. But it seems likely that the change produced by *The Wagon Mound* was less drastic than it seemed in 1961. At that time the test of foreseeability was regarded as a more stringent one than that of 'natural and direct' consequences. Nowadays the truth of this must be doubted. The foreseeability test is subject to important exceptions and, in any case, is commonly treated as equivalent to conceivability. The result is that the test can lead to tortfeasors being held responsible for consequences a long way removed from the tort. In practice there is a lot of evidence that courts have managed to avoid the more bizarre results. They have done this by emphasising that 'policy' issues are raised; by saying that the test is one of 'reasonable foreseeability' rather than 'foreseeability' and by recourse to 'instinctive, robust common sense'. Again the process at work is one of judicial discretion hidden behind what might appear to be a carefully controlled scientific test.

The foreseeability test applies only to differences in the kind of damage suffered. Damage of an unforeseeable extent but a foreseeable kind is recoverable as is damage of a foreseeable kind inflicted through an unforeseeable sequence of events. These rules, which place a serious qualification on the *Wagon Mound* test were established by *Hughes v The Lord Advocate* (1963). In that case the plaintiff, an eight year old boy, was seriously injured when playing with some unguarded paraffin lamps which had been left surrounding an open manhole by Post Office employees. The defendants were held negligent because they should have foreseen the risk that a child might drop one and burn itself. In fact the child was severely injured when he knocked a lamp into the manhole and escaping paraffin vapour ignited and caused a powerful explosion. The defendants argued that although they ought to have foreseen damage by burning they could not have foreseen injuries caused in this fashion. The House of Lords rejected this because the risk to be guarded against was that the child would be injured by burning. This had occurred and damages were recoverable, albeit that the injuries suffered were of an unforeseeable extent and had been produced in an unforeseeable fashion.

The distinction between kinds and extent of damage is firmly entrenched in the law. However, it is not free from difficulty; particularly because there is no agreed classification of the kinds of damage. For example, it is not clear whether all personal injuries amount to injuries of the same kind. The difficulty was emphasised by *Doughty v Turner Manufacturing Co Ltd* (1964) when an employee was injured as a result of an asbestos cover being knocked into a vat of hot liquid. An unforeseen chemical reaction occurred which caused the liquid to erupt and burn the employee. His claim that the eruption of the liquid differed from a splashing, which was foreseeable, only in terms of extent was rejected. An eruption was held to be different in kind from a splash. It is difficult to reconcile this with the decision in *Hughes* that the explosion merely produced damage of a different extent to a burning.

The foreseeability test is also qualified by the rule, commonly referred to as the 'egg shell skull' rule, that a defendant who causes personal injuries must take the plaintiff as he finds him. It is not possible to argue that there should be no liability because the plaintiff suffered from a peculiar vulnerability. An injury which causes minor bruising to a normal person may prove fatal to a haemophiliac. In the leading case an employer was held liable when a tortiously caused burn promoted a cancer which killed an employee who had a pre-disposition to cancer. The rule, which is basic to the compensatory role of tort, has been applied to hold tortfeasors liable for mental disorders and for attempts at suicide. In practice, it makes irrelevant the question whether different personal injuries are classified as different 'kinds' as it overrides the kind/extent distinction in relation to such damage. However, it does not seem to extend to forms of damage other than personal injuries.

Duty of care

In most situations in which the defendant's carelessness has been responsible for damage to the plaintiff, the defendant will be liable. Thus, there is no doubt that a negligent driver may be liable to fellow road-users or a negligent employer to employees. But there are a few situations where for one reason or another the courts have decided that there should be no liability. The concept used to distinguish between liability and no-liability situations is known as the duty of care. Where a duty is owed there may be liability and where no duty is owed there can be no liability despite the defendant's negligence and responsibility. The pivotal point in the courts' approach to the duty of care was the great 1932 case of *Donoghue v Stevenson*, arguably the best known legal decision in the English language.

Prior to *Donoghue* the courts had no general test for determining whether a duty of care existed. Instead, each situation was considered in isolation as it came before the courts. The result was a complex list of situations where there was and was not a duty. It all depended upon the particular relationship of the parties, for example, whether it was a manufacturer, salesman or landlord on the one side and a customer, tenant or stranger on the other. No general reason linked the decisions in one category or relationship to another. This was what changed with the speech of Lord Atkin in *Donoghue*. The facts were trifling. The plaintiff and a friend went to a cafe where the friend ordered a bottle of ginger beer for the plaintiff. The beer, which had been manufactured by the defendant, was supplied in an opaque glass bottle which made it impossible to see the contents. The plaintiff consumed part of the beer and claimed that when she poured the rest into the glass she was confronted by the decomposed remains of a snail. She claimed that this sight and the beer which she had already drunk rendered her ill and she sued the defendant manufacturer in tort. The claim raised important issues of principle concerning a manufacturer's liability in tort to persons who had not contracted with him but its relevance for present purposes lies in the well known dicta in Lord Atkin's speech.

'(I)n English law there must be, and is, some general conception of relations giving rise to a duty of care, of which the particular cases found in the books are but instances. The liability for negligence ... is no doubt based upon a general public sentiment of moral wrongdoing for which the offender must pay. But acts or omissions which any moral code would ensure cannot in a practical world be treated so as to give a right to every person injured by them to demand relief. In this way rules of law arise which limit the range of complainants and the extent of their remedy. The rule that you are to love your neighbour becomes, in law, you must not injure your neighbour; and the lawyer's question who is my neighbour? receives a restricted reply. You must take reasonable care to avoid acts or omissions which you can reasonably foresee would be likely to injure your neighbour. Who then, in law, is my neighbour? The answer seems to be – persons who are so closely and directly affected by my act that I ought to have them in contemplation as being so affected when I am directing my mind to the acts or omissions which are called in question.'

As Lord Atkin went on to explain, there were two elements in this formulation. The first was the test of reasonable foresight. A duty would exist only where injury was reasonably foreseeable. The second was the neighbour principle, namely that the duty was limited to 'persons so closely and directly affected' by the defendant's act that they should be in his contemplation. Lord Atkin equated this second requirement with the concept of proximity understood, not in narrow sense of physical proximity, but in the wider sense of 'close and direct relations' between the parties.

This general test of foreseeability plus proximity gave the courts a basis on which to identify new situations in which a duty of care could be owed. As a result, by the 1960s the scope of the duty of care had extended to cover new types of conduct such as the provision of services, new types of defendant such as public authorities, and new types of loss such as pure economic loss as opposed to physical damage. However, this expansion led the courts to realise that an additional element needed to be added to the duty test, that of policy. Many of the new relationships being considered, such as whether a barrister representing his client in court should owe a duty of care to that client, raised difficult questions of policy. In the case concerning the barrister, *Rondel v Worsley* (1967), the House of Lords had concluded that although the barrister could foresee damage to his client if he presented the case negligently and there was close proximity, there were powerful policy reasons for denying a duty: the imposition of a duty would deter barristers from representing 'difficult' clients and would lead to criminal cases being retried in the civil courts when convicted clients sued their barristers for negligence. In many of the new situations, like that in *Rondel*, being considered by the courts in the 1960s and 1970s policy considerations were clearly relevant. In the mid-1970s in *Anns v Merton London Borough Council* (1977) Lord Wilberforce suggested a new two stage test for duty, incorporating a policy element. The first stage of the test was whether there was a sufficient relationship of proximity such that damage was foreseeable by the defendant, in which case there was a prima facie duty. If there was such a prima facie duty, then the court moved to the second stage and considered whether there were any policy reasons for denying a duty. The problem with this formulation was that it seemed to merge the separate criteria of foreseeability and proximity into a single test in which foreseeability was *the* test for proximity. In the late 1970s and early 1980s courts extended the duty of care to a number of new situations on the simple basis that the damage was foreseeable and there were no policy reasons against imposing a duty. However, from the mid-1980s onwards the appeal courts began to reassert the importance of proximity in an attempt to control the scope of potential duties. Finally, in *Caparo Industries v Dickman* (1990) Lord Bridge formulated a new, three stage test for duty. The first stage was foreseeability, the second was proximity and the third was 'whether the situation was one in which the court considers it fair, just and reasonable that the law should impose a duty'.

This last stage gives the courts an opportunity to consider policy matters as well as the narrow issue of justice between the parties. The case of *The Nicholas H* (1995) is a recent example of the House of Lords applying this three stage test. The Nicholas H was a cargo ship which developed a crack in the hull whilst on a voyage. At its next stop in port, it was inspected by a marine surveyor employed by the defendant who inspected the safety of ships on behalf of an association of shipowners. The surveyor approved a temporary repair and allowed the ship to continue its voyage but the repair failed and it sank with loss of cargo worth $6 million. The plaintiff was the owner of the cargo and alleged that through its surveyor, the defendant had been negligent. The issue in the case was whether the defendant owed the plaintiff a duty of care. The majority of the House of Lords held that no duty was owed. The defendant could reasonably foresee that negligently allowing the ship to sail might result in its sinking and the loss of the cargo. There was uncertainty whether there was sufficient proximity given that the damage had not been directly caused by the sinking and only indirectly by the surveyor's conduct. But the majority were sure that imposition of a duty would be unfair, unjust and unreasonable. The reason was that the international rules limited the liability of the shipowner to the cargo owner for loss of its cargo to $500,000. The cargo owner was expected to protect itself from greater losses by taking out insurance. Allowing the cargo owner to recover the full loss against the defendant would undermine the international limit on liability. True, the limit expressly protected just shipowners but the defendant was owned by a group of shipowners and hence its liability would be passed back to the shipowners who should have been protected by the limit. Complex reasoning which did not convince the dissenting judge, Lord Lloyd, who considered that it would be just to impose a duty as it would provide an incentive to marine surveyors to improve their standards.

The *Nicholas H* presented a new problem situation to the courts, one that had not been considered before. However, there are a number of problem situations where the courts have had a full opportunity to settle the line between duty and no duty situations. We will consider four such situations each raising rather different issues. They are the liability for nervous shock, liability for omissions, liability for the decisions of public authorities and liability for pure economic loss.

NERVOUS SHOCK

Cases on nervous shock deal with psychiatric illness inflicted through the medium of the mind, rather than by physical impact. They commonly involve a person being shocked by seeing an injury inflicted on another. There are two reasons why the law has developed special rules to limit the scope of the duty of care in such a circumstance. The first is the need to place a limit on the wide liability that could result from a shocking disaster such as Hillsbrough or the Piper Alpha tragedy. This limit has been achieved by requiring the shocked plaintiff to be related in some way to a victim of the shocking event. The second is the need to draw a line between those suffering psychiatric illness as a result of witnessing a shocking event involving a relative and those suffering the illness as a result of grieving for the death of a relative. This line has been achieved by the requirement that the plaintiff witness the shocking event or its immediate aftermath with his own 'unaided senses'. Applying this limit, a plaintiff would not be able to recover if he merely heard about the shocking events from a third party.

These limits are well illustrated by the leading case of *Alcock v Chief Constable of South Yorkshire Police* (1991). Due to the negligent failure of the police to control the crowd at the Hillsborough football ground some 95 spectators were crushed to death. The fifteen plaintiffs all claimed to have suffered nervous shock as a result of a relationship with a victim of the disaster. The relationships included parent-child, spouse, fiance, sibling, grandparent-child, brother-in-law and in one case, mere friendship. Most had witnessed the events on live television, some had identified the bodies of relatives in the mortuary, and a couple had witnessed the horror first-hand in the stadium. The House of Lords held that no duty of care was owed to any of the plaintiffs. Those who watched on television were not owed a duty because the Lords considered that whilst the pictures would give rise to feelings of the deepest anxiety and distress, they were no more shocking than information from a third party and not the equivalent of witnessing with one's own unaided senses. Those who identified the bodies in the mortuary some nine or more hours later were not owed a duty because they were not within the 'immediate aftermath' of the shocking event. It could not be said that they had witnessed something which formed part of 'the accident as entire event'. The suspicion in relation to both classes of plaintiff may have been that they suffered illness through grief rather than shock. The two who saw the crush at first hand might well have suffered illness through the shock but their relationship with the victims for whose safety they feared, was that of brother and brother-in-law. The Lords held that there was insufficient evidence that these two plaintiffs had 'such a close and intimate relationship (with the victim) as gave rise to that very special bond of affection which would make shock-induced psychiatric illness reasonably foreseeable.' Only in the case of parental or spousal relationships would it be assumed that there was such a bond. In all other relationships it had to be proved.

These restrictions on the scope of liability have been criticised as too arbitrary. The Law Commission has suggested that there should be no distinction between spousal and parental relationships on the one hand and other close relationships such as that of siblings. It has also suggested that where there is a close relationship, there is no need to insist on the plaintiff witnessing the events through his own unaided senses and he should be able to recover, for example, through being shocked by seeing the event on television or reading about it in a newspaper. One argument against these suggestions is that the arbitrary restrictions provide a 'bright line', that is they enable lawyers to predict with some accuracy whether a claim would succeed of not. Adopting the more flexible approach proposed by the Law Commission might lead to more litigation in the areas of uncertainty. Other critics go further than the Commission and suggest that there should be no special restrictions on liability. This would mean that a mere bystander who was shocked by seeing a horrific road accident could recover from the negligent driver. One argument against liability in such a situation is that it might vastly increase the number of claims brought for shock resulting and thereby lead to higher insurance premiums for motorists. Finally, it should be noted that there is just one situation in which a bystander can recover under the present law. That is where he also participated in an attempt to rescue the victims of the accident. Because rescuing is regarded as something to be encouraged, the courts have felt that the 'shocked' rescuer should be allowed to recover against those responsible for the shocking accident. This raises an interesting question in relation to *Alcock*: should the police who helped rescue the victims of the crush and themselves suffered psychiatric illness as a result be able to recover damages for negligence against their officers whose negligence was to blame for the shocking incident? To allow them to recover might seem a little ironic in view of the failure of the relatives to recover. However, they were rescuing and unless one argues that police officers must put up with being shocked as part of their job, it would seem a little unfair to prevent them recovering. The issue has not been decided as in 1996 the police claim was settled.

OMISSIONS

In *Home Office v Dorset Yacht Co* (1970) Lord Diplock explained the position in these terms:

> 'The very parable of the good Samaritan which was evoked by Lord Atkin in *Donoghue v Stevenson* illustrates, in the conduct of the priest and Levite who passed by on the other side, an omission which was likely to have as its reasonable and probable consequence damage to the health of the victim of the thieves, but for which the priest and Levite wold have incurred no civil liability in English law. Examples could be multiplied. You may cause loss to a tradesman by withdrawing your custom though the goods which he supplies are entirely satisfactory; ... you need not warn (your neighbour) of a risk of physical danger to which he is about to expose himself ...; you may watch your neighbour's goods being ruined by a thunderstorm though the slightest effort on your part could protect them from the rain ...'

Two grounds are often given to justify the principle that there should be no duty of care in respect of omissions. The first is that a duty to act affirmatively would impose an unreasonable burden on the bystander, for example in making the effort to rescue. But critics argue that this should go to the standard of care expected not to the existence of the duty and that in many cases, for example where a warning would suffice, very little effort is required. Second, it is said that such a duty would require the defendant to benefit the plaintiff. Morally, it is argued that the defendant should only be responsible for activity which makes the plaintiff's position worse. But critics suggest that this laissez-faire, individualist ideology needs to be balanced by that of social responsibility.

The tension between these two principles has resulted in a compromise. Whilst starting from the basis that there is no duty of care in respect of omissions, the law increasingly recognises exceptions where the nature of the defendant's responsibility justifies the imposition of a duty. Thus, someone who has assumed responsibility for the care of another may be liable for failing to provide proper care. For example, in *Barrett v Ministry of Defence* (1995) the Ministry was held not to be under a duty to prevent a naval airman from drinking too much alcohol at the mess bar because such a duty would dilute the need for self-responsibility by individuals. But it was held to be under a duty once the airman had collapsed and naval personnel had taken responsibility by carrying him back to his room. The Ministry was held liable for failing to keep him under sufficient observation to prevent him asphyxiating from inhaling his own vomit. Again, a person occupying land is under a duty to others to control dangers arising on that land. For example, in *Goldman v Hargrave* (1967) a fire started acc-idently on the defendant's land and he was held liable, having failed to prevent it spreading to the plaintiff's land. A third example of a duty based on a specific responsibility is where the defendant has a responsibility to prevent a third party causing damage. Thus, in *Home Office v Dorset Yacht Co* (1970) the prison officers' responsibility for prisoners under their control justified the imposition of a duty of care in respect of damage caused by such prisoners during an escape. That is a clear example of liability for an omission, for failure to control the activities of third parties for whom one is responsible. But there are more difficult cases. One that has not been litigated concerns doctors with patients known to be suffering from the HIV virus. Suppose the doctor knows that his patient is having unprotected sex with his partner without telling her that he has the virus and, as a result, she develops the virus. Could she sue the doctor for failing to take care and warn her of the danger? Is the doctor's control over his patient analogous to that of the prison officer over an inmate? Would imposition of such a duty of care undermine the doctor's duty of con-fidentiality to his own patient? If it became know that doctors were under a duty to warn partners, would this deter patients with the virus from going to see their doctors. On the other hand, failure to warn the partner may result in that person's death. There is no easy answer.

PUBLIC AUTHORITY DECISIONS

In the case of nervous shock, there are practical reasons for restricting the scope of the duty of care. In the case of omissions, there are both practical and ideological reasons. In the case of the decision-making role of public authorities, there are practical and political reasons. The practical problem stems from the fact that unlike the private sector, the public sector is not free to raise its own funding but has to rely on limited resources allocated from public revenue. Imposing a duty may lead an authority to feel that the wider the service provided, the more it is likely to be liable. Hence, it may act defensively and restrict services to the detriment of the public as a whole. Alternatively, if it does provide a service which is subject to a duty of care and is found liable for negligence, it will have to divert resources from the provision of services to litigation and compensation. The political problem stems from the fact that public authorities are generally given their powers to take decisions by the electorate and they are ultimately answerable for those decisions to the electorate. It is for the electorate and not the judges to decide whether the authority exercised its discretion properly when making decisions. Imposing a duty of care in respect of such discretionary decisions might undermine the political accountability of the authority.

The leading case dealing with these problems is *X v Bedfordshire* (1995), a House of Lords decision involving a number of different claims some of which concerned child abuse decisions. To illustrate the problem, one of the decisions was to take a child away from its mother on the mistaken ground that the mother's partner was the abuser and in another, the decision was to leave a child with its parents despite clear evidence of abuse. In both cases it was alleged that the conduct of social services was negligent and physical harm had resulted to the children. In holding that no duty was owed by the authorities, the House of Lords used a two stage, discretion and justice approach which reflected the political and practical considerations. First, no duty would be owed if the authority had acted within the discretion given to it. The right place to questions such decisions was in the political arena and not the courts. If the authority's conduct did not involve discretion or was outside the scope of its discretion (this is know as an 'ultra vires', literally 'outside powers', decision), then it could owe a duty but it had to be remembered that in deciding whether it had acted 'ultra vires', the courts could not question 'non-justiciable' decisions. These are decisions based on economic or social policy which the court is not competent to question. Hence, in the case of a policy decision based on lack of resources, the court cannot examine whether that decision was beyond the authority's powers. Rather, it must simply accept that no duty is owed. In *Bedfordshire*, no discretion seemed to be involved in the decision. The authorities had made simple mistakes. They did not exercise judgment or discretion. Hence, a duty was not precluded at this first stage. This took the House of Lords to the second stage of asking whether the imposition of a duty would be just and fair. They decided that it would not be just to impose a duty on the social services for a number of reasons: Social services work closely with the police and doctors and it would be difficult in any given case to establish which member of the multi-disciplinary team was to blame: The task itself involved treading a difficult line between taking action too soon and not taking it soon enough: Faced by potential liability, social services might adopt a more cautious and defensive approach to their duties, waiting for concrete evidence before acting with the possible result that children are left longer in danger: The imposition of a duty of care in such a difficult area would be bound to lead to many cases being brought with scarce resources having to be diverted from providing care to defending cases: Finally, parents already have statutory rights to complain against social services. The reasons seem convincing but perhaps one should ask what the difference is between the 'social diagnosis' and decision of a social worker and the medical diagnosis and decision of a doctor working for the health service. The doctor is undoubtedly under a duty of care.

Following *Bedfordshire* it is clear that public authorities will not often owe a duty of care in relation to their decisions. For example, it is now well established that the police do not normally owe a duty of care to the members of the public in relation to decisions about when to arrest a suspect, how to control public disorder or how to handle a traffic hazard. If a member of the public is injured as a result of a wrong decision by the police on such a matter, he is unlikely to be able to establish liability. But there are some situations in which a duty has been imposed. In *Home Office v Dorset Yacht Co* (1970) the House of Lords held the prison authority liable for a careless decision of its officers which led to the escape of young offenders who caused damage to the plaintiff's property whilst escaping. The Lords considered that decision involved no element of discretion. The officers made a simple mistake when deciding on the level of supervision required to ensure that the offenders did not escape. The argument that imposition of a duty would lead to the adoption of defensive policies by the authority was rejected on the ground that prison officers were made of 'sterner stuff'.

Finally, it should be noted that if an authority goes further than making a decision and gives a member of the public advice, then a duty of care is much more likely to be imposed. For example, in *T v Surrey County Council* (1994) a four month old baby was physically abused by a child-minder. Before hiring the child-minder the mother had contacted the local authority to check that this minder was registered on its list of approved minders and was told not only that she was registered but also that it would be safe to leave the baby in her care. The authority had been negligent because although it had grounds to suspect the minder of child abuse on a previous occasion, it had failed to deregister her. The court held that the authority owed no duty of care in relation to its decision not to deregister as the registration system was not intended to protect the public as a whole and not to give individuals the right to sue. But it also held that the authority did owe a duty of care in respect of the advice it gave to the mother and was liable for its negligence in this respect. The moral for the citizen is clear: Never rely on registration schemes as such; always ask for specific advice. Whether there is really much sense in this distinction is another matter.

PURE ECONOMIC LOSS

This area has led to the most difficult case law concerning the scope of the duty of care. We consider it in detail in Chapter 19.

Strict liability

The concept of the duty of care binds together all the situations of potential negligence liability into a single tort. But there is no similar unifying concept linking the areas of strict liability. Instead, there are a number of separate situations in which a defendant may be strictly liable. Some have been developed by the common law, others by legislation and the justification differs in each area. This section will consider in outline the main common law and statutory areas of strict liability.

Common law strict liability

The two most important forms of strict liability at common law both have the effect of imposing strict liability on employers.

VICARIOUS LIABILITY

This is the principle under which an employer is strictly liable for torts committed by its employees. A number of the cases studied above involved vicarious liability. For example, in *Wilsher* it was the hospital authority rather than the negligent registrar that was sued and in *Dorset Yacht* it was the Home Office which was sued because it was the employer of the negligent prison officers. When the employer is sued as vicariously liable for the negligence of its employees, it is no defence for it to claim that it took all reasonable care in selecting and supervising its staff. It is strictly liable for their conduct. Of course, if the employer had itself failed to take care, for example, by failing to provide adequately trained staff, then it will be liable in negligence as well as being strictly liable under the vicarious principle. The most important justification for the imposition of vicarious liability is financial. Liability rests with the person best placed in terms of resources to insure the risk. The employer, rather than the employee, is likely to have the knowledge required in order to obtain the correct amount and kind of insurance. There is also an attractive logic in the idea that the employer, who obtains the benefits of the employee's work, should meet the responsibilities created by it.

Vicarious liability may also assist the plaintiff by providing a defendant to sue. It may be impossible to identify the employee whose fault caused the damage, but the employer will still be liable if it can be shown that the damage was caused within his enterprise by one of his employees. It should be noted that although the employer is vicariously liable, it is generally thought that the employee remains personally liable for his conduct. In practice, a plaintiff rarely sues a negligent employee personally because such an employee will not normally have insured himself against liability and may not have the resources to pay much compensation. Now that the courts are placing such weight on it being fair and reasonable to impose a duty, it is perhaps arguable that it is not fair to place a duty and potential liability on the uninsured employee when the insured employer is vicariously liable.

Vicarious liability only applies where the wrongful conduct was that of an employee. It does not apply where it was that of a self-employed independent contractor engaged by an employer. Many workers, particularly in the building trades, now purport to offer their services as self-employed contractors mainly because of the tax benefits. However, the courts, in a desire to preserve the scope of employers' strict liability, have looked at assertions of self-employed status rather sceptically. They insist that the worker be genuinely in business on his own account and taking financial risks, before being prepared to accord a self-employed status which will free the employer from a strict regime of vicarious liability. A further limit on vicarious liability is that the employer is not liable for torts committed by his employee which are unconnected with the job. The tort must have occurred within the course of the employment for there to be vicarious liability. But once again to preserve the scope of strict liability, the notion of the course of employment is interpreted liberally. If this were not the case it might be possible for an employer to subvert the purpose of vicarious liability by pleading that he did not employ the employee to misconduct himself. This kind of argument was raised in *Century Insurance v Northern Ireland Road Transport Board* (1942) which concerned an employer's liability for the acts of a petrol tanker driver who caused damage by smoking whilst offloading petrol. In one sense it is difficult to conceive of the employer employing the driver to do this act. But the law does not accept this. It distinguishes the actions which an employee was employed to perform from the manner in which they were performed. Only the first issue matters. In the *Century Insurance* case the driver was actually doing his job at the relevant time because he was offloading petrol, albeit in an exceptionally negligent manner. His acts therefore fell within the course of his employment. It is a question of fact whether an employee's acts have reached the point at which he is doing something which he is not employed to do. Fairly extreme facts would seem to be required. In one case a bus conductor's assault on a passenger was held to fall outside of the course of his employment. The argument that he had merely chosen an extreme and unauthorised mode of performing his duty of keeping order on the bus was rejected. This might seem the correct result but it does leave a seriously injured person to his, probably worthless, remedies against the employee.

It is possible that courts will regard even an express prohibition on the doing of an act as merely directed to the methods by which a job is done. Prohibitions on drivers giving lifts fall into this category. Older cases allowed the employer to restrict the course of a driver's employment in this way and even classified such passengers as trespassers on the vehicle. However, the Court of Appeal's approach in *Rose v Plenty* (1975) seems likely to be followed in the future. That case concerned a milkman who disobeyed instructions not to have children assisting him in delivering the milk and not to carry passengers on his milk float. The plaintiff, a boy aged thirteen, was injured by the milkman's negligence whilst riding on the float in the course of helping on the round. The majority of the Court of Appeal clearly appreciated that the child's rights could only be secured by making the employer's insurance available to meet the claim. They held that the milkman was doing his job, he was delivering the milk, albeit that the was acting in a prohibited fashion. It seems likely that the employer would only have escaped liability if it could have been shown that the employee's activities at the relevant time were unconnected with the employer's business. Indeed, the employer may be liable even when the employee acted to benefit himself. Employers have been held responsible for frauds and thefts committed by employees at work if the employer has given the employee a job which involved handling the transaction or items at issue.

BREACH OF STATUTORY DUTY

A person is liable in tort if he breaks a statutory duty which was impliedly intended to confer a civil right to sue on anyone suffering damages because of the breach. Some statutes confer an express right to sue, for example the Consumer Protection Act 1987, and in this case the plaintiff simply sues under the provisions of the statute. In most cases where the statute does not expressly provide for a civil action, it will be inferred that its purpose was to benefit the public as a whole rather than to give an individual a right of action. Thus, in *X v Bedfordshire* (1995) the House of Lords held that although the social service authority might have been in breach of the child care legislation, that legislation was designed to promote the welfare of the community as a whole and not to provide individuals with the right to sue the authority. The most important example of a statute which has been interpreted as impliedly giving rise to a civil action is the Factories Act 1961 which imposes duties on employers in relation to safety at work. If a such a duty has been broken with the result that an employee has been injured, that employee may sue the employer not under the provisions of the statute (because it says nothing about civil liability) but for the tort of breaking the statutory duty. This form of liability is strict because the employer is liable if it has broken the duty irrespective of whether it took care or not. The best illustration of the strictness of this form of liability is *Summers v Frost* (1955) which concerned section 14 of the Factories Act which provided that 'every dangerous part of any machinery ... shall be securely fenced'. The employee was injured when his hand touched a grinding wheel which he was operating. He sued on the ground that the grinding wheel was not securely fenced, that is protected from contact, all the way round and it was the fact that there was a gap in the fencing which had allowed his injury to occur. Of course, the gap was also essential to allow the grinding wheel to be used for grinding objects. Fencing it all the way round would certainly prevent any injury but would also make it useless. Despite this, the House of Lords held the employer to be liable. In effect, the Lords were holding that grinding wheels could be used but only if the employer paid for any injuries resulting from their use. The justification for this strict liability is obvious. We all benefit from industry and it is only fair that we all pay for the injuries caused to industrial workers. Strict liability achieves this because the employer's liability will be met by his insurer which will raises premiums on all such insurance policies to meet the cost of claims. The cost of the higher premiums will be passed on by the employers to the public at large through an increase charge for the product or service provided.

Statutory strict liability

A number of statutes impose strict liability for particular hazards. For example, the Nuclear Installations Act 1965 imposes strict liability for damage caused by radiation leaks from nuclear plants, the Prevention of Oil Pollution Act 1971 imposes strict liability on shipowners for damage caused by oil pollution and the Environmental Protection Act 1990 imposes strict liability for damage caused by waste disposal subject to the defence of having taken all reasonable precautions. There are two more general statutory regimes to be considered: the Consumer Protection Act 1987 which imposes strict liability for defective products and the Animals Act 1971 which imposes strict liability in relation to dangerous animals.

THE CONSUMER PROTECTION ACT 1987

The Consumer Protection Act 1987 introduced strict liability for damage caused by defective products. Several arguments were given for doing this. A person injured by a defective product faces a heavy burden in trying to prove a manufacturer negligent because he is likely to lack information on the cause of the defect and to have no expertise in relation to the design and production process. The doctrine of privity of contract places the primary legal responsibility for defective products on the supplier. This had the advantage of giving the injured person rights against a person with whom he was likely to have had dealings. However, it was argued that strict liability should be imposed on the manufacturer who had control over the design and production process and who could account for the risks created by the product in the price charged for it. Strict liability for defective products combines the strictness of contract liability with tort's ability to give remedies beyond privity of contract. Irrespective of the contractual position any injured consumer is given similar protection to a person who purchases directly.

The Act covers cases of personal injury and death as well as some areas of property damage. However, damage to the item itself or to another item of which it forms a component is excluded. In such a case the remedy against the supplier under the Sale of Goods Act has to be used. Strict liability may be imposed on a number of parties to the production process; the manufacturer, the person who abstracted the item or who processed it, a person who by his presentation of the item holds himself out as the producer, the person who imported it into the EC and a supplier who fails to identify the producer when requested to do so. An item is defined as defective if its safety 'is not such as persons generally are entitled to expect'. The safety of the item is judged at the time that the item is placed on the market. The definition of safety recognises the fact that many everyday products are unsafe if abused. It takes into account the marketing and packaging of the item, the use reasonably to be expected of it and the time at which it was supplied. It is specifically stated that the fact that products marketed at a later date were safer does not raise an inference that earlier examples were unsafe. In practice the most dangerous products are likely to be drugs. Over recent years it has been discovered that drugs such as Opren marketed for the elderly and Thalidomide which was prescribed to pregnant women, may cause serious damage. It is now alleged that some tranquilisers may have damaging consequences. Large numbers of people may be affected. However, the pharmaceutical industry lobbied hard and successfully to have a special defence added to the legislation. This is the development risks defence, which states that there will be no strict liability if the state of scientific and technical knowledge at the time when the item was put into circulation was not such that a producer of the kind of product in question was not able to discern the existence of the defect. Critics argue that this re-establishes a standard of care and may lead to injured consumers, such as the thalidomide children, obtaining no benefit from the legislation.

THE ANIMALS ACT 1971

The keeper of an animal can be liable in negligence for damage done by the animal if he carelessly failed to keep control over it. Thus in *Draper v Hodder* (1972) the owner of a pack of Jack Russell terriers was held liable when they attacked a young child. It was said that, as an experienced breeder of such animals, he ought to have been aware of the risk that a pack of these dogs would attack any moving object and was careless in failing to keep the dogs behind secure fencing. The Animals Act 1971 imposes additional strict liability in respect of dangerous animals. The Act divides animals into two classes according to their species. Strict liability is automatic if damage is caused by an animal which belongs to a 'dangerous species'; that is, one which is not normally domesticated in the British Isles and whose fully grown animals may, unless restrained, cause severe damage. If the animal in question belongs to such a species it does not matter that it appeared to be tame or had characteristics which seemed to render it harmless. Strict liability also applies even though the damage was not caused by the animal's dangerous characteristics. Strict liability may apply to damage done by an animal which does not belong to a dangerous species if certain conditions are satisfied. Its keeper must have had actual knowledge that the animal was likely to cause damage and this likelihood must have been caused by characteristics of this animal which are not normally found in the species or by those which are normally only found in particular circumstances. Strict liability therefore extends to cover bad tempered examples of normally safe species and those animals which are known to be dangerous on particular occasions, such as when they are rearing young. In *Cummings v Granger* (1975) strict liability was imposed on the basis of 'particular circumstances' in respect of the perfectly normal reaction of an untrained alsatian, which had been left to run free in a yard at night, to attack persons who entered the premises.

Defences

Under the Consumer Protection Act, the Animals Act and at common law for breach of statutory duty or vicarious responsibility, liability is strict but not absolute. It is still possible for the defendant to argue the defences of contributory negligence and consent. These defences also apply to negligence liability and need to be considered along with the defence of illegality and that of limitation of action which applies where the plaintiff has failed to sue within the permitted time period.

Contributory negligence

A plaintiff whose own fault was a partial cause of damage suffered in an accident will be held to be contributorily negligent. The damages which are recoverable will be reduced by section 1(1) of the Law Reform (Contributory Negligence) Act 1945 which provides that:

> 'Where any person suffers damage as the result partly of his own fault and partly of the fault of any other person or persons ... the damages recoverable in respect thereof shall be reduced to such an extent as the court thinks just and equitable having regard to the claimant's share in the responsibility for the damage.'

Proof of contributory negligence depends on a simple finding that the plaintiff failed to take reasonable care of his own safety. The standard of care is an objective one, an individual's view that a safety precaution is unnecessary or positively harmful will be discounted if the court holds that a reasonable person would use it. However, the courts have not allowed contributory negligence to be used to justify a hypercritical evaluation of a plaintiff's conduct. It may be possible to show that the reactions of a plaintiff when confronted by a situation of danger actually increased his loss. But a defendant who put the plaintiff in a position in which he made what proved to be the wrong decision, cannot be allowed to criticise reasonable reactions to the danger. Courts have similarly been wary of arguments that a child should be held to be contributory negligent and have applied a test which asks what dangers a child of the particular age could be expected to appreciate. Contributory negligence is available in cases of industrial injuries, but the balancing of responsibility between employer and employee has been influenced by the argument that it is the employer's responsibility to provide proper safety equipment, to instruct that it is used and to guard against employees becoming casual in the face of risks. This is particularly so when an employer is held to be in breach of a statutory safety duty. The courts are conscious that a finding of a high percentage of contributory negligence against an employee, would undermine the policy behind imposing strict liability for breach of a statutory duty.

A plaintiff's unreasonable conduct may be either a partial cause of an accident or increase the consequences of an accident caused wholly by the negligence of another. This is particularly important with regard to failures to use safety equipment. A motorist who failed to use a seat belt may have driven with all reasonable care and only have been involved in an accident because of the fault of another. However, if the failure to wear the belt increased the injuries suffered a reduction in the injured party's damages will be made on account of contributory negligence. This was established in *Froom v Butcher* (1975), a case decided before it became a criminal offence to fail to wear a seat belt when driving a car. The reasonable road user is taken to know that there is a risk that other people will cause a road accident. Lord Denning in *Froom* summarised the position in the following terms

> 'The question is not what was the cause of the accident. It is rather what was the cause of the damage ... in seat belt cases the cause of the accident is one thing. The cause of the damage is another. The *accident* is caused by the bad

driving. The *damage* is caused in part by the bad driving of the defendant, and in part by the failure of the plaintiff to wear a seat belt.'

The reduction in damages made on account of contributory negligence is a question of fact which is left to the discretion of the courts. Two issues are considered. The causal effect of the plaintiff's act and the blameworthiness which can be attributed to him. A child's conduct may be identical to that of an adult in contributing to the accident but its blameworthiness is likely to be much less, if not non-existent. Usually the court will compare the plaintiff's conduct with that of the defendant. However, in 'seat belt' cases the Court of Appeal removed the possibility that many road accidents would require a detailed consideration of the conduct of the parties by imposing a rule of thumb whereby 25% of damages are deducted if wearing the belt would have protected the plaintiff from all harm and 15% if it would have provided partial protection. This must have simplified the proceedings in many cases, but is open to the objection that it substitutes a detailed inquiry as to the cause of the injury for the comparison of the conduct of the parties. In one case a person injured in a road accident lost 20% of his damages because he knew that the driver of the car in which he was travelling had been drinking heavily. He would have lost 25% if it could have been shown that his failure to wear a seat belt was a cause of the damage. In fact it was impossible to prove that wearing the belt would have made any difference to his injuries and the 20% deduction applied.

There is a superficial fairness in the notion that a person who has contributed to causing the damage for which compensation is being sought should be met by a defence. Further thought, however, reveals some problems. There are difficulties with the argument that the defence has an important role in accident prevention. It is said that if people could obtain compensation from those who injure them irrespective of their own conduct there would be no incentive to make use of safety equipment and the number and severity of accidents would rise. The difficulty with this is that the available evidence suggests that most people are unaware of the role of the defence and do not govern their conduct according to it. The majority of drivers did not wear seat belts until their conduct was made a criminal offence. This happened more than six years after *Froom v Butcher* deemed it to be contributory negligence. If drivers did not use a safety precaution to guard against the clearly appreciated risk of suffering personal injuries they were hardly likely to be influenced by the remote and barely understood possibility that any damages awarded several years later on account of such injuries would be reduced. Second, the effect of contributory negligence differs from that of a finding of negligence. A finding of liability rarely imposes a direct loss on a defendant because the insurance company stands behind him. In contrast, contributory negligence denies a plaintiff money which the rules on damages deem to be needed to cope with the injury. This deduction is uninsurable. Contributory negligence provides the only example of a situation in which the quantum of compensation is calculated according to the degree of fault. It is wholly at variance with the supposed compensatory purpose of tort. In addition, it is certain that the existence of contributory negligence gives insurance companies a powerful weapon with which to pressure a plaintiff into settling a claim for a low sum. But despite these criticisms the defence is deeply embedded in English law.

Consent

Consent provides a complete defence as opposed to an apportionment of damages. It may result from an express agreement to run a risk or be implied from the plaintiff's conduct. The implied form of the defence is normally referred to by its latin tag, *volenti non fit injuria* (literally: consent does not make a wrong). The basis of this form of the defence is that the plaintiff's actions were so stupid that it must be inferred that he agreed to discharge the defendant from the consequences of his conduct. As contributory negligence is available on similar grounds to provide the lesser result of a partial reduction of damages, it is not surprising that a heavy burden needs to be satisfied before the defence operates.

The two factors which are relevant to this defence are knowledge and consent. Knowledge, in the sense that the plaintiff knows of the risk which is being run, must be proved. A person cannot consent to run risks which he does not know about. This severely limits the role of the defence in negligence cases because the plaintiff will commonly have had no knowledge of the negligence before the accident. In *Slater v Clay Cross Quarries* (1956) the defence did not operate in the case of a person injured by a train whilst using a railway tunnel in a quarry as a short cut. The court held that the plaintiff's conduct was sufficient to imply an acceptance of the risk of injury from the normal running of trains, but not from those which were driven negligently. On the facts it was held that the driver had acted negligently and the defence failed.

Knowledge of the existence of a risk does not, on its own, establish the defence. For example, the fact that an employee continues to work knowing that his employment creates risks does not establish the defence. The additional requirement which must be proved is that a consent was freely given. Consent, here, does not mean that the plaintiff knowingly put himself in a position of danger. It must be established that the plaintiff willingly consented to exempt the prospective defendant from any legal liability. A person may take the risk of crossing a busy city road, but it does not follow that he agrees to exempt any motorist who negligently injures him while he is doing this. Modern courts have tended to regard the question whether consent to accept the legal responsibility is established as an issue of fact. The level of disregard of safety involved in embarking on a pleasure flight in an aircraft piloted by a person who was known to have been drinking heavily was held in *Morris v Murray* (1990) to establish the existence of consent, whereas travelling as a passenger in a car with a driver who consumed a moderate amount of alcohol in the course of the journey is only likely to raise the defence of contributory negligence (*Dann v Hamilton* (1939) but note that for motoring cases volenti was abolished anyway by a 1972 statute). If these conditions are not sufficient to ensure that the defence can only rarely be established, there is a further requirement in that a valid consent can only be given if the plaintiff had complete freedom of choice. This is the rule which excludes the defence from any role in industrial injury cases. It is said that the pressures on an employee to obey the employer's orders and to earn a living remove his freedom of choice as to whether to run risks created by the job.

It must be asked whether the defence has any role to play in modern law. It is based on the plaintiff's conduct. Contributory negligence is similarly based and operates in parallel with volenti, with the latter defence being far more difficult to prove. Volenti does not usually operate in industrial injury cases and it is excluded by statute from motoring claims. However, Parliament has encouraged its survival by making a number of statutory torts (for example, those arising under the Animals Act 1971 and the Occupiers' Liability Acts 1957 and 1984) subject to it. Furthermore, consent does have a role to play as a defence to intentional torts such as trespass to the person. It makes lawful both medical procedures and those contacts incurred in sports, such as boxing or rugby, in which physical contact is within the rules of the game. In such cases the consent will be limited, in the medical case to the procedures agreed to, and in the sporting context, to injuries incurred within the rules of the game. The consent will not extend to negligent conduct and it is difficult to envisage a court supporting the view favoured by some commentators that sportsmen consent to a certain amount of intentional foul play. In the medical sphere this species of the consent defence differs from normal volenti insofar as full disclosure of all risks created by the procedure is not required. Only the basic nature of the treatment need be disclosed. If the stricter rule was used doctors would be strictly liable whenever medical treatment went wrong unless they could show that they had disclosed all the risks that it entailed, however remote. The consequences of this for patient autonomy are discussed later in Chapter 18.

A second form of defence based on consent is the exclusion clause or notice. It is somewhat fictitious to regard such a defence as based on the plaintiff's express consent to waive rights. In most situations in which an exclusion clause is used it is the defendant's idea to draft and use the clause which removes the plaintiff's rights. However, the best theoretical justification for the efficacy of such clauses is that the plaintiff's consent to become subject to the clause can be inferred.

The great majority of exclusion clauses which purport to remove rights in tort derive their force from incorporation in a contract. Clauses of this kind, the judicial methods of interpreting them and their statutory regulation are discussed elsewhere in this book (Chapter 24). The discussion in this section is confined to the small number of clauses which operate outside of contract. The great majority of these are notices erected on land and disclaimers of liability in respect of negligent misstatements (p 444). One point which must be clearly appreciated is that is that not all notices are drafted to perform the same function. Some will purport to exclude liability. Others may merely warn of risks, in which case they will not provide a complete defence but may mean that the defendant's duty has been discharged or, if less effective, give grounds for a plea of contributory negligence. The final possibility is that the notice simply ensures that a person who enters the property is classified as a trespasser and is thus subject to a less favourable level of protection. For a notice erected on land to be effective all that a landowner has to do is give reasonable notice of the exclusion. If this is done all entrants are bound by the clause, whether or not they actually appreciated or understood its significance. Thus, in *White v Blackmore* (1972), a case concerning injuries suffered by a person while watching a motor race, an exclusion notice proved to be more effective than the standard volenti defence. The fact that the deceased did not know of the negligence which produced the fatal accident meant that he could not be held volenti to the risk. However, an exclusion notice placed at the entrance to the ground removed his rights irrespective of his knowledge. The only common law rule which limits the operation of such clauses is that which requires the plaintiff to have had a free choice whether to become subject to the clause. Persons entering property in the course of their employment are regarded as lacking such freedom and are not subject to the clause.

These rules obviously have the capacity to produce unfairness and the balance has been redressed by a number of statutory controls. The Road Traffic Act 1988 invalidates any attempt by owners of cars to use such clauses. Before this provision was first enacted in 1972 it was not unknown for drivers who had not insured their liability to passengers to attempt to exclude it by attaching exclusion notices to the dashboards of their cars. The 1988 Act makes such insurance compulsory and, logically, renders any such clauses invalid. A more comprehensive attack on exclusion clauses exists in the Unfair Contract Terms Act 1977 which, in spite of its title, extends its controls to notices which are not enforced as part of a contract. The Act renders inoperative clauses which 'restrict or exclude' negligence liability for personal injuries or death and makes the validity of clauses which exclude or restrict liability for other forms of loss or damage turn on whether they are shown to be reasonable. These controls are imposed by section 2 of the Act. They do not apply to all exclusion clauses and notices. Their operation is confined to situations of 'business liability', that is, where the clause excludes liability for breach of obligations or duties arising from things done in the course of a business or from the occupation of premises used for business purposes. It follows that the controls do not extend to exclusions used by private persons and other non-business activities. In those areas the results established by the common law survive. The precise definition of business is a matter of some contention. The Act provides no definition, but the term is commonly thought to entail the carrying on of trade with a view to profit. The Act seems to confirm this by including within the term the activities of professional persons, those of government departments and of local and public authorities which might fall outside of a restrictive definition. An exception was created in 1984 to allow businesses which grant access to their property for recreational or educational activities to use exclusion clauses if the granting of access does not form part of the occupier's business purposes. Farmers can therefore exclude their liability to ramblers and potholers. The exceptions are not likely to prove to be of great significance. For the most part the Act places powerful controls on the use of such clauses.

Illegality

If a person is injured whilst committing a criminal offence the defence of illegality (known in Latin as *ex turpi causa non oritur actio*) may bar any tort claim which is brought. This defence has been held to be capable of barring claims brought by a person injured in a road accident while escaping from the scene of a crime, by a person injured while encouraging another to drive dangerously and by a person injured in the course of a fight provoked by his initial assault. However, it is unclear which criminal offences are capable of invoking the defence and how closely related to the offence the tort has to be for the defence to operate. The fact that an injured person was committing an offence at the time of his injury cannot invariably bar a subsequent claim in tort. Many motorists injured in road accidents may have been committing criminal offences such as breaking speed limits or driving carelessly. Employees involved in industrial accidents may have committed criminal offences under the Health and Safety at Work etc Act 1974. The approach generally adopted in such cases is to reduce the plaintiff's damages on grounds of contributory negligence. This is surely correct. To completely bar a claim because of a minor illegality would be exceptionally harsh. The financial consequences suffered by even a moderately injured plaintiff might dramatically exceed the maximum penalty which the criminal law would impose.

A different issue arises where the plaintiff has been injured whilst trespassing on the defendant's land. The law used to take the view that as an occupier was entitled to exclude its liability to visitors, logically it should owe no duty of care to trespassers who were unwanted visitors. But this view had harsh consequences, particularly where the trespassers were children injured by serious dangers left unguarded by the occupier. The Occupiers' Liability Act 1984 was passed to strike a balance between the interests of the occupier and the trespasser. It does this through the definition of both the standard of care and the circumstances in which a duty is owed to a trespasser. An occupier will only owe a duty in respect of a risk if three conditions are satisfied. He must be aware, or have reasonable grounds to believe, that a risk exists because of the state of his premises or because of things done or omitted to be done on them; he must know, or have reasonable grounds to believe, that the trespasser is in the vicinity of the danger or may come into it and, third, the risk must be one against which, in all the circumstances of the case, he may reasonably be expected to offer some protection. If these factors impose a duty on an occupier towards a trespasser it is one 'to take such care as is reasonable in all the circumstances of the case' to see that the trespasser does not suffer injury by reason of the danger. It is expressly stated that a warning may suffice, in an appropriate case, to discharge the duty. It seems likely that the duties created by the Act vary greatly according to such factors as the nature of the risk, the character of the entrant and the cost of providing protection. An obligation to provide significant protection for the safety of burglars is unlikely to be recognised.

Limitation of actions

It may be possible for a defendant to plead limitation of actions as a defence to a tort claim. A plaintiff has a limited period in which to commence proceedings. Proceedings are commenced by the issue of a writ rather than by getting the case to trial. The standard limitation periods applied are three years in a case which involves personal injuries or death and six years in other forms of contract or tort action. A claim started outside of these periods will fail because it is time-barred.

The need for some limitation period is obvious. Evidence will be lost with the passage of time and defendants have a legitimate interest in being able to close their books on work long completed. Time periods should encourage plaintiffs to expedite the commencement of proceedings. On the other hand, the period should not be so short that it prejudices the plaintiff's ability to obtain advice on bringing proceedings. It may take time for the true extent of the damage to become clear. The law has been particularly troubled by issues of latent damage. At common law time runs from the date that damage occurs, not from the date at which it could reasonably have been discovered. This may be unfair because the limitation period may expire before the plaintiff could know that he had suffered damage. An employee exposed to a dangerous industrial process may only develop symptoms of consequential illness some years later, although it can be proved that he must have suffered damage at an earlier date. Similarly, poor quality construction work may result in a slow and progressive failure of a building the seriousness of which is not immediately apparent to the owner. A number of legislative attempts have been made to achieve a fair balance between these competing interests. The result is an exceptionally complex piece of law.

The limitation rules concerning personal injury claims modify the common law rules considerably. The three year limitation period runs from the date that the plaintiff suffered damage, or (if later) from the date that he first had knowledge that he had suffered significant injury which was attributable to negligence. This latter rule is designed to assist plaintiffs who have suffered from latent damage. In addition, the court has a general discretion to allow a claim to proceed in spite of its being started outside of the standard limitation period. The court has an unfettered discretion to do this, except that it must look at the position of the parties and consider the extent to which they would be prejudiced by the application of the normal period or by its being waived.

Negligence cases which do not involve personal injuries are subject to a different regime. Typical examples are professional negligence cases concerning negligent advice. As a result of the Latent Damage Act 1986 three periods operate. The basic rule is a six year period which runs from the date of the damage irrespective of whether it was discoverable. A secondary period running from the date of knowledge of significant injury may add to this or start a new period running if the basic period is exhausted. But, as the secondary period is only a three year one it does not assist a plaintiff who discovers the fact of his injury within three years of the date of suffering damage. Finally there is an overriding 'cut off' period of fifteen years which runs from the date of the negligence. This period sets a final limit to liability even though the primary and secondary periods have not yet run out. There is no discretion to extend the limitation periods beyond these limits.

Postscript: liability for injuries caused by road traffic accidents

The extent of tortious liability for physical damage is determined by a balance of fault and strict liability principles developed over a period of time. The balance reflects the importance society attaches to different interests. The fault principle gives priority to the freedom to engage in activities without liability provided care is taken. The strict liability principle gives priority to the need to protect individuals from risks stemming from activities which benefit society as a whole. Domestic accidents fall on the fault side of the line and industrial accidents on the strict liability side of this line. Where should road accidents fall? At present liability for road accidents is based on fault. But there are grounds for thinking that liability should be strict. In the first place, road transport is central to our modern economy and on this ground it might be thought that road users should meet the full cost of road accidents caused by their driving whether they were at fault or not. Second, all road users are covered by compulsory insurance and so a system of strict liability would not ruin the individual driver but would shift the loss to road users as a group through higher insurance premiums. Third, higher insurance premiums might lead to fewer vehicles using the road than would otherwise be the case and, consequently, to fewer accidents with a net saving to society. As against this, it is said that liability based fault has a deterrent value, that is, drivers are more careful because they fear being to blame for an accident and facing a resulting increase in insurance premium. Other critics would argue that the whole liability system is inefficient and should be replaced by a system of state compensation for accidents. This suggestion is considered at length in the next chapter.

Chapter 16
Physical damage: tort compensation and state compensation

Whether liability for personal injuries is strict or fault based, there remains the question whether tort provides the best means of compensating accident victims. Some would argue that compensation for personal injuries should be provided by the state irrespective of whether anyone was at fault or was in anyway responsible for the accident causing the injury. This approach is sometimes known as a 'no-fault' scheme but it is really a no-responsibility scheme in the sense that the victim will recover from the state even though no other person was responsible for causing the accident, for example where the victim falls asleep at the wheel of his car and crashes. New Zealand has introduced such an accident compensation scheme and abolished the right to bring a tort action for personal injuries. The UK already provides limited state compensation for accident victims through the social security system. The critics of the tort system argue that it should be replaced by an improved social security system which would provide a more efficient and fairer means of providing compensation. This chapter will outline the principles upon which tort compensation is calculated and the present system of social security benefits, before moving to the broader question of whether a wider scheme of state compensation would be preferable to the present mix of tort and social security.

Tort compensation for personal injuries or death

The approach adopted by English law when assessing tort damages is to provide full compensation for financial losses suffered by a victim. The aim is to replace every £1 lost and to keep the victim in the state to which he had become accustomed or, conceivably, in the state to which he aspired. The tort system is unique in insisting that the victim's means are not to be reduced by an accident. Tort also awards 'fair' compensation for non-financial losses such as pain and suffering. Non-pecuniary losses comprise a significant proportion of many awards of tort damages and can add greatly to the overall value of the award. It has been argued that their nuisance value leads to insurers settling many small claims for more than they are truly worth. The research has shown that more than half of the money paid as tort compensation was for non-pecuniary losses.

Tort damages are awarded as a lump sum, on a 'once and for all' basis. There are obvious advantages for insurers in a system which enables them to close their books on a case. However, there are disadvantages for the small number of victims estimated at about 8%, whose losses will continue into the future. Damages awarded to such persons will be intended, in a large part, to replace regular income and expenditure. The court which calculates the award will take account of contingencies, such as that the victim might have gained promotion or been disabled by a naturally occurring illness. But such speculation has its limits and is almost certain to prove inaccurate.

There are some limited exceptions to the lump sum approach. First, a plaintiff may seek an interim payment. This is an award intended to help meet losses incurred before the final calculation of the damages is made. It is particularly useful as many accident victims incur the greatest part of the additional expenses and have the most difficulty in tailoring their commitments to a reduced level of income immediately after the accident. A final award of damages may still be some way in the future at this time even if liability is not disputed. A court may award an interim payment if satisfied that the defendant is liable to the plaintiff for a substantial sum and has the means to enable him to make the payment. An interim payment will not exceed a reasonable proportion of the damages which the court believes will ultimately be recovered. Second, the problem of future contingencies may be answered, to an extent, by an award of provisional damages. If a chance exists that the plaintiff will as a result of the tort develop a serious disease or suffer serious physical or mental deterioration, the court may assess damages on the assumption that the contingency will not occur but declare that, if it does, he will be entitled to a further award. The procedure is a split lump sum award rather than a system of periodic payments and is only of use in a limited number of cases. It does not cover claims in which the victim's job prospects deteriorate beyond the normal deterioration which can be expected to follow from certain injuries. However, when it does apply, it produces a more accurate result than guessing the rate of deterioration.

Calculation of damage awards

A plaintiff is compensated for two different types of loss: pecuniary and non-pecuniary. Pecuniary loss is the damage capable of being directly calculated in money terms and is normally made up of the amount of earnings lost and the expenses incurred as a result of injury. Non-pecuniary losses are such immeasurable items such as pain and suffering and loss of amenity.

Non-pecuniary losses

The criterion of 'fair' compensation for non-pecuniary losses accepts that no sum of money can be exact compensation for such losses. Sympathy for the victims of accidents must not lead to the award of massive damages against a defendant. It is also important to achieve consistency between the awards made to different plaintiffs who suffer similar injuries. As a result a 'tariff' of conventional awards has developed to govern the fixing of the appropriate figure. But the tariff provides a range of possible awards and a plaintiff will recover at the high end of the range if she can show that the injury has a particular impact upon her life. Thus, injury to a hand will result in a higher award to a plaintiff whose hobby was playing the piano.

The different areas of non-pecuniary loss, pain, suffering and loss of amenity, are usually represented by a single award of damages. However, exceptional cases do occur in which it is necessary to distinguish between them. Awards of damages for pain and suffering are made on a purely subjective basis. The greater the pain suffered, whether as a result of the injury or of the consequential treatment, the higher the award. If the pain is controlled by drugs or if the victim has periods of unconsciousness the award will be reduced or eliminated. The element of suffering can be important even if the victim experiences no pain. It covers the whole disruption of the victim's life consequential on the injury and includes elements such as loss of marriage prospects and the opportunity of having children, distress at the physical indignities suffered by a crippled person or by someone who receives a disfiguring scar and the appreciation that one's expectation of life has been shortened. Awards for loss of amenity (also referred to as loss of faculty) represent the fact of physical injury and impairment of bodily function. An award of this kind is assessed objectively and is thus independent of the victim's knowledge of his fate. As a result large awards for loss of amenity have been made to plaintiffs who have suffered catastrophic injuries, survive on a life support machine and have little or no appreciation of their injuries. It is difficult to see any justification for this. The award is made in addition to awards for loss of earnings and care and can only be a windfall for the victim's relatives.

Pecuniary losses

EARNINGS

It is easy to calculate what the plaintiff has lost prior to the trial or settlement of the action. The real problem is to estimate what will be lost in the future. The method the courts use is based on calculating the net annual earnings loss incurred by the plaintiff (a net basis is used because damages are tax free) and to multiply it by a figure representing the number of years over which the loss will run (the multiplier). The figure chosen as the multiplier will be less than the number of years over which the loss is estimated to run for two reasons. First, it is assumed that the money awarded as damages will be invested and produce income. The plaintiff's needs should be met from a combination of capital and income, the aim being to exhaust the fund at the end of the period. A successful plaintiff receives capital to replace earnings which would have been made in the future and credit must be given for this. Second, it cannot be assumed that the plaintiff would, in the absence of the accident, have avoided contingencies such as unemployment or natural illness which might have reduced his earning capacity. The multipliers used by the courts, which tend to be limited to a maximum of 17, take account of these factors. Where the plaintiff had no earnings at the date of the accident but was likely to have had some in the future, the courts will award damages for loss of earning capacity. Examples include children, students, and non-employed housewives. Calculating such awards can be very much a matter of guesswork.

The difficulty involved in protecting the value of a lump sum award of damages against the declining value of money produced by inflation has caused much discussion. However, attempts to increase the multipliers awarded to allow for inflation were rejected by the House of Lords in *Cookson v Knowles* (1978) where it was said that the interest generated by investing the lump sum award would tend to outstrip the effect of inflation. A similarly robust response has been given to the argument that the multiplier should be increased to take account of the higher rates of tax likely to be levied on the income on a large award of damages. In *Hodgson v Trapp* (1988) the House of Lords rejected this contention on the ground that the rate of taxation to be levied on income in the future is only one of the many imponderables taken into account by the traditional range of multipliers. Lord Oliver summed up the attitude of the courts when he said: 'to assess the probabilities of future political, economic and fiscal policies requires not the services of an actuary or an accountant but those of a prophet.' It is for this reason that the courts have preferred to trust their own judgment rather than that of expert witnesses claiming to provide 'scientific' predictions of life expectancy, earnings growth, inflation, taxation rates and the rest.

Damages for lost earnings are awarded in full up to the expected date of the victim's death or retirement, whichever comes first. What happens if the accident has reduced the plaintiff's life expectancy? It used to be the law that the plaintiff could not recover what he would have earned in his lost years, that is the years he would have lived but for the accident. This was most unfair as it seemed to reward the defendant who managed to shorten the plaintiff's life. In *Pickett v British Rail Engineering Ltd* (1979) the House of Lords altered the law to allow the victim to recover what he would have earned in this lost years. But this recovery for the lost years is subject to one rather macabre qualification: the victim will not be alive during the lost years and hence, he will 'save' the amount of money he would have spent on himself during those years. For this reason, he can only recover the amount of money he would have earned in the lost years and would not have spent on himself. The family man who saves money for the children's future will do better than the single man who spends his money on cars.

EXPENSES

The main expense which may be incurred as a result of an injury is the cost of medical care. If the victim is treated by the National Health Service, there is no charge – yet! But the victim is completely free to choose private health care instead and can then claim the cost as an expense resulting from the accident. Rationally it might be argued that claims for the cost of private health care should be limited to situations where it was reasonable to opt for private as opposed to NHS care but ideologically this has never been acceptable. There are other types of expenses which can be claimed such as the cost of home nursing, travel, special clothing and equipment. The expenses claim is calculated in the same way as that for loss of earnings, that is, the annual cost is calculated and multiplied by whatever multiplier is appropriate. The case of *Hunt v Severs* (1994) illustrates this process and also raises one difficult issue. Severs negligently crashed his motorbike and as a result his pillion passenger, Hunt, was rendered paraplegic and needed constant nursing care. Severs looked after her and, indeed, they later married. Hunt claimed damages against Severs, damages which would be paid by his motor insurers. It was agreed that her life expectancy was 25 years and at the trial the judge discounted to a multiplier of 14. He then estimated the annual cost of nursing care had if not been provided by Severs, and multiplying that by 14 produced the figure of £60,000 for future care expenses. To this was added much larger sums for loss of earnings and non-pecuniary losses and the final award came to over £600,000. But the case was appealed on the ground that it was against public policy for an award of £60,000 to be made, in effect, to the wrongdoer. Hunt argued that the basis of the award was her need and that the court should not be concerned with how she met the need. The House of Lords rejected this argument. It held that the central objective of the care element of the award was to compensate the voluntary carer to whom the plaintiff was entrusted to pass on the award. Consequently, it would be wrong for the court to require the wrongdoer to pay the plaintiff damages which she would have to return to the wrongdoer. Of course, this eminently logical reasoning completed ignored the reality that it would be the insurer paying the award. It also resulted in the couple being £60,000 worse off because Severs had relied on her husband's care. The message to someone in her position is:

hire private nursing care so that your husband's time is free for work. Whether this makes sense is a different matter.

COMPENSATING BENEFITS

An accident victim may receive payments and services intended to alleviate hardship and it must be decided whether their value should be deducted from any damages awarded. A deduction reduces the tortfeasor's liability; whereas, if it is not made, the victim, is over compensated. English law has used a number of techniques to answer the problem. It has asked whether the payment was 'too collateral to' or 'too remote from' the loss to be taken into account. Attention has been paid to the source of the money and to whether it was intended to replace the kind of loss suffered. So, if an injured employee continues to receive payments from his employer this reduces the losses incurred and the tortfeasor's liability. Payments from insurance policies which the victim had effected to protect himself against the risk are not deducted from damages. They derive not from the accident but from the victim's wisdom in contracting the insurance. Deduction would create a disincentive to insurance by giving the benefits of any payments made to the tortfeasor (or his insurers). Double recovery is an acceptable price for avoiding the victim being a net loser by expending premiums on the policy for no return. Payments, such as disability pensions, made by pension funds are treated similarly as an element of insurance is commonly present. Payments from charities and disaster funds are not deducted as those giving to the fund did not intend their generosity to benefit the tortfeasor by reducing his liabilities.

Accident victims may receive a variety of social security benefits (p 416). These benefits go some way to compensating the victim for his loss of income and expenses and it is arguable that they should be taken into account when damages are calculated. The law on this was complex and somewhat inconsistent with different rules for different benefits. But it has been simplified by section 22 of the Social Security Act 1989 which introduces a uniform scheme for all benefits and applies to both damages awarded by courts and out-of-court settlements. If an award or settlement of more than £2,500 is to be made, the person paying the compensation (usually an insurance company) is obliged to deduct the value of any social security benefits which have been paid to the victim over the first five years after the injury or paid up to the date of settlement if that comes earlier. Benefits which are paid after the five year period are not deducted from the damages. In the case of damages of £2,500 or less a different system applies under which the person making the payment is entitled to deduct from the damages paid half of the value of any benefits paid, or to be paid, to the victim in the five years from the accident. In such cases the tortfeasor's liability is simply reduced and the DSS gets no credit for having paid benefit to the victim. The scheme is a complex but fair compromise.

For the victim of a serious accident, a major state benefit is likely to be free medical treatment from the National Health Service. To the extent that the victim has received such free treatment prior to the award of damages, he will not be able to claim medical expenses. If he is likely to receive such free treatment in the future, the award for future medical expenses will be reduced to take account of this and the award for loss of earnings will be reduced to take account of the fact that the NHS will provide him with the food and accommodation for which he would otherwise have had to pay out of his salary.

DEATH OF THE VICTIM

If the accident victim dies before being able to obtain damages from a court or a settlement, there are three types of claim which can be brought. First, the victim's estate, though his legal representatives, can bring a claim for all his losses prior to death. So the estate can sue for his pain and suffering, loss of amenity, loss of earnings and medical expenses, all of which are losses incurred before death. Obviously the quicker the victim dies, the less the possible claim under this head. Indeed, someone killed instantaneously, for example in a road accident, will have no claim at all. The second claim can be brought by the victim's dependants under the provisions of the Fatal Accidents Act 1976. The Act provides that a wide range of relatives may make a claim but to be successful the relative must prove the fact of dependency on the deceased. This means the receipt of some benefit from the deceased which can be measure in financial terms. This covers earnings spent on the dependants, savings made for their future use, non-essential items, such as holidays and the value of services rendered. The Act covers losses other than a deceased's husband's earnings; loss of a non-earning housewife's services to her family justify an award. Awards under the Fatal Accidents Act are calculated according to the general principles relating to financial losses in personal injury cases outlined previously. The result is that damages in dependency claims often come to a sizeable element of what would have been awarded had the victim lived. The 'saving' to the defendant through killing the victim rather than leaving him badly injured comes primarily from avoiding damages for medical expenses and non-pecuniary losses.

The process of calculating the dependency is well illustrated by *Spittle v Bunney* (1988) in which the defendant's negligent driving had resulted in the death of the mother of a three-year-old child, Kate, who brought a dependency claim. The Court of Appeal took the view that Kate would probably proceed to tertiary education and hence, her dependency on her mother's services in some form would have lasted until the age of 22. So the period of dependency would be 18 years. As in personal injury claims the actual period over which losses are incurred must be discounted to produce the multiplier and here the court thought that 11 would be the appropriate multiplier. Calculating the annual dependency was more difficult. At trial, the judge had taken the yearly net wage of a nanny at £4,250 as the basic multiplicand which produced an award of close to £47,000. The Court of Appeal spotted the obvious weakness in this approach: once Kate had started at school she did not need a full-time nanny. Indeed, as she got older, her need for 'motherly' services progressively diminished. The court did not suggest a precise multiplicand for each year of dependency but took a 'ball-park' approach and held that £25,000 would be a fair figure for the total dependency. In fact, Kate's aunt had taken her into her own family and would look after her as a daughter free of charge. The court ignored this, just as it would ignore the voluntary caring of a relative when calculating expenses in a personal injury claim (save where the caring relative was also the defendant: see *Hunt v Severs* p 410). Kate's father was not married to her mother but they did live together and the legislation provides that cohabitees count as relatives. So he could have had a claim for dependency, for example, on the mother's domestic services. But he had disappeared, so no such claim was brought. If Kate's mother had been earning, then the dependency would have been expressed more directly in terms of the amount of money earned which would have been devoted to the child. Exactly the same process applies where a father has been killed. But there is one difference between fathers and mothers. If the mother has been killed, the court will consider the widower's prospects of remarrying. If the prospects were good, for example because of his job prospects, charm etc, then the court will reduce the dependency award to both father and any children on the assumption that a substitute wife/mother will appear on the scene. However, if the father has been killed, the court is barred by legislation from considering the remarriage prospects of the widow which might be dependent upon her looks etc. An outpost of chivalry, an outdated gesture or a denial of equal treatment?

The third type of claim on death is for bereavement. The amount of the claim is fixed under the provisions of the Fatal Accidents Act and is currently for £7,500. But only two categories of person can claim; the husband or wife of the deceased and the parents of a deceased unmarried minor. Thus, in the Hillsbrough disaster which resulted in the *Alcock* case discussed earlier (p 386), the siblings, grandparents, fiances and friends could not claim for their grief at the death of their loved one. The bereavement award is a gesture towards those most likely to suffer extreme grief but by denying 'equal treatment' to others suffering from intense grief, it simply added to their feelings of outrage.

An illustrative problem: *Lim v Camden Health*
Authority (1979)

The rules for calculating damages are complex and often hide the underlying issues of policy. One case which well illustrates the complexity but
also faces the underlying issues is *Lim v Camden*. Dr Lim suffered
irreparable brain damage during a routine operation due to the negligence
of the defendant's hospital staff. She was an unmarried 36 year old and
would spend the rest of her life a helpless invalid with little appreciation
of what had happened to her. At trial she was awarded £254,000 damages,
a then record for an English court. Camden's appeal against the damages
reached the House of Lords. There were three grounds of appeal. The first
was against the award of just over £100,000 for the cost of future care in
private institutions. It was argued that she should have chosen National
Health Service care. Lord Scarman, giving the judgment of the House of
Lords, sympathised with the argument but could not accept it as the
plaintiff's right to choose was enshrined in legislation passed at the time
the NHS was created. However, a second point succeeded. This was the
fact that being cared for in a private institution would save Dr Lim an
estimated £1,600 per year in living expenses. Yet her loss of earnings
compensation was based on the assumption that she would be spending
some of her earnings on living expenses. She was being compensated twice
over for her living expenses, once as part of her earnings compensation
and twice as part of her care expenses. The House of Lords accepted that
this duplication was wrong and reduced her care expenses by £15,600
(£1,600 per year times the agreed multiplier of 12). It would have made
equal sense to have reduced her loss of earnings by this amount. It did not
matter which head of loss was reduced but one certainly had to be to
prevent the duplication.

The third ground of appeal was in relation to the £20,000 awarded for
loss of amenity. The argument was that no sum should have been awarded
as Dr Lim was not aware of her loss. The House of Lords sympathised
with the argument but felt that the previous case law permitting such
awards could only be over-turned by the legislature and not by the judges.
From the perspective of the judges, the justice of being consistent outweighed the justice of reducing the award. The third ground was in relation
to nearly £100,000 awarded for loss of earnings. Here the argument was
based on the dissenting view of Lord Denning MR in the Court of Appeal,
that 'fair compensation' meant an award sufficient to pay for the costs of
Dr Lim's care but should not include anything for her loss of earnings as
she did not need the money and had no family in need. Lord Scarman
rejected this argument on the ground that 'fair' compensation meant
'proper' compensation and Dr Lim was properly entitled to her loss of
earnings. Her relatives would have expected to inherit her money had she
died wealthy after years of well-paid medical practice, so what is wrong

with them inheriting her unused damages when she died? So the overall result of the appeal was only a small reduction in the damages to take account of the duplication.

Lord Denning coupled his view that loss of earnings should not be awarded with the equally radical suggestion that Dr Lim should be allowed to return to court if her reduced damages proved to be insufficient for her care. In other words, the expenses award should be regarded as an interim figure capable of adjustment later in the light of need. Lord Scarman also thought that the 'lump sum' principle of awarding 'once and for all' damages produced insuperable problems and referred to the reforms proposed by the 1978 Royal Commission under Lord Pearson. This had proposed that compensation for seriously injured plaintiffs should be awarded in the form of periodic payments varying with the needs of plaintiff. But Lord Scarman argued that such a change in the law could only be introduced by the legislature after appropriate investigation of the range of social and economic consequences, and could not be introduced by the judges. (p 190).

In fact, the legislature has not introduced a periodic payment scheme because the Pearson proposal was rejected by liability insurers on the ground that it would prevent them from closing their books. Somewhat ironically, these very same insurers are now promoting a periodic payment scheme of their own, known as a structured settlement. The explanation for this change of heart does not lie so much in an appreciation of the problems of the lump sum system for the victim, but rather in a tax concession introduced by the Inland Revenue. Put simply, the concession is that if the victim and the insurer settle on the basis that the insurer will invest the settlement sum to produce a periodic income for the victim, those payments will not be taxed. By contrast, if the settlement takes the form of a lump sum payment which is invested by the victim, the periodic income received by the victim will be taxed. Why should the insurer bother to invest the settlement sum to produce an income for the victim? Because by offering to settle on this basis it will be able to persuade the victim to accept a lesser sum. For example, if the victim's claim was worth £500,000 and he invested that sum to produce an income of £50,000 per year, taxation would absorb roughly £15,000 of that sum leaving him with an income of £35,000 per year. But if he accepted a lesser sum of £400,000 to be invested in a structured settlement by the insurer, then his income would average a tax-free £40,000 per year. The insurer gains because it can settle for less. The victim gains because he benefits from an invested settlement which can be structured to guarantee him sufficient money for each year. It is no wonder that since structured settlements were first approved in *Kelly v Dawes* (1990) they have grown greatly in popularity and have received the enthusiastic blessing of a Law Commission report in 1994. Both insurer and victim win. Who loses? The Revenue. Does this matter? Society has only a certain resource it can devote to caring for the victims of accidents and illness. The tax concession for structured settlements provides more of this resource for the minority of victims who are able to bring a tort action. Ultimately, it may do this at the expense of the much larger group of victims who depend upon state compensation alone. This is a point to which we return after considering the scope of state compensation.

State compensation for personal injuries

State compensation comes in the form of social security payments. The philosophy of the social security system differs from that of tort. It does not aim to achieve full compensation, but merely to provide a level of income which will meet a claimant's basic needs. It also provides hardly any benefits in relation to non-pecuniary losses. When first set up the system was regarded as based on insurance principles; benefits depended on the claimant having contributed to the National Insurance Fund. However, the growth of non-contributory benefits has eroded this principle substantially.

Social security benefits, although they cannot rival the highest tort awards paid, have advantages for many accident victims. They are payable immediately after the accident as a matter of entitlement rather than of dispute. They are paid in a regular, inflation linked form. They may be supplemented by sick pay and are not always fully deducted from any award of tort damages ultimately made. It has been argued that the low wage earner is adequately protected by social security benefits and has little incentive to sue in tort.

Protecting the accident victim is only a small part of the task of the social security system. The Pearson Commission reporting in 1978 estimated that £468 million out of the £11,885 million then expended in total on social security supported accident victims. Areas of benefit such as unemployment and retirement benefits, which play a limited role in relation to accident victims, will not be discussed here. Concentration will be placed on sickness and death benefits, industrial disablement benefit and income support.

Two kinds of benefit are paid to those who are unable to work because they are ill. A short term benefit (Statutory Sick Pay or SSP) is paid for the first 28 weeks of illness suffered in any tax year. This benefit is administered and paid by employers who are in turn, recompensed by the Benefits Agency which is the body responsible for administering the social security system for the state. The 1995 rate for SSP was £52.50 per week. No additional payments are made on account of dependants and the benefits are subject to income tax and National Insurance contributions. A claimant who exhausts his entitlement to SSP is likely to be transferred to incapacity benefit, known as ICB. This is a long term benefit which, if the claimant remains unable to work through sickness, is payable until retirement age. It is different in character to SSP. It is administered by the Benefits Agency and is only payable to a claimant who has made a minimum number of National Insurance contributions. The basic rate of benefit is supplemented if the claimant has dependants and by an allowance which varies according to the claimant's age when the incapacity first occurred. The 1995 weekly rates for long term ICB payments were £58.85 for the disabled person plus £35.25 for an adult dependant such as a spouse and £11.05 for each child dependant. This would make a total of £116.20 per week for the stereo-typical two child family.

In addition to these basic income support benefits a number of additional benefits exist designed to cover particular needs. The Disability Living Allowance helps to meet the increased expenditure which disablement may require. It has two components which cover the cost of regular nursing (1995 weekly rate of £46.70 for the most serious disabilities) and of special transport needs (1995 weekly rate of £32.65 for the most serious disabilities). Two other benefits provide income support. Severe disablement allowance is available to those who are unable to work, but who do not satisfy the contribution conditions needed for incapacity benefit. Invalid care allowance (1995 maximum weekly rate of £32.25) is payable to those who lose earnings in caring for a relative who is in receipt of the disability living allowance.

For many years the industrial injuries scheme was separate from the main social security scheme and offered significantly higher levels of benefit paid in the form of a lump sum for minor injuries and a pension for more serious disabling injuries. Nowadays it is but a shadow of its former self and is limited to providing special pensions for those disabled as a result of an industrial accident or disease. An industrial accident is one which arises 'out of or in the course of ... employment'. The industrial disease category recognises that health may be damaged by long exposure to a process. It operates on the basis that certain diseases are prescribed risks of particular employments and anyone who develops that disease while working in such a job is presumed to have contracted it from the employment. The disablement may be permanent or temporary but must last for more than 15 weeks and be caused by the industrial accident or disease. Provided the disablement remains, the pension is payable even though the claimant continues working or returns to work. The level of benefit is assessed according to a tariff. All injuries are allocated a percentage on the tariff and the claimant is awarded the corresponding level of benefit. For example, for 100% disablement the 1995 weekly rate was £95.30 whilst for 20% disablement, it was £19.06. Persons in receipt of a disablement pension may also be entitled to additional benefits, a constant attendance allowance and exceptionally severe disablement allowance may be available to those assessed as 100% disabled.

The basic social security benefit paid on death is a lump sum of £1,000 payable to a widow. Additional long term pensions are payable to widows who have children to maintain when their husband dies or who are widowed, or cease to maintain children, when they are over the age of 45.

Underpinning these benefits are the means tested ones which are designed to ensure that everyone has a minimum level of income. In the case of those who are unable to work Income Support payments will be made to bring income up to the stipulated level. Family Credit payments have the same objective for those who are working but at low pay levels. The level of benefit varies according to whether the claimant has dependants, is disabled or is a pensioner. Housing Benefit may assist both the unemployed and employed. Finally, a claimant can seek additional support from the Social Fund. This Fund has a discretion to make loans to claimants, repayable from future benefit, to meet particular items of expenditure.

Only around 6% of the total social security budget goes to accident victims but it is the major source of compensation meeting the needs of over 1.5 million accident victims per year and paying out more than double the amount that the tort system pays each year to the 200,000 who are able to bring a claim. The social security system is highly complex and most accident victims will need expert advice, often from the Citizens' Advice Bureau rather than a solicitor, as to the payments to which they might be entitled. But one strength of this complex system is that once the details of the victims personal circumstances have been ascertained, the rules will fix the amount of benefit to be paid. There is no question of estimating future losses or the extent of pain and suffering. Everything is settled by the rules. The result is that the system is efficient with over 90% of the social security budget being paid to claimants with the remainder spent on administration. In contrast, research has shown that only 55% of the money paid into the tort system as insurance premiums was ultimately paid to accident victims as damages. The remaining 45% went on administration and much of that on lawyer's fees. The comparative inefficiency of the tort system is not the only criticism levied against it. The problems of litigating personal injury claims were discussed in Chapter 3. The overall result is reflected in the findings of a 1994 Law Commission report: fewer than 12% of accident victims recover compensation; of those that do, a substantial number have to wait more than four years for a payment, four years of financial hardship and psychological pressure; when the payment is received it is often inadequate partly because claimants tend to under-estimate the long-term impact of injuries on their health and capacity for work, and partly because claims get squeezed by the settlement process. These problems have led critics to call for the replacement of the tort system with a so-called 'no-fault' system of enhanced state compensation for accident victims.

No-fault compensation

New Zealand provides the model for a no-fault compensation scheme. In 1972 it abolished the right to sue in tort for personal injuries and substituted a compensation scheme financed from general taxation and from levies on car owners, health care professionals and employers on the ground that their activities were a major cause of accidents. The scheme compensates all those who suffer a 'personal injury by accident' irrespective of how the accident occurred, where it occurred and who caused it. Under the scheme, victims are entitled to 80% of their loss of earnings and a scaled allowance for those with a permanent disability of 10% or more. The resulting levels of compensation are more generous than those provided for under the UK's social security system. This level of compensation has been achieved by adding to state funding, the 'levied' money which under the tort system would have been paid in liability insurance premiums and then distributed to relatively few victims. The majority of 'no-fault' accident victims have gained at the expense of the minority whose accident was caused by fault.

The original New Zealand scheme was even more generous, providing for substantial payments for pain and suffering. But this level of compensation proved to be too much for the economy to support and was abolished in 1992. The cost of the scheme has not been the only problem. There has been considerable difficulty in defining what is meant by 'a personal injury by accident'. For example, a heart attack sustained whilst walking is regarded as an illness and is not covered by the scheme but an attack sustained by a teacher whilst playing in a school game has been regarded as an injury by accident because it resulted from unusual stresses. The injury/illness line is fraught with difficulty. Finally, there has been some concern that the apparent increase in accident rates in New Zealand might be related in some way to the abolition of liability in tort and, at a broader level, that the notion of individual responsibility has been weakened.

This last issue was a major concern for our own Royal Commission on Civil Liability and Compensation chaired by Lord Pearson which reported in 1978. The Commission rejected the proposal to abolish tort liability and adopt a no-fault scheme on the New Zealand model. One reason was the belief that individual's responsibility for the consequences of fault was an important moral principle. A second reason was the view that the existing state compensation system provided a basic level of compensation and that the focus should be on upgrading that system rather than introducing a totally new no-fault system. The Commission had one specific upgrading proposal and that was to extend the scheme of higher social security payments for industrial injuries to cover road accident injuries. This proposal along with others for minor improvements to the social security system, has not been adopted. Instead, the conservative government which took office in 1979 shortly after the Pearson report, has concentrated on controlling rather than expanding social security benefits. Both lump sum benefits for short-term disablement and the earnings-related element of long term disablement benefit have been abolished. Instead of focusing on improving the social security system, the government has looked to private insurance as a way forward. In 1991 it put forward a proposal for a compulsory personal injury insurance for motorists. Under this proposal a motorist would be covered by his own insurance policy (this is known as first party insurance) for the first £2,500 worth of his injuries. He would only be able to recover losses above £2,500 if he had a claim in tort against a third party whose liability insurance (known as third party insurance) would meet the claim. A number of American states and Canadian provinces do operate somewhat similar road accident schemes through private insurance companies or public insurance agencies. Such schemes entail motorists paying higher premiums. The political pressure required to persuade motorists of the wisdom of this is lacking in the United Kingdom and hence, nothing has come of the proposal.

Postscript: the medical malpractice problem

The themes of this chapter are well illustrated by the problem of how to deal with medical accidents. Claims for negligence against hospitals more than doubled over a five year period from 1983 to 1987. In 1990 the NHS spent £45 million on meeting negligence claims against hospitals and in 35 cases that year, the damages were in excess of £300,000. With the advent of structured settlements, the level of awards have risen still further. It was originally intended that the Trust Hospitals established by the NHS reforms would meet liability claims out of their own budgets but this proved so damaging to their finances that a central fund has been established to meet claims. The level of claims not only affects hospital finances but also attitudes. It is said that it has led to 'defensive medicine'. An often cited example is the preference for a caesarian rather than a forceps delivery of a baby based on the view that, although a caesarian may carry a higher inherent risk of damage to mother and baby because of the anaesthesia, the forceps delivery carries the higher risk of litigation because the mother will assume that any brain damage to the child must be due to a negligent use of the forceps. Whether there is any real evidence of defensive medicine of this kind is doubtful, but undoubtedly fear of litigation is one of the reasons for the lack of trust between doctors and patients and the reluctance to fully inform patients.

All this has led the doctors' professional body, the BMA, to suggest the introduction of a no-fault compensation scheme for accidental medical injuries. However, the proposed scheme excludes compensation for diagnostic error which could only have been avoided by hindsight and unavoidable complications arising however carefully the procedure was carried out. Exclusions such as these mean that far from covering all accidents, the scheme would cover little more than those accidents which can already give rise to a negligence claim. Sweden operates a much wider Patient Insurance Scheme which is funded by public authorities providing health care and private sector clinics and doctors. As a percentage of population, the Swedish scheme compensates ten times as many patients as the tort system, paying them about a fifth the amount of the tort system but at a much lower overall cost. The scheme is attractive but not to the government which has continued to support the tort system although it did propose in 1991 that the operation of that system could be improved by the use of a cheap, voluntary arbitration system for settling claims. As the main objective of such a scheme would be to avoid legal expense, it is not surprising that lawyers have been unenthusiastic and the proposal seems to have died a death.

A final proposal is that of Professor Atiyah who is perhaps the UK's leading academic expert on personal injury compensation. After years of advocating first a New Zealand no fault system and failing that, strict liability systems, in 1996 he came out in favour of abolishing tort liability for personal injuries and leaving it to individuals to provide themselves with protection by taking out first party insurance against injury. Most of us take out such insurance when we travel abroad, so why not take it to cover against injuries at home where accidents are just as likely to occur? Again, pregnant women may insure against the possibility of having twins. So why not take out insurance against the other accidents of childbirth? Why not go further and have a system under which hospitals asked patents to complete an insurance form prior to admission or patient's associations negotiated block policies with insurers on behalf of their members. To the critics who say this is right-wing, Thatcherite ideology, Atiyah responds by pointing out that the present tort system in effect redistributes money from the lower paid to the higher paid. How so? All motorists pay insurance premiums based on related claims experience but not to income. The lower income groups pay as much the higher income groups (save for the fact that the more expensive cars of the higher paid may result in a higher premium). But the higher income groups benefit far more than the lower income groups. Why? Because much of the money paid out by insurance policies goes to compensate victims for loss of earnings. The more the victim earned, the more he will receive as compensation from the negligent driver's insurance company. It is in this sense that the present system redistributes from the poor to the rich. Atiyah argues that from the point of view of distributive justice, the whole system is grossly unfair.

Chapter 17
Interference with the use of land

'A man's house is his castle'. So wrote the great Jacobean judge and father of the common law, Sir Edward Coke. Indeed, for much of its history the common law was more concerned with protecting a person's right to use his land than with his right to physical security. Such protection kept at bay both the power of the state and the social and economic demands of individuals. It preserved the status and freedom of the landed. The central problem today is that of adapting the law to meet new social and economic problems, whether they be the need for planned economic development of land, the need to preserve the environment, or the more mundane interest of the householder and his/her family in clear TV reception uninterrupted by high rise developments. The framework of protection is based around the old tort actions of trespass and nuisance, supplemented by the more recent development of negligence and the action known as *Rylands v Fletcher*, named after the nineteenth century case from which it originated. The availability of an injunction to prevent interference in addition to the normal remedy of damages, further complicates the picture.

The framework of protection

Trespass

The tort of trespass to land provides a remedy against those deliberately invading another's land. Squatters in empty local authority housing commit a trespass to land and may be both liable for damages and subject to an injunction prohibiting the occupation. Neither remedy is likely to be of much use against the penniless and homeless, and tougher criminal law provisions have been introduced to deal with the problem. But in other situations, the tort may provide an effective remedy. Consider the use of tower cranes on building sites. Such cranes frequently overhang neighbouring sites. Technically, that amounts to a trespass because the crane has invaded the usable airspace of the neighbouring site. It might prevent the neighbour from using a crane himself. But even if it causes no such interference, it still gives rise to liability because trespass is actionable *per se* ie without any need to show damage. In the leading case, *Anchor*

Brewhouse v Berkley House (1987), the defendant's crane overhung the plaintiff's neighbouring site but did not cause any interference. The plaintiff sought an injunction ordering the defendant to stop the trespass. The defendant argued that as the trespass caused no interference and was essential for its building operation, the only remedy for the trespass should be damages. If this argument had been successful, the plaintiff would have probably recovered nothing as the trespass had caused it no loss. But Scott J rejected the argument and held that the plaintiff was entitled to the injunction. Of course, the plaintiff did not want to stop the defendant's work. It simply wanted the defendant to make a payment in return for permission to continue trespassing.

Nuisance

Trespass liability is based on *direct* invasion of the plaintiff's land and does not depend upon whether the invasion is *unreasonable* in any way. The invasion itself is the wrong. The second protective tort, nuisance, differs from trespass in both respects: nuisance is committed where there is an indirect interference with the plaintiff's land and that interference has been unreasonable. Take the example of a building site. The work on that site may indirectly interfere with the ability of a nearby owner to enjoy the full use of his land. The wind may blow dust from the building site onto the nearby owner's land and damage, say, washing drying on a line. Or noise coming from the building site might keep the nearby owner awake at night. These are instances of indirect interference rather than direct invasion and hence, the possible liability will be in nuisance rather than trespass. Whether such interference amounts to a nuisance will depend upon whether it was unreasonable. If the interference causes physical damage eg to the washing, it is normally regarded as unreasonable. However, if it simply affects the enjoyment of the land without causing tangible damage, for example by creating noise or smells, then the question is more difficult and the court must balance the interests of defendant and plaintiff to determine whether the interference is unreasonable. Thus, the operator of a building site in a development area may not be liable for interference to nearby landowners caused by the noise of pile-driving during day-time hours. The nearby landowners have to accept this interference as the price of owning property in a developing, urban area. But if the pile-driving were to be conducted at night, it might be thought that this was unreasonable and constituted a nuisance. Again, in a quiet rural area it might be thought that pile-driving all day long was also unreasonable. Those living in noisy manufacturing areas are expected to put it with more than those living in leafy residential areas. As one Victorian judge put it: 'What would be a nuisance in Belgrave Square would not necessarily be so in Bermondsey'. In a modern context, it has been held that whilst the sleazy atmosphere and clientele created by a sex shop might be acceptable in the environs of Victoria Station, it could amount to a nuisance when placed in the nearby residential area of Pimlico.

Apart from the location in which the interference occurred and its duration, other factors may be relevant in determining whether the interference was unreasonable. In one case, a vicar claimed that the noise of the defendant's power station interfered with the peace of mind he needed to write his sermons. The court took the view that it was his sensitivity which was the problem. The level of noise would have been acceptable to the normal person and could not be regarded as an unreasonable interference simply because of his special need. Along with any special sensitivity of the plaintiff, the motive of the defendant may be relevant. For example, if the defendant made the noise with the intention of disturbing the vicar, then the interference which might otherwise have been regarded as acceptable, might now be regarded as unreasonable. Conversely, if the motive of the defendant's activity is to benefit the general public, this may support the view that any resulting interference is reasonable. But there are limits. In *Miller v Jackson* (1977) the defendant was responsible for a village cricket club which for many years had been the heart of the community. The plaintiff purchased a house on the edge of the small ground. Her garden was only 30 yards from the centre of the pitch and despite the protection of a 14 foot fence, half a dozen balls landed in her garden each season. She claimed that the playing of cricket amounted to a nuisance as it unreasonably interfered with her enjoyment of the garden. Lord Denning rejected her claim on the ground that the public interest in playing cricket outweighed the private interest of the houseowner in the privacy of her garden. He also considered that the plaintiff should be disbarred from claiming as she 'came into the nuisance' ie she bought her house knowing of the risk of being bombarded by cricket balls. However, the majority of the Court of Appeal held there to be a nuisance. In their view, the real danger of the plaintiff or her house being hit outweighed the benefit of playing cricket. They also considered that nineteenth century precedent prevented them from taking into account the fact that the plaintiff had come into the nuisance. They awarded the plaintiff £400 compensation for any past and future damage caused by the cricket. But whilst one of the majority judges was prepared to grant an injunction stopping the playing of cricket, the other was not, arguing that the villagers should 'not be deprived of their facilities for an innocent recreation'. As Lord Denning had held there was no nuisance anyway, this gave a majority against granting an injunction. So the result of the case was that the club could continue playing in return for paying £400 to the plaintiff. *Miller* is an interesting case and can be argued either way. Indeed, subsequent cases have suggested that the an injunction ought to be granted in such circumstances. Thus in *Tetley v Chitty* (1986) the plaintiff was granted an injunction to stop the constant high level of noise created by the activity of a nearby go-kart club. What these cases illustrates above all, is that liability for nuisance involves striking a fair balance between the interests of the plaintiff and defendant.

Negligence

In *Miller*, the club was also held liable for negligence on the ground that the risk of injury was so great that any failure to prevent incidents happening would be inexcusable and hence, 'on each occasion when a ball came over the fence and causes damage to the plaintiffs, the defendants are guilty of negligence.' The decision illustrates that the tort of negligence may also contribute to the framework of protection for the landowner. But it also illustrates three important differences between negligence and nuisance liability. First, negligence liability rests on the fact that the defendant's *act or omission* was careless. The negligent conduct in *Miller* was each failure to prevent a ball coming over the fence. Each failure would be due to careless conduct because we would expect a reasonable man to prevent each incident by some means. Nuisance liability rests on the fact that the defendant's *activity* interfered unreasonably with the plaintiff. The playing of cricket was an unreasonable interference because the interests of the plaintiff outweighed those of the defendant. Although both forms of liability rest on a reasonableness criterion, in negligence that criterion refers to a standard of care whilst in nuisance it refers to a balancing exercise. The second difference is that negligence liability can only arise if the careless conduct has caused an item of damage eg a ball had broken a window in Mrs Miller's house. But nuisance liability arises from the interference with the plaintiff's enjoyment of her land. The fact that Mrs Miller was too scared to sit in her back garden during the cricket season was sufficient to constitute the interference. The third difference follows from the others. Because nuisance results from an activity the plaintiff may obtain the remedy of an injunction which orders the defendant to cease the activity which has caused the interference. But an injunction is not relevant to negligence liability which is based on the careless conduct causing damage. The plaintiff is entitled to compensation for the damage done but cannot obtain an injunction to prevent future negligence. Hence, although in many nuisance cases the defendant may also be liable for negligence, the plaintiff will prefer to claim in nuisance to obtain the more powerful remedy of the injunction. Once the injunction has been obtained, the plaintiff could always agree not to enforce it in return for a substantial payment from the defendant. In *Miller*, for example, if the court had granted an injunction, Mrs Miller might have been prepared to waive her right to stop the cricket in return for a payment from the club. But she might have expected a lot more than £400. An injunction is a more powerful remedy than mere damages. It enables the plaintiff to negotiate her own level of compensation.

Rylands v Fletcher

In the nineteenth century a fourth form of tortious liability developed to protect landowners. It became known as *Rylands v Fletcher* liability after the name of the 1868 case from which the principle stems. We discussed the decision in some detail in Chapter 6 (p 146). Briefly, the *Rylands* case concerned a landowner who employed a contractor to construct a reservoir on his land. Unfortunately water from the reservoir escaped into old mineworkings and spread to the plaintiff's land causing considerable damage. The defendant was held liable on these facts. As we noted earlier, the judgment of Lord Cranworth suggested that the basis of liability might be the principle that one who carries on an inherently dangerous activity such as maintaining a reservoir (several collapsed in the nineteenth century), should be strictly liable for any damage resulting from that activity. But it was the narrower principle proposed by Blackburn J and Lord Cairns which prevailed in later caselaw. This was that liability was limited to situations where there had been an escape of something 'likely to do mischief' from the defendant's land and the defendant had been making a 'non-natural use' of his land. Building a reservoir was a non-natural use and water was likely to do mischief if it escaped. Hence, there was liability in *Rylands*. However, the courts soon began to interpret 'non-natural user' in a narrower way as meaning, in the words of Lord Moulton in a 1913 decision, 'some special use bringing with it increased danger to others and not merely the ordinary use of the land or such a use as is proper for the general benefit of the community.' This trend reached its highpoint in *Read v Lyons* (1946) where it was suggested that the manufacture of explosives might not amount to a 'non-natural user' and hence an escape of material following an explosion at the plant would not give rise to liability under the *Rylands* principle. For many years after this decision it was thought that the principle was of little significance, a historical oddity. But new life has been breathed into it by the recent decision of the House of Lords in *Cambridge Water v Eastern Counties Leather* (1994).

In *Cambridge Water* the defendant was a leather manufacturer which used a chemical solvent in its tanning process. During this process small amounts of the solvent inevitably spilt onto the concrete floor of the tannery. Over the years the solvent seeped through the floor and down through the soil and bedrock until it reached an aquifer ie an underground water flow. The aquifer carried the solvent into neighbouring land where the plaintiff water company extracted 1.5 million gallons a day from a borehole. Soon this water was polluted by the solvent and the plaintiff could no longer use it for domestic supplies. It had to spend a million pounds developing a new borehole site and it claimed this sum as damages from the defendant under the *Rylands* principle. At trial it was held that the tannery was a natural use of the land because the employment created by the tannery was for the 'general benefit of the community'. Hence, there could be no *Rylands* liability. But the House of Lords reversed this finding. Lord Goff considered that Lord Moulton's criterion of the 'general benefit of the community' was far too wide, that the employment benefits of an activity should be ignored, and that the storage of chemicals was a 'classic case' of non-natural use. Following this approach, most industry is likely to be regarded as a non-natural use and potentially liable under *Rylands* for damage caused by an escape. However, whilst reviving *Rylands* liability with one hand, Lord Goff restricted it with the other. He held that for there to be liability under *Rylands*, the kind of damage caused must have been reasonably foreseeable. The defendant escaped liability in *Cambridge* because it could not possibly have foreseen the pollution to the plaintiff's water supply.

The requirement that the kind of damage be foreseeable is known as the 'remoteness' test and, as we have seen, it applies to negligence claims. But negligence claims are based on the defendant's fault and it makes sense to say that the defendant is only to blame for the kind of damage he could foresee. Where, as under *Rylands*, the defendant is liable even if he exercised all possible care ie he is strictly liable, it is not obvious why his liability should be limited to just the foreseeable kind of damage. Lord Goff justified his decision in two ways. First, he referred to the original judgment of Blackburn J in which he said there was liability for 'anything *likely* to do mischief if it escapes'. He argued that the use of the word 'likely' indicated that the kind of damage had to be foreseeable for there to be liability. Second, he argued that *Rylands* liability should be seen as an extension of nuisance liability to situations where the interference had been caused by a one-off escape. Then he argued that nuisance liability had always been limited to situations where the interference was reasonably foreseeable. From there it was a simple step to argue that the same principle of foreseeability should apply to *Rylands* liability. If this were not so, there might be cases where the defendant was not liable in nuisance because the interference was caused by some unforeseeable form of pollution spreading from the defendant's land, but liable under *Rylands* because the pollution was caused by a non-natural user resulting in an escape. The coherence of the common law required the same remoteness limit to apply to both nuisance and *Rylands* liability.

The reasoning seems logical. But Lord Goff did have a choice. He could have argued that *Rylands* liability should not be treated as an extension of nuisance but as a separate principle of strict liability rather along the lines suggested by Lord Cranworth. Indeed, some courts in the United States have taken this approach and allowed the tort a greater role in the control of dangerous and polluting activities. Lord Goff recognised the importance of protecting the environment and the introduction of legislation to make the polluter pay, but concluded that:

> 'It does not follow from such developments that a common law principle, such as the rule in *Rylands*, should be developed or rendered more strict to provide for liability in respect of pollution. On the contrary, given that so much well-informed opinion and carefully structured legislation is now being put in place for this purpose, there is less need for the courts to develop a common law principle to achieve the same end, and indeed it may well be undesirable that they should do so.'

He has a point. But much of the legislation is concerned with regulating pollution in the public interest and imposing fines on those breaking the regulations. The common law is concerned with protecting the private interest of land owners by awarding compensation. Perhaps there is room for both approaches.

Postscript: Eastenders

This chapter has sketched the role of the four torts which protect the use of land. The most important of these are nuisance and negligence. We end the chapter by examining one recent case which both illustrates the significance of this protection and explores some new issues. The case is *Hunter v Canary Wharf Ltd* (1996). At the time of writing it had just been decided by the Court of Appeal but there is to be a further appeal to the House of Lords and readers should watch for the outcome.

The plaintiff and several hundred co-plaintiffs lived in the East End of London. They claimed that negligent construction of a new road by the defendant had led to excessive dust in the area and that the construction of the 700 foot Canary Wharf Tower constituted a nuisance because it interfered with their TV reception. In relation to the dust, the defendant argued that no damage had been caused and hence, no action in negligence was possible. The Court of Appeal rejected this argument on the ground that the excessive dust could have led to fabrics having to be cleaned more often, electrical apparatus failing more often etc. To the extent that such articles were rendered less useful or valuable, they had been damaged and there could be negligence liability. Of course, there could have been nuisance liability as well based on the dust interfering with the plaintiffs' enjoyment of their property but this was not an issue in the litigation.

Three more difficult issues arose in relation to the interference with TV reception. The first was that many of the plaintiffs did not own the property in which they lived. Indeed, many such as wives and children were not even the tenants of the property. They were simply family members. Historically nuisance has only protected the interests of land-owners or tenants. Citing the rights to residence given to both spouses and children by recent legislation, the court held that occupancy now provided a sufficient link with the property to enable a person to sue for nuisance. Nuisance now protects occupants as well as owners. The second problem was that the defendant had planning permission to build the tower. It argued that this permission conferred an immunity from nuisance liability upon the tower; that, in effect, it 'licensed' the nuisance. It is the case that if a construction has been authorised by legislation (and many major projects such as oil refineries are authorised in this way), then that statutory authority does confer an immunity from nuisance liability. But the building of the tower was not authorised by legislation and the court refused to extend the immunity to planning permission which is granted by local administrators rather than the legislature. The final question was whether interference with TV reception could ever constitute a nuisance and on this, somewhat surprisingly, the plaintiffs lost. The court accepted the importance of television in the lives of many people. But it equated viewing television with viewing one's surroundings. It has long been accepted that you cannot sue for nuisance if your view of the countryside is blocked by a building such as the Canary Wharf Tower. The court reasoned that if 'loss of view' was not actionable in nuisance, neither was loss of TV reception. Loss of both may be the price to be paid for modern developments. Is the analogy between loss of view and loss of TV reception a good one? Having extended nuisance protection from the land owner to the ordinary family member, it may seem odd not to recognise the basis of family entertainment as worthy of protection.

The plaintiffs did have one final legal shot to fire. They claimed in public nuisance. The tort of nuisance we have considered so far is known as private nuisance. A public nuisance is a crime. It is committed by conduct which annoys or inconveniences a large number of people. Conduct as varied as swimming in the nude and obstructing the River Thames have been held to constitute the crime. Where the conduct causes an individual 'special damage', that is, something over and above the inconvenience suffered by the rest of society, then the specially affected individuals can bring a civil action in tort. In the *Canary Wharf*, the plaintiffs argued that although 100,000 people suffered some annoyance due to TV interference, only a small minority including plaintiffs suffered the special damage of being totally unable to receive a coherent TV picture. The argument raised the interesting question of what constitutes a special group: if all 30,000 whose TV picture fell below acceptable standards had sued, would the damage have been too widespread to be special? In the event the court ducked the question by holding that interference with TV reception did not constitute damage for the purpose of public nuisance liability. The reason was simply: it had held that such interference did not constitute a private nuisance and therefore it could not constitute a public nuisance.

Chapter 18

Infringement of personality

Men used to duel not about physical injuries, nor about interference with their land, but about insults to their honour or occasionally that of a woman. An honourable reputation was the essence of being. Not surprising then that the law of tort has afforded that reputation the most strict protection under the tort of defamation. Other torts also protect reputation. In some ways negligence can give more protection than defamation. False imprisonment provides a remedy for both an insult to reputation and an affront to liberty. But personality interests are broader than mere reputation. Arguably, the privacy of persons should be protected by the law of tort. In the medical sphere, the autonomy of individuals, that is their right to choose for themselves, may also merit protection.

Defamation and the protection of reputation

A person commits the tort of defamation if he publishes an untrue statement about the plaintiff which will tend to lower the reputation of the plaintiff in the estimation of right-thinking members of society. Stating that a businessman cheated or a surgeon was careless or even, that a politician lied, may amount to defamation. What about a statement that a person is homosexual? A case in the 1970s suggested that such a statement would almost certainly be defamatory. But times have changed and in the Jason Donovan case in 1992 the judge considered that it was debatable whether such a statement was defamatory. Donovan, the ex-*Neighbours* actor, won his case as he had previously denied being homosexual and hence the magazine article labelling him as gay was, in effect, accusing him of hypocrisy and lying and that is defamatory. As that example shows, it is sometimes what is implied in rather than expressly stated by a statement that is defamatory. Indeed, a statement may be defamatory even if only a few people with special knowledge would draw the implication. For example, in *Cassidy v Daily Mirror* (1929) Mrs Cassidy recovered damages against the paper which had published a picture of her husband with another woman with an announcement of their engagement. To millions of readers that publication was not defamatory of anyone. But the few who knew Mrs Cassidy might have inferred from the publication that she had been lying and had never actually been married to her husband. A statement which is defamatory only on the basis of such special knowledge is known as an innuendo.

Whether the statement is said to be defamatory in express terms, by common implication or by innuendo, the test remains that of the reasonable reader. Neighbours stars once again provide a good illustration of the point. In *Charleston v News Group Newspapers* (1995) the News of the World had run a banner headline 'Strewth! What's Harold up to with our Madge?' and below was a second line, 'Porn Shocker for *Neighbours* Stars'. Between the two lines were photographs of the apparently naked stars having sex. The article below the headlines quickly made it clear that the photos were taken from a pornographic computer game and that without their consent, the stars faces had been superimposed on to the photos of naked models. The stars sued the paper for defamation on the ground that some readers would read only the headline and form their view of the stars reputation on that basis. However, Lord Bridge held that 'the ordinary, reasonable, fair-minded reader' would read on, realise that the stars were, in the words of the article, the victims, and think nonetheless of their reputations. Hence the action failed. What would have been the outcome had most of the article continued with a hyped description of the game and only ended with the real explanation? Lord Bridge indicated that such an article might have been defamatory as the reasonable reader might not have read the full piece. The decision whether or not such an article was defamatory would have been taken by a jury. Defamation is one of the few civil actions that is tried by a jury. But a judge may only allow the issue to be determined by the jury if the statement was capable of being defamatory. In *Charleston* Lord Bridge held that it could not be defamatory because the reasonable reader would go beyond the headlines. If the article could be regarded as defamatory, as in the example of an article leaving the real explanation to the end, then a jury will decide the issue.

Liability for defamation is strict. The publisher of the statement in *Cassidy* was liable although it did not know of the facts which made the statement defamatory. A publisher may be liable although he does not know that the statement will be taken to refer to the plaintiff. Thus in *Hulton v Jones* (1910) a newspaper publishing a fictional account of the antics of one 'Artemus Jones' was held liable to a barrister of the same name although it seemed not to have know of the existence of the barrister. Unfortunately, the paper had not stated that its report was fictional and the barrister was able to show that some colleagues thought the account referred to him. The Defamation Act 1952 now provides some protection in both *Cassidy* and *Jones* situations by providing that in innuendo cases (*Cassidy*) and unintentional cases (*Hulton*) the publisher will not be liable provided it acted with reasonable care and offered sufficient apology. In other situations liability remains strict. If the publisher proves that the statement about the plaintiff was true, that establishes the defence of justification and there will be no liability. But it is no defence to show that the publisher had investigated with care and relied on believable but mistaken witnesses. Thus, in *John v Mirror Group* (1996) the newspaper was held liable for publishing a 'world exclusive' stating that Elton John was hooked on a bizarre diet involving spitting out food and had been observed doing this at a Hollywood party. The paper had relied on the story of two eyewitnesses at the party but they must have been mistaken as Elton John had not been at the party. The fact that the paper had relied on two witnesses rather than just gossip, had published the article in good faith and had offered to apologise was of no avail. It was liable for defamation and the jury awarded £350,000 damages.

Huge damage awards such as that in the *John* case have caused concern because they far exceed the level of awards made in personal injury cases. More than that, whilst in a personal injury much of the compensation will be for actual losses, for example earnings and medical expenses, in a defamation case a plaintiff does not normally have to show any damage. The only exception is where the defamation has resulted from an oral statement (known as a slander) rather than a written statement (known as a libel). In the case of slanders, the defendant must prove damage. But in the case of libels, the fact that the statement would have the affect of lowering a person's reputation is enough. The reason for the high awards in such cases is simple: the awards are made by the jury rather than by the judge. Juries are not in the position to make comparisons with personal injury awards. Furthermore, in defamation cases juries may award damages not simply to compensate the plaintiff for loss of reputation but also to punish the defendant for acting badly. In the *John* case, £75,000 was awarded as compensation and £275,000 to punish the paper for deliberately promoting the article in order to increase sales. Concern about the high level of awards led Parliament to include a right of appeal to the defendant in the Courts and Legal Services Act 1990. It was hoped that the lower levels of damages set by the Court of Appeal would lead to juries being less generous but the jury award in the *John* case demonstrated that this might not be so. Consequently, when that case was appealed, the Court of Appeal not only decided that the damages should be reduced from £350,000 to £75,000 (£25,000 as compensation and £50,000 as punishment) but also that judges in defamation cases should indicate to juries the appropriate level of award based on comparisons with personal injury claims where £125,000 is the maximum award for non-pecuniary loss in the most serious case of quadriplegia. As Sir Thomas Bingham, the then Master of the Rolls, said 'juries may be properly asked to consider whether an injury to reputation should fairly justify any greater compensation'.

The media's exposure to strict liability and high awards in defamation cases is balanced by two important defences: fair comment and qualified privilege. The defence of fair comment protects honest expressions of opinion on matters of public interest. Provided an assertion is a comment on facts, it can be highly damaging to reputation and yet give rise to no liability in defamation. Establishing that the assertion is one of comment rather than fact is the key to the defence and can give rise to problems. In *Telnikoff v Matusevitch* (1991) the plaintiff wrote an article in the Daily Telegraph suggesting that the BBC Russian service employed too few individuals who associated themselves 'ethnically, spiritually or religiously with the Russian people'. The defendant, a Russian Jew, read the article and then wrote a letter to the paper which it published and in which he stated that the plaintiff 'is stressing his racialist recipe by claiming that no matter how high the standards of "ethnically alien" Russian staff might be, they should be dismissed'. The plaintiff claimed for defamation on the ground that being called a 'racialist' lowered his reputation. The defendant argued that his letter should be considered alongside the original article and that when read together, it was clear that his statement was simply a comment on the content of the article. The Court of Appeal agreed but the House of Lords rejected the argument. The Lords held that as readers of the letter might not have read the article, the assertions of the article had to be considered in isolation. The jury was left to take the final decision on whether the 'racialist' assertion was comment or fact but clearly the Lord's decision made it less likely that it would be regarded as a mere comment.

The defence of qualified privilege applies where a person was under some kind of duty to provide information which contained the defamatory statement. Thus, a teacher providing a reference on a student to a potential employer can plead qualified privilege if the reference contains a defamatory statement. There are other situations in which the defence applies, for example where both the maker and the recipient of the statement have a common interest such as being members of staff discussing a pupil. But in all these situations there is an important qualification to the defence: it cannot apply where the maker of the statement was malicious. A person acts maliciously if he makes the statement knowing that it is untrue or with the motive of harming the plaintiff. The same qualification applies to the defence of fair comment so that if in *Telnikoff* it had been shown that the motive for making the 'racialist' assertion was personal spite towards the plaintiff, then the defendant would not have been able to plead fair comment as a defence. In the United States a broader form of qualified defence is available. A defamatory statement about a public figure will not give rise to liability unless the maker of the statement knows it is false or is reckless as to its falsity. This defence gives the media much greater freedom to criticise politicians but at a cost; the dignity and reputation of individuals who enter the public arena.

Perhaps the real problem with the tort of defamation is that it protects defamation with an award of damages. Because so much money is at stake with the high damage awards, defamation litigation is very expensive. Only the rich can afford to protect their reputations. But it costs the media too. The legal cost to the Daily Mirror of unsuccessfully defending the Elton John case may well have come to more than the £350,000 initially awarded as damages. These costs have led the media to press for wider defences to balance the strict liability. But these defences prevail at the expense of individual reputations. The 1996 Defamation Bill seeks to switch the emphasis from damages to apology. It provides that where the defendant concedes that he has published a defamatory statement, he will be able to offer an apology. A judge will determine the terms of the apology and also assess what monetary compensation, if any, should be awarded. The court will also have powers for summary disposal of cases with relief for the plaintiff in the form of an apology and damages of up to £10,000. If enacted, the result might be cheaper and a more effective protection for remedies. There would then be less need for the present wide defences to liability.

Negligence and the protection of reputation

With strict liability for injury to reputation under the tort of defamation, it might be thought that there is no role for negligence to play in relation to reputation but the case of *Spring v Guardian Assurance* (1994) proves otherwise. Guardian had provided a reference on Spring, an ex-employee, to another insurance firm. The reference stated that Spring had acted dishonestly. Spring did not get the job but learnt of the reference and sued Guardian for loss of the chance of employment. At trial it was found that Spring had merely been incompetent and that Guardian had acted negligently in stating that he was dishonest. As Guardian had not acted maliciously in providing the reference, it was protected from liability in defamation by the defence of qualified privilege. Hence, Spring based his claim in negligence. The Court of Appeal held that no duty of care was owed by Guardian to Spring on the policy ground that any liability in negligence would undermine the defence to defamation provided by qualified privilege. The House of Lords reversed that decision arguing that liability in negligence was quite different from that in defamation as it required the proof of careless conduct and some damage such as loss of a job. The restricted scope of negligence liability meant that it could not be said to undermine the principles of defamation which balanced strict liability with defences such as qualified privilege.

False imprisonment and reputation

Being detained for committing a criminal offence will inevitably have a most damaging effect on a person's reputation. If that detention is wrongful, there is a special tort which provides a remedy, the tort of false imprisonment. An example of the kind of situation which can lead to liability is provided by *Davidson v Chief Constable of North Wales* (1994). A store detective thought that the plaintiff had stolen a cassette from the store. He called the police and they arrested the plaintiff and detained her at the police station until the store telephoned to say that a mistake had been made and the cassette had not been stolen. The police were not liable for false imprisonment because they are entitled to arrest and detain an individual where there were reasonable grounds to suspect that a crime had been committed. Neither was the detective liable as he had not personally detained the plaintiff. But if he had detained the plaintiff prior to the police arriving, he would have been liable because ordinary citizens, such as store detectives, can only arrest where a crime has actually taken place (p 84). In fact, the majority of false imprisonment claims are brought against the police on the ground that they have detained without arresting or arrested without having proper grounds. In this way the tort plays a vital role in protecting civil liberties, a role perhaps more important than that of protecting reputation.

Privacy

The European Convention on Human Rights provides that 'everyone has the right to respect for his private and family life'. As the UK has signed the Convention, one might think that this right would be protected by the law of tort but it is not. As the activities of the 'paparazzi' show, a person in public life can expect little respect for her privacy and still less protection from the law. Aside from situations where the invasion of privacy also involves a publication giving rise to defamation liability, the only real protection is provided by the tort of nuisance. The leading case is *Korasandjian v Bush* (1993). After their relationship broke up, the defendant harassed the plaintiff, an 18 year old girl, with phone calls, abuse and threats. The plaintiff was living at home with her parents. Previous authority had suggested that the tort of nuisance only protected owners of land but in this case the Court of Appeal decided that its protection should extend to occupiers of homes like Miss Khorisandijan. The court also held that the defendant's conduct did unreasonably interfere with the plaintiff's enjoyment of her home and granted an injunction restraining the defendant from pestering or communicating with the plaintiff in any way. Following this decision, it is possible that the activities of the media in laying siege to the home of a celebrity with their cameras etc, could be regarded as a nuisance and be subject to a similar injunction. But the protection would be limited to the plaintiff's enjoyment of her home. Nuisance would not protect from other invasions of privacy. It would not protect individuals from having their past affairs etc raked up in the tabloid press simply for sensationalism and profit. Every so often when this happens in a particularly gross way and especially when a politician is the victim, there are calls in Parliament for some wider protection to be afforded to privacy and each time, the press responds by suggesting that it can regulate itself. Finally, the pressure led to the Calcutt review of press self-regulation in 1993. Calcutt recommended that the law should be toughened by making it a criminal offence to enter private property to obtain personal information for publication, and to take photographs of an individual on private property with a view to publication. This proposal focuses on invasion of property rather than privacy and utilises the criminal law rather than tort. The alternative approach might be to follow US law which provides a tortious action where there has been an intentional and offensive intrusion into a person's private life. Jackie Kennedy was able to use this action to stop the paparazzi shadowing her and her children to parks, restaurants and schools. In the postscript we consider further the case for tort of infringement of privacy along these lines.

Autonomy

A different kind of personal interest is the right to self-determination or autonomy. We have considered the significance of this value in relation to the right to die which was discussed earlier in Chapter 8. In that context, the wishes of the patient was one of the factors to be considered in determining when it may be lawful to withhold treatment and allow a patient to die. But those wishes are also relevant in determining what treatment should be given to a patient. It is arguable that if the patient's views are not properly taken into account then his autonomy has been infringed and he has suffered a wrong which should be remedied by the law of tort.

The law of tort does provide a remedy if the patient is treated without consenting at all to the kind of treatment involved. The remedy is provided by the tort of battery. If a woman consents to an exploratory gynaecological operation and during the operation the surgeon decides to go further and conduct a hysterectomy, the woman will be able to sue the surgeon for battery because she did not consent to the kind of treatment involved. If she consented to the hysterectomy but had not been informed of all the risks involved and so had not given her fully informed consent, she cannot sue for battery even if one of those risks, for example a stroke provoked by the anaesthesia, eventuated. But she might be able to sue for negligence if the operation had led to damage such as a stroke. She would have to establish that in failing to inform her of all the risks the surgeon had acted negligently and that this negligence caused damage because if she had been informed she would have refused the operation and not suffered the stroke. Neither negligence nor causation are easy to establish. In *Sidaway v Bethlem Hospital* (1985) the House of Lords decided that the test for negligence was what would be expected of the reasonable doctor. If the reasonable surgeon would not have warned of the risk of a stroke then there can be no negligence in failing to warn. In contrast, both Canadian and Australian courts have adopted a reasonable patient test and held a doctor to be negligent in failing to warn of risks which a reasonable patient would have wished to consider. This reasonable patient approach gives more support to the notion of patient autonomy but does not answer the problem because the patient must still establish causation. The hysterectomy patient must still show that if warned of the risk of a stroke she would have declined the operation and avoided the damaging stroke. If there was a good reason for the hysterectomy such as the elimination of a cancer risk, then it will be very difficult for the woman to show that she would have declined the operation if warned of the lesser hazard of a stroke. As with defamation, the real problem is that the law of tort has failed to grasp the real reason for providing a remedy. In defamation the objective of the remedy should be the restoration of reputation through an apology. Here the objective should be the valuing of patient autonomy. This cannot be achieved through the tort of negligence which is tied to the notion of physical damage. Instead, it is arguable that the law should recognise that autonomy like reputation has a value but, unlike reputation, a value which cannot be adequately protected by an apology. Rather, infringement of autonomy should be marked by an award of a limited level of compensation, perhaps akin to the lowest level of award for pain and suffering.

Postscript: Gorden Kaye and the Sunday Sport

Many of the issues discussed in this chapter are brought together in the case of *Kaye v Robertson* (1991). Gorden Kaye, the star of the TV series 'Allo! Allo!', suffered head injuries after being hit by a falling tree during the great storm of 1989. Whilst in a critical state in hospital, he was visited by a journalist and photographer sent by the defendant, the editor of the lurid Sunday Sport newspaper. They entered Kaye's private room despite a notice on his door asking visitors to contact a member of the hospital staff before entering. They took a photograph of Kaye who was barely conscious and purported to conduct an interview. The paper proposed to publish both the photograph and 'interview' with a statement that Kaye had consented to both. Acting on his behalf, Kaye's agent tried to obtain an injunction to prevent publication. The problem lay in finding legal grounds for such an injunction. As Bingham LJ said in the Court of Appeal: 'If ever a person has a right to be let alone by strangers with no public

interest to pursue, it must surely be when he lies in hospital recovering
from brain surgery and in no more than partial command of his faculties.'
He continued: 'It is this invasion of privacy which underlies the plaintiff's
complaint. Yet it alone, however gross, does not entitle him to relief in
English law.' The court decided that only the legislature could provide
for the enforcement of a right to privacy. It was beyond the powers of the
common law.

The Court of Appeal also considered whether defamation might provide
a remedy. If the proposed article and photograph would certainly have been
defamatory of Kaye, the court could issue an injunction. It was arguable
that publication would have been defamatory on the basis that it would
have associated Kaye with the Sunday Sport and its sex stories, and that
would have lowered Kaye's reputation in the eyes of ordinary people. But
the court did not think it was inevitable that a jury would have found
publication to have been defamatory and hence, could not grant an
injunction on this ground. But they did grant an injunction on the ground
that the defendant would certainly be liable for the tort of malicious
falsehood if he published. This tort is committed if the defendant deliberately published false words about the plaintiff which will cause him
actual damage. The defendant knew that Kaye had not consented to the
interview and hence malice and falsity were established. The damage
would be the loss of a valuable story to Kaye. He could sell his story to
other papers for large sums but if the Sunday Sport published its story,
his own would be worth far less.

So in the end, it was Kaye's right to freely market his story rather than
his right to reputation or privacy that provided the basis of his protection.
In the United States he might well have succeeded on the basis of offensive
intrusion into his private life. If the European Convention had the force
of law in the UK, he might have been able to succeed on the ground that
the conduct of the paper infringed his right to respect for his private life.
Does Kaye's case illustrate the strength of the common law in being able
to find a remedy from the clutch of possible tort actions or its weakness in
not developing a central principle of privacy?

Chapter 19
Economic loss

Negligently injuring someone can cause economic loss, for example, loss of earnings and medical expenses. So may interfering with someone's enjoyment of land or defaming someone's reputation. But in these situations the economic loss is suffered because something else has been damaged, whether it be a person, property or a reputation. The economic loss is recoverable because that other thing has been damaged. The problem we consider in this chapter is to what extent a plaintiff can recover economic loss when nothing other than his economic interest has been damaged. A classic example would be where a surveyor negligently advised that the house the plaintiff intended to purchase needed no repairs was worth £100,000 when it needed extensive repairs and was only worth £75,000. If the plaintiff purchased the house at £100,000, he would have suffered an economic loss of £25,000. It might look as if that economic loss is due to damage to the house. But that damage was not caused by the surveyor. He simply advised the purchaser to buy a defective house and that is what has caused the economic loss. Lawyers call such loss 'pure economic loss' to distinguish it from economic loss which results from the defendant negligently damaging something. There is a limited right to recover pure economic loss in tort where the defendant's conduct has been deliberate and a still more restricted right where his conduct has been negligent. The reasons for this should become fairly obvious.

Deliberately causing pure economic loss

Part of the objective of most businesses is to cause loss to their competitors. True, businesses generally leave negative advertising to politicians but a range of devices from price cutting to hyped promotion are regarded as perfectly fair means of attracting business from rivals and causing them economic loss. A general tort action for intentionally causing economic loss would completely undermine the market economy. Instead, the law picks out particular kinds of intentional conduct as being tortious. Thus, knowingly making a false statement with the intention that the plaintiff act upon it will give rise to liability for the tort of deceit if the plaintiff does rely on it and suffers economic loss. It is often difficult to prove that a defendant has acted fraudulently in this way but sometimes deceit actions against salesmen whether of cheap cars or expensive investments do succeed. Another example is the tort of intentionally interfering with the performance of a contract. This can be of particular relevance to businesses, like football clubs, which headhunt new managers. If the business persuades a manager to break his contract with his present employer by not giving the required period of notice, then the business will be liable to the ex-employer for the tort of inducing breach of contract. Of course, if there is no evidence of contact between the business and the manager and all that can be established is that the manager left without the required notice and subsequently joined the new business, then although the manager would be liable for breach of contract the business would not be liable for the tort. There are two other torts in this group: conspiracy which applies where the defendants combine together with the motive of causing the plaintiff loss rather than furthering their own interests; and intimidation which applies where the defendant threatens to do something unlawful to a third person to persuade him to cause loss to the plaintiff. The detail of these tort actions is complex but the overall picture is not; the circumstances in which liability for deliberating causing economic loss can be established are rare.

Negligently causing economic loss

Pure economic loss is often the foreseeable result of negligent conduct. For example, a valuer valuing a house for a building society can foresee that his report may be passed to the purchaser who will then suffer economic loss if the valuation was negligently too high and the purchaser bought at the overvalued figure; an auditor who negligently fails to detect and report that a company is bankrupt can foresee that an investor will suffer economic loss through relying on the audit report and purchasing shares in the company; a negligent builder working for a developer can foresee that a subsequent purchaser of the defective building will suffer economic loss through having to meet the cost of repairs. In all these examples the victim pays for something worth less than he thought and this is the foreseeable result of the other's negligence. The relationship between the parties may also be sufficiently proximate to give rise to a duty. This would be the case if the valuer or auditor knew that its report was being passed to the particular purchaser or investor, or if the builder knew who was to purchase the building from the developer for whom the builder worked. Despite the existence of foreseeability and proximity, courts have decided in many instances that the imposition of a duty in respect of pure economic loss would not be fair and reasonable. Why? What differentiates cases of pure economic loss from those of physical damage?

Instinctively we may feel that our physical security is more important than that of our bank account. As we have seen, the importance of our physical security justifies both the wide protection of negligence liability and limited strict liability protection. But the fact that it is more important does not entirely explain why negligence protection is rarely afforded to our bank account, to our purely economic interests. Part of the explanation lies in the different way in which physical and economic damage is caused. The typical physical injury, for example the road or work accident, results from a relationship which is imposed. The plaintiff does not choose his fellow car drivers or workers. But economic loss generally does result from a relationship which was chosen. The purchaser of the overvalued house, the worthless shares or the defective building had a choice. Instead of relying on the valuer engaged by the building society or the auditor engaged by the company or the builder engaged by the developer, the victim could have protected himself by paying for his own valuer, his own accountant or, in the case of the defective building, his own surveyor to check for defects. If he had done this and the mistake had still been made, he would have been able to sue his own adviser in contract. So the question now becomes: why should the victim be able to sue a negligent valuer, accountant or builder in tort when he had not paid for the service and yet could have paid for his own adviser? In a sense, to allow him to recover in tort would be to allow him to 'free ride', that is, take advantage of a service without paying for it. It is for this reason that the law will only impose a duty of care in relation to pure economic loss where it can be said that the third party has assumed a moral responsibility to the victim.

The case in which the courts first accepted as a general principle that a duty of care could be owed in relation to pure economic loss was *Hedley Byrne v Heller* (1963). There the defendant bank had given a credit reference on one of its customers to the plaintiff who was considering doing some work on credit for the customer. The plaintiff did not pay the defendant for the reference. Indeed, it had no direct contact with the defendant but had asked its own bank to obtain the reference from the defendant. The reference was satisfactory. The plaintiff did the work but the customer went bankrupt and could not pay. It was obvious that the defendant had acted negligently in preparing the satisfactory reference. The plaintiff sued the defendant but lost because the reference clearly stated that it was prepared without responsibility on the part of the defendant bank. However, the House of Lords held that the defendant would have owed a duty of care if the reference had not been subject to that disclaimer of responsibility. The basis of the duty would have been the fact that the defendant had assumed a responsibility to the plaintiff. Evidence of this was the fact that it had undertaken to use its skill to assist the plaintiff and that the relationship between the parties was 'equivalent to contract' but for the lack of payment for the service.

The test of assumption of responsibility has been criticised by both judges and academics on the ground that it is artificial because no one really asks whether the defendant consciously decided to assume a legal responsibility to the plaintiff. Instead, the question is really whether the circumstances are such that it is fair to impose responsibility on the defendant and that is just another way of asking whether there should be a duty. Indeed, this criticism led some members of the House of Lords in the 1990 case of *Caparo Industries v Dickman* to suggest that the test should be abandoned and that each case should be decided on its own facts without reference to a general test. This pragmatic case-by-case approach seems to avoid the problems attached to using a general test but it is hardly helpful. It tells us nothing about the general approach to be taken to the duty question. At least the assumption of responsibility test indicates that it is a moral question to be viewed from the perspective of the defendant. In more recent decisions in the 1990s, the House of Lords has returned to assumption of responsibility as the governing principle. We will trace the way in which the principle applies to a number of economic loss situations.

Assumption of responsibility

The examples of the valuer and the auditor provide a helpful contrast. In *Smith v Bush* (1989) a valuer providing a valuation of a house for a building society was held to have assumed a responsibility to the plaintiff who purchased the house with the building society loan and who had been given a copy of the valuation. The valuation report had negligently failed to identify a defect in the house and the plaintiff was put to the expense of repairing the defect. He recovered this sum from the valuer. The House of Lords based the finding of assumption of responsibility on the fact that the valuer knew that the fee he received from the building society had been paid to the society by the plaintiff and that his valuation would determine whether or not the plaintiff purchased the house. These two factors led the Lords to consider that the relationship between plaintiff and valuer was 'akin to contract'. The contrasting decision is *Caparo Industries v Dickman* (1990) where it was alleged that the defendant had negligently audited the accounts of a company giving the impression that it was more profitable than was the case, and that by relying on the accounts the plaintiff investor had suffered loss by purchasing the shares at an over-value. The House of Lords held that the auditor owed no duty of care to the investor. The key distinction between *Caparo* and *Smith* was that although in *Caparo* the auditor could foresee investors such as the plaintiff relying on the audit, its purpose in providing the audit report to the company was not to assist investors but solely to enable the shareholders of the company to take informed decisions about the management of their company. Although the Lords did not express their conclusion in terms of assumption of responsibility, it is clear in the light of the limited purpose of the audit report that the auditor could not possibly be said to be assuming a responsibility to the investor. Their relationship could not be said to be akin to contract as the purpose of the auditor's report was to advise only the shareholders about company management.

Cases concerning building contractors provide another interesting contrast. In *D & F Estates v Church Comrs for England* (1988) the House of Lords held that a contractor did not owe any duty of care to a subsequent purchaser of the building who was put to expense in repairing defects for which the contractor's negligence was to blame. The contractor was responsible to his employer who might be another contractor or the developer of the property, but did not have a responsibility to subsequent purchasers of the property of whom he would have no knowledge. It was for the purchaser to protect himself by having the property surveyed prior to purchase. However, in *Junior Books v Veitchi* (1982) the Lords had been prepared to find a duty in a situation where the subsequent owner of the building, a factory in that case, had chosen the defendant contractor to work on the site. The plaintiff owner had engaged a builder to construct the main fabric of the factory but instructed the builder to engage the defendant as the specialist subcontractor for the flooring work. The defendant negligently laid the floor and the plaintiff was put to expense in replacing the floor. The plaintiff could not sue the defendant in contract as the defendant's contract was with the builder, but did succeed in negligence. The Lords stressed the fact that the defendant had been chosen by the plaintiff and knew that the plaintiff was relying on its skill. Although the Lords did not use the terminology of 'assumption of responsibility', subsequent cases have explained the decision on that basis.

The same principle has been applied to the services provide by public authorities. In *Murphy v Brentwood District Council* (1990) the House of Lords held that an authority responsible for inspecting the building of houses did not owe a duty of care to subsequent purchasers of those houses. Such purchasers could not sue the authority for the expense of repairing defects in the house due to inadequate construction which the inspection should have prevented. The Lords concluded that there was no assumption of responsibility as it was not part of the purpose of the authority's inspection powers to prevent economic loss to subsequent purchasers. On the other hand in *X v Bedfordshire County Council* (1995), the House of Lords did consider that an authority might be liable in respect of advice to parents about the educational needs of their children provided by its teachers and educational advisers. Schools, teachers and advisers do assume a responsibility to pupils in relation to their educational needs.

Perhaps the most difficult problem to face the courts has been that of the disappointed beneficiary in *White v Jones* (1995). The plaintiffs were two daughters who had been excluded from their father's will after a family quarrel. Eventually, the father relented and sent a letter to the defendant, his solicitor, instructing him to draw up a new will giving the girls £9,000 each. However, the defendant negligently failed to carry out the instruction and when two months later he contacted the father to arrange a meeting, he discovered that he had died three days earlier. Under the law relating to wills, the girls received nothing from their father. They were disappointed beneficiaries, disappointed due to the negligence of the defendant. They each sued the defendant for the lost £9,000. By three votes to two, the House of Lords held that the defendant owed the plaintiffs a duty of care. The problem lay in the fact that the express assumption of responsibility by the defendant solicitor was solely to his client, the testator, that is the father. In many cases the beneficiaries may be just names, people or institutions like charities, about whom or which the solicitor knows nothing and cares less. It was on this ground that the two minority Law Lords held as a general principle it could not be said that there was any assumption of responsibility to the intended beneficiary. The argument clearly weighed with one of the majority Lords, Lord Nolan, for he emphasised that the duty was justified in *White* because the defendant was the family solicitor and knew all about the position of the daughters. The other two majority Lords also found an 'assumption of responsibility' to the intended beneficiaries but by slightly different routes. Lord Goff argued that the court had to find that the assumption of responsibility extended 'in law to the intended beneficiary' because otherwise such a person would have no remedy and the negligent solicitor would go unpunished. Obviously the testator could take no action as he was dead, but neither could the representatives of his estate, because it had lost nothing. Lord Browne-Wilkinson was more subtle, arguing that the solicitor had assumed responsibility for the task of drawing up the will and this justified a duty to those intended to benefit from proper performance of that task, that is, the intended beneficiaries. The issue can be argued both ways. Some critics say it demonstrates the artificiality of using assumption of responsibility as the governing principle. But the fact of the situation was that it was always going to be on the borderline of liability, whichever tests were used to determine the existence of a duty. The fact that all the Law Lords were able to use the terminology perhaps indicates that it provides a satisfactory framework for deciding such cases.

Problem cases: disclaimers and concurrent liability

There are two situations where the assumption of responsibility test has been seen as raising a conceptual problem. The first is where, as in *Hedley Byrne*, the provider of the service disclaims responsibility. At first sight it would appear that there can be no duty in such a case. The second is where the parties are already in a contractual relationship. Here, although it might appear that there must be a sufficient assumption of responsibility to justify tortious liability for negligence, there have been fears that the resulting concurrent liability, that is in both tort and contract, might undermine the principles of contractual liability.

The problem of the disclaimer has been met by the provisions of the Unfair Contract Terms Act 1977 and the interpretation given to it by the House of Lords in *Smith v Bush*. The detail of the Act is dealt with later in the contract section (p 538) but essentially it provides that a provision excluding negligence liability is only effective so long as it is reasonable. In *Smith* the valuer's report contained a disclaimer of his responsibility to the house purchaser. The Lords held this to be unreasonable mainly on the ground that the purchaser was given no choice about accepting the disclaimer in a report for which he had indirectly paid the fee. However, the valuer argued that the disclaimer had the effect of preventing any assumption of responsibility arising and hence, it prevented there being a duty rather than excluding the liability for breach of the duty. An ingenious argument but one which the Lords managed to defeat by noting that the wording of the Act applied to clauses which prevented duties arising as well as to exclusion clauses. Hence, the Lords held that the correct approach was to ask whether, disregarding the presence of the disclaimer, there would have been an assumption of responsibility and if so, then ask whether the disclaimer was reasonable. It seems likely on this approach that the outcome in a *Hedley Byrne* situation would now be different and that a bank would be liable for a negligent credit reference even if it had disclaimed responsibility.

The concurrent liability problem stems from the different time limits for suing applicable to the actions in tort and contract. In contract the time limit of six years for bringing an action runs from the date of the breach of contract. In tort the six year time limit runs from the date when the damage occurred and that may be longer after the original breach of duty. In the leading case of *Henderson v Merrett Syndicates* (1994) the defendants were agents responsible for managing the investment of money by Names in the Lloyd's insurance market. It was alleged by the Names that in each year of management during the 1980's the agents had carelessly exposed the Names to excessive risks of liability under insurance policies, most notably in covering asbestos liability risks in the USA. Clearly the Names could sued the agents for breach of contract but as they had only started their legal action in the 1990s, their contract action could not apply to losses due to breaches of contract occurring in the early 1980s. More than six years had passed between those breaches and the legal action being started and hence, a contract action in respect of losses caused by those breaches was barred. However, a tort action for negligence in respect of those losses might not be barred because the time period in tort runs from the date of the loss and not the breach. Here, it was arguable that many of the losses resulting from the breaches in the early 80s did not occur until the late 80s. This was because although the breach was the exposing of the Name to the risk, the loss only occurred when the risk materialised; when, for example, the asbestos claims started to come in. So it was vital for the Names to establish that they could claim against the agents in tort as well as contract. As there was a contractual relationship between the agents and Names it seemed obvious that the agents must have been assuming responsibility to the Names for managing their affairs carefully. But some previous authorities had held that where there was a contract between parties there could be no concurrent tortious liability. In other words, a contracting party was limited to his remedy in contract. The reason was obvious: to hold otherwise would enable the contracting party to take advantage of the more favourable time limit rules applicable to tort actions. In *Henderson* Lord Goff, leading the House of Lords, held these authorities to be wrong. He argued that rather than the law of tort being 'supplementary to the law of contract, ie as providing for a tortious liability in cases where there is no contract', it was 'the general law out of which the parties can, if they wish, contract'. As there was no clause contracting out of tortious liability in the agreement between the agents and Names, the latter were free to sue in tort and take advantage of the more favourable time limits.

Strict liability for pure economic loss

In view of the very limited recovery of pure economic loss in negligence, it may seem somewhat surprising that there is any strict liability for such loss but there is under the provisions of the Defective Premises Act 1972. Section 1 of this Act provides that a person who takes on work 'for or in connection with the provision of a dwelling' owes a duty to 'every person who acquires an interest' in it to see that the work 'is done in a workmanlike or ... professional manner, with proper materials ... so that as regards that work the dwelling will be fit for habitation when completed'. Under this provision a subsequent purchaser of a house may claim against anyone such as a builder or architect who was responsible for a defect rendering the house unfit for habitation. The purchaser may claim the cost of remedying such a defect, ie the economic loss, and he may claim where the builder or architect has not been negligent. This is because the section provides that the duty is to '*see that*' rather than to *take care that* the work is done so that the house is habitable. The reason for the strict duty in this context is partly to promote habitable, healthy housing but partly because the purchase of a house is the biggest investment made by the ordinary person and if any economic interest needs the protection of strict liability, it is this one.

Part IV
Contract

Contract

Chapter 20
What contract law is all about

The purpose of this chapter is to provide a setting for the next six chapters which contain an account of what the law of contract is. In order to understand this body of rules it is helpful to consider first the nature of the transactions which the rules are designed to control. It may by useful to point out that the word 'contract' contains an element of ambiguity. Lawyers usually use the word to mean an agreement to which the law will give effect; non-lawyers often use the word to mean a document in which the agreement is contained. So a non-lawyer who had been into a shop to buy goods for cash might say 'I bought the goods but there was no contract' by which he would mean that there was no written record of the transaction. A lawyer would not describe what has happened in the same way as he would know that in general, there is no need in English law for an agreement to be in writing to be binding.

Once it is appreciated that the law of contract is concerned with the whole range of agreements which are binding, it will be seen that its scope is vast. It embraces simple everyday transactions like catching a bus or train, buying food from a supermarket; important family transactions like buying a house or taking out policies of life insurance and major commercial enterprises like taking over a company or building the channel tunnel.

One may well ask whether a single body of rules can possibly be appropriate for such disparate arrangements. There are at least two reasons for giving an affirmative answer to this question. One is that one of the major purposes of the law of contract is to provide contract makers with a flexible array of tools capable of handling a wide range of very different situations. The second is that the law of contract is supplemented by a second set of rules which govern all the major contracts that are repeatedly made. So there are special rules for contracts for sale of goods, sale of land, for employment, insurance and so on. Of course the boundary between those questions which are governed by the general law of contract and those which are controlled by special provision is rather fluid and difficult to mark out precisely. However, we can say that there are certain questions such as how contracts are made which receive the same answer for virtually all contracts and are, therefore, part of the general law of contract, whereas there are other matters such as the content of the parties' obligations which tend to develop special rules on a contract by contract basis. When lawyers talk about the law of contract they usually mean that body of general rules which applies to all, or at least to most, contracts.

Why should contracts be enforced?

This is a complex and difficult question to which no single answer can be given. One answer would be that contracts are enforced because promises are morally binding. However, this may simply transfer the problem to the moral philosophers. Although most people feel intuitively that most promises are binding, philosophers find it quite hard to explain why. It is also clear that few, if any, legal systems actually enforce all those promises which the average person finds morally binding. So if I promise one of my daughters who is about to start her 'A' level course that I will support her through university if she works hard, that is certainly not legally binding, but most people would feel that it created some form of moral obligation. Before you conclude that the law is quite amoral, note that most people would probably also feel that my moral obligation was reduced or removed if I lost my job, but the law is both slower to impose contractual liability and also slower to release parties from liability because of subsequent disasters.

It is fairly clear that one of the major practical reasons why contracts are enforced is that it would be very difficult, if not impossible, to run a developed modern capitalist economy in which promises were not binding. So the authors of this book would not have spent time writing it if they had not had a binding promise from the publishers to publish it on completion. Many contracts are of this kind, involving performance spread out over a long time; examples include not only the building of office blocks or ships or aircraft, but long-term loans and policies of life insurance. Of course people entering into such transactions do not usually consciously rely on the law of contract, but rather on their confidence in the reliability and reputation of the other party. Nevertheless, a society in which none of these transactions was legally binding would be very different.

English law did not wake up one morning and decide that contracts should be enforced for this reason. The English law of contract was developed through the decisions of the judges and English judges do not ask themselves questions of this kind. Nevertheless, English law reached the position that an informal exchange of promises was binding very much earlier (by the early seventeenth century) than continental systems, and it is plausible to suggest that this was both cause and effect of England's early development into a capitalist industrial society. This phenomenon was described by Sir Henry Maine as the move 'from status to contract', that is from a society in which the obligations of individuals to other members of society were largely dictated by their position in society, to one in which it was largely determined by the agreements into which they entered. A simple example of a status is marriage. Getting married is a consensual act requiring the agreement of the parties but the obligations of the parties to each other are largely determined by the fact that they are married and not by their agreement.

Contractual behaviour

We can divide the contracts people make into a number of groups. Probably the largest in number are informal cash transactions such as buying goods in the supermarket or catching a bus. These transactions are normally accompanied by a minimum of negotiation, indeed the parties may often not even speak but indicate their assent by gestures. At first sight it might appear that legal enforceability is an irrelevance in such transactions because agreement is immediately followed by performance. However, if things go wrong, for example if the goods are defective or the bus crashes owing to the driver's negligence, the law of contract will come into play. A major technique here is the use of implied terms which fill in many of the gaps which would otherwise appear in such contracts (this is discussed in Chapter 22).

Another group consists of standard transactions which are entered into on the basis of a standard form written contract. The use of standard forms has great practical advantages in that it saves the time which would otherwise be needed to draft the contract and enables contract making to be entrusted to relatively junior levels: in other words, the advantages of mass production transferred to the contract making process. In some cases the standard form may be one produced by a third party and adopted by the parties. So most building contracts are on one of the forms produced by the Joint Contracts Tribunal (JCT) (this body is, despite its name, a standing committee of representatives of those groups most closely concerned with building contracts such as architects, surveyors, contractors and sub-contractors) and contracts between traders in the sugar trade are usually on the terms of the Sugar Trade Association. In some cases, such as building contracts, it seems to be the usual practice to adopt one of the standard forms with little or no amendment: in other cases, such as the chartering (hiring) of ships, it seems common to use the standard form simply as a basis for negotiation which will lead to the adoption of the form in a heavily amended version.

In other cases, standard forms are produced by one of the parties and routinely used by that party for all transactions of a particular kind. Such contracts are often called 'contrats d'adhesion' on the ground that the other party has only the choice to take it or leave it. This is in some ways an oversimplified view in that in many contractual situations there is flexibility in some areas and not in others. Typical examples would be the policies produced by insurance companies. Insurance companies compete vigorously in certain areas such as premium rates and a well-informed insurer (or one assisted by a skilled broker) can shop around effectively on such questions but is likely to find that the insurance company will insist on sticking precisely to the policy wording. Obviously one reason for this is that the contract wording produces results which are favourable to the insurance company, but another would be that negotiating on such matters would not fit into the bureaucratic structure of a large organisation like an insurance company and therefore produces costs which seem unacceptable unless there is a sufficiently wide demand.

Even where one party produces a standard form it does not necessarily follow that the other party cannot negotiate away from it. In contracts of sale between businesses it is very likely that the seller will try to contract on his printed standard terms but alert buyers will commonly refuse to accept the seller's terms or even try to contract on their own (the so-called battle of the forms, see p 461). The resolution of such questions will depend partly on the relative skill and experience of the negotiators, partly on how much each side needs the transaction and partly on whether the sums at stake justify spending a lot of time on negotiations.

Freedom of contract

Discussions of the development of contract law usually involve references to the part played in such development by the idea of 'freedom of contract'. This may be described as the notion that parties should enjoy a wide freedom to make contracts without interference by Parliament or the courts. This is sometimes associated with the doctrine, popular in the early nineteenth century, of laissez-faire, that the state should adopt a minimal role and that the best interests of all will be best served by each person pursuing his own self-interest. In his important work, *The Rise and Fall of Freedom of Contract*, Atiyah has suggested that earlier conventional accounts were oversimplified and that the period during which such minimalist views held sway was, at least as far as the law of contract is concerned, quite short. This view has in its turn not gone unchallenged.

For present purposes it may suffice to say that in any given period, an uneasy balance is struck between rules based on freedom of contract and paternalistic doctrines designed to protect those too weak to protect themselves, and that the general thrust of development over the last 150 years has been to increase the proper sphere of paternalism. In this, the law of contract has no doubt followed prevalent political and social doctrines though at a respectful distance. More will be said about this later, particularly in Chapter 24. We may, however, note three factors here.

Firstly, there are certain kinds of imbalance which the law of contract can hardly attempt to control. One example is real monopolies. If only one body controls the telephone service, whether this be a public or private body, individual telephone users will have little chance of negotiating with it successfully. In such cases protection of the individual is largely dependent on effective public regulation, or on breaking up the monopoly so that there is effective competition. (Note that there are not too many real monopolies because many apparent monopolies have competitors who provide an alternative service. So, until recently, British Rail had a monopoly of rail travel, but was in competition for long distance passenger carriage with coaches, cars and in some cases airlines.)

Secondly, many of the legislative interventions, though very important, take the form of abrogating freedom of contract in respect of particular contracts. For instance, there has been legislation for over 80 years regulating the relationship between the landlord and tenant of residential housing. This has been based on the belief that the shortage of rented accommodation has put tenants in an unduly enfeebled position to neg-otiate with landlords so that it is necessary to regulate some of the terms and in particular the rent. This is clearly a derogation from freedom of contract, but contract lawyers tend to treat the result as part of the law of landlord and tenant rather than of general contract law. Of course to treat the rule as part of general contract law and the exception as part of the law of particular contracts can give a misleading impression!

Thirdly, even today it is clear that freedom of contract is very important in many areas of contract practice. Most of the contract disputes which are litigated are between businesses and within very wide limits, courts tend to approach such cases on the basis that businesses are better able than courts to decide what is in their own self-interest and to take appro-priate steps to protect those interests. Further, the courts are very reluctant to protect the business which seeks to escape from a contract simply because it is a silly contract for them to have made. There are at least two reasons for this. One is that the training and experience of judges does not equip them to decide, except in the most obvious cases, whether an agreement is (or rather was at the time it was made) silly. The second is that taking a broad view, it is much more flexible and efficient to leave those decisions to those who are most closely concerned with the results.

Chapter 21

How contracts are made

The place of writing

As we noticed in Chapter 20 many non-lawyers assume that contracts have to be in writing and signed. This is in fact the complete reverse of the truth. In English law, there is no requirement that a contract be in writing, except where so provided by statute (see below). This has been the position since the early seventeenth century.

A common response from a person told this is to ask how you can prove that there is a contract if there is nothing in writing. The technical answer is that if a plaintiff alleges that there is a contract and gives evidence to that effect which is believed, that will suffice, and if the defendant gives evidence to the opposite effect, the judge will have to decide which story is more believable. In practice contract disputes are rarely about people going into sealed rooms and emerging quarrelling about what has just been said; it is much more likely that the dispute will not arise until acts have been done in pursuance of the contract which tend to confirm one party's story or the other – goods have been transferred, money has been paid, work has been done. A prudent contract maker who makes a contract over the phone would make a contemporary note of it which he would produce later to 'refresh his memory' or he would write a letter to the other party confirming what had been said. If left unchallenged this is very likely to be believed later. This illustrates an important point that although the contract may not be in writing, there may be written evidence of it.

Of course in practice, many contracts are in writing and it is often prudent to put contracts in writing, not so much to prevent disputes as to whether there has been an agreement at all, but to minimise disputes as to what has been agreed. The greatest danger in relation to agreements which are not in writing is that apart from the simplest agreements which are to be quickly performed, there is a risk that the parties will have different recollections as to what exactly was said.

The great advantage of the rule that writing is not usually required is that it is not open for the defendant to say 'I know I agreed but there is nothing in writing'. In practice, it seems that many people will raise this defence if it is available who would hesitate to tell lies in the witness box.

454

Historically, the great exception to the general rule was the Statute of Frauds 1677 which required six classes of contract to be evidenced in writing. In practice, this statute gave rise to much litigation and many unsatisfactory cases. In 1954, four of the six classes were removed from the list so that there then remained only contracts of guarantee and contracts for 'the sale or other disposition of land or any interest in land' (which were now in fact controlled by section 40(1) of the Law of Property Act 1925 which had restated the relevant part of the Statute of Frauds in slightly more modern language). A contract of guarantee occurs when one party guarantees the obligation of another, as where a father guarantees his daughter's overdraft at the bank. Since the guarantor usually has nothing to gain from such an agreement, there is much to be said for a requirement that it be in writing. Similarly with contracts for the sale of land, it is the nearly invariable practice to make the contract in writing. However, both with guarantees and sales of land, the requirement of the Statute of Frauds is not that the contract be in writing but that it be evidenced in writing by a note or memorandum, 'and signed by the party to be charged therewith'. So a memorandum containing all the terms of the contract and signed by one party and not by the other could be enforced by the non-signer against the signer, but not vice versa. The note or memorandum need not have been created for that purpose and indeed it was possible to add documents together so as to constitute a memorandum if one started from a document signed by the defendant and found in it an express or implicit reference to another document which contained the balance of the terms.

This is still the case with contracts of guarantee but section 40 of the Law of Property Act has been repealed by section 2 of the Law of Property (Miscellaneous Provisions) Act 1989. Section 2(1) provides that 'A contract for the sale or other disposition of an interest in land can only be made in writing and only by incorporating all the terms which the parties have expressly agreed in one document or, where contracts are exchanged, in each'. It is further provided that the contract must be signed by or on behalf of each party. This section applies to contracts made on or after 27 September 1989. Section 40 of the Law of Property Act continues to apply to contracts made before that date. It will be seen that the new section requires the contract to be made in writing and not merely to be evidenced in writing.

There are other contracts which are required either to be in writing or to be evidenced in writing under later statutes. So a lease for more than three years must be under seal, and under section 61(1) of the Consumer Credit Act 1974, a regulated consumer credit agreement, for example a contract of hire purchase, must be in the prescribed form.

Agreement, consideration and intention to create legal relations

Introduction

We have seen that writing is not essential to the creation of a contract in English law. What are the essential ingredients? The answer lies in a threefold combination – agreement, consideration and intention to create legal relations. Before we consider these three requirements in turn, it is important to note that the three requirements are interrelated and not wholly independent. Quite a few problems can be approached by using more than one of these techniques, but this does not usually matter since all three requirements must be present for there to be a binding agreement. The reason for the overlap is that the doctrines entered English law at different times. Historically, consideration is the oldest requirement and goes back to the early development of modern contract law in the sixteenth century. The analysis of agreement through the techniques of offer and acceptance (see below) only emerges in the nineteenth century, as a means of solving the problems which arise from the then new practice of contracting through the post. There was little, if any, mention of a requirement of intention to create legal relations until the twentieth century.

Agreement

THE MEANING OF 'AGREEMENT'

At first sight it seems obvious that agreement is necessary for contract since in lay usage, the two words are nearly synonymous. Indeed judges often say that there must be agreement or *consensus ad idem* (agreement on the same thing).

It is, however, clear that there can be a contract in English law even though the parties are not and never have been in agreement. Take this simple timetable:

July 1st	A posts letter to B offering to sell A's car to B for £2,000.
July 2nd	A posts letter to B withdrawing his offer.
July 3rd	A's first letter arrives at B's office and B immediately posts a letter accepting the offer.
July 4th	A's second letter reaches B.
July 5th	B's letter of acceptance reaches A.

As we shall see, it is clear law that there is a binding contract on these facts as soon as B's letter is posted, but it is clear that at this moment the parties are not actually agreed since A has already changed his mind. The result is sensible, however, since at the time he accepted A's offer, B reasonably believed that it was still open and he ought to be able to rely on this.

This is an aspect of what lawyers call the *objective test* of agreement. (Compare criminal law where tests of intention are usually subjective, see p 244.) In principle, each party is bound by what the other party reasonably believes that he meant. A good example is *Tamplin v James* (1880), where a pub was advertised for sale by auction. The particulars of the auction described clearly the boundaries of what was being offered. Adjoining the pub was a field which had often been used in conjunction with the pub, but the particulars made it clear that the field was not being offered for sale. The defendant made the highest bid and the pub was knocked down to him. Subsequently he sought to argue that he had only bid such a high price because he believed that the field was being offered too. This argument was rejected by the Court of Appeal since even if true it was irrelevant. The auctioneer was entitled to proceed on the basis that the defendant was bidding for the pub as clearly described in the auction particulars.

The objective test means that arguments such as 'I didn't really mean that' or 'I made a mistake' do not usually succeed. In general this is sensible because the process of contracting is essentially bilateral and all each party has to go on is what the other party appears to be saying. Hidden reservations normally count for nothing. This means that in the law of contract there is only a limited scope for a *doctrine of mistake*. For present purposes mistakes are of two main kinds. In one kind the parties are agreed but their agreement is based on some shared false assumption (these cases are discussed in Chapter 22). In the other kind which we consider here, it is argued that the effect of the mistake is to prevent the parties being agreed at all.

Tamplin v James demonstrates that it is not enough to show that one of the parties has made a mistake. However, there may be exceptional cases where the confusion is so great that even the reasonable onlooker cannot spell a contract out of what the parties have said. Such a case is *Scriven Bros v Hindley* (1913) where an auctioneer was engaged to sell both hemp and tow. The catalogue specified two separate lots one of 47 and the other of 176 bales. The catalogue did not state that the second lot was of tow which was much less valuable than hemp. Both lots bore the same shipping mark indicating on what ship the goods had been brought to England, and there was undisputed evidence that Russian tow and Russian hemp had never previously been landed from the same ship under the same shipping mark. There were samples of both lots at the auction but the defendant did not inspect them as he had already seen samples of the hemp at the plaintiff's showrooms. The defendant was the highest bidder for the second lot, bidding a price which was extravagantly high for tow though reasonable for hemp. It was held that there was no contract. It was clear that *subjectively* the plaintiff intended to sell tow and the defendant intended to buy hemp, but this alone is not sufficient. The decisive factor was that circumstances were such that each party not unreasonably thought as he did.

In these cases where two contracting parties, A and B, are at cross purposes, there are three conceivable answers – that there is a contract on A's terms, a contract on B's terms, or no contract at all. The decisive test will be whether an objective analysis leads to either of the first two possibilities; if not there will be no contract. A critical case is *Raffles v Wichelhaus* (1864) where A agreed to buy and B agreed to sell a cargo of cotton which was to arrive 'ex Peerless from Bombay'. In fact there were two ships called Peerless sailing from Bombay, one in October and one in December. The case is only reported on a preliminary hearing as to whether the buyer was bound to accept a delivery off the December ship and it was held that the case should go to trial. At the trial the defendant would have been entitled to seek to prove either that there was no contract at all, or that the contract was for delivery off the October ship (in which case the seller would have been in breach for tendering goods off the December ship); the seller would have been seeking to prove that the contract was for a December shipment. The critical question would then be whether there was anything in the negotiations or surrounding circumstances to resolve the ambiguity.

In these cases, the parties have been unaware that they are at cross purposes. In another group, one party is aware of the other's mis-understanding. There will be many cases where one party is mistaken to the other's knowledge but there is still a contract. The typical example is where one party is mistaken as to the value of the contract. Suppose you go into an art gallery and see a picture which you recognise as a genuine Picasso marked at £50. It is clear that the art dealer has made a mistake as to its value, but this would not invalidate a contract by you to buy the picture for £50. On the other hand, if one party makes a mistake not only as to value, but as to what some vital term of the contract is to be and the other party realises it, there will be no contract. A good example is *Webster v Cecil* (1861) where Cecil, who had already refused to sell his land to Webster for £2,000, wrote a letter in which he offered to sell for £1,250. Webster purported to accept the offer, but it was held that he could not do so since in the circumstances it was clear that Cecil did not intend to make an offer as to £1,250 and the price was clearly a vital term.

Perhaps the most difficult cases of this kind are where one party is mistaken as to the identity of the person with whom he is dealing. In *Cundy v Lindsay* (1878), a rogue called Blenkarn wrote from an address '37 Wood St, Cheapside' to order goods from the plaintiffs. There was an established firm called Blenkiron & Co which traded from 123 Wood St, Cheapside, Blenkarn signed his letters so that his signature looked like Blenkiron. The plaintiffs supplied goods to Blenkarn/Blenkiron on credit and he sold them to the defendants and disappeared. The plaintiffs sued to recover the goods from the defendants. Whether they could do so depended on whether there was a contract between the plaintiffs and Blenkarn. If there was then Blenkarn would have become owner of the goods and would have been able to transfer ownership to the defendants. The House of Lords held that there was no contract since the plaintiffs intended to contract with Blenkiron only and knew nothing of Blenkarn. On the other hand in the very similar case of *Kings Norton Metal Co v Edridge, Merrett & Co* (1897), where a rogue called Wallis sent orders using notepaper headed Hallam & Co, it was held that Hallam & Co was simply an alias for Wallis and that the sellers did intend to contract with the sender of the letter whether he be called Wallis or Hallam.

Similar fine distinctions have been drawn in cases where the parties actually meet but one assumes a false identity. In *Lewis v Averay* (1972) the plaintiff had advertised his car for sale. A rogue called to look at it and said that he was Richard Greene the film actor, producing a pass to Pinewood Studios. The plaintiff accepted an offer of £450 for his car and accepted the cheque which proved to be worthless. 'Greene' sold the car to the defendant and the plaintiff sued to recover it. The Court of Appeal held that there had been a contract between the plaintiff and 'Greene' and that therefore the latter had acquired ownership which he had transferred to the defendant.

It seems that in order to establish that there was no contract in such case, it must be shown that there was some definite third person with whom there was an intention to contract, different from the person with whom the contract was apparently made; that the identity of the other party to the contract was an essential matter; that the mistake was known to the other party and that adequate steps were taken to investigate the identity.

OFFER AND ACCEPTANCE: OFFER

In many cases it will be obvious that there is an agreement. When the existence of an agreement is in dispute it is often helpful to ask whether there has been offer and acceptance. It is important to emphasise that the absence of offer and acceptance does not mean that there is no contract – it is the absence of agreement which has this result. There are certainly cases where no one doubts that there is a contract but it is difficult to analyse the situation in terms of offer and acceptance. A good example is the process of exchange of contracts which normally precedes the coming into existence of a contract for the sale of land. Under the normal conveyancing practice two copies of the contract are prepared, one signed by each party, and the copies are exchanged, the intention being that there will be no contract before the exchange and that the parties will be bound the moment the exchange is complete.

The words offer and acceptance are frequently and naturally used in relation to the contract making process, but there is no need for any particular words to be used. An offer can perhaps be defined as a statement of the terms on which a party is prepared to contract, accompanied by a clear indication that all that is needed for a contract to arise is that the terms be accepted. There are many cases holding that typical transactions are or are not offers. So it was held in *Grainger & Son v Gough* (1896) that a price list or mail order catalogue was not an offer; in *Fisher v Bell* (1961) that display of goods in a shop window was not an offer and in *Pharmaceutical Society of Great Britain v Boots Cash Chemists (Southern) Ltd* (1952) that display of goods in a self service store was not an offer. In each of these cases, the terms on which the goods were to be sold were adequately clear, and the stumbling block was the possibility that if the transaction was treated as an offer the seller would be flooded out with acceptances not all of which he could meet.

In an auction it has been held that the offers are made by the bidder and the contract comes into existence if and when the auctioneer accepts the highest bid. Similarly, in a contract by sealed competitive tender, the tenders are the offers and the contract comes into existence when one of the tenders is accepted. In this situation there is usually no obligation to accept a bid or tender and indeed in *Harris v Nickerson* (1873) it was held that one who advertises an auction is under no liability to hold it. It has long been doubted what the position is where the auction is advertised as 'without reserve' (that is that the goods will be sold to the highest bidder however low), but this question now seems to be resolved by the decision of the House of Lords in *Harvela v Royal Trust of Canada* (1986) where a promise to sell to the highest tenderer in a sealed competitive tender was binding.

In *Blackpool & Fylde Aero Club v Blackpool Borough Council* (1990) the Court of Appeal held that the defendant Council, which had invited tenders for the provision of pleasure flights from the municipal airport, was bound seriously to consider all the tenders which had been properly submitted even though it had made it clear that it would not necessarily accept the highest or any tender. (The Council had by accident overlooked the plaintiff's tender.) The Court of Appeal thought that the adoption of a formal and structured tendering process carried with it an implied under- taking to operate the process exactly according to the rules.

Where the transaction is a non-standard one, it is necessary to examine the facts closely to see whether things have reached the stage of an offer. A good example is *Gibson v Manchester City Council* (1979). In this case, the council, while Conservative controlled, decided to sell council houses to tenants. In pursuance of this policy, the City Treasurer wrote to Mr Gibson saying that the Council 'may be prepared to sell the house to you at the purchase price of £2,725 less 20% = £2,180 (freehold)'. The letter invited Mr Gibson to make a formal application which he did. Control of the Council then passed to the Labour Party which reversed the policy of sale. The Council had no power to escape from a binding contract and the question was whether there was a binding contract. The letter from the City Treasurer was not an offer (note especially the expression 'may be prepared'), but was designed to get Mr Gibson to make an offer (such a pre-offer is often called an invitation to treat). Mr Gibson had made an offer, but it had not been accepted when the change of control took place.

OFFER AND ACCEPTANCE: ACCEPTANCE

The basic rule is that for an acceptance to be effective it must be an acceptance of the precise terms of the offer. So if I receive an offer and write back saying 'I accept your offer subject to the following modifications', this is not an acceptance at all but rather a counter-offer, that is an offer to contract on different terms which will only give rise to a contract if it is itself in due course accepted.

Neither offer nor acceptance need be in any particular form. All that is necessary is some form of words or conduct which sufficiently show an intention to offer or to accept respectively. In many simple cases this may be done by little more than nods and grunts. Usually silence alone will not amount to acceptance because silence is usually equivocal though there may be exceptional cases where this is not true.

The case most commonly discussed in this context is *Felthouse v Bindley* (1863). In this case, an uncle and a nephew had been discussing the possible sale of the nephew's horse to the uncle. The uncle wrote to the nephew offering to pay £30 and 15 shillings and saying 'if I hear no more about it, I consider the horse mine at that price'. The nephew did not reply to the uncle's letter and told the auctioneer who was selling his property to keep the horse out of the sale. The auctioneer forgot to do this and sold the horse. It was held that there was no contract between uncle and nephew. It seems quite likely that the nephew intended to accept the offer, but his instruction to the auctioneer was capable of other explanations and therefore equivocal. What the case really decides is that silence in the face of the uncle's (friendly) ultimatum did not amount to acceptance.

When the offer is met by a counter-offer, whether explicit or disguised as 'acceptance', the original offer becomes dead and no longer available for acceptance. There may, of course, be a whole series of counter-offers and so on, but there will be no contract until the latest counter-offer is accepted. This process is most vividly exemplified by the so-called 'battle of the forms'. This takes place when each party is trying to contract on its own standard form, and steadfastly ignores the other party's form. A typical situation would arise when a buyer wishes to procure a supply of widgets for delivery in six months' time and writes to the seller to ask for a quotation. The seller sends a quotation and the buyer sends an order. Normally the seller's quotation would be an offer and the buyer's order would be an acceptance, but nowadays it will often be the case that both seller and buyer are writing on stationery which has on its reverse the seller's and buyer's standard conditions of sale and purchase respectively. If this is so, the seller's quotation will still be an offer, but the buyer's order will be a counter-offer. In the leading case *Butler Machine Tool Co Ltd v Ex-cell-O Corpn (England) Ltd* (1979), the seller replied to the buyer's order by returning a tear-off acknowledgement slip supplied by the buyer which referred back to the buyer's conditions. This was held tantamount to an acceptance of the buyer's terms. To return the slip was obviously a tactical error by the seller and more commonly sellers use their own acknowledgement slips to refer to their terms. Orthodox opinion holds that in this situation there is no contract unless one party weakens and accepts the other party's terms. This may not be until the goods are eventually delivered and accepted, so that either party is free to withdraw before that.

OFFER AND ACCEPTANCE: COMMUNICATION OF ACCEPTANCE

It is usually said that not only must the offer be accepted, but the acceptance must be communicated to the offeror. Where the parties are negotiating face to face, this presents no problem since the acts or words which manifest acceptance will also communicate it. Where the parties are negotiating at a distance by post, telephone, telegram, telex, fax or messenger the principle obviously has important applications.

However, in the case of postal acceptance, perhaps numerically the most common case, the rule is subject to an exception. It was decided in *Adams v Lindsell* (1818) that a postal acceptance was effective as soon as it was posted and in *Household Fire and Carriage Accident Insurance v Grant* (1879), this rule was applied even when the letter of acceptance never arrived. No doubt the rule would not apply when the letter of acceptance was inadequately stamped or wrongly addressed, and it is open to the offeror to say expressly that he will not be bound until he receives the acceptance. In *Holwell Securities v Hughes* (1974), the Court of Appeal held that such a requirement could be implied from the nature of the contract (exercise of an option).

On the other hand the communication rule was applied to contracts of telex by the Court of Appeal in *Entores Ltd v Miles Far East Corpn* (1955) and by the House of Lords in *Brinkibon v Stahag Stahl* (1982). In these cases, the telex machines were in the offices of the parties and messages were sent during office hours. Communication, therefore, was practically instantaneous as it is on the telephone, which is assumed to be covered by the same rules. The position where telex messages are sent out of hours or through telex agencies remains unclear.

The rule that acceptance must be communicated is designed for the protection of the offeror so that he will know where he stands. It is open to the offeror, therefore, to prescribe the way in which acceptance is to be communicated (for example, by return of post), or to waive the need for communication. So if in *Felthouse v Bindley* (above, p 461) the nephew had clearly accepted and had then sought to enforce the contract against the uncle, it is very doubtful if the uncle could have complained of the lack of communication. When the offer calls for the offeree to accept by doing some act such as walking to York or finding the offeror's lost dog, it has been held that the offeree can simply do the act, and need not first tell the offeror that he is doing so (*Carlill v Carbolic Smoke Ball Co* (1893)).

OFFER AND ACCEPTANCE: CERTAINTY

There may be cases in which there is certainly, in a sense, offer and acceptance, but the court will nevertheless hold that there is no contract because the agreement is insufficiently certain. A good example is *G Scammell and Nephew Ltd v Ouston* (1941), where it was agreed that the plaintiff would buy a new lorry from the defendants, trading in an old lorry and paying the balance 'on hire-purchase terms' over two years. The House of Lords held that there was no contract because the expression 'on hire-purchase terms' was too vague and indefinite, since it left in the air such questions as whether instalments were to be paid on a weekly, monthly or quarterly basis; whether there was to be a cash deposit; what the rate of interest was to be and so on.

This decision is no doubt correct, but it is probably a mistake to read too much into it. Courts often enforce agreements where many details have been left in the air. This may be because they can fill in the gaps by implying terms (see Chapter 22), or because the contract is made against the background of trade usage or previous dealings which enable the gaps to be filled in, as in the earlier House of Lords decision in *Hillas & Co Ltd v Arcos* (1932).

One of the major difficulties in this area is that the common law has adopted an all or nothing approach to the question whether there is a contract, which leaves little or no room for a finding that there is three-quarters of a contract. This approach does not correspond with the way in which parties actually negotiate, which often involves a series of negotiated stages, such that it would be regarded as sharp practice to go back on what had been agreed at one of the earlier stages. It is this gap between practice and law which has aroused so much public concern in relation to 'gaz-umping'. In the normal practice of house purchase, the seller and the buyer agree on a price and then hand the completion of the transaction over to their solicitors. The solicitors normally proceed on a 'subject to contract' basis, that is that the parties have agreed that they shall not be legally bound until the lawyers have completed and they have signed a formal agreement. (There is no legal requirement to handle house purchase in this way – it is simply the practice which has grown up amongst conveyancing solicitors.) This arrangement is normally beneficial to the buyer, as it gives him time to have the property surveyed, and to raise a mortgage, and it gives the buyer's lawyers time to make the appropriate pre-contractual enquiries (to make sure, for instance, that there is no plan to build a motorway through the back garden). However, this process usually takes at least a month and often longer. If house prices are rising fast, the seller may announce at the last moment that he will not sign the contract unless he receives a better price. There is no doubt, under the existing law, that the seller is entitled to do this, but it is not surprising that it causes fury to the buyer who will often have wasted money on lawyers' and surveyors' fees and so on. This has naturally led to calls, so far unanswered, for a change in the law.

There are various techniques which can be used to deal with this kind of situation. The buyer could have entered into an option contract with the seller under which, for an immediate payment by the buyer, the seller promises to keep his offer to sell open. This protects the buyer against the seller changing his mind; it does not protect the seller against the buyer changing his mind and deciding not to buy, but the option payment is designed to compensate the seller against this risk. (This is likely to make the transaction more expensive to the buyer. Can you see why?) Another possibility would be to enter into a contract conditional on the survey being satisfactory or a mortgage obtained. This possibility will be considered later (see p 492).

In England, the option technique is not much used in conventional house purchase, but it is quite common in leases, where the lessee may be granted an option to buy out the interest of the lessor. An instructive case in this context is *Sudbrooke Trading Estate Ltd v Eggleton* (1982). Here the lease granted the lessee an option to purchase the lessor's interest 'at such price not being less than £75,000 as may be agreed upon by two valuers, one to be nominated by the lessor and the other by the lessee, or in default of such an agreement by an umpire appointed by the said valuers'. The lessee exercised the option, but the lessor argued that the provision for fixing the price was uncertain because he had not appointed a valuer, and, therefore, the valuation machinery could not be operated. Such arguments had repeatedly been accepted by the Court of Appeal but the House of Lords rejected them. The majority of the House took the view that since valuers were now an established profession bound to apply professional standards, the provision for fixing the price by professional valuation was implicitly a provision for a reasonable price, which could, if necessary, be determined by the court in other ways. This decision is consistent with a greater willingness in courts to discover a binding contract, even though there are a few loose ends left untied.

Even where there is no contract, a party may be entitled to payment for services rendered on some other theory. In *British Steel Corpn v*

Cleveland Bridge and Engineering Co Ltd (1984), the defendants were subcontractors engaged in construction of the steel framework of a bank to be built in Saudi Arabia. For this purpose they needed some nodes of an unusual kind which had not previously been manufactured in the United Kingdom. They entered into discussions with the plaintiffs and there were complex legal, financial and technical negotiations. It was clear during these negotiations that neither side was willing to contract on the other's standard terms, but technical discussions continued and in due course the nodes were completed, delivered and accepted. The plaintiff sued for the value of the nodes and the defendants counter-claimed for late delivery. Robert Goff J held that there was no contract as the parties had never agreed on the terms, but that the plaintiff could recover the reasonable value of the nodes as the defendant had requested and accepted them. The practical result of this was that the plaintiff's claim succeeded, but the defendant's counter-claim for late delivery failed. As there was no contract, there could be no agreed delivery date and, therefore, delivery could not be late.

The plaintiff's claim in this case is an example of what is often called a quasi-contractual claim. This name is one of the many misleading labels in English law since the basis of the claim is not agreement, but that it would be unfair to allow the defendant to keep the nodes and not have to pay anything for them. The reason for the name is that under the procedure by way of cause of action which operated until the middle of the nineteenth century, the same form of action was used for claims of this kind and for contractual claims.

Difficult problems can arise as to precisely in what situations a claimant is entitled to recover money on this basis for work he had done in pursuance of a contract which has never come into existence. In *William Lacey (Hounslow) Ltd v Davis* (1957) the plaintiff had tendered for work and had then been led to believe that he would probably receive the contract and had been encouraged to do further work. The judge held that, although the costs of tendering were a business overhead at the time which normally fell on the tenderer, the extra work was of a kind which the plaintiff would not normally have done without an expectation of payment and that in the circumstances he was entitled to be paid. This case can be explained either on the basis that there was an implied contract to pay for the extra work or on the basis that the plaintiff had a claim in restitution. In *Regalian Properties plc v London Dockland Development Corpn* (1995), Rattee J refused to apply this reasoning to a situation in which the plaintiffs spent over £3 million on development work for a project in the London Docks area which had eventually come to nothing because of the collapse of the property market. In this case, although the parties expected to reach a contract, the whole of the negotiations had been expressly on a 'subject to contract' basis and the judge held that the plaintiffs had taken the risk that the transaction would never come to fruition.

The parties may seek to provide for some of the difficulties by agreements made as to the conduct of the negotiations. In some legal systems, the doctrine has developed that there is a duty to negotiate in good faith. In *Walford v Miles* (1992), the House of Lords held that even an agreement by the parties to negotiate in good faith created no legal obligation because it was impossible to give consent to what the parties had undertaken. This decision has been strongly criticised. Although it is no doubt the case that the parties, by promising to negotiate in good faith, do not promise to reach a contract, it does not necessarily follow that they have not agreed that one party should compensate the other for wasted expenditure which arises out of a failure to negotiate in good faith (for example, because one party never intended to contract and simply wasted time or because one party was secretly negotiating with two potential partners and intended only to contract with one of them). In *Walford v Miles* the House of Lords suggested that it would be legally permissible and enforceable to make an agreement that, for a defined period, one or both of the parties would not negotiate with anyone else (a shut out clause) and this view was applied by the Court of Appeal in *Pitt v PHH Asset Management Ltd* (1993).

TERMINATION OF OFFERS

Not all offers are accepted of course. Sometimes when an offer is accepted the offerer is sorry that he made it and wishes to argue that the offer is no longer open for acceptance. This may be the case for a variety of reasons.

Rejection
Once an offer is rejected it cannot be accepted unless it is renewed. This rule applies not only to specific rejections, but also to implicit rejection by making a counter-offer, *Hyde v Wrench* (1840). Merely to enquire whether better terms (for example, longer credit) might be available is not, however, a rejection, *Stevenson v McClean* (1880).

Revocation
The general rule is that an offer can be revoked at any time until it has been accepted. This is so even where the offeror has promised to keep the offer open, *Routledge v Grant* (1828), unless that promise is itself the subject matter of a binding contract (such contracts are common in relation to land, shares and commodities and are called options).

In practice, this rule is limited by another rule that the offeror's revocation of his offer is not effective until it has been communicated to the offeree. This was held in *Byrne & Co v Van Tienhoven and Co*(1880), on facts very similar to those set out in the hypothetical example given above on p 456. The slightly earlier case of *Dickinson v Dodds* (1876) is usually taken to have decided that such communication may be indirect, that is via a third party who tells the offeree that the offer has been withdrawn (at least if the information appears reliable).

There has been much discussion as to whether this unrestricted revocation rule applies to cases where the offer is made in return for the offeree performing an act. Suppose A offers B £100 if B would walk from London to York, and A purports to revoke the offer when B has arrived at Doncaster. One argument is that B has not promised to walk to York and is free to stop at any time and that A should therefore be free to revoke his offer at any time. This kind of reasoning has been applied to the standard estate agent arrangement which is that the estate agent will be paid a commission if he finds a buyer and nothing if he does not. In the leading case of *Luxor (Eastbourne) Ltd v Cooper* (1941), the House of Lords held that the owner was not obliged to keep his property on the market so as to give the estate agent the chance to earn his commission. However, the reasoning of the House of Lords assumed that the result would be different if the offeror had expressly or impliedly promised to keep his offer open. (It was held that there was no such implied promise in the standard estate agent situation since it is inherently speculative – that the houses the estate agent sells pay for the ones that he does not.) It is easy to think of cases where the offeree could not reasonably be said to be taking his chances on the offeror changing his mind. A good example is *Errington v Errington* (1952), where the father bought a home for his son and daughter-in-law to live in. The father bought the house in his own name with the aid of a building society mortgage. He told the son and daughter-in-law that if they paid the mortgage instalments he would convey the house to them when the mortgage was paid off. The Court of Appeal held that even though the son and daughter-in-law had never promised to pay the instalments, the father could not revoke his offer so long as they in fact continued to do so.

Lapse of time

Many offers are explicitly made for a fixed period. In such a case, the offer automatically comes to an end when the period runs out. If there is no express time limit, the court will usually hold that the offer is open for a reasonable time and decide what a reasonable time is. It may well be a very short time as, for example, in an offer to sell shares on the Stock Exchange which is only open for minutes, if not seconds. Clearly in other situations, a reasonable time may be measured in days, weeks or even months.

Death

A contract does not automatically come to an end on the death of one of the parties. So if A contracts to sell his house to B and dies before the house is conveyed, the contract will be binding on A's executors. It is different where the contract calls for personal performance as in a contract of employment or to write a book. It is clear that further performance would usually be impossible in such cases, though even so there may be contractual rights which survive death, such as pension rights in the contract of employment or royalty payments in the case of an author.

The effect of death on a contract as yet uncompleted is less clear. Probably the position is that the offer cannot be accepted after the offeree's death, and that the offeree cannot accept after the offeror's death, at least once he knows of it.

Failure of condition
In *Financings Ltd v Stimson* (1962), the defendant decided to acquire a second-hand car which he had seen at a dealer's showroom. He wished to take the car on hire-purchase terms. For this purpose two documents were used – one was an offer by the dealer to sell the car to the plaintiff finance company, and the other was an offer by the defendant to enter into a hire-purchase contract with the plaintiff. (Finance companies commonly supply such forms in blank to car dealers, but do not give them authority to contract on their behalf.) The plaintiff was allowed to take the car away before the paperwork had been completed. He decided that he did not want the car after all and returned it to the dealer. The majority of the Court of Appeal held that this was not an effective revocation as the dealer was not the agent of the finance company to receive notice of the revocation. (This decision was subsequently reversed by statute.) The car was then stolen from the dealer's premises and seriously damaged. The next day the plaintiff purported to accept the defendant's offer. The Court of Appeal held that the offer was no longer open as it was conditional on the car staying in substantially the same condition from offer until acceptance.

SOME SPECIAL CASES

As we said above, offer and acceptance are only a useful technique and not an essential ingredient in the formation of contract. In each case the court has to decide whether the parties have agreed and it may reach this conclusion even though it is difficult to analyse the situation in terms of offer and acceptance. A good example is *Clarke v Earl of Dunraven* (1897), where the parties had both entered for a yacht race by completing the entry form. It was held that this created a contract between them even though there had been no direct dealings. Responsibility for accidents was therefore governed by the race rules.

In practice, this state of the law gives the court considerable flexibility to discover contracts where this seems a desirable result. So, in *Carlill v Carbolic Smoke Ball Co* (1893), the defendants advertised their smoke ball as a preventive for flu and undertook to pay £100 to anyone who bought the smoke ball, used it according to the instructions and still caught flu. Mrs Carlill bought a smoke ball, not from the Smoke Ball Company but from a pharmacist, and caught flu. It was clear that she had made a contract with the pharmacist, but the pharmacist had not guaranteed the efficacy of the smoke ball. The Court of Appeal held that the terms of the advertisements were sufficiently specific to create a binding contract with anyone who bought the smoke ball and later caught flu. This could be explained by saying that the advertisement was an offer to the whole world, capable of being accepted by buying and using the smoke ball.

Usually manufacturers of products avoid making such definite undertakings, but a modern example is *Shanklin Pier Ltd v Detel Products Ltd* (1951) where the plaintiffs, owners of the pier, made a contract with decorators for the painting of the pier with a paint to be chosen by the plaintiffs. The defendants assured the plaintiffs that their paint was very suitable for painting piers and the plaintiffs instructed the decorators to use it. In fact the paint was quite unsuitable. The plaintiffs had clearly made a contract with the decorators but the decorators had simply done what they had been told. The decorators had made a contract with the defendants but the decorators had suffered no loss. The court solved the problem by holding that there was a contract between plaintiffs and defendants which could perhaps be spelt out as 'if you choose our paint and tell the decorators to use it, we will guarantee that it is suitable'.

If offer and acceptance is not essential, it may be asked whether a contract can be made where two identical cross offers are made simultaneously. It is usually assumed that *Tinn v Hoffmann & Co* (1873) requires a negative answer to this question, though some of the judges, in fact, decided the case on the ground that the cross offers were not in fact identical. The assumption is probably correct, however, for the situation speaks of coincidence rather than agreement. Of course in practice, it is very likely that one of the parties will accept one of the offers before the other party withdraws his.

Another conundrum which has been much discussed is whether one can create a contract by accepting an offer of which one is unaware. A typical situation which presents this problem is where A advertises a reward for the return of his lost dog and B, unaware of the offer, finds the dog and returns it to A. The purist view expressed in the American case of *Fitch v Snedaker* (1868) and the Australian case of *R v Clarke* (1927) is that there is no contract on such facts unless B knows of the offer and intends to accept it when he returns the dog. On the other hand, it must be admitted that it makes no difference to A whether B is ignorant when he returns the dog, and it is perhaps not wholly surprising that in the leading, but unsatisfactorily argued, English case of *Gibbons v Proctor* (1891) the reward was recovered.

Consideration

INTRODUCTION

The modern English law of contract developed during the fifteenth and sixteenth centuries, and by the beginning of the seventeenth century it was in a recognisably modern form. By this stage consideration was already established as a requirement. The process by which this came about is still the subject of dispute amongst legal historians. The leading modern account is that of Simpson. He says that sixteenth and seventeenth century lawyers thought not of the enforceability of contracts but of promises. When informal promises became generally enforceable, it was necessary to distinguish between those promises which were enforceable and those which were not. This was done by requiring the promise to be 'supported by a consideration', that is, a good reason for enforcing it. So in origin, the doctrine of consideration was concerned with reasons for enforcing promises and there were 'good' considerations and 'bad' considerations. A leading modern scholar, Atiyah, in a famous article has argued that in essence that is the function which the doctrine still performs.It is a feature of the development of law through the cases that particular instances precede general principles. So there were many cases considering whether particular considerations were good or bad, but already by 1588 Sir Edward Coke tried to summarise them by saying 'every consideration that doth charge the defendant in an assumpsit must be to the benefit of the defendant or charge of the plaintiff, and no case can be put out of this rule'. This anticipates an antithesis between benefit and detriment which dominated nineteenth century accounts of the law. According to this analysis, consideration must consist of something which was either of benefit to the promisor (the person who made the promise) or a detriment to the promisee (the person to whom the promise was made). However, this analysis only fits the law if one gives a highly technical meaning to the words benefit and detriment. So if I agreed to sell my Rolls Royce to you for £100, the transaction is in fact highly detrimental to me and highly beneficial to you, but it is undoubtedly binding. This result can be explained by saying that it is beneficial to me to receive your promise to which I was not previously entitled but this seems very artificial. It seems simpler to say that a binding promise must have been bought by some counter-promise or action.

In most cases, the price of the promise will be a counter-promise by the other side. In such cases the consideration is said to be executory. The classic example is an engagement to marry (treated by English law as a binding contract until 1970) where there is inevitably a time gap between promise and performance. In some cases, such as the promise of a reward of £5 for the return of my lost dog, consideration is the act of returning the dog and is said to be executed. This distinction between executory and executed consideration is also sometimes put as a distinction between bilateral and unilateral contracts. In a bilateral contract both parties assume obligations (the word bilateral is strictly inaccurate since there is no reason why a contract should not be multilateral – a partnership of three or more partners is a good example), whereas in a unilateral contract only one party assumes obligations (so the estate agent does not usually promise to sell your house or even to try to do so, but you promise to pay him a commission if he does).

'PAST' CONSIDERATION

If consideration is the price of a promise, it must usually have been given in exchange for it. A promise to pay for something which has already been done would not usually be in exchange for it and will not do. It is a 'past consideration' – a classic example of a 'bad' consideration. A good example is *Re McArdle* (1951), where work was done to improve a house and the defendants, who were entitled to the house after the death of their mother, promised to pay their sister-in-law for the work. The Court of Appeal held that as the work had been completed before the promise was made there was no consideration for it.

There is a well established exception to this rule where the work was originally done at the request of the promisor. This goes back to the old case of *Lampleigh v Brathwait* (1615), where the defendant asked the plaintiff to secure a royal pardon for his having killed a man. The plaintiff spent much time and effort in obtaining the pardon and the defendant promised him £100. It was held that the defendant's promise was binding.

This decision was explained by the Court of Appeal in *Re Casey's Patent* (1892) and by the Privy Council in *Pao On v Lau Yin Long* (1980), on the basis that the original request carried with it an implied promise to pay, of which the later promise was only an explicit recognition. It is undoubtedly the case that a request to do something often carries with it an implied promise to pay a reasonable price for doing so. So if I go to a solicitor and ask him to carry out the conveyancing of the purchase of my house I am impliedly promising to pay him a reasonable fee for doing so. Of course, it is not always the case that a request has this effect, as when I go to my next door neighbour and ask him if I may borrow his lawnmower as my own lawnmower has broken down. On which side of the line the behaviour of the plaintiff in *Lampleigh v Brathwait* fell, it is perhaps impossible for those in the twentieth century to tell.

CONSIDERATION MUST MOVE FROM THE PROMISEE

From an early stage it was said that consideration must move from the promisee. Translated into more modern English this means that the person who seeks to enforce the promise (usually the plaintiff) must be the person who provided the consideration for that promise. In this context it is important to remember that where, as is usually the case, the contract is made by exchange of promises, each side will have made promises and so each party will be a promisor in respect of its own promises and a promisee in respect of the other party's promises.

In a straightforward contract, say for A to sell his car to B for £5,000, if there is consideration at all it will have been provided by the person to whom the promise was given. So the consideration for A's promise to sell is given by B and the consideration for B's promise to buy is given by A.

However, there are important classes of contract where promises are made to third parties, for instance, as part of X's employment by Y it is agreed that on X's death Y will pay a pension to X's widow, Z. Clearly Z would not have provided consideration for this promise; indeed if X has worked for Y for many years, he may not even have been married to Z when the promise was made.

The rule that consideration must move from the promisee overlaps here with another doctrine, called the doctrine of privity of contract (discussed below). There is a dispute of some theoretical interest, but little practical importance, as to whether these doctrines are in fact distinct or merely different ways of saying the same thing. It is clear that they are distinct in the sense that one could imagine a system which did not have a doctrine of consideration but did have a doctrine of privity of contract; it is equally clear that in a system which adopts both rules, they overlap at least as to 99% of cases.

ADEQUACY AND SUFFICIENCY OF CONSIDERATION

The basic rule is quite clear. The court will not enquire into the adequacy of consideration but only as to whether there is consideration. So, in general, a contract to sell a car worth £1,000 is valid whether the price be £10,000, £1,000 or £1. This statement in fact contains two policies of judicial self-denial. The court will not inquire into either the *fairness* or the *genuineness* of the bargain. To say that the court will not consider the fairness of the agreement is true, but it is not the whole truth. It will not do simply to attack the question of fairness head-on, but many unfair contracts may be upset because they fall within the ambit of rules as to mistake, misrepresentation, duress, undue influence and so on. In applying these rules, the court may well be influenced by considerations of fairness, but lack of equality in the exchange, however great, does not in itself make the contract invalid.

The refusal to enquire into genuineness is an important feature of the doctrine, since it means that anyone who knows the law can dress up a gift as a contract by reciting a nominal consideration. In one sense this may seem odd, but English law has always been very tolerant of those who organise the facts to fit into legal pigeonholes. In any case, there is a substantial, and not merely formal, difference between my promising my daughter that I will give her a car on her 21st birthday and promising that if she gives me £1 today I will transfer to her a car free of further payment on her 21st birthday. In the second case, I have deliberately adopted a form which makes the transaction legally binding. (Note that I could have made the transaction binding by making it under seal, as in the covenants which many people make in favour of charities – promises under seal being a survival from medieval forms of contract making.)

Another very important consequence of the rule that normally anything given in exchange will do, is that although the requirement of consideration is technical and unknown to most contracting parties, it is nearly always satisfied in practice. Unless the transaction is wholly gratuitous something will usually have been given in exchange for the promise. Contract litigation is largely dominated by disputes between businessmen. Businessmen rarely make wholly gratuitous promises which they intend to be binding. (A major exception is agreements designed to vary the effects of existing agreements where gratuitous concessions are much more common. The problems presented by this are considered in Chapter 25.)

There are, however, some important exceptions. One is the rule discussed above (p 466), that a promise to keep an offer open is not binding unless it is itself part of a binding contract. Another arises in relation to requirements contracts. Suppose a hospital asks suppliers to tender against a list of supplies for the following year and X writes offering to supply disposable cups at £5 a hundred. He receives a letter indicating that his price has been accepted. Is there a contract? There clearly would be if the hospital has indicated how many cups it requires, but it is very likely that the hospital will not wish to bind itself to a firm figure 12 months in advance. There would also be a contract if the hospital had undertaken to take its entire supply for the year from X, but in many cases there would be no contract because although the hospital had indicated that the price was acceptable, it had not yet in fact ordered a single cup. In such cases the supplier is sometimes said to have made a standing offer and a series of contracts comes into existence each time the hospital sends an order. The hospital would not be bound to give any orders and the supplier would be free to revoke his offer at any time except in relation to orders already given.

There remains a group of cases where the courts have characterised certain acts and promises as insufficient to count as consideration. The common feature in these cases is that in each case the consideration consists of doing something, or promising to do something, which there was already a duty to do. The problem is well illustrated by the decision of the House of Lords in *Glasbrook Bros Ltd v Glamorgan County Council* (1925). In this case, a mine owner during a coal strike in South Wales asked the police to station a guard at the colliery. The police took the view that the colliery could be adequately protected by a mobile force, but a garrison was provided after the mine owner had promised to pay £2,200. After the strike the mine owner refused to pay, arguing that it was the duty of the police to protect the property and that they were not entitled to demand payment for carrying out their duty. The House of Lords accepted the principle but held that it was inapplicable on the facts. The police were bound to defend property, but the means adopted was to be decided by them and not by members of the public. If they were bona fide and reasonably thought that the garrison was not needed, they were entitled to charge to provide something more. The same principle has recently been applied to justify charging for the provision of police officers at Football League matches.

In this case, the duty which was owed was one imposed by the general law and it was held that a contract to go beyond the duty was valid, but one which simply involved the performance of the existing duty was not. The same approach has been applied where the duty is one which is imposed by an existing contract between the parties. In *The Atlantic Baron* (1979), the defendants, a Korean Shipbuilding Corporation, had contracted to build a ship for the plaintiffs. The price was expressed in US dollars and was payable in instalments as different parts of the ship were completed. There was a fall in the value of the dollar which made the contract less profitable for the defendants. It was clear that under the terms of the contract they had taken this risk, just as the plaintiffs had taken the risk of a rise in the value of the dollar, but the defendants told the plaintiffs that they would not finish the ship unless they were paid 10% more. The plaintiffs were particularly anxious to have the ship as they had made a very profitable contract to charter it and they therefore agreed to pay the extra 10%, and in due course did so. Some months later, they sued to recover the extra payment. Mocatta J held that if these had been the only facts the money would have been recoverable. However, under the terms of the original contract, the defendants were obliged to provide a letter of credit for repayment of the instalments if the ship was not completed. When the defendants asked for extra payment they agreed to increase the size of the letter of credit. This was held to be sufficient consideration to support the change in the terms of the contract.

This account of the law probably needs to be revised in the light of the decision of the Court of Appeal in *Williams v Roffey Bros & Nicholls (Contractors) Ltd* (1990). The defendants were a firm of builders who had entered into a contract for the refurbishment of a block of flats. They had sub-contracted the carpentry work to the plaintiff for £20,000. Midway through the contract, the plaintiff discovered that he was in financial difficulties, partly because he had underestimated the cost of the work and partly because he had not managed his workforce well. The plaintiff had a meeting with the defendants at which the defendants agreed to pay the plaintiff a further £10,300 at a rate of £575 per flat to be paid as each flat was completed. The plaintiff carried on work and finished some eight further flats but only one further payment of £1,500 was made. It could perhaps have been argued that there were additional obligations assumed by the plaintiff here since the payment arrangements under the revised deal were arguably more specific and detailed than under the original contract. However, this was not the way in which the Court of Appeal approached the contract. They thought that the decisive factor was that the plaintiff had not been guilty of economic duress and that there was sufficient consideration for the rearrangement in the fact that the defendants obtained a significant extra practical undertaking that the work would be finished. Glidewell LJ stated the law in the form of the following proposition:

'The present state of the law on this subject can be expressed in the following proposition:

(i) if A has entered into a contract with B to do work for, or to supply goods or services to, B in return for payment by B, and

(ii) at some stage before A has completely performed his obligations under the contract B has reason to doubt whether A will, or will be able to, complete his side of the bargain, and

(iii) B thereupon promises A an additional payment in return for A's promise to perform his contractual obligations on time, and

(iv) as a result of giving his promise B obtains in practice a benefit, or obviates a disbenefit, and

(v) B's promise is not given as a result of economic duress or fraud on the part of A, then

(vi) the benefit to B is capable of being consideration for B's promise, so that the promise will be legally binding.'

Just as a contracting party may seek to get paid more for completing the contract, he may also seek to discharge his liability by offering something less than a complete performance. The simplest case is the debtor who asks for discharge from a debt of £100 by paying £90. Creditors often accept such offers, but English law has repeatedly held in decisions culminating in the decision of the House of Lords in *Foakes v Beer* (1884), that such an acceptance is not binding on the creditor and that he can take the money and then sue for the balance. In *Re Selectmove Ltd* (1995), the Court of Appeal held that this rule was not effected by the decision of the Court of Appeal in *Williams v Roffey Bros* (above).

This is subject to important exceptions, however. It does not apply where the amount which is owing is the subject of a genuine dispute. So where the parties make an agreement to compromise a claim (whether the dispute is as to the very existence of the claim or as to its amount), the agreement is binding even though if the matter had been litigated one party or the other would have done better than the compromise.

The rule also applies only where it is obvious that the offered performance is less valuable than what was due as with money which bears its value on its face. So if I offer you my car in satisfaction of my debt of £1,000 and you accept, this is binding whether the car is worth £10,000 or £1,000 or £100 because the court will not enquire into the value of the car, just as it would not have enquired if I had sold the car to you for £1,000. Clearly if a car will do, £900 plus a car will do just as well, and if £900 plus a car will do, £900 plus a peppercorn will do equally well. This means that if a debt of £1,000 is owed, a creditor who agrees to take £900 in full settlement is not bound, but one who agrees to take £900 plus a peppercorn is bound. At least one great judge, Sir George Jessel, has thought this logical but absurd; on the other hand, the second form of transaction is perhaps unlikely to be adopted except by a creditor who knows the law and means to be bound.

A final possibility is that the existing duty is one imposed by a contract which one of the parties has made with a third party. After long uncertainty this was resolved by the decision of the Privy Council in the *Eurymedon* (1975). In that case, a firm of stevedores had contracted to unload a cargo from a ship first with the ship owners and then with the cargo owners. It was held that the promise to unload was good consideration for the contract with the cargo owners. The difference between this situation and the earlier one is that the cargo owners gained something – the stevedores' promise to unload – to which they were not previously entitled.

Intention to create legal relations

Of the three requirements for a binding contract, intention to create legal relations is clearly the most recently developed and the least practically important. The reason for this is simple. In the English system, most of the trivial agreements which would otherwise be excluded by this requirement are already excluded by the need for something bargained in exchange under the doctrine of consideration. The requirement only comes into play when there is consideration, but nevertheless, it is desired to argue that the agreement is not a contract. In practice this is relatively unusual.

When we talk about intention to create legal relations, it is important to bear in mind that in the law of contract 'intention' is objectively ascertained. So the question is not what the individual parties intended (unless they have made this clear), but whether the court thinks the transaction is of a kind which the reasonable man would have intended to be binding. This is brought out by the decision of the House of Lords in *Esso Petroleum v Customs and Excise Comrs* (1976). Esso launched a marketing scheme which involved producing millions of 'coins' bearing the head and shoulders of the members of the England 1970 world cup squad. Motorists were told by television advertisements and by posters at filling stations that they would receive a 'coin' for each four gallons of Esso petrol which they bought. For tax reasons, it became necessary to decide the legal position of a customer who bought four gallons. Did he have a contractual right to a 'coin'? Obviously the transaction was trivial and it was very unlikely that the average motorist sought to analyse the legal effect of the transaction. Equally, it was not likely that the motorist who was told that coins had temporarily run out would resort to litigation. Nevertheless, the majority of the House of Lords thought that the commitment to provide a coin for every four gallons was legally binding. This decision reflects the earlier refusal of the Court of Appeal in *Carlill v Carbolic Smoke Ball Co* (1893) to accept the argument of the promoters of the Smoke Ball that their advertisements were not intended to be taken seriously.

The position is different if the parties expressly agree that their agreement is not to be legally binding. It has been clear since *Rose and Frank Co v JR Crompton & Bros Ltd* (1923) that such an agreement is effective to deprive what would otherwise be a binding contract of legal effect.

In principle, what can be expressly agreed can be implied, but in practice, courts have been reluctant to infer that legal relations are not intended outside the field of family and social relationships. Within this field, it is clear that many agreements between husband and wife are not binding. The leading example is *Balfour v Balfour* (1919), where it was held by the Court of Appeal that a promise by a husband to pay his wife a monthly allowance while they were living apart owing to his wife's inability to return to Ceylon with him after a period of leave was not binding. Similar arguments have been adopted between parent and child as, for example, in *Jones v Padavatton* (1969), where the mother's promise to support a daughter while she was studying for the Bar was held not binding. Even within the family, it is certainly not the case that agreements are never treated as legally binding. This is most obviously the case where a marriage is breaking up and it may be expected that husband and wife will negotiate at arms length. So in *Merritt v Merritt* (1970), an agreement by a husband to transfer his share of the family home to the wife, made after he had left home to live with another woman, was held binding. Viewed from the prospective of today rather than 1919, *Balfour v Balfour* looks close to this line on its facts. Even where an agreement between husband and wife is not legally binding, it may not be without legal consequences. In modern marriages where both partners are working, it is very likely that agreements will be made as to whose pay is to be used for household expenses and whose to pay the mortgage. Such arrangements would usually not be binding, but in *Pettitt v Pettitt* (1970), their performance was held by the House of Lords to be capable of effecting the rights of husband and wife in the matrimonial home.

The one situation with a commercial flavour where intention to create legal relations has been denied by English law is a collective labour agreement, that is an agreement between an employer or a group of employers and a union or a group of unions. Such agreements are legally binding in most legal systems, but in *Ford Motor Co Ltd v AUEFW* (1969), Geoffrey Lane J held that such an agreement was not intended to be legally binding. This decision was based primarily on evidence from experts in labour relations that such was the suspicion among trade unionists of law and lawyers, that they would not wish such agreements to be legally binding (although collective bargaining does affect the terms of individual contracts of employment which are undoubtedly legally binding). This decision was reversed by the Industrial Relations Act 1971, section 34(1) but that was reversed in its turn by the Trade Union and Labour Relations

Act 1974, section 18, which provides that collective agreements are presumed not to be intended to be legally binding unless they expressly state that they are intended to be binding.

Privity of contract

Statement of doctrine

Even where there is a contract, questions may arise as to who has rights and duties under it. In principle, English law has a very simple answer to this question; contracts give rights to, and impose duties upon, contracting parties and no-one else. This is the result of the doctrine of privity of contract and its doppelganger, the rule that consideration must move from the promisee.

This result seems to flow naturally from what contract is about – the regulation by parties of the relationships between them, and a similar result was adopted by classical Roman law and by the Code Napoleon. Nevertheless, in modern economic conditions the rule has been found strikingly inconvenient and it has been abandoned both by French law and by the version of the common law that prevails in the United States.

The critical problem arises when one of the parties' aims is to create contractual rights in someone who is not a party. It is against this that English law has so far set its face. So in *Tweddle v Atkinson* (1861), the father of the plaintiff made a contract with the father of the plaintiff's bride-to-be that each of them would pay money to the plaintiff. The contract expressly provided that the plaintiff was to be entitled to enforce it, but the court held that the plaintiff had no right to do so. Similarly in *Dunlop Pneumatic Tyre Co v Selfridge & Co* (1915), a contract between Dunlop, a manufacturer of tyres, and Dew, a wholesaler, had a clause requiring Dew to have a clause in their contract with retailers requiring the retailer not to sell below list price. Dew duly inserted such a clause in the contract which they made on selling tyres to Selfridge, who were then found to be selling tyres below list price. The House of Lords held that although this clause was inserted entirely for the benefit of Dunlop and in pursuance of Dew's contractual obligations to Dunlop, Dunlop could not bring an action to enforce it.

Dunlop v Selfridge illustrates another important aspect of the doctrine. Even when we have a series of contracts which are closely linked economically, we are required to treat them as legally separate and distinct. *Dunlop v Selfridge* was concerned with the chain of distribution – manufacturer, wholesaler, retailer and customer. The doctrine of privity of contract imposes a pyramidal or hierarchic form upon such relationships so that there are contracts only between the adjoining parties. Normally (apart from unusual cases such as *Carlill v Carbolic Smoke Ball*) there will be no contract between customer and manufacturer, and if the goods are defective, there will be no contract claim against the manufacturer. The customer may well have a contract claim against the retailer and the retailer may in turn have a contract claim against the wholesaler who may have a contract claim against the manufacturer. So by this process the claim may be shunted up the line to the manufacturer, though the claim may fall off the rails because the terms of the contract between manufacturer and wholesaler are different from those between customer and retailer, or because as in *Lexmead (Basingstoke) Ltd v Lewis* (1982), the retailer cannot remember from which wholesaler he bought the goods though he knows the name of the manufacturer.

A similar hierarchical analysis applies in the arrangements which are typically made for the handling of construction projects of any size. A main contractor is engaged for the work, but he will usually sub-contract large parts, and often sub-contractors will in turn sub-subcontract. There will normally be no contractual relationship between customer and sub-contractor, or between contractor and sub-subcontractor. So the customer will not usually be able to sue the sub-contractor in contract for bad work, or the sub-contractor sue the customer because he has not been paid; again claims must usually be shunted through the contractor. Most of the time this simply makes life a little more complicated, but it has very important practical results if the contractor becomes insolvent. Can you see why?

Three general points may be made here. The first is that the doctrine of privity of contract only bars contract claims; in many cases a plaintiff may have a tort claim. So if the goods are defective, the customer may be able to sue the manufacturer in tort, but often he will have to prove that the goods are not only defective but that the manufacturer was negligent. (This is discussed more fully in Chapter 26.)

Second, it is important to see that in the construction example, the main contractor does not escape liability by subcontracting. This is because he will usually have undertaken that the building will be correctly built and so if the sub-contractor does his work badly, this would usually be a breach not only of the sub-contractor's contract with the main contractor, but of the main contractor's contract with the customer. This is an illustration of the principle that although one can usually delegate performance of one's contractual obligations, one cannot transfer (assign) the duty to perform them. (There are some contracts where personal performance is so important that even to delegate performance is not permitted. A good example would be the contract to write this book which called for personal performance by the authors.)

A third point is that the combined effect of the doctrines of consideration and privity is not only to bar certain kinds of claim but to shape our very concept of a contract. So in some systems of law the banker's reference given in *Hedley Byrne & Co Ltd v Heller & Partners* (1964) (see p 441)

would be thought to give rise to a contract claim, but an English lawyer
would tend to classify this situation as tortious without a second thought.

Some exceptions to privity of contract

LAND LAW

On the border between land law and contract, the doctrine of privity has
proved so inconvenient that it has been subjected to major exceptions.
Suppose X sells off a plot of land at the bottom of his garden to Y so that
Y can build a bungalow there. It would be prudent for X to require Y to
promise not to build a factory there instead, as this would obviously affect
the value and amenities of X's house. X will want to be sure, however,
that the promise is binding not only on Y, but on anyone who buys from
Y and so on; similarly, it is desirable that the promise is enforceable not
only by X, but to anyone to whom X sells his house. In fact, such *restrictive
covenants* (that is covenants not to do something) are enforceable by and
against succeeding owners providing they are registered in the land
register.

In the same way, the covenants made in a lease between lessor and
lessee are enforceable by and against successive lessors and lessees
provided the covenant is one which concerns the property and is not of a
purely personal nature. There is much technical learning outside the scope
of this book as to details of these rules which are partly the product of
common law and partly of statute.

TRUSTS

If I am the owner of Blackacre, I can declare that I hold it on trust for X,
or I can transfer it to A to hold on trust for X. X's rights depend on the
equitable rules governing the creation of trusts and clearly do not depend
on any form of contract. Any form of property can be the subject of a trust,
including rights under a contract which are themselves a form of property.
So under the contract for the writing of this book, the authors are entitled
to royalties on the sales. One of the authors could declare himself a trustee
of the royalties to which he was to become entitled for the benefit of X
(for the sake of completeness it should be said that he could also transfer
(assign) this right outright to X). No special form of words is needed to
create a trust, and at one time it looked as if a number of cases had
established that a court could, in appropriate cases, hold that where a
contract was made for the benefit of the third party, a constructive trust
came into existence under which one party to the contract held his contract
rights in trust for the beneficiary: *Tomlinson v Gill* (1756); *Gregory and
Parker v Williams* (1817); *Lloyds v Harper* (1880); *Walford's Case* (1919).

However, from the mid 1930s onwards, the courts, for reasons which are still not entirely clear, have retreated from this position: *Vandepitte v Preferred Accident Insurance Corpn of New York* (1933); *Re Schebsman* (1944); *Green v Russell* (1959). The position now seems to be that although it is still possible expressly to create a trust of a promise, the court will only imply such a trust in some wholly exceptional case.

OTHER PROPERTY TRANSACTIONS

These doctrines operate at the difficult margin between the law of contract and the law of property, made more obscure for present purposes by the fact that the law of property is outside the scope of this book. It has been the subject of long, and still unresolved, controversy whether similar rules can be applied to property other than land. Suppose A, the owner of a ship, charters (hires) it to B for two years and then sells it to C, who knows of the contract. Is C bound to respect the contract? The Privy Council thought so in *Lord Strathcona SS Co v Dominion Coal Co* (1926), a decision regarded as incomprehensible and wrong by Diplock J in *Port Line Ltd v Ben Lin Steamers Ltd* (1958) but as correct by Browne-Wilkinson J in *Swiss Bank Corpn v Lloyds Bank Ltd* (1979).

INSURANCE

Insurance is an area where the privity doctrine creates substantial difficulty, since there are many situations where one person may legitimately wish to take out an insurance policy for the benefit of another. An important exception created at common law was that a carrier might properly insure the whole value of the goods he carries and not merely his own interest in them. It is obviously commercially convenient that there should be a single contract to cover all the goods rather than require all the goods' owners to take out separate policies (of course if the goods are all lost or damaged, the carrier has to account to the goods' owner for what he receives from the insurers).

By statute it has been provided that a husband or wife may take out a life insurance policy for the benefit of the other or of the children (Married Women's Property Act 1882, section 11), and that the owner of a car may take out a policy which covers other people driving the car with his consent (Road Traffic Act 1972, section 148(4)), a result which the Privy Council held not achievable by use of the trust concept in *Vandepitte's* case (above p 480).

ENFORCEMENT BY THE OTHER CONTRACTING PARTY

The doctrine of privity of contract does not forbid the making of promises for the benefit of a third party, but simply refuses to help the third party enforce the promise. So if A promises B to do something for C and fails to do so, he has broken his contract with B and in some circumstances B may have an effective remedy. This was clearly shown in *Beswick v Beswick* (1968), where Peter Beswick sold his coal merchant's business to his nephew John, in return for John's promise to pay Peter £6 and 10 shillings a week for the rest of Peter's life, and to pay Peter's widow £5 a week during her life after Peter's death if Peter died before her. John kept his promise during Peter's life but after Peter's death, he paid only one instalment and refused to pay any more. He did not offer to return the coal merchant's business or any part of it! The House of Lords held that the widow had no personal right to enforce the promise as she did not fall within any of the exceptions to the doctrine. However, they held that the promise could be enforced by Peter's estate, of which his widow was administratrix, and that suing on behalf of the estate, the widow could obtain specific performance of the contract. (See Chapter 23.)

A major problem in this respect is that specific performance is often not an available or appropriate remedy. The most common remedy for breach of contract is an action for damages and usually the plaintiff recovers only the damage that he (the plaintiff) has suffered. In many cases, it will be the third party and not the plaintiff that suffers the loss. This was said not to be a difficulty by Lord Denning in *Jackson v Horizon Holidays* (1975), where the plaintiff booked an expensive and disastrous holiday in Ceylon for himself, his wife and two children and was awarded damages to compensate him for the loss that his family had suffered as well as his own. In the later case of *Woodar Investment Development Ltd v Wimpey Construction (UK) Ltd* (1980), the House of Lords said that Lord Denning's reasoning was wrong though the decision in *Jackson* could perhaps be justified on other grounds. The same view was taken by the House of Lords in *The Albazero* (1977).

However, it is now clear that the position is not so simple. In *St Martins Property Corpn Ltd v Sir Robert McAlpine Ltd* (1994), the two plaintiffs were associated companies both of which were part of the Kuwait financial empire. For simplicity, we will call them *St Martins 1* and *St Martins 2*. *St Martins 1* entered into a building contract with the defendants for a major shopping development project. Shortly after doing so, they purported to assign the contract to *St Martins 2*. This assignment was ineffective because, as the House of Lords held, it was prohibited by the terms of the building contract. In due course, after the work had been finished and paid for, it was alleged that some £800,000 worth of defects had been discovered. Both plaintiffs sued. The trial judge held that *St Martins 1* could not sue because it had not suffered loss since the building belonged to *St Martins 2* and that *St Martins 2* could not sue because the purported assignment to it was invalid. The House of Lords agreed with the second view but not with the first. It held that *St Martins 1* could recover the cost of remedying the building work even though this was a loss which in fact was suffered by *St Martins 2*. The distinction between this case and the early cases appears to be related to the nature of the contract. It was always foreseeable that the building might be transferred to a later owner and that he would be damaged if it was defective. In the circumstances, it was appropriate to allow the original contracting party to recover damages for the benefit of those who suffered from defective performance. This reasoning was followed and somewhat extended by the Court of Appeal in *Darlington Borough Council v Wiltshier Northern Ltd* (1995). In this case, the plaintiff local authority wished to build a new recreational centre. Because of government restrictions on local authority borrowing, this was arranged by a complex transaction in which a subsidiary of the merchant banker Morgan Grenfell entered into the building contract with the defendant contractors for the erection of the building. It was always intended by all parties that the building and the benefit of the building contract would in due course be transferred to the plaintiffs. In due course this happened and then it was alleged that the building was defective. It was accepted by both sides that, as the plaintiffs were suing on the contract originally made by Morgan Grenfell and assigned to them, they could be in no better position than Morgan Grenfell would have been if they had kept the building. The defendants argued that Morgan Grenfell had never suffered any loss because it was never intended that they would have use of the building and they had never accepted any responsibility for the condition of the building towards the plaintiffs. Nevertheless, the Court of Appeal held that, in the circumstances, Morgan Grenfell could have recovered damages for defects in the building which reflected the full damage and not merely their own loss and that therefore the plaintiffs were in the same position.

Agency

It is common to talk as if contracts were always made between individuals. In practice, however, one party, at least, to the contract is usually a corporate body – a company, a nationalised industry, a local authority or the Crown. Such bodies have of necessity to operate through human beings who act as their agents. It is necessary therefore to say something here about the law of agency.

The law of agency has a cast of three characters: P, the principal; A, the agent; and T, the third party with whom A deals on P's behalf. We are concerned here only with the way in which A can create a contract between P and T. The usual effect of this will be that P and T have a contract and that A drops out of the picture. There will usually (except where A acts gratuitously) be a contract between P and A, but we will say nothing of this or of the ways in which A can make P liable in other areas of law.

WHO IS AN AGENT?

It is important to understand that the word agent is used more narrowly in the law of contract than in commerce. So a car dealer might well describe himself as a Ford Agent, but in the eyes of the law of contract, he would not be an agent at all because he is selling cars on his own behalf and not on behalf of Ford. For present purposes, the essence of an agent is that he acts on behalf of his principal and not on his own behalf. Even so, it may be very difficult to tell in particular cases whether someone is an agent or not. A good example is the case of *Financings v Stimson* (discussed at p 468), where the Court of Appeal were divided as to whether a car dealer was the agent of a finance company, a question which also divided the House of Lords in *Branwhite v Worcester Works Finance* (1969).

In other cases, it may be clear that A is an agent but unclear who is his principal. Take the case of an insurance broker procuring a policy of motor insurance. Clearly he is an agent and his activities usually produce a contract between insurer and insured. But is he an agent for the insurer or insured? This may be important for various reasons. Suppose he issues a cover note – is the insurer bound? Suppose the insured tells him about an accident he had last year and the broker does not pass this information on to the insurer. Suppose the insured pays the premium to the broker who disappears with this and other motorists' premiums. In all these cases, the legal analysis depends on whether the broker acts for one side or the other, but the cases give a confusing and indecisive answer to this question.

THE AUTHORITY OF THE AGENT

The basic principle is that the agent binds his principal so long as he acts within the course of his authority. This principle is wider than it looks, however, because of the meaning which has been given to the concept of authority. Authority may be either actual or apparent. Actual authority is what the agent has actually been authorised to do, but this again is wider than it looks since it is treated as including not only express authority, what the agent has been expressly authorised to do, but implied authority, that is what the law regards as implicit in what he has been expressly authorised to do. In practice, this will turn as much on how the law has treated similar transactions in the past as on the intention of the particular parties. So cases have decided that a solicitor engaged by the seller of a house to conduct the conveyancing, has implied authority to accept a deposit, whereas an estate agent does not. This does not depend at all on what the particular principal and agent have in mind except that it would be open to them to agree something else.

Apparent (or ostensible) authority consists of the authority which the agent appears to have. Clearly this has some degree of overlap with implied authority, since an agent will appear to have the authority which an agent of his kind would usually have been implicitly given. This is well illustrated by *Waugh HB v Clifford & Sons Ltd* (1982), where a firm of solicitors was engaged to carry on litigation. It is well settled that a solicitor so engaged has implied authority to settle the litigation (that is, to negotiate a compromise with the other side), but in this case, P had told A not to settle without reference to him. This instruction was not, of course, known to the other side. A vital message went astray in A's office and A accepted an offer of settlement from the other side which he had been told not to accept. The Court of Appeal held that A's implied authority had been terminated, but P was bound because A still had apparent authority.

A may have apparent authority either because he is doing something which an agent in his position would usually be authorised to do, or because he has been held out by P as having authority to act in a particular way. So in the leading case of *Freeman and Lockyer v Buckhurst Park Properties (Mangal) Ltd* (1964), the company allowed someone who had never been appointed as its managing director to act as if he were, and the Court of Appeal held that it was as bound by his acts as it would have been if he had been its managing director.

RATIFICATION

If A makes a contract outside his actual authority but within his apparent authority, P is bound by the contract but he is not entitled to enforce it. However, it is open to P to ratify a contract made by A outside his actual (or even outside his apparent) authority, provided that A was purporting to act on behalf of P at the time he made the contract and that P was competent to make the contract at that time. This latter requirement has given rise to difficulty where A purports to act on behalf of a company about to be, but not yet formed. In such cases, it was held at common law that the company could not ratify it, but under section 9(2) of the European Communities Act 1972 (now the Companies Act 1985, section 361(4)), A will be liable on the contract personally unless it was expressly agreed in the contract that he was not to be.

UNDISCLOSED PRINCIPALS

In the most common case, A will make it clear who his principal is. There are many commercial situations, however, where it is clear that A is acting as an agent, but the identity of the principal is not revealed. This is particularly likely where A is buying and selling on behalf of P. It may suit P to keep his identity concealed; it may also suit A since he may be worried that otherwise T will deal direct with P. It is also possible that A is in fact acting as an agent, but behaves as if he is contracting as a principal. English law has (unlike many other systems) permitted P to come into this contract and enforce it, even though T had no idea that he was dealing with P and not with A. Many writers have thought this doctrine of the undisclosed principal anomalous (particularly in view of the strictness of the doctrine of privity) but it is well established.

The doctrine is, however, subject to certain limitations. Since T thought he was dealing with A, he is allowed to choose whether he will enforce the contract against P or against A and his choice will not finally bind until he has obtained a judgment against one of them. There may be cases where it is so clear that T would not have contracted with P, that P will not be allowed to take over the contract, *Said v Butt* (1920). It is not possible to add together the doctrines of ratification and undisclosed principal, so if A, while acting as agent for P but without disclosing that he is an agent, makes a contract with T which is outside his actual authority, P cannot ratify it, *Keighley, Maxsted and Co v Durant* (1901).

WARRANTY OF AUTHORITY

A may purport to make a contract on behalf of P when he thinks that he has authority, but in fact he has neither actual nor apparent authority. Does T have any remedy on such facts? It was held in *Collen v Wright* (1857), that on such facts, it may be possible to hold that A has contracted with T that he does have authority. The same result can be reached where A had authority but his authority has been terminated, as in *Yonge v Toynbee* (1910), where unknown to A, P had become insane. (It being held that insanity automatically terminates agency even if unknown to the agent.)

Chapter 22

Discovering what the contract is

This chapter is concerned with the process of analysing what the parties have agreed. This process cannot be separated completely from the process of discovering whether there is a contract at all, since if we cannot tell what the contract is with adequate certainty there will be no contract. Nevertheless, for purposes of exposition it is convenient to take the two questions separately.

The primary question to answer is what are the terms of the contract? However, many things which are said during negotiations may be classified as not being terms of the contract, but legal effect may be given to them under the rules relating to misrepresentation. It is also desirable to consider at this point the rules about situations where the parties' agreement is based upon some shared but erroneous assumption (common mistake), or where it is overtaken by some unexpected cataclysmic event (frustration), since the solution to these problems lies largely in an analysis of what precisely the parties have agreed and how they have allocated the risks between them.

Terms of the contract

Express terms

The terms of the contract may be either expressly agreed or implied by the courts. There is no difference in effect between express and implied terms; the distinction relates simply to the historical process by which the term became part of the contract.

It might be thought a simple question, apart from evidential disputes, what the parties have expressly agreed, but English law has succeeded in making it much more complex than it needs to be. There are a number of reasons for this. One is the division of function between judge and jury, which obtained when contract disputes were tried by juries and which still affects the shape of the law. Under this, judges held that the effect of written documents was a question of law and, therefore, a matter for them, while what had been said was a matter for the jury. The second factor was the so-called parol evidence rule, which for a long time was thought seriously to restrict reliance on oral undertakings which qualified or contradicted written documents.

The simplest situation is where there is nothing in writing and the whole negotiations have been conducted orally (using the word oral widely to include conduct). It is then necessary to decide what was said, but that does not conclude matters since the court may decide that what was said was not intended by the parties to be a term of the contract. The test of what the parties intended is not one which is easy to apply to the sort of informal, unstructured negotiation which is likely to precede an oral contract, and the cases are, therefore, not easy to reconcile. A striking example is *Oscar Chess Ltd v Williams* (1957), where the majority of the Court of Appeal held that a statement by the seller of a car that it was a 1948 Morris was not a term of the contract. The car was in fact a 1939 Morris, and the seller had received a 1948 trade-in price rather than the lower 1939 trade-in price against his new car. It was clear that the seller was honest (the log book had been altered by a previous owner) and the majority were much influenced by this and by the fact that he had no relevant expertise in dating cars. These arguments seem nicely balanced against the minority view that the date was a very important matter and that because of his assertion, the seller had got a better price.

Quite often, the contract is the product of a combination of oral conversations and the attempts by one party to incorporate terms by reference to a notice or a ticket. In such cases, the notice or ticket must appear before the contract was concluded and in such circumstances as to give reasonable notice of the terms (*Parker v South Eastern Rly Co* (1877)). This test has usually been applied in a way rather indulgent to the ticket giver. So in many railway cases it has been held sufficient that the booking clerk delivered the ticket bearing the magic words 'for conditions see back', and that the reverse of the ticket bore the words 'for conditions see company's timetable' – the timetable containing some hundreds of pages of densely printed conditions. In practice, it is clear that very few passengers would be aware of the conditions in such cases – probably the decisions rest in part on the fact that the railways seldom, if ever, had conditions which would have surprised lawyers!

The unusualness of the terms (to the lawyer's eyes) played a part in *Thornton v Shoe Lane Parking Ltd* (1971), where the ticket produced by an automatic car park barrier referred to conditions displayed inside the car park. The conditions in fact purported to exclude liability, not only for damaged cars (usual) but also for damage to drivers (unusual). It was held that in the circumstances reasonable notice had not been given. In this case, the clause was one which sought to exempt liability but the Court of Appeal in *Interfoto Picture Library Ltd v Stiletto Visual Programmes Ltd* (1989) held that the doctrine that surprising terms required extra efforts to communicate them to the other party was of general application. In that case, the plaintiffs had lent photo transparencies to the defendants under their general conditions which provided for a rent free loan period of 14 days, followed by a charge of £5 per transparency per day thereafter. This was regarded by the Court of Appeal as requiring a special notice. Since there is nothing surprising about the notion of having to pay something for having to return photos late, it seems that what was surprising was the large amount of the charge. This illustrates a general point that whether a term is surprising may require inquiry into what is normal in a particular trade or locality.

These problems about notice do not apply where there is a written contract (which includes typewritten or printed) signed by the parties, since it has been held that a person who signs a contract cannot complain that he signed it without reading it, unless he was induced to sign it by misrepresentation as to its contents (*L'Estrange v Graucob* (1934)). If there is a written contract, the parties cannot give evidence of what they understood it to mean, since its meaning is a question of law on which their views are of no interest! Further, evidence of the pre-contract negotiations cannot be given to explain what the contract means, as opposed to establishing that there is a contract. In the same way, evidence of how the contract has been operated in practice is excluded if its purpose is to explain the contract rather than show that the parties have agreed to change it. This rigorous exclusion of evidence which many people (and other legal systems) might think relevant can be seen as a logical application of the objective view of contract, that what the parties have agreed to is whatever the court holds their written words to mean.

For much of the nineteenth century, it was thought that the parole evidence rule went further, and excluded pre-contract dealings which qualified the written words. It is now clear, however, that the courts have escaped from this cul-de-sac by developing two alternative options. It is permissible to argue that what looks like a written contract is in fact a contract partly in writing and partly oral. Alternatively, it is possible to argue that there are two contracts, one written and one oral, and that the oral contract qualifies or even contradicts the written one. Both of these approaches were applied by different members of the Court of Appeal in *J Evans & Son (Portsmouth) Ltd v Andrea Merzario Ltd* (1976). In this case the plaintiffs, an engineering firm in Portsmouth, were in the habit of importing machinery from the continent. For this purpose they employed the services of the defendants, a firm of forwarding agents (that is, specialists in arranging for the carriage of other people's goods). Business had always been done on the defendant's standard conditions. In 1967, the defendant's decided to switch their business largely to containers. This was discussed with the plaintiffs who agreed, subject to an assurance, that their goods would be carried below deck. (Far more of the cargo is carried above the deck line in a container ship than in an old fashioned cargo ship with holds.) Numerous transactions followed, all on the defendant's revised standard conditions, which purported to permit carriage above deck. In due course, a container containing goods being imported for the plaintiffs was lost when it slid overboard. The Court of Appeal held that the plaintiffs could recover on the basis of the oral assurance that their goods would be carried below deck. It will be seen that this oral assurance continued to regulate the relations between the parties, despite the many transactions which had intervened and the repeated use of formal written conditions.

Implied terms

It would be impossibly demanding of resources if every contract were carefully and explicitly negotiated down to the last detail. Only a few very important contracts receive this Rolls Royce treatment; most come off the production line. The two great organs of mass production are the standard form contract and the implied term.

The implied term is one of the major techniques developed by English law for filling in gaps in the contract making process. Terms may be implied on a number of different theories. It may be possible to show that the term should be implied by *custom* as in *Hutton v Warren* (1836). This involves demonstrating that the contract was made in a particular trade or locality, and that it was clearly understood in that trade or locality that all transactions were subject to certain implicit terms unless expressly excluded. A good example is transactions on the Stock Exchange, where what is said is, because of pressure of time, very brief, but where transactions are subject to customs of Stock Exchange, which have been elaborated over many years.

It is increasingly common for Parliament to provide by *statute* the terms to be implied. So Parliament may provide that it is an implied term in certain kinds of lease that the landlord should do the repairs. Parliament might have simply provided that the landlord should do the repairs; to do so by means of an implied term means that the tenant is given a contractual remedy. The decision to adopt the implied term technique has important consequences, therefore, for the way in which the right is enforced.

Some statutes have simply given legislative form to the work of the courts. A good example is the Sale of Goods Act of 1893 (now replaced by the Sale of Goods Act 1979), which was intended by its draftsman to be a statutory statement of the common law of the sale of goods as it had developed by 1893. Under this statute there are, for instance, implied terms which lay down the seller's obligations as to the transfer of ownership and as to the quality of the goods (this is discussed more fully in Chapter 26). Similar terms are implied in hire-purchase contracts by the Supply of Goods (Implied Terms) Act 1973 and in other contracts under which goods are supplied by the Supply of Goods and Services Act 1982. So in everyday simple transactions in a shop or supermarket, there are implied terms as to the quality of the goods and so on.

Apart from custom and statute, the court may imply a term on general common law principles. In recent years it has been recognised that there are really two different processes at work here. In one, the court is building up a body of rules which are applicable to contracts of a particular type, say employment. Terms developed by this process will be implied in all contracts of employment unless they are expressly excluded, but are effectively independent of the particular contract makers. So by this process, the courts have held that it is an implied term of the contract of employment that an employer takes reasonable care to provide a reasonably safe system of work and there are many cases working out in detail what this involves.

The leading modern example of this kind of implication is *Liverpool City Council v Irwin* (1977). In this case, the defendants were tenants of a maisonette in a high-rise council block in Liverpool. The council had allowed them into possession and handed them a copy of the council rules for tenants. The block was persistently and successfully vandalised so that the lifts seldom worked, the stairs were unlit, and the rubbish chutes were inoperative. The defendants withheld payments of rent claiming that the council were in breach of contract. The council argued that it had no obligations at all as there were no express or implied terms. This argument succeeded in the Court of Appeal (Lord Denning dissenting), but was rejected by the House of Lords. All their lordships thought that a landlord who let property of this kind must be under an implied obligation of some sort to provide access and so on. However, their lordships thought that the appropriate implied term was one which required the landlord to take reasonable steps, which the council had in fact done.

Alternatively, the court may look at a particular contract and decide that a term must be implied into it to give it business efficacy as was said in *The Moorcock* (1889). In practice, this is a much more restricted process, since courts have repeatedly said that terms must only be implied when it is necessary to do so to make the contract work: it is not sufficient that to imply a term would improve the contract.

In principle, implied terms should not be implied where they are inconsistent with express terms. However, in modern times Parliament has often provided that implied terms are mandatory, that is that the parties are not free to exclude them. A good example is sections 12, 13, 14 and 15 of the Sale of Goods Act 1979 which cannot be excluded in consumer sales, so that all consumers get the benefit of implied undertakings as to title and quality of the goods. This is an important measure of consumer protection.

Even where there is no prohibition on exclusion, they will be difficult questions as to whether the express and implied terms are in fact inconsistent. A good example is *Johnstone v Bloomsbury Health Authority* (1991). In this case the plaintiff, a junior hospital doctor, sued his employer alleging that the employer was in breach of the implied obligation to take reasonable care to provide a reasonably safe system of work. He alleged that the employer had been requiring him to work such long hours that his health was threatened. There is no doubt that such a term is normally to be implied but the employer argued that, as far as working hours were concerned, it would be inconsistent with the express terms of the contract of employment, which provided that the plaintiff should work 40 hours every week and an average of 48 hours overtime. One judge in the Court of Appeal agreed that this express term excluded the implied term, as far as it extended to working hours but the majority disagreed. The two judges in the majority gave different reasons. The best explanation of the majority judgment is that the express and implied terms were not necessarily inconsistent. The court was ruling at a preliminary stage when the precise working practices had not been investigated. It was therefore possible that the express term as to working hours could be qualified by implied terms which restricted the way in which the employer could require the overtime to be worked. Many professional people, who control their own lives, commonly work 80 or 90 hours a week in some weeks but they usually make sure to have time for adequate amounts of sleep and recreation. The implied term might have permitted some such working practices but prevented the employer from requiring the plaintiff to work 168 hours every fourth week, which would clearly have been damaging to his health.

Relative importance of terms

Until 1962, most contract lawyers would have said that there were two types of contract terms: conditions and warranties. Conditions were the more important terms, and breach of condition entitled the injured party to terminate the contract and to sue for damages. Warranties were less important terms, and the remedy for breach of warranty was only an action for damages.

This distinction was not without difficulties. As is often the case with English law, the terminology was not consistently used. In contracts of insurance, the word warranty was used to mean an important term; in other situations it was used to mean guarantee. The word condition was used in even more senses. One in particular demands discussion here before we carry the story beyond 1962. That is the use of 'condition' to mean something upon which the contract is dependent. This usage has been known at least since Roman law, and the same usage will be familiar to many readers of this book who may have received offers by universities of places conditional on getting specified grades at 'A' level. In this situation, the candidate does not contract to get particular grades, but if he obtains them, the conditional offer becomes absolute and the university is bound to honour its offer. Similarly, once the offer has been made, it cannot be withdrawn until it is clear that the condition will not be met.

The condition may operate in a number of ways. It may be such that the contract does not come into existence until the condition comes about, as in *Pym v Campbell* (1856), where the contract was conditional on an invention being approved by a named third party. Alternatively, there may be a contract, but one party may not be obliged to perform one of his obligations until the other has performed his. So in a contract of sale where the seller has agreed to give credit, we can say that the buyer's duty to pay is conditional on the seller's delivery of the goods, and it would be a breach of contract for the seller to demand payment on delivery. Another possibility would be that the contract was subject to a condition which would bring the contract to an end. Although clearly recognised as permissible, this seems a very unusual type of clause in reality. In all cases it is necessary that the condition is expressed with sufficient certainty, so that the court would know whether it has come about. This has been a fertile source of disputes where there is a contract to sell land subject to the buyer obtaining a satisfactory mortgage. Some courts have held such conditions adequately certain; others have not.

Let us return to 1962. In that year the Court of Appeal decided the *Hong Kong Fir* case. In this case the defendants had chartered a ship from the plaintiffs. It was a term of the contract that the ship was seaworthy. In fact the ship was unseaworthy, owing to the combination of an ancient engine room and a less than first class engine room staff. This led to repeated breakdowns and the ship was frequently in port for repairs. This was undoubtedly a breach of contract and the defendants would have been entitled to bring an action for damages; instead they elected to terminate the contract. The plaintiffs claimed that although they (the plaintiffs) were in breach of contract, the breach was not one which entitled the defendants to terminate, and that, therefore, the defendants had repudiated the contract by a wrongful termination.

The traditional way to answer this question would have been to ask whether the term as to seaworthiness was a condition or a warranty. In fact one judge did this and held that the term was a warranty. However, in an historic judgment, Diplock LJ said that two-fold analysis into conditions and warranties was incomplete, and that there were intermediate terms (now often called innominate terms, terms without a name) where the effect of breach depended on the importance of the breach. He thought the term as to seaworthiness was such a term because it could be broken in a wide variety of ways and with a wide variety of effects. On the particular facts of the case, he thought that the breaches were not such as to entitle the defendant to terminate the contract.

This was undoubtedly an historic judgment. However, as with many historic judgments, it took time for it to be absorbed into the law. For a time, there were those who thought that investigation of the importance of the breach had supplanted characterisation of the importance of the terms. It is now clear that this is wrong and that what is called for is a two-fold approach. If a contract is broken and one party claims to be entitled to terminate, the first question to ask is whether the term broken is a condition. This question may receive an affirmative answer for a variety of reasons. The term may be characterised as a condition by a statute, as in the Sale of Goods Act. The same term may have been characterised as a condition by previous cases. So in *The Mihalis Angelos* (1971), a charterparty provided that a ship was 'expected ready to load . . . about 1 July 1965'. The Court of Appeal held that although arrival by 1 July was clearly not a condition, it was a condition that at the time of the contract the ship owner expected the ship to arrive by 1 July; if, as was the case, he knew of facts which made it certain that the ship would not arrive by 1 July, this was a breach of condition. In coming to this conclusion, the court relied heavily on the fact that in previous cases involving sale of goods, such undertakings had been construed as conditions.

Another possibility is that the court may see the undertaking as very important because of the way it falls in with the other obligations in the contract. A good example is *Bunge Corpn v Tradax SA* (1981). In this case the seller had to ship the goods during June 1975 (this was certainly a condition). The buyer had to give 15 days' notice of the readiness of the vessel but only gave notice on 17 June. Clearly the seller might have been able to complete his obligation to load in 13 days rather than 15, but the House of Lords held that as the seller's obligation to load in time was certainly a condition, so that the buyer could terminate if loading was not completed until 1 July, it necessarily followed that the buyer's obligation to give notice was a condition since it would be unfair to deprive the seller of his full period of notice in the context of a contract of this kind.

Finally, the parties may expressly agree that an obligation is a condition. In a document drafted by a lawyer the use of the word condition would usually have this effect, as would any expression indicating that the obligation was 'fundamental', 'went to the root of the contract', 'was of the essence' and so on.

If the court decides that the term which is broken is not a condition, the injured party may still be entitled to terminate because the contract has been broken in a very important way. This is discussed more fully in Chapter 23.

Misrepresentation

The nature of misrepresentation

We have seen that a quite important statement made by one party to the contract may be characterised by the court as not being a term of the contract. So, in *Oscar Chess Ltd v Williams* (above, p 488), the statement that the car was a 1948 model clearly and directly affected the price which was offered for it. Although such statements are not terms of the contract, they may nevertheless give rise to liability as misrepresentations. This is because the common law of contract has been supplemented in this area by an amalgam of rules, drawn partly from the law of tort and partly from equity and now supplemented by the Misrepresentation Act 1967. The result is very untidy and confusing. We need to consider three problems here – what is a representation? What kinds of misrepresentation are there and what are the remedies for misrepresentation?

For present purposes, a representation may be defined as a statement of fact made by one party to the contract to the other party, which while not a term of the contract, induces the other party to enter the contract and which turns out to be untrue.

In principle, the terms of a contract are not statements of fact but promises. Promises may be, and often are, about future actions – I will pay you £2,000; I will deliver this car to you tomorrow; but they may also be promises about present or past facts – I promise you that this car is a 1984 model and it has only done 50,000 miles. Clearly there is an area of overlap between contractual terms and representations as far as statements of fact are concerned. In principle, if a seller says 'this is a 1948 Morris', this can be either a promise (contractual term) or a statement (representation). If it is a contractual term, the only question will be whether it is true or false; if it is a representation it will be necessary to enquire not only whether it is true or false, but also whether the representor knew or ought to have known that it was true or false (see below).

There is another less obvious area of overlap. Suppose I borrow money from you, saying that I intend to use the money to expand my business. This is a statement of my future intention. Clearly future intentions may be and often are the subject of promises. But English law has also held that a statement as to future intention carries within it a statement of present fact – that the intention is actually held. So in *Edgington v Fitzmaurice* (1885), the borrower had made the statement above, always intending to use the borrowed money to pay off existing debts. This was held to be a misrepresentation of existing fact as to the borrower's state of mind, Bowen LJ made a famous and often quoted observation that 'the state of a man's mind is as much a fact as the state of his digestion'. The critical distinction to observe here is that if a statement of future intention is a contract, a change of mind will be a breach of contract, whereas if it is being treated as a representation, the only question will be whether the intention was actually held at the time the statement was made and a later change of mind will not give rise to liability.

This rule that a statement as to your state of mind is a statement of fact also means that liability may attach to a statement of opinion if the opinion is not in fact held. Indeed, the cases go a little further than that and hold that if the opinion is given in circumstances where the person stating the opinion looks as if he knows facts upon which the opinion can reasonably be based, then there is a representation that such facts do in fact exist.

It is necessary to show not only that a representation has been made which has turned out to be untrue, but also that it was one of the factors which led the representee to enter into the contract. So in some nineteenth century cases where false statements were made in company prospectuses, it was held that investors who had never read the prospectus had not been induced by it. Similarly, if it is clear that the representee has entirely relied on his own judgment as in *Attwood v Small* (1838), then there has been no actionable misrepresentation. Obviously if the representee always knew that the statement was untrue, he has not relied on it, but it is not enough for the representor to show that he provided the representee with the means of discovering the untruth of what he had said. So in *Redgrave v Hurd* (1881), a solicitor said that his practice was worth £300 a year and invited the representee to examine the papers in his office. Careful analysis of the papers would have shown that the practice was not worth more than £200 a year, but the Court of Appeal held that the representee had relied, as he was entitled to, on the representor's word.

The position of silence

In principle, English law makes a clear analytical distinction between misrepresentation and non-disclosure. It is one thing to tell the other party to the contract that the painting I am selling is by Constable; it is quite another thing not to tell him that it is not by Constable when I know that he is only buying because he believes it is. The latter would amount only to what Cockburn C J called in *Smith v Hughes* (1871) 'the passive acquiesence of the seller in the self-deception of the buyer'.

There are three exceptions to this general rule. The first is not so much an exception as a qualification. Selective silence may amount to a mis-representation when the combined effect of what has been said and what has been left unsaid is misleading. In other words, a half-truth may easily contain a lie. Further, if one makes a statement which was true when made but becomes untrue before the contract is concluded, one is under an obligation to amend the statement. So in *With v O'Flanagan* (1936), the seller of a doctor's practice made a statement about its value which was true when made. Negotiations for the sale lasted a long time and before they were concluded the seller knew that the value of the practice had dropped dramatically. It was held that he should have revealed this.

The second arises in the group of contracts that the law characterises as *uberrimae fidei* (of the utmost good faith). In these contracts, of which insurance is by far the most important example, each party is under a duty to reveal to the other party all the facts known to it which are material. So if you wish to take out a policy of life insurance, you will need to tell the life insurance company any facts known to you which would affect the judgment of the reasonable insurer as to whether to issue the policy or what premium to charge. This could include not only obvious facts such as a weak heart, but also perhaps such matters as the age at which your parents died, if the insurance company could persuade the court that this was taken into account by reasonable insurers. In practice, life insurance companies often ask questions, but the insurer is still under a duty to reveal material facts even though no questions have been asked about them. It should perhaps be emphasised that if there is failure to disclose a material fact, the policy is voidable even though the risk is brought about by some quite different circumstances. So, if a life insured fails to reveal that he has cancer and is then killed in a car accident, the policy cannot be enforced.

The third exception arises when there is such a relationship between the contracting parties that equity imposes a duty on one party to make disclosure to the other. So, if a solicitor makes a contract to buy his client's house, he would be under a duty to tell the client any material facts which would influence the client's judgment. This is because equity says that a solicitor stands in a fiduciary relationship to his client. The list of fiduciary relationships is not closed, but includes such relationships as parent and child, principal and agent, and trustee and beneficiary. Furthermore, it is always open to a party to show that although the relationship between him and the other contracting party does not fall within one of the recognised categories, nevertheless it is such 'that, while it continues confidence is necessarily reposed by one, and the influence which naturally grows out of that confidence is possessed by the other'.

Types of misrepresentation

From at least the eighteenth century, common law gave a remedy in respect of fraudulent misrepresentation. The innocent party could rescind the contract and maintain an action for damages. The damages action was essentially a tortious action in the tort of deceit, which consists in knowingly making a false statement of fact to someone who suffers loss by relying on it. In this case, the loss consists of the plaintiff making a contract with the defendant. (In practice, this is a rather common result of fraud and this tends to obscure the tort/contract borderline in this area.) The mental element of deceit was not finally resolved until 1889, when the House of Lords held in *Derry v Peek* that a defendant could only be liable in deceit if he did not believe that the statement he was making was true. Negligence, however gross and morally culpable, would not do.

After 1889, it was assumed that all misrepresentations which were not fraudulent were to be treated alike, and the only remedy for them would be recission in equity (see below). This view was generally held until the House of Lords in *Hedley Byrne v Heller* (1963) (see p 441) held that in principle it was possible to have a tortious action for negligent statements. It is now clear since *Esso Petroleum Co Ltd v Mardon* (1976), that a *Hedley*

Byrne type action can be maintained where one contracting party is induced to enter into the contract by a negligent statement by the other party upon which he reasonably relies. In that case, Mr Mardon entered into a lease of a petrol station because of a careless forecast by Esso executives as to the likely sales. The Court of Appeal held that he was entitled to damages to compensate him for his loss in entering into the transaction.

This decision makes it clear that there are at least three types of misrepresentation: fraudulent, negligent and innocent (that is, neither fraudulent nor negligent). However, in 1967, Parliament decided that three categories were not enough and created a fourth category under section 2(1) of the Misrepresentation Act 1967. By this, damages can be recovered by a misrepresentee who has entered into a contract as a result of a misrepresentation by the other party, unless the other party can prove 'that he had reasonable ground to believe and did believe up to the time the contract was made that the facts represented were true'. Essentially this introduces a type of negligent misrepresentation, but with the burden of proof reversed so that the person making the statement has to prove that he was not negligent.

Obviously it makes no sense at all to have two slightly different categories of negligent misrepresentation. The reason for this bizarre arrangement is that the 1967 Act is based on a report produced in 1961, at a time when it was thought that there could be no liability in tort for negligent misrepresentation. This assumption was falsified by *Hedley Byrne v Heller* and the report ought to have been, but was not, reconsidered. Obviously this says a good deal about the efficiency of Parliament as a legislative machine.

Remedies for misrepresentation

RESCISSION

During the nineteenth century, Equity gradually developed a general rule that if the contract had been induced by misrepresentation, the innocent party could rescind, that is, undo the contract and go back to the original position. In many situations this would be a perfectly satisfactory remedy because all the misled party wants is to escape from the contract. However, there will be cases where the representee suffers loss of a kind which cannot be repaired by rescission. Suppose a farmer buys a weedkiller having been assured that it is very good at killing a particular weed and instead it kills all his crop. He will not be very impressed to be told that he can return the weedkiller and get his money back. Such a loss cannot be compensated for except by a money award, that is, damages.

Equity steadfastly refused to grant damages as such, though it did give monetary awards to compensate for loss which necessarily followed from entering into the contract. Such awards were described as indemnities. The distinction between damages and indemnities is well illustrated by the decision in *Whittington v Seale-Hayne* (1900), in which the plaintiff took a lease of a chicken farm, relying on a representation that the drains were satisfactory. In fact they were not, and as a result, the manager of the farm became seriously ill, the poultry died or became valueless, and the local council ordered the plaintiff to repair the drains. It was held that the plaintiff could recover the cost of repairing the drains as this was a necessary consequence of taking the lease, but he could not recover for the illness of the manager or the loss of the poultry since these losses, though readily foreseeable, were not necessary since the lease imposed no obligation to appoint a manager or stock the premises with poultry. (Such losses could be recovered if it had been a term of the contract that the drains were sound, or if the lessors had been fraudulent. Today the lessee could recover damages if the representation as to the drains had been negligent.) It will be seen that this is a restrictive rule.

Rescission is not an automatic remedy. The representee has a choice whether to rescind or not. In many cases the representee may decide that although there has been some misrepresentation which makes the transaction somewhat less attractive, going on is still to be preferred to going back. This is particularly likely to happen where the contract has been carried out and unscrambling it will be tedious and complicated. Since 1967, the court has had a general power to order damages instead of rescission, which could be usefully used in this type of case (Misrepresentation Act 1967, section 2(2)).

If the representee decides not to rescind, once he knows that he has been misled, he cannot subsequently change his mind. He is said to have affirmed the contract. This can be done either expressly or by doing something which would be inconsistent with an intention to rescind. A typical example would arise where a man buys shares as the result of a misrepresentation and when he discovers the truth, he tries to sell them to someone else. Strictly speaking, doing nothing at all does not amount to an affirmation, but the courts have been quick to treat quite small acts combined with a lengthy period of inaction as affirmation. In *Leaf v International Galleries* (1950), a period of five years between the contract and discovery of the truth was held to bar rescission in the case of innocent misrepresentation.

Affirmation is often described as a *bar* to rescission. Other bars arise where it is impossible to restore the parties to their original position – an obvious example is where the subject matter of the contract has been consumed – or where the rights of third parties are involved. This latter rule is of considerable importance. A contract procured by misrepresentation is not void but voidable, that is, valid until it is avoided. It follows that such a contract is capable of creating rights in the period between formation and rescission. Suppose that A sells his car to B because B has fraudulently misrepresented that he is C, a well known and credit-worthy person and that B, having obtained possession of the car, sells it to X who buys it in good faith. If the sale to X takes place before A has rescinded the contract, X will become the owner and his rights will prevail over those of A. (The position is different where the transaction is said to be void for mistake. See pp 458–459 above.) In a case of this kind, it is obviously vital to know when A has rescinded. Normally it has been assumed that rescission involves telling the other party to the contract, but in *Car and Universal Finance v Caldwell* (1965), it was held that, at least in the case of a fraudulent misrepresentation, the representee has effectively rescinded when he has done all he can reasonably do (such as telling the police and the motoring organisations in the case of a car).

DAMAGES

The representee has a right to damages either if he can establish fraud or negligence at common law, or if the representor cannot disprove negligence under section 2(1) of the 1967 Act. The most important point to note here is that these claims have all been characterised as tortious and not contractual and that, therefore, damages are to be calculated according to the rules of the law of tort. Contract damages are discussed in Chapter 23. The most important practical difference is that calculation of contract damages involves, in principle, carrying the plaintiff forward to where he would have gone if the contract had been performed, whereas tort damages involve taking the plaintiff back to where he was before the tort was committed.

This sounds fearsomely complex, but can perhaps be explained by a (relatively) simple example. Let us suppose that A sells to B a painting said to be of Lady Hamilton by Romney for £50,000. Let us further suppose that the market value of such a painting is £40,000, but B has paid over the odds because of his passion for collecting Nelsoniana and that the painting is in fact by a student of Romney's and worth only £5,000. On these facts the contract damages would be £40,000 minus £5,000 and the tort damages £50,000 minus £5,000. The reason for this is that if the contract had been performed, B would have paid £50,000 for a picture worth £40,000 and if he receives £35,000 and keeps a picture worth £5,000, he is as nearly as money may do it in the same position as if the contract had been performed. On the other hand, if B claims in tort then he will get £45,000 which with a picture worth £5,000 will take as him as nearly as possible back to where he started from. It will be noted that if a genuine Romney were to be worth £50,000 (contract price), the tort and contract damages would be the same and if £60,000, the contract damages would be greater. This is because contract damages vary according to whether B has made a good or a bad bargain.

It is sometimes said that because tort damages seek to take the plaintiff back to his initial position they prevent the plaintiff recovering damages for loss of profit, which he might have earned in the future. This is an oversimplification. In *East v Maurer* (1991) the plaintiff bought a hairdressing salon from the defendant, who fraudulently represented that he was going to open a salon abroad. In fact the defendant continued to work at a salon in the same town and took many of his customers with him. The Court of Appeal did not award the plaintiff the profits which he would have received if the defendant had contracted to go abroad, but did hold that but for the fraud of the defendant the plaintiff would have received a return on his investment and that the damages should reflect this.

In *Doyle v Olby (Ironmongers) Ltd* (1969) the Court of Appeal held that a plaintiff in an action for damages for fraudulent misrepresentation, could recover for loss which directly resulted from the fraud, even though it was not foreseeable. In *Royscot Trust Ltd v Rogerson* (1991) the Court of Appeal held that the same rule applied to damages recovered under section 2(1) of the Misrepresentation Act 1967.

Common mistake

Suppose A sells to B for £100,000 a painting which both of them believed to be by Picasso, but which is in fact a skilful copy. What remedies might B have?

One possibility is that A has contracted that the painting is by Picasso, for instance because there is a written contract which so describes it. In this case, B will have an action for damages for breach of contract. Another possibility is that A has represented that the painting is by Picasso. In that case, B, if he acts quickly, will be able to rescind and may have a claim for damages under the rules we have just discussed. Yet another possibility is that A may have taken advantage of B in circumstances where A stands in a fiduciary relationship with B. (This is discussed further in Chapter 24.)

Still A may not have contracted that the picture is by Picasso, or represented that it is, or taken advantage of B in any way of which the law takes account. Can the law do nothing for B then? One further possibility which requires examination here is that the contract is void for mistake, because the parties based their agreement on some shared but flawed assumption. We have already discussed some cases of mistake in Chapter 21. In these cases, the mistake arose because the parties were at cross purposes; in the present situation the parties are agreed. Both parties intend to make the same contract but their agreement is based on a shared (common) mistake that the picture is by Picasso.

It is clear that if English law ever permits a positive answer to this question it only does so in a narrow range of cases. Indeed this example is taken from the leading judgment in the leading case, that of Lord Atkin in *Bell v Lever Bros Ltd* (1932), where he said 'A buys a picture from B;

both A and B believe it to be the work of an old master, and a high price
is paid. It turns out to be a modern copy. A has no remedy in the absence
of representation or warranty'. Nevertheless, it is possible that there are
very exceptional cases where the common mistake is as to some matter
so fundamental that the contract should be treated as void.

Any analysis must start with the great case of *Couturier v Hastie*
decided by the House of Lords in 1856. In this case there was a contract
for the sale of a cargo of corn which was supposed to be on a ship
sailing from Salonica to England. In fact, at the time that the contract
was made, the cargo had commercially ceased to exist as the master
of the ship had sold it in Tunis because it was fermenting. The sellers
nevertheless claimed that they were entitled to the price, on the grounds
that the buyers had agreed to pay for the rights which they would have
against the carrier and the insurance company if the goods failed to
arrive. (This would have been the position if the contract had been made
the day before the goods were sold in Tunis.) This argument was
rejected by the House of Lords.

One possible explanation for the result of the case is that it is an example
of common mistake as to a fundamental matter – the existence of the goods
– but there are other explanations. The decision is consistent with a
narrower principle – that there is no contract if the subject matter of the
contract does not exist. There are a number of other cases of non-existent
subject matter: *Strickland v Turner* (1852) (sale of annuity on a life of
person already dead); *Pritchard v Merchant's and Tradesmen's Mutual
Life Assurance Society* (1858) (life insurance policy on person already
dead); *Galloway v Galloway* (1914) (separation deed between the parties
not in fact married).

In 1893, Parliament stated the decision in *Couturier v Hastie* in statutory
form when it provided in section 6 of the Sale of Goods Act that 'where
there is a contract for the sale of specific goods and the goods without the
knowledge of the seller have perished at the time when the contract is made,
the contract is void.' Although this provision only deals with the special
case of goods which have perished, it has been taken by many to support
a general proposition that the key factor in these cases is whether the subject
matter of the contract exists.

Couturier v Hastie is therefore the starting point for two separate
controversies. The first concerns a debate as to whether it is always the
case that if there is no subject matter there is no contract. Section 6 of the
Sale of Goods Act supports this view. An alternative view is that although
the usual rule will be that if there is no subject matter there is no contract,
nevertheless there are two other possibilities which may be found in
particular contracts. One is that (as argued unsuccessfully in *Couturier v
Hastie)* one party is taking his chance on whether the goods exist; the other
is that the contract is one where one party in fact contractually undertakes
that the goods exist. This latter possibility was held by the High Court of

Australia to be the correct analysis of the famous case of *McRae v Commonwealth Disposals Commission* (1950), where the defendants sold to the plaintiff a wrecked oil tanker which was said to be on Jourmand Reef. In fact neither the tanker nor the reef existed, but the plaintiff did not discover this until he had spent considerable time and money mounting an expedition to look for the tanker. The plaintiff brought an action to recover the money he had wasted on this futile search. The defendants argued that as there was no tanker, there was no contract. This view was rejected and it was held that the Commission had, in the circumstances, contracted that there was a ship.

Granted that the Commission was, to put it mildly, very careless, this result seems eminently desirable and sensible, but it has been much discussed whether English courts would reach the same result by the same reasoning. An alternative path would be to hold the Commission liable in tort for having negligently represented that the tanker existed.

A second controversy is whether there are any cases where common mistake operates to make the contract void, other than the cases where the subject matter of the contract is non-existent. In the leading case of *Bell v Lever Bros Ltd* (1932), this possibility was certainly recognised in theory. For instance, Lord Atkin said that the contract would be void if there were a common mistake 'as to the existence of some quality which makes the thing without the quality essentially different from the thing as it was believed to be'. This principle was applied by Steyn J in *Associated Japanese Bank (International) Ltd v Crédit Du Nord* (1988).

In the last 40 years, Lord Denning has suggested in a series of cases starting with *Solle v Butcher* (1950), and culminating with *Magee v Pennine Insurance Co Ltd* (1969), that the correct way to handle cases of this kind is to hold that if the parties are agreed, even though their agreement is based upon some mistake of a fundamental character as to the subject-matter of the contract, the contract should be treated as valid at common law, but that equity should be prepared to intervene where there is a fundamental mistake. The advantage of approaching the question in this way is that equity is more flexible than the common law, and in particular may impose terms upon which it is willing to give relief. This is well illustrated by the decision in *Grist v Bailey* (1967), where the plaintiff agreed to buy the defendant's house subject to an existing tenancy. Both parties assumed, wrongly, that the existing tenant was protected by the Rent Acts and could not be turned out. On this basis the house was worth £850, but with vacant possession the house was worth £2,250. The tenant left and the defendant refused to deliver possession. Goff J held that the mistake as to the protected nature of the tenancy did not make the contract void at common law, but did provide a basis for setting aside the contract in equity. However, he only set aside the contract on terms that the defendant would enter into a new contract to sell at the appropriate vacant possession price.

Rectification of written documents

There is an undoubted equitable jurisdiction to rectify written documents which do not correctly record the parties' agreement. In principle, this is only applicable where the parties have agreed A, but the document has recorded B. Suppose, for instance, that X has agreed to sell his house to Y for £213,200, and that the typist preparing the written contract types £212,300 and that the parties sign the contract without either of them noticing the mistake. Undoubtedly, X can apply to the court for the document to be rectified so as to record the actual agreement.

Rectification is not available where the written document accurately records the agreement, but the agreement is based upon a mistake. This is the effect of the decision in *Frederick E Rose (London) Ltd v William H Pim Jnr & Co Ltd* (1953), where the plaintiffs and the defendants made an oral contract for the purchase by the plaintiffs from the defendants of 'horse beans' which was later turned into writing using the same term. Both parties thought that 'horse beans' were a synonym for 'feveroles' which the plaintiffs had contracted to sell to third parties. In fact that was not the case, and the third party sued the plaintiffs. The plaintiffs sought to rectify the written contract between them and the defendants, but this application was refused since the written contract accurately reflected the parties' agreement.

At one time it was believed that rectification was only available in cases where both parties failed to notice the mistake in the document. It is now clear, however, that in the example above, X could sue for rectification even if Y had noticed the mistake before he signed the document, provided that the court thought that it would be inequitable to allow Y to take advantage of X's mistake, *Thomas Bates & Son Ltd v Wyndham's (Lingerie) Ltd* (1981). In *Commission for the New Towns v Cooper (Great Britain) Ltd* (1995) the Court of Appeal held that where the defendant had pursued a cunningly devised strategy to mislead the plaintiff as to the legal effect of the document which the plaintiff was being invited to sign, though without any actual misrepresentation, the plaintiff could secure rectification without proving that the defendant knew that the plaintiff had been misled. It was sufficient to prove that the defendant hoped and expected that the plaintiff had been mislead and that in the circumstances it was inequitable to allow the defendant to resist rectification.

Frustration

Suppose that A contracts to hire a hall from B for two days so that he can arrange for a concert to be given in the hall. Unknown to both parties, the hall is burned down the day before the contract is made. On the principles discussed in the last section it can be plausibly argued that the contract is void. Let us suppose instead that the hall is burned down the day after the contract was made. We can no longer apply the rules because at the time the contract was made the hall was in existence, but there is a strong intuitive perception that the burning down of the hall should effect the contract. These are essentially the facts of *Taylor v Caldwell* (1863), in which it was held that the contract was brought to an end by the destruction of the hall. English lawyers call the rules under which this result is brought about the doctrine of frustration.

The rules as to common mistake and frustration are in a sense dealing with the same problem – the allocation of risks. This is a central problem in contract making. Suppose I am a large oil company and wish to charter a ship to carry oil for the next five years. Suppose also that I believe that the freight rates are moving down so that it will be cheaper to charter in twelve months' time. Clearly it would not be sensible to charter a ship for five years at today's rates, but is it better to charter for a year at today's rates and hope to charter at a lower rate next year, or should I try to charter at a lower rate for five years, as I should be able to do if the other people in the market share my perception of which way it is moving? In a situation of this kind money is obviously made and lost by the skill or lack of it shown in taking risks. People who have taken the wrong view of the risk will look for ways of escaping from contracts, but one should not in general permit people to escape from contracts simply because things have not turned out as they expected.

Not all contract makers like to take risks. Many contract makers are what is called risk averse, that is they wish to minimise their exposure to risks. A trivial domestic example is provided by the large number of people who prefer to rent rather than to buy TVs. All the available evidence suggests it is cheaper to buy than to rent if a new set lasts for as long as three years and that most sets do last substantially longer. Nevertheless, many people prefer to rent because they have been persuaded (probably correctly) that they will get quicker and more reliable service if they rent. Such people are more concerned to make sure that they don't have to survive a single evening without their TV than to make the best possible financial deal. Similarly at the commercial level, there are contracts which one party makes in order to avoid or minimise risks. Suppose I am an English business which is buying goods from an American company for a price payable in US dollars in six months' time. I can wait until the day before payment and buy the dollars then, but I may not wish to take the risk that the dollar will appreciate against the pound. I can go out today and buy dollars for delivery in six months' time. Of course the price will not be the same as if I bought dollars for delivery today because it will reflect the market's view of the future prospects of the dollar-pound exchange rate. (Of course the person who has sold the dollars for delivery in six months to me appears to be taking a risk, but he is probably a bank or currency dealer who can spread the risk over many transactions and perhaps has American customers who are buying pounds for delivery in six months?)

English law starts in relation to both common mistake and frustration from the position that one should in all ordinary circumstances respect the parties' allocation of risks. This produces results which can look hardhearted, but it encourages and rewards those who consider carefully those risks which they are assuming. It is very dangerous to assume that litigation would provide a satisfactory system for the retrospective reallocation of risks. Nevertheless, it is clear that there are some cases where the change has been so great and surprising that intervention is justifiable.

When are contracts frustrated?

It is possible to gather the cases into a number of groups.

PHYSICAL IMPOSSIBILITY

One obvious example of physical impossibility is destruction of the subject matter as in *Taylor v Caldwell* (1863). There are also countless cases where contracts of personal service have been held terminated by the death, imprisonment or serious illness of one of the parties.

SUBSEQUENT LEGAL IMPOSSIBILITY

There are many cases in both the 1914–1918 and 1939–1945 wars where contracts, perfectly legal at the outbreak of war, have been frustrated by legislation introduced in order to promote the war effort. A good example would be a building contract which could not be carried out because the government had forbidden building work under powers given it by Parliament.

PARTIAL IMPOSSIBILITY

If one has a sudden cataclysmic event which renders the contract wholly impossible of performance, the argument that the contract has come to an end is very strong. But what of events which made the contract impossible only in part? It seems clear that in some cases impossibility may excuse non-performance, although it does not discharge the contract. So in a modern employment contract, an employee who is off work for a week because he had flu does not break the contract but the contract is not frustrated (whether he is entitled to pay for the time he was off work is a separate question). Nevertheless, it is clear that there may be impossibility so substantial though not total as to terminate the contract. One question is how big a part will do for this purpose. Another difficulty is to decide the time when the question has to be considered. It is often said that frustration operates automatically at the moment of the frustrating event, but in some cases there is no single moment when a frustrating event takes place. This has caused very considerable difficulty in relation to contracts of employment where the employee develops an illness, which initially looks as if it will only last a few weeks and grows and grows until he is away from work for months or even years. A leading example of the difficulties likely to be encountered in this case is *F A Tamplin SS Co Ltd v Anglo-Mexican Petroleum Products Co* (1916). In this case a tanker was chartered for five years from December 1912. In February 1915 she was requisitioned by the Government. In February 1915 no one knew how long the requisition would last because no one knew how long the war would last. The House of Lords held that the question – frustration or not – had to be decided as at the date of requisition. (By the time the case reached the House of Lords the prospects of an early end to the war had vanished but this was to be ignored.) By a majority of three to two, the House of Lords held that the charter party was not frustrated. (Possibly the majority were effected by a somewhat bizarre feature of the case. The charterer, although denied the use of the ship, argued that the charter party was not frustrated as the government compensation for requisition was greater than the amount of the charter party hire that the charterer had to pay the owners.)

FRUSTRATION OF THE VENTURE

Although cases of impossibility are the most common, it is clear that the doctrine of frustration is not limited to cases where the contract becomes impossible to perform. In the leading modern judgment in *Davis Contractors Ltd v Fareham UDC* (1956), Lord Radcliffe said that it was sufficient to show that 'the circumstances in which performance is called for would render it a thing radically different from that which was undertaken by the contract'. A classic example is *Krell v Henry* (1903), where the plaintiff let a room in Pall Mall to the defendant for a day on which the coronation of Edward VII was to take place. The room had a view of the coronation procession and the defendant intended to sell space in the room as a commercial venture. The contract contained no explicit mention of the coronation but the agreed price reflected the significance of the day. The coronation was postponed owing to the illness of the King. The Court of Appeal held that although the contract was still capable of literal performance, it was frustrated. On any view this case is close to the line, as it is likely that if postponement had been discussed by the parties, the plaintiff would have said that the defendant must take his chance on that. Perhaps a relevant factor was that the coronation was not actually cancelled but was merely postponed, so that the plaintiff did not lose his chance to cash in on the attractive location of the room.

An instructive example on the other side of the line is *Tsakiroglou &
Co Ltd v Noblee Thorl GmbH* (1962) where there was a contract for the
sale of Sudanese ground nuts cif Hamburg for shipment during November
or December 1956. (Under a cif contract, the seller quotes an inclusive
price to cover the goods, carriage cost to the nominated port, and the cost
of insurance during transit.) At the time of the contract, the natural route
from the Sudan to Hamburg was via the Suez Canal. On 2 November 1956,
the Suez Canal was closed and the seller argued that the closure of the
canal frustrated the contract. The House of Lords rejected this argument.
Undoubtedly the closure of the Canal would make it more expensive for
the seller to perform because the goods would now have to be shipped by
the longer route round the Cape, but it is clear that in a cif contract the
seller takes the risk that freight rates will go higher just as he takes the
benefit if they fall. So the risk, higher freight rates, is one which the contract
had allocated though the event which brought it about was not one which
had been foreseen.

FORESEEN AND UNFORESEEN EVENTS

Discussions of frustration tend to talk about unforeseen events and most
of the decided cases involve events which the parties do not appear to have
foreseen. It has been asked, therefore, whether only unforeseen events can
frustrate. The answer is probably in the negative. Certainly there are cases
where the frustrating event was pretty clearly foreseeable at the time the
contract was made, and there are also cases where what has happened was
a more spectacular example of something which was explicitly mentioned
in the contract – requisition by the Government, outbreak of war, perils
of the sea and so on. Obviously where it is clear that the parties have
foreseen something and not dealt with it explicitly, this points to some
extent to it not being a frustrating event, but it would be too mechanical
to convert this into a rigid rule.

LEASES

In the same way, the old view that leases could not be frustrated has been
replaced as a result of the decision of the House of Lords in *National
Carriers Ltd v Panalpina (Northern) Ltd* (1981), by a rule which says that
frustration is legally possible but factually unusual. The reason is that the
lessee assumes, as a result of the lease, most of the risks of ownership. So
if I take a 99-year lease of a house, I assume the risk of the house being
burnt down just as much as if I had bought the freehold of the house. This
is sensible because the lessee is the person who should insure against such
risks. Nevertheless, there may be exceptional cases where there is an
arguable case for frustration, say, where the lease is for a single permitted
use which is later forbidden by legislation.

SELF-INDUCED FRUSTRATION

All the discussion so far assumes that the frustrating event was not brought about by the party claiming that the contract was frustrated. So in *Taylor v Caldwell* (1863), it was the owners of the hall who claimed that the contract was frustrated. Their argument would have failed if they had burnt the hall down. This is certainly true if they had deliberately burnt the hall down; it appears to be true also if they had negligently done so (though the burden of proving negligence would have been on the plaintiffs, *Joseph Constantine SS Line Ltd v Imperial Smelting Corpn Ltd* 1942)). It is true that in the *Constantine* case Lord Russell of Killowen said that if a prima donna lost her voice by carelessly sitting in a draught this would not be self-induced frustration, but it is not clear whether he regarded this as an example of carelessness falling short of technical negligence, or thought that there were different degrees of negligence for this purpose.

Often a frustrating event will, if self-induced, be a breach of contract but this is not necessarily so. In *Maritime National Fish Ltd v Ocean Trawlers Ltd* (1935), the appellants chartered from the respondents a steam trawler which could only be used if fitted with an otter trawler. Both parties knew that such a trawler required a licence from the Canadian government. The appellants applied for five such licences but were granted only three and used these to license three of their own trawlers. The Judicial Committee held that the decision to use the licence to license the chartered trawlers was self-induced frustration. Clearly in this case the appellants had not contracted to use the ship or to license it; they had simply contracted to pay the hire, but they could not complain that they were not able to use the ship if the reason for this was one that they had brought about themselves.

In the above case, the appellants had chosen to license their own ships rather than the ones they were chartering. It is obviously possible, however, that a party may find himself in a position where he is able to perform some but not all of the contracts he has made because of some supervening event. Some commentators have thought that this would not be a case of self-induced frustration but the Court of Appeal disagreed in the *Super Servant Two* (1990). In this case, the defendants had agreed to carry the plaintiffs' drilling rig from Japan to Rotterdam using what was described in the contract as the 'transportation unit'. The defendants had two suitable vessels, the Super Servant One and the Super Servant Two, which were very highly specialised forms of ocean transport. Under the contract, the defendants were entitled to use either of the vessels. On 29 January 1981, Super Servant Two sank in circumstances which were not the defendants' fault and which it was assumed would have frustrated the contract between the defendants and the plaintiffs if that contract had required the use of the Super Servant Two. The Court of Appeal held that it was not open to the defendants to argue that the contract was frustrated by the sinking of the Super Servant Two even though the defendants had a more than adequate number of contracts to keep the Super Servant One fully employed without performing the contract with the plaintiffs.

EFFECTS OF FRUSTRATION

Frustration brings the contract to an end from the time of the frustrating event. It does not make the contract void from the beginning and there are therefore, as we shall see in a moment, problems as to the legal effects of acts done before the contract is brought to an end. The contract is said to come to an end automatically without any choice on the part of the parties. So it is open to either party to argue that the contract is frustrated. (In some cases, as for instance the *Tamplin* case above, the party who makes this allegation is not the one who at first sight one would expect to make it.) Obviously if neither party claims that the contract is frustrated then no question will arise. Equally, if the parties agree what is to happen in the light of the frustrating event, no problem will come before the court. As we have already seen, the rule that the contract comes to an end automatically upon the frustrating event is difficult to apply where the scale of the frustrating event is uncertain at the beginning. This can happen not only with an illness, but also with an industrial event like a strike which may last for 24 hours or a year. In theory, it appears that one should decide at the beginning how long the alleged frustrating event is to run, but in practice, it certainly looks as if the courts sometimes take into account what has actually happened.

Two major problems arise in relation to the effects of acts which have already taken place under the contract. The first is where money has been paid in advance. At one time it was thought that as this had been a valid payment at the time, it could not be recovered. So in *Chandler v Webster* (1904), the facts were very similar to those in *Krell v Henry*, but the parties had agreed for a price payable immediately on the making of the contract. The plaintiff who was hiring the room had paid £100 with the signing of the contract, but a further £41 15s was payable. The Court of Appeal held that not only could the plaintiff not get back the £100 he had paid but he was also bound to pay the £41 15s. Their reasoning was that this obligation had crystalised before the frustrating event and the frustrating event did not make the money recoverable. This result was much criticised and eventually reversed by the House of Lords in *Fibrosa Spolka Akcyjna v Fairbairn Lawson Combe Barbour Ltd* (1943). In this case, the House of Lords held that if money had been paid in advance and there had been a total failure of consideration (that is the payer had received no benefit under the contract at all) then the money could be recovered. On the other hand, if money had been paid in advance but the payer had received some benefit under the transaction, though not as much as he had paid for, then the money could not be recovered because of the decision in *Whincup v Hughes* (1871). The House of Lords recommended that legislation should be introduced to remedy this defect and with remarkable speed in the middle of an enormous world conflict, Parliament passed the Law Reform (Frustrated Contracts) Act 1943. This Act confirmed the *Fibrosa* case but extended it to cases where there had been only a partial failure of consideration. Simply to allow the recovery of money paid in advance, or to provide that money payable in advance should cease to be payable would, however, reverse the balance too far. It might well be that although no benefit had been conferred on the payer, nevertheless the payee had incurred expenses. This was in fact so in the *Fibrosa* case where goods were being manufactured. No goods had been delivered to the payer, but the payee had incurred expenses for manufacturing the goods and might well have had difficulty in reselling them and recovering his expenses. Section 1(2) of the Act, therefore, gives the court a wide discretion to enable the payee who has incurred expenses to recover such part of those expenses as the court considers just.

The other problem dealt with by the Law Reform (Frustrated Contracts) Act arises where one party has performed the contract in part and conferred some benefit on the other party but there is no provision for payment in advance. As we shall see in Chapter 23, the general rule of the common law as set out in the great old case of *Cutter v Powell* (1795) (see below, p 516) is that a person who contracts to complete a job for a lump sum payment is not entitled to part payment if he completes part of the job. This rule, whatever its other merits, appears particularly unfair where the reason for non-completion of the job is that the contract has been frustrated part way through the performance. Section 1(3) of the Act, therefore, gives the court a wide discretion to award to the person who has conferred the benefit any sum which it considers fair up to but not exceeding the value of the benefit.

Section 1(3) was the subject of the only case so far reported as having arisen under the Act, *BP Exploration (Libya) Ltd v Hunt (No 2)* (1982). In this case, the defendant, a wealthy Texan, owned an oil concession in Libya. Although very wealthy, he could not afford the enormous costs of the exploration himself and entered into a deal with the plaintiffs under which the plaintiffs were to take the risk of exploration, but the parties were to share the profits if the oil concession turned out, as it in fact did, to be valuable. Unfortunately, before the full exploration costs incurred had been recovered, the concession was cancelled by the Libyan Government which clearly frustrated the contract. At the stage of the cancellation of the concession, BP had paid about 10 million dollars to Hunt, and had spent about 87 million dollars on exploration and had recovered about 62 million dollars as their share of the royalties of the oil. In an exceptionally careful and full judgment, which was later affirmed by the Court of Appeal and the House of Lords as to those parts which were appealed against, Robert Goff J held that in a case of this kind, the benefit to Hunt did not consist in the services of exploration, since the act of looking for the oil did not itself confer benefit, nor did it consist in the oil which was already his under the terms of his concession from the Libyan Government. The benefit consisted in the increase in the value of the concession produced by the discovery of the oil. However, in valuing the increased value of the concession, it was necessary to take account of the effect of the frustrating event. It followed that the benefit conferred on Hunt consisted of the value of oil removed, together with any claim against the Libyan Government, that is 10 million dollars plus 87 million dollars. However, the plaintiffs' loss was less than this since they had recovered 62 million dollars already, and the judge, therefore, awarded the sum which he considered just, which was 10 million dollars plus 87 million dollars minus 62 million dollars.

Chapter 23
Remedies

Introduction

This chapter is concerned with the problems which arise where the contract has been broken. The primary question is what remedies may be available to the party who has not broken the contract, but we also need to consider whether the party who has not performed the contract perfectly may nevertheless be entitled to payment for the work which he has done.

Perhaps the first point to make is that it by no means follows that because the contract has been broken there is an effective remedy. The reason for this is that the common law thinks primarily in terms of financial compensation for breach of contract and many breaches of contract do not cause any significant financial loss although they may cause considerable distress and worry. Suppose for instance that a school or college hires a group to play at their annual dance and that a week before the dance the group announce that they are not coming. This is a clear breach of contract, but if it is possible to hire another group at the same price then there will be no financial loss. If one has to pay a significantly higher price in order to get a replacement group at such short notice, then this extra cost can normally be passed on to the contract-breaker. This latter statement, however, though true in principle, may be less than the whole truth. In many cases, the cost of embarking on litigation would seem wholly disproportionate to the amount that one is likely to recover. Undoubtedly many people break contracts in the quite correct belief that it is very unlikely that the other party will sue them.

Remedies may be classified in a number of different ways. The discussion in this chapter will basically be about the standard remedies which the law provides – termination, damages, specific performance and injunction. However, it is important to note that where the contract has been carefully drafted, the parties may well have designed their own additional scheme of remedies. It is very common, for instance, for one party to structure the contract so that if the other party wrongly withdraws, he will be protected. To take a simple example, most companies selling package holidays require the customer to pay a significant sum when booking and another significant sum, say, a month before the holiday is due to start. This means that if the customer announces the day before the holiday that he is not after all going to go, the travel agent will have a substantial sum of the customer's money in his hands which he need not return. This will obviously be much more satisfactory to the travel agent than to contemplate the possibility of having to sue the customer for the money which has been lost by his wrongful cancellation. In practice in this situation, the travel agent would almost certainly not bother to sue and it is, therefore, sensible for him to have structured the contract so that he does not need to.

It is common, even for lawyers, to talk about enforcing the contract. It is important, therefore, to see that in fact, remedies which are given often do not amount to enforcing the contract. The basic common law remedy is an award of damages, designed to compensate the plaintiff for the financial loss he has suffered and to put him in as good a position, so far as money can do, as if the contract had been performed. But this is not enforcement. There are two main exceptions to the principle that on the whole one does not enforce the contract literally. The first is that if one party has completely performed his side of the contract and all that remains is for the other party to pay, then the common law has no difficulty in permitting an action for unpaid debts. Clearly in this case the end result is that the contract is enforced albeit payment is late. (A not unimportant point since there is no automatic right in the absence of agreement to interest on debts which are paid late.) The other qualification is that, as we shall see, in a rather restricted group of cases, equity will intervene to order specific performance compelling the defendant to perform the contract, or will grant an injunction ordering the defendant not to break the contract in some specific way. In the case where equity will intervene in this way, the contract or the relevant part of it will in effect be enforced.

This distinction between damages on the one hand and specific performance and injunction on the other is one of the ways in which the great distinction between law and equity has affected the law of contract. Up until the 1850s, the common law courts had no power to order specific performance or grant injunctions, and the Court of Chancery no power to give an award of damages. These remedies are now available in all divisions of the High Court, but it is still normal to distinguish between legal and equitable remedies.

Withholding performance, termination and cancellation

The order of performance

A layman will often think that the sensible way to encourage the other party to perform his side of the contract is to withhold one's own performance. Undoubtedly this is often true as a common sense perception. Nevertheless, the law on whether one party can withhold his performance is complex and difficult to understand. The first point to examine is the order in which the parties have to perform their obligations. The contract may well be structured so that one party has to perform some obligations before the other party has to perform some of his obligations. Alternatively, it may be the case that the obligations have to be carried out at the same time, when they are often said to be 'concurrent'. This can be simply illustrated by taking the contract of sale. In such a contract, the seller will be under an obligation to deliver the goods and the buyer will be under an obligation to pay the price. The Sale of Goods Act says that these obligations are concurrent unless there is agreement to the contrary. This means that the seller cannot complain that the buyer has not paid unless he was at the relevant time able and willing to deliver the goods and conversely, the buyer cannot complain that the seller has not delivered the goods unless he was at the relevant time able and willing to pay the price. (We put it in this rather elaborate way because in most cases, the seller will not be able to deliver without the co-operation of the buyer, or the buyer to pay without the co-operation of the seller.) In many contracts of sale, however, the parties will have reached a different agreement. For instance, in commercial sales in this country, it is very common for the seller to supply on standard trade terms, which typically allow the buyer 28 days' credit or payment at the end of the month in which the goods are invoiced. It is quite clear that if this is the agreement, the seller is not entitled to demand payment on delivery. Conversely the buyer may have agreed to pay in advance. For instance, in contracts for international sales, it is very common for the buyer to agree to procure a banker's letter of credit and the courts have held that the seller is not obliged to do anything until the letter of credit has been opened. These results are often expressed by using the language of conditions. So we may say that paying the price and delivering the goods are concurrent conditions if the standard Sale of Goods Act rule applies or that, if the seller is to deliver first, delivery by the seller is a condition precedent to the buyer's obligation to pay.

It is by no means the case that all the obligations of one party will be conditioned on obligations of the other party. So, for instance, the seller's obligations as to the quality of the goods do not depend on whether the buyer has paid for them. A buyer who is late in paying and is in breach of contract can still complain that the goods are defective. Similarly, in a contract of employment, the employee's right to be paid wages is normally dependent on his having completed the week's or month's work (depending on whether he is paid by the week or by the month), but the employer's obligation to take reasonable care to provide a reasonably safe system of work applies the day the employee starts work. Where the obligation of one side is not linked to the performance of obligations on the other side it is often said to be independent.

How do we tell in what order the contract should be performed? Obviously the parties would usually be free to make their own agreement.

In many cases, however, this agreement will be inexplicit; the courts will have a clear view in many cases as to what the natural order of performance is. So in a contract to do work, it is normal to expect the work to be done before payment is made unless there is contrary agreement.

Claims by those who have performed defectively

Suppose that one party to the contract embarks on performance and does some of what he has agreed to do, but does not do all of it. In this situation the other party would normally have an action for damages and we shall discuss this below. An important question, however, is whether the defective performer is entitled to be paid for the work he has done. The general answer that English law has given to this question is in the negative. This was laid down in the great case of *Cutter v Powell* (1795). In this case, Cutter signed on as a second mate on a voyage from Jamaica to Liverpool for 30 guineas for the voyage. The voyage began on 2 August and Cutter died on 20 September. The ship reached Liverpool 19 days later. It was held that Cutter's widow had no right to recover a proportion of the 30 guineas. This obviously looks like a very tough decision, though it should be noted that Cutter had deliberately chosen to accept a rate for the voyage rather than a rate for the day or the week. Of course in this case Cutter did not commit a breach of contract by dying; this was an early example of what later came to be recognised as the doctrine of frustration. In relation to frustrated contracts, the rule has been reversed by the Law Reform (Frustrated Contracts) Act 1943 (see Chapter 21). In relation to contracts where the failure to complete the performance is a breach of contract the rule remains. A modern example is *Bolton v Mahadeva* (1972). In this case, the plaintiff contracted to install a central heating system in the defendant's house for £800. He installed the system, but it worked very inefficiently and the defendant refused to pay for it. It was held that the defendant need pay nothing. In this case, the evidence was that for about £200 the system could be got to work properly. The result of the case was, therefore, that the defendant in effect made a profit of £600, since by spending £200 he could acquire a central heating system worth £800. In the same way the employer in *Cutter v Powell* got Mr Cutter's services free. It should be noted that in both cases, however, the benefit was of a kind which could not be readily restored. In *Cutter v Powell*, the employer could not give Mr Cutter's services back to him; in *Bolton v Mahadeva*, the defendant could only return the constituent parts of the central heating system by tearing them out of his house which he was not obliged to do. In the case where the results of a defective performance are readily returnable, an injured party will not usually be entitled to keep those results and refuse to pay. So where a seller delivers defective goods or less than the contract amount, the buyer will often be entitled to reject, but he will not be entitled to keep the goods and refuse to pay for them.

This rule can undoubtedly be regarded as somewhat harsh; on the other hand, it has the great merit of encouraging performance and providing the innocent party with a simple and cost-free remedy. On any view, the rule is subject to substantial qualification. In many contracts the arrangement which the parties have made for payment excludes or qualifies the rule. So if Mr Cutter had agreed to be paid by the week, he would have been entitled to payment for each completed week's work; if he had agreed to be paid by the day, he would have been entitled to payment for each day's completed work. In contracts of employment such arrangements are, of course, almost universal. In other contracts, where a great deal of work has to be done before payment is due, it is very common to provide for payment by instalments. So in a building contract of any size, there would usually be arrangements for payment at monthly intervals according to a certificate by the architect of the value of the work done.

It is also clear that the right to payment does not depend on perfect performance of every obligation in the contract. If Mr Cutter had reached Liverpool but had committed some trivial breaches of contract during the voyage, he would have been entitled to payment and the employer would have had to bring an action for damages for any loss arising from the breach. This result is often expressed by saying that *Cutter v Powell* does not apply where there has been substantial performance. This is really an oversimplification. It is more a question of looking at the particular obligation which has not been performed than at the contract as a whole. It may well be that Mr Cutter would not have been entitled to payment even if he had died within sight of the Mersey, because the court might have held that complete performance of the voyage was a prerequisite for payment. They would certainly not have said the same about each of his duties as a mate.

The rule certainly does not apply where the reason why performance has not been completed is that the other party does something which prevents performance. So in *Planché v Colburn* (1831), the plaintiff was commissioned to write a book for a fee. When he had written part of the book, the publishers decided not to publish the series of which his book was to be part. He brought an action to recover compensation for the value of the work he had done. The publishers argued that he was not entitled to payment because he had not finished the book. This argument was rejected because the only reason he had not finished the book was that the publishers had told him that they no longer wanted it. (It should be noted that the author could perhaps have gone on and finished the book and sued for the fee. He might also have maintained an action for damages. He probably chose not to do so because it would be difficult to quantify the loss that he had suffered by the non-publication of the book, whereas it was relatively easy to set out the amount of time and effort that he had put in to write the proportion that he had written.)

Termination

When one party fails to perform the contract without some lawful excuse, the other party will have an action for damages. In addition, in some cases the injured party will be entitled to terminate the contract. One possible situation where he can terminate is where the term which has been broken is classified by the court as a condition. (We have already discussed this in Chapter 22.) Termination may often be a very attractive remedy as compared to damages. This can be illustrated by the case of *Re Moore & Co and Landauer & Co's Arbitration* (1921). In this case, the seller agreed to sell tins of fruit and to deliver them in cases containing 30 tins to the case. He delivered the right number of tins and as far as we know, there was nothing wrong with the fruit, but some of the cases contained only 24 tins. It was held that the number of tins to the case was part of the description of the goods and that, therefore, the buyer could reject under them section 13 of the Sale of Goods Act, which provides for an implied term that where the goods are sold by description, the goods shall correspond with the description. It is clear that in this case, if the buyer had brought an action for damages, he would have had difficulty in demonstrating any loss, other than perhaps the cost of re-boxing the tins into cases of the right number. The inquiring reader may well ask why the buyer was so fastidious about the casing arrangements. The answer in cases of this kind is usually that the buyer is anxious to escape from the contract for some other reason. The most likely reason is that there has been a change in the market which means that the transaction is now unprofitable, for instance because the price of tinned food has fallen and the buyer can buy the fruit more cheaply elsewhere. Of course the fall in the price of food has nothing to do with how many tins there are to the case, but that does not prevent the buyer terminating if there has been a breach of condition.

The innocent party may also terminate even where the term broken is not a condition if the contract-breaker has either repudiated his obligations, or has committed a fundamental breach of the contract.

The contract-breaker will be treated as having repudiated either where he has explicitly said that he will not perform, or where he has done something which makes it clear that he will not perform. In practice, the latter is a more frequent occurrence. A classic example is *Short v Stone* (1846), where the defendant having promised to marry the plaintiff went off and married another lady. A more complex modern example is *Federal Commerce and Navigation v Molena Alpha Inc* (1979). In this case there was a dispute between a shipowner and the charterer of the ship. The shipowner instructed the master of the ship not to issue freight prepaid bills of lading. The reason for this was that they knew that the charterers had an overwhelming commercial need to be able to issue freight prepaid bills of lading in respect of the goods which were being carried in the ship, and that this would, therefore, have a coercive effect on them and make them come to heel in settlement of the dispute. The shipowners had been advised by their lawyers who were a well-known London firm that they could take this step. This advice was regarded by the House of Lords as manifestly wrong, but the question arose whether the shipowners, who had acted honestly on apparently competent advice, could be committing a repudiation of their contractual obligations. The answer given by the House of Lords was resoundingly in the affirmative. If a contracting party refuses to perform in circumstances which are immediately coercive of the other party, he will be treated as repudiating if it in fact turns out that the course of action on which he is involved is not legally justified. The position would be different where the dispute was as to how the contract was to be performed at some future date. Merely to indicate a view as to what are one's contractual obligations, which is later held to be wrong, does not amount to repudiation (*Woodar Investment Development Ltd v Wimpey (Construction) UK Ltd* (1980)).

A party may announce that he is not going to perform and thereby repudiate his obligations in advance. English law has said that where this happens the injured party does not have to wait until the actual date for performance arrives. This is well illustrated by the classic case of *Frost v Knight* (1870), where the defendant promised to marry the plaintiff on the death of his father. He then broke the engagement off and when sued by the plaintiff argued that he could not be sued until his father died. This argument was rejected. Although the date for performance had not yet arrived, it was clear that the defendant did not intend to perform and it would have been very unfair to keep the plaintiff waiting until the date of the defendant's father's death before she could sue.

The innocent party may also terminate the contract if the contract-breaker commits what has been called a 'fundamental breach' or a 'breach which goes to the root of the contract' or other similar metaphors. The idea is that even where the contract-breaker is trying to perform the contract and does not repudiate his obligations, nevertheless there are some performances which are so defective as to be little, if any, better than no performance at all. It is really, therefore, a question of comparing what the innocent party would have been entitled to if the contract had been properly performed, and considering whether he has been substantially deprived of what he would thus be entitled to. It is worth noting that sometimes arguments may be based on the extent by which the performance falls short of what has been promised; in other cases, the breach may be quite small but may have such striking effects as to qualify as a fundamental breach. This concept of fundamental breach has been much discussed in relation to the regulation of exemption clauses and is further discussed in Chapter 24.

It is necessary to say something specifically about late performance. To perform late is obviously not to perform strictly according to one's contract. Nevertheless, in many cases late performance may be little, if any, less satisfactory than performance on time. In the other cases, late performance may be no better than no performance at all. This has been reflected by saying that the effect of later performance turns on whether 'time is of the essence of the contract'. This expression is often misunderstood. In every contract it is a breach to fail to perform on time and damages can be recovered for any loss which results from late performance (*Raineri v Miles* (1981)). What is meant by saying that time is of the essence is that in such a case, late performance even by a day will justify the injured party in terminating the contract. So if a contract of sale of goods calls for shipment in June and the goods are shipped on 1 July, the goods can be rejected even though in every other respect they are as per the contract, because it is well established that in a commercial sale of this kind shipment in the right month is of the essence.

How do we determine whether time is of the essence? There are three possibilities. The contract may expressly say that the time is or is not of the essence. Second, the contract may be of a kind where time is normally of the essence or normally not of the essence. So, in commercial contracts of sale, time is normally of the essence, whereas in contracts for building, time is normally not of the essence. However, the particular circumstances of a particular contract may negate this prima facie rule. Time is usually not of the essence for a building contract, but if the building is being put up for some specific purpose time may become of the essence. So if the building is being erected to house the 1992 Olympics, it will hardly do to finish it the day after the closing ceremony. In the leading modern case *United Scientific Holdings v Burnley Borough Council* (1978), it was said that there was a third possibility. Even where the contract is one where time is not initially of the essence, it is open to the innocent party, after the contractual date for performance is passed, to call upon the contract-breaker to perform within a reasonable time. If he does not perform within a reasonable time, the innocent party may terminate the contract. (Clearly the operation of this requires the court to share the innocent party's view of what would be a reasonable time for completion.)

Where there has been a repudiation or a fundamental breach, the contract does not come to an end at once. The innocent party has a choice either to keep the contract alive or to terminate. In principle, the innocent party is fully entitled to keep the contract alive, but if he elects to do this it is kept alive for the benefit of both parties. So if, as in *Avery v Bowden* (1855), after there has been a repudiation by one party, which has not been accepted as terminating the contract by the other, there follows a frustrating event, the contract-breaker can allege successfully that the contract has now been terminated by the frustrating event. He could not have done that if the innocent party had earlier accepted the repudiation as terminating the contract.

In practice, of course, if one party resolutely insists on not performing and the situation is not one where specific performance is available, then eventually the innocent party will be compelled to acquiesce in the contract coming to an end. Nevertheless, termination depends on the decision of the innocent party to treat the contract as at an end. The contract comes to an end when the innocent party decides to terminate it. (This can have important effects as to the calculation of damages by fixing the relevant date.) At one time it used to be said that where the innocent party brought the contract to an end he was rescinding it. However, the House of Lords in *Johnson v Agnew* (1980), made it clear that it was inappropriate to use the word rescission in this context. The word rescission should be used to describe those cases where the contract is undone as it were from the very beginning, as in the case of rescission for misrepresentation. In the case of termination for breach of condition, repudiation or fundamental breach, the contract is not retrospectively made invalid; the effect is to terminate the obligations to perform for the future. The court will recognise that there were obligations up to the date of termination and these may play an important part in consequential calculations of damages.

It should perhaps be emphasised that the discussion in the preceding paragraphs concerns termination under general common law principles. It is in practice very common for a contract to contain express provisions for termination in certain circumstances. So the contract may well provide for termination on an event which would not otherwise be a ground of termination. A classic example is late payment. The courts are usually very reluctant to hold that a failure to pay punctiliously entitles the other party to terminate the contract. Creditors, however, often put provisions in contracts entitling them to terminate or to accelerate the payment of outstanding balances if money is not paid on time. In a series of decisions of which the *Laconia* (1977) is the most important example, the House of Lords has held that it is perfectly permissible for a party to take advantage of a short period of delay in payment, even though it is very likely that the delay in payment had in fact caused no significant loss. The House of Lords have taken the view that if the parties have agreed to such a scheme, effect should be given to it even though in most cases one suspects that the party terminating is doing so because of some movement in the market which makes it commercially advantageous to terminate.

A contract may also provide for unilateral termination without the contract having been broken in any way. At first sight this sounds surprising, but there are many contracts which are designed to run for an indefinite period but which ought to be terminable and which if well drafted will contain a provision for termination. An obvious example is a partnership which is very commonly made and intended to run for a long and indefinite period, but where it would be very foolish not to make some provision for termination by notice. Termination by notice is also common in some kinds of government contracts, particularly in the defence procurement industry, where the government may well decide later that resources should be allocated in some different direction. In cases of this kind, the contract usually provides for compensation for the work which has been done, but usually not for the profits which would have been made if the project had been brought to completion.

Damages

Types of loss

In a famous American law review article, Fuller and Perdue pointed out that a plaintiff in a contract action may calculate his loss in a number of different ways. It is often said that the purpose of damages in contract actions is to put the plaintiff in the position he would have been in if the contract had been performed. This was described by Fuller and Perdue as the expectation interest, that is what the plaintiff expects to get. This means that if the plaintiff is buying goods with the intention of reselling them, he may be able to recover the profit which he would have made by reselling the goods (subject to the rules of remoteness discussed below). There may well be cases, however, in which it is very difficult for the plaintiff to establish with any precision what he hoped to get if the contract was performed. He may, nevertheless, have suffered loss from relying on the defendant's promise. He may, therefore, seek to quantify his loss in this way, which has been christened the 'reliance interest'. A good example of this distinction between expectation loss and reliance loss is provided by the case of *Anglia Television Ltd v Reed* (1972). In this case the defendant, an American actor, was engaged by the plaintiffs to play the leading role in a film which they were planning to produce. Sometime later, before shooting had actually started, he decided to accept another engagement and did not honour his contract. In this case the plaintiffs hoped that the film would be successful and that they would be able to sell it to other television channels and so on. But everybody knows that film-making is an extremely speculative business and that many films lose money. Clearly, therefore, the plaintiffs would have had formidable difficulties if they had tried to establish what their profit on the film, which had never been made and never would be made, would be. However, it was clear that the plaintiffs had suffered loss because they had spent considerable sums of money in preparing for the shooting of the film. No doubt scriptwriters had worked on the script, arrangements had been made for the suitable locations to be examined, contracts had been entered into with other actors and so on. The Court of Appeal held that the plaintiffs could recover this loss which they would not have suffered if they had not relied on the defendant's promise. (More controversially, they allowed the plaintiffs to recover losses of this kind which they had actually incurred before the contract with the defendant. This is perhaps justifiable on the basis that if the defendant had not broken his promise, the film would at least have been sufficiently successful to cover all the plaintiffs' expenditure of this kind whether before or after the contract.) Later cases have shown that the plaintiff has in effect a choice of whether to formulate his claim on an expectation or reliance basis, provided only that if the defendant can show that the contract which the plaintiff made was in any case such a bad one that it would have made a loss, the plaintiff cannot transfer this loss to the defendant by calculating on a reliance basis.

There is a third type of loss which the plaintiff may have suffered. He may have transferred money or property to the defendant. The plaintiff may of course wish to recover this money or property. Such a claim is restitutory in effect, that is it is designed to make a restitution to the plaintiff of property or money which was transferred to the defendant. Historically, English lawyers have described this as a quasi contractual claim. Quasi contract is outside the scope of this book but something briefly is said about it below.

Remoteness of damage

Whether the plaintiff calculates his loss on an expectation or a reliance basis, it is clear that he cannot necessarily recover the full amount of the loss. Certain kinds of loss will be excused as being too remote. Basically this is the same problem as has already been discussed in the section on tort, although the answer which contract law gives is slightly different. The starting point of all discussion is still the case of *Hadley v Baxendale* (1854). In this case the plaintiffs owned a mill and the millshaft was broken. The plaintiffs needed to send the shaft to the manufacturers as a model for the making of a new shaft. While the shaft was being made, the mill was out of operation. The plaintiffs contracted with the defendants, a firm of carriers, to carry the shaft to the manufacturers and bring the new shaft back. The defendants broke this contract by taking longer to perform it than they should have done. Undoubtedly this caused the mill to be out of operation longer than it otherwise would have been, and undoubtedly this was a form of expectation loss. Nevertheless, the court held that the plaintiff could not recover for this loss. This was because the court thought that the loss was not the sort of loss which would naturally arise from the breach which had taken place. For this purpose, the court distinguished between two possibilities which are often called the two rules in *Hadley v Baxendale*. The first possibility was that the defendant should be treated as having that knowledge which a defendant in his position would normally have, and should be responsible for that loss which would naturally arise in the light of that knowledge. The carrier would obviously often not know what he was carrying and, therefore, would lack a great deal of relevant knowledge. In this case, the defendants knew that they were carrying a broken shaft, but the court thought that the ordinary carrier would not assume that there was no spare shaft and would, therefore, expect that there would be no loss of profits in the ordinary course of things. Obviously the plaintiff might have told the defendant that he had no spare shaft and this leads on to the second rule which is that if the defendant has special knowledge over and above that which any person in his position ought to have, then he is responsible for loss which would naturally arise in the light of the knowledge which he actually has.

Everything turns, therefore, on the knowledge which the defendant has at the time of the contract, either because he is treated as having the knowledge which people in his position customarily have, or because it can be shown that he actually has it. Obviously in some cases, without the relevant knowledge, the defendant would have no idea that a loss might take place. In other cases an imaginative defendant might see that the loss is a remote possibility. It is obviously vital to try to define the degree of likelihood which marks the boundary between that loss which is so likely that it ought to be recovered and that loss which is not so likely. Much pen and ink has been spilt on this question. In *Victoria Laundry (Windsor) Ltd v Newman Industries Ltd* (1949), Asquith LJ, in a judgment which for 20 years was regarded as the leading modern restatement, said that the test was one of foreseeability. This had the attraction that the same test was being applied in tort and contract which looks neat and tidy. However, in *The Heron II* (1969), the House of Lords disapproved of the use of the word foreseeable in this context though they suggested, between the five members of the House, a bewildering variety of alternative formulations. The House of Lords were objecting to the use of the word foreseeability because they thought that was too favourable to the plaintiff. They suggested some words suggesting a significantly higher degree of like-lihood such as 'contemplate as liable to result'. It seems fairly clear that in practice the courts have been applying such a higher standard even when they have been using the word foreseeable. For instance, in *Hadley v Baxendale*, the reasonable carrier, knowing that he was carrying a broken shaft, could foresee that somewhere in the United Kingdom there would be a mill owner so careless as not to have a spare shaft, but it is clear that the court did not think this was an appropriate form of reasoning. Similarly, in the *Victoria Laundry* case, the plaintiffs, who were buyers of a boiler for their laundry and dry cleaning business, which was delivered late and in breach of contract by the defendants, were held able to recover 'ordinary' loss of profits, but not loss of profits from an extraordinarily lucrative contract of which the defendants knew nothing. Again, it is clear that an extraordinarily lucrative contract is not inconceivable, but it is not some-thing that arises in the ordinary course of things. It is no doubt impossible to produce either a verbal or a mathematical formula which exactly catches the appropriate degree of probability, but it is clear that there has to be a significant chance that the loss will flow from the breach of contract.

Provided the loss is of a kind which is liable to result, it does not matter that the extent of the loss was quite unforeseeable. So in *Wroth v Tyler*, a buyer of a house recovered, by way of damages for the seller's refusal to complete, the sum he needed to go out and buy a similar house in the market, although the extent of the rise in house prices during the relevant period was quite unforeseeable.

Damages are normally assessed as at the date that the contract is broken. The reason for this is that that is normally the date on which the plaintiff takes consequential action. So if a seller fails to deliver goods, the buyer can go out into the market on the date when the goods should have been delivered and buy substitute goods. Prima facie, the buyer should recover the difference between the price he had to pay for the substitute goods and the contract price. However, it is clear that in some circumstances, it would be unduly favourable to the defendant to do the calculations at this point because the plaintiff has good reasons for putting off remedial action.

Contract law has tended to take the position that the only damages which can be recovered in contract are for loss which is measurable in financial terms. So in *Addis v Gramophone Co* (1909), the plaintiff was wrongfully dismissed in humiliating circumstances. The House of Lords held that although there had been a clear breach of contract the plaintiff could only recover his out of pocket loss. He could not recover exemplary damages as a compensation for the humiliating aspects of his dismissal. Some inroads have been made on this principle in recent years. In particular courts have been willing to compensate those who have suffered rotten holidays as a result of breaches of contract by tour operators by giving awards of damages which were in excess of the cost of the holiday and were therefore clearly not limited by consideration of out of pocket loss. On the other hand, the Court of Appeal held in *Hayes v James & Charles Dodd* (1990) that damages for distress could not be recovered in an action arising out of breach of an ordinary commercial contract. In *Watts v Morrow* (1991) the plaintiffs had bought a holiday home relying on a negligent survey by the defendant. They had not only paid more than the house was worth but also had assumed that there would be no major structural flaws in the house and that they could move into it at once to secure relaxation from their busy and stressful jobs. In fact the house had major defects, which meant that the plaintiffs had to live amongst builders for a substantial time. The Court of Appeal held that the plaintiffs were entitled to a modest award (£750 from each) for the physical inconvenience and discomfort, arising from living as it were on a building site but not for the distress which this caused.

Reasonableness, mitigation and causation

It is commonly said that the plaintiff is under a duty to mitigate his loss. This means that in calculating the recoverable loss, the court will look to see what steps the plaintiff took to reduce his loss, and will consider whether these steps were reasonable and whether there were other reasonable steps which he might have taken. Strictly speaking, it is wrong to describe this as a duty since this is not a duty which the plaintiff owes to anyone. He is perfectly free to do what he likes, *but* he will not be compensated for losses which he could have avoided by taking reasonable steps. A simple example would be a company director with a five year contract, who is dismissed in breach of contract after a year, because his company is taken over by another company, which does not wish to retain his services. It is clear that he ought to take reasonable steps to find alternative employment. Of course in practice, very difficult questions may arise as to what jobs he ought reasonably to be expected to consider, since many of the alternative posts will be at a much lower salary.

Reasonableness considerations are not limited to mitigation. In *Ruxley Electronics and Construction Ltd v Forsyth* (1995) the plaintiffs were suing for the price of a swimming pool, which they had erected in the defendant's garden and he counter-claimed for damages. It was clear that the pool was not strictly built to contract, because the contract required a pool which was 7ft 6in deep at the deep end and the pool actually erected was only 6ft 9in at the deep end and only 6ft at the normal diving point. The trial judge held that the pool was perfectly safe for diving; that there was no difference in value between the pool as actually built and as it should have been built but that it would have cost £21,560 to rebuild the pool perfectly in accordance with the contract. He also held that if Mr Forsyth received £21,560, it was very unlikely that he would spend it on the remedial work and that in the circumstances it would not be reasonable for him to have done so. He accordingly decided that the primary measure of Mr Forsyth's loss was the difference in value but awarded him £2,500 damages by way of compensation for loss of amenity. The Court of Appeal, by majority, reversed this decision but the House of Lords unanimously reinstated the trial judge's decision. The House of Lords thought it would be wholly unreasonable to spend £21,000 remedying the defect in the pool and that if Mr Forsyth had been awarded such a sum he would have been significantly over-compensated.

Difficult questions can arise as to whether the plaintiff's loss has wholly flown from the defendant's breach of contract. In *Banque Bruxelles Lambert v Eagle Star* (1995) the plaintiffs had lent large sums of money to commercial property developers against mortgages, which were based on negligent over-valuations of the property by the defendant valuers. The property market collapsed and the borrowers were unable to repay the loans. The mortgaged property was insufficient to cover the loans, partly because of the over-valuation and partly because it had in any case fallen in value because of the collapse of the market. The defendant argued that the plaintiff should only recover the loss which flowed directly from the over-valuation and not that part of the loss which flowed from the fall in the market. This view was rejected by the Court of Appeal, which held that in the circumstances the plaintiffs would not have entered into the loan transaction at all if it had not been for the defendant's negligence and that accordingly the whole of the plaintiff's loss should be treated as flowing from that negligence. The House of Lords allowed the defendant's appeal and excluded loss flowing from the collapse of the property market from the plaintiff's recovery.

Agreed damages

The parties may agree in advance on a mechanism for deciding what the damages are to be. This is particularly common in relation to late performance. So in most building contracts, it is provided that the builder shall pay so much a week for each week of delay in completing the works. A provision of this kind is described as one for *liquidated damages*, as opposed to unliquidated damages, which are those which are not fixed in the contract and are calculated according to the principles discussed above.

However, English law has not allowed the parties complete freedom of action in this respect. It was held for over 300 years that some such provisions are invalid as *penalties*. The distinction between liquidated damages and penalties does not depend on the words used to describe the agreed sum, but on the real nature of the process for deciding it. In order to be a valid liquidated damages clause, the sum must represent a reasonable pre-estimate of the damage likely to flow from the particular breach for which it is to compensate. It does not appear to be necessary to show that the parties actually made a reasonable pre-estimate, provided that the sum they have agreed is no more than a reasonable pre-estimate might have been. If, for instance, the parties have agreed that in the event of failure to pay a sum of money, a larger sum should be payable, or have agreed that a single sum should be payable in respect of a large number of different breaches of different kinds, it will usually be a reasonable inference that this is not a reasonable pre-estimate of the loss. If the agreed sum is classified by the court as a penalty, this does not mean that the plaintiff cannot recover any damages; it means that he cannot sue for the penalty but must pursue a claim for unliquidated damages. These rules only apply, however, where the agreed sum is payable on an event which is a breach of the contract between the plaintiff and the defendant. This has caused great difficulty in relation to hire-purchase contracts where sums are often made payable not only on the failure by the hirer to keep up the instalments, but also on the other events which are not breaches of contract, like the death or insolvency of the hirer or his decision to exercise a contractual right to return the goods. Nevertheless the general principle that a sum could only be classified as a penalty if it was payable on a breach of contract was reaffirmed by the House of Lords in *Export Credits Guarantee Department v Universal Oil Products* (1983).

In *Workers Trust and Merchant Bank Ltd v Dojap Investments Ltd* (1993) the Privy Council held that where a seller of land required the buyer to pay a deposit which was well above the traditional rate of 10%, it was open to the buyer to argue that the deposit was, in effect, a penalty since it had no reasonable relation to the seller's likely loss in the event of the buyer's breach of contract.

Specific performance and injunction

Specific performance and injunction are often described as equitable remedies because they were remedies which were granted by the Court of Chancery, when this was a separate court, operating a separate system of rules known as Equity. These remedies are said to be 'discretionary'. This does not mean, however, that the court is quite arbitrary in deciding whether to grant specific performance or injunction. There are law books containing the cases on specific performance and injunctions that are just as complex and full of rules as those books dealing with damages. When we say that the remedies are discretionary, we mean that the plaintiff is not automatically entitled to specific performance or injunction just because he can show that the defendant has broken the contract. There will be other factors to be taken into account. Nevertheless, these factors can usually be expressed in the sort of categories that lawyers are used to employing.

The basic rule about specific performance is that it will not be granted where the common law remedy of damages is an adequate remedy. Historically, the Court of Chancery regarded the most obvious example of damages as an inadequate remedy as being in the case of contracts for the purchase of land. It took the view that a buyer would not be able to go out in the market and buy the same piece of land with a damages award and ought, therefore, to be given specific performance. (This principle is perhaps slightly unreal as applied to a house on a typical twentieth century housing development, but is probably too well established to be reconsidered even in this context.) On the other hand, a court would not normally grant teh specific performance of a contract for the sale of goods, because the buyer could go out and buy equivalent goods in the market. There can be exceptional cases, however, as in *Behnke v Bede Shipping* (1927) (sale of a ship), and *Sky Petroleum Ltd v VIP Petroleum Ltd* (1974) (contract for the sale of petrol to a filling station at a time when other petrol companies were only supplying regular customers).

If we revert to the case of the contract for the sale of land, the seller would normally be adequately compensated by damages, since he could normally sell to another buyer and if no other buyer would pay such a high price he could recover the difference as a damages award. However, it was thought unfair to give specific performance to buyers and not to sellers, and this is one example of the principle of mutuality which is often said to underlie specific performance. In this case, the argument is that the seller should have a right to specific performance because the buyer has, which is a positive form of mutuality. In some other cases, it has been said that the plaintiff should be denied specific performance because specific performance would not be granted to the defendant. A classic example of this is *Flight v Bolland* (1828), where specific performance was refused to an infant who had contracted with an adult on the grounds that the adult would not have been granted specific performance against the infant. (The contract being one which was enforceable by the infant but not by the adult.)

The court will usually be reluctant to grant specific performance where the contract involves a long series of actions, because specific performance is enforced by committal for contempt in the event of failure to perform. The court would not usually wish to open the possibility of repeated applications by the plaintiff to commit the defendant for contempt. Nevertheless, in *Beswick v Beswick* (1968) (discussed above p 481), the House of Lords ordered specific performance of a contract to pay a sum every week.

An injunction is an order by the court to do or not to do something. Injunctions are commonly sought where the contract contains a provision promising not to do something. So if the seller of a business agrees not to open a competing business and this is a valid agreement (see discussion in Chapter 24, p 548), the natural remedy for the buyer if the seller breaks his promise is an injunction to restrain him. This would in practice be a much more effective remedy than damages, both because it is much quicker and also because in cases of this kind it is often extremely difficult to establish what the real financial loss is. In *Doherty v Allman* (1878), it was said that injunctions should normally be readily available in support of negative covenants (that is covenants not to do things).

One of the classic examples of an area where specific performance will not be granted is contracts for personal services. Equity will not order an employee to go on working for an employer even when leaving is a breach of contract. This is sometimes justified on the grounds that to enforce such a contract by specific performance would be to establish a form of contractual slavery, though this is perhaps an overdramatic rationalisation of the rule. Applying the mutuality principle, Equity also refused to compel the employer to honour the contract of employment, though it must be said that the reasons for this seem much weaker. There is a difficult line of cases on the borderline between specific performance and injunction here. This starts in the old case of *Lumley v Wagner* (1852), where an opera singer had promised to sing for the plaintiff and not to sing for anyone else. It was held that the singer could not be compelled by specific performance to sing for the plaintiff, but could be restrained by injunction from singing for anyone else. Of course the practical effect of restraining the defendant from singing for anyone else would be to give the defendant very great encouragement to sing for the plaintiff, since, no doubt, the defendant could earn a great deal more by singing than by doing anything else. This has been said to amount to giving specific performance by the back door when it would not be granted at the front door. In a typically murky English compromise, the courts have eventually settled on a rule which says that an injunction will be granted in such cases, but only if the contract contains an express promise not to work for someone else (even though an implicit promise not to work for anyone else will usually be inherent in the express promise to work for the plaintiff).

Actions for contractual sums

It is important to see that in many cases, all the plaintiff will be seeking is the agreed contractual sum. The most obvious example of this will be where the plaintiff has provided the goods or services on credit and is carrying out a debt collecting operation. However, there are many other examples where the claim that the plaintiff makes is that the defendant has agreed in certain circumstances to pay money. An obvious example is the royalties which publishers have agreed to pay authors, commonly expressed as a percentage of the sale price of the book in relation to each book sold.

Quasi contractual actions

For historical reasons, English law came to describe certain kinds of action as quasi contractual, because they were enforced by means of the writ of assumpsit, which was also used to enforce contractual claims. To modern eyes, the common feature of these cases is that the plaintiff has paid over money or transferred property in circumstances which have enriched the defendant, either because he has paid it to the defendant or because payment has discharged some obligation of the defendant. The details of these actions are outside the scope of this book, but their existence should be noted here since they may well be relevant in contractual situations.

For instance, if money is paid in pursuance of a contract which comes to nothing, it can be recovered if there has been a total failure of consideration, that is, if the person who made the payment has received no benefit under the contract, but not if there has only been a partial failure of consideration. The application of this rule in the case where the contract has been frustrated has been amended by the Law Reform (Frustrated Contracts) Act 1943 (see above, p 511), but it continues to apply when the contract has been broken, and there are also special rules about money paid in pursuance of illegal contracts which are discussed in Chapter 24.

Chapter 24
Interference by the law with freedom of contract

Introduction

This chapter is concerned with situations where English law will interfere with what is in some sense at least a freely negotiated contract. The subject matter of the chapter covers in effect two very different grounds for interference. One is that the contract is unfair; this involves the next two sections. The other is that the contract is, although fair between the parties, contrary to public policy. This is the subject of the final section. (Restraint of trade which is discussed in the final section also has elements of unfairness within it as we shall see.)

In discussing unfairness, it is useful to adopt the distinction drawn by the American scholar, Arthur Leff, between procedural unfairness and substantive unfairness. By procedural unfairness, we mean unfairness in the contract negotiation process, for example, that one party was holding a gun to the other's head while the contract was being negotiated. By substantive unfairness, we mean that the contract arrived at is in some sense unfair to one of the parties because he has been over-charged or underpaid and so on. It should be noted that although this distinction is very useful for the purpose of analysis, in practice, in most cases where the law intervenes there tends to be some element of both procedural and substantive unfairness. The doctrines discussed below, duress, undue influence, unconscionable contracts, inequality of bargaining power, are primarily related to procedural unfairness. A most important example of intervention on the grounds of substantive unfairness is in the treatment of exemption clauses which is discussed post. We shall see, however, that the treatment of exemption clauses in its present form involves distinguishing between consumer transactions and non-consumer transactions. This assumes that consumers, as a class, lack the ability adequately to protect themselves in the contracting process against the imposition of unfair exemption clauses (in so far as this is true, it is a kind of procedural unfairness).

Interference on the grounds of public policy is a quite different matter. If a Mafia godfather hires a hit-man to eliminate a rival, this contract may be perfectly fair as between godfather and hit-man and it does not lack adequate certainty, agreement or consideration. Our objections to enforcing this contract are entirely external to the parties and derive from its subject matter. Quite simply, the law should not be in the business of enforcing such agreements. This particular example is perhaps hardly likely to give rise to many disputes, but as we shall see, the ambit of subject matters to which the law objects is much wider than this.

Duress, undue influence, inequality of bargaining power

It goes without saying that a contract which is procured by the threat of force on one side to which the other party yields is invalid. It is sufficient to show that the threat was one of the reasons why the threatened party entered into the contract; it need not be the main or decisive reason. This was confirmed in *Barton v Armstrong* (1975), where the respondent had threatened to kill the appellant if he did not enter into the contract, but there was clear evidence that there were also good commercial reasons for entering into the contract.

In the last 20 years, it has been recognised that the doctrine of duress need not be limited to threats of force, but can be extended to other forms of wrongful threat which exert improper coercive pressure on the threatened party. This has led to the recognition of a doctrine of economic duress. A good example is *The Atlantic Baron* (1978) (discussed above p 474). A threat to break one's contract is one of the most effective forms of such pressure, in many cases, though clearly not the only form. There is obviously a line which may be difficult to draw in practice between pressure and economic duress. It is necessary to show that there was pressure of a kind which compels the victim to submit from the realisation that he has no other practical choice open to him, and it must be shown that the pressure was illegitimately exerted. This is clearly stated in the House of Lords' decision in *Universe Tank Ship of Monrovia v ITWF* (1982).

Alongside the common law, Equity developed some further doctrines which provided relief in certain cases. One was the doctrine of undue influence. This doctrine is not limited to contracts, but can be applied also to gifts and other transactions. It is part of the wide equitable doctrine of constructive fraud. Basically, this involves showing that one party to the contract was in a dependent position on the other and that the other took unfair advantage of the dependence. A relationship between the parties from which the courts will infer that dependence is usually present in cases such as parent and infant child, religious superior and inferior, solicitor and client, or because one party is able to establish that there was a particular relationship of dependence which had been developed between the parties even though the contract did not fall within one of the recognised heads of dependence.

A classic example of dependence in this second sense is provided by the case of *Lloyds Bank Ltd v Bundy* (1975). In this case, old Mr Bundy had been a customer at Lloyds Bank for many years, and relied exclusively on his local bank manager for the time being as a source of financial advice. Mr Bundy owned a farm and lived in the farm house which was effectively his only significant asset. Old Mr Bundy had a son who also banked at Lloyds Bank, and who was an optimistic but unsuccessful businessman. Young Bundy borrowed from the bank and his father gave guarantees of his son's overdraft. By a series of successive transactions, the father was persuaded to increase the amount of the guarantee and to give mortgages over the farm to underwrite the guarantee. The final transaction involved a guarantee and mortgage equivalent to the whole worth of the farm. The documents relating to this transaction were signed by Mr Bundy in his house, the manager having brought them to him to sign. The manager did not point out, as any independent financial adviser would have been bound to do, that the transaction was a very foolish one for Mr Bundy to enter into, since there was a significant risk that he would lose all his assets and be turned out of his home. In due course, the son's business failed and the bank attempted to call in the guarantee and the mortgage. It was held that this was a classic example of undue influence because the bank manager was in a conflict of interest situation. He had an interest on behalf of the bank, and indeed on behalf of his personal reputation within the bank, to secure that the loans to young Bundy were recovered. He also had a duty as Mr Bundy's financial adviser. He should have realised that he could not perform this duty in this situation, since he could not hope to take a dispassionate view of whether the transaction was sensible from the point of view of Mr Bundy, because it was so attractive from the point of view of the bank itself.

In the last ten years there have been a number of what may be called three party undue influence cases. A typical scenario involves a husband borrowing from a bank to support his business. The bank presses for security for the loan and the husband offers the family home or a guarantee by his wife as security. The family home is owned partly by the husband and partly by the wife and clearly mortgaging the home therefore requires the consent of both parties. Similarly the wife's consent is of course required if she gives a guarantee. It is not necessarily in the best interest of the wife to mortgage her share of the family home to support the business because she risks losing the home. Some people, of course, may consider that in some circumstances their standard of income is so dependent on the success of their partner's business that it is worth throwing their share of the house into the pot. Obviously these decisions are difficult and in principle the partner should make the decision after a calm analysis of where their best interest lies. In a number of the cases the husband has persuaded the wife to enter into the transaction either by bullying her or by telling her lies about the underlying financial position. In some of these cases the business has still collapsed and the bank has sought to enforce its security. The wife has then said that the security is invalid because of the husband's fraud or undue influence.

In the earlier cases the Court of Appeal developed a doctrine that the result of such cases depended on whether the lender had made the husband its agent for the purpose of getting the wife to sign the relevant documentation. In *Barclays Bank v O'Brien* (1993) the House of Lords held that this was the wrong test. The question was whether the bank had notice. Lord Browne-Wilkinson said 'where a wife has agreed to stand surety for her husband's debts as a result of undue influence or misrepresentation, the creditor will take subject to the wife's equity to set aside the transaction if the circumstances are such as to put the creditor on enquiry as to circumstances in which she agreed to stand surety.' In a transaction where the borrowing is to support the husband's business the bank will normally have notice. In such a situation it should take effective steps to see that the wife has independent advice from a solicitor as to the risks she is taking by entering into the transaction. Later cases say that the bank need not double check the advice which the solicitor has given but is, in all normal circumstances, entitled to assume that the solicitor will act professionally and give appropriate advice.

This doctrine would not apply in this form in the standard case where the husband and wife are buying a home to live in because there is no conflict between the husband's interest and the wife's interest. Both have a shared interest in acquiring a home. This notion was applied by the House of Lords in *CIBC Mortgages v Pitt* (1993) decided at the same time as in *O'Brien*. In this case Mr and Mrs Pitt owned a family home worth some £270,000 and subject to a Building Society mortgage for £16,700. Mr Pitt wanted to borrow against the family home in order to invest on the stock exchange. Mrs Pitt was opposed to this proposal but eventually gave in because of bullying by Mr Pitt. Mr Pitt approached the plaintiffs but did not tell them the truth. He said that he wanted to borrow money to buy a holiday home and the plaintiffs agreed to make such a loan for £150,000 subject to the paying off of the earlier mortgage. Mrs Pitt signed all the forms and received no independent advice. Once Mr Pitt had the money he spent it on buying shares and then borrowed money against the shares to buy more shares and so on and so on. Eventually there was a fall in the stock market and all of the money was lost. The House of Lords held that Mrs Pitt could not resist the enforcement of the mortgage by the plaintiffs on the grounds of her husband's undue influence since the transaction was not one which put the plaintiffs on enquiry. It appeared to be a transaction which was for the benefit of both parties and there was nothing to alert the plaintiffs to the possibilities of undue influence or fraud.

In the books, there are a miscellaneous collection of cases where Equity has intervened on the ground that the transaction was an 'unconscionable bargain'. One group of such cases involve purchases from poor and ignorant people of their property at substantial undervalues. *Evans v Llewellin* (1787), is perhaps the best known example. Perhaps a larger group involves transactions with extravagant members of the aristocracy, who hoped to have substantial estates on the death of their fathers. In the seventeenth, eighteenth and nineteenth centuries, such people often fell into the hands of money lenders, who were glad to lend them money at extravagant rates of interest against their expectations. Such transactions were equally frequently struck down by Equity as unconscionable.

In *Lloyds Bank Ltd v Bundy*, Lord Denning MR, while not disagreeing with the conventional way in which the majority of the Court of Appeal solved the problem, embarked on a broad ranging review in which he expressed the view:

> 'through all these instances there runs a single thread. They rest on "inequality of bargaining power". By virtue of it, the English law gives relief to one who, without independent advice, enters into a contract upon terms which are very unfair, or transfers property for a consideration which is grossly inadequate, when his bargaining power is grievously impaired by reason of his own needs or desires, or by his own ignorance or infirmity, coupled with undue influences or pressures brought to bear on him by or for the benefit of the other.'

This broad approach has produced widely different reactions. Overseas, particularly in Canada, it has been regarded as a bold and creative piece of reasoning. In England, on the whole, it has been received with scepticism and suspicion. However, in most of the cases in which the argument has been raised, judges have been careful to demonstrate that the transaction involved is in fact substantively fair, before expressing marked reserve about the status of any general doctrine of inequality of bargaining power (*Alec Lobb (Garages) Ltd v Total Oil GB Ltd* (1983); *Burmah Oil v Governor of the Bank of England* (1981)). The most important case is *National Westminster Bank plc v Morgan* (1985), where Lord Scarman, delivering the only reasoned opinion in the House of Lords, certainly expressed grave res-ervations about the need for any general doctrine. On the other hand, Lord Scarman had earlier spent considerable time analysing the transaction by which Mr and Mrs Morgan borrowed money from the bank in order to pay off a building society mortgage on their house, and had concluded that the transaction was not unfair.

Exemption clauses

This section is concerned with clauses which seek in some way to exclude or limit or qualify some liability which would otherwise fall on one of the parties. Such clauses come in fact in a wide range of forms, and it is almost certainly a mistake to treat all forms in the same way, a mistake which is in fact frequently made both by courts and by commentators.

The category of exclusion or exemption clauses includes not only clauses which purport to exclude liability altogether for certain types of breach of contract or for certain types of behaviour such as negligence, but also clauses which limit the amount of compensation, eg to a thousand pounds; or exclude certain types of loss, eg consequential loss; or exclude certain remedies, eg the right to reject the goods; or which impose limitations on remedies, eg by requiring complaints within a short time limit; or by requiring complaints to be pursued in a particular way, eg by arbitration, and so on. There is also a category of clause which in principle is not so much an exclusion clause, but a clause defining what it is that has been promised. Suppose for instance that a horse is entered for an auction described as 'warranted sound except for hunting', this can be regarded as a clause seeking to exclude liability for the horse not being suitable for hunting, but is more properly to be regarded as making it clear that no undertaking about its soundness for hunting has ever been made. This distinction is important in principle, but again it has often been lost sight of in practice.

Common law controls

Although the attitude of the courts to exemption clauses has been far from wholly consistent, many judges, especially Lord Denning, in the last 40 years have shown very considerable hostility to exemption clauses, particularly in relation to consumer contracts and clauses excluding liability for personal injury. A number of techniques have been used for this purpose. One is to examine whether the exclusion clause has been effectively incorporated into the contract. This has already been discussed in Chapter 22 (see p 488). The second technique is to use what are called rules of construction, that is, rules for helping the court to construe the contract, that is, to decide what it means. It has been said, for instance, that clear words are needed to exclude liability for negligence, or to exclude liability where a very serious breach of contract has been committed, or where the behaviour of one party goes outside the four corners of the contract. It has also been said that where one party has drafted the contract, it is permissible to resolve ambiguities in the drafting in the sense least favourable to the person who is responsible for the drafting of it. Obviously, these principles may readily overlap. Many cases have been decided using these rules, because people who use exemption clauses are often not anxious to be brutally frank about their purpose. They are prone, therefore, to use obscurities and equivocations which open the door for a court to apply these rules of construction.

A critical question is whether, where the contract is clear and explicit as to its desire to limit or exclude liability, it is subject to any common law control. At one time, it was thought that the answer to this might be in the affirmative. In a series of cases in the Court of Appeal, of which *Karsales (Harrow) Ltd v Wallis* (1956) was the leading example, that Court appeared to state a doctrine that no words, however clear, could exclude liability for breach of a fundamental term or fundamental breach of contract. In *Karsales v Wallis*, the contract was a hire-purchase of a second-hand motor car under a standard hire-purchase contract which purported to exclude all liability in the finance company for the condition of the car. The car, when delivered, was fundamentally different from its condition when inspected in the showroom and in particular, had a cracked cylinder block and would not start. The Court of Appeal held that the exemption clause was ineffective, because what had been delivered was not a 'car', since it lacked the fundamental quality of a car, that is the capacity for self propulsion. This case was followed by other decisions which considered whether vehicles which would start but not stop, or which would only drive in straight lines and not around corners were cars. All of these cases were obviously motivated by an entirely understandable desire to protect those who bought shoddy second-hand cars. However, the House of Lords in two cases, *The Suisse Atlantique* case (1966), and *Photo Production Ltd v Securicor Transport Ltd* (1980), held that this principle was wrong. The House of Lords thought that the hire-purchase cases were correctly decided on grounds of construction, but held that there was no substantive doctrine that liability for fundamental breach could not be excluded by clear words. This is clearly illustrated by the *Photo Production* case. In this case, the plaintiffs engaged the defendants to make regular visits to their factory for the purposes of reinforcing their fire precautions. Unfortunately, the defendants engaged for this purpose an employee who set fire to the plaintiff's factory and burnt it down. The Court of Appeal held that this was a fundamental breach of contract and that liability could not be excluded by words, however clear. The House of Lords, however, held that the words used in the Securicor standard form were perfectly clear and were adequate to exclude Securicor's liability. (This result is not as surprising as it looks at first sight. It is important to remember that it is extremely probable that both parties were insured, so that the real dispute was between the plaintiffs' loss insurers and the defendants' liability insurers.)

Legislative controls

It has gradually come to be felt that the regulation of exemption clauses is probably a matter best left to legislation. Legislation to control exemption clauses is not new. Statutes controlling particular trades or industries or commercial areas have been common for over a hundred years. Previous statutes, however, have not been of general application. The first statute to be applicable to all contracts was the Misrepresentation Act 1967 which, as amended in 1977, provides that any contractual provision which purports to exclude liability for pre-contractual misrepresentation is subject to a test of reasonableness. In 1973, the Supply of Goods (Implied Terms) Act imposed major restrictions on contracting out of liability in relation to contracts of sale and hire-purchase. It introduced a general test of reasonableness and special treatment of consumers, two of the major features of the Unfair Contract Terms Act 1977, which is now the leading source of statutory law in this subject. This Act is complex and mis-leadingly titled. It is not concerned with unfair contract terms generally, but only with a limited class of potentially unfair terms, that is exemption and exclusion clauses. Furthermore, it does not anywhere apply a test of fairness, though it does in some cases, as we shall see, apply a test of reasonableness, which may be similar. The Act does not apply to all contracts, and indeed it is somewhat confusing and difficult to disentangle to which contracts the Act does in fact apply. For the purpose of English law the main sections are sections 2 to 7 which only apply to business liability (except for section 6(4)). 'Business' is not defined anywhere in the Act, though section 14 extends 'business' to include a profession and the activities of any government department or local or public authority. Schedule 1 excludes a number of contracts including contracts of insur-ance; contracts for the creation or transfer of interests in land; contracts for the creation or transfer of most forms of intellectual property (such things as patents, copyrights and so on); contracts relating to the formation or dissolution of a company and most contracts for the carriage of goods by sea. Section 26 excludes international supply contracts, and section 27 excludes contracts where English law only governs, because the parties have chosen to make English law the governing law and but for that choice, some other law would apply.

Types of control

The Act makes certain types of clause totally invalid and subjects others to a test of reasonableness. The clauses which were made totally ineffective are: clauses including liability for negligently caused personal injury or death (section 2(1)); the implied undertakings as to title in contracts for sale and hire-purchase (section 6(1)); the implied obligations as to title in contracts for the supply of goods other than sale or hire-purchase (section 7(4)); the implied undertakings as to quality in consumer contracts for sale and hire-purchase (section 6(2)); and the implied undertakings as to quality in other contracts for the supply of goods (section 7(2)).

Clauses subjected to a test of reasonableness are clauses excluding or limiting loss or damage arising from negligence other than personal injury or death (section 2(2)); the implied undertakings as to quality of the goods in non-consumer contracts of sale or hire-purchase (section 6(3)); and in other contracts for the supply of goods (section 7(3)); and contracts falling within the scope of section 3. Section 3 is a wide and complex clause which applies where one party deals as a consumer, or where one party contracts on 'the other's written standard terms of business'. It is clear that consumers often contract on suppliers' written standard terms of business and therefore these two limbs overlap. It is also clear that many businesses contract on the standard written terms of business of other businesses. Such contracts also fall within section 3. However, there is considerable ambiguity as to the scope of this, since the Act does not define what is meant by written standard terms of business. This obviously applies to situations where company A has had drafted for its own use, standard terms which were incorporated into all company A's contracts. But what if the situation is one where company A deals with company B, and both companies are members of a trade association and use the standard terms of that trade association. Are these the standard terms of company A or company B, or both or neither? This is really wholly unclear. Also unclear is the situation such as that of a builder, who commonly builds on standard terms designed by the JCT over which he has no personal control. Are these his standard terms because he always uses them, or not because he has no control over them? Again the position is not clear. Once one has decided that the contract is one to which section 3 applies, then certain types of clause within such a contract are subject to the test of reasonableness. These include not only clauses which exclude or restrict liability, but also clauses which permit one party to substitute a different performance, or in certain circumstances to tender no performance at all. Obviously substituting a different performance or tendering no performance would often be a breach and, therefore, already covered. This clause, however, is obviously aimed at ingenious draftsmen who try to draw up the contract in such a way as to make what is in substance an exemption clause, a contractual option to substitute a performance. It is probably easier to understand the thrust of this provision if one can take an example. A good case would be a holiday company, who sold a package holiday with conditions which provided that in certain circumstances they could move the customer to a different hotel, or to a hotel in a different resort in the same country, or to a hotel in a wholly different country, or which provided that in certain circumstances, such as a strike by air traffic controllers, they could simply return the money and provide no holiday at all. All of these provisions would be subject to a test of reasonableness. It can be seen that many such provisions might pass the test, but that is of course another question.

The central innovation made by the Act, following on the structure of the 1973 Act, was to subject consumer contracts to different rules and to introduce a wide test of reasonableness. Dealing as a consumer is defined by section 12. This requires that one party should be a consumer and the other a non-consumer. Transactions between two consumers are not consumer transactions for this purpose. A party is defined as a consumer where he 'neither makes a contract in the course of a business nor holds himself out as doing so'. A very wide view of who is a consumer was taken by the Court of Appeal in the controversial case of *R & B Customs Brokers Ltd v United Dominions Trust Ltd* (1988) where the plaintiffs were a company owned and controlled by Mr and Mrs Bell which ran a business as shipping brokers and freight forwarding agents. The company bought a second-hand car from the defendants. Although the company only existed for the purpose of carrying on the business, the Court of Appeal held that it was a consumer. The decisive argument in the Court of Appeal was that the company was not in the business of buying cars since it only bought one car at a time and had only previously bought one or two cars. Where the contract involves goods, they must be of a kind which are 'ordinarily supplied for private use and consumption'. There is no similar rule in relation to services, probably because it was thought impossible to make any clear distinction between consumer and non-consumer services.

Reasonableness

Reasonableness is dealt with by section 11 and also by Schedule 2. Schedule 2 sets out a number of 'guidelines' for the application of the reasonableness test, which strictly only apply to sections 6 and 7, but which have, in practice, been treated as relevant also to questions of reasonableness which arise under sections 2 and 3. Section 11 lays down that the time for judging reasonableness is the time when the contract was made. Section 11(4) contains a special treatment of clauses which limit liability to a specified sum of money. In judging whether such a clause is reasonable, it is permissible to have regard to the defendant's financial resources or to his ability to cover himself by insurance. Most of the cases which have arisen under the Act have been concerned with the exploration of the concept of reasonableness. A leading case is *George Mitchell (Chesterhall) Ltd v Finney Lock Seeds* (1983). In this case, the defendants were seed merchants who agreed to supply the plaintiffs with 30lbs of Dutch winter cabbage seed for £192. The plaintiffs, who were farmers, planted 63 acres with the seed, but the seed was both of the wrong kind (being spring cabbage seed) and also defective in quality. The result was that the crop was a total failure and the plaintiffs claimed compensation for some £60,000, the value of the crop which they had lost. The defendants relied on a clause on their invoice, which purported to limit liability to replacing the seed or refunding the price. The House of Lords held that the defendants' clause was unreasonable. They attached considerable weight to the fact that the defendants had themselves led evidence that in such situations they had commonly made *ex gratia* payments to compensate farmers who had suffered losses. This was designed by the defendants to show that they were reasonable chaps, but the House of Lords held that it showed that they lacked confidence in the reasonableness of their own clause. Probably this was unfair, since businessmen often think it is sensible to make concessions, even when their lawyers tell them they have technically a good case. Other factors which were thought relevant to the case were that the defendants had been very careless and had committed a very serious breach of contract by delivering the wrong kind of seed, and that the evidence was that it was easier for the sellers to insure against this risk than for the buyers. Other factors which are relevant in general in a case such as this, are the relative bargaining powers of the parties, which in this case appear more or less equal; the availability of different terms from other suppliers and the extent to which the terms were surprising. (Apparently, virtually all seed merchants use terms similar in extent to those of the defendants, so that on the one hand, the buyer could not have got better terms elsewhere, but on the other hand, he should have been rather familiar with the risk.)

In *Smith v Eric S Bush* (1990) the House of Lords thought that it was not reasonable for a valuer to seek to disclaim liability for the valuation which he had made of the house bought by the plaintiffs since as between the valuer and the plaintiffs, who were first time buyers of a house at the bottom of the market, it was much easier for the valuer to bear the loss, against which he could insure, than it was for the buyers. In this case the buyers were suing the valuers in tort since they were relying on the fact that they had received an advance from the building society showing that the valuer's report was favourable. Where a house was more valuable a court might perhaps be more willing to give effect to a disclaimer which suggested that the buyer should commission his own structural survey. The House of Lords clearly thought this was unrealistic in the circumstances of this particular case.

Other interesting points which have come out of other cases on reasonableness include the following. In *RW Green Ltd v Cade Bros Farms* (1978), a clause requiring the customer to complain within a short time limit was held unreasonable where the defect could only be discovered by planting potatoes and waiting to see whether the crop came up; in *Woodman v Photo Trade Processing Ltd* (1981), a photo processing contract which provided that if the film was lost the customer should simply be entitled to a new film or the cost of the old film was held unreasonable, but it was suggested that the clause might be reasonable if the processor also offered a premium service, where he took the risk but charged a higher rate (the reasonableness of this would depend in part on the difference between the lower and higher rate); in *Walker v Boyle* (1982), where a clause in the National Conditions of Sale, one of the two standard documents commonly used by solicitors for conveying houses was held unreasonable, even though the clause was extremely well known and both parties had been represented by solicitors throughout the negotiations.

The European Directive

The position has been dramatically developed by the Unfair Terms in Consumer Contracts Regulations 1994 which came into force on 1 July 1995. These Regulations gave effect to the European Directive on unfair terms in consumer contracts. They have a confusing relationship with the Unfair Contract Terms Act. Some clauses are struck by both the Act and the Regulations. Others are struck by the Act and not by the Regulations and still others by the Regulations and not by the Act. In a perfect world the Government would have introduced legislation which combined the Act and the changes needed to give effect to the directive but this would have taken a substantial amount of legislative time. Instead the Government decided to bring the directive into force by using secondary legislation. This was quicker but much harder for everyone to understand.

The Regulations only apply to consumer contracts. The definition of consumer contracts is slightly different from the Act and in particular it is clear that companies cannot be consumers for the purpose of the Regulations. So the Act is wider in one respect in that it deals also with many business contracts.

The Regulations only apply to contracts for the supply goods and services. On the other hand they do apply to a number of contracts which were excluded from the Act. This is particularly important in relation to the contract of insurance since there is a vast market in the supply of insurance to consumers which was left outside the Act but is powerfully effected by the Regulations.

The Regulations only apply to standard form contracts. They do not apply at all to individually negotiated contracts. However, the Regulations recognise that even where the parties start with the standard form it will be common for there to be some negotiation even in consumer contracts, particularly about price. So a certain amount of negotiation does not take a standard form contract outside the Regulations provided that an overall assessment of the contract indicates that it is nevertheless a pre-formulated standard contract. Here again the Act is in principle wider though it must be said that virtually all the cases that have actually been litigated under the Act have involved a standard form of contract.

The most striking way in which the Regulations are wider than the Act is that in respect of the contracts to which they do apply, they apply in principle to all contract terms and not simply to terms which exclude liability. There is an important qualification to this in that terms which relate to the central purpose of the contract cannot be challenged and so for instance it is not open to a consumer to argue that he has paid too much for a second hand car because the price was too high. However this exemption of the central purpose only applies where the contract is expressed in plain intelligible language. In effect this will mean that all well advised people supplying goods and services to consumers will have to re-draw their contracts into plain intelligible language. Neither the Directive nor the Regulations define what is meant by plain intelligible language but it must presumably mean something more than intelligible to lawyers. There will obviously be important cases working out the scope of this requirement in real life.

The test which the Regulations supply is that a term shall not be binding on a consumer if it is unfair. In the first instance unfair terms will be struck out, though if this leaves the remainder of the contract unworkable the whole contract may collapse. Unfairness is defined to mean 'any term which, contrary to the requirement of good faith, causes a significant imbalance in the parties rights and obligations arising under the contract to the detriment of the consumer.' The Regulations marked a major development in English contract law by the adoption of notions of unfairness and good faith. The Regulations contain a long list of types of clause which are suspect. It is not a black list of clauses which are prohibited but a grey list of clauses which courts will need to look at carefully to see if they are justified. This list is not exhaustive but it does appear to be comprehensive.

Illegality

As we have said, the basic principle behind illegality in relation to contract is that the subject matter of the contract is such that the law wishes to distance itself from the enforcement of the contract. Of course, in many cases this process has little practical effect; the refusal of the law of contract to allow a prostitute to sue for her fees has little noticeable effect on the volume of prostitution.

The underlying basis of illegality is the concept of *public policy*. Public policy is notoriously difficult to define, and the reports are full of cautionary statements by judges about the dangers of allowing the concept of public policy too wide a scope. One can perhaps approach the definition by saying what public policy is not. There is clearly a difference between policy and public policy. The general policy of the law of contract is concerned with reasons why agreements should be enforced (see the discussion in Chapter 19). This involves such matters as protection of reasonable expectations, reliance and so on. Public policy is concerned with reasons why what would otherwise be enforceable contracts should not be enforced; in other words, it is concerned with cases where the general policy in favour of enforcing agreements is abandoned. This abandonment is based on some perceived judicial exposition of society values. Clearly, public policy is not the policy of any particular government or political party. It is concerned with the defence of widely held society values, and these values are likely, on the whole, to be independent of the views of any of the main political parties. On the other hand, since the decisions as to what these values are lie in the hands of the judges, there is likely to be a rather cautious and conservative approach to this question. This is accentuated by the fact that it is not the practice to tender or admit evidence on public policy issues, so that they tend to be resolved by *a priori* reasoning, which is sometimes of a somewhat simplistic kind.

It is sometimes said that the heads of public policy are closed and that new heads cannot be discovered. It seems doubtful, however, whether this can really be true. It is certainly the case that in the past, what had formally been regarded as heads of public policy, have a generation later been held not to be. So in *Cowan v Milbourn* (1867), the court held that a contract for leasing a hall for an atheistic meeting was illegal, because Christianity was part of the law of England, a view spectacularly demolished 50 years later in *Bowman v Secular Society* (1917). It would be a possible position that heads could be closed down, but that the new heads could not be discovered. However, since society's values, whatever they are, undoubtedly change at different times and places, it would seem very odd to apply the doctrine of precedent in its most rigid form in an area most in need of flexibility. An obvious candidate for recognition as a new head of public policy would be the prohibition of racial, religious and sexual discrimination. Religious discrimination was actually enforced by statute until the early nineteenth century, and equally undoubtedly, Victorian judges would have had no doubt that women were inferior to men and should be kept in their place (one of the most articulate of them, Sir James Fitzjames Stephen, actually wrote a book devoted to this proposition). It seems equally clear that these values have been reversed, and that there is now a strong community sense that discrimination on these grounds is abhorrent. (Of course, it is not necessary to show that everyone shares this abhorrence.) Some forms of discrimination are explicitly outlawed by statute, but there are forms of activity not outlawed by statute which could lie within the grasp of the doctrine of public policy. An obvious example would be an agreement between the owners of houses in a particular street that they would not sell a house to a person from a particular race or religion. If an owner wished to make such a sale, and the other owners sought an injunction to restrain him, the court would be called upon to decide whether enforcement of such a covenant was or was not contrary to public policy. There would seem to be strong arguments for holding that it was contrary to public policy. This notion receives some support from the decision of the Court of Appeal in *Nagle v Feilden* (1966) that in this case there was a good arguable case that the Jockey Club could not lawfully decide, as a matter of policy, not to give trainers' licences to women.

What are the illegal contracts?

The traditional way of describing which contracts are illegal has been to list a number of subject matters or 'heads' which are protected. A detailed account of the cases would be quite out of place here, but let us give some heads and some examples. Agreements to commit crimes (the contract with a hit-man, supra); agreements to commit torts (agreement by A and B to practise a deception on others, for example, by driving up the price of shares during a takeover battle); sexual morality (agreements between prostitutes and clients); trading with the enemy (contracts with nationals of enemy countries during wartime); good relations with friendly states (contracts to smuggle whisky into the United States during prohibition); administration of justice (agreement not to prosecute, for example a criminal offence in return for payment); corruption in public life (agreement for the sale of honours); defrauding the revenue (agreement to pay a salary bogusly described as expenses); agreements to keep confidential information which should be publicly revealed; and agreements in restraint of trade (agreement not to open a business competing with the other contracting party). All of these examples are taken from decided cases.

It is worth emphasising that questions of public policy can arise in a wide range of different ways and not only in relation to a range of different heads. It is unlikely, for instance, that an agreement to commit a crime will be the subject matter of direct litigation, but this head has been the subject of a number of very interesting and instructive cases in relation to insurance. For instance, in *Beresford v Royal Insurance Co Ltd* (1938), the House of Lords held that a life insurance policy which clearly contained a promise to pay if death was caused by the suicide of the life insured more than two years after the policy was taken out, was contrary to public policy, because suicide was still a crime then. On the other hand, it has been repeatedly held that a motor insurance policy which indemnifies a driver when he commits a crime is enforceable even where the crime is a very serious one, such as motor manslaughter, as in *Hardy v Motor Insurers' Bureau* (1964). The real reason for this is probably that the beneficiaries of compulsory motor insurance are not so much the drivers, as the people whom they run into. It would be a serious gap in the mandatory third party insurance scheme if victims could not look forward to compensation in the case when the drivers had committed serious criminal offences.

It is worth saying a little more about *restraint of trade*. The purpose of striking down agreements in restraint of trade is to promote competition. There is now an elaborate statutory system for the promotion of competition, both as part of English domestic law and as part of the EC law. This has not entirely replaced, however, the common law rules in relation to restraint of trade. At one time, it was thought that all agreements which involved restraints on competition should be treated as bad per se, but by the early eighteenth century it was recognised that there were certainly some cases where it was desirable to allow a person to bind himself not to compete. The classic example is where someone is selling a business. In many cases, much of what one has to sell consists of the intangible asset of goodwill, that is the relationship with the customers. The seller can only give the full value of the business if he can make a binding promise not to open a competing business next door. Obviously, the purchaser will not pay for goodwill if in fact the seller can take it away with him. It is, therefore, in both the buyer's and seller's interests that such policies can be legally binding. It is also, in general, in the public interest, since it is in the public interest that businesses should change hands and that new and more enterprising people should come in to run businesses of those who are old or wish to move on. These considerations led to the adoption of a rule that covenants in restraint of trade are valid if reasonable. In the developed modern form, which starts from the decision of the House of Lords in *Nordenfelt v Maxim Nordenfelt Guns and Ammunitions Co* (1894), reasonableness is tested in two ways. The agreement must be reasonable as between the parties to it, and it must be reasonable in the public interest. In practice, most cases have turned on whether the agreement is reasonable as between the parties, and that is why we said earlier that contracts in restraint of trade lie across the border between unfairness and public policy. Courts have been particularly careful to analyse transactions between employer and employee, because it is very easy for an employer to insist on a covenant in restraint of trade as a condition of engaging the employee. On the other hand, it would be going too far to prohibit employers from ever imposing restraints. What the law has done is to say (and indeed this is true in all other cases) that the covenant can only be enforced if it is no wider in territorial scope and time than is needed to protect the covenantees' legitimate interests. In the case of an employer, the only legitimate interests which he may seek to protect are his connection with customers and his trade secrets. Restrictions designed simply to prevent competition are not allowed.

The second requirement that the agreement should be reasonable in the public interest has received more attention recently because of a whole series of cases about the petrol marketing arrangements in this country, of which the most important was *Esso Petroleum Co Ltd v Harper's Garage (Stourport) Ltd* (1968). It is standard practice for owners and lessees of filling stations to enter into arrangements with petrol companies under which they agree to take all their supplies of petrol from a particular petrol company, in return for getting a rather bigger retail mark up than they would if they took supplies from two or more petrol companies. The House of Lords held that such an argument was a covenant in restraint of trade. They also held that as a rule, covenants for five years or less would be treated as reasonable, but covenants for longer than five years would be treated as unreasonable. This decision represents a balance of the interests of the petrol company and of the public. Petrol companies have a legitimate interest in a stable distribution system, since they have to move vast quantities of petrol around the country and plan ahead to do so. The public has an interest in lively competition between petrol retailers, which will help to keep prices down. The argument was that if the average length of tie is five years, then on average, 20% of filling stations will come on the market each year, which would enable newcomers to the market to bid for contracts, but at the same time would not lead to total chaos.

The effects of illegality

Normally an illegal contract cannot be enforced. However, there will be cases where the contract is innocent on one side, because one party is quite unaware of facts which make the contract illegal. So, for instance, if a landlord lets a flat to a prostitute, quite unaware that she is planning to take her clients there, the contract will be illegal as far as the prostitute is concerned, but legal and enforceable as far as the landlord is concerned. Clearly the position would be quite different if the landlord knows the prostitute's intentions. Usually the size of the rent will give an irresistible clue to this. In some cases, it may be possible to excise the improper part of the contract and enforce the balance. So, for instance, a contract of employment, which contains an invalid covenant in restraint of trade, is certainly valid as to the rest of the contract (unlike a contract of employment which contains an invalid provision for the payment of bogus expenses, which is certainly not enforceable – the difference lies in the much greater moral culpability of evading tax, than of agreeing not to compete). It is also possible in some cases (particularly where this can be done simply by striking out a few words) to repair a covenant in restraint of trade which is excessively wide, but could be rendered acceptably narrow by deletion.

More commonly, problems arise about unscrambling the effects of illegal contracts. The general rule is that where the parties are equally at fault, the person in possession is stronger. As a rule, if an illegal contract collapses half way through, partly performed, the court will not order one party to restore money or goods that he has received from the other. However, there are a number of exceptions to this. It does not apply if the parties are not equally at fault in the technical sense. Under this rubric, exceptions have been made where one party has fraudulently led the other to believe the contract was perfectly valid, or where the rule which makes the contract invalid was designed to protect a class of people of whom the plaintiff is one, against another group of whom the defendant is one. It is also said that if one party repents of the illegality before the contract is carried out, he can change his mind and get his money or property back. The cases are, however, extremely confused as to the last moment at which he can safely claim to have changed his mind.

The plaintiff can also recover property where he can set up a title to the property which is wholly independent of the contract's illegality. The classic example of this is *Bowmakers Ltd v Barnet Instruments Ltd* (1945). In this case, there were a number of hire-purchase contracts which were in fact invalid for having contravened some statutory regulations. This would have meant that the plaintiffs could not have sued to recover the sums which the defendants promised to pay in monthly instalments, because this would be enforcement. However, the defendants had wrongfully sold some of the goods and it was held by the Court of Appeal that in doing so, they created a right of action in the plaintiff quite independent of the validity or invalidity of the contract.

In *Tinsley v Milligan* (1993), Tinsley and Milligan were two women who were lovers and who bought a house in which they lived and where they operated lodgings. The income from the lodgings made up the major part of their income. The house was put exclusively into Tinsley's name though it was bought with money provided by both of them. The reason for this was that it made it easier for Milligan to make false claims on the Department of Social Security.

In due course Milligan repented of the frauds on the DSS and admitted them. A settlement was reached with the DSS. Later the parties fell out and Tinsley left the house. Tinsley then started an action for possession. It was clear that on these facts there would, but for the escapade with the DSS, have been a division in the equitable ownership of the house between the two parties because Milligan had contributed financially to the purchase price. Tinsley argued that it was not open to Milligan to use this argument because the transaction had been put in this way in order to facilitate the fraud on the DSS. The House of Lords by three to two rejected this argument. The majority view was that Milligan did not need to rely on the fraud on the DSS as any part of the reasoning supporting her claim. Her claim was based on the fact that she contributed financially to the purchase of the house and there was a presumption therefore that the house is held on resulting trust for those who have contributed to the purchase price in proportion to their contributions. It was Tinsley and not Milligan who had to seek to rebut this presumption. Some people have criticised this reasoning as excessively formalistic. Certainly it means that if a husband and wife buy a house and both of them contribute to the price the result will be different according to whether the house is put into the husband's name or the wife's name since there is a presumption of advancement between husband and wife, that is a presumption that husbands make gifts to wives whereas there is a presumption of resulting trust between wife and husband so a husband who puts the house into his wife's name in order to defraud the Inland Revenue or the DSS will be in a different position from a wife who puts the house in her husband's name for exactly the same purpose.

Chapter 25
Variation, waiver and determination by agreement

Introduction

Parties may well decide during the running of an agreement that they wish to change the terms, or to bring the agreement to an end. This is particularly likely where the agreement is one which is designed to run for a long time. Indeed, it has been remarked that contract lawyers tend to use as examples agreements which are relatively simply and discrete, such as contracts to sell a car or horse, whereas many contracts are complex and contain many-sided relationships. Even if one is talking about sale, there is all the difference in the world between a contract by a car dealer to sell a car, and a contractual relationship between a component supplier and a manufacturer of cars. The possibility of change in some long-term contracts is so obvious that the parties may build this into the contract and provide mechanisms for change. So it is very common in long-term contracts for there to be a mechanism for an increase in the price to take account of inflation, and in long-term construction contracts, it is normal to give the architect or engineer wide powers to give variation orders, that is, to order additions or deletions from the work. This is because what is needed to complete the works often becomes clearer as the works progress.

In this chapter, we are concerned with the mechanisms by which parties can change a contract for themselves during its running. English law has succeeded in making this an unnecessarily complex area of the law. This is primarily because the starting point is a rule which says that any agreement designed to terminate or vary the contract must itself have all the legal ingredients of a contract. The classic example of this is the decision in *Foakes v Beer* (see above, p 475). where the House of Lords held that an agreement to settle a debt by paying part of it was not binding because it was not supported by consideration. The decision that consideration was necessary not only for the initial formation of agreements, but also for their variation or discharge, looks, in retrospect, very like a mistake. The reason is that while parties will not very often want to make serious binding contracts where there is in fact no consideration, it is an every day occurrence for parties to want to alter the terms of a contract without there being any consideration. Gratuitous contracts are unusual, but gratuitous adjustments to contracts are commonplace. The rule that consideration is necessary has, therefore, been subjected to considerable pressure, because it does not fit the needs of contracting parties. A number of qualifying doctrines have, therefore, been developed. Even so, it is still necessary to start from the principle that consideration is necessary for bringing the contract to an end or changing its terms.

In order to discover whether consideration is present, it is necessary to look carefully at what agreement the parties have actually made. There are a number of different possibilities. One is that the parties have agreed to bring the contract to an end. Consideration will normally present no problem here, where each of the parties has been released from some of his obligations, because each party's agreement to release the other will normally be a consideration for the release of his own obligations. On the other hand, if the parties agree to bring the agreement to an end when one party has already performed the whole of his side of the agreement, consideration is much more difficult to find. Obviously, there is no problem where the parties are aware of the rules of consideration and desire to manipulate them, since they can make the agreement to terminate the contract in return for the delivery of a rose at mid-summer, or some other nominal, but effective consideration.

Variation

Another possibility is that the parties intend to change what is to be done to perform the contract. Here again there will usually be no problem if what each of the parties is to do is to be changed, or if the change is one which is capable of benefiting both parties. So, for instance, in *WJ Alan & Co Ltd v El Nasr Export and Import Co* (1972), the original contract was for the sale of coffee beans and the buyer was to arrange the payment by opening a bankers' letter of credit payable in Kenyan shillings. Instead, the buyer opened a letter of credit payable in pounds sterling. This was undoubtedly a breach of contract, and the seller could have insisted on a credit in the correct currency being opened before he shipped any goods (see above, p 515). In fact, the seller shipped the first half of the coffee, because at that time the pound sterling and the Kenyan shilling were standing at par and the difference probably did not appear important. However, there was then a devaluation of the pound, unaccompanied by a parallel devaluation of the Kenyan shilling. The result was that a differential of 15% appeared between the currencies, and it became of critical importance whether the seller continued to be bound to accept payment in sterling for the second part of the delivery. It was held that he was. One explanation that was given for this was that the parties had tacitly changed the contract from a Kenyan shilling contract to a sterling contract, and that there was consideration for this in that, at the time of change, it could not be known for certain whether the pound would move up or down against the shilling and therefore the change was potentially for the benefit of either party, depending on currency movements.

The distinction between bringing the contract to an end and changing its terms can be important not only in relation to consideration, but also in relation to any requirements of written evidence. Usually, it is permissible for a contract which is required to be in writing or evidenced in writing to be terminated by an unwritten agreement. It is not, however, permissible to change the terms by an unwritten agreement. English courts have in fact recognised three possibilities in this area: outright termination, variation of terms, and termination followed by a new contract. The point of this distinction is that variation of the contract which is evidenced by an oral agreement is ineffective, but termination followed by a new unwritten contract is effective to terminate the old agreement, though the new agreement being unwritten will not be effective, *Morris v Baron* (1918).

Waiver

An early qualification to the requirement of consideration came with development of a notion of *waiver*. A good example is the case of *Hickman v Haynes* (1875). In this case, a buyer asked the seller to delay delivery of the goods and then later, when sued by the seller for refusal to accept delivery, argued that the seller had broken the contract by failing to deliver on time. The court naturally rejected this argument, since the seller had only failed to deliver on time at the buyer's request. It is easy to see that where there has been a change at one party's request, that party should not normally be able to complain without giving the other time to put things right. This was how a failure to open a credit of the right kind was treated in *Panoutsos v Raymond Hadley Corpn of New York* (1917), and this line of reasoning could have been applied in *WJ Alan & Co Ltd v El Nasr Export and Import Co*. If the seller had told the buyer in time that he insisted on a credit in Kenyan shillings, the buyer would have been able to make this arrangement without any cost. The loss in the transaction only arose because the seller did not respond sufficiently quickly to the situation, and could, therefore, be said to have waived his rights. The notion of waiver is also extremely important in relation to remedies. Some remedies, particularly termination and rescission, need to be exercised promptly, and the courts are, therefore, often quick to infer that one party has waived an undoubted right to terminate or rescind because of his inaction. Such waiver would not, by itself, remove the injured party's right to damages.

Promissory estoppel

In 1946, Lord Denning suggested in the *High Trees* case an alternative basis which has come to be known as the doctrine of promissory estoppel. In this case, there was a lease for 99 years of a block of flats. The lessees intended to let the individual flats and use the rents in order to pay their rent on the head lease, and no doubt to make a profit. During the 1939-1945 war, many of the flats were unlet, because tenants had left London. The parties agreed that for the time being, the lessees would only pay half of the normal rent. This agreement continued to be operated for the whole of the war, but at the end of the war, the lessors argued that the agreement was only intended to run until the end of the war or until the flats were let. As both these events had happened, they argued that they were entitled to full payment. Denning J, as he was then, agreed. Most judges would have stopped there, and if they had, the case would never have been heard of, since the decision at this point is obviously correct. However, Denning J went on to consider what the position would have been if the landlord has sued in 1945 for the half-rent which had been unpaid in each quarter since 1940. (There was another question which he did not discuss, which was what the position would have been if the landlord in 1942 had said that he wanted the full rent to be paid thenceforth, even though the flats were still not full.) Denning J held that the landlords could not recover all the rent which was unpaid during the war. He argued that they were estopped from putting forward such a claim, as they had promised to accept part-payment and the tenants had relied on this. Clearly, there was no consideration for the landlord's release of part of the tenants' obligations, but Denning J found authority in an old decision of the House of Lords, *Hughes v Metropolitan Rly Co* (1877). In that case, under the terms of the lease, the landlord was entitled to give tenants six months' notice to repair the premises and on failure by the tenant to repair, to forfeit the lease. The landlord gave the appropriate notice, but the tenant responded by starting negotiations with a view to selling the lease to the landlord. During the negotiations, the tenant, to the landlord's knowledge, did not start the repairs. When the negotiations eventually broke down, the landlord claimed to be entitled to forfeit the lease, because the tenant had not completed the repairs within six months from the original notice. The House of Lords held that the landlord was not entitled to do this, but must give a fresh six-month period of notice to run from the breakdown of negotiations. Undoubtedly, this was a case in which the one party was not entitled to insist on the strict terms of the contract because of the way he had conducted himself in relation to the other party. However, although the reasoning of Lord Cairns LC in the House of Lords was expressed in very wide terms, the decision itself was quite narrow, since the landlord was not prevented from having the premises repaired, but simply prevented from gaining the much more valuable extra right to forfeit the lease, until the tenant had a full six-month period to do the repairs. So the landlord's rights were not terminated, but simply suspended for a short while.

If one were to apply this reasoning to the facts in *High Trees*, it would undoubtedly support an argument that the landlord could not turn the tenant out for not paying the rent, when he told him the day before that he need only pay half the rent. It leaves completely in the air, however, the question whether the landlord could, by giving adequate notice, revive his right to the rent either in 1942, as to rent after 1942, or in 1945, as to rent unpaid between 1940 and 1945. It is clear that Denning J read a good deal more into the case than was, strictly speaking, there. Nevertheless, it is also clear, 40 years later, that to a large extent this wider reading has been accepted. It is not easy to be dogmatic about the precise state of the law, because most of the later cases consist of decisions of the Court of Appeal in which Lord Denning approves his doctrine and other judges decide the case on rather different grounds (*Combe v Combe* (1951); *D & C Builders v Rees* (1966); *WJ Alan & Co Ltd v El Nasr Export and Import Co* (1972), or decisions of the House of Lords which carefully avoid the main issue, *Tool Metal Manufacturing v Tungsten Electric* (1955); *Woodhouse A C Israel Cocoa v Nigerian Produce Marketing* (1972)). Perhaps the best general guide to current judicial thinking is the statement by Robert Goff J in *The Post Chaser* (1982); that 'the fundamental principle is . . . that the representor will not be allowed to enforce his rights where it would be inequitable having regard to the dealings which have thus taken place between the parties'.

Chapter 26
Consumer protection

Introduction

Since the war, consumers have become a recognisable social group able to organise, to lobby and to press for legislation and decisions of the courts which they see as protecting their interests. Consumers are not yet a body as forceful as producers or organised labour, but they have become much more effective at presenting their views. We now have a junior minister, one of whose major functions is to look after consumer affairs, and an important appointed official, the Director General of Fair Trading, one of whose major functions is to keep a general oversight on the protection of the consumer.

Consumer protection has been an important motivating force in a number of developments in the law of contract. In particular, it has been of great importance in relation to exemption clauses. The desire to protect the buyer or hirer of tatty second-hand cars was an important feature in the development of the doctrine of fundamental breach and that in turn, revealed the need for a wider piece of legislation. Although the Unfair Contract Terms Act 1977 spreads well outside the field of consumer protection, the desire to protect the consumer and specifically, the explicitly separate treatment of the consumer, is the most important feature of the Act.

Implied terms

The other major technique used by the law of contract to protect the consumer is through the development of implied terms. Although the implied terms in a contract of sale apply equally to commercial buyers and consumer buyers, the movement from the position in which the seller was only liable when he had explicitly warranted the goods as having particular qualities, to one where he impliedly undertakes major responsibility for the condition of the goods, because the law routinely imposes an implied term upon him, has proved of inestimable advantage to the consumer.

Under section 13 of the Sale of Goods Act 'where there is a contract for the sale of goods by description, there is an implied condition that the goods correspond with the description'. It was under this provision that the buyers in *Re Moore & Co and Landauer & Co's Arbitration* (1921) (see above, p 518) were able to reject improperly packed tins of fruit. Similarly, in *Andrews Bros (Bournemouth) Ltd v Singer & Co Ltd* (1934), a buyer was able to reject as a 'new Singer car', a car which had already been driven for several hundred miles in an abortive attempt to deliver it to an earlier purchaser. In practice, the concept of a sale by description is very wide, so as to exclude only those few contracts where the parties agree on a specific article without attaching any words of description to it. So, for instance, goods sold in a supermarket with a label on, are sold by description and must comply with that description.

Since 1994, section 14 (2) of the Sale of Goods Act, has provided that 'where the seller sells goods in the course of business, there is an implied condition that the goods supplied under the contract are of suitable quality'. Between 1893 and 1994 the same provision had provided that the goods must be of merchantable quality and the 1994 Act not only changes the language but also widens somewhat the circumstances which make the goods of unsuitable quality. It appears to be the case that all goods which were unmerchantable before 1994 are now unsuitable but that the converse is not the case. In *Rogers v Parish (Scarborough) Ltd* (1987), the Court of Appeal held that a new Range Rover which developed a number of defects, none of which actually made the vehicle undriveable or unsafe, but which were very irritating for a new car at such an expensive price, made the vehicle unmerchantable. Basically, goods lacked merchantable quality if the buyer would not have bought them at that price if he had known what their true condition was. For this purpose, the price and the description may both be important factors. So in *B S Brown & Sons Ltd v Craiks Ltd* (1970), cloth was bought for resale, the buyer intending to sell it as dress material but not having told the seller this. The cloth was in fact not suitable for dress material, but was suitable for industrial use. The House of Lords held that as the goods had not been described as dress material, and as the price paid was more appropriate to an industrial than to a dress use, the cloth was merchantable. Clearly, the result would have been different if a higher price had been charged, or if the goods had been described as dress cloth. In *Henry Kendall & Sons v William Lillico & Sons* (1969), there were sales of Brazilian groundnut extraction which was suitable for cattle food but not for compounding into poultry food. The evidence was that compounded groundnut extraction commands much the same price whether compounded as cattle food or as poultry food. The House of Lords held that the goods were merchantable because they were being sold under the description of groundnut extraction, and under that description they were fit for the purpose of cattle food, a purpose for which they were commonly bought. This case was decided under the 1893 version of the Sale of Goods Act, which contained no definition of merchantable quality. The 1979 version, following the statutory amendment of 1973, defined goods as being of merchantable quality 'if they are as fit for the purpose or purposes for which goods of that kind are commonly bought, as it is reasonable to expect having regard to any description applied to them, the price (if relevant) and all the other relevant circumstances'. The 1994 Act makes a further revision of the statutory definition so as to make it clear that goods which have serious cosmetic defects, such as cigarette burns on the seat of a brand new car, or which work when they are bought but lack adequate durability, are not of suitable quality.

Section 14(3) provides that:

'where the seller sells goods in the course of a business and the buyer, expressly or by implication, makes known:

... any particular purpose for which the goods are being bought, there is an implied condition that the goods supplied under the contract are reasonably fit for that purpose, whether or not that is the purpose for which such goods are commonly supplied, except where the circumstances show that the buyer does not rely, or that it is unreasonable for him to rely on the skill or judgement of the seller'.

In practice, the courts have given a wide scope to this provision because they have been willing to infer in any case where goods have one single predominant purpose, that they have been bought for that purpose. So in *Preist v Last* (1903), the buyer went into a shop and asked for a hot-water bottle and this was held sufficient to make it clear that he wanted a bottle which would hold hot water, without bursting, for warming his bed. Similarly, it has been held that tinned salmon and milk must be reasonably fit for the purpose of eating and drinking respectively. Where goods have several possible purposes and the buyer requires them for one specific purpose, then his position is very much better if he makes this known.

Law of tort

Consumer protection is also effected through the law of tort. In this sense, the line of cases starting with *Donoghue v Stevenson* (1932), which says that a manufacturer of goods is under a duty of care not to put goods into circulation which may damage the ultimate consumer is of the greatest importance. This line of cases is now, of course, being supplemented by the introduction of a statutory regime protecting the consumer against personal injury and certain limited kinds of property damage which arise from defective products, even if the manufacturer is not negligent in producing the products (see above Chapter 15).

Criminal law

In many ways, however, the most important protection of the consumer comes through the criminal law. This is because protection through the law of contract and tort requires the consumer himself to be aware of his rights, and to be prepared to give the time and money needed to protect them through the courts if necessary. The tradition of criminal law intervention in the area is very old. It goes back to measures designed to make sure that tradesmen used accurate weights so that they gave fair value. Cheating by tradesmen in giving short weight can be traced back to Ancient Egypt, and in England there are provisions in the Magna Carta requiring there to be uniform measure for wine and ale and so on. It also became recognised that it was desirable to have officials whose duty it was to check that tradesmen did in fact comply with these requirements.

The present law contains a number of measures. Under the Consumer Protection Act 1961, the Consumer Safety Act 1978 and the Consumer Safety (Amendment) Act 1986, powers were taken to make regulations to ensure that particular categories of unsafe goods were not put on to the market. This was reinforced by the Consumer Protection Act 1987, Part II of which introduced a general requirement of safety which supplements all the specific requirements introduced in relation to specific goods.

Under the Fair Trading Act 1973, machinery was set up to keep under constant review certain types of trading practice, and an Office of Fair Trading was created which is headed by the Director General of Fair Trading, who is neither a political appointee nor a career civil servant. The Director General of Fair Trading has powers, amongst other things, to act against traders who persistently act in ways which are unfair or detrimental to consumers.

Under the Trade Descriptions Act 1968, it was made an offence for any person who, in the course of a trade or business, (a) applies a false trade description to any goods, or (b) supplies or offers to supply any goods to which a false trade description is applied. This act is the centre-piece of consumer protection in the criminal law, and there may be over 30,000 prosecutions a year under it. It catches, for instance, the well known dishonest practice of car dealers turning back the clock which amounts to a description that the car has done the turned-back mileage. Only the most clear and explicit statements that nobody is to pay any attention to or to rely on the mileage will be effective to exclude liability. The Trade Descriptions Act also dealt with the particularly intractable problem of misleading price indications such as 'just reduced', which are the salesman's delight. It has proved exceptionally difficult to design effective legislation in this area, and Part III of the Consumer Protection Act 1987 represents the latest attempt to deal with this.

Index